# Educational
# Psychology

# Glenn Myers Blair

PROFESSOR OF EDUCATIONAL PSYCHOLOGY
UNIVERSITY OF ILLINOIS

# R. Stewart Jones

CHAIRMAN, DEPARTMENT OF EDUCATIONAL PSYCHOLOGY
UNIVERSITY OF ILLINOIS

# Ray H. Simpson

PROFESSOR OF EDUCATIONAL PSYCHOLOGY
UNIVERSITY OF ILLINOIS

# Educational Psychology

---

## THIRD EDITION

The Macmillan Company

Collier-Macmillan Limited,
*London*

50

THE MACMILLAN COMPANY
866 THIRD AVENUE, NEW YORK, NEW YORK 10022
COLLIER-MACMILLAN CANADA, LTD., TORONTO, ONTARIO

Printed in the United States of America

# Preface

Education in the United States has grown to be one of the nation's largest enterprises. At all levels of instruction, enrollments have burgeoned and teaching personnel has enormously increased. New programs have been introduced to provide for children and youth of widely differing backgrounds and educational and vocational ambitions. Teaching and teaching methods are being scrutinized by both lay and professional groups. Probably at no time in our history has there been greater need for expert teaching and efficient learning in our schools. The improvement of educational programs will depend heavily upon the ideas that educational psychology has to offer.

The modern teacher no longer is merely a hearer of lessons or an officer who maintains discipline in the classroom. Instead, he is an individual who is concerned with the total development and adjustment of children in a very complex society. He is vitally interested in having each child acquire the basic skills of our culture, and in addition is sensitive to the child's development in the areas of health and personal adjustment. He needs to understand the special problems of children from culturally deprived surroundings, and those with individual handicaps of many kinds. He also must be aware of the tremendous technological advances of our age, and the increasing knowledge in his own field.

The old adage that "teachers are born and not made" may contain a germ of truth, and may have been useful in characterizing teachers of an earlier date, but it is very misleading and inappropriate today. The present-day teacher, who would succeed with such complex tasks as guiding and directing learning, diagnosing and alleviating personality maladjustments, and evaluating the outcomes of his work, must be a specially trained expert. Among the subjects of greatest relevance in this program of training is obviously that of educational psychology. Teachers need thoroughly to understand the basic principles of psychology governing the behavior of children, and in addition to possess skill in methods of child study.

The present book has been written in an effort to supply teachers and prospective teachers with those facts and principles and methods of procedure which have maximal usefulness in the classroom and in other educational situations. The materials have been gathered from many sources, including the psychology laboratory, classroom experimentation, clinical

experience, and from such related fields as cultural anthropology, psychiatry, biology, and sociology.

It is the plan of the book first to present a view of the child as he progresses toward maturity; second, to show the forces which influence and produce change in the child's learning and adjustment; third, to illustrate how the methods and tools of psychology can be used to evaluate the effectiveness of the educational program; and finally, to discuss some of the psychological factors which influence the professional growth and mental health of the teacher. The book has a developmental emphasis throughout and is particularly oriented in terms of the needs of children and the forces which motivate them to learn and adjust.

A distinctive feature of the book is the deliberate effort which has been made to illustrate psychological theories by using actual classroom examples, so that teachers may gain clear insight into the fundamental values which psychology has to offer. Also of a unique nature is the section dealing with the psychology of the teacher. Books in the past have frequently given the impression that all one needs to know in order to teach is understanding of children. Recently, however, an awareness has developed that to be effective the teacher must know himself—be able to diagnose his own assets and liabilities, his own personality, and his own teaching methods. Hence much attention has been given to the teacher's role in the learning process, and to the nature of teacher-pupil relationships.

This third edition incorporates the new research and recent advances which have been made in the field since the two previous editions appeared. The text has also been expanded to include many new illustrations and exercises at the ends of the various chapters, to be worked out by students. Although the book has been written by three authors, it is, in every sense, a joint and integrated effort. The entire manuscript was read, revised, and put in final shape by all three authors working as a team.

The writers are indebted to many individuals for the part they have contributed toward the substance of this volume. These include research workers and colleagues in psychology and related fields who have augmented the rapidly growing body of experimental evidence, and thousands of experienced teachers in the writers' classes who have helped them build a bridge between theory and practice. Gratitude is also expressed to the many publishers who have generously given permission to quote from copyrighted works, and to the schools of Champaign, Illinois, St. Louis, Missouri, and Culver City, California, which supplied many of the photographs of classroom activities.

G. M. B.

R. S. J.

R. H. S.

*Urbana, Illinois*

# Contents

## PART ONE
### Introduction

## PART TWO
`50`
### Growth and Development

## PART THREE
### Learning

## PART FOUR
### Adjustment and Mental Hygiene

## PART FIVE
## Measurement and Evaluation

## PART SIX

## The Psychology of the Teacher

# List of Illustrations

# List of Tables

# PART ONE

## Introduction

# Chapter 1

## Psychology and the Work of Teaching

The complexity of teaching and the many problems inherent in the process require the most refined skills on the part of teachers. Psychology cannot solve all of these problems, even with the aid of other related disciplines, but it is an essential tool that must always be at hand. In this chapter some of the situations that face education and teachers are presented, as are suggestions for making the applications of psychological principles as functional as possible. Changing the behavior of teachers, children, and other learners so that they may successfully meet the problems of living is the major concern of this book.

### EDUCATIONAL CASUALTIES AND THE NEED FOR TALENT

People who can learn efficiently, who can think, and who can generate new ideas, are the most precious of our resources; yet it is this wealth of the human mind and spirit that we squander away more recklessly than we do any of our other resources. It has been popular in the past decade to seek a scapegoat for this waste, and the American teacher, whose own education can be shown to be wanting, has been a favorite target. More sober reflection will certainly reveal that the problems of education grow out of diverse

problems within society as a whole, and that human casualties, while manifest in the school, stem from a variety of sources.

The term "educational casualty," first used by Pressey,[1] vividly expresses one of these major problems of education. In its original sense, the phrase was used to describe those students who began an educational program that they never finished. In the broader sense, as it is used here, it embraces all those who, because of cultural or economic disadvantage, adverse attitudes, or inefficient schooling, fail to acquire the learning and intellectual development which they and society rightfully expect. In this sense, there are educational casualties at all levels from kindergarten to graduate school.

Some of the various kinds of educational casualties and their bases will now be described. They are presented from the point of view that one of the first orders of business in a book that deals with teaching and learning is to obtain a proper perspective of the scope and magnitude of the problems faced by the profession of education. Only through the concerted effort of all who are connected with the educational enterprise can we hope to maintain the present rate of progress and achieve needed improvements in teaching. Educational psychology is a basic foundation for understanding and treating the problems that follow.

## DROP OUTS AND PUSH OUTS

Fifty percent of the students in the United States colleges drop out of their degree programs within four years following matriculation.[2] Every year 50,000 students with the ability to finish college drop out of high school and do not even enter college.[3] In some universities, the attrition rate in the freshman and sophomore years is as high as 75%, and in many high schools, the drop out rate is nearly 50%.

In going over the graduating classes of one large high school, one of the writers found the top five students in four successive years to be girls all of whom had IQ scores on the California Test of Mental Maturity of 140 or higher. A follow up of these five girls showed that not one had entered college. One had dropped out of high school in the senior year because of an untimely pregnancy. Two had married within a few months after graduation, were raising families, and had no intention of continuing their schooling, and the remaining two were working as sales clerks in the local

---

[1] Sidney L. Pressey, and Francis P. Robinson, *Psychology and the New Education*, New York, Harper and Row, 1944.

[2] Lehymann F. Robinson, *Relation of Student Persistence in College to Satisfaction with "Environmental" Factors*, unpublished doctoral thesis, Graduate College of the University of Illinois, Urbana, Illinois, 1967, p. 1.

[3] Glen Stice, "50,000 Potential College Graduates Quit High School Each Year," *ETS Development*, Vol. 8, No. 2, January 1960.

community. Only one of the five said that if the opportunity were available she would like to continue her education. These girls happened to live in a community where there was no expectation that lower class or middle class girls would continue their schooling.

The number of pupils entering the fifth grade who drop out before finishing high school is shown in Table 1.[4] It can be seen that for the high school graduation year of 1964 one-third of these children were no longer

### TABLE 1
#### Estimated Retention Rates, Fifth Grade Through High-School Graduation in Public and Non-Public Schools, 1924–32 to 1956–64

| School Year Pupils Entered Grade V | Number in Grades | Number of High-School Graduates Eight Years Later | Year of Graduation |
|---|---|---|---|
| 1924–25 | 1,000 | 302 | 1932 |
| 1934–35 | 1,000 | 467 | 1942 |
| 1944–45 | 1,000 | 522 | 1952 |
| 1954–55 | 1,000 | 642 | 1962 |
| 1956–57 | 1,000 | 667 | 1964 |

in school. Many of these no doubt left as soon as they reached the school leaving age, 16 in most states. Some were unquestionably expelled and certainly large numbers left after much discouragement in school.

These drop outs and expulsions are occurring at a time when our demands as a nation for more highly trained workers and more intelligent citizens are greater than ever before.[5] While there are millions of recipients of relief and public aid there are many hundreds of thousands of jobs unfilled because of the unavailability of trained applicants.[6]

Finally it should be noted that frequently the children who drop out of school are the very ones who have the most to gain from continuing. On the average, the poorer (financially speaking) the student is, the sooner he will leave school. Those who most need what the school can offer to compensate for inadequate home backgrounds, with limited ability to learn directly from experience, are the least likely at the present time to receive it.

---

[4] *Digest of Educational Statistics*, pp. 120–21. United States Department of Health Education, and Welfare, Office of Education Bulletin, 1964, No. 18 (OE 10024-64), Washington, D.C.: United States Government Printing Office, 1964.

[5] See *The Educationally Retarded and Disadvantaged*, Part I, 66th Yearbook of the National Society for the Study of Education, University of Chicago Press, Chicago, Illinois, 1967, pp. 211–236.

[6] Grant Venn, *Man, Education and Work*, Washington, D.C., American Council on Education, 1964.

It is not appropriate to the purpose of this book to discuss in detail the problem of the school "drop out," or of the able student who does not go to college. Excellent discussions can be found elsewhere.[7] Suffice it to state here that even with the most excellent program of scholarships and financial aid, there will still be a large residue of our most talented youth who refuse higher education, even when it is offered to them. As it is, the combination of such factors, as low socio-economic status, low intellectual values in the community, poor elementary and high school preparation, false images given by the mass media, and mismanagement of higher education, results in a tremendous waste of intellectual potential. We can take little comfort in the fact that we are probably doing a better job in education at all levels than ever before, because the discrepancy between what we ought to do and what we are doing is clearer than ever before.

## THE "NEVER INS"

An even more severe problem than the drop out is represented by those people who never obtain schooling, or receive only bits and fragments so that essentially they are illiterates. Taking a world view, rather than thinking only of our own educational system, the problem is almost overwhelming. In 43 of the world's large countries in which there are 880 million adults there is a total of 600 to 640 million adult illiterates.[8] A quarter of a century ago, such facts might have been viewed as interesting but not highly relevant to a discussion of this kind. Today they are not only relevant, but perhaps crucial to survival. Whatever knowledge we have about learning and intelligence must quickly be put to work, if we are to help ourselves and others upon whom we depend to find a fingerhold to climb out of the abyss that mankind's ignorance has created.

In our own country, the rate of adult illiteracy is only 3%, and in the future may be even less. However, such gross figures may be deceptive. For example, about one million children of migrant workers receive only haphazard schooling at best, and large segments of our population in the great cities, while they receive some schooling, may profit little from it. Many are there in body only. In a recent visit to a junior high school in a prosperous community, one of the writers noticed in a study hall three Negro boys who were looking at pictures in one corner away from the rest of the children. When asked about them, the teacher replied that they disturbed the other children if left in their proper places, so to keep them quiet she put them in a corner with pictures. When asked about their assignments, she said they could not read. The next question, which

---

[7] Daniel Schreiber (Editor), *The School Dropout*, Washington, D.C., National Education Association, 1964.
[8] UNESCO, *World Illiteracy at Mid-Century*, Paris, 1957.

seemed sensible, was how they were doing in remedial reading. The teacher said that remedial reading was only for those pupils who could learn to read and could profit from the instruction, and not for these children. Results of attitudes such as these are clearly evident on every hand. Here for example are the written reports of a group of junior high school pupils (ninth graders) in New York, who were assigned the task of briefly describing the television programs of the night before.

"1. The main part of the picture. I like sent the man sick go ham to the - girl.
2. My television was Booke and I dip go to the . . . in a line time.
3. I like Rock Pretty Baby the pitcher was vevery nice. the actors did they part vevery Nice. the made good Reansor." [9]

## THE MISDIRECTED AND MISGUIDED

Another waste of potential that creates unhappiness, frustration, and ineffectiveness, both in school and in work, is that which results from misdirection in educational and vocational plans. Bill's troubles are a case in point:

Bill as a child seemed very much interested in art, and developed good aptitude for further work. In high school his paintings were frequently on display, and he won several prizes for his work. Bill's father, himself a business man, was not impressed by this "extracurricular" activity, and when the time came for Bill to go to college, insisted that since he, the father, was paying for it, the boy enter a college of commerce. Seeing no other choice Bill did so. Within a semester he was on academic probation, and at the end of the first year was dropped. Now with a record of failure he found it impossible to be admitted to any other state college. For awhile he did nothing, but eventually got a job as a baggage clerk in a hotel. He tried one more small college, but its requirements were too stringent, and he failed again. Since then he has drifted from job to job never being happy or very effective in any of them. Worst of all he has completely given up his art work, even as an avocational pursuit.

There are a variety of reasons for cases such as this. In many instances young people acquire distorted views of the world of work and of their own capabilities. For the past several decades it has been clear that many young people aspire to vocations for which they are not fitted. The status levels, and the hierarchical arrangement of occupations and of courses in school, create frustration and feelings of insignificance for large portions of our population. Even granting that the stated aspirations of juniors in high school show vain hopes of impressing friends and student advisers, they are still indications that certain things are the "right" things to do,

---

[9] George Allen, *Undercover Teacher*, New York, Doubleday & Co., Inc., 1960, p. 73.

and they may stand in the way of clear-cut goals that could be used to direct energies toward courses and experiences that could be much more rewarding than the daydreams of a tomorrow that never comes. On the other side of the coin, we find some young people of good abilities whose aspirations are entirely too low. In both city and rural slums, for example, students, especially from minority racial groups, do not even consider the possibility of college or of a professional life.

A further misdirection may arise from the attitudes prevalent in many high schools that the important students take courses preparing for liberal arts college. Many young people are inappropriately influenced by this attitude, even though specialized programs in commercial subjects or vocational programs are available. The tyranny of the college preparatory curriculum, with its emphasis upon languages, mathematics, and science, has made courses of art, music, and the vocational fields seem second-class. One sad result has been the use of these latter courses as a dumping ground for the malcontents, and for the students of low ability. Some teachers trained in art, music, and the industrial arts have either quit teaching, or where possible have changed to a minor teaching field. Able students, who might profit greatly from such courses, shun them even though they may have high aptitudes in the areas represented by such courses.

Finally there is a large percentage of students for whom no adequate guidance facilities are available. One of the writers recently interviewed several dozen high school juniors in some of the better schools in his state, and found they had had only cursory contact with their counselors or advisers. In general they had these contacts only if they were in some kind of academic or disciplinary difficulties. Otherwise, they were pretty much on their own. Present standards of the American Personnel and Guidance Association specify one full time and well-trained counselor for each 300 students. Few schools meet this standard, and even if they tried, they would not find a sufficient number of counselors with the proper training.

## THE CULTURALLY DISADVANTAGED

At a time of apparent great abundance, of conspicuous consumptions and "planned obsolescence," it may be difficult to realize the growing numbers of our people whose living conditions deny them minimal material advantages and educational opportunities adequate for even the basic requirements of an independent life in our society. In his book, *The Culturally Deprived Child*, Riessman [10] maintains that in 1950 about one child out of every ten in the fourteen largest cities of the United States was culturally deprived, but in 1960 this figure had risen to one in three. He

---

[10] Frank Riessman, *The Culturally Deprived Child*, New York, Harper & Row, 1962.

goes on to show that between 1950 and 1957, 97% of our population growth as a nation took place in and around these same large cities where about one-sixth of the total population resides. That these culturally deprived children are truly educational casualties, that is, are educationally deprived as well, has been shown in numerous studies.

How does this deprivation come about, and how does it manifest itself? First of all, these children gain less stimulation perceptually and verbally from their parents, other adults, other children, and from their surroundings than do their more fortunate peers. Too rarely does the language they encounter include abstractions, relational thinking, or concepts from the modern world of science. Moreover, they do not obtain a good model for grammar and pronunciation, or corrective feedback from adults or others in their community. In the second place, they have too many opportunities to learn defeat and failure, both by comparing themselves with other more fortunate children, and in school, where they have difficulty with such basic subjects as reading and arithmetic. More often than not, they are members of a minority racial group which may add to their low self-esteem. Thirdly, these children find themselves in school situations that are inadequate to their needs. At one point, the Board of Education of New York asked for volunteers to staff the "difficult" schools. Only 25 out of 40,000 teachers stepped forward, and no principal volunteered. In the same year, 22% of the new teachers assigned to "difficult" schools failed to report to their jobs.[11] Only rarely do prospective teachers receive much in the way of special training to deal with the culturally deprived, or to provide the remedial help which they so often require. (If some of the critics of education have their way, teachers will receive no training in these matters at all.) All too often the wealth of the community is used in the construction and equipping of the schools in better neighborhoods, while the slum area schools receive neither adequate physical facilities nor special services that are badly needed. The cost of providing sufficient plant and services for these disadvantaged children (if real progress and change are to be effected) will undoubtedly be double or triple what the costs are in suburban communities. As it is now, these cost figures are reversed.

Results of these adverse influences, which are apparent from the first grade on, are seen in aptitude tests, school achievement, and even ineptness in the daily problems of living. These children drift farther and farther away from what society expects them to accomplish, so that they may go through their entire period of schooling with material and methods never pitched at their level of ability nor in consonance with their interests. Frequently an active anti-intellectualism develops. There is not just a failure to learn but an active hostility toward schooling and learning.

---

[11] George N. Allen, *op. cit.*, p. 187.

## VICTIMS OF INADEQUATE
## LEARNING SITUATIONS

The comparison of two adjacent school districts, each in moderately "well off" sections of the U.S., reveals the great disparity of educational opportunity which depends upon the accident of place of birth.

### TABLE 2
### Comparison of Curricular Offerings of Two School Districts *

| Unit District with High School Enrolling 200 | Unit District with High School Enrolling 1,000 |
|---|---|
| Past 5 years—19.53% Drop Outs | Past 5 years—14.8% Drop Outs |
| Two of the 14 staff members teaching on temporary approval | No temporary approvals out of a total of 67 teachers |
| Curricular Offerings | Curricular Offerings |
| French—2 units | Latin—4 units |
|  | French—3 units |
|  | Spanish—3 units |
|  | German—3 units |
| Science—3 units | Science—6 units |
| Mathematics—5 units | Mathematics—6½ units |
| Art—0 units | Art—4 units |
| Business Education—5 units | Business Education—14½ units |
| Vocational Education | Vocational Education |
|    Agricultural Education |    Distributive Education |
|    Home Economics Education |    Diversified Occupations |
|  |    Practical Nursing |
|  |    Home Economics |
|  |    Machine Shop |
|  |    Electricity |
|  |    Cabinetmaking |
|  |    Drafting |
|  |    Nursing |
|  |    Commercial Art |
|  |    Auto Mechanics |
|  |    Building Trades |
|  |    Plumbing |
|  |    Sheet Metal |
|  |    Factory Maintenance |
|  |    State Approved Guidance |
| Music—Band and Chorus | Music—Band, Chorus, Orchestra, Theory |
| Special Education—Limited to home bound classes for physically handicapped | Special Education—Physically Handicapped, Speech Correction, Deaf, Partially Sighted, Socially Maladjusted, Educable Mentally Handicapped, Gifted |

* Committee on Illinois School Administrative Structure, *Modern School Administrative Structure*, Mount Zion, Illinois, 1962.

It takes no penetrating analysis to see the difference between the two schools shown in Table 2. Even with good teaching, the high school with 200 students offers far too little choice for the complex and diverse needs of both students and of the society that is to accept them. These adjacent school districts were in a prosperous section of a state that is one of the leaders in educational opportunity. What of the less fortunate areas of the country?

One of the writer's students a few years ago was principal of a small elementary school in Mississippi. It was a segregated Negro school in a rural area. According to his description the school was housed in the basement of a small church. Two naked electric bulbs hung from the gloomy ceiling and cast their feeble light upon the ramshackle chairs and desks. The total equipment for the primary grades in this school consisted of 28 outmoded primers (there were 32 pupils) whose passage from hand to hand over the years had left them grimy and torn, and in spots barely legible. Prior to the time when the student described his school, the writer had discussed with his class the values of various reading series and supplementary books within the classroom in addition to the collection of materials in the school library. How ridiculous it must have seemed to this student who did not even have enough worn out readers to go around.

The prestige of James B. Conant has alerted the public to facts about our schools which educators have known for a long time, *viz.*, that to serve adequately the various requirements of entire student bodies a comprehensive program is necessary.[12] Few schools today, with the exception of the larger city and suburban ones, are able to do so. To provide a comprehensive program for both precollege and vocational training is exhorbitantly expensive for schools of small size. The one room school for its time undoubtedly had many advantages, but the nostalgia for such arrangements should not keep us from seeing the radically changed demands of the society in which we live today.

Inadequacies should not be thought of only in terms of lack of physical facilities. Other factors of even greater importance exist. They include, failure to take account of differences among children, failure to provide adequate remedial help, outmoded curricula, poorly trained teachers, and a host of others. All such observations are, of course, relative—relative to what better schools are doing, and relative to what is perhaps an ideal situation. The preponderance of schools are doing a good job. But the job is growing more difficult, the need for well educated and professionally minded teachers is greater, and this at a time when schools are under attack, and good teachers and prospective ones are driven from the profession by unbridled and unhealthy criticism.

---

[12] James B. Conant, *Slums and Suburbs*, New York, McGraw-Hill Book Company, 1961.

## ATTITUDINAL FAILURES

At all levels of schooling, and among all social groups there are numerous individuals whose attitudes toward education in general or toward certain subject matter in particular are hostile. This situation practically guarantees that pupils will learn little more than a bare minimum. These negative attitudes are reflected in diverse ways, and will be further discussed in a later section of this book. The following are a few examples of the origin and results of negative attitudes toward school learning.

1. Studies of underachievers in school have revealed a sizable number, perhaps a fourth, whose home situations or family relationships are unsettled and where concealed hostility exists toward one or both parents. There seems to be an unconscious motivation to "get even" with parents by doing poorly in school. The hostility, even though displaced, may be active toward school, studying, and teachers who may be viewed as parent surrogates.

2. Trauma may account for another group of negative attitudes. Sometimes teachers unwittingly embarrass, ridicule, or hurt a child to the extent that he is alienated from the subject matter being taught. A university student related the following anecdote about his early schooling:

> Miss Wilson, our music teacher, labeled the class as bluebirds, robins and sparrows. The bluebirds got to sing all the time, the robins most of the time, and the sparrows occasionally. As a sparrow, I joined in the chorus vigorously, but with results that probably offended Miss Wilson's musical ear. During one song when I was likely way off key, she stopped the class and said, "We now have one more kind of bird, a listening bird who must not sing, but instead listen to the other birds so he will learn how." Needless to say I was demolished not only by my public demotion, but by the titters of the smug bluebirds and robins whom I hated vigorously. From that time until now, I have never tried to sing again. Many times I have avoided social affairs where I knew they were likely to have group singing.

3. Some negative attitudes arise from the groups of which the child is a member. The culturally deprived child may simply reflect the anti-intellectual attitudes of his home. The popular boy in school may find his popularity jeopardized unless he adopts a "devil-may-care" attitude toward school work. The girl may discover more social and dating opportunities in extracurricular activities than she does in classwork. Boys frequently find it quite acceptable to be interested in science and mathematics, but it may be considered somewhat effeminate to show an interest in writing and in the humanities. In all these cases the child is naturally moved by strong forces of identification and imitation to be like another person or group. These attitudes are woven into the culture and cannot easily be erased.

4. A most serious attitude failure in our country arises from the too common belief that schooling is for children and that once a period of schooling is completed, that's the end of it. Learning is seldom viewed as a lifetime activity, one which never ceases. Experts in adult education rate this as one of their most serious roadblocks to continuing education, so badly needed, particularly in our urban areas.

## THOSE WHO FAIL TO REMEMBER MINIMUM ESSENTIALS

In a university class composed of juniors and seniors, the difficulties of a particular eight-year-old boy, whose IQ was reported as 120, were being discussed. Students were asked what his mental age would be. No one knew. They were then given the rough formula for determining this, i.e., IQ is $\dfrac{MA}{CA} \times 100$. It shortly became clear that even with paper and pencil, less than half were able correctly to calculate this boy's mental age. Some professors view such facts with outrage and ask what such students are doing in college? A more moderate view would be that such instances merely reflect a general condition among all of us who have to some extent or in some area learned things in school which did not take, which were, but should not have been forgotten. Moreover, most of us, when confronted with a situation that calls for intelligence or for thinking, will find our performances below that of which we know we are capable, and most of us, if we are honest with ourselves, realize many things we were supposed to have learned are almost completely forgotten. Some cases in point will now be presented:

1. "When a group of 126 college students were asked to define in any way they could the 20 most common units of measure (such as mile, gallon, peck or millimeter) it was found, on an average, 58 per cent of these students showed no knowledge of the unit even though grading was liberal. The following sample errors make clear the grossness of the ignorance. Acre was defined as one square mile, 2½ square miles; mile as 352 feet, 11,550 feet; degree as a measure of weakness or strength, the smallest unit of distance measurement; meter as an English measure of distance with reference to our mile, a tiny unit in an inch, 27 inches, about three miles." [13]
2. A friend of one of the writers who is a woman of superior intelligence and highly successful in the advertising business remembered that Rio de Janeiro was at the mouth of the Amazon River.
3. A faculty colleague who was about to go on a long vacation trip purchased an extra tire tube so as to have a spare tube in case of a blow out. He drove in to one of the local filling stations and instructed the attendant

[13] S. L. Pressey, and F. P. Robinson, *op. cit.*, p. 545.

to put 32 pounds of air in the tube, as he would have no way to inflate it should he have occasion to use it on his trip.

These examples highlight one of the greatest educational casualties of all, for they serve to show us that misconceptions, and unlearned and forgotten essentials exist among all people, and as we grow more specialized in our fields of knowledge the problem will probably increase.

Opportunities for more intelligent behavior exist in every field and in every aspect of our lives. The way one reads the newspaper, how he uses ingredients in cooking, the way he disciplines his children, the way a doctor diagnoses and treats illness, and how the mechanic repairs our car are all activities that more intelligent behavior could easily improve.

This book cannot give comprehensive attention to all the educational casualties, nor to the conditions that spawn them. It will in the chapters that follow try to show how psychology provides knowledge about the strategies for attacking them, and will show how some of the present educational research gives designs for action in the improvement of our schools.

## EDUCATIONAL PSYCHOLOGY
## AND DECISION MAKING

First, and perhaps foremost, educational psychology helps teachers make wise decisions. Every day, and in many ways, teachers make decisions that influence the pupil, school, and community. Learning how to make judgments and to take decisive action, at times planfully and carefully, but often forced speedily by the demands of the situation, require the teacher to understand himself, his pupils, and the processes of learning and intellectual development. These understandings are essential parts of educational psychology which selects from the total field of psychology those facts and principles that have a direct bearing upon the growth, learning, and adjustment processes. Educational psychology draws heavily from such areas as developmental psychology, the psychology of learning, clinical psychology, abnormal psychology, and social psychology. While employing findings and relevant research from these areas, it does not confine itself to them. Educational psychologists have done research in the teaching of reading, spelling, arithmetic, and other school subjects. They have also developed and evaluated guidance practices and remedial programs and have contributed notably to the better understanding of the atypical child, the social psychology of the classroom, and measurement of the more intangible outcomes of education. Since the turn of the century educational psychology has probably contributed as much to general psychology as it

has had occasion to borrow.[14] Educational psychology also utilizes relevant materials from such fields as anthropology, medicine, psychiatry, biology, and sociology. Thus the teacher who has a good grounding in this field finds a rationale for the problems he faces and for the decisions he must make.

Following is a sample of some specific problems teachers face. The statements are in the teachers' own words.

1. What textbook to select in my elementary social studies work
2. What to say to a student kept after class for a misbehavior
3. How to handle a freshman who left my class without permission
4. What to do about a junior boy in study hall obviously copying his English
5. Deciding what method to use in reteaching a group which failed an important grammar test
6. Deciding whether or not to talk over a health problem of one student with her parents
7. Whether to remove a hyperactive student from the class group
8. Deciding whether or not to allow sophomores to register for beginning typewriting
9. Whether to give children extra help in phonetics or in other forms of word attack
10. How to set up an accelerated course of study in biology for advanced classes
11. How to assign work (and what work) to a student with a great emotional problem (student had attempted suicide last semester)
12. Selection of appropriate teaching aids
13. Whether to start 6th-grade pupils on term papers and what length they should be
14. Whether to divide children into two classes on the basis of IQ scores
15. Whether or not to promote a child whose reading and arithmetic competence was very low
16. How much time to spend on making assignments and how specific should I be
17. Whether to let the class have a hand in determining the methods of discipline to be used

Three short case studies may serve to illustrate further some of the types of problems that continually face teachers. In the instances de-

---

[14] Glenn M. Blair, *Educational Psychology, Its Development and Present Status,* Urbana, Bureau of Research and Service, College of Education, University of Illinois, 1948, p. 13.

scribed here, the teachers were poorly trained and hence unable satisfactorily to solve the problems.

### GEORGE—A POTENTIAL DELINQUENT

George is an attractive looking eleven-year-old boy who spends most of his time annoying the teacher or the other pupils in his sixth-grade class. He jiggles the desks, talks out loud, and throws objects around the room. On the school grounds, he pushes little children and throws dirt on their clean clothing. He occasionally breaks windows by throwing rocks. Frequently he brings to his teacher flowers which he has stolen from neighboring yards. George comes from a poor home. He is neglected by his parents. Seldom does he have adequate clothes or food. Although he has an IQ of 110, he is reported to be failing in his school subjects. Recently he has been accused of damaging street lights and of stealing articles from other children's lockers. His teacher and principal are considering the possibility of sending him to a reform school. His teacher has never understood what makes George misbehave. She has sent him to the principal to be punished, has asked him to apologize to the class, and has kept him after school, but none of these methods has been effective.

### LUELLA—A SOCIAL ISOLATE

Luella is a nine-year-old girl in the fourth grade who never causes her teacher any trouble. Although her IQ is 139, her school grades are only slightly above average. When the teacher asks questions, she hides her head behind the pupil in front of her to avoid being called upon. She daydreams much of the time, and blushes when she speaks. The slightest criticism brings her to the verge of tears. Luella has no friends and does not play with other children during recess or after school. Her chief form of recreation consists of helping her mother develop a stamp collection. Because her school work is satisfactory, and because she is a "good" girl, her teacher gives her no special thought or attention. Luella, however, is developing in a most unwholesome manner. Every day she is becoming more fearful, shy, and unsocial.

### HAROLD—A RETARDED READER

Harold is a high school sophomore who has serious difficulty in reading. His English teacher was amazed when she discovered that he was unable to answer the simplest questions covering the content of *Silas Marner*. When the class moved on to a consideration of *Julius Caesar*, Harold again showed a complete inability to comprehend what he was reading. Not knowing what to do the teacher took Harold to the principal. She received no help from him other than a suggestion that she consult a Miss X in the neighboring school who was reported to have worked with such cases. After some difficulty, arrangements were made for this teacher to come to Harold's school to study him and to make recommendations.

Each of the above illustrations poses problems requiring decisions. These decisions can be made emotionally, with insufficient data, and in accord with the personal bias resulting from the teacher's own experience as a pupil, or they can be made rationally with a proper weighing of relevant

variables and related experimental evidence. A course in educational psychology will not guarantee a thoughtful approach to such problems, but it can provide many of the tools that will make such an approach possible.

## EDUCATIONAL PSYCHOLOGY AND
## THE AIMS OF THE SCHOOL

In at least three ways educational psychology helps the teacher and school better handle the objectives provided by educational philosophy and society.

1. It helps define these objectives operationally, i.e., to translate them into terms of implied action and measurement. Take the objectives of school as they have been stated. One group, the Midcentury Committee on Outcomes in Elementary Education,[15] listed nine areas of instruction which schools should endeavor to improve. These include such aspects of development as health, emotional and social adjustment, knowledge of the physical world, and quantitative relationships. Such terms are so general that without further clarification they may be of little value. But objectives like these come to life and can be implemented when stated in such behavioral terms as: (1) can identify and name the foods that contain each of the important vitamins and minerals, (2) can cite examples of the kinds of crystals appearing in various mineral substances, and can perform experiments necessary to produce crystals. One promising approach to the clarification of objectives in operational terms is that of Bloom and others whose *Taxonomy of Educational Objectives* [16] illustrates how the educational psychologist may contribute to the more careful and understandable statement of the aims of schooling. This topic will be discussed further in Chapters 9 and 17.

2. It provides experimental methods and evidence yielded therefrom as to how objectives may be achieved. Using objectives from secondary education [17] one finds items such as the cultivation of useful work habits and study skills, and the acquisition of important information. Illustrative of how educational psychologists have made possible the better implementation of such objectives is the work of Professor F. P. Robinson, whose study habits laboratory developed a method of study (Survey, Question, Read, Recite, Review), that has aided young people and adults to im-

---

[15] Nolan C. Kearney, *Elementary School Objectives*, New York, Russell Sage Foundation, 1953.

[16] Benjamin S. Bloom (Editor), *Taxonomy of Educational Objectives, The Classification of Educational Goals, Handbook I, Cognitive Domain*, New York, Longmans, Green and Co., 1956.

[17] Eugene R. Smith and Ralph W. Tyler, *Appraising and Recording Student Progress*, New York, Harper and Brothers, 1942, p. 18.

prove their work and study habits, their reading comprehension, and incidentally their school grades.[18]

3. It gives various means whereby the attainment of aims can be measured. By increasing the skill of the teacher in the construction of better evaluative instruments and by providing the school with carefully constructed standardized tests, educational psychology has provided better means of judging student progress and diagnosing students' difficulties.

## MAKING EDUCATIONAL PSYCHOLOGY FUNCTIONAL

Traditional textbooks and courses in educational psychology have frequently failed to make the contribution they should to teacher education. Teachers have been known to have taken one or more courses in the field of educational psychology and yet have been unable to apply effectively the knowledge gained to their teaching. Too often they have seen but slight connection between what is discussed in the textbook or in the educational psychology course and what goes on in the classrooms where they work. To them educational psychology has appeared to be just another academic subject whose facts must be learned for test purposes and then just as quickly forgotten. There are probably several reasons for this. In the first place, the topics chosen for treatment in some textbooks in educational psychology have been only remotely related to the actual on-the-job behavior of teaching. Certain fairly recent books, for example, discuss at length such topics as microscopic features of the nervous system, visceral processes, the synapse theory of learning, the neural basis of imagination, the Muller-Lyer Illusion, and the ergograph test. In these books, actual children or teaching situations seldom if ever make their appearance. For the course in educational psychology to function in the work of the teacher, only that content should be selected and emphasized which has maximal educational applicability.

Another reason why courses in educational psychology may fail to influence greatly the behavior of teachers is that principles and theories are often learned apart from their application. *Individuals learn to do what they do.*[19] If teachers or prospective teachers commit to memory facts and principles of educational psychology, they should be able to repeat them verbally at some later date provided forgetting does not set in too rapidly. However, a teacher's ability to recite psychological facts or principles gives

---

[18] Francis P. Robinson, *Effective Study*, Revised Edition, New York, Harper and Brothers, 1960.

[19] For a thorough elaboration of this principle see E. R. Guthrie, *The Psychology of Learning*, Revised Edition, New York, Harper and Brothers, 1952.

no assurance that he will be able to utilize them when educational problems are encountered in the schoolroom. If the educational psychology course is to have important and lasting effects upon teaching procedures and techniques, it will have to tie up theory and practice in a very definite way. Specific educational implications of psychological facts and principles should be pointed out both in the text and in class discussions. Students should be given abundant opportunity to study, from a psychological viewpoint, typical educational problems. The educational psychology class itself may be studied. Public school classrooms may be visited and the activities evaluated in terms of sound principles of educational psychology. Whenever possible, observation and study of individual children should be undertaken by members of the class.

The teacher who would successfully guide the development, learning, and adjustment of children must (1) possess a comprehensive and integrated set of psychological principles which explain human behavior, (2) possess a technique for studying the individual child in order to determine which principles explain his behavior in a given situation, and (3) be able to analyze his own teaching and learning procedures. The teacher who knows psychological principles, but who does not know the particular facts regarding a given child will be ineffective in his work. Equally ineffective will be the teacher who knows numerous facts about an individual child, but who does not possess a well-formulated set of principles to explain behavior. The teacher's position is similar to that of the medical practitioner who must first study his patient before prescribing for him. The teacher who knows his pupils, knows psychological principles, but does not know how to diagnose and improve his own behavior and his relationship with his pupils will also be ineffective. In short, if educational psychology is to function in the work of the teacher, it will have to assist him to develop competence in studying children, in utilizing psychological principles, and in evaluating his own teaching methods.

## ORGANIZATION AND PLAN OF THE BOOK

The book contains six units or parts as follows: Part I, Introduction; Part II, Growth and Development; Part III, Learning; Part IV, Adjustment and Mental Hygiene; Part V, Measurement and Evaluation; and Part VI, The Psychology of the Teacher. In Parts II, III, and IV, the basic facts and principles of child and adolescent growth, learning, and adjustment are presented together with applications to school practice and problems for psychological study. Part V is devoted to a study of instruments, methods, and procedures teachers may use in evaluating the results of the educational programs with which they are concerned. The purpose of Part VI is to acquaint the student with professional and

personal problems of a psychological nature which teachers face in the course of their work. This section is designed to help teachers understand themselves and the teaching-learning situations of which they are or will be a part.

### References for Further Study

Anderson, Richard C., "Educational Psychology," in *Annual Review of Psychology*, Palo Alto, California, Vol. 18, 1967, pp. 103–164.

Blom, Gaston E., "Psychoeducational Aspects of Classroom Management," *Exceptional Children*, Vol. 32, February, 1966, pp. 377–383.

Bloom, Benjamin S., Davis, Allison, and Hess, Robert, *Compensatory Education for Cultural Deprivation*, New York, Holt, Rinehart, and Winston, 1965.

Bowers, Norman D., "Psychological Forces Influencing Curriculum Decisions," *Review of Educational Research*, Vol. 33, June, 1963, pp. 268–277.

*Education for Socially Disadvantaged Children*, Review of Educational Research, American Educational Research Association, Vol. 35, No. 5, December, 1965.

Gage, Nathaniel L. (Editor), *Handbook of Research on Teaching*, Chicago, Rand McNally and Company, 1963.

Hendrickson, Gordon, and Blair, Glenn M., "Educational Psychology" in Monroe, W. S. (Editor), *Encyclopedia of Educational Research*, Revised Edition, New York, The Macmillan Company, 1950, pp. 346–352.

Hershey, Gerald L., Shepard, Loraine V., and Krumboltz, John D., "Effectiveness of Classroom Observation and Simulated Teaching in an Introductory Educational Psychology Course," *Journal of Educational Research*, Vol. 58, January, 1965, pp. 233–236.

Jones, R. Stewart (Chairman), *A Handbook for Instructors of Educational Psychology*, Urbana, Illinois, College of Education, University of Illinois, 1965.

Justman, Joseph, "Responsibilities of the Educational Psychologist for Teacher Training," *Peabody Journal of Education*, Vol. 44, November, 1966, pp. 160–164.

Kvaraceus, William C., Gibson, John S., and Curtin, Thomas J. (Editors), *Poverty, Education, and Race Relations*, Boston, Allyn and Bacon, Inc., 1967.

Miller, Harry L. (Editor), *Education for the Disadvantaged*, New York, The Free Press, 1967.

Miller, Harry L., and Smiley, Marjorie B. (Editors), *Education in the Metropolis*, New York, The Free Press, 1967.

Roberts, Joan I., *School Children in the Urban Slum*, New York, The Free Press, 1967.

Seagoe, May V., "Educational Psychology," in *Encyclopedia of Educational Research*, Third Edition, New York, The Macmillan Company, 1960, pp. 403–407.

Shoben, Edward J., Jr., "Psychology in the Training of Teachers," *Teachers College Record*, Vol. 65, February, 1964, pp. 436–440.

Symonds, Percival M., *What Education Has to Learn from Psychology*, New York, Bureau of Publications, Teachers College, Columbia University, 1958.

Tyler, Ralph W., "The Behavioral Sciences and the Schools," in *65th Yearbook of the National Society for the Study of Education*, Part II, 1966, pp. 200–214.

Watson, Goodwin, "What Psychology Can We Feel Sure About?" *Teachers College Record*, Vol. 61, February, 1960, pp. 253–257.

Wiseman, Stephen, "Trends in Educational Psychology," *British Journal of Educational Psychology*, Vol. 29, June, 1959, pp. 128–135.

Witty, Paul A. (Editor), *The Educationally Retarded and Disadvantaged*, The Sixty-sixth Yearbook of the National Society for the Study of Education, Part I. Chicago, The University of Chicago Press, 1967.

## Questions, Exercises, and Activities

1. What are your views regarding compulsory education? Should pupils be required to attend school until they are 16 years of age or 18, or what age? Should every one receive a college education? Defend your answers.

2. What in your opinion are the chief causes of school drop outs? Suggest changes in our schools or society which would help solve this problem.

3. Write an analysis of our schools today. Include a statement of their good points and also their less favorable ones. You may wish to consider such things as subjects taught, methods of teaching, and school organization.

4. Select one of the cases described in this chapter—George, Luella, or Harold—and indicate what procedures you would consider following in dealing with the situation.

5. What is the chief distinction between educational psychology and general psychology? Is it proper to state that educational psychology applies the findings of general psychology to school problems? Explain.

6. Do you believe that teachers "are born and not made"? Discuss this issue and support your position with whatever evidence you have.

7. Do you know of any facts or principles from the areas of sociology or anthropology that may be of value to a classroom teacher? List as many as you can.

8. How do you think an educational psychology class should be taught in order for the material to have greatest applicability to actual teaching?

9. Suggest several reasons why we are failing to develop a sufficient number of skilled workers and professional people at the present time.

10. In any one of your present college classes select one class period and make an appraisal of the instructor's method. What decisions has he made regarding his method of operation? Why do you think he made those decisions?

11. How do the functions of educational psychologists and educational philosophers differ with respect to what should be the nature of the curriculum?

# PART TWO

## Growth and
## Development

# Chapter 2

# The Biological
# and Social Bases
# of Behavior

An individual at any stage of his development is the product of organic and environmental factors working hand in hand. What he is, what he does, what he becomes, in short, how he reacts and behaves in all life situations, can be explained in terms of these two interacting forces. The teacher should understand the nature and mechanisms of these two bases of behavior in order properly to diagnose and guide the growth and development of children. For example, a child may misbehave in school because of an abnormal glandular condition or he may misbehave because he comes from a home where good manners are not stressed. A child may fail to learn because of a vitamin deficiency or because he is not sufficiently motivated.

The behavior of a human being is obviously, to a large extent, dependent upon his biological inheritance.[1] Children, for example, can perform many acts which are impossible for lower animals to perform just because they have the organic equipment of human beings. Man's large and complex cerebrum makes possible the use of abstraction and enables him to develop symbolization and language.

On the other hand it is equally clear that there could be no develop-

---

[1] George W. Beadle, "Genes, Culture, and Man," *The Columbia University Forum*, Vol. 8, No. 3, Fall 1965, pp. 12–16.

ment whatsoever without environmental stimulation. No organism could live or grow in a vacuum. A basic property of protoplasm (living substance) is irritability. Without stimulation no modification or differentiation of protoplasm would be possible. Changes in both structure and function of the body are dependent upon physical and chemical changes within its protoplasm.

A few of the differences which exist between human beings and some of the lower animals may even be traceable to environmental differences. For example, apes when reared in the same environment with children learn to play ball and tag, and to work with the form board and to scribble. Home-raised chimpanzees have learned to say "mama" and to use in a meaningful manner the words "papa" and "cup." Certainly many of the differences which exist between human beings of a given chronological age can be attributed to differences in environmental conditions. Persons of similar heredity reared in different environments clearly grow differently and behave differently. The aboriginal who is reared in the United States becomes civilized and takes on forms of behavior which are unknown to his brother who remains in the primitive society. City children play games which differ from those of country children. People in different geographical locations possess distinctive language accents. Children from different social classes learn different forms of behavior with regard to family relationships, sex, aggression, and work, and acquire different codes of right and wrong.

Although it is probably impossible to attribute any specific act or form of behavior entirely to either organic or environmental causes, it is possible to discuss each separately and to note the important role each plays in the growth of behavior.

## PHYSIOLOGICAL FACTORS

### The Mechanism of Heredity

Each child begins life as a one-celled organism known as a *zygote*. This first speck of life which is about $\frac{1}{125}$ of an inch in diameter is formed from the union of a *sperm* from the father and an *ovum* from the mother. In this fertilized cell there are twenty-three pairs of *chromosomes*, half of which have been contributed by the father and half by the mother. Each chromosome consists of a string of tiny particles arranged in linear fashion known as *genes*. These genes appear to be the ultimate bearers of heredity. The zygote or fertilized ovum contains all the hereditary potentialities the individual will ever realize.

There is considerable evidence that physical traits such as eye color, skin color, blood types, color blindness, and tendencies to be tall, short, heavy, or light follow the laws of heredity. It is not known to what extent

mental traits are inherited. A discussion of the factors related to mental growth and development will be found in later sections of this chapter.

### The Human Organism

The one-celled organism or zygote, described in the previous paragraph, grows by a process of cell division and specialization, and in time (approximately 280 days) reaches a stage of growth which makes it unnecessary to remain *in utero*. It emerges into the outside world and is known as a *neonate* or new-born child. This human organism is equipped with receptor organs (such as those for seeing, hearing, smelling, tasting, and feeling), effector organs for making movements (muscles and glands), and an integrating system (the nervous system). Without this equipment it would obviously be impossible for the child to grow or to develop new forms of behavior.

### Physical Needs of the Child

The individual at birth, and at later stages of development, possesses a wide variety of physical needs or drives which demand satisfaction. These bodily, or tissue needs create a state of restlessness or tension in the organism which is only reduced when the appropriate goal [2] or satisfier is reached. The physical needs or drives of the individual serve as potent motivators of behavior. A child whose basic physical needs are severely frustrated will not develop or behave normally. Frequently such children become problems in school. Among the major physical needs of the child which teachers and parents should keep in mind are the following:

*The need for food, air, liquid.* The hungry or malnourished child is frequently restless, irritable, and inattentive. Mid-morning lunches and feedings in schools have been known greatly to reduce the amount of nervousness and restlessness in school children. The child who is denied adequate amounts of fresh air or liquid is also tense and unadjusted and hence unable to carry forward his schoolwork in an effective manner.

*The need for proper temperature.* A schoolroom which is too hot or too cold creates a condition which interferes with the well-being of the child and makes effective study well nigh impossible. The human organism strives to preserve its body temperature from threatened change. Cannon introduced the word "homeostasis" to apply to those constant states which the organism seeks to maintain.[3] The individual becomes ill or dies when his blood temperature varies a few degrees above or below 98.6°F.

*The need for activity and rest.* A rhythm of activity and rest seems to be a biological essential in the development of the child. The young child who is forced to remain inactive very long becomes bored, unhappy, and frequently unruly. On the other hand, too extended periods of activity are

---

[2] The term *goal* as used here refers to any object or condition which satisfies a need.

[3] W. B. Cannon, *The Wisdom of the Body*, New York, W. W. Norton & Co., Inc., 1932.

detrimental to the child's physical and emotional well-being. The tired or overfatigued child is often cranky, stubborn, irritable, and in no condition to profit from learning experiences.

*The need for elimination.* Regular and adequate elimination of the waste products of the body is an important biological need. Children who have irregular habits in this matter and who suffer from constipation are often irritable, physically ill, and unsuccessful with their school work. There are school teachers who will not permit children to leave the room to take care of this physical need regardless of the urgency. Other teachers are known to the writer who permit pupils to leave the classroom in case of necessity, but who require everyone who does so to stay fifteen minutes after school as a punishment. Needless to say, such lack of insight on the part of teachers with respect to this basic need may cause both physical and mental harm to children under their control.

*The sex drive.* The psychologist Freud and others of the psychoanalytic school have held that frustration of this basic need is a chief cause of personality maladjustments and nervous disorders.[4] This contention contains much truth, since we know that the frustration of any basic need may lead to maladjustment. Small children are curious about sex and should receive straightforward and accurate information from teachers and parents. Appropriate sex instruction should also be given to older children who are at more advanced stages of sexual development. In our society, as in most others, numerous conventions and taboos are enforced with regard to expression of the sex drive. It is, therefore, necessary for most young people of adolescent age to "sublimate" or develop substitute outlets for this energy until such a time as marriage is possible. School activities such as sports, parties, dances, and plays provide wholesome outlets of importance.

### What About Instincts?

At one time it was a very common practice of psychologists and educators to explain much human behavior in terms of "instincts." Instincts were thought of as inborn tendencies to respond in certain definite and somewhat complicated ways without previous experience or training. James,[5] one of America's first great psychologists, listed twenty-eight human instincts with nine subordinate varieties. McDougall[6] recognized seven principal instincts in man: the instinct of flight, the instinct of repulsion, the instinct of curiosity, the instinct of pugnacity, the instinct of self-abasement, the instinct of self-assertion, and the parental instinct. Thorndike in 1913[7] enumerated forty or more different types of instinctive reactions of which the following are samples: hunting, collecting and

[4] Sigmund Freud, *New Introductory Lectures on Psychoanalysis*, New York, W. W. Norton & Co., Inc., 1933.

[5] William James, *Principles of Psychology*, Vol. II, New York, Henry Holt and Company, 1890, p. 440.

[6] William McDougall, *Introduction to Social Psychology*, Boston, John W. Luce Company, 1923, Chap. 3.

[7] Edward L. Thorndike, *Educational Psychology*, Vol. I, *The Original Nature of Man*, New York, Teachers College, Columbia University, 1913.

hoarding, fighting, motherly behavior, gregariousness, rivalry, cooperation, greed, ownership, kindliness, teasing, imitation, cleanliness, and play.

Research on infant behavior and on children in nursery schools seems to point to the conclusion that human instincts are either relatively few or do not exist at all in any pure and unmodified form. Watson, the behaviorist, was one of the first of modern-day psychologists to question the existence of elaborate and numerous instincts in man. He says,

> Everything we have been in the habit of calling "instinct" today is a result largely of training—belonging to man's *learned behavior*. As a corollary from this, I wish to draw the conclusion that there is no such thing as the inheritance of *capacity, talent, temperament, mental constitution and characteristics*. These things again depend on training that goes on mainly in the cradle. The behaviorist would *not* say, "He inherits his father's capacity or talent for being a fine swordsman." He would say: "This child certainly has his father's slender build of body, the same type of eyes. His build is wonderfully like his father's. He too has the build of a fine swordsman." And he would go on to say: "—and his father is very fond of him. He put a tiny sword into his hand when he was a year of age, and in all their walks he talks sword play, attack and defense, the code of dueling and the like." A certain type of structure, plus early training—slanting—accounts for adult performance. . . .
>
> So let us hasten to admit—yes, there are heritable differences in form, in structure. . . . These differences are in the germ plasm and are handed down from parent to child. . . . But do not let these undoubted facts of inheritance lead you astray. . . . The mere presence of these structures tells you not one thing about function. . . . Much of our structure laid down in heredity would never come to light, would never show in function, unless the organism were put in a certain environment, subjected to certain stimuli and forced to undergo training.[8]

Too often in the past the term "instinct" was used as a cover up for ignorance as to the precise cause of some specific behavior pattern. If a child or group of children were observed to perform some act for which a scientific explanation was unavailable, the behavior was apt to be labeled instinctive. The same general practice prevailed in the past in the field of animal study. Cats were supposed to have a rat killing instinct because they were observed to have killed rats. Birds were said to have a migratory instinct because it was known that they flew away at certain seasons of the year. Young salmon were supposed to possess some mysterious instinct or "ancestral memory of the sea" which caused them in their second year of life to leave the headwaters of inland streams and to journey downstream to the ocean depths from which their parents came.

As the result of carefully controlled experimentation, it is now believed

---

[8] John B. Watson, "What the Nursery Has to Say About Instincts," *Journal of Genetic Psychology*, Vol. 32, June, 1925, pp. 293–327.

that rat killing behavior on the part of cats is an acquired response. Kittens who are brought up with rats and who have never seen their mothers kill rats learn to "love" them and to play with them, and do them no bodily harm. On the other hand, kittens who have been raised in a more traditional environment in which they have observed their mothers killing rats almost always develop into rat killers.

Controlled experimentation with birds has shown that migration either in a northerly or southerly direction is caused by endocrine changes which are controlled by the amount of daily illumination which acts upon the birds.

In the case of young salmon, it is now known that a loss of skin pigmentation, which occurs as the result of normal growth, is the cause for their downstream migration. The disappearance of the pigment makes their skin extremely sensitive to light. In the shallow waters of the inland streams, the illumination from the sun becomes so irritating that the salmon seek relief in deeper pools or are rendered inert and carried by the current tail first downstream. Over a period of time they reach the sea where they spend the next three or four years of their life.

The word instinct, at least as it applies to human beings, has become so misused and has carried so many unscientific connotations that it has been almost entirely dropped by psychologists. Instead of labeling certain forms of behavior "instinctive," and closing the matter at that point, there is an increasing tendency to try to discover what environmental or biological conditions produce the activity in question.

The child seems to begin life with a few basic physical needs or drives as have been mentioned earlier, and a few somewhat undifferentiated and not too specific reflexes (sucking, swallowing, etc.). He is also equipped with receptor organs (sense organs), effector organs (muscles and glands), and a nervous system. From this simple beginning more complex behavior is developed as the result of the child's interaction with his environment. This further growth and development involve changes due both to maturation and learning.

### The Effect of the Glands upon Behavior

There are two types of glands—the duct glands and the ductless (endocrine) glands. The duct glands or glands of external secretion, as they are sometimes called, convey their secretions through tubes (ducts) to some opening on the surface of the body or the mucous lining. Among the more important duct glands are the following: salivary glands, gastric glands, liver (in part), pancreas, kidneys, sweat glands, sebaceous glands, tear glands, and sex glands. The salivary and gastric glands and the liver and pancreas serve primarily in the digestion of food. The kidneys serve an important excretory function; the sweat glands and sebaceous (oily) glands also excrete waste products from the body, and in addition condition the

skin, and help regulate the body temperature. The tear glands lubricate the eyes, and the sex glands serve in reproduction.

The ductless or endocrine glands (glands of internal secretion) are the ones about which so much has been written for popular consumption and which seem to be so strikingly connected with normality and abnormality of behavior. The endocrine glands have no special ducts or outlets, but instead secrete their products directly into the blood stream, which carries them to all the tissues of the body. The products of the endocrines are powerful drug-like substances known as *hormones*. The chief endocrine glands are the thyroid, pituitary, parathyroid, adrenal, sex (in part), pineal, thymus, pancreas (in part), and the liver (in part). In Figure 1 the location of these glands is shown.

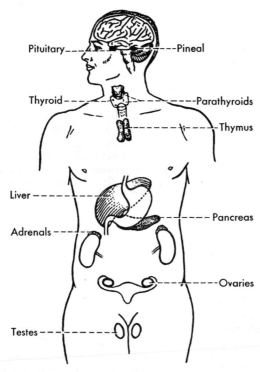

**Figure 1.** Locations of the Principal Endocrine Glands.

THE THYROID GLAND. Of the endocrine glands, probably more is definitely known about the thyroid gland and its effects upon behavior than is known about any of the others. This gland, which is about the size of a walnut, consists of two lobes which are situated in the neck on either side

of the windpipe. The functioning of the thyroid gland has marked effects upon the growth of intelligence, on the rate of metabolism, and on behavior in general. If this gland is defective at birth or wastes away while the child is very young, a condition known as *cretinism* results. The cretin is stunted in height, exhibits feeblemindedness at the imbecile or idiot levels, possesses little emotional color, and is incapable of taking care of himself. Underfunctioning of the thyroid gland in school children and adults tends to produce, among other things, lethargy, diminished metabolism, and overweight. A striking case of a fifteen-year-old boy whose thyroid gland was not functioning properly is reported by Lawrence, a Boston physician.[9] This boy, who had previously done excellent work in school, all of a sudden began to fail miserably. His teachers reported that he had lost interest in his studies, and was very uncooperative. As a result, the principal recommended that he be dropped from school. At this point the parents brought the boy to see Dr. Lawrence who comments as follows on the case:

> We went to work and we found that for some reason Johnny's thyroid had left him flat. His basal metabolism, which is one of the important measurements of thyroid function, was about 35 per cent below the normal range. He had a very slow pulse. He had a low blood pressure. He was gaining weight. What had happened to Johnny was this: because of a thyroid gland disturbance he was not burning his fuel to give him energy to study and to understand. He was laying it all away in the form of weight.
>
> I called up the principal of the school, and told him the story, and said, "I wish you would agree to take Johnny in next fall, and just to make this a sporting event, I will bet you he passes his courses all the year long." The principal, who was a friend of mine said, "If you have got something you think you can do, we will give him a try."

The boy went to the school, and under thyroid medication took honors in every subject.

Mateer describes a six-year-old child whose behavior was also adversely affected by lowered thyroid activity. She says,

> This child, reared with the assistance of a pediatrician, properly handled by intelligent parents, and given an excellent environment, had been under preschool and kindergarten training for two years with no perceptible gain in self-reliance, initiative, or even normal social responses. Careful scrutiny of every phase of her life revealed only minute deviations of a physical nature that might be due to lowered thyroid activity. The personality traits, however, confirmed the possibility of subnormal glandular functioning. Entrance into first-grade work brought no better response, and after one month in that work a very small daily dose of thyroid extract was started. In three weeks the child was taking a normal and very active part in all group activities, and

[9] Charles H. Lawrence, M.D., "The Endocrine Factor in Personality Development," *The Educational Record*, Vol. 23, Supplement No. 15, January, 1942, pp. 88–89.

within the next month she had asserted herself to the point of exercising leadership which was readily accepted by her group.[10]

In the two cases just described marked improvement in behavior was noted as the result of feeding the individuals thyroid tissues or extracts. Many individuals suffering from a shortage of thyroxine, including cretins, have been brought up to normal or near normal as a consequence of such treatment. The feedings, however, must usually be continued in order for the individual to maintain the gains he has made.

Overdevelopment or hyperfunctioning of the thyroid gland creates a condition of increased nervous tension, accelerated pulse, loss of body weight, and increased oxygen consumption. In short, the body tissues are overstimulated throughout. The results in the life processes are comparable with those of opening the draughts of a furnace. The basal metabolic rate that mirrors this forced draught may be doubled.

A good example of a case of hyperthyroid activity is that of Alice, a fifth-grade child in the Winnetka schools. She bothered children around her by continually whispering; she talked out loud when the class was supposed to be quiet; she interrupted; she was constantly out of her seat wandering around the room to sharpen her pencil needlessly, to drop a piece of paper in the wastebasket, or perhaps without any reason whatever. The teacher worked for months trying to get Alice to be still and to "behave herself," but she was unsuccessful. Treatment of her thyroid gland by a physician and the teacher's improved methods of dealing with her in school, which were suggested by the physician, however, brought marked changes in Alice's behavior. By the end of the school year she had ceased to be a problem child.

In treating hyperthyroidism it is necessary to decrease the amount of glandular secretion that is pouring into the blood stream. The usual method is to remove part of the thyroid gland by a surgical operation, although some practitioners destroy a portion of the gland by means of X-ray or radium treatments.

THE PITUITARY GLAND. Malfunctioning of the pituitary gland in a child frequently creates conditions which may have important effects upon his personality and behavior. This gland, which is about the size of a large pea, is located in a small pocket near the center of the head. Underfunctioning of the gland leaves the child short, and physically and sexually underdeveloped. Pituitary deficiency also plays a more or less definite part in the production of "Frohlich's disease." Individuals suffering from this disorder are extremely fat. Overfunctioning of the gland may result in *gigantism* and precocious sexual maturity.

---

[10] Florence Mateer, "The Correction of Special Difficulties through Glandular Therapy," *The National Elementary Principal*, Vol. 15, No. 6, Fifteenth Yearbook, pp. 543–544.

It is well known that marked physical deviations of the type just mentioned greatly affect the personal-social adjustment of children. Stolz and Stolz report that lack of size, excessive height or weight, and other physical deviations greatly disturb adolescent boys and girls.[11] The same holds true with respect to elementary school pupils. Pressey's statement [12] that "anomalies of physical development explain many a 'problem child' " is a most apt and accurate observation. There is evidence that the course of physical growth and development may be altered, and that personality changes may be brought about as the result of medical treatment involving the pituitary gland.

THE PARATHYROID GLANDS. These small glands are located upon the thyroid gland, but have no known connection with the thyroid's activity. Removal of the parathyroid glands or marked deficiency in their function causes cramps and convulsions (tetany) which may result in the death of the individual. Less marked deficiency of function produces hyperexcitability, lack of agreeableness, mental depression, and numerous other disorders. In treating a parathyroid deficiency a solution of calcium salt is usually injected into the subject's muscles or veins. Also used are parathyroid extracts and foods containing high calcium content.

THE ADRENAL GLANDS. The paired adrenal glands are small yellowish bodies located at the top or "pole" of each kidney. Each gland consists of two parts—a central portion known as the *medulla* and a surrounding portion known as the *cortex*.

The effects of adrenal cortical deficiency are many. These include fatigue, lethargy, weak heart action, low blood pressure, and general interference with the growth process. Overactivity of the adrenal cortex or the existence of tumors on the gland may create a condition known as *adrenal virilism*. This disorder is characterized by precocious growth and sexual maturity. Girls suffering from this disorder may develop excessive facial hair, a deep voice, and other masculine characteristics. Abnormalities resulting from the dysfunction of the adrenal cortex can be treated and ameliorated by means of medication or surgery.

The *medulla* secretes a substance known as "adrenin" or "epinephrin." This substance acts upon the tissues of the body in such a way as to prepare a person to meet emergency conditions. The proper functioning of the medulla is thus of the greatest importance for the individual's survival and for his adjustment to an ever changing and sometimes hostile environment.

---

[11] Herbert R. Stolz, M.D. and Lois Meek Stolz, "Adolescent Problems Related to Somatic Variations," Forty-Third Yearbook of the National Society for the Study of Education, Part I, *Adolescence*, Chicago, The Department of Education, University of Chicago, 1944, pp. 80–99.
[12] Sidney L. Pressey, Francis P. Robinson, and John E. Horrocks, *Psychology in Education*, New York, Harper and Brothers, 1959, p. 9.

THE SEX GLANDS or GONADS. The *sex glands* serve both as organs of internal secretion (ductless) and external secretion (duct). As duct glands their function is reproduction. As ductless glands they play an important role in the development of personality and behavior. The male glands are known as *testes* and the female glands as *ovaries*. Inadequate functioning of these glands in either boys or girls may make normal development of the secondary sexual characteristics impossible. Children, especially of adolescent age, are extremely sensitive to differences which exist between them and their peers. Either precocious sexual development or greatly retarded development is a source of great concern and anxiety to them and may have far-reaching effects upon their adjustment to school and to other life situations.

OTHER ENDOCRINE GLANDS. The functions of the *pineal gland,* which is located at the base of the brain, and the *thymus gland,* which is located in the upper thorax, are at present not well known. It is believed, however, that both produce hormones which help to regulate the rate of bodily growth and the onset of puberty. The *pancreas* have small parts located in them known as the *Islands of Langerhans* which secrete *insulin.* Underfunctioning of these glands causes *diabetes.* The liver also possesses endocrine functions which are of great value in supplying energy to working muscles.

In this discussion the different endocrine glands have been listed one by one, and some of their chief functions have been pointed out. It must not be inferred from this, however, that they work independently of one another. Many bodily conditions are created by the joint actions of several of them. For example, the secretions of the thyroid, pituitary, pineal, and sex glands all seem to contribute definitely to the control of growth. Extreme obesity may result from dysfunction of one of several glands, or it may be caused by the interaction of two or more glands. Similarly, sex development seems to be influenced in part not only by the gonads, but also by the action of the pituitary, pineal, thymus, adrenal, and thyroid glands.

The evidence is clear, however, that the glands do produce marked effects upon the physique and behavior of individuals. Teachers should be on the alert for physical or mental signs of glandular disorders in pupils. Any pupil who is a scholastic or behavior problem in school should, when possible, be given a thorough physical examination which includes an endocrine diagnosis. This examination, of course, must be conducted under the personal direction of a medical expert.

### Physical and Sensory Defects

The effects of malfunctioning glands upon behavior have just been mentioned. There are many other physical defects or disorders which greatly influence the learning and adjustment of school children. Among

these are the following: poor eyesight, defective hearing, diseased tonsils and adenoids, diseased teeth, physical deformities, skin blemishes, defective speech organs, malnutrition, and encephalitis. The child who possesses some physical defect or disease frequently is as much affected by the psychological consequences of the condition as he is by the physical. A child with a hare lip, for instance, might suffer but little in the way of speech disturbance from the defect, but be greatly tormented by oversensitivity to imagined rejection by his playmates. He might even withdraw from association with other children and fail to learn the social skills necessary for later adjustment.

POOR EYESIGHT. Statistics show that as many as 30 percent of all school children possess some defect of vision. Most of these defects are correctable, but in many school systems only a small percentage of the children who need ocular attention receive it.

> Some time ago the writer was administering a mental test to a group of ninth-grade pupils in an English class in a high school in the West. He noticed that one little girl had apparently fallen asleep because her head seemed to be reclining on her desk. He, therefore, went to the section of the room where she was, with the intention of waking her up. To his surprise he found that she was not asleep but was working intently on her test. She was so near-sighted that it was necessary for her to place her face not more than an inch from the material she was attempting to read. The writer made a mark on her test blank to remind him not to compute an IQ from data gathered under such unfavorable conditions. He also called the teacher's attention to this pupil. The teacher replied that there were undoubtedly many pupils with severe visual defects in the school but that so far as he knew no tests had ever been given, or no effort had ever been made to find out who they were or to do anything about them.

The child whose eyes do not function properly may have difficulty in learning to read, may suffer from headaches, or may in some instances develop unwholesome personality adjustments. Children with crossed eyes or with other forms of vertical or lateral imbalance are often very sensitive about the defect.

DEFECTIVE HEARING. The child with defective hearing may develop undesirable forms of behavior. He may avoid talking to people, be sensitive, aloof, and suspicious. Furthermore, he may have difficulty in acquiring effective speech patterns, and have trouble with reading and spelling, especially when these subjects are taught with an emphasis upon phonics. It has been estimated that about 14 per cent of school children have defective hearing. Thus in any typical classroom there would normally be at least five out of thirty-five pupils with some hearing defect. Such children often are unnoticed and neglected by their teachers because of the inconspicuousness of this defect.

PHYSICAL DEVIATIONS, DEFORMITIES, AND BLEMISHES. In a study by Stolz and Stolz [13] it was found that physical anomalies of various types greatly disturb boys and girls of adolescent age. Boys were chiefly worried and upset by such manifestations as: lack of size (particularly height), fatness, poor physique, lack of muscular strength, unusual facial features, unusual development in the nipple area, acne, skin blemishes, scars, bowed legs, obvious scoliosis,[14] lack of shoulder breadth, unusually small genitalia, and unusually large genitalia. Physical conditions which bothered girls were: tallness, fatness, facial features, general physical appearance, tallness and heaviness, smallness and heaviness, eye glasses and strabismus, thinness and small breasts, late development, acne, facial hair, big legs, one short arm, scar on face, and brace on back.

Just how such physical defects or deviations may affect the behavior and adjustment of children can be seen from the following letters [15] which were sent by boys to a doctor who conducts a section in a boys' magazine dealing with problems of physical development.

> . . . I have been bothered since the last year of high school with pimples and blackheads on my face, and that is what I want to ask you about. I probably could not tell the whole story to a doctor in person even if I had the opportunity, so I am taking this means to put into effect my determination to suffer no longer, but to do something about it. . . .
>
> Time and time again I had thought that I had rid myself of them, only to have another bunch of pimples break out. I know you have read the advertisement of . . . yeast in . . . magazines. Very likely some people laugh at the idea of a boy's complexion keeping him from mixing with people, going places, having a normal life, but everyone of those ads is a reminder of something I have endured. And it's serious; if I thought that I had to live the rest of my years with my trouble, or even many more years, I would rather die today. I'm not afraid of death. I am afraid of life handicapped with pimples. . . .

> I am a boy twelve years of age and am very skinny. I am in the seventh grade. In school when we have gym periods and we get in our gym suits, when they see me with my gym suit on they say, "lookit skinny over there," and I hate them to call me that. So I decided to let the fellow have a sock!
>
> The other fellow grabbed me by the arm and said, "skinny, better take it easy because I might sock you and you'll dry up and blow away."
>
> I want your advice on how to get strong with big muscles, and when I get in my gym suit to look like a second Max Baer. Will you please answer

---

[13] Herbert R. Stolz and Lois Meek Stolz, "Adolescent Problems Related to Somatic Variations," Forty-Third Yearbook of the National Society for the Study of Education, Part I, *Adolescence*, The Department of Education, University of Chicago, 1944, pp. 85–86.

[14] A lateral curvature of the spine.

[15] E. D. Partridge, *Social Psychology of Adolescence*, New York, Prentice-Hall, Inc. These letters are used with the permission of *Boys' Life*, the original publisher.

this letter and tell me how to be strong. . . . I don't want the boys to call me skinny. . . .

I am fifteen and a half years old, weigh 96 pounds, and am only five feet in height. I still talk in a high-pitched, girlish voice. I am several inches shorter than anyone in my class—third year high school.

I have been told that it is just a case of delayed development, but just the same, I am beginning to worry as I show no signs of "sprouting." . . .

Do you think there is anything I can do besides just waiting?

Although the cases which have just been presented show a connection between physical deviations and behavior patterns, it is clear that the social implications of the physical conditions have played a major role in the resultant adjustment of the individuals involved. Pimples in and of themselves, for example, would have little effect upon the behavior of young people if it were not for the attitudes of other individuals toward this condition. In some societies a scarred face is a mark of distinction and is greatly cherished by the possessor.

## ENVIRONMENTAL FACTORS

In previous pages of this chapter, some of the biological and organic factors which influence the growth, development, and behavior of children have been pointed out and discussed. It has constantly been reiterated, however, that there is a continuous reaction between the organism and the environment.[16] The individual makes changes in the environment and the environment in turn produces profound changes in the individual and in his behavior. In some ways, however, it might be said that the environment possesses the "last word." No organism, regardless of its potentialities and basic qualities, can survive in the absence of a favorable environment. Two children of equal constitutional capacities or characteristics may develop in entirely different ways depending upon the nature of the environment in which they are reared. In this connection the sociologist Lynd makes the following comment:

Persons in the great modal mass of our population are endowed with what we call "normal (i.e., most customary degrees of) intelligence." From the moment of birth, the accidents of cultural status—for instance, whether one

---

[16] In this discussion of the effect of environment upon behavior, it is well to remember that environment affects the child as *he* perceives it, not as parents, teachers or others see it. It would not be amiss to say that in a given schoolroom, there is not one environment but forty, and in a given home, not a single set of external circumstances, but as many as there are persons in the family. It is crucial, in attempts to understand children, that teachers find out how the child perceives the situations that surround him. Such a procedure should greatly facilitate the prediction and control of youngsters' behavior. For additional discussion of this point, see Arthur W. Combs and Donald Snygg, *Individual Behavior*, Revised Edition, New York, Harper and Brothers, 1959.

is born "north or south of the tracks"—begin to play up and to play down the potentialities of each person. As life progresses, culture writes cumulating differences recklessly into these individual lives.[17]

Terman's 1528 gifted children did not turn out equally well. Although many of them became successful and distinguished adults, 15 committed suicide, 13 became alcoholics, 6 had encounters with the police or served prison sentences, 28 developed homosexual tendencies, and 271 have been divorced one or more times.[18]

The average teacher probably does not realize the tremendous significance of environmental and cultural factors as they affect the attitudes, adjustments, and behavior of children. In the next few pages a brief résumé will be made of some of these non-biological conditions and the ways they influence behavior and personality of growing individuals.

### Effect of the Environment on Prenatal Development

Actually the environment begins to affect the course of development of the individual as soon as he is conceived. This belief is reinforced by studies from the field of experimental embryology which have clearly shown that by altering the chemical environments of salamanders, squids, and other animals, marked changes in bodily structures can be brought about. In the case of the squid which normally has two eyes, a one-eyed specimen can be obtained by exposing the embryo to a solution of one per cent LiCl in sea water from twelve to forty-eight hours. For obvious reasons no such experiments have been performed with human embryos. Several studies have been made, however, of the effects of external stimulation upon the behavior of the human fetus. In one such study it was shown that it is possible successfully to condition the unborn fetus. It is possible that left-handedness and other human characteristics may be in part due to prenatal conditioning.

### Some Effects of the Environment on Mental Development

An increasing number of investigations have clearly shown the remarkable way that mental growth may be facilitated or retarded by factors present in the environment.[19] Of particular interest are those studies which have been made of children reared in foster homes, isolated and backward communities, and various ethnic groups.

---

[17] Robert S. Lynd, *Knowledge for What?* pp. 229–230. Copyright, 1939, by Princeton University Press, Princeton, New Jersey.

[18] Lewis M. Terman and Melita H. Oden, *The Gifted Group at Mid-Life: Thirty-Five Years' Follow-up of the Superior Child*, Stanford, California, Stanford University Press, 1959.

[19] See Samuel A. Kirk, "Diagnostic, Cultural, and Remedial Factors in Mental Retardation," in *The Biosocial Basis of Mental Retardation* (Edited by S. F. Osler and R. E. Cooke), The Johns Hopkins Press, 1965, pp. 129–145. Also see J. McV. Hunt, *Intelligence and Experience*, The Ronald Press, 1961, pp. 19–34.

STUDIES OF CHILDREN REARED IN FOSTER HOMES. Studies by Skodak,[20] Speer,[21] and others have all shown the beneficial effect upon IQs of children who have been taken from poor homes and placed in superior adoptive homes or boarding houses.

Skodak's investigation was based upon 154 children, 140 of which were illegitimate, and all of whom were placed for adoption under six months of age, the average age being 2.8 months. The average IQs of the true mothers of these children was 88 as revealed by the Stanford-Binet test. The occupational levels of the true fathers were markedly below that found in the general population.

Both true mothers and fathers were found to be on the whole socially inferior, shiftless and irresponsible. The foster homes in which the children were placed were distinctly superior to the average run of homes, and in each case the home was rated as a good place in which to rear a child. Since the children were mere infants (average age, 2.8 months) at the time of adoption, no mental tests had been given them at that time. However, they were tested after they had lived with their foster parents nearly two years, and again after they had lived with them approximately four years. On the first test, when the children were about two years old, the average IQ was found to be 116; on the second test, when the children had reached a mean age of four years and four months, the average IQ was 112. Both of these figures are well above the averages for the general population of children of the same ages. In referring to the Skodak study, George D. Stoddard states: "Children like these, if left in their own homes, would on the average show a mental retardation." [22] Yet, we find these children early reaching a most satisfactory intellectual level.

Speer made a study of 68 dependent children all of whose mothers were definitely feebleminded as judged by mental test results and social criteria. He says: "All but one of the mothers were committed to state institutions for the mentally defective. The mean IQ of the mothers is 49.0, with a range from 38 to 64. The children have been placed in boarding homes [23] selected and supervised by the Children's Service League." [24]

---

[20] Marie Skodak, "Children in Foster Homes: A Study of Mental Development," *University of Iowa Studies of Child Welfare*, Vol. 16, No. 1, 1939, 156 pp.

[21] George S. Speer, "The Mental Development of Children of Feeble-minded and Normal Mothers," Thirty-Ninth Yearbook of the National Society for the Study of Education, Part II, *Intelligence: Its Nature and Nurture*, 1940, pp. 309–314.

[22] George D. Stoddard, *The Meaning of Intelligence*, New York, The Macmillan Company, 1943, pp. 356–357.

[23] Speer says: "The age at which these children have been placed has not been influenced by any factor other than the need for care. When the mother died, deserted, or was declared incompetent, *all* children in the family under sixteen years of age were declared dependent and placed in boarding homes." G. S. Speer, *op. cit.*, p. 311.

[24] *Ibid.*, p. 310.

The Children's Service League is the child caring agency responsible for all dependent children in Sangamon County, Illinois. The fathers of the children are described as being either unemployed or engaged in unskilled labor and as being "irresponsible, alcoholic, epileptic, mentally ill, or venereally diseased."

In analyzing the mental test scores of these 68 children, Speer made the amazing discovery that children who were taken from their feebleminded mothers and impoverished environments very early in life had approximately average intelligence quotients while those children who remained in their own homes with their feebleminded mothers for more extended periods of time were either mentally retarded or feebleminded. The amount of mental retardation was proportional to the number of years spent in the unfavorable environments. The exact figures for the Speer study are given in Table 3. It is seen that the twelve children who were taken from

### TABLE 3
#### Distribution of IQs of 68 Children of
#### Feebleminded Mothers *

| Age at Placement, in Years | Number | Median IQ |
|---|---|---|
| 0 to 2 | 12 | 100.5 |
| 3 to 5 | 19 | 83.7 |
| 6 to 8 | 12 | 74.6 |
| 9 to 11 | 9 | 71.5 |
| 12 to 15 | 16 | 53.1 |

* From Speer.

their own homes before they were three years old had, at the time of the testing, on the average, IQs of 100.5. On the other hand, the sixteen children who remained from 12 to 15 years in their definitely poor environments scored an average IQ of only 53.1 on the tests.

In commenting upon his study, Speer says: "The data presented here do not support the position of agencies in refusing to place for adoption children of mentally deficient mothers. Insofar as the data of the present study are concerned, there is no reason why physically normal children of feebleminded mothers may not be placed for adoption, from their own home, provided this is done before the third birthday." [25]

STUDIES OF CHILDREN REARED IN ISOLATED AND BACKWARD COMMUNITIES. The effect of the environment on the mental development of children is further illustrated by studies which have been made of children who

---

[25] George S. Speer, *op. cit.*, p. 314.

have been born and reared in extremely atypical communities. Two very striking examples of such studies are those conducted by Gordon [26] and by Sherman and Key.[27]

Gordon tested 76 English canal boat children ranging in ages from 4 to 14. For this purpose he used the Stanford-Binet Scale. In describing these unique people he says, "The Canal Boat population, as a rule, is born, lives, and dies on the boats. . . . These people appear to live very isolated lives with very little social intercourse. . . . When the boats remain in a town for loading and unloading, the children do not appear to mix readily with other children." He also states that the children only attend school "about once a month for one to perhaps two and a half days."

The test data secured for these 76 underprivileged children reveal two most interesting facts. In the first place it was found that the entire group was very much retarded as measured by the tests—the average IQ being 69.6. In the second place, it was found that the extent of the dullness was proportional to the age of the child. Younger children who had spent fewer years in this impoverished environment had higher IQs than their older brothers and sisters. The correlation between chronological age and IQ is usually zero, but for the canal boat children it was −.755, meaning that the older the child the lower the IQ. How the IQs of the children dropped with age can be seen from the data presented in Table 4.

### TABLE 4
#### IQs of 76 Canal Boat Children *

| Age of Children | Number of Cases | Average IQ |
|---|---|---|
| 4, 5, 6, 7 | 21 | 84.4 |
| 8, 9, 10 | 27 | 66.1 |
| 11, 12, 13, 14 | 28 | 58.4 |

\* Adapted from Gordon.

At the conclusion of his study, Gordon states: "The fact that there is a marked decrease in 'intelligence' with an increase of age, and that this is especially noticeable among children in the same family, suggests very convincingly that the low average 'intelligence' of these children is not due to heredity. It may be due to environment, or to the lack of schooling, or

---

[26] Hugh Gordon, *Mental and Scholastic Tests Among Retarded Children, Physically Defective, Canal Boat and Gipsy Children and Backward Children in Ordinary Elementary Schools*, Educational Pamphlets, No. 44, London, Board of Education, 1923, 92 pp.

[27] Mandel Sherman and Cora B. Key, "The Intelligence of Isolated Mountain Children," *Child Development*, Vol. 3, 1932, pp. 279–290.

to both combined." [28] The present writers would classify schooling as being part of the environment and hence conclude that the trends shown in Table 4 are due primarily to environmental factors.

Sherman and Key [29] tested 102 isolated mountain children and compared their intellectual ratings with 81 children who lived in a little town (Briarsville) only a few miles distant. They also studied the relationship of chronological age to IQ for these groups. The mountain children lived in four hollows—Colvin, Needles, Oakton, and Rigby—which are located about 100 miles west of Washington, D.C., in the Blue Ridge Mountains. In Colvin Hollow, there is no road to the outside world with the exception of a small trail; all the adults are illiterate except three; school is held most irregularly (a total of sixteen months over an eleven-year period), and many of the children do not know their last names. "They identify themselves, for example, as Sadie's Benny or Dicy's Willie." In the other three hollows the conditions though roughly comparable are probably somewhat superior to those of Colvin Hollow. For example, in Oakton Hollow the school term is approximately four months each year; there is a combined general store and post office and "many of the inhabitants receive mail and an occasional magazine." The town of Briarsville is located at the base of the mountains to the south of the hollows, has hard surface roads connecting it with principal cities of Virginia, has a four-room modern school with three well-trained teachers, has a good general store, telephones, and receives newspapers.

On the mental tests which were administered, the average intelligence quotient of the Briarsville children was higher than that of the mountain children in every instance. For example, on the *National Intelligence Test*, the average IQ of the mountain children ($N = 24$) was 61.2, while the average IQ of the Briarsville children ($N = 50$) was 96.1. An analysis of relationship of age to IQ showed for the mountain children a tremendous drop in IQ with increasing age. For the Briarsville children there was a slight drop in IQ with increasing age but not nearly so marked as for the mountain children. Of the mountain children those living in Colvin Hollow had the lowest mental ratings. From the standpoint of social development it should be remembered that Colvin Hollow also ranked lowest.

Sherman and Key conclude that the expression of intelligence, as measured by standardized tests, depends in a large measure upon the opportunities to gather information and upon the requirements made upon the individual by his environment.

In both the Gordon study and the one by Sherman and Key, the average IQs of the underprivileged groups were much below the norms for typical children. Furthermore, the older children had lower IQs

[28] Hugh Gordon, *op. cit.*, p. 44.
[29] Sherman and Key, *op. cit.*

than the younger children. This of course does not mean that these children were "dull" or "feebleminded" as these terms are generally used. These data, in the opinion of the writers clearly show instead that these groups were greatly retarded in skills which have been mastered by children reared in more favorable environments.

ETHNIC DIFFERENCES IN INTELLIGENCE AND ACHIEVEMENT.[30] The existing studies in this field show that children reared in superior economic and cultural environments have on the average higher IQ scores and achievement test scores than children from disadvantaged groups regardless of their ethnic backgrounds. Klineberg,[31] in a specific discussion of Negro-white differences in intelligence, concluded that there is no scientific evidence for the view that any ethnic group differs from any other in innate ability. This position is the only one that the present authors feel is tenable in the light of current knowledge.

### Effects of the Environment upon Personality

Environmental factors not only play a most important role in the mental development of the individual, but also have much to do with the type of character and personality he will develop. The effects of the culture upon the attitudes, ideals, and behavior patterns of individuals have been clearly shown by social anthropologists [32] who have studied various primitive peoples.

The mountain-dwelling Arapesh of New Guinea,[33] for example, are a highly cooperative, peaceful, docile, and unaggressive type of people. Their children seldom show temper tantrums or steal and lie. One hundred miles away from the Arapesh, however, lives the river-dwelling Mundugumor tribe. These people are highly competitive, suspicious of one another, aggressive, and violent. Among the lake-dwelling Tchambuli, also a tribe in New Guinea, the roles of men and women are completely reversed from what they are in American culture. The women do the farming, fishing, hunting, and other heavy work, while the men stay at home, look after the children, and devote themselves to artistic pursuits. The women thus develop typically masculine personalities and the men appear effeminate

---

[30] For several studies in this area see George A. Ferguson, "Human Abilities," in *Annual Review of Psychology*, Vol. 16, Palo Alto, California, 1965, pp. 51–62.

[31] Otto Klineberg, "Negro-White Difference in Intelligence Test Performance," *American Psychologist*, Vol. 18, 1963, pp. 198–203.

[32] Beatrice B. Whiting (Editor), *Six Cultures: Studies of Child Rearing*, New York, John Wiley and Sons, 1963.

John W. M. Whiting, and Irvin L. Child, *Child Training and Personality: A Cross Cultural Study* (Paper back), New Haven, Yale University Press, 1962.

For a study of non-primitive cultures see R. J. Havighurst, M. E. Dubois, M. Csikszentmihalyi, and R. Doll, *A Cross-national Study of Buenos Aires and Chicago Adolescents*, New York, Karger, 1965.

[33] Margaret Mead, *Sex and Temperament in Three Primitive Societies*, New York, William Morrow and Company, 1935.

according to our standards. These differences in temperament and personality found to exist between the Arapesh, Mundugumor, and Tchambuli peoples can be traced very definitely to their respective systems of social organization and methods of child rearing.

Even in our own society, we have subcultures or classes each of which leave their marks on the personality of the individuals belonging to them. Davis brings this out very clearly in discussing the relationship of the caste and class structure of American society to the personality development of adolescents. He says:

> Lower-class culture, white or Negro, organizes adolescent behavior with regard to aggression, sexual relations, age roles, and family roles, to mention only a few of the basic types of relationships, into patterns which differ radically from those of middle-class adolescents. . . . In the middle class, aggression is clothed in the conventional forms of "initiative," or "ambition," or even "progressiveness," but in the lower class it more often appears unabashed as physical attack, or as threats of and encouragement of physical attack. . . . The lower classes not uncommonly teach their children and adolescents to strike out with fist or knife and be certain to hit first. Both girls and boys at adolescence may curse their father to his face or even attack him with fists, sticks, or axes in free-for-all family encounters. Husbands and wives sometimes stage pitched battles in the home, wives have their husbands arrested, and husbands try to break in or burn down their own homes when locked out. Such fights with fists or weapons, and the whipping of wives occurs sooner or later in many lower-class families. They may not appear today, nor tomorrow, but they *will* appear if the observer remains long enough to see them.[34]

Much evidence in recent years has also clearly shown the effect of family influences upon the personality development of the child. Neurotic parents are often directly responsible for similar traits found in their children. Children who are rejected by their parents are very likely to be aggressive, negativistic, quarrelsome, rebellious, or untruthful. The over-protected child is likely to be submissive, anxious, and lacking in self-reliance. The Viennese psychologist, Alfred Adler, and his students have also stressed the importance of such other family members as brothers, sisters, and grandparents as factors influencing the character and personality of the child. For example, Dreikurs, who studied with Adler states:

> The child's position in the family entails a great variety of trials and stimulates the development of certain traits and qualities. The second-born child

---

[34] Allison Davis, "Socialization and Adolescent Personality," in Forty-Third Yearbook of the National Society for the Study of Education, Part I, *Adolescence*, 1944, p. 209. Quoted by permission of the Society.

For additional studies of the effect of social stratification on behavior see Harold Proshansky, and Bernard Seidenberg (Editors), *Basic Studies in Social Psychology*, New York, Holt, Rinehart and Winston, 1965, pp. 318–373.

is generally more active in good and in evil; he acts as if he had to make up for lost time. The first-born, on the other hand, may be troubled his whole life long by the feeling that his position is under threat.[35]

Although the evidence with respect to birth order *per se* and personality is somewhat confused and unconvincing, there is little question but that certain situations and relationships resulting from a child's position in the family order of succession do have marked effects upon his behavior and personality.

In concluding this chapter, the writers would like to cite the excellent statement of the psychologist Lewin. He says:

> One can say that behavior and development depend upon the state of the person and his environment, $B = F (P, E)$.[36] In this equation the person $P$ and his environment $E$ have to be viewed as variables which are mutually dependent upon each other. In other words, to understand or to predict behavior, the person and his environment have to be considered as one constellation of interdependent factors.[37]

The teacher who would understand, control, and predict the behavior of children must, therefore, (1) know the child, his physical condition, needs and abilities, and (2) know the environmental, social, and cultural forces which are acting upon him.

## SUMMARY

The behavior of a child at any given moment is the result of biological and environmental factors operating simultaneously. The child behaves as he does because he is a human being with needs, and because he is surrounded by environmental and cultural forces which determine how these needs shall be met. In this chapter the effect upon child behavior of various physical, biological, and social conditions has been traced. It has been shown, for example, how the action of the glands affects personality, and how sensory and physical defects may alter behavior. Equal attention has been given to the effects of cultural variations upon personality and conduct. Children from isolated and backward communities have been shown to deviate downward from the usual norms on standard tests of intelligence. Children taken from "poor" homes and placed in "superior" foster homes have shown marked increases in mental test scores.

---

[35] Rudolph Dreikurs, *Manual of Child Guidance*, Ann Arbor, Michigan, Edwards Brothers, Inc., 1946, p. 27.

[36] This equation is read: behavior $(B)$ is a function $(F)$ of the person $(P)$ and his environment $(E)$.

[37] Kurt Lewin, "Behavior and Development as a Function of the Total Situation" in Leonard Carmichael (Editor), *Manual of Child Psychology*, Second Edition, New York, John Wiley and Sons, Inc., 1954, p. 919.

In the realm of personality, evidence has been presented that children from the lower socio-economic classes show characteristics which are markedly different from those of children in the middle class. The effects of interfamily relationships on the child's development have also been noted.

The point has been amply documented that what children are to become depends in no small part upon influences arising from the school and other educational agencies. Human nature is highly modifiable and teachers have a crucial role to play in the process of producing desired changes in children's behavior. To understand the child the teacher must (1) know him as a biological organism with needs and goals, and (2) must know the social and psychological environment of which he is a part.

## References for Further Study

Bloom, Benjamin S., Davis, Allison, and Hess, Robert. *Compensatory Education for Cultural Deprivation*, New York, Holt, Rinehart, and Winston, 1965.

Bloom, Benjamin S., *Stability and Change in Human Characteristics*, New York, John Wiley and Sons, Inc., 1964.

Carter, C. O., *Human Heredity*, Baltimore, Penguin Books, 1962.

*Education for Socially Disadvantaged Children*, Review of Educational Research, American Educational Research Association, Vol. 35, No. 5, December, 1965.

Ferguson, George A., "Human Abilities," in *Annual Review of Psychology*, Vol. 16, 1965, pp. 39–62.

Hsu, Francis L. K., *Psychological Anthropology: Approaches to Culture and Personality*, Homewood, Illinois, The Dorsey Press, 1961.

Hunt, J. McV., *Intelligence and Experience*, New York, Ronald Press, 1961.

Montagu, Ashley, *Human Heredity*, Cleveland, The World Publishing Company, 1963.

Montagu, Ashley, *Man's Most Dangerous Myth: The Fallacy of Race*, 4th Edition, The World Publishing Company, 1964.

Mussen, Paul H., Conger, John J., and Kagan, Jerome, (Editors), *Readings in Child Development and Personality*, New York, Harper and Row, 1965.

Newcomb, Theodore M., Turner, Ralph H., and Converse, Philip E., *Social Psychology*, New York, Holt, Rinehart, and Winston, 1965.

Parsons, Talcott, *Social Structure and Personality*, New York, The Free Press of Glencoe, 1964.

Proshansky, Harold, and Seidenberg, Bernard, *Basic Studies in Social Psychology*, New York, Holt, Rinehart, and Winston, 1965.

Scheinfeld, Amram, *Your Heredity and Environment*, Philadelphia, J. B. Lippincott Company, 1965.

Steiner, Ivan D., and Fishbein, Martin, *Current Studies in Social Psychology*, New York, Holt, Rinehart, and Winston, 1965.

Stern, Curt, *Principles of Human Genetics*, Second Edition, San Francisco, W. H. Freeman and Company, 1960.

Turner, Clarence D., *General Endocrinology*, Third Edition, Philadelphia, Sanders, 1960.

Whiting, Beatrice B. (Editor), *Six Cultures: Studies of Child Rearing*, New York, John Wiley & Sons, 1963.

## Questions, Exercises, and Activities

1. Do you agree with John B. Watson, the behaviorist, that there is no such thing as the inheritance of talent and temperament? State your own position and support it with what facts and observations you have.
2. Read a recent article on the effect of the glands upon personality. Write a brief summary and also give a critical evaluation of the article.
3. Do you believe children should be assigned to classes on the basis of their IQs? Give a list of reasons why they should or should not be so grouped.
4. Are children of some races mentally inferior to those of other races? Defend your answer with evidence from research.
5. Summarize some of the differences in behavior you yourself have noticed between middle-class children and those from the lower class.
6. It has sometimes been said that Italians are unusually musical, that Scotchmen are stingy, and that Englishmen lack a sense of humor. Do you believe this? Explain your answer.
7. Should a teacher try to change the personalities of some of the children in his room? If so, how can this be done?
8. Do you believe the school can change the tested IQs of certain children? Give examples and facts to support your conclusion.
9. Read two or three articles on birth order and its effect upon intelligence or personality. What do they show?
10. Statistics show that both men and women are taller today than they were fifty years ago. What are some possible explanations?
11. Is there any correlation between the brain sizes of races and the ability to learn? What are the facts? Consult such sources as Ashley Montagu's *Man's Most Dangerous Myth: The Fallacy of Race* which is listed among the references for this chapter.
12. Utilizing the library, summarize the findings from several recent articles on the effects of "head start" programs and programs for the culturally disadvantaged on the mental development of children.

# Chapter 3

# Growth and Development During Childhood

The events of childhood and the developmental trends in these early years cast long shadows into the future. The teacher, whatever the age of his pupils, will do well to study these formative years. He should do so, first, because he may have an important part in shaping future development; second, because he can only understand the person as he is now by knowing what has gone before; and, finally, because he will inevitably work with children whose early development has been impaired and who will need skillful help and guidance to overcome their difficulties.

The period of childhood may be divided into five stages, viz., the neonatal period (birth to about four weeks), infancy (four weeks to two years), preschool period (two to six years), middle childhood (six to nine years), and preadolescence (nine years to puberty which of course ushers in adolescence).[1]

This chapter will focus attention upon the period of childhood, particularly upon middle childhood, and the next chapter will deal with the adolescent. In each chapter, major developmental trends will be noted, and the meaning of these trends for education will be discussed. Additional work with primary resources in child development and child psychology

---

[1] David P. Ausubel, *Theories and Problems of Child Development*, New York, Grune and Stratton, 1957, pp. 17–18.

as represented in footnotes and bibliographic material is needed by the prospective elementary teacher just as the prospective high school teacher must pursue further the material about adolescents presented in Chapter 4.

## GENERAL NATURE OF GROWTH

There are a number of principles regarding growth which should be understood by teachers and others who work with children.

1. Structure generally precedes function, i.e., the structure of a muscle group is intact and ready for use before it is competently used, and brain weight is complete by seven or eight years of age, but the child may not yet be ready to do certain types of abstract thinking. Although growth is always continuous and not saltatory there are asynchronies in the process of development.
2. The direction of growth is from the general to the specific, i.e., from general and diffuse responses to more differentiated and specific ones. Thus coordination of large muscle groups precedes fine muscle movements.
3. There is a sequence of development in general and specific traits and in various systems of the body. Children babble before they speak, crawl before they walk, and develop incisors before they walk. They use egocentric language before they use other-directed language, and develop a concrete schema for thinking before engaging in abstract thinking.[2]
4. Within a given child various types of development occur at different rates, even though there is some correlation among various traits. Thus one child may be tall for his age, but only average or below in vocabulary development.
5. Even though the sequence of events in developments is the same or nearly so for all children, the rates will vary depending upon the child's genotype, and the environmental conditions which together produce development.

The fact of continuity of growth makes it possible to project curves and to make predictions regarding future growth with some degree of accuracy. Bayley,[3] for instance, has developed a set of tables which can be used for predicting adult height from the child's present height and skeletal age. A child's mental capacity at age 9 or 10 is also a fairly reliable indicator of what it will be at age 12 or 13 provided the environment is held reasonably

---

[2] For a fuller discussion of the predictable pattern of development see Elizabeth B. Hurlock, *Child Development*, Fourth Edition, New York, McGraw-Hill Book Co., 1964, pp. 18–31.

[3] Nancy Bayley, "Table for Predicting Adult Height from Skeletal Age and Present Height," *Journal of Pediatrics*, Vol. 28, 1936, pp. 49–64.

constant. Although growth in a given trait can be predicted to some extent, it is most difficult if not impossible to predict growth in one aspect of personality from the rate of growth in another. The typical child has many "ages." Thus a child who is 10 years old chronologically might have a mental age of 12, a social age of 8, a dental age of 9, a reading age of 7, and a weight age of 13.[4] The teacher who wishes to match teaching with the developmental level of the child, must clearly understand that unevenness of growth in the several traits is more often the rule than not. A curriculum based upon chronological age alone or on mental age alone, for example, will fall short of ministering to the needs of the whole child.

## FUNDAMENTAL NEEDS OF THE CHILD

In Chapter 2, reference was made to the physical or tissue needs (drives) of the child, e.g., need for food, air, liquid, activity, and rest. In addition to these biological needs, every child in our society (and possibly in all human societies), possesses certain social or personality needs.[5] These latter needs are sometimes referred to as sociogenic or learned needs. They are, however, among the most powerful of the human needs. No child can develop properly or learn effectively whose personality needs are disregarded. The teacher should constantly ask himself if the activities of the classroom are ministering to these needs of children. Among the important personality needs are the following:

1. *Need for status.* Every child wants recognition and attention. He craves the esteem of his teachers, parents, and peers.
2. *Need for security.* Children desire regularity and stability in their lives. Too much uncertainty as to how they stand in their group or excessive anxiety as to whether they will pass or fail a course creates a very unwholesome condition for them.
3. *Need for affection.* Everyone craves love. The good teacher is one who genuinely likes his pupils. A child becomes uneasy and restless when he discovers that he is not liked by his teacher.
4. *Need for independence.* Children want to take responsibility and to make choices which are commensurate with their abilities. The wise teacher will give children an opportunity to satisfy this need in the many classroom activities which are arranged.

As just noted, children learn social and personality needs, and it is the very fact that they are learned that makes each child's motive-need system

---

[4] A social age of 8 means that a child is as advanced socially as the average 8-year-old; similarly a dental age of 9 indicates that the child is as advanced in dentition as the average 9-year-old.

[5] Muzafer Sherif and Carolyn Sherif, *An Outline of Social Psychology*, Revised Edition, New York, Harper and Brothers, 1956, Chapter 11.

somewhat unique. For example, one child's need for security or affection may be higher than another's. In an illustrative study pre-school aged children who were denied adult company for just a short period of time showed intensified efforts to secure attention. In other words, they had, in a manner of speaking, acquired a new need from the experimental circumstances.[6]

The needs of the child and the needs of society come together in what Havighurst [7] labels "developmental tasks." His proposition is that at each period of life, there are certain accomplishments expected of the person by society. Thus in early childhood, the child must learn to walk, talk, and acquire sexual modesty, and in middle childhood to get along with peers and to read. In the sense that these tasks are demands of the family and society they may be thought of as needs created for the child, and linked to more basic needs, because it is through the successful accomplishment of these tasks that the child finds the status, security, and independence which he seeks.

## PHYSICAL DEVELOPMENT

Health, energy, rate of growth, and general physical fitness contribute both directly and indirectly to success in school and to mental and personality development. Knowledge about a child's physical nature may be revealing in studying his behavior in his home and at school, and may give clues about his attitudes toward himself and others. The child who is fatigued may be irritable, the child who is malnourished may lack energy required by school tasks and, as already noted in Chapter 2, the child whose level of physical development is at variance with that of his friends may feel insecure or ashamed. One of the writers knew a woman student who, when in junior high, was over six feet tall. On the first day of school in the eighth grade, this student, as was the custom, stood by her seat until the teacher entered the room; whereupon the teacher reprimanded the girl for standing on her chair instead of the floor. Such remarks, involving physical deviations of any kind may cut deeply into a sensitive child. A better understanding of physical development and of normal variations may help to avoid such obvious psychological damage.

### Use of Height and Weight Norms

Comparisons of children with others of the same sex and age or with their own past growth trends can be helpful indicators of acute or chronic

---

[6] J. L. Gerwitz, D. M. Baer and C. H. Roth, "A Note on the Similar Effects of Low Social Availability of an Adult and Brief Social Deprivation on Young Children's Behavior," *Child Development*, Vol. 29, 1958, pp. 149-152.

[7] Robert J. Havighurst, *Human Development and Education*, New York, Longmans, Green and Co., 1953.

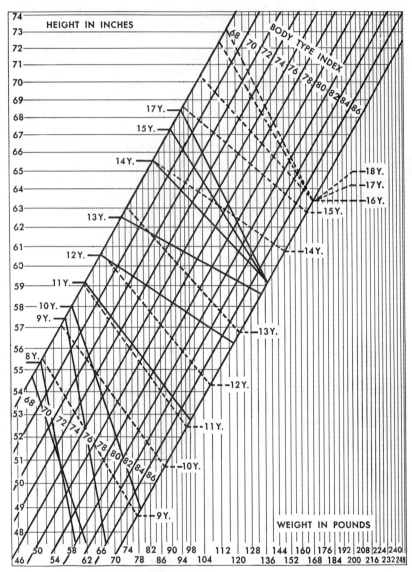

**Figure 2.** Body-Type Growth Chart.

physical disorders. One obvious difficulty in the use of norms is that they may be based on average body builds, and may mistakenly assume that what is average is optimal.[8] Simply because a child is smaller or shorter than

---

[8] D. M. Hall, "Determining Healthy Growth for 4-H Club Members," *Research Quarterly*, Vol. 24, 1953, pp. 284–294.

others may have no significance at all. Consequently it is common for schools and pediatricans to use predictive schemes based upon a child's past growth and body type. Wetzel,[9] Massler,[10] and Hall [11] have all devised charts and graphs for this purpose. Note on the chart in Figure 2 that a teacher or the child himself may record successive growth points according to the legend accompanying the figure. As may be seen, a ten-year-old boy who was 53 inches tall and weighed 66 pounds would have a body type index of 76 and would be near the average (solid line marked 10 y) for all boys at that age. A ten-year-old girl who weighed 94 pounds and was 54 inches tall would fall in the channel for a body type index of 84, and would be as heavy as the average twelve-year-old girl (dotted line marked 12 y). When successive measurements show that a child has crossed channels, a physical examination is indicated. Hall, who devised the chart shown in Figure 2, maintains that, though there are exceptions, he does not generally find a child below channel 72 or above 80 who is physically fit as far as physical strength is concerned.

If the school does not use devices as those shown in Figure 2, the most sensitive single measure for successive check points would be body weight, for it is a fairly sensitive indicator of environmental conditions such as disease, nutrition, and emotional factors.[12]

## Motor Development

At all ages many school activities are posited on the assumption that practice and growth have yielded sufficient development to allow for active participation by all pupils. Everything from the early use of scissors and crayons to the fine hand-eye coordination demanded by mechanical drawing necessitates a certain degree of motor development. It therefore behooves teachers and curriculum builders to be aware of normal developmental expectations. For example, Ausubel [13] has asserted that we should not expect handwriting of any reasonable quality before age nine.

Following are some generalizations about motor development that should be useful guides for teachers.

1. Children (especially boys) place a high premium upon physical strength, vigor, and coordination. In fact there is probably a closer re-

---

[9] Norman Wetzel, "Physical Fitness in Terms of Physique, Development and Basal Metabolism," *Journal of the American Medical Association*, Vol. 116, pp. 1187–1195. For a discussion and lucid explanation of the use of the Wetzel Grid, see Horace B. English, *Child Psychology*, New York, Henry Holt and Company, 1951, pp. 282–286.

[10] M. Massler and T. Suher, "Calculation of 'Normal' Weight in Children," *Child Development*, Vol. 22, 1951, pp. 75–94.

[11] D. M. Hall, *op. cit.*

[12] Ausubel, *op. cit.*, p. 505.

[13] *Ibid.*, p. 515.

lation between popularity and strength, than between popularity and IQ.[14]

2. Growth of muscle mass precedes its functional development, hence it is not uncommon to find children who look big enough to be well coordinated but who are in fact functionally immature. This is truly one of life's hazards for the larger child for whom the world has unreasonable expectations.

3. Motor skills in one area (such as running, jumping, etc.) do not correlate highly with those in other areas such as manual dexterity.

4. There is also only a slight relationship between a child's mental ability and his motor skill.

5. Lack of self-confidence may preclude a child's receiving sufficient opportunities for the necessary practice in developing motor skills, e.g., the child who is over-protected at home often shrinks from contact games, thus losing the opportunity both for the learning of the physical skills involved, and for important social contacts. The direct means of helping this sort of child is to help him acquire motor skills.

### Physical Fitness

While health and growth of children have greatly improved during the past quarter century, physical fitness seems to have deteriorated.[15] Too many children are overweight, and too few acquire muscular strength and tonus anywhere near the level of which they are capable. Awareness of this problem is reflected in the Presidential Conferences on Fitness of American Youth.[16] In these conferences, leading authorities on physical education, medicine, and recreation have suggested means by which schools and communities can improve physical fitness. Many schools now give a diagnostic test of fitness just as they give tests of mental growth and school achievement.

Just how clearly physical fitness relates to mental alertness, energy, and health is largely undetermined. In any case there is evidence as noted before that the physically inept and weak child is unduly penalized by his age mates. Fitness is thus both a goal to be sought as a recognized part of the school's responsibility, and as a remedial measure to help children gain acceptance by their social group.

---

[14] L. W. McCrow and J. W. Talbert, "Sociometric Status and Athletic Ability of Junior High Schools Boys," *Research Quarterly*, Vol. 24, 1953, pp. 72–80.

[15] D. M. Hall, "The Value of Exercise and Physical Fitness" in L. M. Fraley, Warren R. Johnson, B. H. Massey (Editors), *Physical Education and Healthful Living*, New York, Prentice-Hall Inc., 1954, pp. 98–117.

[16] National Conference on Fitness of Secondary Youth, *Youth and Fitness*, Washington, D.C., American Association for Health, Physical Education and Recreation, 1959.

## MENTAL DEVELOPMENT

Growth in mental ability is very rapid during early childhood and the intermediate years, and gradually tapers off in late adolescence; hence it is a negatively accelerated curve whose exact form has never been determined. In Figure 3 is shown schematically what the curve might look like. This curve is postulated on the supposition that half of an individual's mental capacity has been attained by the age of three, and that the terminal point occurs at about 21 years of age. Both E. L. Thorndike and Florence L. Goodenough [17] have gathered evidence which seems to support the shape of the mental growth curve in Figure 3.

**Figure 3.** Theoretical Curve of Mental Development.

A moment's reflection should make clear that mental development is always an inference based upon observable behavior that includes such a wide array of possible items for observation as: size of vocabulary, language structure, problem solving, perceptual speed, and immediate memory. Therefore, actual scores on any test could be placed into a normal curve, or be used for drawing a curve to show mental development, but the curves mean little unless one knows what mental functions are being tapped by

[17] Florence L. Goodenough, "The Measurement of Mental Growth in Childhood," *Manual of Child Psychology* (Leonard Carmichael, Editor) New York, John Wiley and Sons, Inc., 1946, pp. 467–468.

the test involved. One can only guess at the relationship between a single test score and the thing called mental capacity. Consequently, some researchers have preferred to study mental development not as a plotting of curves derived from a composite of many (sometimes ill-defined) mental functions, but by analyzing the separate processes such as memory, problem solving, and concept attainment. The work of Piaget in this regard can be appreciated in perspective when one realizes that his descriptive analyses of language concepts and perceptions took place at the time when the single IQ score was very popular as a representation of intelligence.

What has just been said is in no way intended as a diatribe against mental testing. Instead, it is a reminder that to understand mental development the teacher should have a clear picture of the developmental patterns of all the elements that go together to make up mental ability. These will not be entirely obtained by looking at the items on an intelligence test.

An example of a study that does give some small insight into how children's mentality develops, and exemplifies the method by which much of Piaget's data were compiled, is the following piece of research by Asch and Nerlove. Their test was designed to determine language abstraction levels for children 3 to 12 years of age. It consisted of a list of double-function words such as soft, sweet, cold, and crooked which mean one thing when applied to objects or conditions and another when applied to people. Their findings were as follows:

Ages

3–4  children's responses indicated little understanding. They said, such things as "poor people are cold," "no clothes," and "no people are cold."

5–6  the terms were defined in terms of physical referents. A cold person was cold.

7–8  47 out of 87 children showed a psychological understanding.

9–10  almost all children tested could see the double meaning of the words.

11–12  the children could see the cogency of dual function words.[18]

### Consistency of Mental Growth

School teachers are usually very much interested in the child's IQ. They feel that this information will provide them with a measure of what the child can do at the present and also provide them with an indication of

---

[18] Solomon Asch and Harriet Nerlove, "Development of Double Function Terms in Children," in Bernard Kaplan and Heinz Werner (Editors) *Perspectives in Psychological Theory*, New York International Universities Press, Inc., 1960.

what the child will be able to do in the future. The IQ of a child, however, does not give a complete answer to either of these questions. In the first place, it must be recognized that the correlation between mental test scores and school achievement seldom is higher than .60. This means that many factors other than intelligence enter into school success. Teaching methods, the child's interests, and emotional security, for example, have much to do with his performance at all educational levels. A child with an IQ of 100 who is highly motivated and who feels secure may do much better work in the first grade, for example, than a child with an IQ of 130 who is uninterested in school or who has severe personality problems. When it comes to predicting what a child's future IQ will be when his present IQ is known, much difficulty and inaccuracy can also result. It is a well known fact that the test scores obtained on children before the age of two bear little relationship to scores obtained on the same children later in life.[19] Even IQs obtained on children at the first- or second-grade levels may be quite different from those obtained on these same children when they are in high school. Data obtained in the Harvard Growth Study, have shown that the correlation between mental scores at age seven and age sixteen is only slightly above .50.[20]

Probably the most thorough study of IQ stability is one conducted at the Institute of Child Development at the University of California.[21] Two hundred and fifty-two children were given mental tests at specified periods over a span of several years. The results showed that between ages 6 and 18, the IQs of almost 60 per cent of the group changed 15 or more points; the IQs of a third of the group changed 20 or more points; and the IQs of 9 per cent of the group changed 30 or more points. The IQs of 15 per cent of the group shifted less than 10 IQ points, but the IQs of some individuals changed as much as 50 points. The authors conclude from their study that the "fluctuations in the scores of individual children indicate the need for utmost caution in the predictive use of a single test score, or even two such scores. This finding seems of especial importance since many plans for individual children are made by schools, juvenile courts, and mental hygiene clinics on the basis of a single mental test score. Specifically it should be noted that a prediction based on a 6-year test would be wrong to the extent of 20 IQ points for one out of three children by the age of 18

---

[19] F. N. Freeman and C. D. Flory, "Growth in Intellectual Ability as Measured by Repeated Tests," *Monographs of the Society for Research in Child Development*, Vol. II, No. 2, Washington, D.C., National Research Council, 1937.

[20] J. E. Anderson, "The Prediction of Terminal Intelligence from Infant and Preschool Tests," *Intelligence: Its Nature and Nurture*, Part I, Thirty-Ninth Yearbook of the National Society for the Study of Education, 1940, pp. 385–403.

[21] M. P. Honzik, J. W. Macfarlane and L. Allen, "The Stability of Mental Test Performance between Two and Eighteen Years," *Journal of Experimental Education*, Vol. 17, 1948, pp. 309–324.

years, and to the extent of 15 IQ points for approximately six out of ten children." [22]

Mental test scores may be altered by emotional conditions, cultural factors, and environmental deprivation. Moreover, since there is no single test scale for all ages it is necessary to equate scales that do not fit together on the same dimension.[23] The result as previously noted is an inability to predict with much accuracy eventual mental development from mental test scores obtained during the early years of life.

The growing concern with the effects on children of poverty and "cultural deprivation," has already been noted in Chapter 1, and the effects of isolated environments upon mental development was discussed in the last chapter. Recent research based upon longitudinal data from intelligence tests,[24] the study of language acquisition,[25] and neural-perceptual growth,[26] has added to the conviction that the major detrimental effects upon mental growth occur in the preschool period. Bloom's analysis led him to believe that an unfavorable environment could depress IQ development by an average of 2.5 IQ points per year in the first four years of life, but between the ages of 8 and 17 only about .4 IQ points per year. The rationale for an early educational intervention before children reach kindergarten or first grade is easy to build with the types of evidence now available.

### Language Development

On the average, children begin to talk when they are about fifteen months of age. Any given child may, however, vary greatly from this general norm. Some children utter their first word as early as eight months of age, while it is not at all uncommon for others to be as old as twenty months or even two years before this happens. The age at which a child starts to talk has often been regarded as symptomatic of his future mental development. Although there is a positive relationship between onset of talking and later mental development, the correlation is far from being perfect. Any parent who attempts to predict his child's future mental abil-

---

[22] This quotation taken from Raymond G. Kuhlen and George G. Thompson, *Psychological Studies of Human Development*, New York, Appleton-Century-Crofts, Inc., 1952, p. 158.

[23] Nancy Bayley, "On the Growth of Intelligence," *American Psychologist*, Vol. 10, 1955, pp. 805–818.

[24] Benjamin S. Bloom, *Stability and Change in Human Characteristics*, New York, John Wiley and Sons, Inc., 1964.

[25] Martin Deutsch, "The Role of Social Class in Language Development and Cognition," *American Journal of Orthopsychiatry*, Vol. 25, 1965, pp. 78–88; and "Facilitating Development in the Pre-School Child: Social and Psychological Perspectives," *Merrill Palmer Quarterly*, Vol. 10, 1964, pp. 249–264.

[26] J. McVicker Hunt, "The Psychological Basis for Using Preschool Enrichment as an Antidote for Cultural Deprivation," *Merrill Palmer Quarterly*, Vol. 10, 1964, pp. 209–248.

ity from the age at which he began to talk is likely to make a very serious error. It is known, of course, that idiots never learn to talk, but on the other hand it is also not uncommon for very highly intelligent individuals to be slow in developing language. In Terman's [27] group of gifted high school children there were some who did not learn to talk until they were two, two and one-half, or even three years of age.

Although the development of vocabulary in the typical child appears to proceed rather slowly at first, there is very marked acceleration in this regard during the last few years in the preschool period. Smith [28] has reported that the average child knows 16,900 basic words by the time he enters the first grade. The growth of vocabulary from Grade 1 through Grade 8 is shown in Table 5.

**TABLE 5**
Size of Vocabulary at Different Grade Levels *

| Grade | Basic | Derived | Total |
|-------|-------|---------|-------|
| 1 | 16,900 | 7,100 | 24,000 |
| 2 | 22,000 | 12,000 | 34,000 |
| 3 | 26,000 | 18,000 | 44,000 |
| 4 | 26,200 | 18,800 | 45,000 |
| 5 | 28,500 | 22,500 | 51,000 |
| 6 | 31,500 | 18,000 | 49,500 |
| 7 | 35,000 | 20,000 | 55,000 |
| 8 | 36,000 | 20,000 | 56,000 |

* From Smith.

The importance of language development in the period of early childhood cannot be too strongly emphasized. It is both a reflection of mental growth and a determinant of mental growth, and some psychologists [29] urge an attack upon language development as the most direct method of alleviating educational retardation.

In addition to the obvious effects of mental and physical anomalies upon the development of the ability to communicate, the following factors are generally cited as related to language development.[30]

---

[27] L. M. Terman, *et al.*, "Mental and Physical Traits of a Thousand Gifted Children," *Genetic Studies of Genius*, Vol. I, Stanford University, California, Stanford University Press, 1925, p. 573.

[28] Mary K. Smith, "Measurement of the Size of General English Vocabulary Through the Elementary Grades and High School," *Genetic Psychology Monographs*, Vol. 24, 1941, pp. 311–345.

[29] D. P. Ausubel, "How Reversible are the Cognitive and Motivational Effects of Cultural Deprivation? Implications for Teaching the Culturally Deprived Child," *Urban Education*, Vol. 1, 1964, pp. 16–38.

[30] R. C. Johnson and G. R. Medinnus, *Child Psychology: Behavior and Development*, New York, John Wiley and Sons Inc., 1965, pp. 130–133.

1. *Sex.* Girls are somewhat superior in vocabulary, articulation, and the amount of speech produced until about the age of 10.
2. *Family Size and Structure. Only* children, probably because of the greater amount of time spent with adults, are, during childhood, somewhat superior in language development to children who have siblings, and twins may be slightly retarded in the development of oral language, presumably because they may develop a "private" language of their own.
3. *Social Class.* Lower class children have poorer vocabularies, more difficulties in reading, and poorer articulation than middle class children. When "lower classness" is combined with cultural isolation, "non standard" dialects may be developed.
4. *Deprivation of Opportunity to Talk with Adults.* Children who are institutionalized in orphanages and in hospitals develop language skills more slowly, on the average, than non-institutionalized children.
5. *Bilingualism.* Children who are brought up in homes where two languages are spoken, particularly where the English learned is of a substandard variety, are often retarded in language functions. For example, in Hawaii many of the children learn pidgin English before coming to school, and their English in the first grade is at about the three-year old level.

## EMOTIONAL DEVELOPMENT

The basic equipment for emotional development (physical and neural) is present at birth, and in a very diffuse way emotional behavior begins at birth, or perhaps even before. Hurlock points out that the infant, even before the end of the neonatal period, will exhibit responses, such as crying and struggling, to painful or unpleasant stimuli, and "pleasant" responses, such as relaxing and sucking, to supportive stimuli.[31] It has also been observed that children whose mothers are anxious and highly emotional for a period prior to childbirth are more likely to have babies who cry more and are more prone to colic. It is believed that the mother's adrenal output has begun to affect the child's "emotional equipment" even before birth.[32]

Before the end of the first year of life, the general excitement observable in the neonate begins to become well differentiated into recognizable expressions of joy, anger, and fear. In infancy these behaviors are quite similar in their manifestations from one child to another, but begin to take on individuality and cultural stereotypy in the pre-school period.

---

[31] Elizabeth B. Hurlock, *op. cit.,* p. 266.
[32] D. P. Ausubel, *Theory and Problems of Child Development, op. cit.*

The elements that together produce emotion are maturation, conditioned response learning, verbal learning, and imitation of the emotions of others.

### Children's Fears

The best available evidence indicates that children are born with few if any specific fears. The psychologist John B. Watson held that the newborn child showed fear or startle reactions only to very loud noises or to loss of support in the act of being dropped. The great number of fears and anxieties held by children at the various age levels must, therefore, be attributed to learning. The child learns to be fearful of objects, persons, or situations in a variety of contexts although the basic principle of learning involved is usually the same. This principle is known as *conditioning*.[33] The child who has had unfortunate or terrifying experiences in the presence of some object, person, or situation tends to be fearful of these same objects or situations in the future. Numerous examples could be cited. The child who possesses an irrational fear of dogs may have been jumped upon by a dog and seriously threatened on a previous occasion. The child who fears school teachers may have been humiliated by a given teacher at some earlier time. The child who fears school examinations is one who has had unsuccessful experiences with such examinations or who has been made to feel insecure with respect to such activities. Such a case described in the subject's own words is given by Wallin.

> As a child in the public school I developed a most pronounced fear of examinations and tests. I am sure this fear was instilled into me by a teacher who always threatened her pupils with the hard examinations she was going to give, and with the fact that if we did not pass we would not be promoted. . . .
> I must confess I have never been able to overcome the fear of tests. To this day examinations and tests almost make me ill.[34]

Through direct contact with disturbing situations or through vicarious experiences such as listening to lurid stories told by adults or by members of one's peer group, children become afraid of an amazing variety of things. These include such things as darkness, snakes, thunder, strangers, high places, dirt, dentists, and water. There is no end to the lists of things which children may learn to fear.

Jersild and Holmes [35] have made an analysis of some of the fears which are held by large numbers of children at different age levels. Jersild has

---

[33] See Chapter 5 for additional discussion of this concept.

[34] J. E. Wallace Wallin, *Personality Maladjustments and Mental Hygiene*, New York, McGraw-Hill Book Company, 1949, p. 80.

[35] A. T. Jersild and F. B. Holmes, "Children's Fears," *Child Development Monographs*, No. 20, Bureau of Publications, Teachers College, 1935.

summarized this study and related ones made under his direction in the following words:

> During the preschool years, more and more of his (the child's) fears are formulated in terms of imaginary or anticipated dangers. At the elementary school age, and from then onward, a large proportion of fears concern misfortunes that never materialize. As the child grows older and abler, there is a decline in his fear of numerous events that scared him at an earlier time, such as noises, unfamiliar persons, places and situations, everyday objects, animals and persons. However, individual children may fail to outgrow such fears, by reason of the harrowing shock of the original experience, or by reason of recurring experiences that strengthen the original fear, or by reason of failures to gain in understanding and mastery of themselves and their environment as they grow older. Certain childhood fears, such as fears of animals, the dark, being alone, criminal characters, ghosts and the like, are likely to persist into adult life sometimes in much the same form, sometimes in a modified version.[36]

The teacher or parent should be concerned with ways and means of helping children overcome their fears. How are fears unlearned? The essential circumstance is that the feared object or situation must be associated with pleasantness, security, success, or other state of well-being. The child who has a deathly fear of cats must gradually be placed in the vicinity of a cat, under conditions where he is secure, happy, and free from threat. After a period of time the cat will lose its terrifying effect. The writer knows of a child who formerly was tense and afraid in the presence of all cats or even little kittens. A kitten was brought in the home. At first the child was unwilling to be in the same room with the kitten. Now the child insists that this kitten, which has now grown into a full-sized cat, sleep at the foot of his bed.

A child who fears school examinations or school teachers needs success experiences with examinations or teachers. The child who dreads or is fearful of such a school activity as reading, needs to have satisfying experiences with reading.

A fifth-grade boy was once brought to the writer at the educational clinic of the University of Illinois because his parents and teachers considered him to be a non-reader. The boy's reaction when the subject of reading was brought up was one of extreme aversion. He stated that he thoroughly disliked reading and felt most uncomfortable to even discuss the subject. He asked that he not be subjected to the terrifying ordeal of trying to read to the writer who was interviewing him. The boy further stated that he was definitely a non-reader and no useful purpose would be served by such an exhibition of his weakness. The writer told the boy

---

[36] A. I. Gates, A. T. Jersild, T. R. McConnell, and R. C. Challman, *Educational Psychology*, p. 98. Copyright, 1948, by The Macmillan Company, New York. Used by permission.

that many people are non-readers and perhaps he was also, but insisted that the boy prove that he was a true non-reader. This the boy reluctantly agreed to do. The boy was given a pre-primer and asked to begin reading. He did very well on this. He was then given a second pre-primer. He was again successful at reading this most elementary material. By this time, his parents returned to the conference room. They were told that the boy was definitely not a non-reader because he had just finished reading two books. In order to demonstrate this fact to his parents, a third pre-primer was placed in the boy's hands and he was asked to read. After he had read three or four pages successfully, the writer reached over to take the book from him, but he would not give it up. He sat there beaming in front of his parents and refused to stop reading until he had finished the entire pre-primer.

This case illustrates how an aversion, dislike, or fear can often be dissipated in a very short time once the activity is associated with need-satisfying experiences. This boy needed success and recognition in connection with reading. His dislike and aversion for reading had developed as a result of his previous humiliating experiences with it. All that was needed to produce a positive reaction toward reading was a sense of achievement and success in connection with the activity.

The efficacy of the method just described for eliminating fears has been subjected to experimental study by Jersild and Holmes.[37] In summarizing this research, Jersild states, "The highest percentage of success was reported for procedures that helped the child to gain increased competence and skill, aided him in finding practical methods of his own for dealing with the feared situation, and helped him by degrees to have active experience with, or successful direct participation in the feared situation."[38]

### Affectional Responses

Children do not display affection simply because they are human. They learn affection just as they learn to tie their shoes and brush their teeth. Affection is not, however, taught directly as are skills, but is rather acquired in the affectional interplay with parents, other adults, and children. The drive for it is so strong that, lacking a mother figure, it may even be transferred to such inanimate objects as a "terry cloth" mother. Most convincing evidence of this fact comes from studies of children,[39, 40]

---

[37] A. T. Jersild and F. B. Holmes, "Methods of Overcoming Children's Fears," *Journal of Psychology*, Vol. 1, pp. 75–104.

[38] A. T. Jersild, "Emotional Development," in *Manual of Child Psychology* (Leonard Carmichael, Editor), New York, John Wiley and Sons, Inc., 1946, p. 768.

[39] J. Bowlby, "Some Pathological Processes Set in Train by Early Mother-Child Separation," *Journal of Mental Science*, Vol. 99, 1953, pp. 265–272.

[40] W. Goldfarb, "Emotional and Intellectual Consequences of Psychological Deprivation in Infancy: A Reevaluation," in P. H. Hock and J. Zubin, *Psychopathology of Childhood*, New York, Grune and Stratton, 1955, pp. 105–119.

primates, [41,42] and other mammals [43] where affection has been denied. In all such cases, the deprivation of affection seems to make the giving of affection more difficult.

In his study, Harlow kept infant monkeys separated from their mothers and from other small monkeys. When these experimentally isolated monkeys were adults, their affectional behavior was very inadequate. They did not mate, except in rare instances, and when females did bear children, they neglected and mistreated them.

The long term effects of maternal deprivation and of the denial of affection in infancy and early childhood are not known with certainty. Some clinical psychologists believe that the psychopath may be produced in homes in which there is little affection.

The writer knew a boy of eight who had been in six different foster homes. His own mother did not want him, and treated him very cruelly. The stepfather brought the child to the Illinois Juvenile Research Bureau as he feared his wife would do the boy serious bodily harm. In each new foster home the same pattern developed. The foster mother would make affectional advances to the boy but they were always rebuffed. Fortunately in this case after two more adoption attempts the boy was finally taken in by a childless couple who lived on a ranch in the Far West, and the boy was able to accept his new mother.

## Aggression

While some aggressiveness is a desirable development in children, it can become a disintegrative emotion when it is not properly controlled. High amounts of aggression in children may be indicative that there has been a failure to learn more adaptive forms of behavior in reaction to anger-producing stimuli; this proposal is substantiated by the observation that highly aggressive behavior is often very stereotyped in its expression.

Aggression may come, first of all, from basic frustrations. This hypothesis has been supported experimentally,[44] and in descriptive studies.[45] A second concomitant of aggression is believed to be the aggressive models which

---

[41] H. F. Harlow, "The Nature of Love," *American Psychologist*, Vol. 13, 1958, pp. 673–685.

[42] H. F. Harlow and R. R. Zimmerman, "Affectional Responses in the Infant Monkey," *Science*, Vol. 130, 1959, pp. 421–432.

[43] W. H. Bexton, W. Heron and T. H. Scott, "Effects of Decreased Variation in the Sensory Environment," *Canadian Journal of Psychology*, Vol. 8, 1954, pp. 70–76.

[44] Nancy B. Otis and Boyd R. McCandless, "Responses to Repeated Frustrations Differentiated According to Need Areas," *Journal of Abnormal and Social Psychology*, Vol. 50, 1955, pp. 349–353.

[45] W. McCord, Joan McCord and A. Howard, "Family Correlates of Aggression in Non-Delinquent Male Children," *Journal of Abnormal and Social Psychology*, Vol. 62, 1961, pp. 79–93.

children find in their environment.[46] The more aggressive the adults in the home, the more aggressive are the children. (The male figure is more likely to be imitated in this regard than is the female adult). It has been postulated that lower class boys are more aggressive than middle class boys because the lower class male, with whom the boys identify, is typically viewed as an aggressive person. Finally, it has been claimed that some aggressiveness may result from treatment received in permissive homes where aggression is allowed, and not quickly punished.

## PERSONALITY AND SOCIAL DEVELOPMENT

### Effect of Early Infant Experience on Personality

Freudians have long held that the experiences of early infancy leave lasting marks on the individual's personality. They have been especially concerned with the effect of infantile suckling, excretory, and genital experience on adult personality.[47] Pediatricians, psychiatrists, and psychologists, who follow Freudian theories have advocated certain systems of infant care which they believe will promote sound personality development.[48] In general, they have advocated breast feeding rather than bottle feeding, late and lenient bowel and bladder training, and lack of rigid scheduling in feeding. The specific conclusions of the Freudians, however, are open to some question in view of the fact that experimental data do not always support their theories. Orlansky,[49] an anthropologist, has brought together an excellent summary of existing objective studies dealing with the effects of such things as nursing experiences, mothering, sphincter training, and restraint of motion on personality development. He concluded that there was no evidence that breast-fed babies were better adjusted in later life than bottle-fed babies, or that children who received early or late sphincter training were particularly different from other children. What seemed to be important was the total context in which the child was reared, rather than some specific method of handling the child. Support for this position can be found in Benedict's [50] study of the effects of swaddling on various groups of European children. She concluded that the child's character is not determined by the overt details of early infant

---

[46] A. Bandura and Aletha C. Huston, "Identification as a Process of Incidental Learning," *Journal of Abnormal and Social Psychology*, Vol. 63, 1961, pp. 311–318.

[47] S. Freud, *New Introductory Lectures on Psychoanalysis*, New York, W. W. Norton & Co., Inc., 1933, pp. 135–140.

[48] See L. K. Frank, "The Fundamental Needs of the Child," *Mental Hygiene*, Vol. 22, 1938, pp. 353–379; and M. A. Ribble, *The Rights of Infants*, New York, Columbia University Press, 1943.

[49] Harold Orlansky, "Infant Care and Personality," *Psychological Bulletin*, Vol. 46, January, 1949, pp. 1–48.

[50] Ruth Benedict, "Child Rearing in Certain European Countries," *American Journal of Orthopsychiatry*, Vol. 19, April, 1949, pp. 342–350.

care, but by attitudes and motives communicated to the child by the mother in connection with the practices employed. It would thus appear that whether a child is to become a well-adjusted adult depends to a great extent upon whether he is loved, accepted, and is made to feel secure in the home rather than whether he is fed from the breast, bottle, or cup.

## Family Relationships and Personality Development

The general conditions existing in homes from which children come have been shown to have marked effects upon children's behavior and personality. An important study in this area was conducted by Baldwin [51] at the Fels Research Institute. He explored the consequences of democracy in the home upon the personality development of 67 children who were approximately four years of age. These children were observed in free play situations in the nursery school. Their behavior was recorded on a rating scale by independent observers who also rated the extent to which the homes from which the children came were democratically or autocratically operated. Democracy in the home was found to produce children who were active, aggressive, fearless, planful, curious, non-conforming, and more likely to be nursery-school leaders than average. Children from authoritarian homes tended to be quiet, well-behaved, socially unaggressive, and restricted in curiosity, originality, and fancifulness. In a California investigation involving the developmental study of 500 nursery-school children over a three-year period, it was reported that children coming from homes where parents *disagree* on methods of discipline are much more often problem cases than are children whose parents *agree* on methods of control.[52]

An extensive survey of the research relating parental characteristics to children's development over a twenty-year period reveals a total of 27 different dimensions or factors that have been identified, but that there is sufficient similarity in the results of the studies to reduce them to two major dimensions: acceptance—rejection, and autonomy—control.[53]

The effects of parental discipline upon personality characteristics in children have been the subject of much speculation, but only a modest amount of factual evidence exists. Three tentative conclusions may be drawn from the available research.

1. There is a positive relationship between aggressive behavior in children and the severity of discipline in the home.
2. Harsh discipline helps build a store of hostility which the child directs toward others.

---

[51] Alfred L. Baldwin, "Socialization and the Parent-Child Relationship," *Child Development*, Vol. 19, September, 1948, pp. 127–136.
[52] Ruth Pearson Koshuk, "Developmental Records of 500 Nursery School Children," *Journal of Experimental Education*, Vol. 16, 1947, pp. 134–148.
[53] Johnson and Medinnus, *op. cit.*, pp. 284–285.

3. Strict discipline by parents often leads to prejudiced and antidemocratic attitudes in the child.[54]

Further evidence of the effect of family influences upon personality has been found in studies of delinquency. In one such study [55] the investigators found three types of delinquent children, (a) an unsocialized aggressive group, (b) a socialized delinquent group, and (c) an emotionally disturbed delinquent group. The unsocialized aggressive boys predominantly came from homes where they had experienced parental rejection; the socialized delinquents were better accepted at home than the aggressive delinquents and came from larger families, but were reared under conditions of extremely lax discipline. The emotionally disturbed delinquent tended to be the unfavored child in his family and to come from a smaller family than either of the other two groups. In another study of problem children, Sloman [56] analyzed the family backgrounds of 62 individuals who were referred to the Chicago Juvenile Court. All the cases in the particular group were "planned for" children, i.e., children who were originally wanted by their parents and whose births were definitely scheduled. The findings revealed that many of these children had been wanted in an effort to remedy marital difficulties. The largest number, however, were children of compulsive and perfectionistic type mothers who liked to plan everything and who were often disappointed when their children failed to meet their expectations as to sex or achievement. This study seemed to imply that whether a child was planned for or not was of little importance so far as the child's character and personality were concerned. The really crucial point was whether or not he was wanted and made to feel secure after he arrived!

### Childhood Friendships

What are the factors that influence children's friendships? Grossman and Wrighter [57] studied the relationship between selection-rejection and intelligence, social status, and personality among sixth-grade children. They found that intelligence was related to selection of friends up to a certain point, that of normal intelligence, but beyond that point no relationship existed. Social status was found to be related to popularity, but the association ceased for levels above the middle class. The more popular children were found to be better adjusted than the less popular as measured by the

---

[54] Johnson and Medinnus, *op. cit.*, pp. 306–308.

[55] Richard L. Jenkins and Sylvia Glickman, "Patterns of Personality Organization Among Delinquents," *The Nervous Child*, Vol. 6, July, 1947, pp. 329–339.

[56] Sophie S. Sloman, "Emotional Problems in 'Planned for' Children," *American Journal of Orthopsychiatry*, Vol. 18, July, 1948, pp. 523–528.

[57] Beverly Grossman and Joyce Wrighter, "The Relationship Between Selection-Rejection and Intelligence, Social Status, and Personality Amongst Sixth-Grade Children," *Sociometry*, Vol. 11, November, 1948, pp. 346–355.

*California Personality Test.* Bonney [58] made an intensive study of five very unpopular children who had been identified by means of sociometric tests. He found that the popular children differed significantly from the unpopular children in conformity and group identification, emotional stability and control, social aggressiveness, adaptability and tolerance, dependability, social service motivation, and several other traits. Thompson and Horrocks,[59] studying the degree of friendship fluctuation for children in Grades 6 to 12, found a trend toward greater stability in the friendships with increasing chronological age. Hare and Hare [60] found that the number of friends possessed by a family increases with length of stay in the community and varies with the presence or absence of children in the home. A negative correlation existed between number of friends and amount of expenditure for recreation outside the home.

There are undoubtedly numerous factors which account for children being drawn together with other children in friendly relationships. The most obvious one, of course, is propinquity. It is very difficult for children who are too widely separated by distance to carry on a close friendship. Age, social class, intelligence, and other traits of personality are also clearly related to the process of forming friendships. It can probably be said that the fundamental reason why two children become friends is that each helps the other satisfy some of his basic social and psychological needs. A child who makes another child feel accepted, secure, and important will likely secure a friend. If the relationship is mutual, a close friendship may be formed and the two children will become confidants—buddies, chums, or pals. This topic will be discussed further in Chapter 11, where the factors that determine children's acceptance and rejection of each other will be presented.

## CURRENT CONTROVERSIAL ISSUES IN CHILD DEVELOPMENT

While there are many theoretical problems, unanswered questions, and controversial matters in the field of child development, the following represent a few that have a direct bearing upon education, and upon decisions about schooling that are being made by governmental agencies.

1. Is there a critical period in childhood for the development of basic mental and personality traits? Some social scientists, particularly those

---

[58] Mark Edwin Bonney, "Popular and Unpopular Children: A Sociometric Study," *Sociometry Monographs*, No. 9, New York, Beacon House, 1947, p. 81.

[59] George G. Thompson and John E. Horrocks, "A Study of the Friendship Fluctuations of Urban Boys and Girls," *Journal of Genetic Psychology*, Vol. 70, June, 1947, pp. 53–63.

[60] A. P. Hare and R. T. Hare, "Family Friendship Within the Community," *Sociometry*, Vol. 11, November, 1948, pp. 329–334.

who study the effects of deprivation on other mammals, claim that once a certain critical time has passed, development in a particular area (language, for instance) will never reach its normal potential. Others, while agreeing that deficits may be cumulative, hold out hope that many faulty developmental trends are reversible; in other words, that educational intervention may be effective at any level of schooling. A sounder position than either of these is that events which occur in early childhood are extremely important; but that most children at any age up to adulthood can learn practically anything they need to know if the proper motivation is acquired, and good educational methods and materials are used.

2. Is intelligence modifiable, and if so to what extent?

The data presented by Bloom and others make it clear that most of today's social scientists believe intelligence to be a modifiable human trait. Bloom's data suggest that only a moderate alteration is possible, and then only if the environmental stimulation comes early in life. Others, as shown in Chapter 2 (Speer) and as will be shown in Chapter 6, believe that gains or losses in intelligence may be considerably higher. The general consensus at the present time, however, is that intelligence as a meaningful, useable concept must be thought of as a trait that is affected not only by such obvious things as genetic and prenatal events, but also by such factors as nutrition, disease, good or bad schooling, and parental encouragement or discouragement.

3. Are the schools, or the general culture, responsible for the educational retardation of children?

Some psychologists [61] and educators [62] believe that the major reason for educational retardation may lie in the schools which too frequently make the assumption at the outset that lower class children, especially those from minority groups, will not learn, and because of these low expectations, the children in fact do conform to the expectations. Others believe that low achievement springs mainly from the disadvantages of the general culture in which the child finds himself; it may be a culture quite different from the one which is represented in the school. Both factors undoubtedly operate in slowing the child's development. There is ample evidence that teachers may prejudge children, and that such prejudgment can have a deleterious effect upon school achievement, but it is also true that even the most skillful and accepting teachers find difficulty in overcoming cumulative

---

[61] Kenneth B. Clark, *Dark Ghetto: Dilemmas of Social Power*, New York, Harper and Row, 1965.

[62] Ernest H. Austin, Jr., "Cultural Deprivations—A Few Questions," *Phi Delta Kappan*, Vol. 67, 1965, p. 67.

deficits that accrue from adverse home and community influences that are to a great extent beyond their control. However, too frequently home conditions are an excuse for ineffective school operation.

4. To what extent should the school be concerned with the personal and social adjustment of children?

While this is partly a philosophical matter, it is nevertheless an important controversial issue of interest to psychologists. It should be clear to the reader that there are powerful voices which have vigorously criticized the schools for giving too much concern to "life adjustment" and not enough to intellectual matters. The fact is that affective and intellectual life are inextricably intertwined, and that educational retardation may be as much a matter of emotion and motivation as of cognition.

## SUMMARY

The period of childhood is one of rapid growth and learning. Starting as it were almost from "scratch" the individual in a few short years develops a most complicated set of behaviors. He learns to talk, read, write, cooperate, distinguish right from wrong, and make thousands of other adjustments to the society in which he finds himself. All children, of course, are not equally successful in mastering the "development tasks" expected of them. Some develop rapidly in some areas of behavior and slower in others. The wise teacher will realize that the typical child is uneven in his abilities and will endeavor to gear instructional activities not only to each child, but also to his several aspects of development.

In judging what a given child can learn, or in predicting what his future growth will be, tests of "intelligence" should be used with extreme caution. Studies have shown marked fluctuations to occur in tested IQs. In one careful investigation it was found that between ages six and eighteen, the IQs of almost 60 per cent of the individuals changed fifteen points or more.

Childhood is the time when the individual's basic outlooks, values, and ideals are to a great extent shaped. The experiences the child has at school and in the home and the larger community during these formative years, will determine, for example, whether he is to be a fearful child or one possessed with confidence in himself, or whether he will be tolerant or intolerant toward others.

No period during the life cycle is more important than childhood from the educational point of view. Teachers who work at this level should understand children—their fundamental needs, their problems, and the forces which modify and produce behavior change. The statement that "the child is father of the man" bears much psychological validity. The patterns of growth, learning, and adjustment established in childhood reach into the future and influence the entire course of life.

## References for Further Study

Almy, Millie, *Child Development*, New York, Holt-Dryden, 1955.

Ausubel, David P., *Theory and Problems of Child Development*, New York, Grune and Stratton, 1957.

Baldwin, Alfred L., *Behavior and Development in Childhood*, New York, Holt-Dryden, 1955.

Baldwin, Alfred L., *Theories of Child Development*, New York, John Wiley and Sons, Inc., 1967.

Baller, Warren R., and Charles, Don C., *The Psychology of Human Growth and Development*, New York, Holt, Rinehart and Winston, 1961.

Carmichael, Leonard, (Editor), *Manual of Child Psychology*, Second Edition, New York, John Wiley and Sons, Inc., 1954.

Charles, Don C. *Psychology of the Child in the Classroom*, New York, The Macmillan Company, 1964.

English, Horace B., *Child Psychology*, New York, Henry Holt and Company, 1951.

Flavell, John H., *The Developmental Psychology of Jean Piaget*, Princeton, New Jersey, D. Van Nostrand, Inc., 1963.

Gesell, Arnold, and Ilg, Frances L., *Child Development*, New York, Harper and Brothers, 1949.

Hunt, J. McV., *Intelligence and Experience*, New York, Ronald Press, 1961.

Hurlock, Elizabeth B., *Child Development*, Fourth Edition, McGraw-Hill Book Co., 1964.

Jersild, Arthur T., *Child Psychology*, Fifth Edition, Englewood Cliffs, New Jersey, Prentice Hall, Inc., 1960.

Martin, William E., and Stendler, Celia B., *Child Development: The Process of Growing up in Society*, New York, Harcourt, Brace, 1953.

Mussen, Paul H., Conger, John J., and Kagan, Jerome, *Child Development and Personality*, Second Edition, New York, Harper and Row, 1963.

Mussen, Paul H. *et al.*, *Readings in Child Development and Personality*, New York, Harper and Row, 1965.

National Society for the Study of Education, *The Education of the Retarded and Disadvantaged*, Part I, 66th Yearbook, Chicago, The Society, 1967.

Olson, Willard C., *Child Development*, Second Edition, Boston, D. C. Heath, 1959.

Pressey, Sidney L., and Kuhlen, Raymond G., *Psychological Development Through the Life Span*, New York, Harper and Brothers, 1957.

Symonds, Percival M., *The Dynamics of Parent-Child Relationships*, New York, Bureau of Publications, Teachers College, Columbia University, 1949.

Thompson, George G., *Child Psychology*, Second Edition, Boston, Houghton-Mifflin, 1962.

Watson, Robert I., *Psychology of the Child*, Second Edition, John Wiley and Sons, Inc., 1965.

## Questions, Exercises, and Activities

1. Should secondary school teachers as well as elementary school teachers be concerned with a study of child development? Why?
2. Which human needs are particularly important in the period of childhood? In our culture, which needs are most frequently unmet?
3. Select a child whom you know and plot his position on the Body-Type Growth Chart in Figure 2. If you remember your own height and weight during some point in childhood, plot that point, and estimate whether or not your body type has remained the same.
4. Read and make a report on a chapter in any one of the books on child development or child psychology that are listed in References for Further Study.
5. The physically handicapped child is often not able to compete with other children at the very time when acceptance by peers may depend more upon physical than personality traits. What problems does this pose for the teacher? What can the teacher do to alleviate these problems?
6. Under what circumstances are children likely to have difficulties in achieving developmental tasks?
7. List school activities that are likely to demand a level of motor development not yet achieved by many pupils of a given age.
8. In this chapter the statement is made that the correlation between tested mental ability and school achievement is rarely higher than .60. What does this mean? If in a given grade or school, the correlation is actually .54, what does this signify?
9. Describe various parental practices in child rearing, and discuss their likely consequences for the development of children's personality.
10. Discuss the teacher's role in dealing with children whose environment and home conditions have failed to meet their sociogenic needs.

# Chapter 4

# The Adolescent Period

Adolescence is that period in every person's life which lies between the end of childhood and the beginning of adulthood. It may be a long period or a short one. It varies in length from family to family, from one socio-economic level to another, and from culture to culture.[1] Its length may even fluctuate in the same society from time to time, depending upon economic or other conditions.

Some primitive societies mature their children into adults almost overnight and thus practically eliminate the adolescent period. In present-day America, however, adolescence usually covers a long, drawn-out span of years.

A girl or boy in a middle-class American family may spend as long as ten years making the transition from childhood to adulthood. An example of this would be a girl who menstruates at twelve, thus ending her childhood, and then continues to be a dependent member of her family until she marries at twenty-two. During this ten-year span she may attend junior high school, senior high school, and college. All this time she is in the process of getting weaned from the family and becoming an independent adult. The same general pattern holds for the boy who may exhibit his first pubic hair at thirteen and then not leave the family nest until twenty-

---

[1] Robert E. Grinder and David L. Englund, "Adolescence in Other Cultures," *Review of Educational Research*, Vol. 36, October, 1966, pp. 450–462.

three. Girls usually begin the adolescent period a year or two earlier than boys, and similarly may finish it a year or two earlier.

In lower-class American families young people are typically "put on their own" much sooner than in middle-class families. These adolescents may thus have only four or five years to spend in the so-called "difficult period" known as adolescence. Many lower-class youths drop out of high school before graduation and leave home, and some even set up families of their own by the time they are seventeen or eighteen.

Every teacher should be aware of the fact that children in the same family or society may vary greatly with respect to the age at which they begin adolescence. Fourth- and fifth-grade teachers often report that they have girls in their classes who have reached puberty and who physically resemble young women while the rest of the class members are immature children. (The special adjustment problems of early- and later-maturing children will be treated in a later section of this chapter.)

## ADOLESCENCE—BIOLOGICAL OR SOCIAL

Adolescence is both biological and social in nature. The beginning of adolescence is marked by biological changes in girls and boys. As a matter of fact, just before puberty there occurs what is known as a pre-adolescent growth spurt. It takes place in girls mostly during the ages of nine to twelve, and in boys between eleven and fourteen. Prior to this time, the rate of growth in height and weight has been slowing down. Now, for a two- or three-year period the rate is greatly accelerated. During this period, and following shortly thereafter, the secondary sexual characteristics emerge. In girls there is typically first the rounding out of the hips, then breast development, the appearance of pubic hair, and menstruation. Typically, the American girl first menstruates when she is about thirteen.[2] Most American girls menstruate initially between the ages of eleven and fifteen. Only 3 per cent menstruate earlier than this, and 3 per cent later. The effect of environmental factors on menstruation, however, has been noted. Data show that girls in the United States menstruate earlier than those in other parts of the world. Also, girls today in America are reaching the menarche a few months earlier than did their mothers. Furthermore, girls from the middle classes menstruate earlier than do girls from the lower socio-economic classes in America. The environmental factors responsible for these differences are not definitely known at this time, but it is believed that better diet and health, and changed habits of activity may have something to do with them.

In boys, some of the secondary sexual characteristics that mark the be-

---

[2] Elizabeth B. Hurlock, *Adolescent Development,* Third Edition, New York, McGraw-Hill Book Company, 1967, p. 36.

ginning of adolescence are appearance of pubic hair, facial hair, and change of voice. These are all biologically induced.

The end of adolescence for both girls and boys is marked largely by social changes and criteria. Such factors as when an adolescent leaves home, gets a job, and can vote determine when his transition from childhood to adulthood is accomplished. The length of the period is thus primarily a social phenomenon.

The problems adolescents face during the long period of growing up have both biological and social roots. Physical changes and deviations can create problems. Society also creates problems for adolescents. Adolescents in America behave very differently than do adolescents in Samoa or New Guinea. Adolescents in the American middle class show markedly different personality characteristics than do those in the lower classes.

The teacher who would help adolescents make good adjustments to school and to life should understand the nature and effects of both biological and social factors in adolescent development.

## WHY ADOLESCENCE REQUIRES SPECIAL STUDY

The general principles of psychology, as they relate to growth, learning, and adjustment, apply to individuals at the adolescent stage as well as to those in any other phase of development. For example, a good course in social psychology, mental hygiene, or learning should help the secondary school teacher deal with adolescents. Yet each stage of life has special and unique problems which must be understood if applications of psychological principles are to be appropriate. The teacher who works with adolescents needs to understand, among other things, the nature of the transition period through which adolescents pass, the special needs and developmental tasks of adolescents, the role of the peer group in influencing adolescent behavior, the effects of somatic variations on adolescent behavior, the special problems arising out of family life, causes of adolescent delinquency, and special problems arising out of sexual maturation. Many of the problems an adolescent faces are new to him and are ones which he may not encounter again if he makes a successful adjustment to them.

## THE ADOLESCENT TRANSITION PERIOD

There are a number of transition or crisis periods in the life span of every individual. For example, the child who goes to school and leaves the security of his home behind for the first time is facing a special crisis period and must make suitable adjustments. At the other end of life, the man who retires from his job faces a crucial period for which radical adjustments must be made. Adolescence represents one of the greatest of these periods

of crisis. In making the jump from childhood to adulthood, great strain and confusion sometimes result.

The psychologist, Kurt Lewin,[3] has held that the adolescent is really in a "no-man's land." He is neither a child nor an adult, but is caught in a field of overlapping forces and expectations (see Figure 4). The child's role is clearly structured. He knows what he can and cannot do. The adult likewise understands pretty well what his role is. The adolescent, however, is in an ambiguous position. He never really knows how he stands.

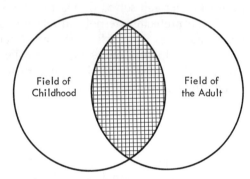

**Figure 4.** The Psychological Field of the Adolescent Is the Dark Space Where the Two Circles Overlap.

One moment he is told by his parents that he is too young to take the family car out of town. The next moment he is chided for not acting like a man and is told that he is as big as his father. It is believed that this uncertainty as to his role causes many an adolescent to be in conflict—to vacillate, to be sensitive and sometimes unstable and unpredictable.

It is a well-known fact that delinquency rates soar during the period of adolescence, that suicides become increasingly prevalent, that drug and alcohol addiction may have their beginning, and that much general unhappiness exists. Adolescence is also a period when satisfactory heterosexual adjustments are facilitated or hindered, when careers are planned, and when philosophies of life become molded. Teachers who understand adolescents and the problems they encounter can do much to help them make a successful transition to adult status. Too often, however, it seems that schools and teachers, because of lack of understanding, actually frustrate adolescents and contribute to their general maladjustment.

---

[3] See Rolf E. Muuss, "Field Theory and Adolescence," in *Theories of Adolescence,* New York, Random House, 1962, pp. 83–102.

## DEVELOPMENTAL TASKS OF ADOLESCENCE

The term "developmental tasks," used earlier in this chapter, refers to those problems that individuals typically face at different periods of their life development. The infant or small child must master the complexities of learning to walk, learning to talk, and controlling the elimination of waste products of the body. In middle childhood such skills as learning to play games and learning to read become of major importance. So far as adolescents are concerned, the developmental tasks represent the vital problems which must be met and solved during the transition from childhood to adulthood. These problems are not entirely unique to the adolescent period, but they are ones upon which the adolescent must work if he eventually expects to achieve a successful adult role. Robert Havighurst [4] has listed ten tasks that are particularly significant for the adolescent and that need much attention during this period:

(1) achieving new and more mature relations with age mates of both sexes,
(2) achieving a masculine or feminine social role,
(3) accepting one's physique and using the body effectively,
(4) achieving emotional independence of parents and other adults,
(5) achieving assurance of economic independence,
(6) selecting and preparing for an occupation,
(7) preparing for marriage and family life,
(8) developing intellectual skills and concepts necessary for civic competence,
(9) desiring and achieving socially responsible behavior, and
(10) acquiring a set of values and an ethical system as a guide to behavior.

If these are, indeed, the important problems of adolescence, schools should gear their curricula to take them into account. The school has traditionally devoted most of its energy to helping the adolescent develop his intellectual skills. This is perhaps as it should be. However, such tasks as achieving socially responsible behavior and preparing for marriage and family life, as well as other tasks on this list, should not be neglected.

## PHYSICAL NEEDS OF ADOLESCENTS

Adolescents the world over possess much the same biological and tissue needs. These are sometimes referred to as biogenic needs. They include hunger, thirst, activity, rest, sex, temperature regulation, evacuation (urina-

---

[4] Robert J. Havighurst, *Human Development and Education*, pp. 11–158. Copyright, 1953, by Longmans, Green and Company, New York.

tion and defecation), and avoidance of physical injury. The way these needs are met, however, varies greatly in different parts of the world. For example, the thirsty adolescent in Italy would probably drink wine, whereas an American youth might prefer a "coke." To satisfy the need for activity, a Cuban youth might engage in the game of *jai alai*, but his American counterpart would probably be much more interested in basketball.

Sex needs of youth are also handled quite differently in various countries of the world and in different subcultures in our own society. In Thailand, for example, young people of high school age would never be allowed to engage in mixed social dancing, but in America our schools feel that school dances provide a very valuable outlet for both boys and girls. In American middle-class society, premarital sexual intercourse is strongly frowned upon; in American lower-class society, attitudes toward such behavior are more permissive, and the behavior may even be condoned.

Although teachers should understand the nature of the physical needs of young people, it is perhaps even more important that they thoroughly understand and take into account the social and personality needs of youth.

## PERSONALITY NEEDS OF ADOLESCENTS

Among the human personality needs that are particularly urgent during adolescence are the needs for status, independence, achievement, and a satisfying philosophy of life.

Perhaps no need is more important for the adolescent than the *need for status*. He wants to be important, to have standing in his group, to be recognized as a person of worth. He craves to achieve adult status and leave behind the insignia of childhood. Thus, it is not at all uncommon to see adolescent boys smoking cigarettes and acting in other ways which seem to them to be grown up and sophisticated. The adolescent girl wants to wear high-heeled shoes, use lipstick, and take on the ways of adult women. Status in the peer group is probably more important to many adolescents than status in the eyes of their parents or teachers, yet recognition from both of these sources is cherished by adolescents. The teacher who directs the activities of the adolescent should always ask himself whether or not the experiences of the classroom are status-producing ones for each individual. The adolescent who is achieving his goals in school and is accorded appropriate recognition is seldom, if ever, a disciplinary problem. Furthermore, he is in the best possible emotional state to continue to profit from the learning experiences of the school.

One of the authors observed the classroom of a teacher who delighted in forcing her pupils, especially boys, to read poetry aloud. Most of the boys were fourteen or fifteen years of age—just at the time when they were try-

ing to throw off the label of "children" and to avoid "sissy" activities. The teacher asked them to read aloud Poe's "The Bells." One section of the poem read, "to the tintinnabulation that so musically wells from the bells, bells, bells, bells, bells, bells, bells." The teacher insisted that each boy rise and read this phrase with different volume and inflection on each "bells." Finally, one of the larger boys could stand it no longer. He slammed his book on the floor in disgust and stamped out of the classroom.

This teacher did not realize how sensitive adolescents are about being treated like youngsters or having to engage in activities they feel to be below their dignity. There is probably no surer way for any teacher to become unpopular with a group of teenagers than for her to call them children or to imply in any other way that they are anything but young men and women.

A second personality need which takes on increasing significance and importance during adolescence is the *need for independence*. The adolescent craves to be weaned from parental restrictions and to become a self-directing person. He wants his own room in the home, where he can be free from younger members of the family and can do his own thinking and plan his own activities. He would like a lock on the door and a private telephone if possible. He desires to run his own life. Young children have no objection to their parents' visiting school and inquiring about their progress, but many adolescents object to this practice, because it implies that they cannot handle their own affairs. The adolescent boy who is a member of the tennis or basketball team in high school usually prefers that his parents, if they attend the matches or games, be not too conspicuous. The normal adolescent does not want anyone to sense or faintly suspect that he is in any way tied to his mother's apron strings.

One of the authors knows of a high school girl whose mother brings her to school every day and insists on helping her carry her books to her locker. On a day that grades were given out, the mother stayed the whole day and visited each class with her daughter. According to the school counselor, this girl is on the verge of a nervous breakdown because of the overprotectiveness of the mother.

Teachers can also be too overprotective of their adolescent students. There is no reason why young people in their teens cannot help plan their programs of instruction, help set up rules for classroom conduct, and take on other responsibilities in line with their increased abilities and maturity levels. Yet, too often, high school teachers "spoon-feed" their students, scold them for little misbehaviors, plan their work for them, and expect little in the way of responsible behavior. If that is what teachers expect that is what they usually get. Adolescents who are treated in a more adult manner will show a more adult behavior, and can be depended upon to take on and carry out highly independent and responsible assignments.

Closely related to the two personality needs just discussed is the *need for achievement*. So far as learning is concerned, this need is of paramount importance. Thorndike, Hull, and Skinner,[5] all leading learning theorists of our time, hold that learning is most effectively accomplished when a student's efforts are followed by a sense of achievement (reinforcement). The way to get pupils to learn rapidly and to like their schoolwork is to take notice of good work that they do. Every pupil at times does something that is worthy of commendation. This should be called to the attention of the student, and perhaps to other members of the class. Slow learners particularly, or adolescents who are not interested in school, need successful experiences if they are to make any worthwhile progress.

Threats and punishments have sometimes been used in efforts to get pupils to study, but this approach may have many bad side effects. The student may learn a little geometry, but at the same time he may learn to hate the teacher and the subject. Numerous experimental studies have shown the superiority of praise over censure as a motivating device in producing learning.

In utilizing this need for achievement, which is present in all pupils, the teacher should carefully gear the classroom activities to the current achievement levels of each individual student. Only in this way can the classroom atmosphere be truly conducive to learning. First-grade teachers and some elementary teachers make an effort to apply this famous principle of readiness, but secondary school teachers quite generally neglect to so differentiate the work in their classes that each student can be a successful achiever.

The final personality need of adolescents (to be mentioned at this point) is the *need for a satisfying philosophy of life*. The young child asks many questions and does some immature speculating about the nature of the universe, but it is not until adolescence that he exhibits a persistent and driving concern about the meaning of life. The adolescent is concerned with questions about truth, religion, and ideals. He has a desire for *closure*. He wants the gaps in his knowledge about the purposes of life to be filled. A satisfying philosophy or set of beliefs tends to provide him psychological security. Data show that in adolescence religious conversion and initial radical political activity reach a peak. Dictators who establish youth movements and religious organizations which sponsor young peoples' societies recognize the importance of this period for attitude formation. The school has a great responsibility to help the adolescent find himself and develop the outlooks on life that are consistent with our democratic philosophy and that will give him stability of character and a sense of security.

---

[5] See Winfred F. Hill, *Learning: A Survey of Psychological Interpretations*, San Francisco, Chandler Publishing Company, 1963, pp. 57–89.

## THE ADOLESCENT AND SOCIAL CLASS

### Attitudes Toward School

No social group in America is more impressed with the importance of an education than is the middle class. This group feels that education is power. The young people who come from the middle class are urged by their parents to finish high school, go on to college, and in a great many instances pursue graduate study. The long-term goals of many middle-class youngsters include entering such professions as teaching, the ministry, medicine, and executive positions in business. As a matter of fact, often greater pressure is exerted on adolescents in the middle class to get an excellent education than on upper-class adolescents.

Middle-class parents, as a rule, are constantly concerned about the scholastic records of their children, attend PTA meetings regularly, visit the schools, save money for their children's college education, and in general leave no stone unturned in attempting to assure success for their children in the educational venture.

Lower-class society, on the other hand, puts little premium on education. Parents will, at times, encourage truancy, belittle education, and show slight or no interest in PTA work or their child's scholastic progress. As a result, many adolescents from the lower class desire to leave school as soon as possible. They want to get a job, get married (or at least find a common-law partner), make some money immediately, and get on with living. They do not see the relevance of the academically oriented school program to their plans.

Teachers are thus faced with a very severe motivation problem so far as many lower-class adolescents are concerned. Courses in shop work, carpentry, beauty culture, and the like may appeal to some, but the college preparatory subjects may leave them unimpressed.

### Attitudes Toward Aggression

Middle-class youth are typically taught by parents that fistfighting is nonproductive—that a clever person can avoid violence in solving personal disputes. Lower-class youngsters, on the other hand, are often encouraged by their parents and other members of their society to "hit the other guy before he hits you." They are instructed to be always prepared against an attack. Lower-class boys and adolescents thus may carry knives, razors, and other weapons in their pockets so that they will be ready when the fight breaks out, as it inevitably will.

Adolescents of both social groups, of course, have observed the behavior patterns of their parents and other adults. The middle-class man who is criticized or insulted may write a letter to the editor of the newspaper, send

a note or rebuttal to a magazine, or ignore the situation entirely. The lower-class man frequently will challenge his tormentor "to come out in the alley and settle the matter right now." In lower-class taverns, fights break out nearly every night. In middle-class taverns (country club and fancy hotel cocktail lounges) such brawls rarely occur.

Teachers need to understand that this basic difference in aggressive behavior exists between middle- and lower-class cultures. The lower-class boys who are fighting in and around school may not be suffering from severe personal maladjustments, but may instead be merely functioning in ways which for them are very normal. Middle-class adolescents who gossip, backbite, and make protests regarding peer behavior which they regard as hostile or obnoxious are also following the accepted pattern of their culture.

### Speech Habits

Teachers are usually well aware that young people from the lower and middle classes bring widely different sets of speech habits to school with them. The lower-class adolescent will use such expressions as "I seen him do it," "He has went home," "I knowed they was coming," "He don't know that I have saw him," "The bell has rang," "I brung my lunch," "The teacher learned me," and "I set on the step while I et my sandwich." A man or youth from the lower classes often refers to his wife as "the old lady" regardless of her age.

Teachers are often disturbed by the great number of "four-letter words" that lower-class boys and girls use with abandon and in the most unlikely places. Teachers, however, often fail to realize that the youngsters have, since infancy, heard these expressions used by their mothers, fathers, relatives, and playmates.

One of the quickest ways to identify the social class of a person is to talk with him for two or three minutes. In that time the speech habits of his subculture will inevitably come to the fore. Young people who are making the transition from the lower class to the middle class will only occasionally make a slip that will indicate their backgrounds.

A large part of the remedial English work in our secondary schools is designed to help lower-class adolescents acquire the speech habits of the middle class. There is much more that they need to learn in order to move up the social ladder, but this is one of the major requirements.

### Race and Social Class

What many people regard as racial behavior is in many cases only social-class behavior. Uninformed whites, for example, often state that Negroes are dirty, carry knives, don't paint their houses or grow grass in their yards. This description, of course, fits many Negroes—lower-class Negroes. The

same behavior is also typical of lower-class whites. In Negro society the class pattern is similar to that of white society. Middle-class Negroes paint their houses, pick crabgrass out of their lawns, scrub their floors, attend the opera, do not carry knives, and send their children to college. Socially, middle-class Negroes have nothing to do with lower-class Negroes. Middle-class Negroes do not want their teenagers to date lower-class Negroes.

One of the reasons that some people confuse "Negro behavior" with social-class behavior is because there is such a large percentage of Negroes in this country in the lower classes.

What has been said about Negroes applies to other racial and national groups in the country. Lower-class Italians behave like lower-class people. Middle-class Italians hold the values and exhibit the behavior patterns of middle-class people.

Teachers should not stereotype the behavior of adolescents on the basis of race, but should judge each pupil for what he himself is. Knowing the social class from which a pupil comes, however, will help explain why he behaves as he does.

### The School and Social Class

Although it is generally recognized that adolescents from the various social classes come to school with widely differing value systems and ways of behaving, it is not always clear to teachers what they should do about it. Should teachers help lower-class youth make good adjustments to the lower class from which they come, or should they help them make the transition to middle-class values and standards? For example, what should be taught in the unit on sex education which is attended by both middle-class and lower-class youth? These are not easy questions to answer.

In America, the middle class is the dominant class. It makes the laws, enforces them, and controls and participates in most of the important activities of the country. Members of the lower classes are in a sense members of a minority group who frequently are discriminated against and who are prevented from realizing themselves fully in our society. Because of this and the fact that mobility from the lower class to the middle class is possible, this author takes the position that schools and teachers should teach middle-class values and behaviors to all pupils. Such a procedure will have an integrating effect on our society and will open vistas and opportunities for many underprivileged pupils. This country has traditionally been a land of opportunity—where the lower-class boy from the "sidewalks of New York" can rise to become a member of the United States Senate or attain other important social positions. Perhaps no agency is better prepared to assist this process than the American school.

## HETEROSEXUAL DEVELOPMENT
## OF ADOLESCENTS

### Dating

Dating customs and practices are, of course, a product of the culture in which the adolescent lives. In certain oriental countries, such as Thailand, boys and girls do not date at all. They are kept separate in social functions, and it is not until the time of marriage that they are brought together by parental arrangement. In the United States dating begins, on the average, at about age fourteen for both sexes, and "going steady" at about fifteen. Many start dating and going steady much earlier. There is much controversy in the current press and anxiety among some parents because of the present practice of "going steady" at such an early age. It is believed that pairing off on a steady basis leads young adolescents into sexual and emotional intimacies long before they are ready for marriage. Anyone attending a high school dance or a dance at a teenagers' club will see fifteen- and sixteen-year-old couples arrive together, refuse to dance with anyone but their own dates, and leave together. Having a steady date makes the adolescent feel secure and accepted by the group, which expects this kind of behavior of him. There is no reason, however, why this pattern of behavior cannot be altered, and there are, perhaps, good reasons for doing so. During the early years of adolescence a boy or girl should make many friends and have social and emotional contacts with many members of the opposite sex.

High schools which sponsor dances, for example, should arrange the evening so that a boy or girl is required and expected to exchange a great many dances. Once the school takes the lead, other agencies such as the church and community clubs should follow suit and encourage boy-girl relationships on a nonsteady basis. Boys and girls would have just as much, or more, fun and at the same time would be developing heterosexual skills and interests that are preferable to those that can be developed with a single, steady association with one member of the opposite sex. As soon as boys and girls find that this new pattern of behavior represents the thing to do, they will fall easily in line. Human nature does not suggest that there is any specified way of dating. When society decides what it wants, that is what it will get.

Dating practices have been intensively studied by Hollingshead, who reported the results in his book *Elmtown's Youth*.[6] Who boys and girls date depends partly on the social class from which they come. The ma-

---

[6] August B. Hollingshead, *Elmtown's Youth*, New York, John Wiley and Sons, Inc., 1949.

jority of dates take place between adolescents of the same social class. When cross-class dates occur, they tend to involve adolescents from an adjacent class. Adolescents in every social class except the highest also try to date persons who are a class higher than themselves in the prestige structure. Conversely, the higher-class adolescent tries to limit his contacts with adolescents who are lower than he on the socio-economic scale. In Elmtown, Class V members (the lowest class) are so repugnant socially that adolescents in the higher classes almost entirely avoid dating ties with its members. About the only time that a date could occur between a higher-class adolescent and a Class V adolescent would be when a higher-class boy would date a Class V girl secretly for sexual purposes. Such a girl would, of course, not be invited to a school picnic, dance, or hayride.

Who an adolescent dates also depends partly on religion and whether the individual dated satisfies the social and personality needs of his partner. Dating among adolescents can serve a very useful purpose in preparing young people for marriage and adult responsibilities. The specific patterns, however, need to be studied and altered by schools and other social agencies in order that this practice may indeed fulfill its purpose.

### Necking, Petting, and Other Heterosexual Activity

Necking and petting among adolescents is not new in our culture, although such practices are probably more prevalent than in former years. Two factors partially explain the increase. First, the number of adolescents who have access to automobiles makes privacy easier to attain, and second, an opinion seems to be developing that a certain amount of sexual intimacy between young people of the opposite sexes is desirable from a mental-hygiene standpoint, and may serve as valuable experience for marriage.

Kinsey's study [7] shows that 85 per cent of boys have engaged in petting by the time they are nineteen. Twenty-two per cent of these have "petted to climax." By the age of eighteen, 81 per cent of girls have engaged in premarital petting. Of these, 15 per cent have "petted to orgasm." Among both boys and girls, premarital petting is somewhat more prevalent among the better-educated classes of society than among those who have had meager educational opportunities.

According to Kinsey, the techniques used by adolescent boys and girls in their petting activities include simple kissing, deep kissing, breast stimulation, mouth-breast contacts, manual stimulation of female genitalia by male, manual stimulation of male genitalia by female, oral contacts with

---

[7] A. C. Kinsey, W. B. Pomeroy, and C. E. Martin, *Sexual Behavior in the Human Male*, Philadelphia, Saunders, 1948. Also see A. C. Kinsey and others, *Sexual Behavior in the Human Female*, Philadelphia, Saunders, 1953.

female genitalia by male, oral contacts with male genitalia by female, and genital apposition.

Many adolescents rationalize that by petting they retain their virginity and at the same time reduce emotional frustration which may lead to personality disorders. The tragedy of premarital pregnancy, of course, is avoided by petting, if the experience stops at that point. Some authorities (Terman, Kinsey) have suggested that premarital petting may actually be an aid to successful marriage. Until more convincing and valid studies are made, however, the present authors take the position that schools and sex-education programs should take a dim view of heavy petting. More personality problems are probably caused by such behavior than are eliminated. Considering the values held by present-day society, the adolescent who engages in many forms of petting runs a real risk of accumulating more guilt feelings and other social problems than he can handle. The school should play an active role in keeping adolescents so occupied with exciting curricular and extracurricular activities that premarital heavy petting will be kept to a minimum.

Kinsey's investigation further revealed that by the age of twenty, 73 per cent of boys have had premarital sexual intercourse. At this same age, only 20 per cent of girls have engaged in premarital coitus. This, of course, reflects the double standard that exists in American society. Some may wonder about the Kinsey statistics. In general, they seem to be on the conservative side. Other studies show adolescent sexual activities to exceed the percentages reported by Kinsey. This may be due partly to the fact that many of Kinsey's subjects were older people who reported their adolescent sex histories, which in many cases were probably less extensive than the activities of present-day adolescents.

As with heavy petting, premarital sexual intercourse between adolescents is not a realistic solution for the emotional problems of youth in present-day society. The sex-education programs of schools should face the problem squarely and help young people make adjustments that will be more rewarding to them in the long run and will at the same time benefit the larger social group.

### Masturbation

Although masturbation seems to be frowned upon in our society, it is almost universally practiced among healthy adolescent boys. By the age of fifteen, according to the study made by Kinsey, between 82 and 90 per cent of boys have masturbated. By the age of twenty, the range is 90 to 94 per cent, depending upon socio-economic status. Among girls the rate is considerably lower. At age fifteen only 28 per cent of girls have masturbated, and by age twenty the figure has risen to only 41 per cent. Ultimately, about 97 per cent of American males and 62 per cent of American females will have had masturbatory experiences.

What should be the attitude of the school toward this sexual practice? In the past, special lectures for boys only or for girls only were sometimes scheduled, at which a religious leader or physician would speak. The alleged evils resulting from masturbation were pointed out, but it is doubtful that these admonitions reduced the practice. In fact, such speeches may have brought the practice to the attention of some adolescents who had previously been unaware of its existence. In recent years the medical and psychological attitude seems to be that masturbation, in and of itself, is not harmful, but may instead provide some relief for pent-up sexual tension that would otherwise interfere with satisfactory schoolwork or the carrying out of other responsibilities.

The fact still remains, however, that many adolescents are in conflict about the advisability of the practice. Kinsey states that "many boys pass through a periodic succession of attempts to stop the habit, inevitable failures in those attempts, consequent periods of remorse, the making of new resolutions—and a new start on the whole cycle. It is difficult to imagine anything better calculated to do permanent damage to the personality of an individual." As for females, he states that approximately half had some psychological disturbance over their masturbatory experiences. Some were disturbed for only a single year or two, but the average female carried her anxiety for six and a half years. Kinsey believes that there is no other type of sexual activity that worries females more than masturbation.

There is no question but that the school counseling and sex-education programs should meet this problem head on. Guilt feelings, where they exist, must be eradicated, and wholesome school activities that will provide substitute outlets for the abundant energies of youth should be encouraged. Perhaps as the mores of society change to fit the facts of human nature, the problem will become less acute. There is some indication that this is taking place.

### Homosexuality

Prior to reaching the period of adolescence, both boys and girls (as was pointed out earlier) are primarily interested in members of their own sex. Freud has called this the "latency period," but it might also be called the "homosexual period." During this pre-adolescent period, not only are boys and girls interested in associating with like sex members in most social activities, but overt sexual activities between members of the same sex frequently take place. Kinsey found, for example, that 29 per cent of twelve-year-old boys engage in such homosexual practices as exhibition of genitalia to other boys, mutual manipulation of genitalia, anal or oral contacts with genitalia, and urethral insertions. Among girls, 33 per cent admitted that they had engaged in homosexual play prior to the onset of adolescence. This consisted primarily of genital exhibitions and examinations (99 per

cent) and manual manipulation of the genitalia of one or both girls (62 per cent).

With the onset of adolescence, boys and girls become increasingly interested in the other sex. However, there is a carry-over into adolescence and adult life of pre-adolescent homosexual play and activities. By the age of forty-five (according to Kinsey), 37 per cent of American males and 13 per cent of American females have had homosexual experiences leading to orgasm.

These figures are much higher than most people would expect. Homosexuality is thus a serious problem for education and for society in general.

Because of the very nature of homosexuality, society has erected severe taboos against it. Males are particularly singled out for persecution and blackmail, although a somewhat more lenient attitude exists toward female homosexuals. It is common in our culture to see girls and women dancing together or rooming together. Most of these associations are not of a strictly sexual nature, but some of them are. With the population explosion what it is, society probably can get along and increase in numbers regardless of the homosexual element. The individual homosexual, however, is subject to great stress and strain. He is constantly in fear of being detected, and suffers from feelings that he is "abnormal." He doesn't like himself as he is, but doesn't see how he can change himself.

The causes of homosexuality are not entirely clear. Freudians believe that parent-child relationships during the formative years (during the Oedipus period) have an important bearing on whether a boy will develop a masculine role and whether a girl will be truly feminine. There is ample evidence, however, from all sources, including the Freudian, that a great share of homosexual behavior is learned. Adolescent boys, for example, who suffer humiliation and lack of success in their associations with girls may turn to boys as the object of their love impulses. Girls who fear pregnancy and are taught that boys are bad may find that a love affair with another girl is much safer than a heterosexual venture.

The school has at least two important functions to perform in assisting the potential homosexual and preventing a wider spread of the practice. The first is to help those pupils with some homosexual feelings or experiences to realize that they are indeed normal individuals. All people, male and female, have hormones of the opposite sex in their blood streams, and all people have characteristics of the other sex in various degrees. Such an assurance will help the individual adolescent to reduce his guilt feelings. Secondly, all boys and girls of adolescent age should be given every opportunity to engage in worthwhile heterosexual activities. Work on the school paper, dramatics, school dances and parties, hikes, and the like will throw young people together in ways that should encourage heterosexual adjustment.

A word of warning should be given to teachers or school counselors who are concerned about the homosexual problem. Students cannot be identified as homosexual by any known physical characteristic. The boy who appears feminine may be extremely masculine, and the boy with a deep voice and heavy beard may be a potential or active homosexual. Only through an interview with the individual who will reveal his feelings and practices, or by direct observation of overt behavior, can the existence of homosexuality be confirmed.

## PERSONAL PROBLEMS OF THE ADOLESCENT

### Problems of Early- and Late-Maturing Adolescents

Jones [8] and associates at the University of California have made an extensive study of the special problems that face early- and late-maturing adolescents. They found that early-maturing girls suffer real handicaps, and that early-maturing boys are not adversely affected but, in fact, are benefited by early physical and sexual development. As for girls, early development results in their feeling conspicuous at a time when conspicuousness is not valued. Many find themselves embarrassingly tall and heavy and possessed of greater breast development than they consider normal for their ages. The early-maturing girl naturally is interested in boys, but the boys of her age or school grade, on the average, are three or four years behind her in physical development and are hence unreceptive.

If the early-maturing girl tries to find associates among the older boys of her school or neighborhood, she encounters other difficulties. Most parents do not want their eleven- or twelve-year-old daughter dating boys who are fifteen or sixteen. Thus, she is caught in a dilemma. If she remains with her own age group, she is frustrated; if she moves into a group much older than she, her lack of judgment and social maturity can create serious social problems, as well as the guilt feelings she may experience if she disobeys her parents' wishes.

To some extent these problems are accentuated by the age-grade systems generally used in our public schools. The early-maturing girl would not be nearly so conspicuous in an ungraded type of program or, in fact, in the old-fashioned country school where children of all ages were in one room. Some authorities have suggested that girls be allowed to enter the first grade of our schools a year earlier than boys. This, of course, would reduce the developmental disparity between the sexes by one year during the remaining years of the school program.

While early-maturing girls have many serious adjustment problems to

---

[8] Harold E. Jones, "Adolescence in Our Society," in *The Adolescent: A Book of Readings, Revised* (J. M. Seidman, Editor), New York, Holt, Rinehart, and Winston, Inc., 1960, pp. 50–60.

face, this is not generally so with late-maturing girls. The studies show that late-maturing girls are superior in many respects to both early-maturing girls and girls who mature at an average age. In the Jones study, the late maturers, on the average, were superior to other girls in personal appearance, poise, cheerfulness, sociability, leadership, and prestige. This advantage is probably partly due to the fact that a longer growing period allows for a more balanced physical development. Late-maturing girls also have longer legs than other girls, which adds to their beauty, according to American standards. Furthermore, the late-maturing girl is more nearly in step with the development of boys in her age group. Thus, her interests in mixed social activities can be more readily satisfied.

When we consider the problems of the late-maturing boy, we find a complete reversal of the situation that exists for late-maturing girls. The slow-maturing boy is too small to gain acceptance in athletics; he is too immature to get dates with girls his own age. He frequently develops inferiority feelings that may persist for a lifetime.

School teachers and counselors should do everything in their power to reassure late-maturing boys that when they reach maturity they will be as tall as earlier-maturing boys and that their rates of growth are perfectly normal. It is important that late-maturing boys not try to adjust by withdrawing from competition and becoming submissive and self-effacing. If late-maturing boys can gain a sufficient feeling of security, many of them will also be less noisy and aggressive and less prone to seek excessive attention.

### Problems Resulting from Physical Deviations from the Norm

It has already been mentioned that early-maturing girls and late-maturing boys suffer from anxieties and worries partly because their physiques vary from the norms of their age mates. Many studies show that practically all adolescents, regardless of their rate of development, are very sensitive about physical defects and somatic variations. Boys and girls worry because they feel they are too thin or too heavy, too tall or too short, or that their hips are too wide or their legs too big. Of great concern to adolescents is their facial appearance. Some of the facial characteristics that worry adolescents are blackheads and pimples, lack of beard, heavy eyebrows, scars, birthmarks, moles, irregular teeth, heavy lips, protruding chin, protruding ears, oily skin, freckles, having to wear glasses, dark skin, and a too long or odd-shaped nose.

Many adolescents would change themselves physically if they could. In a study made in Arizona by Frazier and Lisonbee,[9] two-thirds of all ado-

---

[9] Alexander Frazier and Lorenzo K. Lisonbee, "Adolescent Concerns with Physique," *The School Review*, Vol. 58, October, 1950, pp. 397–405.

lescents queried wished to change their appearance in one way or another. Following are some of the verbatim statements of the boys.

> I would make my chest bigger than it is now and also my shoulders. I would like to weigh a little bit more, say about twenty to twenty-five pounds more.
> I would make myself look handsomer and not fat. I would have wavy black hair. I would change my whole physical appearance so that I would be handsome with a good build.
> Well, I would start off by putting on some meat, next I would get rid of my pimples, then get some muscles, then get rid of my glasses.

The way adolescent girls feel about physical deviations can be seen by some of their comments:

> My hips and legs are too large and fat. If I could have smaller hips and legs, I'd have a much better figure. I'd also like to be a little more developed above the waist than I am, but I am not too flat. I wish I didn't have so many pimples or have to wear glasses.
> I would first of all change my nose, as it is large. I think some day I will go to a plastic surgeon and get my nose changed. . . . I would like a clear, unscarred complexion. I have blackheads and pimples. I may go to a dermatologist.
> I would like to be three inches shorter and have smaller feet.

There is no question that many adolescents consider themselves to be abnormal in physical characteristics when in reality they are well within the normal range. For example, girls are sometimes known to worry because their menstrual cycles vary from the so-called norm of 28 days. A study made by Fluhmann [10] of 76 healthy young women showed that their menstrual cycles varied from 11 to 144 days, the great majority falling between 18 and 42 days. Only five of the girls showed absolutely regular cycles. A certain amount of variation is to be expected. Marked deviations, of course, should be checked, and a metabolism test should be made by a qualified physician, who may recommend medication.

Adolescent boys are known to be sometimes concerned about the size of their genital organs and to develop personality disorders because of their anxieties. Yet, such concern in most cases is groundless, because the boys are in all likelihood well within the limits of normality. If adolescent boys and girls could be supplied with appropriate information regarding the great range of individual differences that typically exists among individuals of their age, a great deal of personal unhappiness could be eliminated. The teacher, psychological counselor, or athletic coach is in a position to offer

---

[10] For details of this study see W. W. Greulich, "Physical Changes in Adolescence," in Forty-Third Yearbook of the National Society for the Study of Education, Part 1, *Adolescence*, Chicago, 1944, pp. 29–30.

sympathetic help and advice to adolescents who are distressed because of real or imagined physical defects or somatic deviations.

### The Problem of Being Normal

When the thousands of worries that beset adolescents are analyzed, one outstanding trend emerges. It is that adolescents want to be normal human beings. To be different is usually considered a bad thing. This is probably a general human trait, but the urge to conform or to be normal seems to be accentuated during adolescence.

Since one definition of "normal" is to be at the "norm," or "average," and since in statistics the "average" is a mathematical number or point, it is obvious that few, if any, adolescents can be really normal, according to this definition. Half will be above average, and the other half will be below assuming a normal distribution. This will apply to any trait that might be mentioned. Weights of adolescents will be too high or too low; breasts will be too large or too small; noses will be too long or too short; feet will be too big or too little; IQs will be too high or too low, and so on.

In dealing with adolescents, it is most important that a different concept of normality from the one defined above be used. No adolescent wants to be thought of as being abnormal. Teachers, counselors, and others who work with children and young people, or other people for that matter, might well take the position that *anyone who falls under the normal curve is normal.*[11] This, of course, includes everyone, for 100 per cent of a distribution will be found under the bell-shaped normal curve. To be different, then, is to be normal. It takes all kinds of people to satisfy this criterion of normality. It is perfectly normal for a high school senior boy to be four feet, eight inches tall, although he is obviously short. It is likewise normal for a girl to be six feet tall. Many are that tall, and if it were not for these tall girls, we would not have a normal curve. Similarly, it is exceedingly normal for an adolescent to have an IQ of 75. Hundreds of thousands of pupils have IQs in this neighborhood, and this value, of course, falls under the normal curve.

No harm can possibly result from persuading each adolescent to feel that he is normal. This will reduce many worries and lessen tensions. After he is reassured that he is normal, then various diagnostic tests or other measures can be used to appraise his achievements, interests, or talents. A profile of his traits can be obtained that will show just what his "normality" looks like. If he is weak in some area, he can be encouraged to improve that particular aspect of his knowledge or personality. If his complete profile shows that he deviates considerably from the average in

---

[11] This definition would obviously not apply to diseases and some severe physical defects.

some physical attribute that is not subject to change or learning, he can at least view his status as being very normal.

This author has interviewed many adolescents who were depressed, discouraged, and worried because they thought they were abnormal in some way. When they were shown that their characteristics fell under the normal curve of distribution, a great load was lifted. Some of them remarked, "This is the first time that I ever knew I was normal." With the pressure and anxiety gone, the student is then in good mental shape to be given sound teaching or educational and vocational guidance that is in line with his achievements, interests, and other traits.

Some who read the foregoing approach to counseling worried adolescents may view this interpretation of normality as being only a psychological trick that can produce effective results and lessen anxieties. There is no question that this approach will reduce worries and anxieties, but it is not entirely a trick. It is a novel interpretation of what normality means, which at the same time takes away the stigma of being "abnormal" when one is really only different.

The preceding discussion of what it means to be normal has definite implications for junior and senior high schools that group their adolescents for instructional purposes. Many schools desire to have at least three levels of instruction in subjects such as reading, mathematics, or science for pupils of a given age or grade level. They want one class for pupils who are low in achievement in the subject, another class or classes for so-called regular achievers, and a third type of class for pupils who are accelerated in the subject. This is a very good idea and is in line with what is known about readiness for learning. Pupils who are homogeneously grouped on the basis of achievement or interest can be better taught than in a group that is too heterogeneous. However, if being placed in a special class implies that a pupil is abnormal or dull, more harm than good usually results.

There is no reason, however, that every pupil in every class in the junior or senior high school, regardless of the level of instruction in the class, cannot be made to feel that he is normal. He can be told that he is very normal and at the same time be informed that he needs special instruction, say, in reading. He will undoubtedly agree with this. He knows that he does not read well, and in most cases he will desire to improve his skills if no stigma is attached to the process. The teacher of a special reading class can point out that anyone can learn to read, just as anyone can learn to tap-dance or play the piccolo. The teacher may cite the cases of famous men, such as President Andrew Johnson who learned to read after he was married.

The school that desires to make all students feel normal and confident should seldom use so-called intelligence tests as a basis of grouping. In

fact, secondary schools would probably be much better off if so-called intelligence tests were not given in these schools at all. These tests do not measure potential ability to do schoolwork well, and in addition they serve in a tremendous number of cases to humiliate and stigmatize pupils and parents. This does not mean that schools should abandon a thorough testing program. Achievement and interest tests serve an extremely valuable function in teaching. The best single indicator of future achievement in an area of instruction is present achievement. "Intelligence tests" themselves are nothing but achievement tests, but they are so general in scope that they make an extremely poor basis for grouping pupils for a specific learning task. The fact that they also imply that they measure native mental ability makes them particularly pernicious when used by schools. Achievement, interest, and aptitude tests for various areas do not have this unfortunate connotation.

## INTELLECTUAL DEVELOPMENT

Many of the basic components of mental development are nearly complete before the adolescent period is fairly begun. Capacities such as perceptual-motor skills, space perception, and the ability to remember show little gain beyond the period of late childhood. This is not to say that intellectual growth stops, but that the groundwork for its development is fairly well completed early in adolescence.[12]

The environmental factors that influence intelligence as well as differences in rate of growth combine to produce wide variations in ability in adolescence. Of course, these same differences exist among adults, but adults are not generally tested, nor do they compete with each other intellectually in the same way that adolescents are forced to do in school. One result of such competition is that adolescents begin to accept their perceived ability as an unchanging trait that forever places them at a given level among their peers. They do not so clearly see, nor do their parents, that intellectual development does continue and relies heavily for its growth upon the interests and attitudes of students—in short, upon their desire to learn.

The idea of intelligence as a general, innate potential that will develop regardless of circumstances has little practical value. The mental capabilities of adolescents are a composite of many influences. By mid-adolescence, interests and abilities have become specialized, interests and motivation have blended in an inseparable way with ability, and habits of

---

[12] For an excellent review of studies in this area see David P. Ausubel and Pearl Ausubel, "Cognitive Development in Adolescence," in *Review of Educational Research*, Vol. 36, October, 1966, pp. 403–413.

thinking, conceptual development, and the strategies used to solve problems have merged into a common pool of attributes that are all reflected by mental test scores. Even the testmakers no longer maintain that they measure potential. Rather, they call their instruments aptitude or scholastic-ability tests, which are designed for the prediction of school achievement.

Even though many of the basic mental processes level off in adolescence, there is continued growth in measured ability or aptitude throughout this period. It is probable that more complex mental activities, such as abstract reasoning, continue to develop into the early twenties. Moreover, it is obvious that learning continues regardless of when the capacity for learning levels off. Continued intellectual sophistication, the accretion of conceptual depth and more complex cognitive structure, and the learning of new skills and methods all become part of the operating or functional intelligence.

## THE ADOLESCENT AND HIS PEER GROUP

Each stage of life brings demands for new social learnings. The infant must learn that his fundamental needs are mediated by his parents. The child learns that his status and his activities are greatly dependent upon his family and his playmates. The adolescent must learn that he can achieve status and maturity only by playing adult roles. He strives for maturity, but is still somewhat insecure; hence he needs alliance with others like himself. In the union thus formed he finds strength and the will to assert himself in the struggle for a place in the adult world.

The social learnings of adolescence, which, of course, build upon the foundation of family relationships formed during childhood, are nevertheless now beyond the direct control of adults. Rarely does an adult have complete access to the teenage group. Instead, the anxious parent, or the teacher who is somewhat suspicious of what goes on in the adolescent "gang," may find active hostility toward his attempts to penetrate or too closely scrutinize the doings of young people.

The peer group is strong and may be imperative in its demands upon its members. But it does serve an important purpose for its adolescent members. It helps them find a role for themselves. It helps them in an insecure period attain the necessary emancipation from the home, and it teaches social skills necessary for living a community life.

Throughout the period of childhood, and continuing on through adolescence, the peer group enlarges in size. From the initial two or three members it often grows to as many as a dozen rather close friends. While the unisexual nature of the group persists to a considerable extent, there is now an obvious crossing of the line. There are parties and dances and

school functions in which boys and girls of a given "clique" are seen together. Almost all children find a group to which they can belong. Those who do not are usually unhappy, oversensitive, and defensive about their lack of social acceptance.

Parents and teachers who desire to change attitudes and values of adolescents will find the peer group to be potentially a powerful ally. A youngster who can be induced to join a group holding a particular viewpoint, will invariably be influenced by the group's opinions. A girl belonging to a clique of youngsters who have no plans for going to college will be difficult to convince that a higher education is desirable. A boy who runs with a group that approves of smoking will nearly always fall in with his peer's standards. Sometimes it is necessary for families to move to new localities or schools in order to find appropriate peer groups for their teenagers.

## ADOLESCENT DELINQUENCY

Statistics seem to indicate that delinquency rates among adolescents are on the increase in this country. This is not true to the same extent in all cultures. No sharp increases have occurred in Denmark, Yugoslavia, Israel, or Poland. Of course, statistics do not tell the whole story. Many punishable acts go undetected or unreported, and what constitutes a delinquent act varies from country to country, and from time to time in our own country.

At the present time, according to official records, boys are involved in "delinquent acts" five times as often as girls. Of young people between the ages of 10 through 17, the most probable age of apprehension is between 14 and 16 years.[13] And among the boys the great majority of antisocial deeds, especially those of theft and violence, are committed in the company of others.

Why is it that many young people are so prone to commit delinquent acts? In the first place, with the coming of adolescence the individual, because of less supervision from the home, is able to get out with the gang and follow either his group or his individual inclinations to a greater extent. In the second place, the adolescent's desire for new experiences together with his only partly developed philosophy of life cause him to make many unwise decisions which an older person would not make.

One basic cause of delinquency, however, is frustration of some type. The adolescent's needs for recognition, security, independence, and affection are frequently thwarted to such an extent that antisocial behavior

---

[13] Muzafer Sherif, and Caroline W. Sherif, *Reference Groups: Exploration into Conformity and Deviation of Adolescents*, New York, Harper and Row, 1964, pp. 274–315.

is employed in an effort to reduce the pent-up tensions. Not all individuals become overtly aggressive when thwarted, but many do. Some of the conditions of life which cause frustrations that may lead to delinquency are poverty, low intelligence, conflict in the family, broken homes, lack of affection from parents, humiliation and lack of success in school, and inferiority feelings arising from real or imagined physical deviations.

A boy may break street lights and put paint on the school building because he receives no recognition around school in either curricular or extracurricular activities. A girl may drift into sexual difficulties because, in this relationship, she is really wanted by someone, and what she has to offer may be for the first time as valuable as what anyone else can offer. Delinquent acts would not be committed if the adolescent did not anticipate that they would satisfy some of his basic needs. The delinquent needs assistance in making adjustments which are socially acceptable and at the same time need-satisfying.

Not all delinquents are personally and emotionally maladjusted. Some are relatively well-adjusted youngsters who in order to satisfy their very normal needs have identified with antisocial groups. Because of group pressures they conform to what is expected of them and thus eventually find themselves in difficulty.

The problem of juvenile delinquency is a real one in our society. Regardless of whether the rates are soaring or are standing still, something must be done to alleviate the situation if possible.

Already some success has been achieved through the early prognosis of delinquency. Studies of delinquency have shown means of early identification, even before the adolescent period.[14] Except in high-delinquency areas, such specific predictive measures have not had widespread use. Their success, though, should indicate that more thorough records and diagnostic techniques would be valuable in all schools to point to adolescents with various problems (many latent), so that whether the problem is academic, emotional, or of a personality type, preventive measures could be taken while there was still a chance of success.

In the training of the average secondary school teacher, the topic of delinquency is covered in only about two or three pages of a textbook in educational psychology. Few ever take a course in juvenile delinquency, yet in some schools delinquents and potential delinquents make up a sizable portion of the classroom. The school counselor may have had a

---

[14] See William C. Kvaraceus, "Programs of Early Identification and Prevention of Delinquency," in Social Deviancy Among Youth, The Sixty-fifth Yearbook of the National Society for the Study of Education, Chicago, University of Chicago Press, 1966, pp. 189–220.

little more training. Social workers and school psychologists have probably had such training, but they exist in such small numbers that they do not even begin to fill the need for trained personnel in this area. At the very least, a beginning should be made to assure that all counselors and supervisory personnel receive education about juvenile delinquency. Along with the development of a core of personnel workers who know and understand the problem, teachers should receive solid work either as a special course or as a major unit of a course in adolescent psychology or educational psychology.

It should be re-emphasized that this is not an area of which we are ignorant. A great deal is known, and we have every reason to believe that such knowledge can be put to useful purposes. It is, however, such an awesome problem, involving our whole social fabric, that schools are likely to say: "What can we do?" "Look at their homes." "Look where they live." "How can we change that?" So long as this attitude persists, it is unlikely that much progress will be made.

New York's program, called "Higher Horizons," [15] in two slum-area schools gives convincing evidence that, among other procedures, intensive counseling of culturally deprived adolescents can produce dramatic results. Although the aim of the program was to produce better schoolwork, there was also a decrease in delinquency.

The paucity of trained workers and the sheer expense of intensive individual counseling argues for the greater use of group counseling, although much more research is needed before its efficacy is clearly established. It seems likely that a realistic program would include individual counseling (even including psychiatric care for the most seriously disturbed), with an adjunctive group-counseling program for the less seriously disturbed. One such program in a suburban school near Chicago,[16] while not aimed at delinquency, did succeed in improving both the personal and social adjustment and the schoolwork of a selected group of academic underachievers.

Every major study of delinquency has shown a close relationship among living conditions, family and community instability, and delinquency. As already noted, teachers in slum-area schools may be so overwhelmed by the problems that children bring to school with them from their homes and neighborhoods that they react with almost cynical despair. It is, of course, naive to expect that a new housing-development program or a new school is by itself going to solve the problem. In short, providing a

---

[15] For a description of this and other programs see Carl L. Byerly, "A School Curriculum for Prevention and Remediation of Deviancy," in The Sixty-fifth Yearbook of the National Society for the Study of Education, Chicago, University of Chicago Press, 1966, pp. 221–257.

[16] Evanston Township High School, Evanston, Illinois.

psychologically unstable family with better material goods, while it may have a palliative effect, does not strike at the roots of the problem. Basic changes of attitudes and motives are required on the part of members of the community. Such changes are most effectively produced by the formation of community action groups in which adolescents are involved. The adolescent who is searching for significance, who has boundless energy and is not yet completely cynical, may become the most valuable ally in any efforts that are made toward better conditions of life.

## SUMMARY

Adolescence is the period of transition which extends from the end of childhood to the beginning of adulthood. It may be long or short depending upon the practices employed by families and larger social groups. In our society children are generally given adult responsibilities very slowly. This results in a prolonged period of semi-dependence for many youths which may continue for as long as eight or ten years.

The adolescent, because of his ambiguous status (being neither a child nor an adult), frequently finds himself involved in emotional conflicts with younger children in the family, parents, teachers, and other members of the community. He wants to be grown-up and sometimes feels that he is not understood or not given enough responsibility for his own acts. Adolescents are particularly sensitive with respect to the opinions of their peers and generally value the judgments of their age mates more highly than those of adults. During adolescence an extreme sensitivity is also exhibited in regard to personal defects, blemishes, or sex characteristics that deviate greatly from the norm. Many adolescents give the impression that they feel insecure. Statistics have revealed that during this period, delinquency and emotional problems of many types reach a high peak. There is no question but that adolescence is a trying time for many individuals. Although adolescence presents numerous problems for young people, there is no reason why under favorable conditions these can not be handled without undue stress or crisis. Teachers are in a favorable position to help adolescents resolve their worries, and plan courses of action which will provide for the satisfaction of their needs. Since adolescents so universally resent being treated as younger children, teachers should make an especial effort to give them responsibilities, and freedom which is commensurate with their maturity. Teachers may also find it possible at times to give guidance to parents regarding procedures to be followed in dealing with adolescents in the family.

It has been shown in this chapter that the adolescent has special problems which he did not have as a child and which are somewhat different from those he will encounter as an adult. He has certain needs which are accentuated, and a series of developmental tasks which must

be mastered. Teachers and parents alike should understand the nature of the unique problems of the adolescents if they are to help them make a smooth transition into adulthood. Knowledge of basic behavior theory plus specialized information regarding the period of adolescence and the individual adolescent are prerequisites for this task.

### References for Further Study

Ausubel, David P. *Maori Youth*, New York, Holt, Rinehart and Winston, 1965.

Blos, Peter. *On Adolescence: A Psychoanalytic Interpretation*, New York, Glencoe Free Press, 1962.

Coleman, James S. *The Adolescent Society*, New York, Glencoe Free Press, 1961.

Crow, Lester D. and Crow, Alice, *Adolescent Development and Adjustment*, Second Edition, New York, McGraw-Hill Book Company, 1965.

Douvan, Elizabeth and Adelson, Joseph, *The Adolescent Experience*, New York, John Wiley and Sons, 1966.

Grinder, Robert E. "Relations of Social Dating Attractions to Academic Orientations and Peer Relations," *Journal of Educational Psychology*, Vol. 57, February, 1966, pp. 27–34.

Havighurst, Robert J., *et al.*, *Growing Up in River City*, New York, John Wiley and Sons, 1962.

Havighurst, Robert J., *Human Development and Education*, New York, Longmans, Green and Co., 1953, Chapters 9, 10, 11, 12, 13, 14, 15.

Hollingshead, August B., *Elmtown's Youth*, New York, John Wiley and Sons, Inc., 1949.

Jones, R. Stewart, "Instructional Problems and Issues," in Educational Programs: Adolescence, *Review of Educational Research*, Vol. 36, October, 1966, pp. 414–423.

Kiell, Norman, *The Adolescent Through Fiction*, New York, International Universities Press, Inc., 1959.

Kinsey, Alfred C., *et al. Sexual Behavior in the Human Female*, Philadelphia, W. B. Saunders Company, 1953.

Kinsey, Alfred C., *et al. Sexual Behavior in the Human Male*, Philadelphia, W. B. Saunders Company, 1948.

Kuhlen, Raymond G., "Adolescence," *Encyclopedia of Educational Research*, Third Edition, New York, The Macmillan Company, 1960, pp. 24–30.

Lewin, Kurt, "The Field Theory Approach to Adolescence," *The Adolescent: A Book of Readings*, Revised Edition (J. Seidman, Editor), New York, Holt, Rinehart and Winston, Inc., 1960, pp. 32–42.

Muuss, Rolf E., *Theories of Adolescence*, New York, Random House, 1962.

Peskin, Harvey, "Pubertal Onset and Ego Functioning," *Journal of Abnormal Psychology*, Vol. 72, February, 1967, pp. 1–15.

Quay, Herbert C., *Juvenile Delinquency: Research and Theory*, Princeton, N.J., D. Van Nostrand Company, 1965.

Remmers, H. H. and Radler, D. H. *The American Teenager*, Indianapolis–New York, The Bobbs-Merrill Company, Inc., 1957.

Richey, Herman G. (Editor). *Social Deviancy Among Youth*, 65th Yearbook of the NSSE, Chicago, University of Chicago Press, 1966.

Schreiber, Daniel (Editor). *The School Dropout*, National Education Association, Washington, D.C., 1964.

Sherif, Muzafer and Sherif, Carolyn W., *Reference Groups: Explorations into Conformity and Deviations of Adolescents*, New York, Harper and Row, 1964.

Staton, Thomas F., *Dynamics of Adolescent Adjustment*, New York, The Macmillan Company, 1963.

Sutherland, Barbara K. "Case Studies in Educational Failure During Adolescence" in *Underachievement*, Milton Kornrick, Editor, Springfield, Illinois, Charles C Thomas, 1965, pp. 376–389.

## Films

*Age of Turmoil*, New York, McGraw-Hill Book Company (20 minutes).

*Meaning of Adolescence*, New York, McGraw-Hill Book Company (16 minutes).

*Meeting the Needs of Adolescence*, New York, McGraw-Hill Book Company (19 minutes).

*Physical Aspects of Puberty*, New York, McGraw-Hill Book Company (19 minutes).

*Social-Sex Attitudes in Adolescence*, New York, McGraw-Hill Book Company (22 minutes).

## Questions, Exercises, and Activities

1. Do you believe that adolescents as a group are really more concerned about their physical appearance (such as being too fat) than are elementary school pupils? Support your position with facts and incidents from your own observations and experiences.

2. It has sometimes been said that a certain amount of conflict between adolescents and their parents is inevitable. Do you believe this? Defend the position you take with facts or theoretical arguments.

3. Adolescents seem to be very much influenced by the opinions of their peer groups. Why do you believe this is so? Do you think that adolescents are more concerned with what their age mates think than are younger children?

4. What were the two or three greatest worries you had as an adolescent? Do you think your worries were typical of other adolescents at that time?

5. People argue as to whether adolescents are more unruly and delinquent today than they were fifty years ago. What position do you take? Secure as much factual information on this controversy as you can.

6. The book *Elmtown's Youth*, as well as other studies, shows that the behavior and attitudes of adolescents in the lower socio-economic class differ radically from those of the middle class. Summarize what these differences are. Why is it important for a teacher to be aware of these differences?

7. What movies have you seen in the past year that provide insight into adolescent behavior? Describe the situations that occurred and point out what psychological principles explain the behavior of the adolescents involved.

8. Look through several issues of your local newspaper and spot articles which deal with adolescent problems. Cut one of these out and bring to class. Also attach to this clipping your evaluation of the article. Are the facts true? Does the writer make a proper interpretation of his facts, etc.?

9. Examine the *Education Index* and look under the heading "Adolescence." Select an article which interests you. Write out and bring to class a short review and critical evaluation of the article.

10. What type of sex education program do you advocate for secondary schools? Should boys and girls receive instruction together, or in separate groups? What should be the content? Visit one or more local schools and evaluate the plans for sex education that are in operation.

# PART THREE

## Learning

# Chapter 5

## Learning:
## Basic Processes

### INTRODUCTION

What is learning? Any change of behavior which is a result of experience, and which causes people to face later situations differently may be called learning. The person not trained in psychology may conceive of learning in a narrow, academic sense. To such a person learning means acquiring skill in reading, spelling, or a trade. Actually, it is much more! Children learn cultural values; they learn appropriate sex roles; they learn to love and to hate and to fear and to be self-confident; they learn wants and interests and character and personality traits. It is not much of an overstatement to say that a person is what he has learned to be.

This chapter will show that while there is little disagreement among psychologists as to the importance of learning and the pervasiveness of learning in nearly all forms of human activity, there is a marked difference in the ways they look at learning. Here for example are two definitions of learning:

> Learning is a change in human disposition or capability which can be retained, and which is not simply ascribable to the process of growth.[1]
> . . . learning is the process of the formation of relatively permanent neural circuits through the simultaneous activity of the elements of the circuits-to-be; such activity is of the nature of change in cell structures through growth in such a manner as to facilitate the arousal of the entire circuit when a component element is aroused or activated.[2]

---

[1] Robert M. Gagne, *The Conditions of Learning*, New York, Holt, Rinehart and Winston, Inc., 1965, p. 5.
[2] B. R. Bugelski, *The Psychology of Learning*, New York, Henry Holt, 1956, p. 120.

These are but two samples of many differing definitions that might have been selected. All definitions have several common elements. They all employ the notion of change. They all exclude those changes that result from innate genetic forces that produce growth. The major points of difference center around what gets changed. To many, the process of change means linking a stimulus and response together, that is, developing an S—R relationship that does not presently exist, or strengthening one that does. To others the important change is in the new connections developed between internal stimuli and responses (mediators), for example, covert kinesthetic stimuli and subvocal responses. Still others view the central feature of learning as the hitching together of stimuli into new combinations as in the linking of the stimulus dog and the stimulus pain to each other. In brief, learning theorists have not settled upon a single model for viewing and studying learning.

The approach taken in this book is that all these changes do occur, all are represented in the neural-physical makeup, and all can properly be described as learning.

## WAYS OF STUDYING THE LEARNING PROCESS

As in other areas of science there are, in the field of learning, various theories which attempt to explain its basic processes. Both in method and conclusion these theories have differed greatly, for they have sharply focused attention on only certain aspects of the total learning process. As a consequence, the behavior which various experimenters and teachers have observed has been different. For example, some workers in this field have so diligently pursued the way in which a stimulus and response are connected that they have ignored the condition of the person or animal with which they were working.

A few of the kinds of experimental situations which have been used to study learning include: (1) A hungry animal is put inside a puzzle box (food outside) from which release is possible only by striking the latch, (2) An animal is put in a box in which there is a bar connected with a source of food pellets which are released one at a time as the bar is pressed, (3) An animal is placed on a platform and forced to jump toward one of a series of doors which are differentiated by shape or color, (4) Nonsense syllables are paired with geometric designs and a person is shown the pairings a number of times until he has memorized them, (5) A person is given a verbal problem, and asked to describe his solution aloud. Obviously the kinds of behavior which are observed will differ greatly. In one case there may be a wild thrashing about in an attempt to escape, in another a seemingly thoughtful or cautious approach. Furthermore, the variation in what is found is not surprising when it is realized that experimenters have worked with animals of nearly every species from one-

celled organisms to man. The result has been the development of at least a half dozen major theories of learning, and a score or more theoretical approaches to the study of behavior.

The educator has much the same relationship to these various theories as the engineer to theories of light, electricity, and matter, or the doctor to theories about genetics or cancer. He uses the ideas where they fit into the practical problems of teaching and he searches for ways of extending theoretical and practical knowledge by testing it against the complex demands of the classroom. Just as in other fields, the gap between a basic idea and its application may be very great. Physicists, for example, have known for perhaps a hundred years that various metals and compounds are endothermic, i.e., absorb a great amount of heat when they change from a solid to a liquid state. But only in recent years has this well-known principle been applied in such practical matters as the construction of brakes for aircraft. (Virtually all large aircraft employ brakes that use this principle.)

Likewise psychologists have known for nearly 60 years of the value of providing immediate knowledge of results to a learner, and even though Pressey [3] forty years ago saw the possibility of applying the idea in education, and developed some means of doing so, the principle is still not in general use in the classroom.

In the following section various ways of studying the learning process and of trying to make order out of the complexities of human behavior will be presented. This material will in part serve as an introduction to the balance of the chapters in this part of the book that deals with learning.

### Learning as a Process of Association

The oldest and most common method of analyzing the process of learning is through a study of the association of ideas, stimuli, and responses. Even the ancient Greeks attempted to describe mental life in this fashion. Aristotle talked of learning as an association of ideas following the laws of (1) similarity, (2) contrast, and (3) contiguity. [4] He believed that people learn and remember those things which are alike, which are striking because of their difference, and which occur together in space and time.

Centuries later, a rebirth of interest in the philosophy of the human mind resulted in a school of thought known as the British School of Associationism. This group had the notion that mind was formed through a lawful process of the association of experiences and ideas. Well-known historical figures such as Thomas Hobbes, John Locke, David Hume, and later, James Mill, and Alexander Bain were represented in this philosophi-

---

[3] S. L. Pressey, "A Simple Apparatus Which Gives Tests and Scores—and Teaches," *School and Society*, Vol. 23, pp. 373–376, 555.

[4] Gardner Murphy, *Historical Introduction to Modern Psychology*, New York, Harcourt, Brace, 1949, p. 9.

cal venture, and the great, revolutionary ideas concerning the original nature of man were developed. For instance, the concept of the new-born infant as having a blank mind (*tabula rasa*) probably gave impetus to the idea that man is a product of his experiences.[5] From these early beliefs came a great concern for the nature of mental life and in turn this concern led to many of the modern ideas about education, child rearing, and even democratic ideals.

Not until the turn of the present century, however, did learning, as a process of association, receive experimental analysis. At that time, two widely separated workers, E. L. Thorndike in America and I. P. Pavlov in Russia, established bases for analytical studies of the process of learning.

CONNECTIONISM. Thorndike's work for a period of over fifty years is recognized as one of the greatest contributions to the psychology of learning, particularly for its educational implications. His psychology of "Connectionism" has had a profound influence upon American education.[6]

Thorndike demonstrated that learning could be analyzed and furnished practical results to educators when he conducted experiments which led to his statement of the "law of effect." In brief, this law tells those who teach that learners will acquire and remember those responses which lead to satisfying after effects.[7] A praised response will be retained longer than one which is not praised or one which is called wrong. This is indeed a practical kind of material, and one which has gained such wide acceptance that the reader may think of it as just common sense.

Another practical venture of the "Connectionists" was their study of the effect of exercise or frequency of repetition on learning. Every teacher in certain types of courses is faced with the problem of how much drill to use in teaching. Thorndike's experiments showed that repetition *per se* did not establish a connection, but that the strength of such connections depended upon the laws of effect and readiness and such secondary principles as belongingness.[8]

Thorndike's work grew directly from the tradition of associationism. His laws of learning, except for the law of effect, were almost identical with the laws of association which were stated two centuries before. Unlike his philosophical predecessors, Thorndike insisted upon experimentation and measurement rather than relying upon introspection and logic.

His observations of animals confronted with the problem of escaping

---

[5] *Ibid.*, pp. 21–29 and pp. 97–110.

[6] An excellent description of Thorndike's contributions may be found in Peter Sandiford, "Connectionism: Its Origin and Major Features" in Forty-First Yearbook of the National Society for the Study of Education, Part II, *The Psychology of Learning*, pp. 97–140.

[7] E. L. Thorndike, *The Fundamentals of Learning*, New York, Teachers College, Columbia University, 1932.

[8] E. L. Thorndike, *Selected Writings from a Connectionists' Psychology*, New York, Appleton-Century-Crofts, Inc., 1949, pp. 62–80.

from a box in order to attain food led first to his description of "trial and error" behavior, and then to his insistence upon motivation (the law of effect) as a central feature in the learning process.

Throughout the years he worked as an educational psychologist, he was a pioneer and maintained an active interest in learning theory, school learning, intelligence testing, and educational measurement. In many respects he is the starting point for both educational psychology, and America's brand of objective psychology (behaviorism).

THE CONDITIONED REFLEX. Intuitively and without labeling specific elements, or measuring them, people have known about associative learning for many centuries, as has been previously noted. Anyone who has a dog may have observed the animal slobbering when he hears the sound of his food being placed in a dish, or even at the sound of the word cookie. An Italian short story written before the time of our Revolutionary War describes an instance of "conditioning." The mother of a young man who had been murdered plotted revenge upon her son's slayer. She secured a large dog, which she taught to feed at the throat of a dummy figure she had built. Soon she placed food at the "dummy's" throat only on those occasions when she tied a scarf around the neck of the home-made mannikin. Then she sent word to the killer that she wished to make peace and forgive him. When he arrived she told him that to show her sincerity she wanted him to have a scarf she had made for him. She proceeded to tie it around his neck and then called her dog.

Just as Thorndike had applied scientific precision to a commonly observed phenomenon (an animal trying to learn how to escape), so Pavlov, a Russian physiologist, applied carefully controlled and systematic study to an anticipatory autonomic reaction (salivation) of dogs.[9] Pavlov's well-known early experiments in what has since come to be called classical conditioning can be detailed as follows:

| | | | | |
|---|---|---|---|---|
| STEP 1. | Original Natural Relationship | Unconditioned Stimulus or Meat Powder | | → | Unconditioned Response Salivation |

STEP 1. Original Natural Relationship — Unconditioned Stimulus or Meat Powder → Unconditioned Response Salivation

STEP 2. Pairing of New Unrelated Stimulus with the Old — Conditioned Stimulus or Sound of a Tuning Fork — Unconditioned Stimulus + Meat Powder → Unconditioned Response Salivation

(SEVERAL REPETITIONS OF STEP 2)

STEP 3. Removal of Unconditioned Stimulus — Conditioned Stimulus Tuning Fork Alone → Conditioned Response Salivation

---

[9] Gardner Murphy, *op. cit.*, p. 255.

If one uses this scheme to analyze the conditioning of a child to a fear of dogs, appropriate substitution would be as follows:

STEP 1. Unconditioned Stimulus → Unconditioned Response
(Pain—Loud Noise)                  (Fear Responses)

STEP 2. Conditioned Stimulus (Dog) and    Unconditioned Response
Unconditioned Stimulus → (Fear)
(Bark or Bite)

STEP 3. Conditioned Stimulus (Dog) → Conditioned Response (Fear)

It should be clear that children can form connections even though there is apparently no "logical" relationship between the ideas and events which are associated. Conditioning does occur in the classroom. For example, there is no logical relationship between a child's feelings of inferiority and arithmetic *per se*. But when, in arithmetic class, he is made to feel inferior enough times, the activities connected with arithmetic become almost inextricably linked with the emotional responses associated with feelings of inferiority. Teachers of remedial reading have often reported cases in which children flinch, tremble, or show other fear responses at the mere sight of a reading book, while a comic book or newspaper fails to elicit these emotional manifestations.

THE ASSOCIATIVE PROCESS IN TODAY'S SCHOOLS. Association as a method of learning and remembering continues as an ever present part of education. Parents teach their children to associate spoken words with objects and persons. Later teachers get them to associate pictures with words, letters with sounds, words with ideas, and ideas with each other. If one were to compose a list of all school activities during the day, a good part of them would be characterized by some kind of associative activity. As a matter of fact, automated teaching and programming of information rely heavily upon this basic view of how learning takes place. For example, the machine shown in Figure 5 was developed to teach hard of hearing children how to associate words with pictures. In this illustration the little girl finds she is right when the electrically-connected stylus makes contact with the correct point to indicate a choice of one of four words, and signals, by sight, that she has indeed chosen the correct alternative. The machine then advances to the next picture-word association.[10]

It is quite possible to argue that too much attention is devoted to this form of learning, or that teachers are concerned with the wrong elements in the process. Nevertheless, it is the most common method of teaching and learning, and would be better used if it were more clearly analyzed and understood. For instance, teachers frequently give their pupils mne-

---

[10] George A. Falconer, A *Mechanical Device for Teaching Word Recognition to Young Deaf Children*, Unpublished Doctoral Thesis, Urbana, University of Illinois, 1959.

**Figure 5.** Association in Teaching-Machine Learning.

monic devices to use in remembering things. The word FACE in music is a good example of a way to remember the spaces in the treble clef. But do teachers know and understand that there are systems of mnemonics that are almost as ancient as Western civilization, systems that can be learned and employed in the rote memorization of any group of things? As early as 500 B.C., there is a report of a Greek poet, Simonides, who devised a system of a specific visualized locality for each of a series of things that he wanted to remember. Both Cicero and Quintilian used the system in preparing their speeches.[11]

In his own classes for several years, the writer has asked students to recall any instance in their own schooling when a teacher has taught them anything about how to memorize. Only two or three out of several hundred students could recall any such teaching in their twelve to fourteen years of schooling. The writers do not argue for more memorization in schools, there is perhaps too much already, at least there is too much of a tendency to substitute memorizing for understanding. Nevertheless when children are expected to do rote memorizing, it would seem obvious they ought to be taught *how* to do it. Suggestions for teaching children how to memorize better are given in Chapter 9.

---

[11] I. M. L. Hunter, *Memory: Facts and Fallacies*, Baltimore, Penguin Books, Inc., 1957, pp. 164–165.

### Learning as a Process of Reinforcement [12]

Another way of looking at the learning process is to focus attention upon the *effect* of the response upon the individual. As previously noted, Thorndike's most important law of learning was his *law of effect*, which has become a basic part of most psychologies of learning.[13]

It is important that educators consider learning in this way, as it is a point of view which alerts them to the characteristics of the learner—the learner's need states, and his past experience (previous reinforcements). There is little doubt that knowledge about the kinds of behavior for which a youngster has been rewarded or from which he has received satisfaction will provide a teacher with the best possible tool for predicting future behavior. Also, this knowledge should offer help in finding ways to change behavior, by changing the patterns of reinforcement.

In a simple form, reinforcement might be illustrated as follows:

$$\text{Rat} - \begin{array}{c} \text{Running} \\ \text{Through} \\ \text{Maze} \end{array} - \text{Food}$$

The receipt of the reward serves to strengthen the responses (making proper turns in the maze) so that on subsequent trials the animal will be more able to go directly to the goal object. The same sort of scheme can be thought of in the learning of children. For example:

$$\text{Child} - \begin{array}{c} \text{Out of School Window} \\ \text{Throwing Paper} \end{array} - \begin{array}{c} \text{Laughter and Enjoyment} \\ \text{of Fellow Students} \end{array}$$

The attention-getting response is strengthened by the receipt of satisfaction, i.e., by the reduction of the need for peer approval.

Most prominent of today's reinforcement theorists is Skinner [14] whose influence upon the contemporary scene in psychology is very great. In his early experimental work he drew the important distinction between the kind of conditioning in which the organism was simply responding to unconditioned and conditioned stimuli, and the kind in which *emitted* behavior was strengthened by positive reinforcement. Pavlov's dog could do nothing but salivate under the circumstances. Bechterev's animals simply stood in their harnesses waiting for a signal which would mean they

---

[12] When an act reduces a need and leads to satisfying consequences that act is said to be reinforced. As used in psychological literature, the concept of reinforcement is roughly equivalent to the notion of reward.

[13] E. R. Hilgard, and G. H. Bower, *Theories of Learning*, Third Edition, New York, Appleton-Century-Crofts, Inc., 1966, pp. 15–16.

[14] B. F. Skinner, *The Behavior of Organisms: An Experimental Analysis*, New York, Appleton-Century-Crofts, 1938.

were going to receive an electric shock unless they raised their right rear paw. Skinner on the other hand concerned himself with freely emitted behavior which through selective reinforcement permitted the strengthening of any response which the animal was capable of making. His system, sometimes called "operant conditioning," allowed for the precise study of many reinforcement variables such as quantity of reinforcing agents, temporal factors, sequences, and the like. In one volume Skinner and his co-worker, Ferster, reported on 70,000 hours of continuously recorded behavior composed of about one quarter of a billion responses.[15]

Applications of reinforcement theory exist in all fields of psychology. Operant conditioning is being used today in classrooms, mental hospitals, animal training centers, and in industry. Further discussion of reinforcement will be found in Chapter 7.

### Learning as a Process of Perception

Much of what is called learning really involves a change in ways of looking at one's environment. The impetus for this point of view comes from Gestalt Psychology.[16] The group of psychologists who established this system began working on problems of perception in Germany about 1912. This group objected to analysis of learning and behavior by breaking it down into specific elements.[17] They contended that such "molecular" analysis destroys the forces which bind experiences into meaningful wholes, and argued that in teaching one must consider the whole situation as a unit, rather than as a series of discrete parts.

For example, these dots and lines [18]

appear to unite into pairs. The "pairness" caused by their proximity is a characteristic entirely apart from the nature of the objects, and any analysis which breaks down this configuration destroys this characteristic.

Conceived in this way, learning may be thought of as a change in cognitive structure, i.e., as a change in the readiness of the individual to perceive objects and situations in a new way. The child who has first

---

[15] B. F. Skinner, "Reinforcement Today," *The American Psychologist*, Vol. 13, 1958, pp. 94–99.

[16] "Gestalt" means pattern or configuration. A good introduction to "Gestalt" learning theories may be found in E. R. Hilgard, *op. cit.*, pp. 229–263.

[17] They objected particularly to a stimulus-response psychology such as advocated by some behaviorists, and the atomism of the psychology of Wundt.

[18] Kurt Koffka, *Principles of Gestalt Psychology*, New York, Harcourt, Brace, 1935, p. 164.

experienced a loss of breath in a wading pool now perceives water in an entirely different manner. Likewise a youngster who for the first time has seen his own story in print, perceives the job of reading as a much different task than before.

The individual's behavior, when looked at in this way, is seen as a "purposive" striving toward goals, the paths to which are marked by signs or cues. The significant feature of the learning process occurs when the learner ascribes meaning or significance to these signs.[19] Experimentation has shown that interference with response sequences is not sufficient to prevent learners from reaching goals by a new series of responses.[20] This supports the notion that what is learned is not primarily a stimulus response connection, but a changed perception in which various stimuli are seen as pointers toward a goal.

### Learning as a Process of Cognitive Organization

For complex learnings, especially when verbal factors are considered, the analysis must include a consideration of such things as meaningfulness, organization, and understanding. This type of analysis is quite similar to the study of learning as a perceptual process. The major emphasis is upon the study of relationships and how people learn to see relationships among various items of experience. Learning of relationships may be clearly seen in the phenomenon of insight. Sometimes pupils work for a long time on a problem or skill with little apparent progress. All of a

---

[19] E. C. Tolman, *Purposive Behavior in Animals and Men,* New York, D. Appleton-Century Company, 1932.

[20] E. C. Tolman, B. F. Ritchie, and D. Kalish, "Studies in Spatial Learning, IV, The Transfer of Place Learning to Other Starting Paths," *Journal of Experimental Psychology,* Vol. 37, 1947, pp. 39–47.

Teaching Mathematics in the Lower Grades by the Use of Manipulative Devices. The Emphasis Is Upon the Discovery Method of Teaching.

sudden there will be a flash of understanding in which the student sees through the problem, or re-forms his responses into a more complex habit. The phenomenon was first widely publicized by the famous German psychologist Köhler,[21] who found that apes, when confronted with a difficult problem, might act as if they were surveying the situation; would then go directly to the goal object (banana) by putting two sticks together, or by piling one box on top of another. It appeared that there had been a sudden perceptual change in which these animals saw the relationship of the sticks or boxes to themselves and the goal in a new way.

The reader who wishes to experience insight might consider the problem shown in Figure 6.

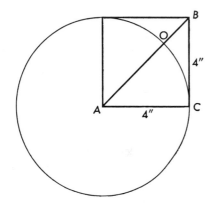

**Figure 6.** What Is the Length of the Line AO?

At first glance many people attempt to apply the Pythagorean theorem or some other inapplicable formula to the solution. Immediately after the line AO is seen as another radius of the circle, a perceptual shift occurs and the problem is solved.

Learning in this sense must also be thought of as a process of problem-solving—a way of thinking, creating, and synthesizing. The point of view that learning is much more than the acquisition of specific skills is made explicit by Brownell, who writes:

> A problem solving attitude, an inquiring and questioning mind, is a desirable educational outcome and it is possible of development. The practice of "learning" by cramming does not produce this outcome, nor does the practice of accepting from others truths and conclusions which ought to be established by the learner himself. The attitude *is* produced by continued

---

[21] W. Köhler, *The Mentality of Apes*, New York, Harcourt, Brace, 1925.

experience in solving real problems, one consequence of which is that the learner comes to *expect* new problems and to look for them.[22]

The important aspect of this view of learning is that it points to the importance of studying the processes in learning—the steps which the learner takes in solving problems, rather than the end-product of learning.

A modern exponent of this idea is Ausubel,[23] whose theory of cognitive structure postulates that concepts grow and become organized through a subsumption process, i.e., as each new concept is acquired, it is categorized and fitted into the existing structure. Experimental support for the validity of his inferences comes from studies in proactive inhibition (see Chaps. 9 and 10 of this volume), and from studies of "advance organizers" which seem to facilitate learning and retention, and reduce proactive inhibition.

### Learning as a Process of Imitation

Not long ago an observer at the Steel Pier in Atlantic City noted that teenagers, who were screaming, bouncing, moaning, and writhing, were spending as much or more time watching each other as they were looking at their then current idol. They seemed to be learning from each other how they were supposed to behave.

Many of our very important learnings, especially those related to emotional expressions and social interaction, come about largely through modeling our behavior after that of someone else. A very fearful mother can easily transmit that fear to a child without any direct teaching of it, or even an awareness that it is happening. A small boy may very much admire his father. The son may have the same swagger in his gait, and similar facial expressions and gestures as those used by his father. Miller and Dollard [24] call this latter kind of imitation, "matched dependent behavior," a form of identification with a person of perceived status. No deliberate attempt is made to copy the behavior of the prestigious figure, but the child develops many of his idol's characteristics.

"Copying" behavior, which Miller and Dollard see as a separate kind of imitation, occurs when the admired adult or a peer performs an action which serves as a model, and which the child knowingly and deliberately strives to duplicate. The piano teacher plays a piece as a demonstration of how it should be played. The piano student uses the teacher's rendition as a model against which he can compare his own performance.

What kinds of models do children choose to imitate? Can deviant be-

---

[22] W. A. Brownell, "Problem Solving" in Forty-First Yearbook of the National Society for the Study of Education, Part II, *The Psychology of Learning*, p. 440.

[23] D. P. Ausubel, *The Psychology of Meaningful Verbal Learning*, New York, Grune and Stratton, 1963.

[24] N. E. Miller and J. Dollard, *Social Learning and Imitation*, New Haven, Yale University Press, 1941.

havior be modified by substituting more socially acceptable models? Questions such as these have been investigated by Bandura [25] and his co-workers by studying the number of imitative responses made by children in various social-role contexts. In one study [26] experimental social groups of three (a man, woman, and child) were formed. In each group one adult was either the controller of rewards, the recipient of rewards from the other adult (consumer), or was ignored. The children were either the recipients of rewards or were ignored. Children were later observed and it was found that they modeled (identified) with the adult who controlled the rewards, the one with power, and not with the consumer, and they did so whether they themselves received rewards from the controller or simply observed him passing them out to the other adult.

### Learning as a Process of Neural Action

At one time the central nervous system, particularly the brain, was considered of such complexity that it was unfruitful even to consider it in relation to learning. Within the past twenty years great progress has been made, and it now seems possible that some day we may understand the brain mechanisms involved in learning.[27] Our definition of learning as a change of behavior due to experience says nothing about the neural processes involved. How is the change maintained over a period of time? Is there an actual physiological change within the organism when it has learned? Why does electrical stimulation at a single point in the human cortex cause a person to "relive" a portion of his life he believed he had long since forgotten? Challenging questions such as these, while still unanswered are the subject of vigorous attack by today's physiological psychologists.

Basic methods employed for studying behavior as it is related to the neural substratum include:

1. Permanent or temporary destruction of neural tissue, to determine the effect upon capacity to learn or upon items of behavior previously acquired.
2. Implantation of electrodes that can feed weak electric currents into various areas of the brain to study effects upon motivation and other forms of behavior.
3. Direct application upon various neural tissues of chemicals such as

---

[25] Albert Bandura, "Social Learning Through Imitation," in M. R. Jones (Editor) *Nebraska Symposium on Motivation,* Lincoln, Nebraska, University of Nebraska Press, 1962, pp. 211–269.

[26] Albert Bandura, Dorothea Ross and Sheila A. Ross, "A Comparative Test of Status Envy, Social Power and Secondary Reinforcement Theories of Identificatory Learning," *Journal of Abnormal and Social Psychology,* Vol. 67, 1963, pp. 527–534.

[27] Donald O. Hebb, "A Neurological Psychological Theory," in S. Koch (Editor), *Psychology: A Study of Science,* Vol. 1, New York, McGraw-Hill, 1959.

metrazol, procaine, epinephrin, and acetylcholine in an attempt to determine the effects when the reaction levels of these tissues are either raised or lowered.

4. Development and refinement of EEG [28] type recorders for measuring the electrical activity generated by the brain itself so as to attempt to relate items of behavior, such as perceiving a visual object, to the underlying electro-chemical force fields generated in the occipital lobes.

5. Electrical stimulation of the cortical areas in human beings during brain operations to locate tumors, but incidentally to help map out the specific functions of various parts of the cortex.

6. Histological studies of neural tissue of organisms which have been highly stimulated (environmentally) and others which have been deprived of stimulation so as to determine the relationship between learning and neural growth and change.

7. Use of electro-convulsive and chemical shocks to study the effects upon learning and memory traces.

8. Analyzing the particular chemical compounds that seem to be related to neural activity (e.g., the acetylcholine-cholinesterase balance) in order to find out if there are any relationships between these substances and observations of such things as deviant behavior and intelligence.

This is necessarily a sketchy summary of new physiological frontiers which furnish hope that in the not too distant future we shall be able to influence learning not only by the external environment but also by neurological manipulation. It was this hope which Herrick expressed when he wrote:

> Our minds are better minds when we understand them and their organs better. In fact, this sort of knowledge is our only hope of gaining satisfactory control over mental evolution. This is worth working for, and is not an impractical ideal.[29]

*Learning Theory and Teaching*

Each of the ways of analyzing the learning process just discussed seems to offer perspectives for better understanding the many types of behavior that occur in the classroom. While the theoretical psychologists may debate the issue of whether or not there are different kinds of learning, or whether one set of principles sufficiently explains all kinds of behavior, the teacher probably is not primarily interested in this argument. He may

---

[28] Electroencephalograph.

[29] C. Judson Herrick, *The Thinking Machine*, Chicago, University of Chicago Press, Second Edition, 1960, p. 361.

for the present, if he desires, work on the assumption that there are indeed various kinds of learning, and different techniques for dealing with them, and in this assumption he will be in good company. Robert Gagne, a leading psychologist in the field of human learning has this to say:

> It is believed therefore that the differences among these varieties of learning far outweigh their similarities. . . . To equate the responding of an animal to a warning signal with the learning of a child asking for a doll, or the learning of a student to identify a chromosome . . . is considered to be a matter of gross disregard for some obvious and simple observations.[30]

Some of the kinds of learning which Gagne believes are suggested by our present observations and experimental evidence include: signal learning, stimulus response learning, and problem solving. It is his belief that each of these kinds of learning requires different conditions for their development, thus the instructive program for each might differ.

In the chapters that follow, the kinds of complex meaningful learning that go on in schools will be presented. The reader will quickly sense the writers' belief that teachers should study learning theory not only to do a better job of teaching the school subjects, but also so they can influence the learnings of motives, attitudes, habits of work, and complex skills such as problem solving and original thinking. It now appears that teaching for such various outcomes may require a number of different strategies and methods of instruction.

### SUMMARY

There are several definitions of learning and many ways of analyzing the processes of learning. Learning may be analyzed as: association, perception, reinforcement, cognitive organization, imitation, and neural action. Various learning theorists have contributed to our better understanding of behavior by focusing particular attention upon one, or sometimes a combination of these basic processes. For instance, the behaviorists have dealt mainly with associationistic kinds of analysis and with reinforcement. The Gestalt psychologists assign perception the major role in explaining learning.

Some teachers may find that each of the ways of viewing learning can contribute to the task of instruction. Others may feel a partiality for one learning theory over another and wish to use it as the predominant tool in their work. The reinforcement theories of Skinner or Thorndike, for example, can be used to engineer the learning of most, if not all, of the kinds of behavior in which teachers are interested. Similarly the Gestalt

---

[30] Robert Gagne, *The Conditions of Learning*, New York, Holt, Rinehart and Winston, Inc., 1965, p. 60.

theory of learning may be used to effectively induce the major types of learning that take place in a classroom. Many of the supposed differences between learning theories may be only differences in semantics (differences in ways of talking about the same process).

The time may come when there will be only one generally accepted learning theory. In the meantime, the successful teacher will use the concepts and theories which he most completely understands and which seem most appropriate to the problems with which he deals.

## References for Further Study

Ausubel, David P., *The Psychology of Meaningful Verbal Learning*, New York, Grune and Stratton, 1963.

Bigge, Morris L., *Learning Theories for Teachers*, New York, Harper and Row, 1964.

Bugelski, B. R., *Psychology of Learning Applied to Teaching*, Bobbs-Merrill, 1965.

Chaplin, J. P. and Krawiec, T. S., *Systems and Theories of Psychology*, New York, Holt, Rinehart and Winston, 1960.

Craig, Robert C., *The Psychology of Learning in the Classroom*, New York, The Macmillan Company, 1966.

English, Horace B., *The Historical Roots of Learning Theory*, Papers in Psychology, New York, Random House, 1954.

Estes, William K., "Learning," in Harris, C. W. (Editor), *Encyclopedia of Educational Research*, Third Edition, New York, The Macmillan Company, 1960, pp. 752–770.

Gagne, Robert M., *The Conditions of Learning*, New York, Holt, Rinehart and Winston, 1965.

Hall, John F., *The Psychology of Learning*, Philadelphia, J. B. Lippincott Company, 1966.

Hill, Winfred F., *Learning: A Survey of Psychological Interpretations*. San Francisco, Chandler Publishing Company, 1963.

Hilgard, Ernest R. and Bower, Gordon H., *Theories of Learning*, 3rd Edition, New York, Appleton-Century-Crofts, 1966.

Lawson, Reed, *Learning and Behavior*, New York, The Macmillan Company, 1960, Chapter 1.

Mednick, Sarnoff A., *Learning*, Englewood Cliffs, New Jersey, Prentice-Hall, Inc., 1964.

National Society for the Study of Education, *Theories of Learning and Instruction*, Part I, 63rd Yearbook, Chicago, 1964.

Travers, Robert M. W., *Essentials of Learning*, New York, The Macmillan Company, 1967.

Wolman, Benjamin B., *Contemporary Theories and Systems in Psychology*, New York, Harper and Brothers, 1960.

Woodworth, R. S. and Sheehan, Mary R., *Contemporary Schools of Psychology*, Third Edition, New York, The Ronald Press Company, 1964.

## Questions, Exercises, and Activities

1. Ask several of your friends who are not taking the course in educational psychology to define learning. How do their definitions vary from each other?
2. Think of all the college courses you have had and are now taking. In which did you learn the most? How would you characterize this course and the instructional methods?
3. Read any one recent article in the *Journal of Educational Psychology* that deals with school learning and write a short précis of its content.
4. Suggest several ways in which the study of comparative psychology and the learning of animals may contribute to a better understanding of classroom learning. What are the dangers of over-generalizing from such comparative studies?
5. Read a list of fifteen words such as bank, cost, stock, to a friend at the rate of about one word per second. Ask him to write them after you have read them. What are the characteristics of the words he remembers? Does the place of the words in the list seem to make a difference? Why?
6. Aside from their both being associationistic theories, what other things do you see in common between Connectionism and Pavlov's study of the conditioned reflex?
7. Which of the various ways of studying the learning process seems most compatible with the goal of fostering intellectual development?
8. Discuss several ways in which learning affects perception, and contrariwise, how perception affects learning.
9. Do you believe that imitation is a basic innate drive, or is it primarily a learned type of behavior which has been developed through reinforcement? Defend your answer. So far as the teacher is concerned, does it make any difference?
10. Describe how you think a teacher would proceed differently in teaching a subject if he adhered to the Gestalt point of view rather than a reinforcement theory.

# Chapter 6

---

# Building Readiness
# and Individualizing
# Instruction

As he faces a class for the first time, the teacher is aware of tremendous differences among his students. But awareness of differences is not enough. If teaching is to be successful, he must know the nature and extent of such differences, how they affect teaching and learning, and the factors which account for such widespread differences among children. The teacher who knows a great deal about learning, but little about the learner, is only half prepared. This chapter will attempt to show the kinds and degrees of differences in learners, the factors which bring about such differences, and the methods which seem best fitted to handle such differences in the classroom. As will be seen in the discussion which follows, learning proceeds best when the instructional program first of all builds readiness within all pupils according to their present deficits and assets, and then provides instructional materials, programs, and methods that are flexible and adaptive to the learner's needs.

If one were to select a class at random, he would find that the readiness of pupils for a given task is so variable that it is inadvisable to expect a single or standard series of lessons and work materials to be effective. Table 6 presents the picture of a single aspect of readiness in only one subject. There it can be noted, for example, that 16 per cent of fifth

graders are not ready for books above the first and second-grade levels;[1] 7 per cent of the sixth graders are also not ready for books above the second-grade level. Seven percent of the fifth graders are ready for ninth-grade books as are 16 per cent of the sixth graders. Such a wide range of differences in all types of school work make attempts to achieve "standardized performance" futile. Readiness for learning must be conceived in terms of individual pupils and the teacher who is aware of differences and knows how to teach accordingly will have a greater chance for success.

**TABLE 6**

**The Percentage of Children in Each Grade Ready for Each Book Level \***

| Book Level | | Grade Level | | | | | |
|---|---|---|---|---|---|---|---|
| Grade | Age | I | II | III | IV | V | VI |
| Nursery School | 5 | 2 | 2 | 2 | | | |
| Kindergarten | 6 | 23 | 8 | 5 | 7 | | |
| 1 | 7 | 50 | 24 | 11 | 9 | 7 | |
| 2 | 8 | 23 | 33 | 20 | 10 | 9 | 7 |
| 3 | 9 | 2 | 24 | 24 | 16 | 10 | 9 |
| 4 | 10 | | 8 | 20 | 17 | 16 | 10 |
| 5 | 11 | | 2 | 11 | 16 | 17 | 16 |
| 6 | 12 | | | 5 | 10 | 16 | 17 |
| 7 | 13 | | | 2 | 9 | 10 | 16 |
| 8 | 14 | | | | 7 | 9 | 10 |
| 9 | 15 | | | | | 7 | 9 |
| 10 | 16 | | | | | | 7 |

\* Willard C. Olson, "Seeking Self-Selection and Pacing in the Use of Books by Children," *The Packet*, Vol. 7, Boston, D. C. Heath, Spring, 1952, p. 7.

## FACTORS WHICH DETERMINE READINESS

### *Maturation* [2]

Children grow into learning. This simple but important fact is often ignored, because the process of growth may be a subtle change which is erroneously attributed to the effects of teaching.

Maturation, which is partly genetically determined, takes place without express efforts to promote it, or even in the face of efforts to prevent it. Maturation and learning operate as dual forces in almost all cases of behavior change. Because of this interdependence, a child who has not

---

[1] Grade level as used here and elsewhere in this book refers to the level of development of the average or middle pupil in designated grades.

[2] For a more detailed discussion of this topic, see G. M. Blair and R. S. Jones, "Readiness" in *Encyclopedia of Educational Research*, Third Edition, New York, The Macmillan Company, 1960, pp. 1081–1086.

reached a sufficient stage of mental and physical development will have difficulties when he tries to perform school tasks which require a higher level of development.

The concept of maturation as a factor in producing behavior change raises several important questions for teachers. First, what evidence is there that maturation does in fact operate to facilitate such change? How important a factor is it in determining readiness for learning? What is the course of growth in various maturing structures and functions? Most important is the question of how teaching can be conducted so as to take account of maturation.

There have been a number of studies [3, 4, 5] of the behavior of infants and preschool children which have shown that such things as sitting up, crawling, walking, bladder and bowel control, and simple manipulative skills are products, mainly, of maturation. Going from infancy to the beginning school years, there is still further evidence that genetically determined growth plays an extensive part in learning.

If maturation is considered an essential prerequisite for learning, the question arises as to what teachers can or should do to speed up the maturational process. Do stimulation and practice alter the capacity to learn in any marked degree? In an experiment with kindergarten children,[6] fourteen pairs of youngsters were used to test the effect of practice in memorizing oral digits. The experimental group of children was given 78 days of practice in this work (the controls were given no practice). At the end of the training period, the experimental group was markedly superior to the controls, but after four and one-half months the superiority of the trained group had completely fallen away. In a similar vein, studies [7] of children who have been taught to read at earlier ages than their peers have generally found no difference in average reading abilities when the early readers are later compared with their age mates.

The extent to which children's development is limited by internally determined stages is, in spite of the above findings still an open question, as will shortly be seen.

It seems certain that some normal "developmental difficulties" can be

---

[3] Wayne Dennis and Marsena G. Dennis, "The Effect of Cradling Practices Upon the Onset of Walking in Hopi Children," *Journal of Genetic Psychology*, Vol. 56, 1940, pp. 77–86.

[4] Myrtle McGraw, "Neural Maturation as Exemplified by the Achievement of Bladder Control," *Journal of Pediatrics*, Vol. 16, 1940, pp. 580–590.

[5] Wayne Dennis, *Readings in Child Psychology*, New York, Prentice-Hall, Inc., 1951, pp. 104–131.

[6] A. I. Gates and G. A. Taylor, "An Experimental Study of the Nature of Improvement Resulting from Practice in a Mental Function," *Journal of Educational Psychology*, Vol. 16, 1935, pp. 583–593.

[7] B. V. Kiester, "Reading Skills Acquired by Five-Year-Old Children," *Elementary School Journal*, Vol. 41, 1941, pp. 587–596.

overcome with proper readiness-building procedures. Studies [8] have shown that less than 10 per cent of kindergarten children correctly handle the b d inversion problem; yet the simple expedient of placing arrows under the letters _b_, _d_ helped children overcome their initial difficulties with these confusable letters.

Teachers should also realize that mental test scores all too often considered equivalent to mental maturation actually provide only a "shaky" inference about neural maturation, which itself is dependent in part upon some kind of stimulation. But even granting some reasonable predictive validity to mental scores, this type of information falls far short of providing all the needed information on educational readiness. It has been estimated that one-fourth of all children who make slow progress in school are of normal or superior intelligence.[9]

Maturation cannot take place in a vacuum. All studies of IQ constancy (and others showing the effect of maturation upon performance) presuppose environmental conditions within a somewhat normal range. There is considerable evidence to the effect that when lack of a normal environmental stimulation is long continued maturing intellectual functions seem to suffer permanent setbacks.[10] Likewise when rich stimulation is provided during early development, mental development seems to be given a boost.[11] The teacher who reads this volume is urged not to take a fixed, one-sided view of the nature-nurture controversy.[12] As before stated, maturation and learning operate together in development, and focusing attention upon one to the exclusion of the other is not only unscientific but impractical. Hiding behind the rationalization that a child is without capacity, as an excuse for poor teaching, and trying to go beyond a child's limits, are equally bad.

The question of limits which are dictated by the level of attained mental and physical maturation is unsolved. Psychologists are sure that for practical purposes such limits do exist but they are not rigid limits for

---

[8] Lois N. Hendricksen and Muehl Siegmar, "The Effect of Attention and Motor Response Pretraining on Learning to Discriminate B and D in Kindergarten Children," *Journal of Educational Psychology,* Vol. 53, 1962, pp. 236–241.

[9] Donald D. Durrell, "Learning Difficulties Among Children of Normal Intelligence," *Elementary School Journal,* Vol. 55, 1954, pp. 201–208.

[10] Mandel Sherman, *Intelligence and Its Deviations,* New York, The Ronald Press, 1945.

[11] For a most thorough research study dealing with a successful attempt to modify tested ability, see S. A. Kirk, *Early Education of the Mentally Retarded,* Urbana, University of Illinois Press, 1958.

[12] During the past few decades, there has been a controversy among social scientists about the degree to which intellectual ability is a function of heredity. Some take the view that mental capacity is largely a matter of genetic potential over which society has little control. Others believe that intelligence is greatly affected by environmental conditions. For an excellent treatment of this topic see J. McV. Hunt, *Intelligence and Experience,* New York, Ronald Press, 1961.

there is evidence that limits assumed to exist are broken. Two children, ages five and six, who would have attempted to swim the English Channel had the English government permitted, were tested by the physical fitness laboratory of the University of Illinois. These children turned in astounding performances. The older, a boy, was able to hold his breath for four minutes, and could swim under water for about 290 feet. The younger, a girl, had swum four miles down the Mississippi River with her hands tied. Both were able to run without stopping for several hours.[13] Feats of this kind are certainly beyond the point which would be expected under previously assumed maturational limits. The writer knows of a mongoloid-type, mentally defective boy who reads with facility and has an unusual memory for certain current events in which he is interested. Roberts [14] reports a case of a mental defective who had suffered serious birth injury and cerebrospinal meningitis. Although his IQ was below 20, and he was completely unable to care for himself, he reputedly knew the day of the week which corresponded with any date since 1915. There are many such cases of individuals who, in spite of seemingly insurmountable handicaps, develop skills and "knock the top off" the level of achievement that could reasonably be expected.

Results of the various experiments that show little persisting effect from early practice should not mislead us into believing that we have certain knowledge about the best time to begin various forms of instruction. Much more research is needed. Investigators have found that skills such as musical and tonal discrimination,[15] and certain mathematical concepts,[16] can be developed much earlier than was once thought possible. It is also quite likely that foreign languages can be profitably studied at a much earlier age than at the high school level where they are now taught. Moreover it should also be clear that the right combination of ability, experience, and motivation make some children ready for a particular kind of learning long before their age mates. For example, some children are ready to read at four,[17] and will do so without much formal instruction so long as they are not discouraged. Even 2½ to 3 year old children have been taught to read with extensive encouragement and imaginative materials (see the description of the Edison Responsive Environment Laboratory, Fig. 12). In all such cases whether teaching a

---

[13] T. K. Cureton, Unpublished Research Data, Physical Fitness Laboratory, University of Illinois, 1952.

[14] A. J. Roberts, "Case History of a So-Called Idiot Savant," *Journal of Genetic Psychology*, Vol. 66, 1945, pp. 259–265.

[15] A. T. Jersild and S. F. Bienstock, "The Influence of Training on the Vocal Ability of Three-Year-Old Children," *Child Development*, Vol. 2, 1931, pp. 272–291.

[16] University of Illinois Arithmetic Project, Project Staff, "Arithmetic with Frames," *The Arithmetic Teacher*, Vol. 4, April, 1957, pp. 119–128.

[17] Dolores Durkin, "Children Who Read Before Grade One," *The Reading Teacher*, Vol. 14, 1961, pp. 163–166.

three-year-old to read, a second grader calculus, or a four-year-old to solve problems, there are some critical questions:

1. How permanent are the effects of training when the child is compared with others at a later time?
2. Are there good or bad side effects as a result of the intensive early training? Does the child gain in self-confidence? Does he acquire an aversion to the activity in question?
3. Will these kinds of learnings preempt time better spent on other activities?

No hard and fast answers can at this time be given to the foregoing questions. Present evidence suggests that we view with some skepticism any claims about the permanence of gains made by very young children in complex learnings of some aspects of reading or using abstractions. At the same time, evidence does exist that deliberate attention to such basic psychological processes as perception, attention, and motivation does in fact produce permanent changes in children's general learning abilities.[18] The crux of the matter may lie in the fact that the children who are not receiving the "formal" training in something such as reading may be getting just as much practice in the aforementioned, basic psychological processes as the "early learners." It also must never be forgotten, however, that some children are as ready to learn to read at three years of age as are others at six or seven. How material is taught also has a direct bearing on how soon knowledge or subject matter can be learned by children.

### Experience

The second major factor in determining a child's readiness for learning is his previous experience. The whole program of prerequisite courses and sequences of learning are predicated upon the assumption that basic skills are necessary before complex tasks are tackled.

Given experiences may make a child more ready for new learnings, but there is no assurance that they will do so. Experiences may be relatively meaningless, and the child's compliance by sitting through a course, or reciting rote material should not be misjudged as assurance that the experience has made a real change in his behavior. A boy who was asked to write the pledge of allegiance to the flag (which he had presumably said dozens of times) wrote, "I led the pigeons to the flag." [19] A student in a biology class asked to give the term which describes the tendency of plants to turn toward the earth wrote, "G. O. Tropism." [20]

---

[18] S. A. Kirk, *op. cit.*

[19] Marion C. Sheridan, "Studying Words," *Teachers Service Bulletin in English*, Vol. 5, No. 4, New York, The Macmillan Company, April, 1951.

[20] Geotropism.

The home and community background are obviously important factors in readiness. To some parents, school is of minor importance. In fact in some communities nearly all adults look with disdain and suspicion at the business of schooling. Few rewards exist in such cases for the child who steps above his group. In language skills, for example, the "fancy" talking child may be rejected both by peers and adults whom he needs to believe care for him. In other communities, as in some of the border areas of the Southwest, the child may start to school in the first grade with an English vocabulary of no more than two hundred words.[21]

That marked community differences do exist is illustrated by the following samples of representative writing drawn from third graders in two widely different communities (age, grade, and mental ability controlled).

Community I:

> I think Americans are honest, good workers, willing, smart and good citizens.
> I think Americans are kind, honest, free and respectful. I think this because they always tell the truth. They are always friendly. It is a free country.
> I think Americans are smart, honest, helpful and brave. If they wanted to be mean, we wouldn't be here today.

Community II:

> I think Americans are kind and hasom. Because the give people stufh.
> I think Americans are clean white flasted people.
> I think Americans are the Best people in the lind. thay are mice people.[22]

The lack of appropriate experiences, today popularly labeled "cultural deprivation," produces a cumulative deficit. The child who is already limited by past deficits can profit less from new and more advanced levels of stimulation.[23] Experiences most crucial to success in school learning are those which center in the development of spoken and written language, and these are the experiences most lacking in the culturally disadvantaged. Obstacles to the acquisition of standard English are isolation from and lack of interaction with the modal culture, interference of one early acquired language structure with another, and a conflict of value systems. In respect to the last factor, Labov, who studied urban dialects in the

[21] Selma E. Herr, "Effect of Pre-First Grade Training upon Reading Readiness and Reading Achievement Among Spanish-American Children," *Journal of Educational Psychology*, Vol. 37, 1946, pp. 87–102.

[22] John Gillis, Unpublished Research Data, College of Education, University of Illinois, 1952.

[23] D. P. Ausubel, "How Reversible Are Cognitive and Motivational Effects of Cultural Deprivation? Implications for Teaching the Culturally Deprived Child," *Urban Education*, Vol. 1, 1964, pp. 16–38.

lower East Side of New York City, found that families with the greatest hostility to middle class norms were the lowest in speech assimilation.[24]

In the face of these experiential deficits in language, it is indeed disheartening to learn from a task force of the National Council of Teachers of English that the common practice in teaching literature to the disadvantaged is the use of anthologies not matched with either reading abilities or interests of students. The Task Force also observed that traditional grammar frequently is being taught to children who are several years behind the norm in reading skills.[25]

### Relevance of Materials and Methods of Instruction

Whereas the capacity of a child at a given time for learning reading, algebra, or physics is not subject to great change, the methods of teaching and materials used are. When we say a first-grade child is not "ready" to read, we generally mean not ready in terms of the kinds of materials and methods that are commonly used.

Evidence that relevance of material to children's interests is a factor in readiness may be found in the superiority of girls over boys in reading achievement. Lecky[26] believes that apparent lack of reading ability of boys may be due to their failure to perceive the consistency between required school behavior and their own self-concepts. For example, primers

[24] William Labov, "Stages in the Acquisition of Standard English," in *Social Dialects and Language Learning*, U.S. Dept. of Health, Education, and Welfare, Office of Education, Cooperative Research Project #F059, Champaign, Illinois, National Council of Teachers of English, 1964.

[25] National Council of Teachers of English, *Language Programs for the Disadvantaged*, Report of the NCTE Task Force, Champaign, Illinois, 1965.

[26] Prescott Lecky, *Self-Consistency, A Theory of Personality*, New York, Island Press, 1945.

Third Graders Learning to Identify Geometric Shapes by Manipulating Concrete Objects.

and other readers may have content which is inconsistent with the masculine role as defined by our culture, and as viewed by boys. Perhaps if boys were given more adventuresome and manly materials, sex differences in reading ability would be reduced.

Children are more ready to respond to material which meets their needs and fits their already established interests. The idea that there should be a dual program, one for rote skill materials and one for developing understandings and meaningful relationships is now regarded as fallacious. "Unless skills are learned while being put to use they are uninteresting and difficult to learn, the resulting learning may not be applicable to real problem solving, and the learning may not be permanent." [27] Children are more ready for skill learning, spelling, reading, and writing, when they are having fun doing it—and in connection with some meaningful project. They may be ready for *this* kind of learning situation and not at all ready for drill material.

What is the relationship of method of teaching to readiness? A case in point is the following situation.

> Observation of a ninth-grade high school class in so-called general mathematics disclosed a teacher (trained in a field other than mathematics) attempting to present to a slow, dull-normal group (more than half of them from foreign language backgrounds and many with reading handicaps) certain solid geometry concepts by merely reading from the textbook, appealing solely to auditory impressions.[28]

It is inevitable that little desirable learning or understanding would obtain in such a situation. But can it be said then that this class was not ready for general mathematics, or even solid geometry? Certainly not. A skillful teacher, using relevant materials and methods commensurate with these children's abilities, could undoubtedly bring at least some measure of success to this work.

A striking contrast to the above description is provided in an experiment by the Luchins.[29] These experimenters, using a 6B class, set out to teach the concepts of geometric area. First they drew a 15 inch by 5 inch rectangle on the blackboard. Then a pupil was given a one-inch cardboard square and asked to determine the area of the figure in square inches. "The pupil laid off the square along the longer base 15 times, repeated this process to obtain a parallel row and was about to start on a third row when he said, 'I don't have to do it again. It will always go 15 times this way

---

[27] Gertrude H. Hildreth, "Skills Develop with Functioning," *Educational Outlook*, Vol. 24, 1949, pp. 13–19.

[28] E. G. Nolan, "Determining the Most Effective Media of Student Learning," *Journal of Educational Research*, Vol. 43, 1950, p. 549.

[29] A. S. Luchins and Edith H. Luchins, "A Structural Approach to the Teaching of the Concept of Area in Intuitive Geometry," *Journal of Educational Research*, Vol. 40, 1947, pp. 528–533.

and it goes 5 times the other way, so it's 15 times 5 squares.'" This student then correctly computed the area as 75 square inches. After all students had practiced this same procedure with various rectangles, they were asked if this was necessary. A number of children replied that the area could be found simply by measuring one side and then the other.

In the next step, each pupil was given a paper parallelogram and asked to find its area. At first they could not solve the problem, but in a few minutes one girl volunteered. She had cut off both ends to make it straight. She was asked what to do with the ends, and after toying with them a moment put them together to form another rectangle. Only after each student made discovery of this process was formal geometric proof presented. The experiment was repeated with nine young girls from five to nine in age, and *all* including the five-year-old learned these processes as above described.

More recently Page and Beberman [30] have demonstrated that with radically altered methods of instruction in arithmetic and mathematics children can learn material once thought appropriate only for college students. Thousands of teachers and other adults who observe these men teaching demonstration classes find themselves knowing less about various mathematical skills and concepts than the young children they are observing.

### Emotional Attitudes and Personal Adjustment

After capacity, experience, and methods of teaching are considered, there still remains a residual of unexplained failure to learn. There are numerous children who have sufficient capacity, and experience, but who are still not ready for a given task in school. A large proportion of pupils who are having difficulties in reading, for example, exhibit forms of emotional instability, and it has been estimated that about a fifth of all retarded readers are rendered so by emotional stress.[31] Thus emotional stress may serve as a factor in lack of readiness or (as is more often the case) be an unfortunate concomitant of a failure to consider individual differences or readiness in setting up school work initially. Emotional disturbance is both cause and effect in children's failure in school. But whichever it is, the chances are that once the pattern of disturbance starts, a circular relationship is built up.

A most dramatic illustration of the reciprocal effects of emotion and

---

[30] For further details concerning the activities of the University of Illinois Committee on School Mathematics see, Project Staff, "Arithmetic with Frames," *op. cit.*, and Max Beberman, "An Emerging Program of Secondary School Mathematics," Inglis Lecture, Cambridge, Harvard University Press, 1958.

[31] A. I. Gates, "The Role of Personality Maladjustment in Reading Disability," *Pedagogical Seminary and Journal of Genetic Psychology*, Vol. 59, 1941, pp. 77–83.

school difficulties is cited by Goldberg [32] who found remedial reading an effective adjunct to psychotherapy with childhood schizophrenics. She reports that many of the children showed marked improvement and were able to return to their schools and communities once they had learned to read.

Common provocations which give rise to emotions and block readiness for learning are: unmet needs, overprotection, and rejection in the home, previous experiences of school failure, and other home difficulties. "The components of emotional patterns leading to reading difficulties are varied and complex. Sibling jealousy, parental overindulgence, excessive negativism, parental rejection, social class differences, general home insecurity, instability and general feelings of inadequacy have all been listed in the literature." [33]

The circular relationship between personal adjustment and readiness creates problems more serious than either maladjustment or lack of readiness alone. Difficulties become intensified as failure to solve either problem continues. Consider the child who enters the first grade and is not ready for reading. By the time he gets to the second grade he is ready for first-grade reading, but now the class is doing second-year work, and so it goes grade after grade until the child is hopelessly behind. This case was reported by a school psychologist:

> John H. was reported to the office as an unmanageable boy of fifteen. In English class, where the trouble was most pronounced, he had crawled on his hands and knees in the back of the room playing bear. He growled and bit several youngsters on the legs. Investigation showed that this class was reading and reciting from *Silas Marner*. Tests of the boy's abilities and achievements revealed that he was almost completely unable to read. (The school psychologist reported that John would have been just about taxed to his limit to pick out such words as "is" and "the" on a page of *Silas Marner*.) Faced with an untenable situation year after year, John had become a behavior problem. Adjustment-wise, he was probably doing about all that was left for him to do—i.e., getting his share of attention in the only way he knew how.

There are many such cases in our schools today. There are emotionally disturbed and maladjusted children who are products of a schooling which continually fails to start their training at their own level or fails to find areas of competency and potential in which they are ready to progress. In the extreme case the student may even reach high school, with years of

[32] Ilsa Goldberg, "Use of Remedial Reading Tutoring as a Method of Psychotherapy for Schizophrenic Children with Reading Disabilities," *Quarterly Journal of Child Behavior*, Vol. 4, 1952, pp. 273–280.

[33] Norman Young and E. L. Gaier, "Implications in Emotionally Caused Reading Retardation," *Elementary English*, Vol. 28, 1951, pp. 271–275.

school experience behind him, and show little progress in mastering the fundamental tools of education.

It is unfortunate that children who are not ready for given tasks are often made even *less* ready through emotional tension induced in the classroom. When 239 college freshmen were asked to describe incidents in their schooling which undermined self-confidence, they gave frequent examples of "punishment and sarcasm in the presence of others; competition or invidious comparison; and ridicule and scorn of personal attributes or background." A specific report of how a teacher actually *interfered* with a student's readiness for learning follows:

> When I was in elementary school, I was rather nervous and high strung. I was tall and very thin. The thing I remember and I shall never forget was an incident that happened in about the fifth grade.
>
> I wasn't a very good reader, and I think that this was partly due to the fact that I was shy and didn't like to be made fun of. I was called upon to read. Things were going along fairly well until I made one mistake and it seemed everyone in the room was laughing at me. This caused me to make more mistakes. My teacher said, "That will do fine, I guess you will never learn to read." [34]

## BUILDING READINESS

### Preschool Experiences

There are important experiences prior to formal schooling which are needed by all children if they are to adapt to the demands of school. They must learn to work and find acceptable channels for aggression; acquire social skills, such as sharing, cooperating, and competing; play group games and follow rules; know about books, pictures, and numbers; and have some degree of motor skills, such as drawing and coloring. Readiness for schooling is thus being built long before the child enters school, as is well stated by Monroe:

> The earliest efforts at reading do not take place at school in the first grade when children are six years of age. Books, magazines, signs, posters, and reading materials of all kinds are so much a part of our American culture that most children have had many experiences with printed materials from early infancy.[35]

That such cultural factors are related to readiness has been shown in numerous studies. Investigators have found that size of family, number

---

[34] Charles Lyman Smith, A *Study of Factors Contributing to Self-Confidence in School*, Unpublished M.A. Thesis, Columbus, Ohio State University, 1950.

[35] Marion Monroe, *Growing into Reading*, p. 3. Copyright, 1951, by Scott, Foresman and Company, Chicago.

of books in the home, and educational level of parents correlate with reading ability.[36] Children who come from "bookless homes" often have difficulty in beginning reading.[37] Such failure should not be blamed wholly upon the home deprivation, but partly upon the school which fails to take account of it.

Kindergarten may be profitably used to build readiness for formal school work without any loss of necessary social learnings (also an important part of readiness). Children from two kindergarten classes were compared to see what effect an arithmetic readiness program would have. One group was conducted in the usual fashion. The other was given a rich and meaningful program which included such things as (1) counting and grouping chairs, pencils, crayons, children, blocks, and toys; (2) comparing and grouping objects and numbers; (3) participating in number games, number stories, number rhymes, and number songs; and (4) measuring with ruler and yardstick children's heights, room dimensions, and tables. Results of this experiment are shown in Table 7.

### TABLE 7
#### Arithmetic and Intelligence Test Data for Experimental and Control Groups [38]

| Group | Average IQ | Av. Arith. Readiness Scores | | Average Gain |
| --- | --- | --- | --- | --- |
| | | Fall | Spring | |
| Experimental | 102.52 | 13.22 | 23.44 | 10.22 |
| Control | 102.59 | 13.59 | 18.74 | 5.15 |

Both groups of children in Table 7 were essentially equal in IQ score and in measured arithmetic readiness (in the fall). However, the group which received special readiness training (experimental) gained 10.22 points in arithmetic readiness, while those who did not get such training (control) gained only 5.15 points. Both the teachers and the experimenter were convinced that the children of the experimental group expressed genuine interest and enthusiasm for this arithmetic experience.

So much of a child's psychological development has occurred before

---

[36] W. D. Sheldon and Lawrence Carillo, "Relation of Parents, Home and Certain Developmental Characteristics to Children's Reading Ability," *Journal of Elementary Education*, Vol. 52, 1952, pp. 262–276.

[37] See M. C. Almy, "Children's Experiences Prior to First Grade and Success in Beginning Reading," *Teachers College Record*, Vol. 51, 1950, pp. 392–393. This writer found a significant positive correlation between success in beginning reading and opportunity for reading prior to the first grade. In studying homes of 106 children, this investigator found some that were almost "bookless."

[38] R. H. Koenker, "Arithmetic Readiness at the Kindergarten Level," *Journal of Educational Research*, Vol. 42, 1948, pp. 218–223.

the first grade, that it seems obvious that the school's concern for children ought to begin long before school entrance. The school which becomes an influential force in a community can and should act as a service agency for parents of preschool children. Services such as nursery schools, home visitation services, and mental hygiene clinics should all be closely coordinated with public schools.

Growing recognition of the importance of preschool years upon the development that is to follow may be seen in such massive attacks upon the problem as Project Head Start, which attempts to provide disadvantaged preschool children with a stimulating environment. In 1965, Project Head Start programs were launched in 2400 communities at a cost that year of about 95 million dollars.[39] The programs (initially eight-week summer sessions, but now extended to eight-month programs) stress language development and social skills and a general broadening of experiential backgrounds. Schools with these programs have also sought various methods of involving parents. Some of the initial attempts to improve parents' attitudes toward education and to obtain permanent improvements in children's abilities were not very successful.[40] An eight-week period of intervention could hardly be expected to produce dramatic results. The programs have now been extended, and from what is presently known about building readiness for schooling it is reasonable to expect major and permanent gains in language skills and attitudes.

### Readiness Programs in School

Readiness training does not stop as the child enters first grade, but should be continued in the first grade and even on into high school for that matter. Training which follows diagnostic procedures to prepare students for further work has successfully reduced educational mortalities at all levels. Results which may accrue from this type of program are shown in a study by Edmiston and Peyton. Fifty-four first-grade pupils, who had made very low scores on a reading readiness test were selected for special help. Under ordinary circumstances, these youngsters would probably have had considerable difficulty in reading. But in this case they were given a program planned to build their reading readiness.[41] Most of the pupils were, as a result of the training, able to move ahead in the reading program without undue difficulty.[42]

---

[39] NEA Journal, *Project Head Start*, Vol. 54, 1965, pp. 58–59.

[40] Harvey F. Clarizio, *Maternal Attitude Differences Associated with Involvement in Project Head Start*, Unpublished Ed. D. thesis, University of Illinois, Urbana, Illinois, 1966.

[41] E. W. Dolch, M. P. Dolch, and B. Jackson, *Readiness for Reading*, Champaign, Illinois, The Garrard Press, 1942, pp. 1–64.

[42] R. W. Edmiston and Bessie Peyton, "Improving First Grade Achievement by Readiness Instruction," *School and Society*, Vol. 71, 1950, pp. 230–232.

Even in college, remedial programs designed to fill in gaps in students' backgrounds have had a good effect upon course work. It was found [43] that college freshmen failing in chemistry and physics (especially veterans of World War II) were not failing through lack of ability, but because they had forgotten (or never obtained) basic concepts of arithmetic. Remedial work in general mathematics was helpful in a number of such cases.

### Building Self-Confidence

The attitude which a child has about himself in relation to school work is a pervasive element in readiness. Children with good ability often have developed such feelings of inferiority that they are defeated before they begin to work. Such children are hardly ready for the tasks they face in formal schooling. These youngsters need, more than anything else, experiences which will build their self-confidence and allow them to approach new situations without fear of failure or ridicule.

How is self-confidence won? Here are some suggestions derived from psychological research:

1. Individual instruction in special skills which are valued by child society gives a direct method of providing children the means of winning their own place in the school.
2. Research in nursery school indicates that children who lack self-confidence may gain it by being placed, for a time, with younger children. In this way the shy or fearful child is inducted gradually into a group of his age mates.[44]
3. College students asked to report instances in which their self-confidence was given a boost during their schooling, named most frequently praise by the teacher, winning in competition, being given a position of trust by the teacher, individual counseling with teachers, and statements by teachers which reflected a desire for the student's well being.[45]

The student's self-confidence and attitude about school are among the important criteria of how well the school has planned for dealing with individual differences and readiness. The centering of attention upon the learner rather than solely upon subject matter has been one of the great educational improvements in this century.

---

[43] J. R. Kinzer and H. P. Fawcett, "The Arithmetic Deficiency of College Chemistry Students," *Educational Research Bulletin*, Vol. 25, 1946, pp. 113–114, 140.

[44] Florence Goodenough, *Developmental Psychology*, New York, D. Appleton-Century Company, 1934.

[45] Charles Lyman Smith, *A Study of Factors Contributing to Self-Confidence in School*, M.A. Thesis, Columbus, Ohio State University, 1950.

## INDIVIDUAL DIFFERENCES

The factors which make children ready for school operate to create widespread individual differences. Before teachers can plan for treating such differences, they must have a clear picture of their nature and extent.

So long as a teacher considers his job as that of teaching individual children, it is necessary to know the level at which each individual operates, and to set up school tasks commensurate with each level. Unfortunately, whether they like it or not, a large part of their work as teachers consists in working with groups and not with individual students. Thus the problem of dealing with differences among children is complicated by the size and heterogeneity of groups which constitute grade levels or subject matter areas. Primary teachers may have as many as forty or more children in a class. Some first-grade classes are so crowded that it has been necessary to change to two half-day sessions of thirty to forty different children in each. An English teacher in high school may have fifty or sixty students in one class, and a physical education or art teacher nearly a hundred. An art teacher in one of the writers' classes has on the average 210 students per day. Under such conditions, providing for differences in the readiness for learning becomes a major problem. Some teachers are attacking this problem vigorously and imaginatively, and with good results.

### Differences in Rates of Growth

Children and adolescents grow at different rates. This differential growth rate is not simply in terms of physical development but includes mental and personality development as well. Growth in many functions varies from one individual to another and rates vary within individuals.

There are "slow growers" and "fast growers" in almost every area of human development. Each child has his own unique growth pattern. "Some children seem 'slow to catch on' in school for several years yet prove later to be excellent students." [46] In fact there may be only a slight relationship between various forms of mental, physical, and social development. Recognition that each growth system operates somewhat independently of others has led to the concept of "organismic age," [47] which is an arithmetical average of various "ages" such as skeletal age, dental age, reading age, arithmetic age, and others.

Variability within school groups increases with age. (This is especially true of higher mental processes.) For example, it was shown in Table 6 that various children in the first grade were ready for books which covered

---

[46] M. E. Breckenridge and E. L. Vincent, *Child Development*, Third Edition, Philadelphia, Saunders, 1955, p. 10.

[47] W. C. Olson and B. O. Hughes, "The Concept of Organismic Age," *Journal of Educational Research*, Vol. 35, 1942, pp. 525–527.

five grades in difficulty level. But by the time these children had reached the third grade, they varied so much that some were ready only for nursery school books, others for seventh-grade books—a range of about *nine* years in difficulty level. Teachers who strive to reduce such differences by insisting on equal preparation for all are bucking against known and immutable facts about growth. Far more effective is effort expended in giving materials and guidance which are commensurate with various rates of development.

The known facts about rates of growth hold several important implications for the educator. Foremost is that each child must be considered in relation to his own level of expectancy (i.e., what is normal development for him) and not in terms of comparisons with other children. Also, it is impossible to predict with anything approaching complete accuracy the extent of terminal development from early developmental patterns. It is poor practice to prejudge a child's eventual potential in terms of early achievement. Since growth is uneven, and varies from one individual to another, the teacher may expect school behavior and school learning to show irregularities and regressions. Such fluctuations should not be viewed with alarm but taken as a matter of course, unless they are long continued.

### Intellectual Differences

The widespread use of mental tests from preschool age through college has provided a wealth of information about differences in mental ability. In summary of some of these differences, Cook has written:

> When a random group of six-year-olds enters the first grade, two per cent of them will be below the average four-year-olds in general mental development and two per cent will be above the average eight-year-olds. Disregarding the extreme two per cent at either end, there is a four-year range in general intelligence.[48]

If one were to follow this group of six-year-olds through the sixth grade, when they were twelve, he would find the range to have increased to almost eight years.

The extent of differences in mental ages at various chronological ages according to Symonds is shown in Table 8 where it may be seen that the range in mental age increases as children grow older. Thus for instance at age 11 one could expect to find some children with a mental age as low as six, others with a mental age of 16, a range of 10 years.

Extensive differences persist on into high school and college, although there is probably an increasing dropping out of students from the lower mental ability levels when attendance at school becomes voluntary. Never-

---

[48] W. W. Cook, "Individual Differences and Curriculum Practice," *Journal of Educational Psychology*, Vol. 39, 1948, p. 141.

**TABLE 8**

Theoretical Distribution of Mental Ages for Groups of
100 Children with Given Chronological Ages *

(Based on a theoretical standard deviation
of IQ of 16.6)

| Mental Age | Chronological Age | | | | | | | | | | |
|---|---|---|---|---|---|---|---|---|---|---|---|
| | 4 | 5 | 6 | 7 | 8 | 9 | 10 | 11 | 12 | 13 | 14 |
| 22 | | | | | | | | | | | |
| 21 | | | | | | | | | | | |
| 20 | | | | | | | | | | | 1 |
| 19 | | | | | | | | | | 1 | 2 |
| 18 | | | | | | | | | | 1 | 4 |
| 17 | | | | | | | | | 1 | 4 | 8 |
| 16 | | | | | | | | 1 | 3 | 7 | 12 |
| 15 | | | | | | | | 2 | 7 | 13 | 15 |
| 14 | | | | | | | 2 | 6 | 12 | 16 | 16 |
| 13 | | | | | | 1 | 5 | 12 | 17 | 17 | 15 |
| 12 | | | | | 1 | 4 | 12 | 18 | 19 | 16 | 12 |
| 11 | | | | | 3 | 11 | 19 | 21 | 17 | 13 | 8 |
| 10 | | | 2 | 11 | 21 | 23 | 18 | 12 | 7 | 4 | |
| 9 | | | 1 | 9 | 22 | 25 | 19 | 12 | 7 | 4 | 2 |
| 8 | | | 7 | 23 | 28 | 21 | 12 | 6 | 3 | 1 | 1 |
| 7 | | 5 | 24 | 31 | 22 | 11 | 5 | 2 | 1 | 1 | |
| 6 | 2 | 24 | 36 | 23 | 11 | 4 | 2 | 1 | | | |
| 5 | 23 | 41 | 24 | 9 | 3 | 1 | | | | | |
| 4 | 50 | 24 | 7 | 2 | 1 | | | | | | |
| 3 | 23 | 5 | 1 | | | | | | | | |
| 2 | 2 | | | | | | | | | | |
| Totals | 100 | 99 | 100 | 99 | 102 | 99 | 99 | 99 | 99 | 101 | 100 |

* P. M. Symonds, "Case Study and Testing Methods" in Ernest
Harms (Editor), *Handbook of Child Guidance,* New York, Child
Care Publications, 1947, p. 311.

theless, tests of academic aptitude or mental ability reveal that even college students may vary to the extent of 100 IQ points.

### Differences in School Achievement

In a typical sixth-grade class, tests in reading comprehension, vocabulary, arithmetic reasoning, and arithmetic computation have shown a range of about eight school years for all these subjects.[49] In other words, in almost any sixth-grade class, there will be a pupil with average second-grade read-

[49] W. W. Cook, *Grouping and Promotion in the Elementary School,* Minneapolis Series on Individualization of Instruction, No. 2, University of Minnesota, 1941, pp. 26–30.

ing ability and one with average tenth-grade reading ability. These differences do not decrease much, if any, in later grades. When a General Culture Battery Test (composed of general science, foreign literature, fine arts, and social studies) was administered to high school and college seniors, the upper 10 per cent of the high-school seniors scored above the college seniors' median.[50] These differences are not extreme cases, they are the kind which any teacher may expect to find in classes in New York, Chicago, San Diego, or most any other place.

Table 9 illustrates the spread of differences in a number of measured abilities and skills for a group of fifth graders and should indicate how futile it is to expect a "standard" performance of every pupil.

Note in Table 9 how few of these pupils were actually at the average of their own grade level. As the investigator indicates, "All of these 240 students were in 5A at the time of measurement but only thirty-six out of 240 or about 15 per cent are at the 5A standards." In the first column of Table 9 (Chronological Age), it may be seen that only one pupil out of

**TABLE 9**

**The Scores of Fifth-Grade Boys and Girls on a Variety of Tests and Measurements ***

**Number of Children Making Each Grade Level Score**

| Grade Levels | C. A. | Height | Weight | No. Teeth Cut | Intelligence Kuhlman-Anderson | Reading Stanford Achievement | Thorndike-McCall |
|---|---|---|---|---|---|---|---|
| 9th and Above | 1 | 7 | 20 | | 2 | 8 | 5 |
| 8A | 2 | 6 | 9 | | 0 | 3 | 0 |
| 8B | 0 | 9 | 15 | | 0 | 7 | 5 |
| 7A | 5 | 36 | 23 | | 7 | 5 | 7 |
| 7B | 6 | 25 | 19 | 18 | 24 | 21 | 10 |
| 6A | 10 | 44 | 29 | 25 | 34 | 22 | 51 |
| 6B | 19 | 18 | 25 | 55 | 64 | 42 | 23 |
| 5A | 34 | 39 | 31 | 44 | 33 | 38 | 31 |
| 5B | 135 | 22 | 23 | 42 | 39 | 43 | 48 |
| 4A | 29 | 19 | 12 | 23 | 17 | 26 | 25 |
| 4B | 7 | 9 | 15 | 14 | 5 | 21 | 17 |
| 3A | | 2 | 11 | 7 | | 7 | 14 |
| 3B | | | | 9 | 1 | | |
| 2A and Below | | 2 | 6 | | | | |
| Total Children Measured | 248 | 238 | 238 | 237 | 226 | 243 | 236 |

* Stuart A. Courtis, "The Rate of Growth Makes a Difference," *Phi Delta Kappan*, Vol. 30, 1949, p. 320.

[50] W. D. Learned and B. D. Wood, *The Student and His Knowledge*, Bulletin No. 29, New York, The Carnegie Foundation for the Advancement of Teaching, 1938.

the 248 is old enough to be at the ninth-grade level or above, while twenty of the pupils weigh enough to be considered at or above ninth-grade averages. Note also that in intelligence one pupil was at the 3B level (first half of the third grade), while two were at the ninth-grade level or above—a range of twelve half-grades or six years.

### Differences in Interests

Perhaps no type of difference among children has been so well recognized and so poorly taken into account in teaching than that of differences among children in interests. The teacher, and rightly so, has seen his job as changing interests, but in order to do this he must start with the child's already existing interests.

Presumably one of the main objectives of schooling is to foster widespread individual interests. In an economy of specialization this is essential, and yet classroom methods more often than not assume common interests. Many teachers still use a single text, a single assignment, and a single class procedure for all. There are, of course, exceptions. In English composition, children are sometimes allowed to write a theme on a topic of their own choosing, and in mechanical arts advanced students often work on their own projects. (See Chapter 8 for a discussion of interests.)

### Sex Differences

Beginning in early life, our culture creates roles which are believed appropriate for each sex. These roles are reflected in the kinds of toys and games which are provided children, and in the kind of behavior which is expected. Also, there are biological determinants which may lead to psychological differences (albeit these biological factors have probably been over-emphasized in the past).

In general, studies of school achievement agree that girls tend to make consistently better scores than boys (particularly in elementary school). Girls are less apt to be retarded readers and spellers and they are less apt to suffer such speech incoordinations as stammering and stuttering (which are often attributed to pushing a child beyond his capacity).[51] Although on the average girls excel in general school achievement, particularly at the elementary level, boys seem to have a slight edge in arithmetic, history, geography, and science. Such differences as do exist seem to parallel so closely what we know about the interests of each sex that it is safe to conclude that a great part of these differences are products of the roles which are set for children and not due to innate factors. A school environment which favors either sex is likely to produce superiority in achievement for that sex.

---

[51] Leona Tyler, *The Psychology of Human Differences*, New York, D. Appleton-Century Company, 1947.

In overall appraisal of differences between sexes in ability, achievement, and readiness, one is forced to conclude that any differences are slight, with almost a complete overlap in distributions. As previously shown in Chapter 3, girls in the early years are probably growing somewhat faster than boys, and since they reach puberty earlier, acquire sex-social interests when younger. The slight difference betweeen sexes is certainly not sufficient to warrant grouping of sexes into separate classes, nor the separation of the sexes in elective classes in high school. Even though boys and girls differ more in interests than they do in ability, there is a considerable overlap of distributions even in this respect. It is common in schools today for boys to take courses in home economics and for girls to be interested in physics and mechanical arts. Special provisions for differences in interests should be on the basis of qualitative differences in needs and not arbitrarily determined on the basis of sex.

By far the greatest differences between the sexes are in factors of personality and value systems.[52] For the most part these differences are also culturally produced. Children learn concepts about themselves which are determined by sex. The girl soon learns that affection, neatness, primness, and a quiet sense of humor are rewarded by adults and by other members of her peer group. On the other hand, boys find rewarding greater aggressiveness, display of fearlessness, and vigorous physical activity.[53] These differences are not due to any innate factors but come about because the child finds rewards, approval, and status in adopting the role which is defined for him.

Present research indicates that men are more aggressive than women, and women are more often neurotic and maladjusted than men.[54] There is little question, however, that the culture is changing and some personality differences now apparent may, within a few generations, virtually disappear. Teachers, in planning work to fit the readiness of pupils, need to be alert to such change. It is a mistake to hold to previously conceived values about the "role of women" and thereby exclude girls from activities once thought of as strictly masculine. School girls of today are probably ready for a much wider range of learning materials than was true even a generation ago.

## INTRA-INDIVIDUAL DIFFERENCES

Teachers may see only a few facets of the total picture of an individual child in school and therefore may not be aware of the great differences

---

[52] Elizabeth Douvan and Joseph Adelson, *The Adolescent Experience*, New York, John Wiley and Sons, Inc., 1966, pp. 342–344.

[53] Caroline Tryon, "Evaluations of Adolescent Personality by Adolescents," *Monographs of the Society for Research in Child Development*, Vol. 4, Serial No. 23, 1939.

[54] Leona Tyler, *op. cit.*, p. 80.

in traits and skills within a given school child. The extent of such intra-individual variation has been summarized as follows:

> Trait variability in the typical individual is 80 per cent as great as individual variability in his age group; trait differences are normally distributed. Some individuals are twice as variable as others, and there is no relationship between general level of ability and the amount of trait variability.[55]

Teachers are sometimes astonished to find a child who they think of as a slow learner doing very well in a specific area. An algebra teacher related the following incident: "My car was stalled on a country road near the town in which I was teaching. I tried in vain to get it started. While sitting there, Bill S. came along. He was the bottom man in my algebra class, but within five minutes he had taken the top off my carburetor, made a minor adjustment, and I was on my way." Psychologists have found that errors in judging persons' total abilities and personality because of specific information is an almost universal weakness. This weakness, known as the "halo effect," operates to reduce the accuracy of such things as personal ratings, because one good or bad feature about a person tends to influence judgment about other aspects of the person. Of all professional groups, teachers have the best reason for avoiding this kind of error.

Even in so-called primary mental abilities, children may show distinct intra-individual differences. In one case, a kindergarten child tested with the Primary Mental Abilities Test,[56] had an IQ of 103, but scored as low as four years, eight months MA on one subtest, and as high as seven years, eight months on another—a range of three-years mental age on these two subtests of intelligence.[57] It is not infrequent for a child to rank at the ninety-ninth percentile in so-called general ability and below the tenth percentile in such functions as pitch discrimination, aesthetic judgment, art, and drawing skills. These differences are apparent also in various school achievements. A junior at the University of Illinois had the following grade record for one semester: Physics A, Integral Calculus B, Descriptive Geometry B, and Rhetoric D. This student's spelling was at the fifth-grade level, and he misspelled such words as "upon, fail, awful and wait." [58]

A profile of a student's aptitudes is often a valuable tool not only in planning his instructional program, but also in counseling him about vocational aims. The profile of a college student with an IQ of 115, who was planning to enter engineering school is shown in Figure 7. This profile indicates the

[55] W. W. Cook, *op. cit.*, p. 143.

[56] Thelma G. Thurstone and L. L. Thurstone, Science Research Associates, 228 South Wabash Avenue, Chicago.

[57] Anne Anastasi, *Differential Psychology*, Second Edition, New York, The Macmillan Company, 1958, p. 344.

[58] G. M. Blair, *op. cit.*, p. 259.

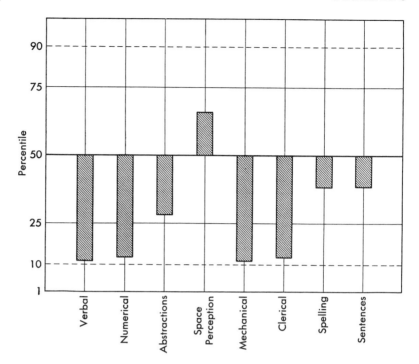

**Figure 7.** Profile of the Aptitudes of a Twelfth-Grade Youth Who Wanted to Study Engineering.

status of this student in relation to other college freshmen who had taken the same test. It is clear that, on seven of the eight traits measured, this student was below the median of college freshmen.

In a consideration of individual differences and readiness for learning, the school needs to recognize such wide differences within students, and, as in Figure 7, these differences may be an instructive pattern for guidance. In this case, as a result of proper vocational counseling, the student decided to change his vocational plans.

### Other Trait Differences

Besides differences in abilities, physique, and interests, there are hundreds or even thousands of other trait differences. Although the distributions of these traits are at this time not clearly or definitely known, there is every reason to believe that most of those which have been identified follow the same normal curves as do differences in abilities and physical factors. In honesty and other measures of character for instance, children probably vary as much as they do in intellectual capacity. Some children are so aggressive that they will try to dominate everyone in their class, while others are so meek that they respond only when they are forced to do so. In sheer

amount of energy, children may show great differences. One child in a class-room may be so restless that he is unable to sit still, while another will be content to let the lesson go by while he spends hours daydreaming about the things he would like to do but never does. One child may have enough self-confidence to try almost anything. He may make decisions rapidly. An-other may approach each new situation with caution and a sense of in-feriority.

### How Differences Appear in School Work

When differences are stated solely in terms of figures representing IQ, MA, or achievement level, one fails to get a full perspective of the nature of such differences and the consequent problems of teaching which are created. The original writing of an eight-year-old boy with an IQ of 180 who began to write a book on astronomy has been described by Carroll. The following is the first paragraph of his first chapter:

> In this book I intend to cover as nearly as I can all that is known of the ten large bodies which form the solar system. But we must remember that the solar system is only a few tiny specks in space, with their parent sun, which in turn, was formed by an immense piece of gaseous nebulae, huge pieces of gas which collect together to form a planet.[59]

When this boy was twelve, he wrote a 75,000 word book on astronomy and when fourteen wrote a letter to an adult friend—part of which is repro-duced as follows:

> Dear ———:
> I was interested in your ideas concerning the "red-shift" or expansion of the galaxies, but I cannot say I agree with it. According to what I read, cer-tain cosmological theories seem to require a contraction or expansion of the galaxies or island universes. Einstein and de Sitter, a Dutch relativist, have found that a certain cosmical constant is necessary for the operation of space-time in the universe as they see it. This cosmical constant is known as lambda. Actually, according to relativity, there is no gravitation and no lambda, but the universal curvature and various other factors working to-gether make these two entities act as if they were forces.[60]

Compare with the above, the work of several eight-year-olds (all were of about average intelligence) who in social studies were asked to tell what they thought about Negroes and Jews:

> I think negroes are real real kind. Because most of them say nice thing I think Jews are pretty. Because they were juwerely and losts of makeup.

[59] Herbert Carroll, *Mental Hygiene*, Second Edition. Copyright, 1951, by Prentice-Hall, Inc., New York, p. 329. Reprinted by permission of the publisher.
[60] *Ibid.*, p. 330.

I thank Jews are just about like us. I thank their just like us because they are huming bings.[61]

Also compare the writing of Carroll's case with that of a fourteen-year-old boy with an IQ of 90. The responses of the latter are answers to a test in arithmetic about insurance. To the question, "What are the three hazards of owning and operating an automobile?" this boy replied, "might go off a cliff," "might bumb into a pole, bumb into another car." To the question, "What is the purpose of comprehensive car insurance?," he answered, "The windle blures up. And its' hard for the windshield wiper to wipe." When asked what factors affected insurance rates, this youth wrote, "gas, oil, keracine." [62]

Such qualitative differences point clearly to the need for *qualitative* differences in the curriculum. Those who expect a given series of learning experiences to be appropriate for such extremes—or even for less extreme cases—are not facing one of the real issues in teaching. A mere change in speed of presentation, or the assignment of extra work (i.e., more of the same problems or study material) falls far short of providing for such differences.

A child who cannot add a column of figures is not ready for studying the formal addition of fractions (yet he may be quite ready to work with simple concepts of fractions), and one who cannot read is not ready to study history. Brownell found when he tested 487 children who had had both subtraction and multiplication, that at least half were not ready for long division.[63] Ordinary measures of achievement fall far short of the requirements of a good check on readiness. A single score on a test or a single letter grade from a previous course or grade level gives very little usable information about a child. In some instances such information may bias the teacher about him before he begins. Often the scores and grades which are available are somewhat meaningless—unless the teacher knows what factors went into the scoring and grading. A grade based on a pupil's standing relative to his group may be of little or no value unless a good deal is known about the group, and a grade derived from some arbitrary standard is useless unless the standard is known and well-defined. Even if the teacher knows these things, he still will not know *why* a student is having difficulties, nor the specific areas of weakness.

In assessing readiness the following information is needed: (1) How does each student compare with a well-defined group? (2) What are the specific

[61] John Gillis, unpublished data, College of Education, University of Illinois, 1957.

[62] Furnished to the writers by David G. Hunt, mathematics teacher, Harlem High School, Rockford, Illinois.

[63] William A. Brownell, "Arithmetical Readiness as a Practical Classroom Consideration," *Elementary School Journal*, Vol. 52, 1951, pp. 15–22.

skills, facts, attitudes, and understandings which each student has or does not have? (3) How consistent are the errors which are made? (4) What personal factors, if any, interfere with his work?

## PROVIDING FOR INDIVIDUAL DIFFERENCES

Knowing about individual differences is the first step. The second step is to try to understand them and to deal effectively with them. People who recall their own schooling and have read anything about teaching will find no novelty in the idea of individual differences. But in spite of all the descriptive knowledge about differential psychology, we have continued to teach children as if they were pretty much alike and all needed the same kinds of learning. The balance of this chapter will present some promising lines of development in the area of individualized instruction.

### Improved Diagnostic Techniques

In the past it has not been uncommon to have a school's psychological examiner present test data that simply confirm what the teacher already knows about a child. Sometimes, of course, the examiner finds things that were missed in the classroom, or can eliminate suspected cases of difficulty. But in the main we still operate with groups of children put together in some very broad categories such as normal, emotionally disturbed, or gifted. Cruickshank [64] highlights this problem when he states that "it would be possible to count on one hand the number of schools in the country that are making a careful discrimination among the subtypes of retarded children and doing something about them."

Before training programs can be devised to build readiness and accommodate to the existing differences among children, a more precise means is needed for pinpointing not only the problems, but the specific elements of them. In the past ten years diagnostic methods have reached out to tap basic psychological processes hitherto inferred from general ability measures. One example is provided by Kirk, who has suggested that some of the basic elements involved in reading include auditory reception, visual reception, associations, vocal expression, motor expression, sound blending, sound discrimination, perceptual speed, and visual closure. Diagnosis must include some measure of each, and not a general measure of reading readiness, if we are to determine the causes of difficulty. Further refinements of these elements, and the blending of them into a theoretically grounded system, led to the development of the *Illinois Test of*

---

[64] William M. Cruickshank, "The Mentally Retarded Child in School," in *The Fourth Yearbook, Association for Supervision and Curriculum Development*, Washington, D.C., 1960, p. 79.

*Psycholinguistic Abilities* (ITPA) [65] which provides subscores on each of the following factors:

1. Auditory decoding—the ability to understand what is heard
2. Visual decoding—the ability to understand what is seen
3. Auditory-vocal association—the ability to educe relationships from what is heard
4. Visual-motor association—the ability to educe relationships from what is seen
5. Vocal encoding—the ability to express ideas verbally
6. Motor encoding—the ability to express ideas by motor means
7. Auditory-vocal automatic—the ability to use the structure of the language automatically
8. Auditory-vocal sequential—the ability to reproduce a series of symbols presented visually
9. Visual-motor sequential—the ability to reproduce a series of symbols presented visually.

While this test is still in the process of being validated, there have been fifty or more studies which show that this multifactor approach gets at processes left untapped by general ability measures.[66] Kirk[67] cites the case of a nine-year-old non-reader who had a high score on visual decoding, but a very low one on auditory decoding. When remedial exercises were aimed specifically at improving the boy's ability to understand what he heard, the boy quickly progressed in reading.

Various other tests of visual and auditory perception together with exercises for developing these basic perceptual processes have been devised. Wepman,[68] for example, has discovered that auditory discrimination, which might be presumed to be a simple and naturally acquired skill, may still not have been sufficiently developed by age six or seven to allow for the discrimination of speech sounds, and this may interfere with both speech and reading.

The importance of early and specific diagnosis is rarely questioned. One study[69] of 10,000 children in a four year survey, shows that pupils

---

[65] For a description of ITPA and its development see: S. A. Kirk and J. J. McCarthy, "The Illinois Test of Psycholinguistic Abilities; and Approach to Differential Diagnosis," *American Journal of Mental Deficiency*, Vol. 66, 1961, pp. 399–412.

[66] Barbara Bateman, *The Illinois Test of Psycholinguistic Abilities in Current Research: Summaries of Studies*, Urbana, University of Illinois Press, 1965.

[67] S. A. Kirk, "Reading Problems of Slow Learners" in Helen A. Robinson (Editor), *The Underachiever in Reading*, Chicago, University of Chicago Press, 1962.

[68] J. M. Wepman, "Auditory Discrimination, Speech and Reading," *Elementary School Journal*, Vol. 60, 1960, pp. 325–333.

[69] Gilbert Shiffman, "Early Identification of Reading Disabilities: The Responsibility of the Public School," *Bulletin of the Orton Society*, Vol. 14, 1964, pp. 42–44.

with reading problems identified by the second grade are ten times more likely to be helped by remedial reading than those discovered at the ninth grade level. Unfortunately, this study goes on to point out even those identified early did not continue to progress when they were returned to a regular program. As Bateman suggests in her excellent review, much further research is needed both to develop more sensitive diagnostic procedures and to find an appropriate matching between diagnosis and remedial procedures.[70]

### Changes in School Policy, Organization, and Structure

Educational schemes for managing differences among children are not new. Educational acceleration was in rather general practice fifty years ago, and a "contract plan" which allowed students to contract for a certain unit of work and to proceed at their own pace goes back to the early twenties. In the era since the first Sputnik, however, virtually dozens of new or revived administrative devices have been proposed and tested. Included are plans for independent study, acceleration, curriculum reform movements, non-graded schools, ability grouping, the radical redesigning of school buildings to permit more individual and small group work, using pupils as tutors for other pupils, work study arrangements, and a host of others.[71]

From a psychological standpoint, administrative innovations have the following advantages:

1. They represent the recognition of a problem; a first step to solving one.
2. When perceived as innovations by the school and its staff, particularly when they are involved in the change, there may be an increased commitment, and a willingness to consider other changes.
3. The individual teacher's freedom to diagnose difficulties and to select varied instructional materials is enhanced in a school whose climate is one of change.

Unfortunately some administrative innovations designed to adapt to individual differences still cling to the idea that all children should cover the same topics, read the same books, and have the same experiences, albeit more slowly. It is not uncommon to find a high school that employs ability grouping requiring all groups to read such classics as Milton's *Paradise Lost*. Little wonder that various forms of homogeneous grouping

---

[70] Barbara Bateman, "Learning Disorders," Chap. V in Education of Exceptional Children, *Review of Educational Research*, Vol. 36, 1966, pp. 93–119.

[71] R. Murray Thomas and Shirley M. Thomas, *Individual Differences in the Class room*, New York, David McKay Company, Inc., 1965.

have failed to live up to the promises made for them.[72] As one writer has put it, "There is nothing so unequal as the equal treatment of unequals." [73] He argues that high school students instead of doing the same things in each of their classes should spend much of their time in independent study.

Within the province of the teacher are also numerous methods of organizing work and the structure of the class so as to meet differences. In their excellent overview of this whole area, Thomas and Thomas suggest various types of acceleration, enrichment, separate assignments, contract plans, and division of classes into groups for special work.[74]

### Improvement in Instructional Materials

In the new "education industry," instructional materials are called "software," and the machines which put them to use such as the talking typewriter and teaching machines are called "hardware." A few observations will be made regarding the instructional materials that have literally flooded the market in the past decade. If treated comprehensively this one topic would more than fill an entire book. Consequently, only a selection of those developments that are especially relevant to providing for individual differences will be treated.

SELF-SCORING EXERCISES, TESTS, AND TEXTS. As already noted in the previous chapter, Pressey devised several methods for providing an immediate knowledge of results during test taking.[75] These materials. have the advantage over more conventional materials by allowing each learner to proceed somewhat independently, and at his own rate. For example, following a unit of study, self scoring tests will reveal immediately to the student the extent to which he needs to review material. Moreover, the test items can be labeled so that when a student misses an item he can proceed directly to the written material from which that item was taken. (For illustration of Pressey's devices see Figures 15 and 16 in the following chapter.) Adkins, has incorporated this procedure in her text in Statistics, a section of which is reproduced in Figure 8.

After the student reads the material, he finds a set of multiple choice questions. By moistening with his finger-tip or with a sponge-tipped pencil

---

[72] J. H. Shores, "What Does Research Say About Ability Grouping by Classes?" *Illinois Education*, Vol. 53, 1964, pp. 160–172.

[73] B. Frank Brown, "The Renascence of Individual Learning," in *New Approaches to Individualizing Instruction*, Princeton, New Jersey, Educational Testing Service, 1965, pp. 63–69.

[74] R. Murray Thomas and Shirley M. Thomas, *op. cit.*, Chap. 5.

[75] For an excellent review of the whole autoinstructional movement see Sidney L. Pressey, "Autoinstruction: Perspectives; Problems, Potentials," in *Theories of Learning and Instruction*, Part I, 63rd Yearbook, National Society for the Study of Education, Chicago, 1964.

the alternative he believes to be right, he can check his own progress. If he was indeed right, the circle in front of the alternative will turn green. If not, there will be no color change and he will moisten one of the other circles and proceed until he finds the correct answer. Thus each reader can test himself and adjust his own pace of study in accordance with his success in dealing with the questions. In Figure 8 the last answer is the correct one.

Ratio scales, as the term suggests, permit comparison of *ratios* of scale values, in addition to having all the advantageous characteristics of other kinds of scales.

Most educational and psychological tests are *not* based upon ratio scales. Suppose that 2 students get test scores of 50 and 100. With the addition of 25 items so easy that both students pass all of them, the respective scores become 75 and 125.

Question   That the scores do not represent a ratio scale is

- not clear without further information

- clear because the scores were changed when items were added

- clear because the ratios of the scores were changed when items were added

Nevertheless the myriad statistical methods that have been developed for interval scales are quite useful and serve for ratio scales as well whenever we are fortunate enough to have them.

**Figure 8.** An Item from the Adkins Self-Scoring Statistics Text.

FLEXIBLE AND INDIVIDUALIZED STUDY MATERIALS. The single primer in the primary grades is becoming a thing of the past. Now most of the reading series include a variety of graded materials, remedial exercises, and special exercises for developing skills such as vocabulary usage, reading speed, study habits, and outlining. At the high school level some of the new curricula are backed up by multiple texts for single courses, each text centering around what are believed to be important concepts, but attacking the concept in different ways.[76]

Several publishing houses are offering books that are individualized for different classes and even for different students. For example, the William

---

[76] John I. Goodlad, Renata Von Stoephasius, and M. Francis Klein, *The Changing School Curriculum*. New York. Fund for the Advancement of Education. 1966.

C. Brown Company publishes an *Introduction to General Psychology: A Self-Selection Textbook.* The material edited by Vernon contains separately bound chapters as individual units on topics such as motivation, symbolic processes, therapy of personality disorders, perception, etc. Each chapter is individually bound and punched to fit a standard three-ring binder.[77]

A similar venture at the junior-high-school level is the Papertext Series of Simon and Schuster, which offers the teacher and his students selection of a number of individual short stories that can be bound in any combination in a special loose leaf cover.[78] Thus far 100 units graded as to difficulty and interest level have been prepared. They include short stories that have been selected as most liked by high school students from more than 800 short stories in high school anthologies. Over 4,000 students participated in the selection.[79] Thus, an attempt has been made first to select stories of high preference value to a large sample and then to prepare them in such a way that individual teachers can make up their own "anthologies."

PROGRAMING. Programing is the blending of input (what the student reads or sees) with (output) students' responses to questions in a logically or psychologically ordered sequence. In a rough sense it is the combining of a text and a workbook into a single intertwined unit which allows the reader to proceed at his own pace. The learner is not only "reciting" as he goes along but is also able quickly to check his answer with a key to see if he is right. He is thus provided information in small bits (often with a high rate of redundancy) in a carefully ordered sequence, and with a continual high rate of reinforcement.

Skinner developed his idea of "autoinstruction" partly because of the contrast he observed between his eagerly performing pigeons and observations in his daughter's schoolroom where he believed many of the children remained only because there were rules which prevented them from leaving.[80] He concluded that what was needed was a means of providing a great deal of positive reinforcement for *all* children, not just an occasional reinforcement for a few. Linear-type programing which grew directly from Skinner's observations and early experimentation with a simple teaching machine (see Figure 9) has these features:

---

[77] Jack A. Vernon (Ed.), *Introduction to Psychology: A Self-Selection Textbook,* Dubuque, Iowa, Wm. C. Brown Co., Publishers, 1966.

[78] *Papertexts,* New York, Simon & Schuster, Inc., 1967.

[79] Ray H. Simpson and Anthony Soares, "Best- and Least-Liked Short Stories in Junior High School," *English Journal,* Vol. 54, 1965, pp. 108–111.

[80] It is interesting to note that Skinner did not at this time, *circa* 1954, know of the previous work of S. L. Pressey, a fellow psychologist, who devised autoinstructional techniques 30 years earlier. If this kind of gap then existed between experimental and educational psychologists, it is little wonder that we have a large gap between psychologists and educators.

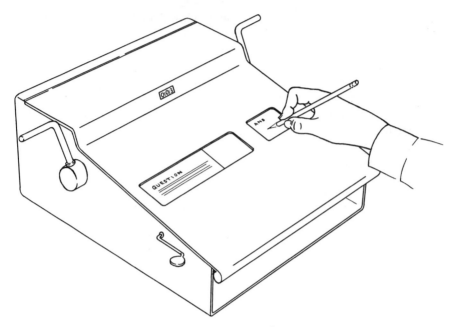

**Figure 9.** A Skinner Type Teaching Machine.

1. All students get the same material, but proceed at their own rates (if they are advanced they may start at a higher point in the program).
2. A deliberate attempt is made to keep error rate low, and reinforcement rate high. Hence each question is only a little different from previous ones, and there are a variety of "prompts" used to assure correct answers.
3. Generally each bit (frame) of the program deals with one specific term, fact or relationship.

Here is a brief example of the way a linear program proceeds:

| | |
|---|---|
| *Frame 1*<br>responses<br>or<br>answers | Programing is a means of combining input and output in a logically ordered sequence. Input is what the reader sees or reads, output consists of the students' _____ to the input. |
| *Frame 2*<br>reinforce-<br>ment | In order to assure a high rate of reinforcement error rates are kept very low in a linear type program. By making each question only a small step away from the previous one a high rate of positive _____ is assured. |
| *Frame 3*<br>interest | Skinner believed that greater effort and increased interest in school could be achieved if all instead of only a few pupils were to receive reinforcement. Here is an assumption that positive reinforcement is related to children's _____ in school. |

The other major type of programing (Crowder) has many similar features to the type just described, however, it is based on the presumption that each learner not only needs to proceed at different rates, but in different directions as well. The terms branching and intrinsic have been applied to programs which ask students questions (usually multiple-choice type) and then as a consequence of their answers send them to a different section of the reading for further explanation and perhaps other questions. If constructed in book form, a student might proceed in his work from page 1, to pages 10, 6, 7, 18, 9, 20, etc. In each instance the text directs him where next to go on the basis of his answers.

Both the linear (Skinner) and the branching-type programs (Crowder) described above have a good deal of logical validity in keeping with psychological theory. Both allow to some degree for individual differences, and both provide for an immediate knowledge of results. Studies comparing the two methods have generally favored branching types.[81]

Programers have made much of the importance of a logical sequence of materials, which they say rarely if ever occurs in a textbook. However, there is some evidence that when frames are presented in a "scrambled" order pupils do as well on a post test as those who follow the "logical sequence." [82]

Pressey, who predicted the technological revolution in education, indeed called for it, has spoken with some alarm about current programing. In his article "Puncture of the Huge Programming Boom," he describes a simple experiment in which 1110 words of a part of Holland and Skinner's program in Introductory Psychology was reduced to 360 words of straight text material. Students were able to read the 360 word text in less than two minutes but an equivalent group spent 22 minutes going through the programed material. The group which received the reading material alone did almost as well as the others on an end test, and when they received a four-minute auto elucidation test over selected difficult ideas (they had now spent 6 minutes as contrasted with 22) they did equally well on the end test.[83] Pressey comments later: "As it is, programing may be saddled for ten years with voluminous, clumsy, thousand-frame write-in programs soon to be discarded, but with one more mark against psychologists as theory-bound and unpractical."

Some form of programing is here to stay. Hopefully the direction it

---

[81] Anderson cites 3 comparative studies favoring branching, 1 favoring linear and two showing no difference. R. C. Anderson, "Educational Psychology," in *Annual Review of Psychology, op. cit.,* 1967, pp. 103–164.

[82] Levin, Gerald R. and Bruce L. Baker, "Item Scrambling in a Self-Instructional Program," *Journal of Educational Psychology,* Vol. 54, 1963, pp. 138–143.

[83] S. L. Pressey, and John Kinzer, "A Puncture of the Huge 'Programming' Boom," *Teachers College Record,* Vol. 65, 1964, pp. 413–418. Also see Pressey, S. L., "Auto-instruction: Perspectives, Problems, Potentials," *Theories of Learning and Instruction, op. cit.,* p. 369.

**Figure 10.** Students Learning by Means of Computer Assisted Instruction.

takes will be partly determined by the readers of this and other educational psychology books. Teachers will be the users. They must make known their reactions.

HARDWARE! To go along with some of the newer educational materials, colleges, schools and industry (particularly electronics and optical firms) have developed numerous devices to aid the teacher. These range all the way from a slide projector rigged to present materials automatically and in a predetermined order to an elaborate instructional station hitched to a high speed computer as shown in Figure 10.

It is difficult at this point, while many of these things are still emerging, to state general psychological principles that would apply to *all* kinds of instructional hardware. Moreover, while the general aim of technological development is to improve the efficiency of education, some are still in experimental stages. Silberman and Carter report early efforts (1958) to develop computer-based instruction at the *Systems Development Corporation*. After some time and several false starts an "automated classroom" was developed with 20 pupil stations tied in to a large high-speed computer, which operated on the branching type of programed material. Their comments about the experience was:

> One of the first things that became apparent in this research was that the potential advantage of the machine was limited by the quality of instructional material. For example, it is a comparatively simple mechanical task to branch a student who is having trouble to remedial material. But it is

quite another thing to design remedial sections that will rectify his difficulty once he is branched to that material.[84]

Industry, foundations, and government are presently investing as much as a half billion dollars a year in technological developments for educational programs. Virtually all the major electronic firms have or are developing instructional systems, and many are merging with textbook publishers.[85] To illustrate the scope of developments three different machines will be briefly illustrated.

The first, a relatively simple device shown in Figure 11 is the Bell and Howell *Language Master* which presents words visually and auditorially, and then allows the pupil to record his own voice and match his pronunciation with that produced by the machine to the word card. As may be

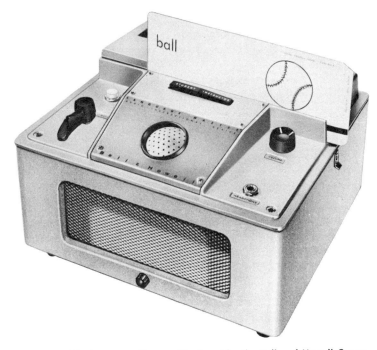

**Figure 11.** The Language Master. (Produced by the Bell and Howell Corporation, Chicago, Illinois)

---

[84] H. F. Silberman and L. F. Carter, "The Systems Approach, Technology and the School," in *New Approaches to Individualizing Instruction*, Princeton, New Jersey, Educational Testing Service, 1965, pp. 71–91. Quote is on p. 75.

[85] The whole issue of *Phi Delta Kappan*, Vol. 68, January, 1967, Big Business Discovers the Education Market.

seen in the figure, the child may work with earphones to shut out noises from the rest of the class and to prevent his disturbing it. Each word card shows the word in large print broken into syllables. A child proceeding at his own pace may practice pronunciation, reading, and checking his own performance against a model to see if he has read and said the word correctly. Monitoring by the teacher is possible through a second pair of earphones. Thus, the child now learns to read new words and to pronounce them properly with only a minimum of supervision by the teacher.

A more sophisticated electronic device for teaching reading is the "Talking Typewriter" or Edison Responsive Environment (ERE) devised in principle by Moore, and manufactured for classroom use by the Thomas A. Edison Laboratories, Division of McGraw-Edison Company, West Orange, New Jersey. Moore's interest in early reading in children led him to develop techniques whereby he taught 2½ and 3 year old children to read by allowing them to "play" with an electric typewriter.[86] Each time the child typed a letter the letter was spoken by an observer and when he accidentally typed a word the letters and word were pronounced. This procedure while successful in developing *very* young readers was cumbersome and required much observational time. The present machine (See Figure 12) has the following capabilities:

1. Pressing any key produces the sound of that key's symbol and instantaneous typing of it.
2. No other key can be depressed until audio is complete.
3. The key board can be prerecorded in several languages.
4. The machine can point out a letter to be typed and wait for the child to type it and pronounce it before proceeding.
5. After words are acquired the audio pronunciation of individual letters is cut out.
6. The machine also can cut out the visual presentation of a word and ask the pupil to type it simply from audio-reception.

In a trial of the ERE at the Freeport Public Schools, Freeport, New York, Martin reports that 25 kindergarten children were taught to read with an average time of exposure to the machine of less than thirty hours. Reading proficiency for the group as a whole was near the second grade level. Several suggestions for further research are mentioned by Martin who believes this one study merely scratched the surfaces of the possi-

---

[86] Omar Khayyam Moore, *Automated Responsive Environments: Part 1* (Motion Picture), Responsive Environments Foundations Inc., 20 Augur Street, Hamden, Connecticut, 1962. See also his "From Tools to Interactional Machines," in *New Approaches to Individualized Instruction*, Princeton, New Jersey, Educational Testing Service, 1965, pp. 5–12.

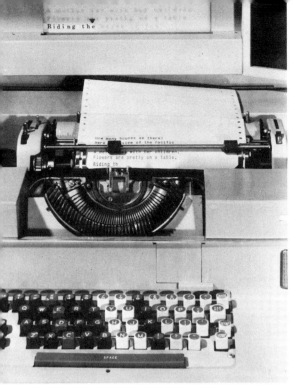

**Figure 12.** The "Talking Typewriter". (Beginners may have their finger nails painted to match the various colored keys. This machine is a multi-sensory computer-based learning system for teaching reading and other skills. Distributed by the Responsive Environments Corporation, Englewood Cliffs, N.J.)

bilities of this machine in combination with research produced "software."[87]

The ERE "Talking Typewriter" is available from Responsive Environments Corporation, Englewood Cliffs, New Jersey, on a sale or lease basis. The company provides programs and programming assistance, trains personnel in ERE operation, installs the equipment and offers the necessary services.

A most ambitious and extensive application of electronic technology to individualizing instruction is the development of the system Programed Logic for Automatic Teaching Operations (PLATO). Developed by the Coordinated Science Laboratory at the University of Illinois, PLATO presents the student a television screen which can give him visual input and a "typewriter" which he can use to respond to the problems or questions set up on the TV screen. See Figure 13. The typewriter keys can be set up so as to represent letters or numbers or any other kinds of symbols required in the response process. Also included are extra keys which the student may use to request supplementary information, check his answers, call for help or review his own previous work. A very large computer is, of course, a central control element in the system. Its capacities are such that 20 students working in different stations as was shown

---

[87] John Henry Martin, A *Report on the Freeport Public Schools Experiment on Early Reading, Using the Edison Responsive Environment Instrument* (Brochure). Responsive Environments Corporation, 21 East 40th Street, New York.

**Figure 13.** Individual Plato Station Showing the Visual Presentation and the Response Keyboard.

in Figure 10 can be dealing with different subject matter and asking for different information all at the same time. The students, however, need not be together. They could be in different rooms, in their dormitories, or even in different cities; and with a modern computer, a system such as PLATO would be capable of handling 5,000 students at a time. Experimentally the system has been used to teach circuit analysis, how to use the library, "fortran" programing, and nursing.[88]

Developments in the technology of education are at a rapid and accelerating pace. While many of the more sophisticated types have not yet made their way into the schools, it seems certain they soon will. Tomorrow's teachers may find a new partner in the school, an educational engineer who can help with the operation and applications of the new machines. To fulfill his professional obligations the teacher must insist upon adequate broad evaluation of the results of all such ventures, and a place in the planning of the objectives which the machines will help achieve.

---

[88] Donald L. Bitzer, Presentation at the Institute of Electrical and Electronic Engineers, New York, March 20, 1967.

## SUMMARY

Children differ widely in the many factors which determine their readiness for learning. To understand learning and teaching one needs a knowledge of the learner. This understanding implies that teachers know the differences among children, as well as the various strengths and weaknesses of each child. It also implies that the teacher understand factors that determine a child's readiness, such as maturation, experience, relevance of materials and methods, and emotional stability.

Much attention has been given to the problem of readiness in the early grades, especially in subjects such as reading and arithmetic. But much less study has been given to the problem as it exists in the higher grades, in spite of the fact that for all levels and in all subjects readiness for learning should be a primary consideration. An eighth-grade child who reads at the second-grade level is not ready to work on eighth-grade reading material, and a college freshman who is not a master of arithmetic is not ready for chemistry.

Class procedures which provide a given text which all must read or a set of exercises which all must do violate the principle of readiness, for there are inevitably great differences among children in abilities, interests, experiences, and personality factors. In a given grade, the teacher is apt to find that children vary in mental abilities from as much as four years in the first grade to as much as eight or ten years in high school. In achievement, interest, and other aspects which contribute to readiness, the differences are equally pronounced. Furthermore, children may be expected to show a great deal of intra-individual variation. A given child may be low on some measures of ability and high on others. All these differences produce unique individuals who are qualitatively different. Any instructional program which is to be successful must plan not only for differences in the quantity of material which is presented, but also for differences in the difficulty and kinds of materials.

A part of every course or grade involves the building of readiness. This process begins before the child ever enters school. Most homes, for example, provide drawing materials, books, and other reading and writing materials, and thus in the experience of nearly all children, there is some knowledge about books, pictures, and rudiments of writing. From that time on through school, children are learning skills both for their immediate usefulness and for their preparation for new learning.

In essence, the building of readiness necessitates, (1) an analysis of the skills, understandings, and knowledges required to study given material, (2) diagnostic pretests or other devices to determine not only the level of each prospective learner, but also the specific areas of strengths and weaknesses, and the nature and origin of errors, and (3) an instructional

program with a good deal of early individual guidance, designed to match teaching with individual needs and abilities.

Individualizing of instruction is finally becoming a major thrust in American schools. Better diagnostic techniques, administrative changes such as the nongraded school, and improvement in instructional materials are developments that hold much promise. Today the learner may find books at his own level of interest and ability, and devices that allow him to do independent work at his own best rate of progress. Tomorrow he may find himself in a computer-assisted classroom which will be even more highly adaptive to his particular needs.

In the meantime much remains to be done. A large segment of the educational profession still operates from the position that all children should learn the same things at the same time and with the same instructional materials. These practices must change if each youth is to profit from his schooling.

## References for Further Study

Anastasi, Anne, *Differential Psychology*, Third Edition, New York, The Macmillan Company, 1958.

Blair, Glenn M., and Jones, R. Stewart, "Readiness," in C. W. Harris (Editor) *Encyclopedia of Educational Research*, Third Edition, New York, The Macmillan Company, 1960, pp. 1081–1086.

Bloom, Benjamin S., *Stability and Change in Human Characteristics*, New York, John Wiley and Sons, 1964.

Brown, B. Frank, "The Non-Graded School," *Bulletin of the National Association of Secondary School Principals*, May 1963, pp. 64–72.

Center for Programed Instruction, *Programs '62*, A Guide to Programed Instructional Materials, Washington, D.C., U.S. Office of Education, 1962.

Cutts, Norma E. and Moseley, Nicholas, *Providing for Individual Differences in the Elementary School*, Englewood Cliffs, N.J., Prentice-Hall, 1960.

Deterline, William A., *An Introduction to Programed Instruction*, Englewood Cliffs, N.J., Prentice-Hall, 1962.

Gagne, Robert M. (Editor), *Learning and Individual Differences*, Columbus, Ohio, Charles E. Merrill Books, Inc., 1967.

Goodlad, John I. and Anderson, Robert H., *The Nongraded Elementary School*, New York, Harcourt, Brace, 1959.

Hildreth, Gertrude H., *Readiness for School Beginners*, Yonkers, N.Y., World Book Company, 1950.

Hunt, J. McV., *Intelligence and Experience*, New York, Ronald Press, 1961.

Hunt, J. T., "What High School Teachers Should Know About Individual Differences," *School Review*, Vol. 60, 1952, pp. 417–423.

Jones, R. Stewart and Pingry, Robert E., "Individual Differences," in Chapter 6 in Twenty-Fifth Yearbook, National Council of Teachers of Mathematics, *Instruction in Arithmetic*, Washington, D.C., 1960.

Lumsdaine, A. A., "Educational Technology, Programed Learning and Instructional Science," in 63rd Yearbook, Pt. I, *Theories of Learning and Instruction*, Chicago, National Society for the Study of Education, 1964.

Markle, Susan M., Eigen, Lewis D., and Komoski, P. K., *A Programed Primer on Programing*, New York, Center for Programed Instruction, 1962.

National Society for the Study of Education, *Programmed Instruction*, Pt. II, 66th Yearbook, Chicago, The Society, 1967.

Pressey, Sidney L., *Educational Acceleration: Appraisal and Basic Problems*, Research Monograph No. 31, Columbus, Bureau of Educational Research, Ohio State University, 1949.

Pressey, Sidney L., "Autoinstruction: Perspectives, Problems, Potentials," 63rd NSSE Yearbook (see Lumsdaine entry above).

Shores, J. Harlan, "What Does Research Say About Ability Grouping by Classes," *Illinois Education*, Vol. 53, 1964, pp. 169–172.

Thomas, R. Murray and Thomas, Shirley M., *Individual Differences in the Classroom*, New York, David McKay Company, Inc., 1965.

Tyler, Leona, *The Psychology of Human Differences*, New York, D. Appleton Century Company, 1947.

Tyler, Fred T., "Issues Related to Readiness to Learn," 63rd NSSE Yearbook (see Lumsdaine entry above).

## Questions, Exercises, and Activities

1. What are some of the specific functions that must mature before a child is ready for reading?
2. From your own experience cite a case in which a person seemed to be performing at a level far beyond that which would normally be expected for one of his age. What factors appeared to be important for this accelerated development?
3. Describe the kinds of research necessary before one could confidently say that foreign language should be taught in the elementary school.
4. List and discuss factors that contribute to the differences among various communities in the degree to which they affect children's readiness for school.
5. Select any one of the following topics and show how through an alteration of method, or a special technique, it might be taught to children younger than the ones who commonly take it at the grade levels specified below.

| TOPIC | PRESENT GRADE PLACEMENT (APPROX.) |
|---|---|
| a. latitude and longitude | 5th or 6th Grade |
| b. square root | 8th Grade |
| c. law of supply and demand | 11th Grade |
| d. evolution | 10th Grade |

6. In the case of John H., described in this chapter, an immediate conclusion might be that John should have been retained in some of the lower grades until he learned to read. What is wrong with this conclusion?
7. Compose a list of at least five methods for giving differentiated instruction in a single classroom, and give the pros and cons of each method.

8. As shown in Table 8 a teacher in any of the upper grades or high school may have in his classroom children whose mental ages vary greatly. Suggest several ways in which a teacher can develop an understanding of the mental characteristics and capabilities of these children.
9. What implications for homogeneous grouping does the material on intra-individual differences have?
10. Compose three sample items that you might include in a pretest for the area or grade level you are preparing to teach.
11. What psychological principles support the use of teaching machines of the type developed by Skinner? Are any principles violated by the exclusive use of teaching machines? Be specific.
12. Describe how a teacher can provide for individual differences by utilizing pupil planned projects and other learning activities which do not involve machines.

# Chapter 7

## Motivation: The Forces Which Energize and Direct Behavior

The control and direction of human energy plays such a vital part in learning and in intelligent behavior that it takes priority over other considerations about teaching. Even with poor teaching methods and badly chosen instructional materials, the student who is aroused and interested may learn a great deal. Speaking of the *Shtetl* culture (Jewish) of Eastern Europe a generation or two ago, Lee describes the schooling as very bad. There were very long hours in the classroom, cruel punishments, and cold and dismal school buildings, and yet to the children of that place and time, learning was an exciting adventure, knowledge was highly prized, and the wisest man of the community was its person of highest status.[1]

Coming to grips with this problem of motivation means learning how to direct appropriately the great energies of which the individual is capable. It is a first step, and perhaps the most important one in being able to control our own behavior and to teach others.

---

[1] Dorothy Lee, "Developing the Drive to Learn and the Questioning Mind," in *Freeing Capacity to Learn*, Fourth Yearbook, Association for Supervision and Curriculum Development, Washington, D.C., 1960.

If behavior is to be understood, it is necessary as Duffy [2] has pointed out to start with the fact that the living organism is an energy system. This energy system has two major qualities, *viz.*, intensity (the degree to which energy is aroused), and direction (a focus in thought or action toward some object or symbolic process).

Energy or arousal level, and the direction of it, play a decisive role in what is received, what is stored as information, and what the individual thinks and does. Even listening intently increases muscular tension, and just the thought of throwing a ball involves muscular reactions, both in the arm that customarily throws a ball, and in other muscles as well.[3] These minimal responses, and the stimuli that they trigger and that are induced by thoughts and words play an important role in maintaining arousal and in keeping our energies directed.

This energy system seems intimately related to the activity portions of the mid-brain, especially the hypothalamus and the reticular formation of the brain stem. Lesions of these structures or temporary alterations of their functions by chemical or electrical changes may radically alter the intensity and direction of energy. More important for our purposes here is the fact that life experiences which link these important physiological structures and their functions to the cerebral cortex will determine the situations for and directions to which energy will be mobilized. It is very likely that these modes of reception and action become habitual fairly early in life. In other words, a person early learns characteristic ways of emoting, of being aroused, and of directing energy.

This chapter will contain three major parts. The first will contain a discussion of some of the basic ingredients that may be involved in the process of motivation. The second will attempt to show how energies acquire direction and individuality, and the third will present suggestions for using knowledge about motivation in the classroom.

## BASIC ELEMENTS IN HUMAN AROUSAL

As with any complex process it is difficult fully to understand all the elements in motivation and the ways in which they interrelate. It may help to start with a concrete example.

During World War II a small advance patrol of American soldiers in Africa was cut off from its outfit when the division to which it was attached retreated during the night. Members of the patrol were left in the blazing desert sun for two days and nights before they were discovered by German soldiers. By then they had nearly died of thirst. The soldier who

---

[2] Elizabeth Duffy, *Activation and Behavior*, New York, John Wiley and Sons, Inc., 1962, p. 17.

[3] Elizabeth Duffy, *op. cit.*, pp. 54–55.

recounted this story described his constant preoccupation with water, and his hallucinations regarding it. When he was given water for his canteen he guarded it fiercely, even to the point of sleeping with it under his pillow. This became such a ritual that later in Sicily where he was in a prison compound with running water, he found the habit of having a full canteen hard to break. On one occasion he failed to fill his under-the-pillow canteen before retiring, and lay awake until 2:00 A.M. Finally he was impelled to fill the canteen; whereupon his tension disappeared and he was able to fall asleep.

Rarely do individuals experience such profound deprivation, but when these events do occur, they provide testimony to the great effect of needs upon behavior. In the case just cited, these effects were not limited to the transitory mobilization and direction of energy toward getting water, but included long-term effects upon habit and subsequent action.

Some of the ingredients of the motivational process will now be discussed.

### Needs and Drives

In order to maintain life, tissues require nutritive substances such as water, oxygen, and minerals, and various chemical substances such as thyroxin and adrenalin produced by other tissues. Even slight variations in the balance of such essential ingredients may cause injury or death. Lack of oxygen for even a brief period may cause destruction of neural tissue. A coronary occlusion very quickly results in the death of the heart muscle, which has been starved of its essential nutritive elements. Since they are so basic to our survival, the drives which grow out of these tissue needs are indeed strong and compelling, and as was shown in the example of the soldier in the African desert may so mobilize energy and thought that there is little left for any other processes. It is sobering to reflect upon the fact that most of the world's population faces a rather constant deprivation of food.

A major element in the release and direction of energy is the internal mechanism that operates to produce drives. The terms *need* and *drive* as noted in a psychological dictionary [4] are frequently used interchangeably in writings about motivation, but it may help in understanding the process if a differentiation is made between the two. A need is the lack of something which if present would further the welfare of the organism. It could be a vitamin deficiency or a less tangible condition such as a feeling of wanting security. Thus needs are descriptive constructs applied to the organism by an observer. They may never find clear expression in any seeking behavior by the organism. A child may have a vitamin deficiency

---

[4] H. B. English and A. C. English, A *Comprehensive Dictionary of Psychological and Psychoanalytical Terms*, New York, Longmans, Green and Co., 1958.

without craving any particular variety of food that would correct it. Likewise he may "need" security without having any clear direction of increased arousal toward achieving it. Drives on the other hand are inferences made from observed behavior and are assumed to be the tensions induced by these "lack-of-somethings," or needs. They may be very specific and closely related to the needs which give rise to them, as when a thirsty person seeks water, or unspecific, and reflected only by a heightened state of energy release, as when a rejected child develops such bizarre psychomotor habits as nail-biting, hair pulling, or tics.

In any case, the presence of a drive increases the tendency to respond and perceive in a selective manner. The child in school who has learned to crave attention and has thus developed a strong drive for it will exert great energy to achieve the satisfaction of his desires. He may seek attention from the teacher, from his fellow pupils, and from the janitor, and if he cannot attain it from these sources, he will seek it in other ways and from other persons. One thing is certain. He will not, except in the most extreme and restrictive situations, go without it. Even in the latter case he may attain it through his daydreams or with imaginary playmates.

### Incentives

From the moment of birth our reflexes and early conditioned responses lead us to attach value signs to substances and situations that reduce the tensions produced by drives. At first, incentives are closely linked with our basic physiological needs, but early in life, objects, persons, and situations become firmly associated with symbols (words, gestures, and the like). Even the very young child can associate his drive state and its satisfactions with appropriate external cues. The management of behavior is based largely upon the manipulation of incentives.

Incentives are the things we want and desire. They may be as tangible as a new car, or as intangible as a word of praise. They may be actual or representational. A person may exert energy for materials such as food and clothing, or he may exert effort to attain money, which he knows he can exchange for the same. They may be immediate or delayed. He may work for either money or the promise thereof. And they can be positive or negative, in that he may either seek or avoid various kinds of stimulation. In the vernacular, incentives are the "carrots and the sticks of our lives, either real or imaginary, that help to energize and direct our behavior."

### Motives

Motives are learned behaviors which have resulted from the reinforcement of responses produced by drives. Once a motive has been developed, it possesses a driving force of its own. Motives are essentially habits, as will be seen in the following section.

Since each person's experiences are somewhat unique, motives may be highly individualized. Even though needs and drives come out of the common elements of our physical makeup and similar cultures, the focus of those drives is often unique. There are, of course, enough similarities among cultures to insure that some motives are almost universally learned. In fact, so common are the presses for accomplishment in school and society in our culture that it is currently popular to refer to an achievement motive.[5]

### Habits as Motives

Professor Moon carries his brief case home every night. He rarely opens it after he gets there, but he would feel ill at ease without it. Mrs. Melvin washes her hands at least fifty times a day. She cannot make a long trip in an automobile because she would then have no way to perform this ritual. Mr. Beam still wants to throw himself to the ground every time he hears a plane overhead, and actually does make a fractional part of that response by flinching. Undoubtedly, each of the behaviors just described had its origin in the early experiences of the people involved. Professor Moon, as a graduate student, brought his brief case home every night. Mrs. Melvin may have washed her hands numerous times in an effort to symbolically wash away a feeling of dirtyness due to guilt feelings. Mr. Beam was strafed and bombed during his military service. In all these instances the behaviors continued even though the original conditions that germinated them had passed. In other words, the very doing of an act over and over seems to invest it with a "drive strength" of its own. Not to perform the act appears to lead to the same kinds of tension that are characteristic of other drives. Allport has called this the "functional autonomy of motives." [6]

William James, one of the early American psychologists, expressed eloquently the force of habit in our lives as follows:

> Habit is thus the enormous fly-wheel of society, its most precious conservative agent. It alone is what keeps us all within the bounds of ordinance, and saves the children of fortune from the envious uprisings of the poor. It alone prevents the hardest and most repulsive walks of life from being deserted by those brought up to tread therein. It keeps the fisherman and the deck-hand at sea through the winter; it holds the miner in his darkness, and nails the countryman to his log-cabin and his lonely farm through all the months of snow; it protects us from invasion by the natives of the desert and the frozen zone. It dooms us all to fight out the battle of life upon the lines of our nurture or our early choice, and to make the best of a pursuit that disagrees,

---

[5] David C. McLelland, John W. Atkinson, Russell Clark, and Edgar L. Lowell, *The Achievement Motive*, New York, Appleton-Century-Crofts, 1953.

[6] John P. Seward, "The Structure of Functional Autonomy," *American Psychologist*, Vol. 18, 1963, pp. 703–710.

because there is no other for which we are fitted, and it is too late to begin again. It keeps different social strata from mixing. Already at the age of twenty-five you see the professional mannerism settling down on the young commercial traveller, on the young doctor, on the young minister, on the young counsellor-at-law. You see the little lines of cleavage running through the character, the tricks of thought, the prejudices, the ways of the 'shop,' in a word, from which the man can by-and-by no more escape than his coat-sleeve can suddenly fall into a new set of folds.[7]

Just as people can learn about drives and motives in their own and others' behavior, so they can discuss, observe, and hopefully learn about the formation and breaking of habits. The contention here and throughout this book is that learning about our behavior and how to control it is equally if not more important than learning about the ideas and tools that allow us to cope with our environment.

## HOW DO ENERGIES ACQUIRE DIRECTION?

Much of the answer to this question has already been implied in the foregoing material. It was said that drives with their arousal function become attached to incentives. But it remains to be explained how this attachment occurs. Obviously, some kind of learning takes place. Often one is not aware of the learning. He may do many things for which he can give no accountable motive or any recollection of the experiences that have led to the motive. The whole theme of the popular book on advertising research, *Hidden Persuaders*, was that awareness of one's own motives is far from complete. The slight aroma of perfume on women's hose at a department store does in fact alter buying behavior. But if asked why she chose one pair of hose in preference to others of equal or better quality the woman buyer often cannot explain her behavior except to say that she likes them better. If, on the other hand, she were to say to herself, how does brand A hose smell as compared with brand B, she possibly could readily detect a difference and proceed to make her selection on more relevant qualities. It is certain that many of our daily decisions spring from motives of which we are only vaguely aware, or from habits which keep us in ruts. A more careful analysis and understanding of motives ought to make our decisions more intelligent, and give us some measure of control over the development of our motives. This is not only a legitimate but a very important goal of education.

### Changes in Perceptions

Needs increase the general level of arousal (neural and muscular activation) and they also operate so as to change perceptual patterns which may

---

[7] William James, *Psychology Briefer Course*, New York, Henry Holt & Co., 1892, pp. 143–144.

increase attentiveness to things that promise some satisfactions. A person who is hungry experiences first some general increase in activation, and then directs his energies and attention toward objects (symbolic or real) likely to satisfy the hunger drive. In addition he will likely be preoccupied not only with food, but also with objects associated with food. A person, for example, who has been on a semi-starvation diet might develop an unusual interest in cookbooks.

Even slight changes in needs seem to change perceptions. Sanford,[8] using a free-association word test (i.e., giving children a stimulus word or picture and asking them to respond with the first word that came to them) found that children gave about twice as many food responses to words *before* meals as immediately after eating. Bruner and Goodman [9] also showed that needs may influence perceptions. Working with ten-year-olds, they asked two distinct socio-economic groups to estimate the size of various coins. One group of children was from a settlement house in a Boston slum area and the other group was from a school attended by children from prosperous business and professional homes. Both groups overestimated the size of coins, but the poor children (to whom the coins presumably represented many unfulfilled needs) consistently overestimated their size more than the rich children, as may be seen in Figure 14.

Children may also reveal their motivational state in such creative acts as drawing, writing, and play activities. For instance, children's drawings of Santa Claus before Christmas are larger and better executed than those after Christmas.[10] One can do more than suspect that the pleasant expectations before Christmas represent a quite different motivational condition than the one after Christmas.

Aside from changing the perceptual framework, needs may affect other responses; in fact may alter the entire manifest personality. For example, prolonged periods of deprivation such as those reported in the University of Minnesota Semi-Starvation Studies [11] created rather major personality and behavior changes. The way in which these food needs manifested themselves in behavior is well expressed in Guetzkow and Bowman's book [12] describing the above studies:

---

[8] R. N. Sanford, "The Effects of Abstinence from Food Upon Imaginal Processes: a Preliminary Experiment," *Journal of Psychology*, Vol. 2, 1936, pp. 129–136.

[9] J. S. Bruner and C. C. Goodman, "Value and Need as Organizing Factors in Perception," *Journal of Abnormal and Social Psychology*, Vol. 42, 1947, pp. 33–44.

[10] Charles M. Solley and Gardner Murphy, *Development of the Perceptual World*, New York, Basic Books, Inc., 1960, p. 166.

[11] A. Keys, J. Brozek, A. Henschel, O. Mikelsen, and H. L. Taylor, *Experimental Starvation in Man*, Laboratory of Physiological Hygiene, Minneapolis, University of Minnesota Press, October 15, 1945.

[12] H. S. Guetzkow and P. H. Bowman, *Men and Hunger, a Psychological Manual for Relief Workers*, Elgin, Illinois, Brethren Publishing House, 1946.

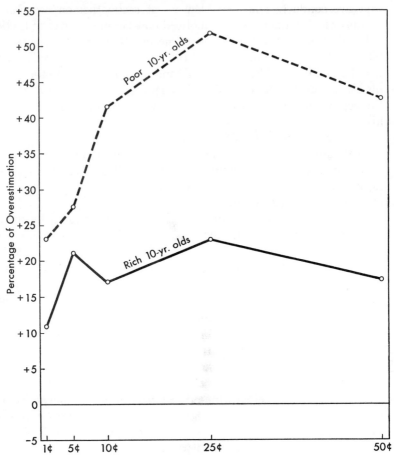

**Figure 14.** How Well-To-Do and Poor Ten-Year-Olds Estimate the Size of Coins. (From J. S. Bruner and C. C. Goodman.)

The intensive preoccupation with food made it difficult for the men to concentrate upon the tasks they had intellectually decided to work on. If a man tried to study, he soon found himself daydreaming about food. He would think about foods he had eaten in the past; he would muse about opportunities he had missed to eat a certain food when he was at this or that place. Often he would daydream by the hour about the next meal.

Perhaps even more important for its implication in school practice (if we assume that other pressing needs would create like results) was the marked change which deprivation produced in the decreased sociability and increased irritability of this semi-starved group. It was reported that "Petty defects became very important and were the source of much irritation. Standing in line at the diet kitchen before being served was the source of

explosive conduct. The men blew up at each other on occasion. Mannerisms which formerly went unnoticed now became sources of friction." [13]

Deprivation or the frustration of needs often produces marked irritability and hostility. For example, the student who gets insufficient sleep may be highly irritable, overcritical, and apt to flare up at the teacher or his classmates. Sherif, a social psychologist, has gone so far as to say that the deprivation of any biogenic need tends to result in frustration mechanisms.[14]

The child who is starved for attention or affection may spend an inordinate amount of school time absorbed in efforts to satisfy these social needs, or when these attempts fail, cut himself off from the teacher and his group, obtaining solace in daydreams, or with other groups, not a part of the school's social situation.

Adjustment to school is fraught with problems created by unsatisfied needs, and consequent distorted social perceptions which in turn give rise to maladaptive behavior. Since an entire section of this book is later devoted to problems of adjustment, such material will not be considered here. At this point it is enough to say that school behavior contains clues of need level which may be valuable aids to the teacher in knowing what kinds of school tasks are appropriate, what manipulations of the social group are desirable, and what kinds of remedial help are necessary to facilitate learning.

### Reinforcement

The second way, perhaps the critical way, in which energies find direction is through the process of reinforcement. In the diffused arousal, before one has found a satisfactory connection between his drives and any external or internal activities that will reduce them, there may be a rather general energy discharge, which may eventually result in the discovery of a means of satisfying the deficit state or drive. Once found, the responses that result in the satisfaction become strengthened and the individual learns to value the objects, persons, and activities that brought the drive reduction.

The concept of reinforcement in learning has had wide acceptance and a tremendous influence upon education. Translating this concept of effect or reinforcement into terms of usable school practices, the principle might be stated: *When a child's responses result in need reduction symbolized by such things as reward, approval, or praise, the responses (activities) perceived by the pupil as having led to these pleasurable consequences are strengthened.*

---

[13] *Ibid.,* p. 27.
[14] Muzafer Sherif and Carolyn W. Sherif, *An Outline of Social Psychology,* Revised Edition, New York, Harper and Brothers, 1956.

A situation from the writer's own experiences is presented to show how reinforcement may operate in a school setting.

> Several years ago in a large West Coast high school some of the teachers were having a good deal of difficulty in handling study halls. One particular incident will illustrate the kind of thing which was happening. The students had been in their seats only a short time, when someone in the back of the room rolled a marble down the steps of the aisle. This was greeted with laughter. The teacher stormed to the back of the study hall in a rage, demanding to know who had rolled the marble. When she received no reply she threatened that when she caught the culprit she would make him pay. This was but one in a series of such incidents—all of which elicited the same fighting response from the teacher. What she did *not* realize was that each episode was a reinforcement for the very kind of behavior which she was trying to stop.

The young man who was sent to replace this teacher began by refusing to fight with the youngsters. There were a few trial episodes which failed to get results. In terms of learning, there was a period of *extinction* due to *non-reinforced trials*. At the same time, this teacher began to reinforce a new kind of behavior. Praise was given for students who worked diligently during the period. Help was given with individual lessons. The new teacher also added a few reference books to the study hall which helped give an outlet for some of the tensions which were built up. Group work was not discouraged so long as it did not interfere with others. In some cases, groups who wished to study something together were sent down the hall to an empty room, where they were placed on their honor to spend their time studying.

There are probably few practicing teachers who are unaware of this principle of motivation. However, only in recent years have school experiences been planned to take advantage of this principle to any great degree, and even now, many opportunities for its application are not utilized. Mistakes in the application of the principle of reinforcement are probably due to failure to consider some of the following specific characteristics of the process:

1. The goals and needs of pupils may be quite different from those which the teacher perceives. For example, a child may make a foolish mistake in recitation and be laughed at by his peers. If this child has a strong need for attention, the laughter quite likely will reinforce this activity—namely, making foolish mistakes.
2. Children's needs are sufficiently individualized so that what is reinforcement for one may not be for another. In one instance a teacher's praise may be a strong reinforcement, while in another that praise will have little or no effect. In fact, for some youngsters the teacher's reproof may be a reinforcement in that it signifies a marking of the pupil as one whose behavior is accepted by his age mates.

3. Punishment and other unpleasant consequences of pupils' activities do not serve as opposites to reinforcements. They do not necessarily weaken response tendencies in the same way that pleasurable consequences strengthen response tendencies.
4. The effect of previous reinforcements is carried into new learning situations. This means that students have an expectation as to what the results of present activities will be.
5. The effect of a particular response must be immediate or at least not long delayed for the reinforcement to be effective. This is particularly true for young children.
6. There must be a consistency in the effect of the response or activity. The learner must not be rewarded for a response one time and then later punished for the same response.

With these principles of reinforcement in mind much of a teacher's guidance of learning should center around the study of the kinds of reinforcement which have previously operated in a student's experience, and also the techniques which he will use as reinforcement in his own teaching program. Understanding of the effect of previous experience is impossible without a knowledge of the kinds of reinforcements which have occurred.

The reader is urged to pause at this point and consider these questions:

1. What are the various ways in which I as a teacher, can reinforce desirable behavior in the classroom?
2. How can the classroom be organized so that the optimum amount of social reinforcement occurs?
3. What can I do to prevent the reinforcement of undesirable behavior?
4. How can I infer from present behavior, the kinds of reinforcement which have previously occurred in the classroom and in the home?
5. How can the effects of undesirable reinforcements be nullified?

Although much of this volume is devoted to just such questions (particularly in this and the following chapter) it is impossible to predict for the reader exactly what kinds of specific techniques of reinforcement will work for every individual. Each child is unique, and requires treatment according to his particular need pattern.

### Set and Intention

As a result of previous reinforcements and punishments and through verbal instructions and self instructions a person builds up expectations as to the drive reducing possibilities of new situations. Moreover, such self instructions as "this is a Mickey-Mouse course," or "the material in

this course will be valuable so I am going to learn it," will make a profound difference in the way in which students direct energies to a new task.

Without purposeful attention to stimuli, or intent to learn, the student may perform rote activities time after time, without acquiring the skills or learnings which represent the teacher's objectives. One psychologist, Sanford,[15] gives an excellent illustration of this fact. He reported that after saying the prayers of the Episcopal service (about 5,000 times in a twenty-five year period) he was unable to recall them unaided.

On several occasions one of the writers has asked his graduate classes how the name of the pen manufacturer, "Sheaffer" is spelled. Invariably well over 90 per cent of the group are unable to give the correct spelling, including those who own Sheaffer pens.

Little wonder that children can read a given word hundreds of times and yet be unable to spell it, or work mathematical problems under the teacher's guidance and be unable to solve similar problems on their own.

What are the factors operating in this important principle of motivation? First, there are attitudes, needs, and desires which lead to an interest in given parts of the pupil's environment. These attitudes are products of experience and guidance and like other kinds of learned behavior are primarily the result of reinforcement. Secondly, these attitudes lead to habits of attention and perception which are learned ways of looking at and looking for something. Even with the desire for information, in a particular area, however, there is the additional question of whether students have enough skill to find what they are looking for.

The perceived usefulness of information and skill is a third factor in the purposefulness of a pupil's approach to school work. Teachers of industrial education, for example, are well aware of increased attention and intent to learn, when class material in motor mechanics relates to the youth's own "hot-rod." An art teacher reports that there was a much greater intention to learn on the part of a settlement house pupil when he had a chance to mould some brass knuckles. In such cases, the learner may be so interested in his own problems that he will go directly to the information of specific concern without bothering to learn other related skills which the teacher may consider essential.

Finally, the kinds of instructions or set given prior to performances such as reading, listening to a lecture, making notes, seeing a demonstration, or taking a test are important variables in determining intent to learn. McGeoch in a summary of considerable experimental evidence has stated that:

---

[15] E. C. Sanford, "A Letter to Dr. Titchener," as reported in J. A. McGeoch, *Psychology of Human Learning*, New York, Longmans, Green and Co., 1942, p. 276.

. . . An active set to learn, with its accompanying active response to the material practiced, is a powerful determiner of learning, whether the learning be the fixation of a verbal series, the establishment of a conditioned response, or the discovery and fixation of the solutions of perceptual-motor and rational problems. The set may be established by formal instructions or it may arise from the experimental situation and the subject's own reaction systems.[16]

One psychologist tested the effect of the preparatory set as a motivational influence by telling student teachers that their grade in his course would be determined by the gains in achievement made by high school students in their individual practice teaching situations. As might be expected, these practice teachers focused their energetic efforts upon their pupils' improvement, and achieved better results in this respect than a control group of practice teachers who had not had this set.[17]

### Personality and the Self Concept as Factors

Another set of determinants affecting the directionality of human energies can be found in personality factors. How a child sees himself in relation to his goals and to others, the kind of person he believes himself to be, and the kinds of fears and aspirations he has, will be major factors in delineating the things for which he strives.

Studies of levels of aspiration have shown that one of the important variables in determining the level of achievement which a child proposes for himself is his previous experience in like situations.[18] A systematic study[19] of aspirational levels has shown the important effects upon future goal setting behavior when the child fails to achieve his stated goals. This same investigation found that a child who thus fails is more apt than the one who succeeds to develop unrealistic aspirations for succeeding performances. More specifically, he estimates his future performance so high as to be wholly impossible, or so low that he is sure to attain the mark. Those children who fall near the level which they have set for themselves are prone to be quite realistic about their estimate for future performances.

Certainly a most important factor in the choice of goals and expected level of performance is the child's self-concept. (This is of course conditioned by such things as previous experiences with stated versus attained

---

[16] John A. McGeoch, op. cit., p. 279.

[17] M. C. Wittrock, "Set Applied to Student Teaching," *Journal of Educational Psychology*, Vol. 53, 1962, pp. 175–180.

[18] R. R. Sears, "Success and Failure: A Study of Motility" in Q. McNemar and M. A. Merrill, *Studies in Personality*, New York, McGraw-Hill Book Company, 1942, pp. 235–258.

[19] P. S. Sears, "Levels of Aspiration in Academically Successful and Unsuccessful Children," *Journal of Abnormal and Social Psychology*, Vol. 35, 1940, pp. 498–536.

goals.) Working with orthopedically handicapped young people, Rotter [20] set up a task involving a simple motor skill. The important finding was that this handicapped group had a lower level of aspiration *even though the task being performed was totally unrelated to their physical handicap.* In Chapter 4 it has already been shown how specific deviations of adolescents (such as minor somatic variations) may be destructive of self-confidence. It is a great misfortune when such minor matters come to spread to a person's entire self-concept. It is clear in such cases what the teacher's job is. The child must be made to realize that a slight handicap may limit him *only* in the specific areas where it is involved. Also the development of a healthy self-concept demands that the youth's notion of normality be in terms of a wide range, rather than conceived as a fixed point.

The over-idealization of goals and of the self in relation to those goals is a disease of our culture. Young people's goals are often unrealistic because of the inadequacy of our language to describe them, and because words are used to take the place of objects. Also influences such as motion pictures, newspapers, fiction, and advertising have given a romantic aura to many goals and ideals sometimes to such an extent that the pupils' aspirations are far from realistic. On top of this idealization of goals, our language is such that we use "either-or" categories in describing, to ourselves, such things as success and attainment. Therefore, if a youth's goals are so idealized as to be non-existent in reality—and therefore impossible of attainment—and if he visualizes success on an all or none basis, he is doomed to be disappointed. One writer describes this process as the cycle of idealization, frustration, and demoralization (IFD). Because he is unable to attain his unrealistic ideals, the youth meets frustration, which in turn leads to demoralization.[21]

Children need to learn to set for themselves goals which are within their ability of attainment and which are realistically perceived. The expectations which build up around goal seeking activities must be met, if reinforcement is to be effective. When achievements fall far short of the learner's expectations the learning process is disrupted. Perhaps even more important, young people need to develop self-concepts which are positive and healthy. In fact this is so important in the person's overall development that counselors and clinical psychologists use, as one measure of the success of their work, the number of positive self references which are made by a client.

When the child is preoccupied with personal concerns and problems and when he is beset by fears and anxieties his energies are directed to

---

[20] Julian B. Rotter, Unpublished information as reported in K. Lewin, *et al.*, "Level of Aspiration" in J. McV. Hunt (Editor), *Personality and the Behavior Disorders*, Vol. I, New York, The Ronald Press, 1944.

[21] Wendell Johnson, *People in Quandaries*, New York, Harper and Brothers, 1946.

these problems and not to the intellectual problems in school. Research comparing children's level of adjustment as rated by teachers with "object curiosity" scores showed a significant negative correlation between degree of maladjustment and curiosity.[22] It appears that anxiety hinders curiosity. Somewhat similar results were obtained by Haywood, who found lower novelty seeking behavior among subjects who were in a relatively high state of anxiety.[23]

## APPLYING PRINCIPLES OF MOTIVATION IN TEACHING

The key to controlling and guiding behavior is the understanding of needs, motives, and interests. Consequently much of a teacher's work centers around problems of motivation. Almost invariably the teacher who fails is the one who is unable to take proper account of motivational factors. Questions such as how to relate school work to pupils' needs and interests, how to appraise the results of teaching methods in terms of their effect upon interest and motivation, how to diagnose interests and motives are persistently raised by teachers. The understanding and proper use of motivational techniques bring interest, good morale, effective learning, and a sense of real achievement to the classroom. Lack of understanding and improper attempts to direct and change behavior often result in increased tension, disciplinary problems, boredom and fatigue, inefficient learning, and a sense that the school activities are little more than busy work.

How important motivation is to school learning has been recently demonstrated by Cattell and his associates. Working in a junior high school, they found that measures of students' personality and motivation contributed more to the prediction of achievement than did scores on measures of general ability.[24]

In an excellent review of research that relates teaching to motivation, Sears and Hilgard suggest that social, ego, and curiosity motives are the major ones to which a teacher can appeal.[25] The balance of this chapter will show how motives such as these can come alive in classrooms where teachers give students a knowledge of their progress, use rewards properly,

---

[22] Paul McReynolds, Mary Acker, and Caryl Pietila, "Relation of Object Curiosity to Psychological Adjustment in Children," *Child Development*, Vol. 32, 1961, pp. 393–400.

[23] H. C. Haywood, "Novelty Seeking as a Function of Manifest Anxiety, and Physiological Arousal," *Journal of Personality*, Vol. 3, 1962, pp. 63–74.

[24] R. B. Cattell, John Butcher, David Connor, A. B. Sweeney and Bien Tsujioka, *Prediction and Understanding of the Effect of Children's Interest upon School Performance*, Cooperative Research Project #701 (8383) Psychology Department, Univ. of Illinois, 1962 (Mimeo).

[25] Pauline S. Sears and Ernest R. Hilgard, "The Teacher's Role in the Motivation of the Learner," Chap. VIII in *Theories of Learning and Instruction*, 63rd Yearbook, National Society for the Study of Education, Chicago, 1964.

understand the function of punishment, build a desire for learning, and apply reinforcement strategically.

### Providing the Student a Knowledge of His Progress

Knowledge of progress seems to be essential for effective learning. The beneficial effects of apprising a learner of the results of his learning activity have been well-demonstrated from the early 1900's to the present,[26] and as a principle of motivation, they have been experimentally tested in a number of school subjects.

There is little doubt that the extent of a pupil's motivation is dependent upon his knowledge of how well he is doing. But probably just as important as this general feeling of attainment is his knowledge of the result of each response, plus some means for the immediate correction of it if he has made an error. This kind of knowledge of progress has been described as follows:

> As illustrative of the value of specific knowledge of progress—of knowing just what is wrong, we may take an experiment by English. A proper trigger squeeze is an important factor in accurate rifle shooting, especially with high powered rifles. Soldiers who were told that they were not properly squeezing the trigger of their guns, showed slow gains with practice; when they were made to feel tactually and kinaesthetically, the difference between adequate and inadequate squeezing, they made much more rapid progress. Likewise it is not enough to be told that one's sentence structure is weak; one needs to be shown where it lacks balance or parallelism.[27]

How may this principle be used in teaching? In one case [28] the simple expedient of showing sixth-grade children progress charts of their reading improvement and emphasizing rapid reading for only a short period of twenty-eight days increased the speed of reading over 200 per cent without a loss in comprehension. This experiment was especially significant in that no other special motivations or skills were emphasized during the period of improvement.

The case which follows was reported to the writer by a basketball coach in an Illinois high school, and will show how this principle was applied in one phase of physical education:

> I had a very poor group of free-throw shooters, and I had tried several means of reward and punishment for improving them, but these methods did not work, so I decided to try something different. Each boy was required to shoot 100 free throws each day. My manager and I kept a record of the number of successful shots but the boys did not know about this. To my

---

[26] J. B. Stroud, *Psychology in Education*, New York, Longmans Green and Co., 1946.
[27] H. B. English, *Learning as Psychotechnology*, Mimeographed Study Guide, Columbus, Ohio State University, 1949, pp. 35a–35b.
[28] J. A. O'Brien, *Silent Reading*, New York, The Macmillan Company, 1921.

dismay, *the practice did not improve their percentage.* So I made a huge chart with each squad member's name on it and the number of successful free throws made each day. I posted this in the gymnasium where all the players could refer to it at any time.

At the end of a week, slow but steady improvement was discernible. I stressed the point that the chart was not to show who had the highest average but rather who was making the most improvement. The chart was continued until the end of the basketball season, and in all but three out of twenty-four cases, the rises were continuous.

Several aspects of motivation are illustrated by this report. First, note that knowledge of progress was effective when other techniques had failed. Secondly, the case illustrates that practice, or repetition, alone, does not necessarily lead to improvement. Finally, it should be noted that the teacher in this case emphasized that pupils should make comparisons with their own previous performance and not with other players.

A general term used to describe the informative character of the consequences of a learner's responses is feedback. Feedback has the dual function of providing motivation and a chance for reinforcement to work, and of giving information that will correct error. Every reaction of a teacher in response to a student's activity is a kind of feedback that has potential for both these functions. The grade on a paper, the marking of specific errors, the verbal reactions such as "that's wrong, try it this way, good," are all relevant examples.

To illustrate the effect on students of teachers' reactions to their work, Page [29] describes a study in which 2139 individuals in 74 classrooms received different types of comments on test papers. For one group, the test papers were graded and simply returned with the letter grade. In a second group, grades were accompanied by comments specified by the investigator. For example for an A, the comment: "excellent keep it up," was written, and for a C the teacher was instructed to write, "perhaps try to do still better." The third group was a "free comment" group which received in addition to their grade whatever comment the teacher himself believed the most appropriate. On a subsequent objective test, the "free comment" students did best, the "specified comment" group next best, and the "no comment" students made the poorest showing.

A specific case may further illustrate some of the problems and questions in the use of feedback. Suppose a student misspells a word in a theme as follows:

On this *occassion* we forded the stream instead of trying to find a bridge.

The teacher could do any one of the following things:

---

[29] Ellis B. Page, "Teacher Comments and Student Performance: A Seventy-Four Classroom Experiment in School Motivation," *Journal of Educational Psychology*, Vol. 49, 1958, pp. 173–181.

sp.
1. occassion        indicate the word had been spelled incorrectly
2. occas$ion        show what the error in spelling was
3. ignore the error
4. write a note at the top of the paper to the effect that there were several misspellings in the theme from which the above sentence was taken

Of the four examples of feedback above, the practice in number 2 has advantages over the other three. From what is presently known, feedback is most effective if immediate and specific. Ideally a misspelled word should be corrected immediately after it has been written. Since this is not possible in most situations, the teacher should make every effort to get work back quickly, and to mark it in such a way that the student knows exactly what his error is, why it is an error, and *especially* important, what he did well in the work. Specificity in the latter instance may be just as important as correcting errors! Continuing the example of theme writing, papers should be returned no later than a day or two after they are written. In fact there ought to be many opportunities for writing sentences and paragraphs that can be appraised by the teacher or other students immediately after they are written.

As learners become more mature they develop models that they can use to judge the quality of their own work. Ideally they gain an internal feedback mechanism that allows for correction of their own errors and provides self-sustaining motivation when they are correct. Thus a boy who is learning to weld has a mind picture of what a good weld looks like. His own attempts can be judged against this standard, and he can find reinforcement of those responses that seem related when his own efforts result in a reasonably good approximation of this mind picture. It is essential that pupils develop these mental pictures. The teacher cannot personally provide feedback to 30 or 40 pupils constantly. Instead he tries to teach what a good theme is like, how to check arithmetic problems by estimation or casting out nines, and how to judge an artistic creation by applying certain rules of balance and design.

As an aid to teachers, psychologists have developed numerous devices designed to provide an immediate knowledge of results. Among the first of these were various "test taking" machines developed by Pressey and described in his writings.[30],[31] One of these is shown in Figure 15, which portrays a machine developed for the Office of Naval Research. This

---

[30] S. L. Pressey, "A Simple Device for Teaching, Testing and Research in Learning," *School and Society*, Vol. 23, 1926, pp. 373-376.

[31] S. L. Pressey, "Development and Appraisal of Devices Providing Immediate Automatic Scoring of Objective Tests and Concomitant Self-Instruction," *Journal of Psychology*, Vol. 29, 1950, pp. 417-447.

**Figure 15.** Pressey's Drum-Tutor Testing Machine.

device allows for multiple choice, or true-false questions to be answered by pressing appropriate keys of the machine. If the student selects the right key, the machine advances to the next question; if not, he must continue selecting alternatives until he does get the right one. An adaptation of one of Pressey's earlier devices is shown in Figure 16. In this device called a punchboard or pocket tutor, students press their pencils into holes in a face plate. If they are correct their pencil goes through the answer sheet. If they are wrong, the pencil makes a mark but does not go through the paper. Here again the pupil keeps at a question until he gets the right answer. The punchboard in Figure 16 was constructed by Mr. George Hilgeneck and Mr. Wayne Butler, teacher and principal of the Stevenson Elementary School, Melrose Park, Illinois. At the same school, a special teaching-testing room has been equipped in which an entire class of pupils can take a test "electronically" as shown in Figure 17. Each desk is wired to the teacher's central control desk. By operating the automatic slide projector, the teacher can project a question on the screen so that it is seen by all the pupils at once. Each of the children then presses a key to indicate his choice of one of the alternatives in the ques-

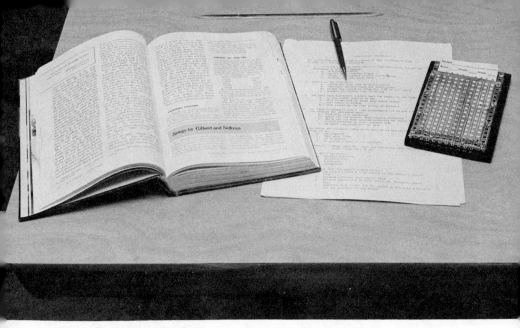

**Figure 16.** A Punchboard Self-Testing Device Used in an Elementary School.

tion. These responses register in a lighted panel on the teacher's desk much like incoming calls on a telephone switchboard.

### Rewards

Whereas reinforcement is generally considered as the pleasant consequence for a specific response, reward is a satisfaction of needs for a whole series of responses. Furthermore rewards (in the form of teachers' rewards to students) may be artificial and somewhat unrelated to the activity for which they are given. The most effective reward (and punishment, for that matter) is that which is a natural consequence of the learning activity. Unfortunately rewards are characteristically given for such things as a well-memorized poem, a correct list of spelling words, or a winning theme.

If reward is thought of in the broad sense of including both material and intangible values which result from performance, such as praise, self-esteem, and adulation of one's fellows, it is then secondary only to physiological satisfactions as a force in human behavior. In fact all other forms of motivation may be thought of as subsidiary to it, and in this sense it becomes synonymous with a previous concept—tension reduction. However, there are various types of rewards, and we are particularly concerned here with the rewards teachers give and their effect upon school behavior.

The use of material rewards in school is not common for obvious reasons, but there is some evidence as to how such rewards affect the learning of children. The important drawbacks in the use of material rewards in school learning seem to be (1) in order to keep performance at a high

**Figure 17.** Testing Room for Automatic and Immediate Scoring.

level it seems necessary to increase rewards periodically, (2) the attainment of the material reward becomes the primary goal, and school learning only an incidental means to an end—a means which is quickly cast aside when the reward is attained, (3) other kinds of incentives are just as effective or more effective and do not lead to the relegation of learning to a secondary position. An Illinois principal gave an illustration of the use of material rewards in his school:

> One teacher who had an outside income, made a habit of bringing presents (generally candy bars) to her classroom. She distributed these to students who, on a given day worked diligently and stayed out of trouble. She was, according to the principal, well-liked by her pupils, and achieved good results in her teaching. However, the other teachers in the school, financially unable to do the same, complained bitterly to the principal who was thus obliged to ask the teacher in question to find other means of rewarding her class.

If learners are to form attitudes about school learnings in which they like school activities for their own sake, stress on material rewards is distinctly out of place.

The use of marks, percentages, and grades; the giving of honors through assemblies, honor societies, and scholarships; and the awarding of prizes in the form of ribbons, cups, or trophies are all ways in which the educator

attempts to foster desirable behavior and promote a maximum of effort toward school goals. Such incentives may be powerful, as they often symbolize the approval and admiration of parents, teachers, or other pupils. However, as is the case with material rewards, these incentives may become the sole purpose or aim of achievement with mastery of subject matter only an incidental step toward the incentive. In such cases, school work itself may be viewed in a neutral way or even as a somewhat unpleasant but necessary task. Even so, the writers take the view that all behavior is purposive or goal directed, hence there is nothing artificial about working for a scholarship or for honors, any more than it is artificial for behavior to be directed toward earning money and the things it will buy. Nevertheless, there is a profound difference between the man who hates his work but does it to earn money, and the man who likes his work and also the financial rewards he achieves for it. In the same way there is an important difference between the youngster who dislikes work, but masters it because of honors, and the one who is engrossed and pleased with his work and achieves honors as a consequence. The important difference here to consider is that the learner in the latter case will be much more likely to remember what is learned and better able to apply it in a new situation. What accounts for the differences in the above cases? What is there about a learning activity which is of intrinsic value to the pupil? Such factors as the following may operate from time to time in the learning situation which possesses intrinsic motivation.

1. There is a pleasant association between material to be learned and the learning situation, e.g., a friendly social atmosphere.
2. The material to be learned allows for a satisfaction of the drive for activity and curiosity and allows the learner to make discoveries for himself and to solve problems. These consequences are rewarding, but are a more natural consequence of the learning activity than teacher-controlled rewards.
3. The student identifies the learning with persons he admires.
4. The consequences of the learning include the opportunity for the student to see how the subject matter works—to see a finished production. For example, he may use a foreign language in another country or with a foreign visitor, or he may build his own radio set.
5. There is novelty or humor in the learning material which serves as a release from boredom and monotony.
6. The learner takes an active part in the planning of the material to be learned, thus gaining a proprietary interest in its completion.

The fulfilling of one, or better, several or all of these conditions, will almost certainly lead to rewards which are an intrinsic part of the learning situation, and the teacher will not have to depend solely upon extrinsic rewards to achieve the school's goals.

### Punishment

Punishment and the fear of punishment are still used as forms of extrinsic motivation in the school room even though the use of punishment has decreased markedly in the last fifty years. There is little question that fear, anxiety, and avoidance of pain are powerful motivating forces. Threats, reproof, and sarcasm build up tensions which are released much in the same fashion as other drive produced tensions. Because of its power, and because of its ease of use, and because it often serves to release tension of the person doing the punishing, this form of motivation, historically, has been among the most frequent forms of man's attempt to train his young. Punishment has been assumed, at one time or another to accomplish these ends: (1) teach the child respect for authority, (2) block undesirable responses, (3) force the child to do something he was not ready to do or did not want to do, (4) set an example for potential offenders, (5) make students pay attention to class work, and (6) motivate students to learn assigned material.

A report of one of the writer's advisees will illustrate the powerful force of punishment:

> When I was in the fourth grade I had a teacher whom I just hated. Once she told me that if I did not learn the "9's" in multiplication by the next day I would fail the course. At that time the idea of failure was terrible, and so I stayed up until twelve that night studying them. I just knew I could never face my parents and friends if I failed, so I really worked that night. I think this is one reason I dislike math so much now. Every time I see a page of figures I get that tense feeling.

This example should show two important facts about the use of threats for purposes of motivation. In the first place, it was a powerful force for this particular child, but it should also be noted that the results of its use included more than learning multiplication. There was also the resulting dislike for the teacher and for arithmetic in general. These too are learnings. For this reason, many psychologists have concluded that while punishment is a potential mover, its results are less predictable than other modes of influencing children and also is often accompanied by undesirable results. These undesirable aspects of punishment include (1) resentment and hostility toward the "punisher," (2) increased emotionality often so severe that any learning during the phase of activity elicited by the punishment is unlikely, (3) learning in order to avoid punishment rather than for the intrinsic value of the material to be learned, (4) fatigue due to tension created by anxiety, and (5) disintegration of class morale.

Psychologists today are convinced that punishment has often been overused in schools and homes. They do not, as a general rule, take the position sometimes ascribed to them by laymen, that punishment should never be used. It might be said, however, as a general principle for teachers

to follow, that as a form of motivation, punishment is crude and relatively ineffective when all factors in the learning process are considered.

Some values of punishment (not primarily for motivational purposes) are shown in the instances which follow:

> The first is when punishment is appropriately combined with reward. Punishment may occasionally be used to redirect behavior so that the desired behavior can occur and be rewarded. Even though the effect of punishment is temporarily disturbing, it may under some circumstances permit the more permanent effect of reward to become operative. For example, a shock through mishandling an electrical appliance in science may be effective if supplemented by help in correcting the hazardous condition.
>
> The second situation in which punishment is appropriate is that recognized clinically as one in which the need for punishment is great. A child sometimes tests the authoritative adult by provocative behavior to see how far he can go. If not punished (in order that the limits may be defined for him), his anxiety mounts as he does things which seem beyond the law.[32]

If the teacher who is confronted by a problem considers the *purpose* for which punishment is meted out, he will go a long way toward eliminating its undesirable aspects and will be far less apt to misuse it. Thorndike suggests several ways in which teachers might improve the results from punishments. They are: (1) make sure in each case that the punishment belongs to the behavior in question, (2) . . . forestall the punishment in cases where the want which led to the offense can be satisfied innocently, and (3) more frequently reward good tendencies in place of repressing bad ones.[33]

Clearly the consequences of punishment upon behavior will vary greatly from one situation to another. Any guiding principles which the teacher formulates for his own use should give cognizance to the following factors. First, there are social relationships between teacher and pupils which are important determiners of the effect of punishment. The slightest reprimand by a very unpopular teacher may be perceived as an injustice. Secondly, there are personality differences among children which make a difference in the effect of various influence techniques which the teacher uses upon them. In one study,[34] it was shown that children who are ap-

---

[32] E. R. Hilgard and D. H. Russell, "Motivation in School Learning" in Forty-Ninth Yearbook, National Society for the Study of Education, Part I, *Learning and Instruction,* Chicago, University of Chicago Press, 1950, p. 50.

It should be noted that the above writers have used as an example that type of punishment which is a natural consequence of the act, and not punishment by the teacher. Also it should be clear that there are times when punishment and restraint are necessary in emergencies for the safety of children.

[33] E. L. Thorndike, *Selected Writings from a Connectionist's Psychology,* Appleton-Century-Crofts, Inc., 1949, pp. 60–61.

[34] G. G. Thompson and C. W. Hunnicutt, "The Effects of Repeated Praise or Blame on the Work Achievement of Introverts and Extroverts," *Journal of Educational Psychology,* Vol. 35, 1944, pp. 257–266.

parently extraverted may respond with greater effort following reproof, while children classified as introverts are more apt to suffer in achievement following reproof. In the third place, the teacher must always try to appraise the child's perception of the punishment. If the student feels he is unjustly singled out for punishment (especially when his transgressions are ones common to his group) he is apt to build a resentment toward the teacher and a desire to "get even" which interferes with learning activities.

Lastly and perhaps most important, punishment must be considered in terms of the total learning situation.[35] The teacher should always be sure that correct or desirable activity is made known and rewarded upon occurrence when punishment is used. Punishment for the *only* thing a child knows how to do will not lead to desirable learning, but may cause emotional disturbance and even a fixation of the undesirable responses.

### Building a Desire for Learning

Learning something, acquiring new skills and knowledge, can in a sense become an end in itself. In his Presidential Address to the American Psychological Association, Jerome Bruner [36] suggests that there is a "psychology of subject matter," and that even young students can be led to see the origins, causes, and effects within a discipline, and thereby obtain a "reward in understanding that grows from the subject matter itself." Bruner further contends that the natural or "intrinsic" problem solving which has high motivational value for students may be suppressed by the extrinsic requirements of the teacher.

In a similar vein, Ausubel states that "instead of denigrating subject-matter knowledge, we must discover more efficient methods of fostering the long-term acquisition of meaningful and useable bodies of knowledge and of developing intrinsic motivation for such learning." One of Ausubel's suggestions is that a teacher with whom children find easy identification can promote intrinsic motivation through his own enthusiasm and excitement about the subject he teaches.[37]

Activity which a child perceives as useful and productive rapidly becomes self-energized. A high school principal furnishes the following illustration from his own experience:

> When I was in high school, I had a learning experience which I shall never forget. It originated in our shop class and involved the study of plywood.

---

[35] For a good discussion of learning theory and punishment see: Richard L. Solomon, "Punishment," *American Psychologist*, Vol. 19, 1964, pp. 239–253.

[36] Jerome Bruner, "The Growth of Mind," *American Psychologist*, Vol. 20, 1965, p. 1013.

[37] David P. Ausubel, "A Teaching Strategy for Culturally Deprived Pupils; Cognitive and Motivational Considerations," *School Review*, Vol. 71, 1963, pp. 454–463.

We actually made plywood. The problem required reading and assembling of facts. We learned about kinds of wood, their strength, durability, and uses. We learned to plane wood to the desired thickness and we made our own glue, and sandpaper, and found the ingredients of these as well as of the finishing agents such as varnish with which we treated the finished product. Although we bought our paint brushes, I enjoyed learning that in primitive times people set combs in the paths frequented by wild boars thus collecting bristles. To this day I like shop work very much, and I attribute this interest to a very understanding and patient teacher. The articles which we made of wood were useful, and I still have some of the things I constructed including a gun rack made from black walnut. Our class actually went to the standing timber, identified the walnut, felled the tree, took it to the saw mill, dried it, and planed it. I would not part with this rack for anything. Needless to say, absences in this shop class were rare, and there were no problems involving discipline.

Aside from the increased meaningfulness and better learning of material which results from making school work relevant, there is the additional consideration here of how such teaching steps serve to increase motivation. Such considerations are particularly important in schools which are relatively isolated from their community. One writer [38] warns that isolation from direct experience is a real danger facing our schools. In large cities, especially, he says "talk about things increasingly takes the place of real experience with things."

The community is full of challenging problems and opportunities for learning, and when students are allowed or encouraged to tackle these problems, their interest and enthusiasm may be tremendous. Following is one example of this kind of well-motivated activity in operation.[39]

> During a class discussion it was found that over half of the persons present had had malaria. The students were amazed and began to wonder whether they were truly representative of the population of Tuscaloosa. A visit to local health authorities revealed a lack of reliable data. By this time class interest was so high, students proposed that they secure answers to their questions through a direct survey.
>
> A questionnaire was drawn up and plans for administering it were discussed. But the city was large. What was an adequate sampling? How should the information be gathered?
>
> It was finally decided that the students would secure training in interview techniques in school and then visit every fifth house in the city with their questionnaire.
>
> Next the data were compiled and charts were drawn. The class found that they were an atypical group. However, the rate of malarial infection was so high that students decided to take some steps to improve the situation.

[38] M. R. Collings, "Exploring Your Community: A Direct Experience Study," *Journal of Educational Research*, Vol. 44, 1950, pp. 225–230.

[39] This is a description of Robert Strang's class in biology in the Tuscaloosa, Alabama High School, reported in The American Association for Supervision and Curriculum Development, 1949 Yearbook, *Toward Better Teaching*, pp. 203–204.

The class studied causes and remedies for malaria and prepared literature for distribution in the school and community. The findings of the study were submitted to the local board of health and to the city newspaper, and a complete report of the study was placed in the high school library.

Here is intrinsic motivation in its mature form. There is little need in such cases for the teacher to be concerned with schemes for prodding students into action, or sugar coating the subject matter to make it palatable. In a sense, activity of this sort is the ultimate for which teachers should strive, because it is the culmination of careful planning which accepts students as responsible self-motivated persons who no longer need the teacher except as a guide and who are now ready to go on learning whether they are in school or not.

### Applying Reinforcement Strategically

Until recently, the precisely scheduled and strategic use of reinforcers to shape behavior had been almost exclusively limited to animals, mainly white rats and pigeons. Reinforcement with animals proved to be highly successful, so much so that it has come to be viewed by some (see Chap. 5) as the central process in the formation and change of behavior. Its wide application in human affairs was forecast by Skinner in his science-fiction utopia, *Walden Two*.[40] In the early 1960's there were isolated reports of the successful use of operant conditioning [41] in the treatment of mental illness, and demonstrations of its use in shaping verbal behavior. In the last five years, however, the application of reinforcement theory has become a major thrust in several areas of applied psychology. Some of the applications in schooling will now be reviewed.

Arthur and Carolyn Staats [42] and coworkers were pioneers in this area. They showed that reading skills could be taught to four-year-olds by the use of tangible reinforcers. They used tokens which children learned could be exchanged for toys and trinkets. The tangible reinforcers kept the young children at their tasks for relatively long periods of time, something the researchers had been unable to accomplish with general rewards, such as praise. An especially interesting case reported by Staats and Butterfield [43] is that of a fourteen-year-old delinquent boy with a history of school failures. His reading achievement was at the second grade level. This boy

---

[40] B. F. Skinner, *Walden Two*, New York, A Macmillan Paperback, 1962.

[41] Operant conditioning refers to the development and strengthening of emitted voluntary behaviors in contrast to the Pavlovian type of classical conditioning in which involuntary responses were conditioned.

[42] Arthur Staats *et al.*, "A Reinforcer System and Experimental Procedure for the Laboratory Study of Reading Acquisition," *Child Development*, Vol. 35, 1964, pp. 209–231.

[43] A. W. Staats and W. H. Butterfield, "Treatment of a Non Reader and a Culturally Deprived Juvenile Delinquent: An Application of Reinforcement Principles," *Child Development*, Vol. 36, 1965, pp. 925–942.

was given a 4½ month period of training in reading via the Science Research Associates Reading materials, and under a token reinforcement system (the tokens could be exchanged for such teen age desirables as pomade, phonograph records, and money). The total value of all the "back-up" reinforcers was $20.31. Results for this case included: (1) 64,307 responses, or single words read, (2) 230 new words learned and remembered, (3) reading achievement increased to the 4.3 grade level, (4) passed all his courses for the first time, and (5) misbehaviors in school decreased to zero.

In a regular school setting, O'Leary and Becker [44] have successfully lowered such deviant behaviors as "pushing, name-calling, and making disruptive noises" by a system of token reinforcements, which could be exchanged for such items as candy, comics, and perfume. Included in their use of reinforcers was a procedure for gradually increasing the delay between the receipt of the tokens and the giving of the back-up reinforcers, in the hope that gradually the normal kinds of social reinforcers would take over. They also gave group points when the whole class behaved well, and these points, when enough had accumulated, could be exchanged for popsicles. Curves showing the rapid drop in deviant behavior are shown in Figure 18.

These studies and others of the same type provide convincing evidence that the strategic control of either tangible or social reinforcers can dramatically alter motivation and behavior. But only sketchy information is given the classroom teacher who handles groups of children. In the laboratory situation there is usually one person for every two or three children, and they are generally well trained in the use of reinforcement techniques. Now psychologists at the University of Illinois have shown how reinforcement can be applied in the classroom by regular teachers.[45] In a recent study, they selected a number of behavior problem children in five classrooms and trained the teachers to use reinforcement procedures as follows:

### GENERAL RULES FOR TEACHERS

1. Make rules for each period explicit as to what is expected of children (remind them of rules when needed).
2. *Ignore* (do not attend to) behaviors which interfere with learning or teaching, unless a child is being hurt by another. Use punishment which seems appropriate, preferably withdrawal of some positive reinforcement.
3. Give *praise* and *attention* to behaviors which facilitate learning. Tell child

---

[44] K. Daniel O'Leary and Wesley C. Becker, "Behavior Modification of an Adjustment Class: A Token Reinforcement Program," *Exceptional Children* (In Press).

[45] Wesley C. Becker, Charles H. Madsen Jr., Carole Revelle Arnold, and Don R. Thomas, *The Contingent Use of Teacher Attention and Praise in Reducing Classroom Behavior Problems*, Report: National Institute of Child Health and Human Development, Psychology Department, Urbana, University of Illinois, 1967 (Mimeograph).

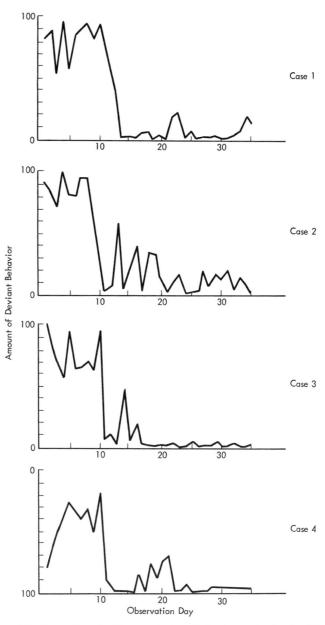

**Figure 18.** Curves Showing Drop in Deviant Behavior as the Result of Reinforcement.

what he is being praised for. Try to reinforce behaviors incompatible with those you wish to decrease.

In general, give praise for achievement, prosocial behavior, and following the group rules.

Besides these general rules, some teachers received special suggestions for their "target" children, such as Alice:

**SPECIAL RULES FOR ALICE**
1. Praise sitting straight in chair with both feet and chair legs on the floor, and concentrating on own work.
2. Praise using hands for things other than sucking.
3. Praise attention to directions given by teacher or talks made by students.
4. Specify behavior you expect from her at the beginning of the day and for new activity. . . .

Deviant behavior of the ten "target" children in the five classes decreased from 62.13% to 29.19%. Teachers who were very dubious about the whole procedure in the beginning became enthusiastic supporters of the reinforcement idea when the experiment ended.

While the cases just mentioned dealt with children who were having special problems, there is sufficient relevance in the techniques for all teaching. The instances and studies cited underline the importance of ensuring that learning for all children has significant results in their lives, so that they may approach each new learning situation equipped both cognitively and motivationally to achieve the success they desire.

## SUMMARY

Motivation, contrary to the popular usage of the term, is not a bag of tricks which the teacher uses to produce learning. Rather it is a process which belongs to the pupil. It is similar to vision, in that it involves external stimulation, appropriate mechanisms of response, and an internal force which energizes the response. The basic substratum of motivation may be found in the needs of the child. The first important characteristic of motives is that they have an energizing function. They stir up behavior. Besides releasing energy, motives have a character of directionality. Energy produced by needs seeks a discharge in relevant incentives, or goal objects which satisfy needs. In brief, motivation may be described as a process in which energies produced by needs are expended in the direction of goals.

An interesting question is why energies take one direction rather than another. Why does one boy do work after school to satisfy his needs for achievement, while another finds satisfaction in his alliance with a gang of lawbreakers? The answer outlined in this chapter was that, first of all, unsatisfied needs change perceptual patterns so that set and attention are selectively controlled. It was next proposed that reinforcements, different for each individual, strengthen certain response tendencies and attach value signs to some objects and not to others. Also, it was suggested that

omething a number of times, the habits thus formed develop
autonomy, a drive property in their own right. Finally, atten-
led to the fact that personality factors and the "self concept"
portant role in the kinds of goals which pupils choose for
and that personal problems such as anxiety restrict curiosity.

It is the job of the teacher to create an atmosphere which provides desirable outlets for needs in the direction of worthwhile incentives—an atmosphere in which interests will as a consequence flourish. How can all this be brought about? This chapter has attempted to answer this question by showing that the teacher should:

1. Treat each child's needs and interests as a unique group of traits, which they are, and plan activities and incentives accordingly.
2. Set up clear-cut goals in which the pupil takes an active part, thereby helping to give the pupil a real intention to learn.
3. Help the child achieve a sense of success and confidence by
   a. providing a clear-cut knowledge of progress.
   b. praising deserving work.
   c. finding special areas of skill, and allowing him to develop these and to display them in the classroom.
4. Give exercises and materials in the context of "real life" so that students see that their work is beneficial and a real achievement.
5. Avoid making school unpleasant by requiring meaningless tasks, by punishment, by over repetition and busy work, or too much drill.

The ultimate goal of teaching should not center exclusively around how many facts have been learned but around the kinds of motives youngsters learn. Surely when students begin to like and want school activities for their own sake a milestone of maturity has been reached. Only when school work offers activities which will satisfy the needs of all pupils will this goal be approached.

### References for Further Study

Atkinson, John W. (Editor), *Motives in Fantasy, Action and Society*, New York, Van Nostrand, 1958.

Bindra, Dalbir, *Motivation*, New York, Ronald Press, 1959.

Berlyne, D. E., *Conflict, Arousal and Curiosity*, New York, McGraw-Hill Book Co., Inc., 1960.

Combs, Arthur W. and Snygg, Donald, *Individual Behavior*, New York, Harper and Brothers, 1959.

Jones, Marshall R. (Editor), *Nebraska Symposium on Motivation*, yearly volumes since 1953, Lincoln, University of Nebraska Press.

Hilgard, E. R. and Russell, D. H., "Motivation in School Learning," Chapter 2 in Part I, 49th Yearbook of the National Society for the Study of Educa-

tion, *Learning and Instruction*, Chicago, University of Chicago Press, 1950.

Marx, Melvin H., "Motivation," in *Encyclopedia of Educational Research*, Third Edition, New York, The Macmillan Co., 1960, pp. 888–901.

Olds, James, *The Growth and Structure of Motives*, Glencoe, Illinois, Free Press, 1956.

Rethlingshafer, Dorothy, *Motivation as Related to Personality*, New York, McGraw-Hill Book Co., Inc., 1963.

Rosenblith, Judy F. and Allinsmith, Wesley, *The Causes of Behavior, II, Readings in Child Development and Educational Psychology*, Chap. X, Motivational Resultants, Boston, Allyn and Bacon, Inc., 1966.

Sears, Pauline S. and Hilgard, Ernest R., "The Teacher's Role in the Motivation of the Learner," in *Theories of Learning and Instruction*, 63rd Yearbook, National Society for the Study of Education, Chicago, 1964.

Sherif, Muzafer, and Cantril, Hadley, *The Psychology of Ego Involvement*, New York, John Wiley and Sons, Inc., 1947.

Thorndike, E. L., *The Psychology of Wants, Interests and Attitudes*, New York, D. Appleton-Century Company, 1935.

Young, P. T., *Motivation of Behavior*, New York, John Wiley and Sons, Inc., 1936.

## Questions, Exercises, and Activities

1. How would you account for the fact that words such as need, drive, and motive are used somewhat interchangeably?

2. One frequently hears statements such as: "If he doesn't want to learn, he doesn't belong in college, and I'll not waste my time on him." Analyze this statement by first describing the motivation of the person who makes the statement, and secondly by analyzing the statement itself.

3. Miss Willis reacts to whispering, coming late to class, and facetious answers of students as if they were personal affronts. She deals severely with offenders and is consequently not well-liked by students even though she is accorded considerable respect because of her competence in history. Develop several hypotheses about the motives that produce such behavior in Miss Willis.

4. Select any one chapter in any of the yearly volumes of the Nebraska Symposia on Motivation, read it, and be ready to discuss the implications for teaching that you see in it.

5. Why do schools and teachers fail to take account of the curiosity drive as a valuable and potent motivating influence? For your own subject matter area or grade level, describe a method, demonstration, or technique that would be likely to arouse this drive.

6. Assume that you wished to develop more cooperative behavior in children. Describe the program of reinforcement you would use to bring about this behavior.

7. As indicated in this chapter, the learner's intent or purpose as he approaches a learning task is an important determiner of how well he will

learn and how long he will remember what he has learned. One source of his "active set" to learn may come from the teacher's instructions.

    a. What can a teacher say or do that will influence this process?

    b. How can a teacher influence the child to incorporate in his own "reaction system" an active set that will transcend a specific assignment and be available for all kinds of learning tasks?

8. What kinds of classroom activities result in an ego involvement of pupils? Why are so many young people *not* ego involved in school work?

9. Just as some effective drugs have undesirable side effects, punishment may have unfortunate consequences. Describe these side effects of punishment, and show how they may be (modified) alleviated.

10. Some people strive to win, whether the activity is of any consequence or not. Explain this behavior. Should schools try to encourage this type of response in children? Why?

# Chapter 8

# Motivation:
# Attitudes
# and Interests
# in the Making

Sometimes the behavior of children, their likes and aversions, the things which they want to do seem strange to adults. Teachers are frequently baffled and may be discouraged when a youngster greets a new venture in the school room with defiance. Likewise the teacher may be frustrated by the enigma of the child who hates him for no apparent reason. In a study,[1] in which teachers were asked to describe those forms of behavior which gave them the most concern or which represented the most serious difficulties, it was found that teachers were most concerned about the existence of negative attitudes, attitudes of indifference, and lack of interest in school on the part of their pupils.

How do teachers handle these important problems? Some answers may be seen in the responses in the following project completed by fifty teachers who had been enrolled in classes in educational psychology at the University of Illinois.

---

[1] E. L. Gaier and Stewart Jones, "Do Teachers Understand Classroom Behaviors?" *Understanding the Child*, Vol. 20, 1951, pp. 104–109.

Think of all the students in your classes in the present school year, and select *one* whom you believe you and the school have helped the most. Then fill out the form below. Please note that the meaning of helped is deliberately left open to your own judgment. Presumably you help children in many ways and finding those ways is one of the main purposes of this study.

Analysis of returns from the above query clearly indicated that while the problems of pupils who were helped varied greatly in severity and type, the *modi operandi* of teachers were directly aimed at changing children's attitudes and interests. (Out of all returns there was no exception to this generalization). There follows, in the teachers' own words some descriptions of the activities that seem to have generated the changes in the children they had selected for their report.

This boy is the fourth child in a family of five. Three of his brothers and sisters have well known police records. He wants to be a good citizen but most of the people have placed a "black label" upon him and he thus has few friends. He enrolled in my World History class as a repeat student. The first few weeks he was very quiet. When we studied the unit on Germany we discussed among others Rudolph Diesel. To make a more practical application I casually asked about the diesel truck, and the principle of diesel engines. I called upon this boy knowing he had some interest in cars. The response was an explanation of great merit. The class members were amazed at the excellent presentation. As a teacher I could see the attitude of the class change from one of "what's this guy know" to one of "this guy's got something." From this point on the boy too has had a changed attitude. This recognition has made the boy a better and much happier student.

This boy (age 13 in grade 6) was held back in second grade because he did not have the capability as determined by reading tests to comprehend more advanced work. He has been in and out of trouble since the early grades. His reading score has steadily improved this year. I have used the method of encouragement. I have always stressed the point that he was very capable, and he has begun to believe in himself. The boy has been given confidence through his interest field which is social studies (world events in particular) in which he is vastly interested. He has also been given the responsibility of being editor-in-chief of the school paper and he has encouraged fellow pupils to help him. He is well liked now; before he had bullied the others in class.

I don't believe there is anything mystical about this student's reorientation. Briefly, this student began his admiration of the "hoodlum element" at the beginning of his sophomore year. His parents were called to the school on many occasions because of their son's behavior (stealing large quantities of towels and selling them to restaurant owners, continual difficulties with teachers, and general anti-social attitude). The only things I can remember doing were (1) making an early contact with the student (I engaged him in conversation the first day of school), (2) I continued this personal contact with him almost daily, (3) I spent many hours outside class with him, (4)

generally I made an attempt to let the student know someone was interested in him. I spoke with this student as recently as a month ago. He has, since leaving high school, maintained a B+ average at a Western university.

The steps I used with this student, as I do with all pupils who may be future drop outs were: (1) explained what dropout means in terms of social life in the future in words they understand, (2) gave them a free hand in choosing what they do in my subject field, (3) gave lots of encouragement regardless of how relatively poor the work was, (4) showed that someone does care (this I think was most important). Scott's grades went from a D to a B in a six-week period and he has maintained a B since then.

These few examples serve to point out that in their formative years, children's attitudes and interests can indeed be influenced by teachers. Methods of intervention that seem most successful include: finding flexible arrangements for rewarding existing interests; nurturing self-confidence through selective reinforcement of children's work in a social context; and building warm human relationships through personal contacts with pupils. In the words of one teacher of vocational agriculture: "No one should teach children unless he has a very deep totally unselfish concern for his fellow man."

In the preceding chapter, motivation was discussed as a process whereby needs create energies, which are directed toward goals. The forces which energize and direct behavior (needs, drives, purposes, goals, and punishment or pain) not only create ongoing behavior, but also help to mould more lasting facets of the child's personality. These forces are the bases of long-time interests and attitudes. This chapter will show how attitudes and interests originate, how they develop, and the methods of controlling and modifying these fundamental human characteristics. These are basic questions in education. They concern the kinds of values which are acquired. One prominent educator has hypothesized that such behavior problems as "apathy, flightiness, overconformity, nagging dissent, extreme uncertainty, underachievement, and great inconsistency," [2] are associated with inadequate value development. He further postulates that "If teachers will work persistently on processes of value clarification, changes will take place in the behavior of children."

## SOME DESCRIPTIVE GENERALIZATIONS

Attitudes and interests are closely related concepts. The broader term is attitude, which subsumes interest. Interests are attitudes which cause

---

[2] Louis E. Raths, "Clarifying Values," Chap. 10 in Robert S. Fleming (Editor), *Curriculum for Today's Boys and Girls*, Columbus, Ohio, Charles E. Merrill Books, Inc., 1963.

a person to seek more activities in a given area; they are positive attitudes about selected aspects of the environment. Both are descriptions of a proclivity of an individual to respond in a certain way toward something. For instance, a child, through experience or through the imitation of admired adults, may have learned to dislike school and academic subject matter. He has thus acquired a readiness to resist actively school materials such as books, and school activities. Children have such a readiness to respond to a large group of objects and abstractions. At early ages youngsters have positive or negative feelings about tangible things such as games, teachers, animals, and people. As they grow older children begin to have definite feelings about such abstractions as honesty, intelligence, and "my country." There are several aspects of attitudes which have special implications for teaching.

### Attitudes Are Learned

Among our most primitive and deep seated human characteristics is the structuring of our phenomenological world into two basic categories, good and bad. Every object, situation and person, and the words we use to describe them fall somewhere on an evaluative dimension.[3] There are "good guys" and "bad guys," bitter and sweet tastes, and painful and pleasant touches. Early in life objects themselves become signals attached to approach-avoidance behaviors, but shortly words become a second-signal system that carries the same abient-adient characteristics.

Attitudes are thus acquired through experiences which have a pronounced affective (feeling) component. More than other forms of learning, they are transmitted through the process of imitation, and many have origins early in life. The parent's revulsion, bodily posture, and facial grimaces toward an object such as a kind of food, or an animal, may be transmitted directly to the child who may even ape the same overt symptoms of avoidance. Others spring from modeling behavior and identification within the peer group in later childhood and adolescence. Witness the great disparity between the attitudes of today's adolescent toward such fads as long hair among boys, and the dominant attitudes of adults toward the same practices.

### Ways of Expressing Attitudes

It should come as no revelation to the reader that people often say one thing and do another. This discrepancy complicates the assessment of attitudes, particularly among adolescents. For purposes of judging attitudes some writers choose to place them in categories as: spontaneous verbal

---

[3] C. E. Osgood, G. J. Suci, and P. H. Tannenbaum, *The Measurement of Meaning,* Urbana, Ill., University of Illinois Press, 1957.

attitudes, elicited verbal attitudes, and behavioral attitudes. This distinction should better alert the teacher to the fact that his students may profess acceptance of an ideal or value, but display behavior quite the opposite. In fact there is even a discrepancy between what adolescents say they believe, and what they *admit* they do. Remmers [4] in his polling of thousands of high school students, found almost all opposed to drinking, yet a quarter of them admitted they drink. Likewise three-fourths of them disapproved of smoking, but 38 per cent admitted to smoking.

### Attitudes Have Both Perceptual and Affective Components

Attitudes help determine not only *what* the child sees, but *how* he sees it. Suppose a pupil has acquired (through parents, other children, or other adults) certain negative attitudes about a particular teacher. He has thus acquired a readiness to respond with those modes of behavior which are characteristic of his particular way of expressing dislike and defense. He may notice the teacher's slightest gesture or suggestion, while other children are unaware of these details. Furthermore, he may see these behaviors of the teacher as evidences of domination, or unfairness. He ascribes motives to the teacher on the basis of his already existing biases. In some cases, children have had such unfortunate experiences that they may see every new person as a threat, and they are constantly ready to flee or strike back.

### Attitudes May Be Resistant to Change

Since they operate in perception, a person tends to see what he is looking for and hence will find reinforcement for already existing attitudes, even though there is evidence to the contrary. They are sometimes highly resistant to change. It is therefore important that desirable social attitudes, attitudes about school, teachers, work, and the like be learned early in life. There are several ways in which we can guard our present attitudes against encroachment by new ones. Watson [5] notes that one method is selective attention. He has observed that on students' tours of foreign countries, Americans who expect to find misery see little else, while those who anticipate finding attractive features perceive what they are looking for. Cannell and MacDonald showed that an article connecting smoking and lung cancer was twice as likely to be read by a non-smoker as by a smoker. [6]

---

[4] H. H. Remmers and D. H. Radler, "Teenage Attitudes," *Scientific American*, Vol. 198, June, 1958, pp. 25–29.

[5] Goodwin Watson, *Social Psychology: Issues and Insights*, Philadelphia, J. B. Lippincott Company, 1966, p. 220.

[6] C. F. Cannell and J. C. MacDonald, "The Impact of Health News on Attitude and Behavior," *Journalism Quarterly*, 1956, pp. 315–323.

Another defense is selective forgetting,[7] i.e., forgetting more rapidly that information which does not jibe with our views and retaining longer that which does. Finally, we may distort a sound argument, or failing that dismiss the information we receive as coming from an untrustworthy source.[8]

With all these defenses for stabilizing existing attitudes, it is little wonder that social psychologists deem it advisable that desirable attitudes and values about work, government, school, and the like be learned early in life while they are still in a state of flux.

### Attitudes Affect Other Learnings

In several ways, the kinds of attitudes which a child has affects school work and learning. If he has positive attitudes about teachers, and likes school work, it is almost inevitable that he will experience some success and through reinforcement (a feeling of achievement) will work more effectively and achieve more nearly up to his capacity. Conversely, negative attitudes toward school and teachers usually signify that his interests and energies are aimed elsewhere, and that he will fight attempts to make him learn.

The orienting function of attitudes, i.e., their influence upon perception, leads to the child's seeing tasks to be learned as pleasant and important, as unpleasant and useless, or as colorless and neutral. The feeling which goes along with such attitudes is an important factor in learning, for experiments have shown that pleasant material is retained longer than that which is unpleasant or neutral. The latter type of material is most poorly retained.[9] Another important factor is that attitudes about oneself are determiners of the kind of approach which a learner makes to a task. It should be recalled that in Chapter 6 it was shown that self-confidence played a major role in determining a learner's readiness for school work.

The way in which attitudes may interfere with learning becomes apparent when one considers the kinds of attitudes which result from school failure. It is safe to say that the majority of school failures seem to disorganize rather than to reorient the child.[10] It is in the nature of a person's ego structure not to accept failure as due to personal inadequacy. Instead the child is forced into the position of attributing lack of success to teachers or schools, and this serves to block future learnings. In re-

---

[7] J. M. Levine and G. Murphy, "The Learning and Forgetting of Controversial Material," *Journal of Abnormal and Social Psychology*, Vol. 38, 1943, pp. 507–517.

[8] P. L. Kendall and K. Wolff, "The Analysis of Deviant Cases in Communication Research," in P. Lazarsfeld and F. N. Stanton (Editors), *Communication Research*, New York, Harper and Brothers, 1949.

[9] H. D. Carter, H. E. Jones and N. W. Shock, "An Experimental Study of Affective Factors in Learning," *Journal of Educational Psychology*, Vol. 25, 1934, pp. 203–215.

[10] Walter H. Worth, "Promotion vs. Nonpromotion: II. The Edmonton Study," *The Alberta Journal of Educational Research*, Vol. 5, 1959, pp. 191–203.

These Children Have Finished a Project Which They Themselves Selected. This Involved the Use of Many Resource Materials.

peated failures when such personal defenses break down, strong feelings of insecurity and inferiority may result.

### The Place of Interests in Schooling

Only in more recent years have the child's interests been given a place in the planning of school activities, texts, and curricula. Earlier ideas of education have been characterized by a leading authority on interests: "The old conception of education based on early philosophy viewed human desires as evil. The first step in educating the child was to break his will. The second step was to force him into the mold of the adult." [11] The present concern for children's interests is a healthy development, but even so, much that goes on in school does not conform with what is known about child development. The beginning teacher could take a lesson in motivation by observing some of the out-of-school activities of youngsters. Under these sometimes near ideal learning situations, which exist outside the classroom, the child's interests are directly related to ongoing play activities. He has spontaneous interests which carry him hour after hour. The boy who wants to drive a car or shoot a gun will devote hours of attention watching adults and imitating them (sometimes in the fantasy of play), and he will learn and retain skills with almost any kind of teaching. Most classroom learning situations are quite different. The goals may be quite abstract or distant from ongoing behaviors and urges. Schools often try to get children to accept as motives and interests those things which, if left alone, they would not seek. They are trying to develop favorable attitudes toward teachers and subject

---

[11] E. K. Strong, *Vocational Interests of Men and Women*, Stanford University, Stanford University Press, 1943, p. 4.

matter, and to use interests as forces to bolster up subject matter learning. This is as it should be. However, motives and interests are far more than tools to be manipulated to the advantage of academic learning. These are objectives of teaching in their own right. The acquisition of socially accepted and worthwhile motives, attitudes, and interests is a major goal of the educative process. Far more than any other factor they determine the kind of a person which the school turns out.

## THE ORIGIN AND DEVELOPMENT
## OF INTERESTS AND ATTITUDES

Attitudes and interests are learned in much the same way that skills, habits, and other kinds of school work are learned. The principles of learning discussed in previous chapters are equally applicable in determining the origin of these behavior determinants. However, the forces which lead to the development of attitudes are not always clearly discernible. Subtle factors such as needs of which the person is not aware, or hidden aggressions and wishes may become cornerstones in the building of attitudes. For example, it was found in one study that young people possessing the most anti-semitism were those who also had a high degree of emotional conflict and insecurity.[12] Commenting about this kind of highly prejudiced individual in the study cited above, Stagner has written, "to such a person, propaganda, educational material, or even casual remarks by teachers suggesting that a certain group is evil or dangerous, provide a welcome outlet for repressed aggression." [13]

### The Function of Needs

A common error made in studying children's behavior is to assume that interests and attitudes are direct indications of needs. The child needs approval, a feeling of importance, security, and independence, and he is likely to develop an interest in *any* activity which brings him a satisfaction of such needs. It might just as well be music or basketball or hopping freight trains or sneaking a smoke of marijuana. All these activities might serve basic needs in some particular societies of young people.

It is deplorable that schools do not allow all children an opportunity to satisfy their ego and social needs through approved school activities. But when rewards are limited to a few students and depend upon a narrow

---

[12] Else Frenkel-Brunswik and R. N. Sanford, "Some Personality Factors in Anti-Semitism," *Journal of Psychology*, Vol. 20, 1945, pp. 271–291; see also Bruno Bettleheim and Morris Janowitz, "Prejudice," *Scientific American*, Vol. 183, October, 1950, pp. 11–13.

[13] Ross Stagner, "Attitudes," *Encyclopedia of Educational Research*, New York, The Macmillan Company, 1950, p. 80.

range of innate abilities there is little chance that all youngsters will experience the achievement necessary to satisfy basic needs. A major function of the school is to find activities which satisfy needs. These activities will then become areas of interest and should lead to positive attitudes about schooling.

### Wishes and Ideals

Valuable clues to what children want and of the factors which influence their modes of behavior and their attitudes can result from a study of their wishes and ideals, their heroes, and their ideas of what is glamorous. The studies which have been made reveal one fact of immediate importance, namely, that what appeals to children most is quite different from the activities which go in the classroom. Young children's wishes are predominantly for material things as pets, bicycles, and athletic equipment. They also have deep concern for family matters such as wanting a new brother or a wish that father would come home. Only a small number wish for materials or activities directly connected with school work.

In contrast with younger children, high school students' wishes are more often in terms of personal improvement, ambition, security, and professional aspirations. Seventy per cent of a large group who were surveyed wished for self-improvement in some form.[14]

In the opinion polling conducted by Remmers and Radler,[15] the wishes and concerns of high school students centered around "wanting to be liked" with a consequent belief that the most important learning in high school was how to get along with people. In this study only 14 per cent of the pupils placed academic learning as the most important thing to be acquired in high school. Clearly attitudes such as these are of concern to teachers. Most likely attitudes and interests are pretty accurately mirrored in the kinds of people with whom children identify. As would be expected, in the early school grades, children's admiration is for people who are close to them. When a group of 344 grade-school youngsters were asked to name the person they would most like to be, the younger ones answered with names of parents, friends, teachers, and other close associates. Older children more often chose characters from books, historical figures, and stars from radio and television. The trend with age of children's identifications away from their immediate environment to the remote environment (radio, books, etc.) is shown below.[16]

---

[14] A. T. Jersild and R. J. Tasch, *Children's Interests and What They Suggest for Education*, New York, Bureau of Publications, Teachers College, Columbia University, 1949, p. 14.
[15] Remmers and Radler, *op. cit.*, p. 27.
[16] M. L. Stoughton and A. M. Ray, "A Study of Children's Heroes and Ideals," *Journal of Experimental Education*, Vol. 15, 1946, p. 157.

|                        | GRADE 2 | GRADE 4 | GRADE 6 |
|------------------------|---------|---------|---------|
| Immediate Environment  | 72%     | 47%     | 42%     |
| Remote Environment     | 25%     | 52%     | 57%     |

In the study just cited boys and girls differed in the kinds of "heroes" which they chose. This is shown, for example, by the fact that no boys out of the primary group (Grade 2) named the teacher as the person they would like to be, while 27.3 per cent of the girls chose a teacher as the person they most wanted to be like. The individuals chosen reveal the type of person these youngsters admire.[17] High on the list were Gene Autry, Roy Rogers, and Shirley Temple. Also named were the Lone Ranger, Superman, Dick Tracy, and J. Edgar Hoover. When these children were asked the reasons for their choice, the most frequent answer was "goodness." For boys, the most important reason was that the character chosen represented adventure. The above choices jibe well with what is known about the reason for children's choices of occupations. Interests revealed in studies of occupational choice show that they are often dominated by the desire for escape, for freedom from humdrum work, and for adventure.[18] Children's wishes and ideals seem to stem mainly from three needs, the need for psychological security, the need for status and importance, and the need for approval. These needs find partial satisfaction through the emulation of those adults whom the child perceives as being highly successful in ways in which he would like to achieve.

### Cultural Influences

The culture plays an important role in shaping our attitudes and developing interests. Social studies teachers express concern when over half their high school students believe that censorship of newspapers and books is all right, and when almost half believe that the mass of people are not capable of deciding what is best for themselves. Though of course the school is a part of the culture, it is only one agency that shapes attitudes. The school's teaching of history, democracy, and the like may have little effect if cross currents in other segments of the culture dictate contrary views. Many view with alarm the increasing pressure toward conformity in our culture. This pressure may be serving to emasculate much that the school is trying to do. In the words of one writer, "As a nation we seem to have a syndrome characterized by atrophy of the will, hypertrophy of the ego and dystrophy of the intellectual musculature." [19] Another psychologist who has studied the effect of group pressure upon judgment comments

---

[17] *Ibid.*, p. 159.

[18] P. M. Freeston, "Vocational Interests of Elementary School Children," *Occupational Psychology*, Vol. 13, London, 1939, pp. 223–237.

[19] Remmers and Radler, *op. cit.*, p. 26.

that, "when consensus comes under the dominance of conformity, the social process is polluted."

Some indication of the effects of different cultures upon the development of attitudes and interests may be seen in the comparison of the interests of American children with those of children from a quite different culture. Table 10 shows some of the findings when interests of American children were compared with those of Egyptian youngsters. A

### TABLE 10
#### A Comparison of Interests of American and Egyptian Children *

| Characteristics of Interests Common to Both American and Egyptian Children | Main Differences in Interests Between American and Egyptian Children |
|---|---|
| 1. Interests in material things declines with age. | 1. American children showed more interest in material things. |
| 2. Expressed interest in academic work declines with age. | 2. More American children expressed interest in improvement of living quarters. |
| 3. Interests in self-improvement increase with age. | 3. A large percentage of American children expressed interest in people outside the family circle. |
| 4. There is an increase in interest in out-of-school intellectual activities with age. | 4. Arts, crafts, and hobbies were reported more frequently by American than Egyptian children. |
| 5. There is more interest in own language and arithmetic than in science or social studies. | 5. A much higher proportion of Egyptian than American children expressed wishes pertaining to religious qualities and social graces. |
| 6. There is a greater interest in people with increasing age. | 6. Less than 1 per cent of American children reported homework as a favorite out-of-school activity, while 40.1 per cent of Egyptian children mentioned it. |
| 7. Sex differences were common to both cultures. Girls expressed less interest in material things. | 7. The American child hardly ever expressed interests pertaining to health, while 12.5 per cent of the Egyptian children did so. |
| 8. There was an egocentric character to interests. | 8. More Egyptian than American children expressed patriotic wishes. |
| 9. There was a disinterest in school courses which did not bear obvious relation to a goal. | |

* Adapted from El-Demerdash Abdel-Meguid Sarhan, "Interests and Culture," *Contributions to Education*, No. 959, New York, Bureau of Publications, Teachers College, Columbia University, 1950.

further example of how a culture influences the values held by its members is provided by Gillespie and Allport[20] who studied the values of college youths in ten nations. They asked students to write their autobiographies of the future ("My life from now until the year 2000"). Commenting upon the results, Allport asserts: "American students were

---

[20] J. Gillespie and G. W. Allport, *Youth's Outlook on the Future*, New York, Random House, 1960.

the most self-centered, the most privatistic in values. They desired above all else a rich full life for themselves and showed little concern for the fate of mankind at large."

The following selections, placed side by side, of a Mexican girl of 18 and a Radcliffe student also 18 years of age illustrate Allport's conclusions.[21]

|  MEXICAN GIRL | RADCLIFFE STUDENT |
|---|---|
| Since I like psychology very much, I wish, on leaving this school, to study it, specializing in it and exercising it as a profession. I shouldn't like to get married right away, although like any woman I am desirous of getting married before realizing all my aspirations. In addition, I should like to do something for my country—as a teacher, as a psychologist, or as a mother. As a teacher, to guide my pupils in the best path, for at the present time they need solid bases in childhood in order in their future lives not to have so many frustrations as the youth of the present. As a psychologist, to make studies which in some way will serve humanity and my beloved country. As a mother, to make my children creatures who are useful to both their country and all humanity. | Our summers will be spent lobster fishing on the Cape. Later we'll take a look at the rest of the country— California, the Southwest, and the Chicago Stockyards. I want the children, when they get past the age of ten, to spend part of the summer away from home, either at camp or as apprentices to whatever profession they may show an interest in. Finally, I hope we will all be able to take a trip to Europe, especially to Russia, to see what can be done about Communism. |

## Opportunities and Experiences

The kinds of opportunities and experiences which a child has are obvious and ubiquitous factors in shaping his attitudes and interests. Even so, it is not uncommon for parents, social workers, and teachers to wonder why a child from a "fine" family has the interests and negative attitudes of a delinquent, when even the most casual investigation would reveal that his youth group (gang) has like interests and attitudes. Likewise, it is not rare to find teachers baffled by a child's lack of interest in reading, when the obvious fact is that in the child's home there has been virtually no opportunity for such an interest to develop.

Table 11 shows the difference in the interests of two groups of boys. Sixty-three delinquents and sixty-three non-delinquents were compared with respect to the kinds of activities in which they were interested. It is clear that delinquency is closely related to an interest in such activities

---

[21] G. W. Allport, "Values and Our Youth," *Teachers College Record*, Vol. 63, 1961, p. 212.

## TABLE 11
### Relationship Between Delinquency and Play Interests *

| Questionnaire Item | Tetrachoric Correlation † |
|---|---|
| Hopping freights | .92 |
| Playing hookey from school | .90 |
| Smoking | .88 |
| Running away from home | .84 |
| Swiping milk bottles | .81 |
| Hitching of rides on wagons, autos or street cars | .72 |
| Seeing historical movies | −.36 |
| Studying schoolwork (at home) | −.39 |
| Making collection of stamps | −.39 |
| Making things with hammer, saw, nails, etc. for fun | −.40 |
| Belonging to school clubs (nature, literary, drawing, farm, citizenship, etc.) | −.40 |
| Imagining you are an explorer or adventurer | −.46 |

* From D. B. Harris, "Relationships Among Play Interests and Delinquency in Boys," *American Journal of Orthopsychiatry*, Vol. 13, 1943, p. 633.

† A measure of the extent of relationship between two dichotomous variables—viz. delinquency, non-delinquency vs. "yes" or "no" on the questionnaire used to discover play interests.

as "hopping freights," smoking, and "swiping milk bottles," and negatively correlated with such activities as seeing historical movies and collecting stamps.

Harris who collected the data shown in Table 17 believes that environmental limitations play a major part in the development of delinquent play interests. In speaking of the delinquent he notes:

> Such a person inevitably uses the materials and methods available to him in his efforts to have a good time. He lives near the railroad tracks and makes them his playgrounds. Locomotives and cars on sidings are intrinsically interesting anyway. He indulges in throwing contests and, lacking the inhibition developed in children reared in homes where more supervision is given their activities, windows and telegraph insulators become his targets. Dodging the policeman constitutes at once an activity indulged in by his fellows and an act of daring and adventure.[22]

Jersild and Tasch [23] note that there are many "wasted potentials" among children because opportunities have not been provided for their development. These deficiencies in opportunity "leave lasting gaps" in the personality of the adult.

---

[22] D. B. Harris, "Relationships Among Play Interests and Delinquency in Boys," *American Journal of Orthopsychiatry*, Vol. 13, 1943, p. 634.

[23] A. T. Jersild and R. J. Tasch, *op. cit.*, p. 64.

## ATTITUDES, INTERESTS, AND TEACHING

### Appraisal of Present School Practices

Schools vary greatly in the extent to which they take into account the attitudes and interests of their pupils. Certainly attitudes and interests are just as much a part of individual differences as abilities and achievements and as such deserve equal attention. But in many instances, these important aspects of learning are at best relegated to a position of secondary importance. Some of the questions which should be answered in appraising the practices in a given classroom are:

1. How are subjects taught so as to correspond with what is known about children's interests? (This implies that some appraisal of interests be made.)
2. How are interests used to facilitate learning of subject matter?
3. To what extent does the school provide information and guidance to meet important interests such as vocational goals, and sex-social matters?
4. Does the school consider as a regular function the teaching of and testing for interests and attitudes?
5. Are children's interests considered in making assignments, choosing reading materials, constructing tests, and planning the curriculum?

That such questions are not given due attention is indicated by the findings of Jersild and Tasch, whose survey of over 2000 children's interests led them to the following conclusion:

> As the average child moves up through the grades, he seems to become less eager about things that distinctly belong to school and scholarliness, more inclined to complain, more interested in the things that go along with school rather than with work in the classroom. He becomes relatively more interested in recess periods than in class periods. He mentions play and sports more often. There is a greater hiatus between his wishes and what the school offers.[24]

Teachers who participated in this major study of children's interests were asked reasons for this "drifting away" of students with increasing age. The most prominent reason given by these teachers was that they believed students too often have a feeling of lack of achievement. High school students liked best those things which led to a sense of personal worth through accomplishment. There is little question that the school has less influence upon a child's primary attitudes and interests than upon many other aspects of his life. The blame for this lack of influence must be

---

[24] A. T. Jersild and R. J. Tasch, op. cit., p. 41.

shouldered, in part at least, by the school because of its failure to meet youths' interests halfway. It is well known that youngsters in high school have an active interest in vocations, yet one survey of high school graduating seniors showed that 58 per cent had received no help in planning a vocational career after graduation and a like number had received no assistance in planning to meet college requirements.[25]

A survey of children's interests in various school subjects and activities shows that several important areas lack appeal. Following are the main results: (1) By far the greatest interests were expressed toward so-called extracurricular activities such as athletics. (2) The subject matters scoring highest were reading and other forms of English usage, and number work. (3) Social studies were recipients of a large number of unfavorable comments, yet it was this area in which children desired more information. (4) There was a great preoccupation with people at all ages (even though the questionnaire used in the survey was not worded to encourage such responses).[26]

A given survey of interests, unfortunately, may not have widespread applicability to children in general, since an appraisal of interests in one community or area, or at any particular time may indicate only a temporary or local condition. Lists of favorite books, games, hobbies can have but temporary usefulness, as fads and interests change from one child generation to another. A few short years ago, science fiction was an esoteric reading interest. Today youngsters find in comic books and on the radio and television, such things as space patrols, interplanetary travel, and ray guns. It is highly doubtful, however, that schools are sufficiently alert to such interests or modify activities regularly to take account of the ever-changing interests of youngsters.

### Forces Which Change Attitudes and Interests

As earlier noted, attitudes once formed may be highly resistant to change. The reader may recall that attitudes are wrapped up with a person's feelings, needs, and self-concept. To let them go requires a change in self. Furthermore, attitudes are easy to maintain because a person sees what he wants to see, and may distort reality so as to find evidence to support any position he wants to hold.

Attempts to modify attitudes will fail unless factors such as the aforementioned are taken into account. Schools often fail in changing attitudes, because their whole program is based on telling and reading. But telling is not teaching. Verbalism alone is not enough. Mere information may do little to change attitudes; in fact one investigator discovered that

---

[25] W. E. Moser, "Evaluation of a Guidance Program by Means of Student's Check List," *Journal of Educational Research*, Vol. 42, 1949, pp. 609–617.

[26] A. T. Jersild and R. J. Tasch, *op. cit.*, pp. 25–40.

information may serve as "so much ammunition," when our dislikes are strong. In other words, the person may use additional information to support a position, to make himself more hostile. It might be said that in some cases, the more we *think* we know, the more hostile we become.[27]

The impact of a well-planned program for changing and building attitudes and interests by means other than "verbalism" is well illustrated in the following case:

> Mr. Turner, a social studies teacher, wished to develop desirable attitudes toward the problem of mental health. He believed this to be a significant social problem, but found that his students neither understood the issues involved nor did they have attitudes that would make for responsible adult behavior in this area. Consequently he planned with his class a unit of study on mental health. First, the students read material about mental hygiene, and the problems in their local community. Next, they invited the head of the local Mental Hygiene Clinic in to describe its work, and to answer their questions. Third, they made field trips to four different institutions including two state mental hospitals, a woman's reformatory, and a state school for the feeble minded. Finally, they prepared an illustrated unit describing all of their own experiences, and presented it to a graduate class in mental hygiene for teachers. Their enthusiasm spread to their community as evidenced by the fact that a state bond issue for the construction of new facilities for state mental hospitals passed by an overwhelming majority in the area in which they lived, while it was defeated in other areas of the same city. Furthermore, many of the students since their work on this unit have decided to pursue careers in fields closely allied to mental hygiene.

An effective program for modifying attitudes should incorporate one or several of the following suggestions in the learning situation.

1. A first step is to know what students' attitudes are. Just as teachers use pretests for cognitive learning, so they may profitably use attitude tests or scales to find out how students feel about various issues. In this regard, it would be quite appropriate to develop tests that contained a number of items such as: [28]

> The government should set minimum wages:
> a) for no one
> b) for women only
> c) for both men and women

Such pretests of attitudes would give the students a preview of the important issues of the course, would give the teacher a basis for developing course material, and might, if the test is given at the end as

---

[27] Harry A. Grace, "Hostility: An Educational Paradox," *Journal of Educational Psychology*, Vol. 45, 1954, pp. 432–435.

[28] Bruce R. Morris and Robert E. Will, "The Student Attitude Survey as a Teaching Aid," *The School Review*, Vol. 67, 1959, pp. 350–360.

well as the beginning of a course, indicate the degree of attitude change that had occurred.

2. Since attitudes are closely linked with the self-concept and with the child's personal identifications, attitudes are more easily changed through group processes. The child may readily accept values of his peer group while rejecting those of the teacher. Even undirected discussion of social issues may be effective.[29] In an experiment with college classes,[30] students working in groups and doing role playing on issues such as heredity and environment, and husband-wife relationships, showed a marked decrease in bias and prejudice toward the issues, while students in the more conventional lecture-discussion classes did not.

3. Firsthand experience is more effective than reading or telling. Delinquent gangs in large cities have changed their attitudes of hate and distrust of the police when these agents of law enforcement have taken part as referees and instructors in athletic programs at youth centers.

4. An appeal to feelings is necessary for change. The affective part of attitudes helps to make them tenacious, and it is only by eliciting different feelings that change can be accomplished. Dramatic movies may bring desirable results; however, in some cases, where a strong negative attitude already exists the attempt may backfire by increasing the negative feeling rather than changing it.[31] In any case, there is considerable evidence that any vicarious experience whether in movies, television, literature, or recordings may, if carefully planned, lead to a desirable change in attitudes.

5. As teachers become expert in anticipating the forces which produce attitudes they may use preventive measures which alert students to propaganda by developing their critical abilities. An experiment with high school students in a unit in child study shows how this may be effective. One group of students was taught the results of studies of various kinds of discipline—a comparable group received no such training. Both groups were then subjected to a radio program favoring the "get tough" method for raising children. The untrained students readily succumbed to the propaganda, while students who had learned experimental evidence about discipline resisted the effects of propaganda.[32]

---

[29] K. M. Miller and J. B. Biggs, "Attitude Change Through Undirected Group Discussion," *Journal of Educational Psychology*, Vol. 49, 1958, pp. 224–228.

[30] Gerald S. Wieder, "Group Procedures Modifying Attitudes of Prejudice in the College Classroom," *Journal of Educational Psychology*, Vol. 45, 1954, pp. 332–344.

[31] William H. Allen, "Audio-Visual Communication" in *Encyclopedia of Educational Research*, Third Edition, New York, The Macmillan Company, 1960, pp. 115–137.

[32] R. H. Ojemann, "Research in Planned Learning Programs and the Science of Behavior," *Journal of Educational Research*, Vol. 42, 1948, pp. 96–104.

6. Children are more apt to accept attitudes which are the result of what they believe to be their own thinking—their own original ideas. Skillful leading of group discussion or planning for information seeking in the community offers opportunities for youngsters to make discoveries, which they will rapidly adopt.

7. Community centered schools may make the development and change of attitudes and interests a project shared jointly by teachers and parents. When the school has to buck values learned in the home or through other sources, the student is placed in a position of psychological conflict and he is more apt to retain community fostered notions than those which are obtained in the classroom. The school which is to have a real effect in a community must concern itself not only with attitudes of the child but also of the adult.

Beginning in about 1930, and continuing at an accelerated rate to the present, there have been many studies of attitude formation and change which have attempted to separate out some of the complex variables that are involved. Table 12 presents a summary of many of these studies, along with ten generalizations drawn from them.

### Suggested Techniques for Using Interests to Facilitate Learning

Many times teachers are faced with the problem of guiding the learning of material which may at first glance not seem to be heavily weighted with intrinsic values for the learner. The teacher must find ways of capturing the energy of his charges and directing it toward desirable school goals. The first-grade teacher who is asked to teach reading may have little choice in the matter. In this situation, there are certain psychological principles in the arousal of interests and the development of favorable attitudes which have been used and found successful by teachers and by experimentation. Suggestions for teaching using such psychological principles are given in the following paragraphs.

The student's perception of the material to be learned may be changed by placing it in a new or different context—one that is pleasant. An example of this principle is found in the reading aids devised by Dolch.[33] One of these is a word bingo game in which the child can play only by recognizing words necessary to complete rows and columns. Another is a "Vowel Lotto Game," which requires the child to know vowels and simple phrases in order to play.

Material to be learned may be placed as a barrier in the path toward a desirable goal. The child may not be interested in reading *per se* but defi-

---

[33] E. W. Dolch, *The Dolch Reading Materials*, Champaign, Illinois, Garrard Press.

TABLE 12
### Generalizations About Attitude Formation and Change with Supporting Experimental Studies

| Generalization | Supporting Experimental Studies * |
|---|---|
| 1. Attitudes are more likely to be formed and to change when the information upon which they are based comes from a source which is perceived as being of high status and credibility. | Hovland and Weiss (1951) <br> Katz (1957) <br> Watts and McGuire (1964) |
| 2. For best results, particularly to fortify one against later counter-propaganda, both pro and con arguments regarding an issue should be presented. | Hovland, Lumsdaine, and Sheffield (1949) <br> Lumsdaine and Janis (1953) |
| 3. Direct experience as a source of information for attitudes may be a highly effective change agent, particularly when that experience is dissonant with previous beliefs and expectations. | Deutsch and Collins (1951) <br> Wilner, Walkley, and Cook (1955) |
| 4. Commitment to an action or to change an attitude (especially if it is public) makes change more likely and strengthens the newly formed attitude. | Brehm (1960) |
| 5. Reference groups with which students identify (particularly their immediate peers) provide fertile soil for the development and change of attitudes. | Sherif and Sherif (1964) <br> Newcomb (1943) <br> Asch (1951) <br> Kelley and Woodruff (1956) <br> Rhine (1958) |
| 6. The amount of information a student possesses on race, politics, and international affairs will be positively related to his assuming a liberal attitude. | Wrightstone (1934) <br> Green (1952) |
| 7. When by force of circumstances a person is made to espouse an attitude discrepant with his own private attitudes, such as playing a role antagonistic to his own beliefs, his attitudes are likely to shift. | Janis and King (1954) <br> Culbertson (1957) |
| 8. Group discussion seems to be more effective in changing attitudes than lectures. | Lewin (1943) <br> Pennington, Haravey and Bass (1958) <br> Mitnick and McGinnies (1958) <br> Miller and Biggs (1958) |
| 9. Resistance to the effects of propaganda may be strengthened by increased information and by providing opportunities for practice of defending existing attitudes. | Ojemann (1948) <br> McGuire and Papageorgis (1962) |
| 10. Persuasible periods in a person's life (times when he is most receptive to new attitudes) come at transition or crisis points such as experiencing a failure of some kind, going from grade school to junior high or from high school to college, or suddenly realizing one is not as competent as he thinks he is. | Davis (1930) <br> Mausner (1953) <br> Bavelas (1942) |

* See end of this chapter for detailed references to these studies.

nitely interested in the stories and activities which the skill of reading will allow him to enjoy. Frequently the child is made to understand that he will gain approval of the teacher only when he has mastered a given skill such as spelling or arithmetic, which are made to become symbols of approval. Perhaps in terms of frequency this technique is most widely used. However, the use of it is based on several assumptions which may not be warranted. First, the teacher in this case is largely the mediator of needs. Second, there is an assumption that the learning activity will, by association with desirable goals, take on some of the affective elements of those goals. Actually this procedure may have the reverse effect. The third assumption is that the material in its own right is not interesting enough to be self-sustaining. Experienced teachers know that it is virtually impossible completely to control rewards either in a teacher dominated class or in a permissive one. With regard to peer approval, for example, pupils may find that various attention-getting devices such as boisterous behavior, note passing, and the like, give sufficient satisfaction of this need without recourse to the means established by the teacher. The assumption that material is not in its own right sufficiently interesting may in some cases be warranted. It is doubtful for instance that arithmetic as sometimes taught, has sufficient relevance to the needs and interests of children. But in this case one should question whether it would not be better to change the whole teaching pattern rather than just the method of arousing interest.

Related material of a high interest value may be inserted into the lesson which is being studied. This technique is based upon the assumption that attention and activity will be maintained at a higher level when the learning material is interspersed with vivid and colorful illustration, demonstrations, anecdotes, personal allusions, and the pupils' own experiences. The following incident, related to one of the writers by a student, is illustrative of the way such devices may be used to stimulate interest.

> After the class was seated, the teacher made his appearance staggering under the weight of what appeared to be a large boulder. When he reached the front center of class he suddenly threw the large object down into the middle of the class. The brief period of pandemonium which ensued subsided quickly when the students saw the "boulder" float harmlessly through the air. It was a large piece of insulating material and the discussion which followed was lively and profitable.

Describing this incident the student remarked that it was this sort of thing which endeared that science teacher to his students. As he put it, "you never knew what was going to happen next. I liked this course better than any I had ever taken." The same student had subsequently taken a

science major in college and largely attributed his choice to this particular high school teacher.[34]

Make the classroom atmosphere a permissive and pleasant one. Interests abound, and attention rarely flags when youngsters are given a proprietary feeling about the doings of a class. Even when the values of what is to be learned are not immediately apparent, children may participate eagerly, because the friendly atmosphere and cooperative work helps satisfy their social needs and their need for feeling important and worthwhile. The following description of a high school class should illustrate how a pleasant yet purposeful classroom atmosphere can stimulate interests.

> In Mr. Eames' high school biology class students were permitted to help with such things as the preparation of specimens, drawings for class use, and the planning of class work. Individual projects were encouraged. One group of students arranged with local dentists for a dental survey of the entire class. Another group took white rats, some fed good diets and others which were malnourished, to nearby grade schools and made talks to the pupils about the effects of various kinds of foods. Class work included a variety of activities many of which were suggested by students. There were debates, biology spelldowns, diet surveys, and numerous demonstrations made by both the teacher and students. Also there were field trips to local bakeries, dairies, nurseries, and the like. The classroom was a center of numerous activities. In a given period one might have found one group of students working with microscopes, another planting seeds in flats, and still another sitting around one of the laboratory tables talking. Mr. Eames traveled from group to group, giving encouragement, making suggestions, and asking help with something he or another student was doing. The total effect of all this was to create an experience which students would never forget. Many believed this the best course they had ever had in high school. Needless to say interest in the work was keen, and there were rarely disciplinary problems.

## SUMMARY

Attitudes and interests are learned dispositions or sets to action. They are highly pervasive and influence personality and personal relationships, as well as having a profound influence upon school learning.

As do motives, interests and attitudes grow out of children's needs. They find voice through children's wishes and ideals. The influence of

---

[34] It might be well here to reemphasize a point stressed earlier, viz., that there is no substitute for the cardinal principle that students' interests center around activities in which they have found need satisfactions. Stimulating episodes created by a teacher may be helpful, but these episodes alone cannot support for long materials and methods which fail to allow each pupil to feel important and to view the learning as worthwhile. It is quite possible in the case just described that for the one student who went on to a career in science, there were dozens of others who had no real interest in science but only in the "antics" of the teacher.

needs upon attitudes may be seen, for example, in the way children identify with persons such as movie stars or other romantic or adventuresome characters. Their identification reflects a desire for escape from the humdrum activities of school. Apparently much school work fails to capture the interest of pupils, and unfortunately the older they become, the less interest youngsters seem to have in what is going on in school.

The major implication for teachers is that interests and attitudes are goals of teaching in their own right, and this means that teachers must know how attitudes are formed and can be changed, and how interests may be used to facilitate learning. The teacher who would change pupils' attitudes should: (1) give group work and group discussion, and provide for improved human relations in classes, (2) provide first-hand experiences with issues about which attitudes are formed, (3) involve the emotional life of the child through dramatics, stories, or episodes, and (4) make the school a real part of the community.

In a number of ways, interests may be used to facilitate learning. By applying the principles discussed under motivation in the previous chapter, the educator ought to be able to transform schooling from drudgery to an exciting adventure. The results of experimentation and of experience of teachers support the greater use of the following techniques. First, material to be learned should be placed in an interesting and sometimes novel context. Sometimes a game will elicit increased interest. Secondly, material to be learned may become more attractive when pupils see it as a necessary step toward a goal. Finally, the learning situation should be one in which there is ample opportunity for active participation of all pupils, and an atmosphere which is friendly and permissive.

## References for Further Study (General)

Allport, Gordon W., "Values and Our Youth," *Teachers College Record*, Vol. 63, 1961, pp. 211–219.

Brown, Roger, *Social Psychology*, Glencoe, Ill., Free Press, 1965.

Cohen, Arthur R., *Attitude Change and Social Influence*, New York, Basic Books, 1964.

Goodman, Paul, *Growing up Absurd*, New York, Random House, 1960.

Green, Bert F., "Attitude Measurement," Chapter 9, in Lindzey, Gardner (Editor), *Handbook of Social Psychology*, Vol. I, Cambridge, Addison-Wesley Publishing Company, Inc., 1954.

Hovland, C. I., and Janis, I. L. (Editors) *Personality and Persuasibility*, New Haven, Yale University Press, 1953.

Hovland, C. I., "Reconciling Conflicting Results Derived from Experimental and Survey Studies of Attitude Change," *American Psychologist*, Vol. 14, 1959, pps. 8–17.

Lehman, Irvin J., "Changes in Critical Thinking, Attitudes and Values from

Freshman to Senior Years," *Journal of Educational Psychology*, Vol. 54, December, 1963, pp. 305–315.

Newcomb, Theodore M., Turner, Ralph H., and Converse, Philip E. *Social Psychology: The Study of Human Interaction*, Chaps. 3, 4 & 5, New York, Holt Rinehart and Winston, Inc., 1965.

Norvell, George W., *What Boys and Girls Like to Read*, Chicago, Silver, Burdett Co., 1959.

Osgood, C. E., Suci, G. J., and Tannenbaum, P. H., *The Measurement of Meaning*, Urbana, Univ. of Illinois Press, 1957.

Raths, Louis E., *Clarifying Values*, Reprint #8410, Columbus, Ohio, Charles E. Merrill Books, 1963.

Roe, Anne, "A Psychologist Examines 64 Scientists," *Scientific American*, Vol. 187, November, 1952, pp. 21–25.

Steiner, Ivan D., and Fishbein, Martin, *Current Studies in Social Psychology*, New York, Holt, Rinehart and Winston, Inc., 1965.

Strong, E. K., Jr., *Vocational Interests of Men and Women*, Second Edition, Stanford University Press, 1948.

Super, Donald E., "Interests," in *Encyclopedia of Educational Research*, Third Edition, New York, The Macmillan Company, 1960, pp. 728–733.

Watson, Goodwin, Chaps. 6 and 7, in Social Psychology: *Issues and Insights*, Philadelphia, L. B. Lippincott and Company, 1966.

Zander, Alvin F., *The Influence of Teachers and Peers on Aspiration of Youth*, Ann Arbor, University of Michigan Press, 1961.

## Detailed Bibliography of Experimental Studies
## Cited in Table 12

Asch, S. E., "Effects of Group Pressure Upon the Modification and Distortion of Judgments," in Harold Guetzkow (Editor), *Groups, Leadership and Men*, Pittsburgh, Carnegie Press, 1951, pp. 177–190.

Bavelas, Alex, "Morale and the Training of Leaders," in Goodwin Watson (Editor) *Civilian Morale*, Boston, Houghton Mifflin Company, 1942, pp. 143–165.

Brehm, J. W., "Attitudinal Consequences of Commitment to an Unpleasant Behavior," *Journal of Abnormal and Social Psychology*, Vol. 60, 1960, pp. 379–383.

Culbertson, Frances M., "Modification of an Emotionally Held Attitude Through Role Playing," *Journal of Abnormal and Social Psychology*, Vol. 54, 1957, pp. 230–233.

Davis, Jerome, "Study of 163 Outstanding Communist Leaders," *Proceedings of American Sociological Society*, Vol. 24, 1930, pp. 42–55.

Deutsch, Morton and Mary E. Collins, *Interracial Housing: A Psychological Evaluation of a Social Experiment*, Minneapolis, University of Minnesota Press, 1951.

Green, Meredith W., "Interrelationships of Attitude and Information," Unpublished doctoral dissertation, New York, Teachers College, 1952.

Hovland, C. I., A. A. Lumsdaine and F. D. Sheffield, *Experiments on Mass Communication*, Princeton, N.J., Princeton University Press, 1949.

Hovland, C. I. and Walter Weiss, "The Influence of Source Credibility on Communication Effectiveness," *Public Opinion Quarterly*, Vol. 15, 1951, pp. 635–650.

Janis, I. L. and B. T. King, "The Influence of Role Playing on Opinion Change," *Journal of Abnormal and Social Psychology*, Vol. 49, 1954, pp. 211–218.

Katz, Elihu, "The Two-Step Flow of Communication: An Up-to-Date Report on an Hypothesis," *Public Opinion Quarterly*, Vol. 21, 1957, pp. 61–78.

Kelley, H. H. and Christine I. Woodruff, "Members' Reactions to Apparent Group Approval of a Counternorm Communication," *Journal of Abnormal and Social Psychology*, Vol. 52, 1956, pp. 67–74.

Lewin, Kurt, "Forces Behind Food Habits and Methods of Change," *Bulletin of the National Research Council*, No. 108, 1943, pp. 35–65.

Lumsdaine, A. A. and I. L. Janis, "Resistance to 'Counterpropaganda' Produced by One-Sided and Two-Sided Propaganda Presentations," *Public Opinion Quarterly*, Vol. 17, 1953, pp. 311–318.

Mausner, B., "Studies in Social Interaction, III, Effects of Variation in One Partner's Prestige on the Interaction of Observer Pairs," *Journal of Applied Psychology*, Vol. 37, 1953, pp. 391–394.

McGuire, W. J. and Demetrios Papageorgis, "Effectiveness of Forewarning in Developing Resistance to Persuasion," *Public Opinion Quarterly*, Vol. 26, 1962, pp. 24–34.

Miller, K. M. and J. B. Biggs, "Attitude Change Through Undirected Group Discussion," *Journal of Educational Psychology*, Vol. 49, 1958, pp. 224–228.

Mitnick, L. L. and Elliott McGinnies, "Influencing Ethnocentrism in Small Discussion Groups Through a Film Communication," *Journal of Abnormal and Social Psychology*, Vol. 56, 1958, pp. 82–90.

Newcomb, T. M., *Personality and Social Change*, New York, Dryden Press, 1943.

Ojemann, R. H., "Research in Planned Learning Programs and the Science of Behavior," *Journal of Educational Research*, Vol. 42, 1948, pp. 96–104.

Pennington, D. F., Jr., Haravey, Francois, and Bass, B. M., "Some Effects of Decision and Discussion on Coalescence, Change and Effectiveness," *Journal of Applied Psychology*, Vol. 42, 1958, pp. 404–408.

Rhine, R. J., "A Concept Formation Approach to Attitude Acquisition," *Psychological Review*, Vol. 65, 1958, pp. 362–370.

Sherif, Muzafer, and Sherif, Carolyn W., *Reference Groups: Exploration into Conformity and Deviation of Adolescents*, New York, Harper and Row, Publishers, 1964.

Watts, W. A. and McGuire, W. J., "Persistence of Induced Opinion Change and Retention of the Inducing Messages," *Journal of Abnormal and Social Psychology*, Vol. 48, 1964, pp. 233–241.

Wilner, D. M., Walkley, Rosabelle P., and Cook, S. W., *Human Relations in Interracial Housing: A Study of the Contact Hypothesis*, Minneapolis, University of Minnesota Press, 1955.

Wrightstone, J. W., "Civic Beliefs and Correlated Intellectual and Social Factors," *School Review*, Vol. 42, 1934, pp. 53–58.

## Films

*Attitudes and Health,* Coronet Instructional Films, Coronet Bldg., Chicago 1, Illinois.

*How to Develop Interest,* Coronet Instructional Films, Coronet Bldg., Chicago 1, Illinois. (11 mins.)

## Questions, Exercises, and Activities

1. Often there is a discrepancy between the way a person says he feels and the way his behavior implies that he feels about something; in short, a difference between a verbal and a behavioral attitude. To what may this discrepancy be attributed?
2. How are attitudes and interests alike? How different?
3. What kinds of attitudes would be most resistant to change? Aside from perceptual distortion, what other measures do people use to help maintain their attitudes?
4. One of the criticisms of American educators is that they try to "play up" to children's interests; consequently, children never learn to discipline themselves to do something unpleasant and difficult. Analyze this criticism and comment upon its validity.
5. It has been shown that many of the attitudes of teenagers represent the beliefs and feelings of their age group, particularly do they reflect the influence of the "gangs'" leaders. Many of these attitudes are in conflict with established social norms, and certainly contrary to what the school is trying to teach. What is the origin of these attitudes? Why do established social norms *not* have more influence upon young people?
6. Why does interest in school seem to decline as children grow older? Is this decline inevitable? If so, why; and if not, what should be done about it?
7. Think of one of your own attitudes that was strongly entrenched at some time in your life, but has now changed to a quite different point of view. How do you account for the change?
8. Select three of your friends and identify their strongest avocational interest. Then ask them how they happened to develop this interest, and the influence that seemed important in maintaining it. What do their explanations have in common?
9. Suppose you were teaching in a school where the dominant attitude toward English literature was one of contempt for anyone who would waste his time with such useless and dry material. Describe the steps you might take to alter this attitude.
10. Often the mass media—television, newspapers, and magazines—seem more effective in influencing attitudes than the school. Why? Does the propagandist have advantages over the school teacher in changing attitudes? If so, what are these advantages? If not, why are not teachers better propagandists?

# Chapter 9

## Teaching for Permanent and Meaningful Learning

In some classrooms children run aimlessly about jumping from one thing to another every few minutes. Lacking guidance, they follow momentary whims and fleeting interests. At the other extreme children are glued to their seats, enthralled by the fear of teacher or of rules. At these extremes may be supporting educational philosophies, but both are blind to important principles of learning. Somewhere between these extremes is an organization of activities mutually shared by pupil and teacher, which will produce optimum learning.

Schooling is more efficient when learning is well-organized and there is a psychologically sound basis for materials, methods, and processes of instruction. So strong is the tendency to learn in an organized way that even when material is presented in a disorganized or relatively meaningless fashion, pupils tend to develop an organization of their own.[1] But when the child is buried under a vast array of apparently unrelated facts, the tendency to organize into meaningful relationships may be partially thwarted by the necessity of repeating those facts on examinations. In such cases, the facts

---

[1] William Brownell and Gordon Hendrickson, "How Children Learn Information Concepts and Generalizations," Chapter IV, Forty-Ninth Yearbook of the National Society for the Study of Education, Part I, *Learning and Instruction*, Chicago, University of Chicago Press, 1950, pp. 92–128.

thus learned are not long retained, nor do they seem to have much effect in changing behavior.[2] As previously shown, developers of teaching machines lay claim to the preparation of very well organized instructional materials, but as Sanford [3] has noted, these innovators may have played into the hands of educators who believe factual content *is* education. There is a large body of convincing evidence which shows how poorly students retain information which is not related to significant problems and which has a low degree of perceived internal relationship. In contrast, results obtained with well-organized and meaningful materials may show actual gain rather than decrease with a passage of time.[4] Ability to apply principles, solve problems, and interpret experimental data are examples of the kinds of activities which are very resistant to the ravages of the forgetting process.[5]

The principles of learning have many implications for pupils, teachers, and school administrators. Answers to questions about assignment making, problem-solving, reviewing, and many others essential to good teaching hinge upon the teacher's understanding of the principles of learning. Teachers' activities should be arranged to fit into a coherent pattern with the activities of pupils. They must know when and how to give guidance, correct errors, introduce new materials, and take part in discussion. No single skill or technique will suffice for the many and often unique educational situations in which a teacher finds himself. Rather he must be able to apply principles and generalizations which have wide usefulness in analyzing each new learning situation as it emerges.

## PROVIDING FOR MEANINGFULNESS

One of the writers once visited a biology class in which one of the major activities of students was looking at slides which the instructor projected upon a screen in front of the class. There were about 250 slides representing various plants and animals and their parts, which students were expected to memorize. These slides were grouped into a logical arrangement following standard classification procedures. Later, on a final examination, newly prepared slides identical with the old ones were substituted and several students who had previously done well, did very poorly. An investigation of these individuals revealed that they had learned to associate specimens

---

[2] G. M. Blair, "How Learning Theory Is Related to Curriculum Organization," *Journal of Educational Psychology*, Vol. 39, 1948, pp. 161–166.

[3] Nevitt Sanford, "Will Psychologists Study Human Problems?" *American Psychologist*, Vol. 20, 1965, pp. 192–202.

[4] Ralph Tyler, "Some Findings from Studies in the Field of College Biology," *Science Education*, Vol. 18, 1934, pp. 133–142.

[5] A. H. Word and R. A. Davis, "Individual Differences in Retention of General Science Subject Matter in the Case of Three Measurable Teaching Objectives," *Journal of Experimental Education*, Vol. 7, 1938, pp. 24–30.

with peculiarities of the old slides such as cracks and other imperfections. When new slides were used, students had lost their cues and were unable to name the specimens. To these students, the learning of these names had been a meaningless task to which they responded with a system which seemed the easiest and best to them. In spite of an organization of materials which seemed very logical and coherent to the teacher, the students learned with an organization of their own.

Understanding and retention are products of that teaching which makes material meaningful to the student. Teachers often take for granted that material "makes sense," especially when youngsters give lip service to the material which is taught. That such assumptions by teachers are not always justified has been often and dramatically illustrated. For example, the drawing in Figure 19 was made by a young child after hearing the poem "Barbara Frietchie." She explained to the teacher that it was "Stonewall Jackson riding a head."

**Figure 19.** A Child's Conception of Stonewall Jackson Riding Ahead. (From Howard Kingsley, *The Nature and Conditions of Learning,* New York. Prentice-Hall, Inc. Reprinted by permission of the publisher.)

Further illustrations are easy to obtain from the work of pupils in almost any school. The reader may recall, in a previous chapter, that the fourteen-year-old who was asked to give the factors affecting the rates of auto insurance replied, "gas, oil, and kerosene." Clearly the work on auto insurance which had preceded this test, as well as the question, as worded, were relatively meaningless to this student. When teaching is characterized by rote learning, meaningless memorizing, and an excessive emphasis upon verbalism, children will almost inevitably make errors such as the following:

"The circulatory system is composed of veins, arteries, and artilleries."

"Socrates died from an overdose of wedlock." [6]

The following well-known anecdote told by William James further exemplifies what happens when meaningfulness is supplanted by meaningless verbalization:

> A friend of mine, visiting a school, was asked to examine a young class in geography. Glancing at the book she said: "Suppose you should dig a hole in the ground, hundreds of feet deep, how should you find it at the bottom —warmer or colder than on top?" None of the class replying, the teacher said, "I am sure they know, but I think you don't ask the question quite rightly. Let me try." So taking the book she asked: "In what condition is the interior of the globe?" and received the immediate answer from half the class at once: "The interior of the globe is in a condition of igneous fusion." [7]

The teacher must know how to avoid such meaningless memorization. He will succeed in proportion as he is able to help youngsters gear material to their vocabulary levels; relate material to their backgrounds; provide activities in context, as they will be used; show relationships among various subjects and concepts; and provide a wide variety of experiences commensurate with the individual differences which he finds in the class.

An excellent example of how modern educational practice incorporates meaningful activity into every step of a learning situation may be found in the new secondary school physics course created by the Physical Science Study Committee.[8] In this course, instead of asserting a law, such as Newton's law of motion, and then illustrating its applicability, the students reconstruct the law in laboratory experiments, in a logical analysis of experiments in their texts, and through observations of experiments on film. Figure 20 shows students applying a constant force to an object, thus allowing them to make a time-distance record motion, and find that changes in velocity are proportional to the time the force acts. Home study provides illustrations such as those in Figure 21 which give further, more precise data for analysis. Help in summarizing and relating ideas is then afforded in films in which a well-known physicist demonstrates the principle or law using equipment which would be too expensive in time and money for the high school to provide. (Figure 22.)

---

[6] H. R. Douglass and H. F. Spitzer, "The Importance of Teaching for Understanding" in the Forty-Fifth Yearbook of the National Society for the Study of Education, Part I, *The Measurement of Understanding*, Chicago, University of Chicago Press, 1946, pp. 10–11.

[7] William James, *Talks to Teachers on Psychology and to Students on Some of Life's Ideals*, New York, Henry Holt and Company, 1899, p. 150.

[8] For further details of this program see *Progress Report*, Educational Services Incorporated, Physical Science Study Committee, 164 Main St., Watertown 72, Massachusetts, 1959.

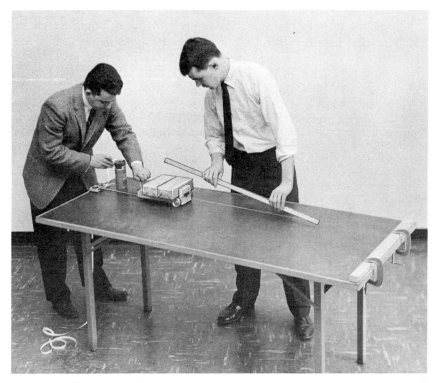

**Figure 20.** Laboratory Experiment on Newton's Law of Motion.

This kind of approach combines the resources of a teacher, laboratory, film, and text so that they supplement one another in developing a carefully organized logical pattern of thought. Errors of recall that often accompany rote learning are minimized, and the student achieves a sense of personal satisfaction in real understanding.

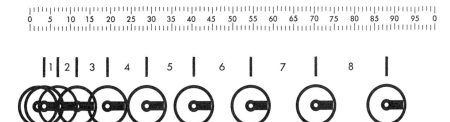

**Figure 21.** Physics Textbook Illustration. (This is a drawing showing the successive positions at one second intervals of an accelerating body. The positions are shown alongside a 100 centimeter scale.)

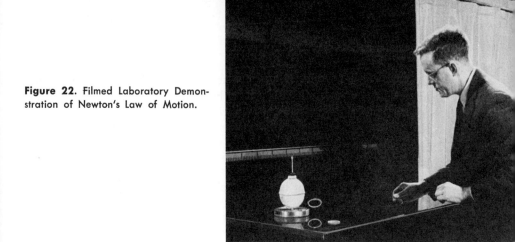

**Figure 22.** Filmed Laboratory Demonstration of Newton's Law of Motion.

## Meaningful Vocabulary

Materials must be commensurate with a pupil's verbal ability. In the past, too little attention was paid to the vocabulary level of school texts. Often grade-school texts were too difficult vocabulary-wise for as much as two-thirds of the entire class using them.[9] In 1938 when thirty textbooks of science were analyzed, it was found that both the technical and non-technical vocabularies of general science, biology, chemistry, and physics were too difficult for most of the pupils for whom the books were written. In this study, it appeared also that too many of the difficult words were non-scientific. In addition, the analysis revealed that too small a percentage of words were defined, and when they were defined it was often only after they had already been used in previous material.[10] The condition reported in 1938 seems not to have improved much by 1951, for an analysis that year of word difficulty in elementary science texts revealed that most, if not all, were too difficult for most of the pupils in the intermediate grades.[11] In 1966, similar observations regarding textual material were made by Ausubel,[12] who describes new texts in biology as "admirably thorough, accurate, and up-to-date, but so ineffectively presented and organized, and so impossibly sophisticated for their intended audience as to be intrinsically unlearnable on a long-term basis."

These vocabulary problems are not limited to textual material. The writer recently visited a fifth-grade class where children were given a word list including such items as: non-protocol, blandly, and syntax. It was apparent

---

[9] E. L. Thorndike, "Improving the Ability to Read," *Teachers College Record*, Vol. 36, 1934, pp. 1–19.

[10] F. D. Curtis, *Investigations of Vocabulary in Textbooks of Science for Secondary Schools*, Boston, Ginn and Company, 1938.

[11] G. G. Mallison, H. E. Sturm, and R. E. Patton, "The Reading Difficulty of Textbooks in Elementary Science," *Elementary School Journal*, Vol. 51, 1951, pp. 460–463.

[12] David P. Ausubel, "An Evaluation of the BSCS Approach to High School Biology," *American Biology Teacher*, Vol. 28, 1966, p. 176.

that many of the children did not understand these words even after they had found them in the dictionary. The following quote may reveal the origins of the "vocabulary gap" in written materials.

> Most textbook writers, one gathers, write as if the grim visages of professional colleagues were leering over their shoulders.[13]

In a similar but somewhat less charitable vein Erasmus wrote:

> My votaries show their refinement by preferring a foreign word to a native one, and when they hear a word to their liking, the more learned laugh pointedly and nod their approval to impress the less well-informed somewhat after the manner of donkeys shaking their ears when they are tickled.[14]

Even in educational writing (journals) in which sensitivity about the necessity to communicate at the appropriate level should be great, there is considerable discrepancy between the language used and the background of many of the prospective readers.[15]

Research has made available to teachers and pupils, methods and materials for increasing the meaningfulness of vocabulary used in schools. Analysis of millions of words which children have used in writing and speaking have given educators several word books, basic vocabularies, and dictionaries written in children's terms. Such sources as Thorndike's list of 30,000 words,[16] The Buckingham-Dolch Combined Word List,[17] the Rinsland List,[18] the Dolch Basic Sight Vocabulary,[19] and the Thorndike Century Junior Dictionary[20] should be available as a part of the school's professional library.

There are several books on the use of language for effective written communication.[21] These sources may be helpful to teachers in showing means of avoiding ambiguity and verbosity in writing. Besides being able to ap-

---

[13] Horace B. English, *Dynamics of Child Psychology*, New York, Holt, Rinehart and Winston, 1961, p. vii.

[14] Desiderius Erasmus, *Moral Encomium or The Praise of Folly*, 1509.

[15] C. M. Garverick and R. S. Jones, "Editors Characterize Professional Journals," Paper, American Educational Research Association, New York City, February 17, 1967.

[16] E. L. Thorndike and Irving Lorge, *The Teacher's Word Book of 30,000 Words*, Bureau of Publications, Teachers College, Columbia University, 1944.

[17] B. R. Buckingham and E. W. Dolch, *A Combined Word List*, Boston, Ginn and Company, 1936.

[18] H. D. Rinsland, *A Basic Vocabulary of Elementary School Children*, New York, The Macmillan Company, 1945.

[19] E. W. Dolch, *A Manual for Remedial Reading*, Second Edition, Champaign, Illinois, The Garrard Press, 1945, p. 438.

[20] E. L. Thorndike, *Thorndike Century Junior Dictionary*, Chicago, Scott, Foresman and Company, 1942.

[21] For example see R. Flesch, *The Way to Write*, New York, Harper and Brothers, 1949.

praise the difficulty of style and vocabulary of textual material, teachers should become apt at direct and clear composition. Examinations, syllabi, and outlines are all too often vague or poorly written.

An attempt to appraise the difficulty of vocabulary has been made through the application of readability formulae.[22] Lorge has indicated that "factors influencing readability are numerous, and many subtle factors have not been accounted for. However, experimental evidence supports the following important elements as determiners of readability: (1) measure of vocabulary such as percentage of different words or word difficulty, (2) sentence form such as length of sentence, number of clauses, etc., (3) appraisal of human interest by determining personal pronouns or vivid words used." [23]

### Experiential Background of Students

To be most meaningful, school work should be related to pupils' backgrounds. Children cannot do real thinking on the basis of abstractions alone. "As long as words refer to objects or situations at some time present to the senses, the meaning is simple and sure. What causes the difficulty is that the higher-order abstractions go farther and farther from realities or concrete experiences." [24] Often teachers rely upon words to take the place of concrete experience, but concepts and real understanding are not formed in this way. The following definition taken from a high school geometry text will illustrate how youngsters may fail to understand ideas which are not based upon concrete experience:

"The word area conveys the idea of space on a plane surface."

Not one of these words is above Thorndike's most common 4000 words in the English language, and yet the above definition can have little meaning to many high school readers because the idea is not rooted in any concrete experience which students have had in dealing with area.[25] *Apropos* is John Dewey's comment: "By rolling an object the child makes its roundness appreciable; by bouncing it he singles out its elasticity; by throwing it he makes weight its conspicuous distinctive factor." [26]

---

[22] See Edgar Dale and J. S. Chall, "A Formula for Predicting Readability," *Educational Research Bulletin*, Vol. 27, January 21 and February 18, 1948, pp. 11–20 and 37–54; Rudolf Flesch, "Marks of a Readable Style," *Teachers College Contributions to Education*, No. 897, New York, Teachers College, Columbia University, 1943; and E. W. Dolch, *Problems in Reading*, Champaign, Illinois, The Garrard Press, 1948, Chapter XXI, as representative of readability formulae applicable for appraising readng difficulty of textbooks.

[23] Irving Lorge, "Predicting Readability," *Teachers College Record*, Vol. 45, 1944, pp. 404–419.

[24] Madeline Scmmelmeyer, "Extensional Methods in Dealing with Abstractions in Reading," *Elementary School Journal*, Vol. 50, 1949, p. 28.

[25] *Ibid.*, pp. 30–31.

[26] John Dewey, *How We Think*, Boston, D. C. Heath, 1910, p. 112.

Generalizations can sometimes be better taught by having pupils verify principles through classroom experimentation.

A student in one of the writer's classes in educational psychology while doing his practice teaching used a number of sailboat problems in his class in physics. He was discouraged by the poor results, but was quick to realize, in class discussion, that the prairies of Illinois offer little opportunity for experience with sailboats.

Following are some suggestions for making material meaningful by gearing it to pupils' experiences: (1) appraise the student's experiences, (2) find problems in the student's immediate environment and help him find solutions to these problems, (3) whenever feasible provide kinesthetic training along with the material presented, (4) use pictorial illustrations, models, or examples frequently.[27]

### Variety of Classroom Experiences

Students should engage in a variety of experiences to increase the depth of meaning of important concepts. Today's schools probably depend far too much upon reading as a data gathering technique. The clever teacher should be able to devise many activities which will give concrete experiences along with verbal abstractions. In one teaching experiment [28] in a general science class in junior high school, it was shown that ideas about atomic

---

[27] Semmelmeyer, *op. cit.*, p. 35.

[28] J. V. Farrell and J. R. Wailes, "Multi-Sensory Approach to Science in the Elementary School," *Elementary School Journal*, Vol. 52, 1952, pp. 271–276.

energy and nuclear physics can be successfully taught with models and demonstrations. In this teaching experiment small building blocks, labeled with appropriate chemical symbols, were used to explain molecular structure. To illustrate the atomic explosion, a number of mouse traps, loaded with corks were placed in a screen enclosure. Then by throwing in one cork, one trap was sprung, hurling its cork to another. This went on until nearly all the traps were set off. This kind of visual analogy, for beginning students, invests school activity with vivid meaningfulness which cannot be achieved solely through the verbal presentation of ideas. Furthermore, the motivation which is likely to occur through such demonstrations is much better than that elicited by a lecture, or even a discussion, where the only tools are words. As will be seen in the next chapter, having a variety of experiences relates also to how well students are able to apply learnings in new and varied situations.

Newer media of instruction such as television, video-taping, films, and telewriters [29] may add variety, and meaningfulness to instruction in the classroom, but have not, as some proponents may wish to believe, demonstrated that they can replace classroom instruction.[30]

## REDUCING INTERFERENCE FOR BETTER RETENTION

Anything that aids learning should improve retention. Conversely, anything that leads to confusion or interference among learned materials decreases the speed and efficiency of learning, and accelerates forgetting. When material is forgotten, it means that either in the process of learning itself, or in previous or subsequent learnings, there have been interferences of some kind. These interferences may exist in the nature of the material itself, in the motive-emotional conditions of the learner at the time of learning or recall, or in the nature of the intellect or organic condition of the learner. The various kinds of interference that cause forgetting will now be discussed. These inhibitions or interferences will be followed with suggestions for increasing retention by overcoming their negative effects.

### 1. Retroactive Inhibition [31]

When anything is learned, the test for or use of that learning usually occurs after the passage of some time. In the intervening period, many other

---

[29] This is a device which will broadcast directly to a receiving set at distant points messages written by an instructor.

[30] Herbert Schueler, Gerald S. Lesser, and Allen L. Dobbins, *Teacher Education and the New Media*, Washington, D.C., American Association of Colleges of Teacher Education, 1967.

[31] It is appropriate also to speak of retroactive facilitation, the situation in which activities following learning, such as review and application, will increase retention. By the same token one can speak of proactive facilitation (the next effect to be discussed).

things are learned. These interpolated learnings interfere with the memory of the original material, and this interference is known as retroactive inhibition. Everyone has had the experience of learning the names of a group of people, as in a classroom, only to find that he has forgotten many of the names when, in an intervening period, he learns the names of a new group. Likewise, many people have had the experience of learning to spell a list of words which later are partially forgotten because in the meantime several new lists have been learned. Obviously the effects of retroactive inhibition will be greatest when there is a large amount of confusability between things that have been learned, and will be minimized when original materials are "overlearned," and when both original and later learnings are meaningful. A very convincing experiment that shows the existence of retroactive inhibition was conducted with college students. One group of students was given a list of nonsense syllables to learn, and then immediately went to bed. Another group learned the same list of syllables, but followed it with their ordinary routine activities for the next eight hours. When retested on the list, the group which slept after learning remembered more than did the group which had been active and awake.[32]

### 2. Proactive Inhibition

Another kind of interference, and perhaps a more important one for meaningful learning is proactive inhibition. Many times when something new is learned, it competes with older learnings, so that when the new learning is required, it is distorted by what had gone before. Illustrative is an experiment in which students were given passages on Buddhism to read. Later tests revealed that the memory of Buddhism had been distorted in a predicted direction because of previous knowledge of Christianity. In speaking of this kind of interference, Ausubel,[33] who conducted the experiment just cited, concludes that conceptualization involves the building of subsumption systems, systems for categorizing newly learned materials, and systems that serve as "storage mechanisms" for our memory. When new materials are not easily assimilated into already existing subsumption systems, or when there is a likely confusability of elements due to undiscriminated similarities, the amount of proactive inhibition tends to be great. Reduction of this kind of interference should be possible when teachers make sure to point out easily confused elements, and see that the category systems and concepts of children are well founded in meaningful experience.

---

[32] J. G. Jenkins and K. M. Dallenbach, "Obliviscence During Sleep and Waking," *American Journal of Psychology*, Vol. 35, 1924, pp. 605–612.

[33] David P. Ausubel and Elias Blake, Jr., "Proactive Inhibition in the Forgetting of Meaningful School Material," *Journal of Educational Research*, Vol. 52, December, 1958, pp. 145–149.

This term is very similar in meaning to negative transfer, to be discussed in the next chapter. Proactive effects are usually thought of as influences upon retention, while transfer effects refer to the influence of a previous task upon learning a new one.

### 3. Motivational and Emotional Interference

In a number of ways, the motivational conditions at the time of learning can either facilitate or interfere with its success. These conditions were discussed in Chapter 7. In a similar way emotion and motivation can interfere with retention. Painful experiences are intentionally forgotten or repressed. High anxiety at the time an individual attempts to recall something he has learned also blocks remembering. All teachers have worked with students whose excessive worry at the time of an examination caused a poor performance. Methods designed to reduce anxiety at the time of examinations have shown significant gains in retention. In one such experiment, students, given the opportunity to defend and explain their answers to objective test items by writing their comments on the back of their answer sheets, made significantly higher scores than students who did not have this opportunity, even when the written comments were given no weight in scoring the test papers.[34] Moreover, it has been demonstrated that when an instructor deliberately creates an atmosphere filled with tension by such remarks as: "Do not raise your hand or attempt to ask any questions once this test has begun"; or, "Cheaters will be automatically expelled from the room," students get lower test scores than when the instructor is more pleasant and relaxed.[35]

Another more subtle motivational influence that serves as an interference to correct recall is the distortion that occurs when a person reports events in which he was personally involved. Frequently, these events are cast in such a way that the individual's own ego is enhanced. This distortion is not to be thought of as lying, but as a normal change in memory when a story gets told a number of times.

In all cases where the interference with retention is a product of emotional stress a change in the classroom atmosphere designed to promote greater self-confidence ought to result in improved work.

### 4. Other Conditions

There are several other conditions that may lead to interference in retention. Included are the physical condition of the individual at the time of recall, organic defects of the neural makeup (e.g., certain forms of brain

[34] W. J. McKeachie, D. Pollie, and J. Speisman, "Relieving Anxiety in Classroom Examinations," *Journal of Abnormal and Social Psychology*, Vol. 50, 1955, pp. 93–98.

[35] W. J. McKeachie, "Students, Groups and Teaching Methods," *American Psychologist*, Vol. 13, 1958, pp. 580–584.

damage interfere with both learning and retention), and normal distortion that results from man's tendency to organize his perceptions and his memories into units having good and stable form.

Attention should be drawn to the fact that the effects of various types of interference may be reduced or increased by features inherent within the instructional materials themselves. An excellent example [36] is furnished by the irregularities of rules for writing and pronouncing different English words and sounds. For example, children must learn that one word "dog" may appear as:

DOG, Dog, dog,

and one phoneme may be spelled in as many as 30 different ways, for example: rule, flue, fruit, grew, move, canoe, moon.

Many of these kinds of interference are inevitable consequences of convention,[37] but others arrive, as earlier demonstrated, by a failure to analyze objectives properly and then to make sure that instructional materials clearly implement them.

As already pointed out in the first section of this chapter, the teacher produces the best defense against forgetting when the material to be learned is well organized and meaningful. Other measures that are effective in promoting permanent learning will now be discussed.

### Working on Units of Optimal Size and Scope

All subject matter, even in a core curriculum, contains elements of various size and complexity. In reading, for example, there are letters, groups of letters which form certain sounds, words, groups of words, sentences, paragraphs, chapters, and so on. In biology there are cells, tissues, systems, members, and organisms, and organisms are grouped into such categories as species, orders, and phyla. In what sequence and in what sized units should this material be learned? Often considerations of this kind are treated as "whole versus part learning," [38] and the general answer by most authorities is that whole learning is frequently superior to part learning. The phrase whole or part learning, however, is somewhat of a misnomer, for in practice, there are rarely parts of anything which are learned which

---

[36] J. A. Downing, "Experiments with an Augmented Alphabet for Beginning Readers in British Schools," Paper at 27th Educational Conference, Educational Records Bureau, New York, Nov. 1 & 2, 1962.

[37] One man's refusal to accept convention has led to the development of the augmented alphabet. Sir James Pitman described it first as the Initial Teaching Medium, later known in this country as the augmented Roman Alphabet, and now known as the Initial Teaching Alphabet. This 43-character alphabet where every character stands for just *one* sound is being widely used in British schools in the first four grades, and is being used experimentally in several American cities.

[38] For a discussion of the "Whole-part" learning controversy see J. A. McGeoch and A. L. Irion, *The Psychology of Human Learning*, New York, Longmans, Green and Co., 1952.

are not "wholes" in their own right. In memorizing poetry, for example, the pupil might learn a stanza at a time or the whole poem. In this case, the pupil is not making a choice between whole or part learning but between two wholes of different size. A tennis instructor who gives concentrated work on the serve is not instructing by a part method, but has chosen a unit smaller than the total game—a sub-whole.

The key principle in choosing units of various sizes for instructional purposes must be based upon the meaningfulness of the units which are to be learned. The learner must be able to see how units fit into a larger, more inclusive whole. Since smaller units will always have to be welded into larger ones eventually, a general principle might be to use the largest whole which the child's developmental level will permit. But the teacher must not become so enamoured of the "whole method" that he loses sight of the importance of various sub-units and skills. When large units are undertaken, such as a whole game, or a whole chapter in physics, special attention to, and additional guidance in, difficult parts should be given concurrently with the larger unit.[39] Likewise in elementary reading, teachers should not lose sight of the necessity for developing skills in word-attack, in order to develop better and speedier readers.

The size of units to be learned has special implications in the field of motor learning and physical education. Many games and manual tasks may be quite novel to an individual. Furthermore, new activities can be very fatiguing due to the involvement of little-used muscle groups. Often there is little relation between various parts of a game. Thus in baseball, there is only a slight relation between batting and catching, and either may be practiced as a meaningful whole. On the other hand, long continued practice on specific parts of the game may fail to capture interest. In such learnings (baseball, football, and basketball, for example) the best approach seems to be an orientation and beginning trials with the game as as whole and then a breakdown into meaningful sub-wholes. This practice should not exclude continuing use of the sub-wholes in actual game conditions.[40]

There is no clear-cut superiority for either whole or part learning when closely knit motor units or skills are learned. For instance, in juggling, there is little apparent difference in eventual skill when the person starts with two balls and works up to more, or begins initially with three or more balls.[41]

---

[39] R. S. Woodworth, *Experimental Psychology*, New York, Henry Holt and Company, 1938.

[40] For a more complete discussion of "management of practice" in motor learning see C. E. Ragsdale, "How Children Learn the Motor Types of Activities," Chapter 3 in Forty-Ninth Yearbook of the National Society for the Study of Education, Part I, *Learning and Instruction*, Chicago, University of Chicago Press, 1950.

[41] C. G. Knapp and W. R. Dixon, "Learning to Juggle: II. A Study of Whole and Part Methods," *Research Quarterly of the American Association for Health and Recreation*, Vol. 23, 1952, pp. 398–401.

Criteria which might serve to determine operating principles for teachers are:

1. First consideration should be given to the development level of the individual learner. Units which are clear to the teacher may be entirely too broad for the learner. Frequent quizzes, discussions, and interviews can serve as check points of understanding and help pace the speed and scope of the material.
2. The meaningfulness of units to be learned should be weighed against the contexts in which such units of learning are to be used. Units artificially or arbitrarily set up such as a unit on the throwing motions in baseball, bowling, and football passing, could be ridiculous. A unit in history on world rulers, if studied in isolation from the events which transpired during their rules might be just as ridiculous.
3. The gross size of the whole to be learned must be within reason. Blind application of the principle of whole learning to all types of material would find teachers having students learn such things as the multiplication tables as a whole.
4. The pupil's own grasp of units to be learned should be given some consideration. Some self-selection on the part of pupils will give clues and direction to the teacher's plans for material to be covered.

### Distributing Learning Activities

Even when learning is made meaningful, and material is presented or studied in the form of comprehensible elements, problems, or units, there still remains the question of spacing and pacing the activity. Learning efficiency varies with the length of study or practice periods and with the spacing of such periods, and with the rapidity with which material is presented.[42] Theoretically for some types of material more profit will be gained from four twenty-minute periods of study than from one eighty-minute period. Distribution of practice has long been regarded as superior to massed practice (or cramming). There is much evidence to support this general principle. In everything from rote tasks such as learning of nonsense syllables[43] to more complex work such as studying a concept in biology,[44] a spacing of relatively short practice periods has proven superior to fewer long periods of study—to periods which are jammed together.

However, teachers may err in either direction. One investigator found

---

[42] B. J. Underwood, "Ten Years of Massed Practice on Distributed Practice," *Psychological Review*, Vol. 68, 1961, pp. 229–247.

[43] C. I. Hovland, "Experimental Studies in Rote Learning Theory: III. Distribution of Practice with Varying Speeds of Syllable Presentation," *Journal of Experimental Psychology*, 1938, Vol. 23, pp. 172–190.

[44] J. H. Reynolds and R. Glaser, "Effects of Repetition and Special Review upon Retention of a Complex Task," *Journal of Educational Psychology*, Vol. 55, 1964, pp. 297–308.

that two-minute practice periods (in hand-eye coordination) were superior to either a one-minute or four-minute period practice group. The four-minute group was poorest of the three.[45]

Because of the dearth of well-designed experimentation in the classroom it is not possible at this time to determine the optimal temporal distribution of practice in a given school subject. The problem is alleviated when there is a good deal of student-teacher planning. When the organization is one of a subject-centered approach the distribution of activities is determined almost entirely by the teacher. When student and teacher work together in defining tasks and setting about to solve problems, the spacing of activities becomes a much less important issue.

However, there are some general principles which will give guidance in appropriate spacing of school activities. The variables which should be considered in determining the distribution of study and work activities are:

1. Monotony, boredom, and fatigue result more quickly, especially in rote learning, than is generally realized. Such factors are obviously deleterious to learning. A college student was able to type errorless speed drills of one-minute duration with an average speed of over fifty words per minute, but when periods of two minutes were tried speed dropped to about forty-two words per minute, and when five-minute periods were used, it was no longer possible to maintain errorless work.[46]

2. Another variable is the retroactive inhibition which results from interference between various parts of a given material or activity. This type of interference increases with the length of the material, the similarity of parts of the material, and the extent to which practice is massed. When there is a good deal of similarity in materials, such as words in foreign language study, practice periods should be short and more widely spaced.

3. The type of material to be learned is another factor. Difficult memorization and complex perceptual motor learning requires short, frequent (more than once a week) practice periods, while well-integrated and interesting material such as problem-solving may be studied or practiced for longer periods without a decrement in motivation or efficiency.

4. Since motivation is a key to performance and learning, self-pacing by the learner seems called for. Predetermined schedules imposed upon the eager student in an effort to make learning more efficient may serve just the reverse purpose by killing interest and initiative. Pupils who work at meaningful tasks matched with their interests and needs

---

[45] R. C. Travis, "Practice and Rest Periods in Motor Learning," *Journal of Psychology*, Vol. 3, 1937, pp. 183–187.

[46] Howard Kingsley, *The Nature and Conditions of Learning*, New York, Prentice-Hall, Inc., 1946, pp. 246–249.

may work arduously and for long periods without any apparent detrimental effects.

## CONCEPTUAL LEARNING [47]

By responding to various objects as both similar and different, the individual is able to organize his environment into meaningful categories. For example, the reader by now has formed a concept about learning. He knows that acquisition of skill, changes in attitudes, and alterations in verbal responses all represent learning. He also knows that changes in behavior resulting from fatigue or organic change do not fall in the category or concept. Thus he has a concept of learning. Without the ability to form concepts, one would have to face each new situation afresh. Concepts enable the person to generalize, discriminate, and label things appropriately so he can communicate with others.

Children learn concepts best when they are given a wide range of experiences with the objects and situations that their developing vocabulary expresses. As already noted in the first section of this chapter, it is possible to play with words without really forming an adequate or correct concept of the things those words represent. One student when asked how to determine the volume of a cube replied that she remembered you multiplied all the sides together. She proceeded to multiply each of the twelve edges of the cube in order to obtain an answer. On another occasion, college students were asked to estimate the diameter of the moon. Their answers ranged from one mile to ten billion light-years, and subsequent questioning revealed that many had only a vague notion of the meaning of diameter.

Modern teachers are sensitive to the inadequacy of sheer verbalism, and the rote application of teacher given rules. They plan activities that allow for a real understanding of what is being learned. Refer to Figure 23 to see how an arithmetic teacher makes concepts of fractions understandable.

Before coming to school, children have developed concepts such as roundness and magnitude, and are beginning to grasp the concept of time. However, abstract concepts such as honesty and courage are probably not well-developed before the average child is in the sixth or seventh grade.[48]

This corresponds with Piaget's period of formal operations, which begins at approximately 11 or 12 years of age. In the stage before (concrete opera-

---

[47] Excellent discussions of concept formation will be found in David H. Russell, "Concepts" in *Encyclopedia of Educational Research*, Third Edition, The Macmillan Company, 1960, pp. 323–333; and in William H. Burton, Roland B. Kimball, and Richard L. Wing, *Education for Effective Thinking*, New York, Appleton-Century-Crofts, Inc., 1960, pp. 162–164.

[48] W. Edgar Vinacke, "The Investigation of Concept Formation," *Psychological Bulletin*, Vol. 48, 1951, pp. 1–31.

**Figure 23.** Studying Fractions with Concrete Objects.

tions) Piaget believes children can see relationships and begin to deal with conceptions symbolically, but that propositional (hypothetico-deductive) thinking does not begin until near the end of the elementary school period.[49]

Even if one accepts the notion of sequential and not-to-be-reversed stages in the development of concepts, it is apparent that conceptualization is not an all or none development. Smedslund has shown that children may appear to have developed the concept of "conservation of weight," but will temporarily "lose" the concept when by trickery the experimenter falsifies the data presented to them for observation.[50]

Conceptualization is not an all or none proposition, but a gradual attainment with experience. A five-year-old who has a good concept of the size of objects in his immediate environment will have little notion of the size

---

[49] J. McV. Hunt, *Intelligence and Experience*, New York, Ronald Press, 1961.

[50] Jan Smedslund, "The Acquisition of Conservation of Substance and Weight in Children," in R. C. Anderson and D. P. Ausubel, *Readings in the Psychology of Cognition*, New York, Holt, Rinehart and Winston, 1965, pp. 581–605.

of sections of the earth. In one instance when a kindergarten teacher told her class that the ocean was bigger than the whole city in which they lived, the children laughed, thinking that it was a joke.

The notion that concepts increase in richness or depth of meaning with experience has serious implications for teaching. As it is now, schooling is often organized into a series of rather discrete areas—a horizontal organization. In the grades, children learn world geography, and in many cases this is a terminal point for such study. Geographical concepts which one would expect to increase in meaningfulness with an increase in age may actually decrease, so that sixth graders sometimes have a better grasp of certain geographical concepts than do college students.[51] There are probably several reasons why certain concepts fail to acquire further meaning with the passage of time. For one thing the number of concepts which children are expected to learn in school may be too large.[52] Another is that concepts are often assumed to have been learned when the child can do no more than define words. But as Brownell has indicated, concepts are far more than words or "arbitrary associations." Most important as an explanation of the failure in concept formation is that teachers have not helped provide a vertical organization which is the natural way in which concepts develop. Instead of teaching fractions once and never again referring to this concept, schools should follow through by creating problems which make use of fractions in a wide range of types of situations. In this sense, every teacher, both at elementary and high school levels, should be an arithmetic teacher when the need arises to use arithmetical concepts.

The evidence on how concepts are learned bears directly upon teaching. The kind of concept for a given child will be determined by the number and kinds of experiences which the child has had with referents of that concept. For example, a child's concept of honesty can grow only as he sees honest behavior in a number of different kinds of situations. Indeed, a child's behavior must be specific to a situation until such abstractions are formed. A child may be honest in one situation and dishonest in another.[53] He has not yet learned the concept of honesty, nor a self-concept which allows discriminations and generalizations. Clearly a teacher cannot expect consistent behavior until maturing concepts make such behavior possible. Behavior will become consistent more rapidly when teachers offer many opportunities for honest behavior, allow pupils to make and correct their own errors, and relate one situation to another.

---

[51] E. W. Dolch, *Studies on Depth of Meaning in Geographical Concepts*, Unpublished Data, University of Illinois, 1951.

[52] Brownell and Hendrickson, *op. cit.*, p. 105.

[53] Hugh Hartshorne and M. A. May, *Studies in Deceit*, New York, The Macmillan Company, 1928.

The following experiment [54] of a psychologist with his son, later repeated with a larger group,[55] illustrates some of the principles of concept formation and the teaching of concepts. The psychologist asked his son the meaning of the word opposite. He refused to accept the boy's negative response and asked him to name the opposite of "good" and "big." For these the son replied "boy" and "man." These were called wrong, and the boy was given the correct answers, and then asked the opposite of "black," "long," and "fat." The boy immediately knew the correct answers.

The teaching of concepts in the classroom has been analyzed by Smith and Meux,[56] who found that of the dozens of ways of presenting and amplifying concepts, only two or three are very extensively used by high school teachers. Smith tape recorded class sessions in various subject matter fields and then isolated several thousand "teaching episodes," or units of classroom discourse. It appeared from this analysis that in presenting and discussing concepts, teachers mainly asked students to describe the concept and give positive instances of situations where it might be used. Teachers did not very frequently use such techniques as presenting negative instances, or showing how the concept fitted into some classification scheme.

In an extension of the work just described, Nuthall and Lawrence [57] have devised a technique they have labeled "incident analysis," which simply classifies teachers' original questions and their follow-up questions about students' responses. The categories are these:

1. Vague questions
2. Questions requiring an opinion
3. Closed questions (Factual in nature or requiring a yes or no answer)
   3.1 Factual
   3.2 Yes or No
4. Open questions (Asking for characteristics of a concept or an example of it)
   4.1 Reference to characteristics of a class or explanatory principles
   4.2 Requiring an example or instance
5. Repeated questions, often by paraphrasing the original question

[54] K. M. Dallenbach, "A Note on the Immediacy of Understanding a Relation," *Psychologische Forschung*, Vol. 7, 1926, pp. 268–269.

[55] G. Kreezer and K. M. Dallenbach, "Learning the Relation of Opposition," *American Journal of Psychology*, Vol. 41, 1929, pp. 432–441.

[56] B. O. Smith and M. O. Meux, *A Study of the Logic of Teaching*, Bureau of Educational Research, University of Illinois, Mimeo, 1962. Also see, M. Meux and B. O. Smith, "Logical Dimensions of Teaching Behavior," in *Contemporary Research of Teacher Effectiveness*, B. J. Biddle and W. J. Ellena (Editors), New York, Holt, Rinehart and Winston, 1964, pp. 127–164.

[57] G. A. Nuthall and P. J. Lawrence, *Thinking in the Classroom: The Development of a Method of Analysis*, Wellington, New Zealand, Council for Educational Research, 1965.

To show how the application of the incident analysis technique may reveal the way in which a teacher handles concepts, see Figure 24, which shows the analysis of one lesson. The teacher in this case asked three vague questions (category 1), three questions requiring an opinion, two factual questions, 20 questions requiring a yes or no answer, and so on.

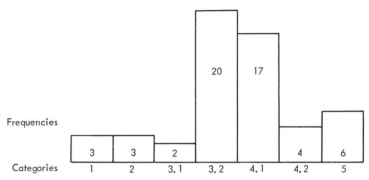

**Figure 24.** Incident Analysis Applied to a Teacher's Lesson.

Nuthall and Lawrence contend [58] that every teacher introduces the child to a variety of patterns of thinking such as defining, inferring, evaluating, and explaining, which can be analyzed by the incident approach. Teachers often do not realize what their own questioning patterns are. Some teachers may concentrate on one type to the exclusion of others. Such techniques as incident analysis just described and episode analysis (Smith and Meux) if widely used would reveal a great deal about the intellectual activities of the classroom.

## PROBLEM-SOLVING

In a rapidly changing world, it becomes imperative that people develop the capacity to adapt to new situations, to make discriminations, think critically and creatively, and make sound judgments. The day-to-day ability to recognize and solve practical problems as well as the concern with and ability to handle intellectual problems has become a major goal of schooling.

An important consideration for teachers is how children learn to recognize and to solve problems as well as how teaching activities can be organized to elicit problem-solving behavior. Problem-solving skill is not learned incidentally as children go through the motions of finding answers to the teacher's questions nor is it learned by watching the teacher or other

---

[58] *Ibid.*, p. 2.

students solve problems. In fact the notion of problem-solving activity as memorized steps, as is apt to occur under these conditions, may actually militate against the learning of problem-solving. On the other hand, problem-solving which is accompanied by examples and explanations, which is marked by active participation of pupils, and which stresses an understanding of method, will be likely not only to last, but also to become functional. One noted experiment in problem-solving compared groups of students who had learned to solve problems by two different methods. Students in one group memorized the solution to a problem which required the moving of lines to make a new geometrical shape. A second group spent the same amount of time as the first in working on several such problems, the solutions to which were explained. Retests of both groups on similar problems showed a decided superiority for the second group which really understood the nature of the problems.[59] In commenting about this and like experiments, the investigator (Katona) wrote: "Pupils should learn to learn—that is the best the school can do for them. They should not merely learn to memorize—they should learn to learn by understanding." [60]

The essential idea in Katona's statement has been reiterated in numerous writings of psychologists and educators over the past twenty years. However, agreement about this important objective is not matched by an agreement among suggestions for ways of attaining it.

### What Is the Case for Stressing Problem-Solving?

The following paragraph, written for mathematics teachers is of such general value that it is presented here:

> If life were of such a constant nature that there were only a few chores to do and they were done over and over in exactly the same way, the case for knowing how to solve problems would not be so compelling. All one would have to do would be to learn how to do the few jobs at the outset.

It is quite clear that the purposes of schooling go beyond the learning of unvarying routines and details which may characterize training in specific jobs. Furthermore, solutions to school problems may be of little value to pupils who will likely face much different problems after they leave school. In short, it is not so much the solution of the problems which is important but the learning of ways to deal with a wide variety of problems which is crucial. There is much evidence in and out of school to show that few persons ever learn to handle their problems very effectively and rationally. Instead it is much more common to find persons facing problems by rote

---

[59] George Katona, *Organizing and Memorizing,* New York, Columbia University Press, 1940, pp. 82–85.
[60] *Ibid.,* p. 260.

memorization of rules or by affective impulse. In one study only 32 per cent of a group of college students, all of whom had studied high school geometry, showed any insight in solving geometrical problems. The rest relied upon habit. Out of 285 test situations, responses of the "oh I see" type occurred only seventeen times.[61] Again college students in one of the writer's classes, asked to find the square root of six digit numbers, attempted to obtain the answer by form (long since forgotten) instead of attacking the problem by the methods of logical thinking [62] or even by trial and error.

The failure of many people to make a direct and straightforward attack upon problems is reflected in difficulties of adjustment, poor judgment, and inability to make decisions. Writers [63] in the field of counseling list decision making as one of the common areas of adjustment problems. Little help comes to such people from rules, bromides, and clichés in newspapers and popular books on adjustment. There is no substitute for actual experience in solving problems, facing difficulties, making errors, and finally discovering a solution which leads to action. The case for learning to solve problems has been well-summarized by Kingsley,[64] who writes: "A good problem is a good motive for learning. Secondly it is conducive to the building up of confidence in one's ability to work things out for himself. This has definite value for the individual's mental health, for one of the first principles of mental hygiene is that difficulties should be regarded as problems to be solved rather than as emergencies to be evaded."

### The Nature of the Problem-Solving Process [65]

A description of the problem-solving process is little more than a reformulation of the learning process. However, there are differences in emphases. Every situation in which a student has a need and a goal, with a barrier between, leads to some kind of learning. A youngster may have a paper route which covers several blocks. One of his problems is to determine the most economical way to cover the territory. In connection with this problem, a good deal of learning can occur. He might continue in a haphazard manner, or he might ask someone to solve the problem for him. In each of these cases he had learned something, viz., habits of avoiding

---

[61] L. K. Henry, "The Role of Insight in the Analytical Thinking of Adolescents," *University of Iowa Studies in Education*, Vol. 9, No. 5, 1934, pp. 65–102.

[62] A few students, for example, went from the known to the unknown. They started with 144 or 625, known squares, and attempted to figure out how the known square roots of 12 and 25 were obtained.

[63] F. P. Robinson, *Principles and Procedures in Student Counseling*, New York, Harper and Brothers, 1950.

[64] Howard Kingsley, *op. cit.*, p. 379.

[65] For detailed accounts of the psychological nature of problem-solving see D. M. Johnson, "A Modern Account of Problem Solving," *Psychological Bulletin*, Vol. 41, 1944, pp. 201–229, 169 titles; Karl Duncker, "On Problem Solving," *Psychological Monographs*, No. 270, 1945; and Carl P. Duncan, "Recent Research on Human Problem Solving," *Psychological Bulletin*, Vol. 56, 1959, pp. 397–429.

such issues or of being dependent upon others. But he has not solved the problem until he has recognized it as a problem, turned energy toward it, arrived at a judgment, and checked his final decision.

Various writers have outlined the steps in problem-solving, and though there is not a complete agreement among them, there are elements which are common in their descriptions. First, there is a *motive* or identification or recognition phase, in which the student sees that he is faced with a problem and has a desire to do something about it. Secondly, there is generally a *planning* phase in which the person considers several avenues of attack upon the problem. Often this consists in the formation of hypotheses which are later accepted or rejected. The third, or *work* phase, consists of testing hypotheses, collecting relevant materials, talking to others about the problem, etc. Finally, there is an *evaluative, action* phase in which the student appraises his solution or ideas, and takes action as a result. The process does not always follow a neat sequence, and it is quite possible that students will be working upon several features of a total problem at once. In fact, undue emphasis upon form may blind students to the necessity for critical appraisal of all steps in the process as they go along.

Problem-solving is a circular process in that facing important issues inevitably leads to further questions. This is especially true when groups as well as individuals work at problems. Various class members should be encouraged to investigate ramifications of questions which individuals raise. As Thorndike notes: "The school is as much concerned with creating problems as it is with solving them." [66]

### How Do Problems Arise?

A practical question for teachers is where and how problems arise in teaching. A first and obvious source is from the teacher, and texts or other reading materials. From the teacher's viewpoint, such problems may be very important. But there is serious doubt that such problems are always real problems or at least significant ones to the student. Furthermore, if the scope of problem-solving activity includes no more than these "set" problems, important steps in the process, namely, recognition and identification of problems are left out. Some problems suggested by the teacher and texts may provide excellent guidance and be a real challenge, but pupils also need activities which cause them to derive problems of their own.

Some of the less obvious but important ways in which problems germinate are through group discussion, trips outside the school, critical self-appraisal, use of a wide variety of class materials, and use of unique equip-

[66] R. L. Thorndike, "How Children Learn the Principles and Techniques of Problem Solving" in Forty-Ninth Yearbook of the National Society for the Study of Education, Part I, *Learning and Instruction*, University of Chicago Press, 1950, p. 194.

ment. In all these activities there is the underlying assumption of existing needs and interests which can be directed toward awareness of problems and their solution, and that the classroom is the place for this kind of activity.

Suggestions for helping students develop problems which are interesting and at the same time profitable have been made by experienced teachers in a class of one of the writers. These teachers suggested:

1. Ask each student to write a list of problems which are of interest to him or which represent needs for him.
2. Have students keep records of difficult words, controversial points, and the like.
3. Provide a rich supply of resource material. One teacher instead of getting fifty copies of the same text ordered fifty different books for study.
4. Use reading interest tests, and provide reading material in the direction of students' interests.
5. Have students score their own quizzes, correct their own written work, and discuss each other's papers.
6. Allow students to participate in making their own assignments.
7. Group students within the class on the basis of common interests and problems.
8. Encourage students to draw problems from the community such as road repair, drainage, police system, and traffic control.

### Selection of Problems

When an individual child or a group of pupils develop a number of questions or problems, they must have some guidance in selecting those most appropriate and valuable for further study.

Each class and each student with the help of the teacher should develop criteria for determining the problems most appropriate for study. In some cases teachers may be unwilling to relinquish this job which they consider their most important prerogative. Other teachers may delegate the whole job to the class leaving pupils without necessary guidance. In either case, children are not learning the important skill of identifying and recognizing important problems in their environment.

Although various class situations are unique, there are several criteria for selection of problems which the teacher should have available. The following are questions which might be asked: Is this the most pressing and important problem at this time? Will solving this problem be profitable and important in developing further learnings? Will there be access to necessary sources of material? Could this problem be more appropriately handled in another class or course? How will solution of this problem benefit the group as a whole?

Mackworth [67] makes the important distinction between problem solvers and "problem finders." He believes the latter kinds of individuals are extremely important to society, for it is they who open up whole new fields of inquiry for the problem solvers to develop and refine. Many times the problem finders are not the experts in a particular area. In a study [68] of the 60 major inventions of the twentieth century, it was found that many came from people in fields quite different from the one in which the invention belonged. The automatic dial telephone was devised by a mortician, the inventor of Xerography was a lawyer, and the pneumatic tire came from a veterinary surgeon.

### Collecting and Using Relevant Materials

Students cannot be expected to solve problems without knowing how to find and use appropriate resources. That students are not generally well-trained in this respect is well documented. It should be noted that "even good students do not know how to find and use source material. Some graduating seniors in college have rarely used any other library resource than the reserve desk where one merely has to ask for the book." [69]

When teachers enrolled in graduate work were given a hypothetical classroom problem dealing with motivation and interests and asked to show how they would go about solving it, *not one* of 231 graduate students suggested the use of bibliographic materials as resources which would aid in solution of the problem. [70] Wiles found in working with a group in college that neither undergraduates nor graduate students had obtained skills in fact collecting. He says, "The chief weakness revealed by the examination was the inability of students to locate reference material in the library." This "glaring deficiency" exists, Wiles notes, in spite of the fact that many of the students had been in contact with about fifty teachers during the years they had spent in school. [71] It is reported that less than 25 per cent of high schools offer training in how to use a library. Even schools which do offer such courses are highly variable in their practices. In one survey of 100 selected schools, three-fourths of which gave formal training in library usage, only one out of the 100 gave work in how to use textbooks, and how

---

[67] Norman H. Mackworth, "Originality," *American Psychologist*, Vol. 20, 1965, pp. 51–66.

[68] J. Jewkes, D. Sawers and R. Stillerman, *The Sources of Invention*, London, Macmillan, 1961.

[69] S. L. Pressey and F. P. Robinson, *Psychology and the New Education*, New York, Harper and Brothers, 1944, p. 608.

[70] R. H. Simpson, E. L. Gaier, and R. S. Jones, "A Study of Resourcefulness in Attacking Professional Problems," *The School Review*, Vol. 40, December, 1952, p. 538.

[71] Kimball Wiles, "Are We Developing Skill in Purposeful Fact Collecting?," *Journal of Educational Research*, Vol. 38, 1945, pp. 617–623.

to check in and charge out books. Only about one-half gave information about the *Readers Guide* and the use of encyclopedias.[72]

### Evaluating the Results of Inquiry

Evaluation should be a continuous process during problem-solving activity. The acceptance or rejection of hypotheses, the appraisal of various source material, incorporation of suggestions from teachers and other students are all essential procedures which can be learned only through guided practice in solving problems. The ultimate goal is to develop habits of critical appraisal so that students can solve problems and make discoveries on their own.

How is this skill developed in the classroom? One simple way is a frequent use of questions of how and why in place of the many what, when, and where questions so often used in our classrooms today. Questions which ask for process and for reasons are challenging, and discourage rote memorization.

Group work and evaluation by students of each other's ideas is another way in which students learn critically to scrutinize problems. Often the most significant classroom problems are those which affect the whole class or even the whole community. Thus appraisal of progress will become a joint venture, each student learning something of appraisal from the activities of others.

### Solution and Action

Unless some action results from the solution of problems, students may see the activity as busy work. For some problems no definite answers will be found, but generally such problems (e.g., consideration of racial intolerance in a social studies class) will lead to other problems, and will result in tentative conclusions which can lead to constructive action.

In a previous chapter an example was given of students who were challenged to find a solution to the problem of malarial control in their community. Activities leading to the solution of the problem involved surveys of the health of the community, of the terrain and breeding places of mosquitoes, and of methods of controlling these insects. Had the class, in this instance, stopped at this point, little would have been gained from the experience. The final test of the effectiveness of their work could only be discovered by these students in trying out methods of preventing and controlling malaria.

For more abstract problems, such as problems in mathematics, the same principle applies. The problems with which students work will take on added significance when their solution can be checked in some practical

---

[72] W. G. Brink, *Directing Study Activities in Secondary Schools*, Garden City, New York, Doubleday, Doran and Company, Inc., 1937.

context—e.g., when they can test algebraic solutions in physics and chemistry.

## CREATIVE THINKING

Originality, inventiveness, and imagination are no longer conceived as intellectual luxuries of a gifted few.[73] The misconception that creative thinking is a special property of the "gifted" can have unfortunate consequences in schooling. It can lead to dull conformity, and passivity in learning. Creative thinking flourishes when teachers realize that all children have the capacity for it, indeed crave to do it. But it has to be learned, just as children learn how to solve problems. It can be killed just as one can kill self-confidence, it can be inhibited just as one inhibits playfulness, and it can be neglected just as one neglects arithmetic or geography. It must not be killed, inhibited, or neglected. "Society will succeed in continuing its creative advance because the alternative to this is irreversible disaster to everyone." [74]

### Motives for Creativity

Somewhere along the line, society and schools have failed to keep alive the curiosity of children and their unconventional and idiosyncratic modes of thinking. Some teachers deliberately encourage originality as this exercise indicates: [75]

Unscholarly, haphazard reading in archaeology is one of my hobbies. I relate it to my class work when I think it will be of interest and value. Class discussion sometimes moves into the fields of historical and prehistorical research. The children often are interested in how historians gather the material which they put in their books. Usually this question comes up, "We understand how research and study can be made of cultures where a written language existed, but how do historians find out so much about peoples where there was no written language or no decipherable language?"

I then spend some time discussing the deductions that can be made from the discovery and evaluation of the artifacts of a vanished culture, i.e., the use of metals implies a knowledge of metallurgy, inscriptions whether decipherable or not, indicate a fairly high level in the culture etc. Most students find this quite interesting and it is not difficult to get a lively question and answer period underway.

At the next meeting of the class, I hand each pupil a sheet of paper and a pencil and a penny. I ask them to imagine that they are people from another planet visiting our world from which all mankind has vanished. I ask them to try to forget their background of culture and environment.

---

[73] J. W. Getzels and R. W. Jackson, *Creativity and Intelligence*, New York, John Wiley and Sons, Inc., 1962.

[74] Henry Eyring, "Scientific Creativity," Chap. I in Harold H. Anderson (Editor), *Creativity and Its Cultivation*, New York, Harper and Brothers, 1959, p. 11.

[75] Furnished by Mr. Omer Tobias, Litchfield, Illinois.

After digging in the ruins of one of the Earth cities, they discover a cache of round disc-like metallic objects. I then ask them to seriously consider the implications of the penny that they hold in their hands, then I ask that they write down their deductions concerning our civilization that could be made from the discovery of a penny.

The results are usually quite interesting. I have each child read his paper, which the class discusses as to the reliability of the perception and the deductions which have been made on the basis of perception. Some of the papers show an amazing insight and logical development.

There are not enough teachers who use their own imagination to pique children's curiosity. The results are that many students go all the way through school and college without developing the attitude that they have the capacity to do creative thinking, as the following excerpt of a letter to the writer indicates.[76]

Psychological Business Research of Cleveland, has enrolled several hundred executives and scientists employed by various corporations across the country in a work shop type course entitled "Creative Problem Solving." Not only has this program received enthusiastic reception, but has on some occasions resulted in immediate gains such as the development of a new synthetic rubber, and a "non-squeaking" metal-to-metal moving surface that does not require a lubricant. Perhaps the real benefit of this kind of training is a change in attitude on the part of the individual participant who realizes that it is possible for him to generate new and useful ideas.

A nascent motive for creativity exists in young children but dull conformity, poor textbooks, and a fear of being different give short life to what should be the school's most precious objective.[77]

### Roadblocks to Creativity

An understanding of the impediments to original thinking should give teachers a better basis for their classroom operations. Foremost among these roadblocks is the acceptance of the teacher and the text as ultimate authorities. Many industries have found that the development of "yes men" and the rewarding of conformity have militated against the development of new ideas. In like fashion the authoritative teacher who permits no deviation from the school solution, fashions an atmosphere of dull routine without spontaneity. In order to tolerate unconventionality and divergent thinking the teacher himself must be a creative person, one who enjoys and rewards originality when it occurs. Equally important in repressing creative thinking is the inflexible program of study with its com-

---

[76] Letter to writer from Dr. J. C. Denton, Psychological Business Research, Cleveland, Ohio.

[77] George D. Stoddard, "Creativity in Education" in Harold H. Anderson, *op. cit.*, pp. 181–202.

pulsion for coverage of material. Often the schedule is so filled with planned activities that there is no time for digression, and no opportunity for the encouragement of individual interests and activities. Important here is the fact that administrators, even more than teachers, are committed to a set program of studies, and teachers are likely to be rated by their administrators on the basis of how well they comply with the predetermined program. It is interesting to note in this connection that schools may not even bother to try to apply the results of educational research in revising their program of studies. Since 1931, there has been rather convincing evidence that teaching history backwards leads to better motivation and understanding in social studies.[78] Yet there are very few schools where this innovation has even been tried.

The fallacy that the gifted are the only ones who have the capacity to be creative has been thoroughly exposed. Yet it continues to exist in classroom operation. The fallacy hurts the gifted, because they get the idea that they do not have to think, and hurts others because they are convinced that they cannot do so. One of the most serious results of this fallacy is the assumption that the bright child will develop this capacity on his own, and that the best the school can do for him is to provide him many facts. Hence memory work is rewarded, and divergence is discouraged. The bright child, partly because he is bright, quickly learns that the "pay off" in examinations goes to the person who can give back to the teacher the "right" answer.

It has been asserted that educational psychologists use selection examinations that pick out efficient verbal reasoners rather than intuitive observers or constructive thinkers.[79]

### Brainstorming and Other Stimulations for Creativity

Whenever anyone seeks the solution for a problem, analytically observes the events around him, and daydreams about a better world, he is likely to be doing creative thinking. Often as previously illustrated, he inhibits the overt expression of these activities and keeps them in his own private world. To unlock the potential for these creative activities and to make them available to others, various stimulating techniques have been developed. Foremost is the technique known as brainstorming.[80] First

---

[78] C. C. Crawford and W. L. Walker, "An Experiment in Teaching History Backward," *Historical Outlook*, Vol. 12, 1931, pp. 395–397.

[79] Sir Cyril Burt, Foreword in A. Koestler, *The Act of Creation*, New York, The Macmillan Company, Inc., 1964.

[80] The origination of the term brainstorming is credited to Alex Osborn, at the time Vice-president of the firm Batton, Barton, Durstine and Osborn. For further details see Alex F. Osborn, *Applied Imagination*, Revised Edition, New York, Charles Scribner's Sons, 1957.

used by advertising agencies, this technique has grown to the extent that it is now widely used by professional groups, and discussion sessions in classrooms. The crux of this technique is that critical evaluation and judicial appraisal must be suspended. It is also important that a group, rapidly producing ideas characteristic of brainstorming, be focused upon the solution of a specific problem. All members must be convinced that *any* idea is acceptable no matter how ridiculous it may appear.

Results of brainstorming sessions are sometimes amazing. The solution to problems reported by Dr. Denton of Psychological Business Research came through sessions similar to brainstorming. In his book, *Professional Creativity*, Von Fange asserts:

> As an example of the value of such sessions, two engineers had spent over a month in conceiving and accumulating twenty-seven embryonic solutions to a difficult control-device problem. When they were finally prevailed upon to conduct a brainstorming session, a group of eleven young engineers with no intimate acquaintance with the details of the problem came up with every one of these ideas plus many others in a short twenty-five minute session.[81]

These brainstorming techniques have been applied in college classrooms by Meadow and Parnes [82] who observe some general gains in mental flexibility as a consequence of the training sessions.

There is no solid body of pedagogical evidence which suggests how to teach in order to induce creativity. Cogan [83] in the field of literature and Reed [84] in science both found creativity related to the teacher's warmth, and in like manner Spaulding [85] observed a negative relationship between creativity in elementary grade children and the formal type of teacher who uses shame to produce conformity. These studies relating creativity to personal qualities of the teacher suggest that its development is as much a product of motivational as of cognitive factors. On the cognitive side we have already seen, in episode and incident analysis, evidence that a greater variety of instructional techniques would offer more "thinking" models to pupils.

Another interesting approach to creative problem solving is that pro-

---

[81] Eugene K. Von Fange, *Professional Creativity*, Englewood Cliffs, N.J., Prentice-Hall, Inc., 1959, p. 51.

[82] Arnold Meadow, and Sidney J. Parnes, "Evaluation of Training in Creative Problem Solving," *Journal of Applied Psychology*, Vol. 43, 1959, pp. 189–194.

[83] Morris L. Cogan, "The Behavior of Teachers and the Productive Behavior of their Pupils," *Journal of Experimental Education*, Vol. 27, 1958, pp. 89–124.

[84] H. B. Reed, "Implications for Science Education of a Teacher Competence Research," *Science Education*, Vol. 46, 1962, 473–486.

[85] R. Spaulding, "Achievement, Creativity, and Self-Concept Correlates of Teacher-Pupil Transactions in Elementary Schools," Urbana, University of Illinois, U.S. Office of Education, Cooperative Research Project No. 1352, 1963 (Mimeo.).

posed by Crutchfield.[86] He has developed a story-telling program in which problems are posed and solved by children with the aid of a kindly, fictitious Uncle John. Uncle John is portrayed as a sort of Sherlock Holmes of the intellectual world, and he starts by giving advice, pointing to clues, and practically solving the problems for the children, but as the program progresses, he becomes only a helper, placing more and more of the responsibility in the hands of the children, who by this time have become his full-fledged partners. Crutchfield reports a measurable increase in creative problem solving ability for children who have completed the program.

Other techniques that have proven useful in stimulating thinking include: the proposing of some ridiculous idea and following it through to a conclusion; providing check lists of processes that may lead to new insights, e.g., one item might be, "when the direct way fails try the opposite"; and exploring the basic conceptual area in which a specific problem falls. [87]

### Implications for Educational Practice [88]

Schools have a growing interest in creativity. Many teachers have tried brainstorming and other techniques just described. However, the implications of what has been said go far deeper than the alteration of classroom techniques. They strike at the roots of how the school is organized, and even at the basic values behind the curriculum. The following suggestions should illustrate the breadth of the changes that seem indicated by present knowledge.

1. The general atmosphere of the school and classroom probably inhibits creative activity. It should be changed to one in which both the teacher and pupil have an experimental attitude. Particularly at advanced levels of schooling is this important. In a discussion of scientific creativity, Eyring [89] gives a vivid description of what he conceives as a good creative environment. It is far different from the conventional classroom or laboratory. The essence of this environment is that everyone is expected to do original research and to be creative. Formal course work is minimal, and the student is accepted into a fraternity of scholars who accept him as an equal partner in a stimulating adventure. In one high school, science students are enrolled with the expectation that they will do original research, and their work is published in a regular bulletin.[90] One volume of

---

[86] Richard S. Crutchfield, "Instructing the Individual in Creative Thinking," *New Approaches to Individualizing Instruction*, Princeton, N.J., Educational Testing Service, 1965, pp. 13–25.

[87] Von Fange, *op. cit.*, pp. 40–58, and Zuce Kagan, *Essentials in Problem Solving*, New York, Arco Publishing Co., 1956.

[88] For further details see references under Anderson and Burton in the bibliography at the end of this chapter.

[89] Henry Eyring, *op. cit.*, pp. 9–11.

[90] *APS Journal*, Vol. II, Urbana, University High School, University of Illinois, 1960.

this publication includes the following titles, together with the students who completed the research.

*Some Properties of Kinetic Friction Between Dry Surfaces,* Richard Bourgin

*Experimental Measurement of the Rates of Oxygen Consumption of Invertebrates,* Nancy Prossor

*An Experiment in the Training of Reptiles,* Jacquie Yates

*The Effects of Hexachlorophene on Bacillus Subtilis,* Carla Zelle

*An Experiment in Stress and Strain,* Dave Williams

*Effects of Currents Through Magnets,* Myla Archer

*The Virus,* Ambrose Richardson

*A Problem in Electronic Computer Design,* John Burgett

*Design of a Binary Counting Circuit,* Louise Barker

*Some Theoretical Studies of the Behavior of Light,* Tom Bestor

*Heat Balance in the Emperor Penguin,* Charles Johnson

*Outline of Pro Chemistry,* Charles Birkeland

It is significant that many of the outstanding scientists of our time first committed themselves to a career in a specific field of science when they found out that on their own initiative they could solve an original problem.[91]

2. Testing and selection of students for advanced placement in various professional fields must include some measure of creativity and originality. The oft-used point-hour ratio or grade-point average reflects more than anything else how well a student was able to memorize and understand what he is told or what he has read. These skills may actually be poorly related or even negatively related to originality and intellectual flexibility. Thus in selection programs in many professional schools we may unconsciously but deliberately deny opportunities to the very people who could do the most toward advancing knowledge. There is convincing evidence that neither point-hour ratio nor the ordinary aptitude tests tap this important trait of creativity.

3. In addition to the use of various techniques already mentioned to stimulate creative thought, the school should make as a recognized goal, the development of intellectual flexibility. Activities to this end would include a great deal more opportunity for self-selection by students, more exercises that require unconventional thinking, and more demonstrations that arouse curiosity.

4. There ought to be time provided and an expectation developed that reflective thinking is a part of the school activity. Quiet times that allow

---

[91] Anne Roe, "A Psychologist Examines 64 Scientists," *Scientific American,* Vol. 187, November, 1952, pp. 21–25.

children an opportunity to try to answer "why" questions and to explain the phenomenon that they observe might regularly be included in the daily schedule. Children should be given the explanation of all these things so that they know the processes they are trying to develop. They should think not only about the problems that arise in the classroom, but also about their own thinking, and they ought to discuss among themselves and with the teacher what this thinking means to them, and how it can be improved.

5. It is most important that reinforcement be given when originality occurs. Grading of papers should include points for creative answers, and the student should be publicly praised when he presents an inventive solution to a problem. Only by making sure that it is perceived as an important objective of schooling can teachers be sure that creative thinking will be fostered. Mearns [92] cites a case that nicely illustrates the effectiveness of reinforcement. He tells the story of a third-grade girl who submitted some original poetry to her teacher who coldly rejected it as "not up to our standards." Later the little girl took the poem to Mearns, an upper-grade teacher in the same building, who duplicated it in the school paper. The child was thrilled to see her poetry in print, took more and more interest in creative writing, and afterwards in high school was made editor of the high school magazine.

6. Finally, it is apparent that many of our school physical plants are poorly constructed and designed for this objective. Bare classrooms with bolted down seats do not lend themselves to the development of discussion, experimentation, and a variety of individual activities. It is to be hoped that schools of the future will include provisions for flexible individual and group work, and that they will make use of the varieties of equipment now available. Figure 25 shows how a school room looks when each child is provided with a portable typewriter. The children shown in the figure were being studied to see what effect upon compositional writing skills would occur when typewriters were used. Results indicated an increase in both the quantity and quality of creative writing.[93]

## SPECIFIC CLASSROOM ACTIVITIES

The teacher should be equipped with working techniques which jibe with psychological principles. A teacher should be an expert in the technology of learning, but as is true of other technologists, must continually appraise techniques in terms of new discoveries and research. It is literally

---

[92] Hugh Mearns, *Creative Power: The Education of Youth in the Creative Arts*, Second Edition, New York, Dover Publications, 1958.

[93] Royal McBee Corporation, *The Manual Portable Typewriter as an Instructional Tool in the Elementary School Classroom*, 1960.

**Figure 25.** Children Using Typewriters to Stimulate Creative Writing.

true that many of today's principles may be outmoded or changed in a few years. It is thus imperative that teachers retain an open-mindedness which allows revision of their teaching methods as new discoveries are made.

Consider these specific examples of current school practice. One teacher makes an assignment by giving a number of problems in the text, or a certain number of pages to be read. Another may spend an hour or so planning a new unit of work. One typing teacher begins work with "frf," "juj" drills, another starts off immediately with business letters, and a third allows students to select their own typing material right from the start. Miss Black has pupils add columns up, Mr. Brown has them add from the top down, while a third has pupils add two digits at a time from the beginning. In the face of so many questions about specific teaching plans and techniques, the teacher must be equipped with psychological principles which are general enough to apply in a number of situations.

That decisions about such simple things as how to frame an assignment may make a major difference in learning is attested to in the following:

> I learned more about modulation via a diminished chord in one week from a teacher who suggested as an assignment discovering how many smooth modulations were possible from a single diminished chord than I did in

three years of learning and following rules from a teacher of music theory who was evidently fearful of her ability to go beyond the book.[94]

### Psychology of Assignment Making

The assignment has been considered as a specification by the teacher of material to be read or studied or of work to be accomplished by the student. This somewhat narrow view of assignment making has resulted in almost complete domination by the teacher of assignments. In one study of one thousand high school teachers 90 per cent of assignments were dominated by the teacher.[95] That this is contrary to the attitudes of pupils about assignments was shown in a study of 1237 high school students who preferred a procedure of democratic assignments to either an autocratic or laissez-faire procedure.[96]

What of present assignment-making procedures? Burton, who has studied such practices writes:

> The meager, vague, unanalyzed, wholly inadequate type of assignment predominates in the secondary school, practically to the exclusion of all other forms.[97]

Still widely used is the procedure of assigning a certain number of text pages or chapters to be read by students and little else. This is done despite the fact that overwhelming evidence supports clear-cut objectives, student participation, and adequately explained assignments as valuable organizing factors in study and learning.

The inadequacy of present procedures may be largely due to a belief that assignments, teaching, practice, and testing are separate entities. These processes are obviously interrelated, and when treated as such should result in better motivation of pupils. The assignment is largely a matter not of information but of motivation, i.e., helping students find a direction for their energy. As such the first principle is that assignments should provide for individual differences.

Assignments should also arouse interest and make for continuing motivation through a unit of work, or problem. Questions, illustrative materials, demonstrations are all a part of the introduction to a new piece of work. Pupils should be involved in the assignment process. The ego involvement which obtains from giving students a proprietary interest in

[94] Communication to the writer from Prof. John N. Maharg, Music Department, Eastern Illinois University, Charleston, Illinois.

[95] W. G. Brink, "Assignment Procedures of One Thousand High School Teachers," *Educational Trends*, Vol. 1, 1934, pp. 6–14.

[96] R. C. Doll, "High School Pupils' Attitudes Toward Teaching Procedures," *School Review*, Vol. 55, 1947, pp. 222–227.

[97] William Burton in Forty-Ninth Yearbook of the National Society for the Study of Education, Part I, 1950, p. 227.

their own course will cause them to identify with the work, and should result in better group morale and enthusiasm. Good assignments give pupils a mental set which makes them anticipate future steps in learning. The youngster learns what to look for, and how to go about doing so. Research has shown that a "set" (i.e., suggestions about how to look at a problem) leads to more rapid and efficient learning.

### Placement and Function of Review

Theoretically the curve of retention of material learned might approximate that shown in Figure 26. In actual practice, however, the shape of this curve is a function of many factors. The goal of education is to change the shape, to avoid the rapid drop-off in retention. As previously

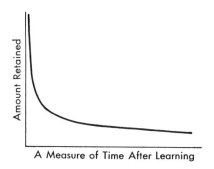

A Measure of Time After Learning

**Figure 26.** A Theoretical Curve of Retention of Relatively Meaningless Material.

discussed, forgetting increases as interference increases. A summary of some of the factors that determine whether forgetting will be rapid or slow follows.

1. The kind of test of retention used makes a difference. A test of pure recall (e.g., completion) would show a more rapid drop than a test of recognition (multiple-choice).
2. The kind of material which is learned affects the shape of the forgetting curve. The more meaningful the material, the less rapid the drop.
3. The thoroughness of the original learning is also a factor. Overlearning produces a retention curve of an entirely different shape, one which may remain at a high level for an indefinite period of time.
4. The kinds of activity which have occurred after the original learning partially determine how rapidly forgetting occurs.
5. Active involvement of the learner in the learning situation also retards forgetting.

Much of a teacher's work is concerned with altering the shape of this curve. Learning which is put away has little chance of being available when it is needed. Point 4 above concerned with review, dictates that after learning there must be some use made of material if forgetting is to be retarded. As Figure 26 shows, the greatest forgetting occurs shortly after learning. Hence it would appear wise to place review activities as close to the original learning as practical. Research bears out this supposition. When several thousand grade-school children read a selection and were given four-minute review tests afterward, the degree of retention was directly related to the placement of the review test. Immediate recall after reading proved the most profitable. Groups which took immediate review tests had over 60 per cent better retention of material read than those who took their first recall test a week later. Furthermore, a group which took an immediate recall test and another one the next day was superior to a group which took an immediate recall test, and a second test a week later.[98] A short test or other form of review at the end of a class period, followed by discussion should do more to retard forgetting than formal reviews which take place several days or even weeks after learning.

### Testing and Learning

More than any other single factor, the kind of testing used in schools determines the organization of class work and materials, the learning of pupils, and often the kind of teaching which is done. Whether teachers admit it or not, the tests they use are statements to students of their objectives and are the forces which direct students' activities. One of the reasons why good teaching methods may fail is probably attributable to the discrepancy between the stated goals of a course and the conventional paper and pencil tests which are used as a means of grading. This discrepancy may be destructive of morale, because the avowed purpose of the school work may be the development of understanding and generalizations, while the tests appraise only the number of facts which the student has been able to amass. As teaching methods are improved, so must testing procedures be revised. As before noted, tests may have a beneficial function in learning (perhaps this is their most important function) in addition to their use in measurement of achievement and diagnosis.

Tests should stress process as well as product. Often the results of the ordinary true-false or multiple-choice test reveal little about the reasons for students' mistakes. An analysis of the reasons back of students' choices of multiple-choice alternatives has shown that many students guess, or

---

[98] H. F. Spitzer, "Studies in Retention," *Journal of Educational Psychology*, Vol. 30, 1939, pp. 641–656.

have a hunch which is the right answer without really understanding why it is correct. Conversely students may miss questions (choose a wrong alternative) and at the same time have a rather good grasp of the issues involved in the questions.[99]

The teacher who wishes to use tests to facilitate learning should provide a wide variety of testing materials. Also the teacher should make use of the group's appraisal of its own work and self-scoring techniques. Much more frequently than now used should be essay or expository questions which require students to organize material and give reasons for their answers. The effect of various types of tests upon the study which precedes the test is also a factor to be considered. In an experiment with college students, Meyer [100] told previously equated groups to study for *one* of the following types of tests: true-false, completion, multiple-choice, and essay. After study periods of like duration, all of the groups were given *all four* types of examinations. The group which had prepared for the essay test earned better scores on *all* types of tests. Students who had prepared for a completion test made the next highest scores on all tests, and the students who had prepared for true-false and multiple-choice tests scored about the same, and were below both the other groups.

What are the characteristics of tests and test items which give rise to learning? Studies of the effect of test items on later performance with similar items show that items which have a high learning value are: (1) high in arousing student interest, (2) those which pose a specific problem, (3) difficult enough to be a challenge, (4) applicational and practical, and (5) those which call for reasoning or judgment and not just for memorized facts. Tests should contain directions which not only tell the student *what* to do, but explain the reasons for doing it.

### Sequence of Activities

Perhaps the most common sequence of activities presently in use is that of—study—teaching—testing, with the first two frequently combined into one process. Generally a reading assignment precedes the study and teaching phase. Sometimes testing follows independent study. This sequence in many ways is contrary to psychological principles of learning. It provides little or no information about individuals prior to the assignment and teaching, and places too much emphasis upon the test as a terminal point in the process. It makes the test the ultimate goal of learning (which it is not) and fails to provide adequate and optimally placed review.

---

[99] R. Stewart Jones, "Process Testing: An Analysis of Students' Reasons for Choice of Alternatives," *Journal of Educational Research*, Vol. 46, 1953, pp. 525–534.

[100] G. Meyer, "The Effect of Recall and Recognition of the Examination Set in Classroom Situation," *Journal of Educational Psychology*, Vol. 27, 1936, pp. 81–99.

It has been suggested [101] that work revolve around problems and that various skills and parts of the course lead to the solution of these problems. The sequence in this case might well begin with a joint planning session of an hour or so, or even several days, in which students and teacher developed overall objectives. The individual and group work which follows should be pointed toward these objectives. In such cases testing would be only incidental to the major goal of action or problem-solving, and the real testing would become an appraisal of performance—only a part of which would be based upon verbal skills.

No single sequence is appropriate for every case. Buswell points out two extremes which are psychologically undesirable. At one extreme, the subject matter sequence of instruction is so highly compartmentalized that few lateral relationships are seen. At the other, are "radical schools" which let the children decide the curriculum. Neither case results in a desirable coherency of material to be learned.

On the basis of present psychological principles, it would seem that the most desirable sequence of activities would be that which takes account of the individual learner and the eventual goals of the work, somewhat as follows:

| Pretest | Assignments | Study | Evaluation | Relearning and Reteaching | Retesting |
|---|---|---|---|---|---|
| (Diagnosis of Needs and Abilities) | (Including Pupil-Teacher Planning) | (Individual and Group Work) | (Quizzes, Recitation, Performance, Out-of-School Behavior, Self-Evaluation) | (Remedial Work in Area of Weakness) | (Evaluate the Reteaching and Effects of Total Learnings) |

The above schema is not one which should be rigidly followed but it does represent a series of steps which apply to many teaching-learning situations. In rare cases there may be no need for remedial teaching. Furthermore, some teachers may combine two or more of the steps in one general activity or process. For example, assignments may be made individually in connection with the development of the work indicated under the heading of "Study." It appears, however, that although there may be a merger of some of the above steps, the essential ingredients of each exist in all good teaching.

---

[101] G. T. Buswell, "Organization and Sequence of the Curriculum," Chap. XIII in *The Psychology of Learning*, Part II, Forty-First Yearbook of the National Society for the Study of Education, Bloomington, Illinois, Public School Publishing Co., 1942.

## SUMMARY

This chapter has shown that what is learned is acquired more rapidly and retained longer when it has meaningfulness, structure, and interrelatedness—in short, possesses *organization*. Too often students are buried under an avalanche of unrelated or isolated facts—facts which do not appear to the learner to bear a relationship to any of his important goals or problems. Little wonder that forgetting takes place on a vast scale. It is not uncommon for students to forget two-thirds to three-fourths of what they learned within a year after a course is completed.

Teaching must take cognizance of the basic principles of learning if it is to produce permanent and usable learning. The implementation of the principles of organization requires that teachers fit learning activities to what is known about perceptual organization, make instructional materials meaningful to pupils, plan for units of optimal size and scope, distribute learning activities intelligently, and elicit a good deal of student activity.

One may see structure and organization at its best in problem-solving. No great deterioration of learning or drop in retention seems to result when learners engage in activities where the objective is to solve problems rather than to learn facts. Furthermore, increased ability to solve problems should help the student to think critically and creatively and to make better judgments. Problem-solving was shown to be a many-sided process which is capable of being learned. In essence, problem-solving to the teacher should mean helping students choose, study and solve problems through their own discovery in contrast to the popular notion that the teacher should give children "pat" solutions or steps to be memorized.

No one who considers the evidence regarding organization in learning should fail to see the many implications of this evidence for teaching method. Surely questions about how assignments are made, how reviews and tests are carried out, and how various activities are related to each other, must be raised in connection with what is known about the principles of organization. The appraisal of present practices shows that teaching method may be based upon conjecture or belief which, in many cases, is not supported by evidence. For example, such outmoded methods of assignment making as: "Read 30 pages and work problems 6 through 17" still persist in the face of overwhelming evidence against their use.

Finally, organization must be considered as it applies to the students' self-directed activities, particularly their methods of study. At the present time there seem to be all too few programs in which a conscious, well-planned effort is made to teach students how to study. One of the features which most clearly distinguishes good from poor methods of study is the degree to which the pupil learns to plan ahead for his study.

The disorganized pupil is the one who has not yet learned the value of making schedules, and of determining the goals and purposes of study before it begins. Ultimately, one who teaches must, if his influence is to persist, help children attain meaningful and purposeful solutions of their own problems.

### References for Further Study

Anderson, Harold H. (Editor), *Creativity and Its Cultivation*, New York, Harper and Brothers, 1959.

Anderson, R. C. and Ausubel, D. P., *Readings in the Psychology of Cognition*, New York, Holt, Rinehart and Winston, 1965.

Burton, William H., Kimball, Roland B. and Wing, Richard L., *Education for Effective Thinking*, New York, Appleton-Century-Crofts, Inc., 1960.

Clark, Charles H., *Brainstorming*, Garden City, New York, Doubleday & Co., Inc., 1958.

Flavell, John H., *The Developmental Psychology of Jean Piaget*, Princeton, N.J., D. Van Nostrand, Inc., 1963.

Harlow, Harry F., and Harlow, Margaret Kuenne, "Learning to Think," *Scientific American*, Vol. 181, August, 1949, pp. 36–39.

Harper, Robert J. C., *et al.*, *The Cognitive Processes: Readings*, Englewood Cliffs, N.J., Prentice-Hall, 1964.

Harris, C. W. (Editor), *Encyclopedia of Educational Research*, Revised Edition, The Macmillan Company, New York, 1960.
    See the following:
        "Concepts," David H. Russell, pp. 323–333.
        "Higher Mental Processes," David H. Russell, pp. 645–661.
        "Methods of Teaching," G. Max Wingo, pp. 848–861.

Hunt, J. McV., *Intelligence and Experience*, New York, Ronald Press, 1961.

Inhelder, Barbel and Piaget, Jean, *The Growth of Logical Thinking*, New York, Basic Books, Inc., 1958.

Johnson, Donald M., *The Psychology of Thought and Judgment*, New York, Harper and Brothers, 1955.

Lawrence, P. J., "A Study of Cognitive Error," *British Journal of Educational Psychology*, Vol. 27, 1957, pp. 176–189.

National Society for the Study of Education, *Theories of Learning and Instruction*, Part I, 63rd Yearbook, Chicago, The Society, 1964.

Piaget, Jean, *The Child's Conception of the World*, New York, Harcourt Brace, 1929.

Russell, David H., *Children's Thinking*, Boston, Ginn and Company, 1956.

Torrance, E. Paul, *Guilding Creative Talent*, Englewood Cliffs, N.J., Prentice-Hall, 1962.

Vinacke, W. Edgar, *The Psychology of Thinking*, New York, McGraw-Hill, 1952.

Wertheimer, Max, *Productive Thinking*, Revised Edition, New York, Harper and Brothers, 1959.

## Questions, Exercises, and Activities

1. Measures of vocabulary, sentence form, and appraisal of human interest are commonly used as components of readability formulae. What other factors would be important in describing the readability of written material?
2. There is sometimes a confusion between what is meaningful and what is practical, e.g., in general science a teacher might show boys how to repair an electric motor on the grounds that this was a meaningful experience. Differentiate between these terms and comment about the general science teacher's approach.
3. When rote learning is necessary in school, how should it be carried out?
4. Give an example of a misconception you have had (a "boner" you have made) and describe the kind of learning (or lack of it) that led to the misconception.
5. It is easy to see how a science teacher could provide for a variety of classroom experiences, and for multi-sensory experiences. How could these things be managed in a class in rhetoric or history?
6. When a project method—or problem-solving method is used—and children are given some opportunity to select their own projects they may choose ones that are too large for completion. What should the teacher do in such cases?
7. Describe how you would go about teaching the concepts of latitude and longitude to a class of fifth graders, and give the psychological rationale for the things you have suggested.
8. What kinds of problems are most likely to generate creative thinking?
9. Try this problem on some friends: Suppose you had a cork, similar to a spherical cork fishing bobber which was ten feet in diameter. How much would it weigh (an estimate will do)? In analyzing the responses answer these questions:
   a. Why are the estimates so much in error?
   b. Are there any *general* learnings or skills that would help prevent such errors?
10. Plan an assignment for the subject- or grade-level you are preparing to teach, and describe it to your class.
11. Suppose it could be shown that the curve of forgetting for material in a required course you are preparing to teach approximates the forgetting curve shown in this chapter (Figure 26). Give the grounds upon which you would argue for retaining the course in the curriculum.
12. Critically appraise the sequence of classroom activities suggested in this chapter.
13. Select one of the methods or techniques given in one of your educational methods courses, analyze it, and show the psychological rationale for it.
14. Suggest several ways in which conventional forms of recitation could be altered so as better to conform with the material given in this chapter.

# Chapter 10

## The Transfer and Application of Learning

### TRANSFER—THE ULTIMATE GOAL OF TEACHING

The ultimate goal of teaching is to produce desirable changes in behavior which will carry over into new situations. Teachers intend training in English composition to produce better writing, mathematics to make pupils better able to solve problems, and civics to lead to better citizenship. At first glance, the attainment of these aims appears simply a matter of providing sufficient training so that what is learned is remembered. But achievement of goals such as these entails much more. Each new situation which confronts the child contains elements of uniqueness, and requires him to use previous learnings in a new way. The child must not only be able to remember, but also must be able to select from his experience those responses which are appropriate in the learning of new and different ideas and skills. When learning thus carries over into new situations, the resulting improvement, or in some cases the interference which is developed, is known as transfer of learning.

There can be little defense of schooling if it does not transfer. Learning for the sake of learning alone is hardly defensible in a system of universal education. All of learning should, of course, not be judged in terms of its "transfer value." Many skills are learned for their own intrinsic worth,

their immediate value in the child's life, or for recreational purposes. In such cases proficiency in relatively unchanging situations may be a legitimate goal of teaching. However, it is impossible to predict for the pupil in exactly what situations he will use the things he has learned. People who learned to drive automobiles fifteen years ago now have to make adjustments to a changed gear shift location, automatic drives, power steering, and the like. The farmer who once acquired skill in the use of horses has been forced to change to machinery, and the pilot who learned to fly by the feel of the plane has had to learn to use instruments.

### The Meaning of Transfer in Teaching

Transfer of learning exists whenever a previous learning has influence upon the learning or performance of new responses. Thus anything which can be learned may be transferred. A simple case of transfer would be the following:

| A pupil learns | $4 \times 9 = 36$ |
| This should help him learn | $9 \times 4 = 36$ |
| and | $40 \times 90 = 3600$ |

Note that in this simple example there are not only associations and discriminations that children may have been presumed to have learned (the numbers themselves and the meaning of $\times$) but rules, viz., the commutative principle [1] and the rule that the same number of zeros must be added to the product as to the multiplier and multiplicand. Evidence in recent years suggests that the way in which these rules are learned and practiced is important in determining whether or not transfer will take place. In short, having learned these simple operations, there is a question of how well a student will be able to use them in long division or in algebraic manipulations.

These apparently simple feats of transfer, are not always easy for the beginner. It has been found, for example, that many students who learn to do algebra problems involving $x$ and $y$ as unknowns may not be able to solve the same problems when $a$ and $b$ are used for unknowns. A specific check of the effect of changed symbols showed that 28 per cent of a group of college students were unable to square $b_1 + b_2$, but of the same group only 6 per cent failed to square $x + y$ correctly! [2]

The above examples of transfer are of a highly specific nature. Suppose a student comes to enjoy arithmetic greatly. Will such attitudes transfer to algebra and geometry? Or suppose the student learns to solve

---

[1] A principle stating that the order in which the elements of certain operations are given is immaterial, as in arithmetic, $4 \times 9$ is the same as $9 \times 4$.

[2] E. L. Thorndike, "The Effect of Changed Data upon Reasoning," *Journal of Experimental Psychology*, Vol. 5, 1922, pp. 33–38.

problems in geometry. Will he, as a consequence, be more likely to use the methods learned in solving other kinds of problems? Immediately one sees that transfer of learning is inextricably bound up with the broader objectives of education. How well the schools are achieving these broader goals is considered in the next section.

### Appraisal of Present School Practices

Most teaching is done with the implicit assumption that what is taught will be available for future use. But research has shown that this assumption is not always warranted. For one thing, the content of school subjects is all too often outmoded and unrelated to students' interests and needs or social usage. For instance, an analysis of spellers from Grades 2 through 8 has shown that many are filled with spelling words typical of our grandparents' day—words that are rare and difficult and must be studied some years ahead of the infrequent times they will ever be used.[3] Surely analyses of this kind should convince teachers and educators that closer attention be paid to the relation between subject matter and the later use of learned materials.

At all levels of schooling the question of relevance of both materials and methods is an important one. Countless examples could be cited of educational programs that are so far divorced from the present levels of ability of learners and from their interests that there is little possibility of transfer.

Even in educational situations, where there is a relatively direct tie-up between content and application, there may be a lack of transfer. In an English medical college, investigators found frequent examples where medical students well trained in diagnostic techniques made errors in their application. In one instance, a case history was being taken of an elderly gentleman who gave all the indications of being malnourished. A medical student asked him if he were eating a normal diet. The old man said he was. Further questioning by a supervisor revealed that to this patient normal meant what he had for some time been eating, viz., treacle and tea. In another example, X-rays showed a collar button in the esophagus. Since this was at the general location where one would expect to find a collar button if a person were wearing one, the students saw nothing amiss when they examined the X-ray plate of a boy who sometime earlier had swallowed one.

Numerous other examples were cited by the writers, who were instructors at this college.[4] Such diagnostic errors were of sufficient concern to

---

[3] Gertrude Hildreth, "An Evaluation of Spelling Word Lists and Vocabulary Studies," *Elementary School Journal*, Vol. 51, 1951, pp. 254–265.

[4] D. W. James, M. L. Johnson and P. Venning, *Testing for Learnt Skill in Observation and Evaluation of Evidence*, London, Lancet, 1956.

lead to the development of a special seminar whose main features were group discussions which focused upon the processes involved in diagnosis and the source of commonly occurring errors. Following are the reported results for students who took the seminar.

1. They discriminated better between facts and conclusions.
2. They drew fewer false conclusions.
3. They considered more than one solution to a problem.
4. They were less adversely influenced in the solution of a problem by experience with a previous problem; in short, they were more objective and flexible in their behavior.

Besides the lack of functionality, school subjects frequently fail to give proper emphasis to the relationships between various learned materials. When the papers (in courses other than English) of 261 college freshmen were analyzed, it was found that only twelve (5 per cent) submitted papers free of misspellings, and 14 per cent contained a number of incoherent sentences. More revealing than this, however, is the fact that when students were given their own papers and were asked to proofread them, they corrected over one-third of their own misspellings and over one-half their punctuation errors. According to Lange, who conducted this investigation, the majority of these students did not expect to be held to good standards of writing in a subject matter assignment. Even more serious is the fact that many of these freshmen not only admitted a lack of communication skills but expressed a fatalistic attitude and believed nothing could be done about it.[5]

The failure of students to see the relationship between English in English classes and English in other subjects or in general everyday usage can often be accounted for by the failure of teachers to make such relationships apparent and to hold students for the use of information acquired in other courses.

An appraisal of the results of inadequate teaching for transfer might be sought by asking: How much does learning in school carry over to later years? There is evidence on every hand that there is far too little carry-over of school learning to out-of-school life—or to other school subjects for that matter. That this is a problem of long standing is illustrated by the following anecdote:

I was in a certain junior high school last week and the principal of the school told me the following story. One of the seventh-grade pupils took the following problem home to her parents, "Find the product of .08 and ⅛." She came back to the teacher on the Monday following and reported that her father said that the problem could not be done, that it did not

[5] Phil C. Lange, "A Sampling of Composition Errors of College Freshmen in a Course other than English," *Journal of Educational Research*, Vol. 42, 1948, pp. 191–200.

make sense. He had worked on it for over an hour and could not do it, so the following morning he took it to his employer, a man who had earned several million dollars in business ventures. The man toyed with the example for some time and asked to take it to a professor friend of his who taught Spanish at a college nearby. The professor could not do the example either, and returned it saying that as far as he was concerned it was ridiculous. The indignant parent sent a note with the youngster to the teacher asking why his seventh-grade daughter was getting work in mathematics which three intelligent adults could not fathom.[6]

Inadequacies in the effects of schooling upon students at all levels and in nearly all subjects are apparent. These inadequacies are not of recent origin. Impermanence of learning, and lack of carry-over of schooling have always been problems of major importance in education. The balance of this chapter will attempt to trace some of the causes of these problems and offer suggestions for their solution through the application of psychologically sound teaching methods.

### Common Misconceptions about Transfer

There are a number of erroneous notions about how children's learning carries over to subsequent tasks, a common failure to clarify teaching objectives as they relate to transfer, and inadequate understanding of issues due to poorly defined terms. For example, mathematicians on the one hand defend geometry as a most excellent means of teaching reasoning— on the other hand they admit that there may be little carry-over of this ability to non-mathematical fields. Some experiments have shown considerable transfer between foreign language study and English vocabulary, others have found little or no effect, and still others have found an actual decrease in understanding of English vocabulary after foreign language study.[7] As positive transfer is the main objective of teaching, it is essential that teachers avoid misconceptions and lay their teaching plans on a groundwork of good understanding of the ultimate purposes of instruction. Some common erroneous views about transfer of training will now be discussed.

The first and most common error in thinking about transfer is that it takes place through a process of "formal discipline." This outmoded idea of education was based on faculty psychology, a theory that separate elements or powers of the mind such as will, memory, and cognition were trained or sharpened by practice. In this view was the assumption that what was practiced was less important than the difficulty or disciplinary value of what was practiced. Also, there was the notion that learning

---

[6] C. O. Richter, "Readiness in Mathematics," *The Mathematics Teacher*, Vol. 37, 1944, p. 69.

[7] A. R. Mead, "Transfer of Training Again," *Journal of Educational Psychology*, Vol. 37, 1946, pp. 391–397.

should be somewhat "painful" if it were to achieve the best results. Thus the hard memory work in classical languages and difficult problems in mathematics and science were viewed as the most promising media for sharpening the mind. Instead of defending these subjects for their own intrinsic worth, teachers of classics, mathematics, and sciences frequently defended them on the basis of their ability (better than other subjects) to improve the mind. Two comprehensive experimental studies which sought to test this hypothesis (that certain subjects or courses are best able to improve the mind) have found no evidence to support it. The first conducted by Thorndike [8] compared the gains in "thinking ability" made by students studying various combinations of subjects. His conclusion was that the subjects studied were of little apparent importance, especially when the influence of the subject was compared with the initial ability of the students. He believed that the apparent superiority of mathematics and science in producing good thinkers was an artifact caused by the fact that better students *take* these courses. If better students were to study vocational arts and social sciences, these subjects would *appear* to produce the best thinkers.

A more recent study (1945) similar to Thorndike's, but in some ways a better designed experiment, found almost identical results.[9] There was no clear-cut superiority for any particular school subject. Students who took the most courses made the greatest gains, and (as shown in Thorndike's work) the bright students made greater gains than the slow ones. Even though the idea of mental discipline has long since been discredited by dozens of experimental studies,[10] it is still a part of the thinking of some present-day educators and is still used as an argument to justify the inclusion of various subjects in the school curriculum. It is unfortunate that certain subjects such as geometry, Latin, and English grammar have most frequently been targets of attacks. There is little question that such subjects can be a rich source of learning for some pupils, and may be taught so that much that is learned transfers. On the other hand, their defense on the basis of the discredited idea of disciplinary value may lead to unrealistic objectives and methods of teaching which are sterile.[11] (The

---

[8] E. L. Thorndike, "Mental Discipline in High School Studies," *Journal of Educational Psychology*, Vol. 15, 1924, pp. 1–22, 83–98.

[9] A. G. Wesman, "A Study of Transfer of Training from High School Subjects to Intelligence," *Journal of Educational Research*, Vol. 39, 1945, pp. 254–264.

[10] A. R. Mead, *op. cit.*, p. 394.

[11] It is important to distinguish between formal discipline and intellectual development. The former implies that practice alone will sharpen the various elements of the intellect, and its proponents view certain subject matters as having the capacity to effect this sharpening by their intrinsic nature. In contrast, the modern view of intellectual development sees "disciplinary value" coming not from substance but from procedure. See Walter B. Kolesnik, *Mental Discipline in Modern Education*, Madison, The University of Wisconsin Press, 1958.

aforementioned subjects are not singled out as representative of this kind of non-functional teaching, for there is probably not a single subject in our schools which would escape this censure to some degree.) When courses are conceived in terms of the values of transfer and on the basis of their own intrinsic worth, there is a greater likelihood that they will be taught in a manner which will make them useful.

The second misconception is just the opposite of the first, and probably grew up as a reaction against it. This is the notion that nothing transfers from one situation to another except specific facts or definite identities. In the extreme, this point of view leads to a curriculum composed only of materials which are believed immediately useful. Transfer is minimized and subjects are all learned only for immediate values. What are the results of such a program? One author notes that special trade courses (as in the vocational-industrial curricula) may *not* prepare students to shift from one vocation to another or one job to another because students have never learned to see relationships or look for similarities among jobs.[12] These students are unable to adjust to the rapidly changing industrial scene brought about by technological advances.

If this idea of transfer (that is, thinking of transfer in its narrowest sense) were followed, education would become largely rote memorization and skill training—a process almost devoid of understanding, generalization, and problem solving.

A third error which emasculates the effect of teaching nearly as much as the first two, is the notion that transfer of learning is automatic. This view puts the main burden of achieving transfer upon the curriculum builder and neglects the important contribution of teaching method. The arrangement of subject matter into related sequences, plans for common learnings or core curricula, and other curricular plans do not guarantee that children will see relationships apparent to the adults who plan the program. (It is certainly true, of course, that such curricular plans may make more likely the teaching for transfer which is so important a function of school.)

The acquisition of information does not guarantee its utility. Most teachers have experienced the disappointment of seeing pupils learn in school but later fail to apply information in situations which call for its use. A well-worn story in educational circles tells of three college professors who were building a cabin in the north woods, and were unable to start with a square corner because they did not have a square. While they were trying to solve this problem, a farmer riding by, stopped, and when told the difficulty suggested that they measure three feet along one

[12] F. T. Spaulding, *High School and Life*, Report of the Regents' Inquiry Into the Character and Cost of Public Education in the State of New York, New York, McGraw-Hill Book Company, 1939.

side, four feet along the other, and if the distance diagonally across the points measured on the sides was five feet, they would have a square corner. All the professors of course were familiar with the Pythagorean theorem, yet were unable to apply it in a practical way. The reader might pause at this point and consider ways in which this theorem could have been taught in the first place so that it would have been more likely to have been recalled under these circumstances.[13]

Finally, the emphasis which books about learning and psychology have given to the topic of transfer has tended to create the impression that somehow transfer and learning are different. Actually transfer is a part of the learning process. There is indeed such a thing as learning to learn,[14] learning how to secure transfer, and learning how to work. There is no learning which does not involve a part of a person's past experience, and in a sense all retention or remembering is a kind of transfer, because original circumstances of learning are rarely, if ever, duplicated in a new situation. Children should learn to expect change—to have the experience of applying even the simplest learnings in a number of different situations. As it is, many times drill precedes understanding and then teachers attempt to teach transfer as a separate step—something different from the initial learning. Actually learning and transfer are best produced when the learning situation offers a variety of experiences so as to better equip the student with the varieties of applications and changed conditions he will find in other school subjects and in out-of-school life.

## HOW AND IN WHAT WAYS DOES TRANSFER OCCUR?

The most obvious form of transfer is that in which an identity carries over from one situation to another. The following are examples:

*Transfer of an identity when a single response is appropriate to two stimuli:*

Stimulus₁ "Casa" (in Spanish) ⟶
                                    ⟶ Response—House
Stimulus₂ "Casa" (in Portuguese) ⟶

*Negative transfer or interference when one stimulus requires two different responses:*

---

[13] For a way in which this theorem can be taught so as to lead to a good understanding of it see: Max Wertheimer, *Productive Thinking*, Enlarged Edition (Edited by Michael Wertheimer), New York, Harper and Row, 1959.

[14] For a theoretical discussion of this point see J. A. McGeoch and A. L. Irion, *The Psychology of Human Learning*, New York, Longmans, Green and Co., 1952, pp. 306–309, and for an excellent description of a series of experimental results that show how "learning to learn" may occur see Harry F. Harlow and Margaret Kuenne Harlow, "Learning to Think," *Scientific American*, Vol. 181, August, 1949, pp. 36–39.

Stimulus "Mas" (spoken) → Response 1 (Portuguese) But
Stimulus "Mas" (spoken) → Response 2 (Spanish) More

This kind of transfer which is a result of stimulus similarity (or identities between two stimuli) was first treated systematically by Thorndike,[15] whose theory held that a function is changed by another only insofar as the two functions have identical or common elements of substance or procedure. Thorndike and his co-worker Woodworth began a series of investigations of the problem of transfer at the beginning of the century. They tested persons in one function, such as estimating the size of geometric figures, then gave practice in another function, such as estimating areas of a quite different magnitude. Finally, they retested them in the first function to see how much improvement was brought about by the intervening practice. They found that the amount of improvement in estimating size was inversely proportional to the degree of change in size and/or shape between the function initially tested and that which was practiced. They concluded that practice did not lead to a general change in such things as discrimination, attention, quickness, and the like, but that it improved these functions with respect to particular sorts of data.[16]

One unfortunate result of Thorndike's early work was an overly pessimistic view of the amount of general gains in mental functioning that could derive from specific learnings. Later work in a score of fields such as concept development, problem solving, mathematical learnings and the like (see generalizations 5, 7, 10, 11, and 13 in Table 13) give reason for being more optimistic. In many of the studies shown in Table 13 there were in fact gains of a non-specific sort which point to the acquisition of new strategies and new forms of mental functioning as a result of experience. Illustrative is the work of Anderson (1965, in Table 13), in which he was able to teach advanced problem solving skills to first graders. Also relevant is further work of Anderson and of Maltzman (Table 13), who demonstrated that original or creative responses could be increased in children through training techniques that reinforced responses high in originality.

### Stimulus Generalization

One may see quite clearly in the Portuguese-Spanish example how an identity transfers (with negative or positive effect) from one situation to

---

[15] E. L. Thorndike, *The Principles of Teaching*, New York, A. G. Seiler, 1906.

[16] E. L. Thorndike and R. S. Woodworth, "The Influence of Improvement in One Mental Function upon the Efficiency of Other Functions," *Psychological Review*, Vol. 8, 1901, pp. 247–261, 384–395, 553–564. More recently a thorough review of the experimental evidence about transfer in the kinds of functions studied by Thorndike and Woodworth has been made by Eleanor J. Gibson in "Improvement in Perceptual Judgments as a Function of Controlled Practice," *Psychological Bulletin*, Vol. 50, 1953, pp. 401–431.

another. In this case the only change is in the situation. But how about the case when the actual stimuli themselves are markedly changed?

One term applied to this kind of transfer is *stimulus generalization*. The young child who learns "dada," at first calls all men "dada." He says ball for his own particular ball and later applies this term to numerous other elastic objects regardless of changes in color, shape, and size. Stimulus generalization is not limited to the development of young children. Numerous studies have shown the same phenomenon in older children and adults.

A child who has become conditioned to fear one reading book, or one text, may show similar reactions when confronted with other books or texts. Likewise the dislike of one teacher may transfer to another teacher in a different classroom. In such cases youngsters overgeneralize from specific cases. They have not learned to make necessary discriminations.

### Transfer and the Learning of Principles

Closely akin to stimulus generalization is the transfer of a general principle from one situation to another. Even before children are aware of it, they begin to generalize or make rules which they apply in several situations. Without ever being told a rule, they learn the generalization that most words form plurals by adding "s," hence "mouses" and "feets" are not uncommon in the speech of young children. Also the fact that "ed" makes the past tense of verbs, leads to such verbs as "runned" and "doed."

One of the earliest experiments (1907) which showed how principles could influence subsequent behavior was that of Judd, who used the principle of refraction of light when it travels from one medium into another.[17] One group of boys was taught this principle, while a second group received no such instruction. Both groups were then given a trial in shooting bows and arrows at underwater targets. Although both groups did equally well when the targets were at a fixed depth, the instructed group excelled the other when the targets were moved to a new depth. The learning of the principle had made them more adaptable under changed conditions.[18] More recently a similar experiment (using air-rifles instead of bows and arrows) obtained like results.[19]

What are the implications of this kind of transfer for teachers? Clearly a general principle has much broader possibilities for use than detailed facts. Also, as shown in the previous chapter, these kinds of learning are more enduring. It would seem then that a major emphasis of schooling

---

[17] When a beam of light passes obliquely from one medium into another it is bent at the surface separating the two.

[18] C. H. Judd, "The Relation of Special Training to General Intelligence," *Educational Review*, Vol. 36, 1908, pp. 28–42.

[19] G. Hendrickson and W. H. Schroeder, "Transfer of Training in Learning to Hit a Submerged Target," *Journal of Educational Psychology*, Vol. 32, 1941, pp. 205–213.

should be upon principles and their use in a number of situations, rather than upon memorization of such details as may be quickly forgotten.

### Set and Transfer

The way in which a person perceives a new situation is a function of previous perceptual learning. He has a certain expectation which conditions the way he sees a situation and the way he responds to it.

The effect of set has been demonstrated as follows. One group of 80 subjects was told that most of the words in a word list they were to see would be the names of animals and birds. Another group of equal size was told that the words had reference to travel or transportation. The following words and pseudo words were then projected tachistoscopically for both groups.

WORD LIST

| | |
|---|---|
| 1. horse | 6. monkey |
| 2. baggage | 7. parrot |
| 3. chack | 8. berth |
| 4. sael | 9. dack |
| 5. whorl | 10. pangion |

The group which had been led to expect names of animals and birds gave 513 "animal-bird" responses such as "seal" for item Number 4 and "duck" for Number 9, while the other group gave only 112 such responses. On the other hand, the group which anticipated items dealing with travel and transportation responded more often (594 to 84) with such terms as "sail" for Number 4, and "dock" for Number 9. Only 4 per cent of the total responses to "unreal" words were seen as what they actually were.

Sometime later, the groups described above were tested with a new kind of list in an attempt to find out if the previously established set would transfer to a new situation. The list (a series of skeleton words), and the expected responses were as follows:

| SKELETON WORDS | EXPECTED ANIMAL-BIRD RESPONSES | EXPECTED TRAVEL-TRANSPORTATION RESPONSES |
|---|---|---|
| ___ oat | goat | boat |
| s ___ ___ l | seal | sail |
| ___ ___ ___ sel | weasel | vessel |

When the groups were compared, the first one, which had been given an "animal-bird" set gave three times as many "animal-bird" responses as the second group, while the second group completed the skeleton words with "travel-transportation" responses four times as often as the first group. Clearly, the kind of set which had been given in the first instruc-

tion was an important determiner of responses, and did carry over or transfer even under altered conditions.[20]

How transfer of set may operate in such complex processes as working problems was shown in an experiment conducted by Luchins.[21] Subjects were given a series of problems such as: You have three vessels with capacities as follows, 21 pints, 127 pints, 3 pints. Show how you would obtain 100 pints of water. The problems were given in this form:

$$A = 21 \quad B = 127 \quad C = 3 \quad \text{Obtain } 100$$

The method of solving this problem is $B - A - 2C$ or, $127 - 21 - 6 = 100$. A series of six such problems were given, all of which could be solved with the formula $B - A - 2C$. Then followed the seventh and eighth problems:

|              | A  | B  | C | Obtain |
|--------------|----|----|---|--------|
| 7th Problem  | 23 | 49 | 3 | 20     |
| 8th Problem  | 15 | 39 | 3 | 18     |

These could be solved either by the same formula as used in the first six problems *or* by the much simpler means of subtracting C from A and adding C to A in the second case. Of eleven graduate students and college instructors, including several Ph.D.'s, not one used the shorter method. They had formed what Luchins calls an *"Einstellung"*—a set, which interfered with the easiest solution, and which carried over to new problems. Perhaps the significant thing for school teachers to know about this experiment is that on further experimentation it was found that the simple injunction, "Don't be blind," served to prevent the formation of this set in many of the cases. In other words, there is evidence here (also from other laboratory work) that a simple direction outlining possible difficulties or alerting students to correct expectations may facilitate the discovery of the correct solution to problems.

### Methods of Work and Transfer

Students who have received practice and guidance in methods of work and study report that such training in one course helps them in other courses. Research dealing with both elementary and high school pupils

---

[20] E. M. Sipola, "A Study of Some Effects of Preparatory Set," *Psychological Monographs*, Vol. 46, 1935, pp. 28–37.

[21] A. S. Luchins, "Mechanization in Problem Solving: The Effect of Einstellung," *Psychological Monographs*, Vol. 54, No. 248, 1942, pp. 1–4. For a fuller description of Luchins' experimental work see A. S. Luchins and Edith H. Luchins, "Rigidity of Behavior, A Variational Approach to the Effect of Einstellung," *Studies in Psychology*, No. 3, University of Oregon Monographs, Eugene, 1959.

showed that time spent in training children how to outline was rewarded with gains in achievement not only in the specific subject in which training was given but also in other subjects as well.[22] Any kind of "how to study" course is predicated on the belief that such training will generalize or transfer to other course material.

As early as 1915 Coover[23] spoke of habits of work and the control of attention as processes which could transfer from one situation to another and since that time numerous research studies have supported this belief.[24] A study which may illustrate how methods transfer was one in which an attempt was made to teach students how to memorize. Three groups of students were given six pretests of memorization. Following the initial testing the groups were treated as follows:

> Group A......No Training (Control)
> Group B......Routine Practice in Memorizing
> Group C......Practice in Memorizing *plus* Instruction
> in the Techniques of Memorizing

Later tests of memorization showed that Group C was clearly superior to the other groups. Practice alone (as Group B had) was not enough to bring a significant improvement.[25]

The pupil who learns a skill in one context should be able to apply it in many contexts. Thus a pupil who has learned in his English class the skills of outlining, note taking, reading, and participation in class discussion should be able to use these proficiencies in all of his courses. These skills are more apt to become generalized when:

1. The teacher uses examples from various subjects and materials as vehicles for the illustration and practice of methods and skills. (The English teacher might ask a student to use his history notes as material to be outlined.)
2. Students are asked (or ask each other) to explain why one method or skill is better than another. In other words, students are led to understand the rationale for various methods of work and study.
3. The class as a whole, with the teacher's guidance, develops criteria for appraising various methods and skills.

---

[22] Rachel Salisbury, "Some Effects of Training in Outlining," *The English Journal* (College Edition), Vol. 24, 1935, pp. 111–116; M. N. Woodring and C. W. Flemming, *Directing Study of High School Pupils*, New York, Teachers College, Columbia University, 1935.

[23] J. E. Coover, "Formal Discipline from the Standpoint of Experimental Psychology," *Psychological Monographs*, Vol. 20, 1916, No. 87.

[24] See J. A. McGeoch and A. L. Irion, *op. cit.*, pp. 330–332.

[25] H. Woodrow, "The Effect of Type of Training Upon Transference," *Journal of Educational Psychology*, Vol. 18, 1927, pp. 159–172.

4. "Situational tests," which call for application of methods, give direction to students' work, and bring more attention to method than tests which deal with facts. A part of the testing program might well involve exercises in which students were asked to point out relationships between solving a problem in geometry and one in social science or physics.
5. Teachers work together toward this important common goal. The English teacher should work with others to determine whether writing skills show improvement in classes other than English.

### Attitudes and Transfer [26]

A complex form of carry-over from previous experiences is the effect of previously formed attitudes upon new learning. The child who has had unpleasant emotional experiences in an English class will not approach the next class in English with the same attitudes as one whose experiences have been gratifying.

This kind of transfer is a special case of transfer of set or expectancy, but in this case perception of *self* plays an important part. Two children of equal mental potential may differ greatly in their ability to solve problems because one has self-confidence and aggressiveness, the other is shy and has a tendency to withdraw from difficult problems. Obviously their previous experiences with work and problems have conditioned the way in which they perform. Children carry to new problems not only skills, principles, and knowledge, but also attitudes and personality traits. These are truly transferable elements and among the most important.

An indirect but neat piece of evidence on how attitudes transfer may be seen in the results of a test in which directions are given not to guess. When this is done, a large part of the measurement is not of knowledge alone, but of personality traits. Students who have had a good share of success and have self-confidence are likely to leave many fewer blank spaces on their answer sheets than those whose experiences with tests and with problems in general have been marked by a lack of success.

Since a person's attitude about himself (his self-concept) is quite likely to become overgeneralized, it is extremely important that youngsters obtain ideas of positive self-reference; that they see difficulties as problems to be solved rather than troubles which call for retreat. Such attitudes are products of successful and gratifying learning experiences. Insofar as such experiences are within the control of the teacher, pupils should receive due praise for their achievement especially when they solve problems under their own initiative.

---

[26] For examples of experimental evidence regarding transfer of attitudes refer back to Table 12, Chapter 8.

## TEACHING FOR TRANSFER

Good teaching always involves teaching for transfer. It is another way of saying that good teachers have a definite objective of making learned material a functioning part of the youngster's response system. It is thus essential that teachers think through their own subject matter and study the generalizations, relationships, and methods which may transfer. The extent to which students learn *how* to transfer will depend on how well teachers can lead students to see the similarities between the subject matter and its applications.

Following is a list of suggestions which should form the basis of teaching for transfer:

1. Have clear-cut objectives. Decide what students should be able to *do* as a result of their work.
2. Study the course content to find what it contains that is applicable to other school subjects and to out-of-school life.
3. Select instructional materials which are best suited to the job of making relationships apparent.
4. Let students know when to expect transfer, what kinds to expect, and the benefits which it can bring them.
5. Use methods of teaching (e.g., problem-solving, discussion, leading questions) which will facilitate transfer.
6. Provide practice in transfer. It is not enough to point out relationships. Pupils should be given practice in finding relationships on their own. Tests of application, guided discussion, and actual class projects ought to provide this kind of experience.
7. Concentrate on the process of learning as well as upon products. Do not be satisfied with a right answer or solution, but probe to find out why a certain answer was given, and discuss with the class the steps which led to their answers.

### Setting the Stage for Transfer

Sometimes opportunities for transfer are lost because teachers do not alert students to look for relationships and to see how material which is being learned can be of future usefulness. One study has shown that the simple expedient of telling students that previous learning might be helpful in other situations increased the amount of measured transfer as much as 16 per cent.[27]

It has also been noted that the kind of test directions which are given

---

[27] M. W. Dorsey and L. T. Hopkins, "The Influence of Attitude Upon Transfer," *Journal of Educational Psychology*, Vol. 21, 1930, pp. 410–417.

may significantly affect the amount of learning and transfer which occurs. One group of students in educational psychology was given a short multiple-choice practice test with the directions "See how the principles involved in these questions might apply in various teaching situations." Another group took the same test without these directions. Both groups made equivalent scores on this first test. Later, the groups were given a second multiple-choice test which called for applications of the principles contained in the previous test. The group which had received the directions made significantly better scores, even though the tests, testing procedures, and discussions following the tests were almost identical.[28]

Effects of expectancy and set have already been shown to have an effect upon transfer. Perhaps equally important is the development of a cognitive structure which will help to avoid negative transfer and proactive inhibition. Ausubel [29] has demonstrated that in the learning of new, meaningful, verbal material interference may be reduced by presenting "advance organizers," e.g., short bits of relevant reading material ahead of a difficult passage so as to provide a means of helping students better discriminate among elements that are easily confused. He found for example, that when American students had read material about Buddhism, these new concepts after a relatively short time merged with their already existing concepts from our Judeo-Christian tradition.

As a practical step, teachers whose students have revealed a tendency to confuse certain concepts might do well to include a brief introduction to regular instruction, which points out salient features that will aid in the discrimination and consequent avoidance of error. Thus a physics teacher who had noticed that students frequently confuse the concepts of force and energy would do well at the beginning to present a brief introduction which points out some of the important differences between the two.

In the last chapter it was shown that the way in which assignments are developed probably has a great influence upon the kind of studying which students do. Teachers who help pupils develop specific questions prior to a reading assignment can expect not only better results in the sections of the reading covered by the questions, but also a transfer of this "seeking-while-reading" activity to other sections of the assignment.

As a result of a series of recent experiments, Rothkopf (Table 13) maintains that the use of test questions in a given area of learning (even ones not related directly to the specific material being read) produce desirable

---

[28] R. S. Jones, *Integration of Instructional with Self-Scoring Measuring Procedures*, Unpublished Ph.D. Dissertation, Columbus, Ohio State University, 1950.
[29] David P. Ausubel, *The Psychology of Meaningful Verbal Learning*, New York, Grune and Stratton, 1963.

instructive and attentional effects. He calls the effects thus attained *mathemagenic* behavior, the behavior that "gives birth to learning."

Programs in curricular improvement as well as experimental studies of children's learning find the cleverly contrived situation for stimulating curiosity a necessary precondition for the improvements they seek. This "stage setting" often becomes an integral part of the newly derived curriculum or experimental method. The reader will recall from Chapter 9, the description of one episode taken from the physics course designed by the Physical Science Study Committee which showed how a laboratory demonstration combined with audio-visual aids created the mental atmosphere for learning and transfer.

The blackboard drawing in Figure 27 exemplifies the way in which one teacher has used a problem situation as a vehicle for eliciting pupil activity. This illustration is one of many such situations that have been used in

**Figure 27.** Stimulating Curiosity as an Aid to Understanding.

A Study of Children's Inquiry Techniques.[30] They are used to set the stage for drawing children out and training them to ask intelligent ques-

[30] J. Richard Suchman, "Inquiry Training in the Elementary School," *The Science Teacher*, Vol. 27, November 1960, pp. 42–47.

tions, an attempt to develop an ability that will transfer to other situations.

### Emphasizing Relationships and Understanding

Teachers who stress understanding tend to stimulate learning of a useful and an enduring nature. On the other hand, emphasis upon facts and memorization of rules and procedures which are not fully understood by pupils, may result in a superficial lip service which has neither permanence nor utility. A study of the learning of mathematics of three thousand pupils reveals that youngsters learn what teachers stress as important in the classroom. The school which glorifies abstract computation in mathematics is likely to produce pupils who excel in this respect, but who may or may not understand what they are doing or be able to use the computations in changing situations. The author of the study just cited concludes that too great a dependence upon formalized paper and pencil problems robs the student of many of the opportunities for transfer which exist in other kinds of mathematical experiences.[31]

In those instances where teaching is specifically designed to emphasize transfer by stressing applications, relationships, and methods, the amount of understanding and usable knowledge increases. Dozens of experimental studies bear out this conclusion.[32] In studies of the transfer value of foreign languages, for example, it has been discovered that the greatest effect on English vocabulary occurs when relationships between English words and their Latin, French, or Spanish roots are shown as a planned part of the teaching procedure. A comparison of four methods of teaching to improve English vocabulary resulted in greater gains for the groups who learned English with word study, or Latin with a study of derivatives, than for the groups taught English and Latin in the conventional manner.[33]

Even when people know principles and understand them they may not be alert to the possibilities of using them. The following problem first used by Szekely[34] and later by three American psychologists[35] in an experiment on teaching method should illustrate this point.

---

[31] B. A. Sueltz, "Mathematical Understandings and Judgments Retained by College Freshmen," *The Mathematics Teacher*, Vol. 44, 1951, pp. 13–19.

[32] A. R. Mead, *op. cit.*, pp. 394–397; and T. G. Andrews, L. J. Cronbach, and Peter Sandiford, "Transfer of Training" in W. S. Monroe (Editor) *Encyclopedia of Educational Research*, New York, The Macmillan Company, 1950, pp. 1483–1489.

[33] R. I. Haskell, "A Statistical Study of the Comparative Results Produced by Teaching Derivation in the Ninth-Grade Latin Classes and in the Ninth-Grade English Classes of Non-Latin Pupils in Four Philadelphia High Schools, Ph.D. Thesis," University of Pennsylvania, 1923.

[34] L. Szekely, "Productive Processes in Learning and Thinking," *Acta Psychologica*, Vol. 7, 1950, pp. 388–407.

[35] Irving Maltzman, Eugene Eisman, and Lloyd O. Brooks, "Some Relationships Between Methods of Instruction, Personality Variables, and Problem Solving Behavior," *Journal of Educational Psychology*, Vol. 47, pp. 71–78.

Suppose you have two metal spheres which are identical in appearance, size, and weight, but one is made of a heavier metal than the other. How could you distinguish between the two without changing them in any way or subjecting them to chemical analysis?

Even though physics students understand the principle of conservation of momentum, they are unlikely to see that rolling the balls down an inclined plane would be an easy and precise means of determining which ball was made of the heavier metal. The quality of mind that permits the extension of a law, generalization, or principle to its many applications is one that we do not yet know how fully to develop. This chapter gives some evidence that bears on this important goal, but much more research is needed. The following section of the chapter describes one modern approach to teaching that may yield results in the hoped-for direction.

### Directing Discovery

Experiments have indicated that the way in which a child learns a generalization will affect the probability of his recognizing a chance to use it. As Hendrix [36] has shown, "persons who know that six times eight is forty-eight, will often count to forty-eight to find the number of chairs in a room containing six rows of eight chairs each." The question of how best to teach a generalization is of utmost importance to the teacher. Evidence shows that one important element may be discovery. One investigator compared methods in which the teacher gave the class a mathematical generalization and then gave several examples of application with methods in which the generalization was a product of the student's own discovery. The latter method proved much more effective in producing transfer.[37] The reader will recall Luchins' [38] method of teaching geometric area to youngsters. In this investigation pupils derived their own principles and formulae and gave evidence of a great deal more understanding than those taught in the usual way. Presumably this understanding makes much more likely the recognition of opportunities to use information or to adapt it to new situations.

Students actually resent too much supervision. It is only natural that teachers should want to help children, but in the very act of helping they may actually be robbing them of the chance to learn how to solve problems and use information.

More recent experimental studies have confirmed the results described by Hendrix and Luchins. These latter studies have dealt with such diverse

---

[36] G. Hendrix, "A New Clue to Transfer of Training," *The Elementary School Journal,* Vol. 48, 1947, pp. 197–208.

[37] *Ibid.*

[38] A. S. Luchins and Edith H. Luchins, "A Structural Approach to the Teaching of the Concept of Area in Intuitive Geometry," *Journal of Educational Research,* Vol. 40, 1947, pp. 528–533.

tasks as decoding,[39] concept formation,[40] and deriving arithmetical principles.[41] All have shown gains when the subjects' activity is guaranteed by their own discovery. Moreover, the experimental findings have been supported by a number of broader investigations of classroom method wherein classes in geometry,[42] mechanical drawing,[43] and industrial education [44] that learned by the "directed discovery" method showed a superiority on transfer tasks to classes in which the teacher gave the rules, facts, and principles.

Exactly what function, psychologically, is served by students' discovery is not at this time clear. Undoubtedly one of the major gains is an increased enthusiasm for the work. Teachers of the University of Illinois Committee on School Mathematics who have used the discovery method in much of their work have all noted the heightened motivation when students work things out for themselves, in fact a major aim of the project is that the study of mathematics be an adventure. Pupils should be encouraged to make their own mathematical discoveries. Some teachers believe the discovery process itself is so exhilarating that it becomes its own motive for academic work. It is likely that zest for work, self-confidence and ego-involvement may all be increased by the discovery process.

Aside from a greater zest for school work, the act of discovering something seems to assure a better understanding. This is not to say that students understand something only when they can manipulate objects as in a science laboratory, or do experimental work on their own. Many insights come from reading and listening. It is probable that the brighter students can make discoveries through verbal media better than can their less bright peers.

Finally, it seems likely that having once discovered something for himself the person achieves a "set" to discover other things. In short, he is applying the scientific method to his own thought processes. If the latter achievement is realized, there are indeed broad values to be attained by courses that allow students to find out things for themselves.

---

[39] G. M. Haselrud and Shirley Meyers, "The Transfer Value of Given and Individually Derived Principles," *Journal of Educational Psychology*, Vol. 49, 1958, pp. 293–298.

[40] Gabriel M. DellaPiana, *Two Experimental Feedback Procedures: A Comparison of Their Effects on the Learning of Concepts*, Doctoral Thesis, Urbana, University of Illinois, 1956.

[41] Bert Y. Kersh, "The Adequacy of Meaning as an Explanation for the Superiority of Learning by Independent Discovery," *Journal of Educational Psychology*, Vol. 49, 1958, pp. 282–292.

[42] Eugene D. Nichols, *Comparison of Two Approaches to the Teaching of Selected Topics*, Doctoral Thesis, Urbana, University of Illinois, 1956.

[43] John D. Rowlett, "An Experimental Comparison of Teaching Methods in Mechanical Drawing," *Industrial Education Teacher*, Vol. 20, September–October, 1960, pp. 14–15.

[44] Willis Eugene Ray, *An Experimental Comparison of Direct and Detailed and Directed Discovery Methods of Teaching Micrometer Principles and Skills*, Doctoral Thesis, Urbana, University of Illinois, 1957.

The teacher who wishes to apply the idea of discovery in teaching might find useful the familiar pedagogical dictum, "Provide the student with an opportunity for active exploration of new situations and content." This simple dictum is violated more often than it is followed. Even in psychology courses (where professors presumably know more about learning than most other teachers) the main emphasis is often upon lectures, discussions, and paper and pencil tests. In a delightful commentary on this state of affairs, which he describes as "teaching in the ivory tower with rarely a step outside," Pressey bemoans the absence of laboratory work, field trips, and direct observation of people. He asks:

> Why not instead come down and open the door, watch what students do outside class, see what psychologists are doing in the wide world, and even venture off campus occasionally to mix with the folks on main street.[45]

However learning comes about, whether deductively or inductively, whether by rule and example given by the teacher or discovered by the student, the process of learning is not satisfactorily completed until the learner has some chance to practice what he has learned. This kind of discovery by the learner of the value of what he has learned is of highest importance in producing long-range behavioral changes.

Transfer is one of the oldest areas of continuous concern to psychologists and educators. Finding a group of reliable generalizations resulting from research on this subject poses considerable difficulty. Different semantic systems are employed by persons of different disciplines, and differences in experimental designs, subjects and materials make comparisons of results extremely difficult. Some valid conclusions, however, now seem relatively clear. Table 13 provides thirteen statements about transfer. These statements together with the studies cited to support them will furnish the educator some guidelines for his development of instructional materials and teaching methods.

## SUMMARY

Transfer of learning is not a new idea to most persons who read this book. It must have occurred to everyone who has given serious thought to teaching, that ultimately class work is designed to equip pupils to solve effectively the problems of living and to make them happier and more effective citizens. These goals are apparent.

Too often, however, teachers and pupils alike neglect to think through the significance of present activities in terms of future usefulness or applicability. One reason for this is that, although everyone shares the above

---

[45] Sidney L. Pressey, "Teaching in the Ivory Tower with Rarely a Step Outside," *Psychological Bulletin*, Vol. 52, 1955, pp. 343–344.

## TABLE 13

### Experimentally Supported Generalizations about Transfer and the Application of Learning

| | |
|---|---|
| **1.** Clear identification of instructional goals and their formulation in behavioral terms is a first prerequisite in devising instructional methods to produce effective transfer. | Mager and McCann (1962) * Wittrock (1962) Silberman (1964) McNeil (1966) |
| **2.** Learners' expectations that transfer will occur and the possession of a set that material may generalize and be useful in new situations increases the likelihood that transfer will occur. | Dorsey and Hopkins (1930) Lange (1948) Jones (1950) |
| **3.** Selective attention and the perception of what is salient can be brought about by proper organization of instructional materials and activities. (An example would be the pointing out of significant cues in a learning situation.) | Sipola (1935) Luchins (1942) Klare, et al. (1955) Judson, et al. (1956) Lumsdaine, et al. (1961) Wittrock and Keisler (1965) |
| **4.** Other things being equal, the learner who makes some form of overt response during the learning experience (particularly when dealing with novel and difficult material) will fare better on transfer tasks than the one who merely listens, reads or watches. | Gates (1917) Gagne and Smith (1962) Krumboltz (1964) Holland (1965) Rothkopf (1965) |
| **5.** Students can learn to apply an abstract principle to a specific task. (They may or may not do so depending upon their age, the complexity of the principle or task, and the nature of instruction.) | Judd (1908) Hendrickson and Schroeder (1941) |
| **6.** Proactive facilitation is enhanced when the first task is thoroughly learned and well understood. In transfer terms, material A must be well in hand before it can be expected to influence material B. | Katona (1940) Underwood (1951) Atwater (1953) Adams (1954) |
| **7.** Variety in the tasks related to the development of a concept, a principle, or a method promises better transfer effects than attempts to elicit generalizations from a single example. | Duncan (1958) Morrisett and Hovland (1959) Gagne and Bassler (1963) Anderson (1965) Stern (1965) Traub (1966) |
| **8.** Transfer of principles, rules, and strategies for using them (as in problem solving), may be increased by actively involving the learner in the discovery of those principles and rules. | Hendrix (1947) Luchins and Luchins (1947) University of Illinois Doctoral Studies (1956–57) Craig (1956) Haselrud and Meyers (1958) Kersh (1962) Wittrock (1963) |

* See end of this chapter for complete bibliographic data on these studies.

## TABLE 13 (Continued)

| | |
|---|---|
| **9.** Calling attention to discriminable elements in different materials to be learned by such means as "advance organizers" can reduce proactive effects (the confusing interaction of one material upon another). | Ausubel (1963) |
| **10.** "Learning how to learn" implies that there are strategies and procedures which have effects broader than those required in a specific category of tasks, and that these broader effects can be learned by direct instruction in appropriate rules, and by opportunities for practice in a variety of situations (see generalization 8 above). | Woodrow (1927) <br> Ward (1937) <br> Salisbury (1935) <br> Harlow (1949) |
| **11.** Making students aware of the common failings of others in applying information, showing the likely genesis of such errors, and providing opportunity for a *discussion* of them may reduce applicational failures and increase transfer. | James, *et al.* (1956) <br> Sassenrath and Garverick (1965) |
| **12.** Just as other responses can be strengthened by reinforcement, so can the responses of making generalizations, problem solving, and creative behavior be reinforced. | Maltzman (1960) <br> Anderson and Anderson (1963) |
| **13.** Some learnings such as making perceptual judgments seem to remain quite specific to the area of training. In these cases, proficiency in a particular skill is attained through direct practice of that skill and not by practicing some general class of skills of which the target skill is a part. | Thorndike (1901) <br> Gibson (1953) |

stated desires about transfer, attempts to reach it are blocked by common, erroneous notions about it. Some of these erroneous notions are: (1) that training *per se* strengthens an ability, (2) that only that which is immediately useful should be taught, (3) that transfer is automatic, in other words, that once a child learns, the learning will lead to transfer, and (4) that transfer and learning are separable elements.

Transfer may occur when there is a similarity between two activities either in substance or procedure. Anything which can be learned can be transferred including such things as attitudes, a feeling of self-confidence, sets, and interests, as well as skills, facts, and other items generally thought of as constituting school work. Transfer may be quite specific, as when elements of one learning situation occur in identical or similar form

in another. In such cases the effects may be either positive or negative, that is, a previous learning may either facilitate a new learning, or may cause interference. Also transfer may be general, in that a given learning such as a principle, a set, or method has influence upon any number of later learning situations.

Teaching for transfer requires that the objectives of schooling be clearly defined, that teachers study content and method to find interrelationships among materials and the applicability to other situations or learned skills, and that the teaching method be such that students are given practice in transfer. Children should learn to expect to see a relationship between present learning and future situations. They should also learn not only to search for such relationships, but also to probe into problems to find reasons for the facts and principles which they are asked to believe. Out of the habit of critical appraisal youngsters will develop the ability to bring past experiences to bear upon new problems and new learning situations.

### References for Further Study (General)

Anderson, Richard C., "Educational Psychology," in *Annual Review of Psychology*, Vol. 18, Stanford University Press, 1967.

Bugelski, B. R., *The Psychology of Learning Applied to Teaching*, Indianapolis, Bobbs-Merrill, 1964.

Ellis, Henry C., *The Transfer of Learning*, New York, The Macmillan Company, 1965.

Ferguson, George A., "On Transfer and the Abilities of Man," *Canadian Journal of Psychology*, Vol. 10, 1956, pp. 121–131.

Gagne, Robert M., *The Conditions of Learning*, New York, Holt, Rinehart and Winston, Inc., 1965.

Grose, Robert F., and Birney, Robert C. (Editors), *Transfer of Learning: an Enduring Problem in Psychology*, New York, D. Van Nostrand Co., Inc., 1963.

Kolesnik, Walter B., *Mental Discipline in Modern Education*, Madison, The University of Wisconsin Press, 1958.

Orata, P. T., "Recent Research Studies on Transfer of Training with Implications for the Curriculum, Guidance, and Personnel Work," *Journal of Educational Research*, Vol. 35, 1941, pp. 81–101.

Osgood, C. E., "The Similarity Paradox in Human Learning: A Resolution," *Psychological Review*, Vol. 56, 1949, pp. 132–143.

Schulz, Rudolph, "Problem Solving Behavior and Transfer," *Harvard Educational Review*, Vol. 30, 1960, pp. FV–GG.

Shulman, Lee S., and Keislar, Evan R. (Editors), *Learning by Discovery; A Critical Appraisal*, Chicago, Rand McNally & Company, 1966.

Stephens, J. M., "Transfer of Learning," in *Encyclopedia of Educational Research*, Revised Edition, New York, The Macmillan Company, 1960, pp. 1535–1543.

Symonds, Percival M., "What Education Has to Learn from Psychology, VII. Transfer and Formal Discipline," *Teachers College Record*, Vol. 61, 1959, pp. 30–45.

Travers, Robert M. W., *Essentials of Learning*, Second Edition, New York, The Macmillan Company, 1967.

## Detailed Bibliography of Experimental Studies Cited in Table 13

Adams, J. A., "Multiple Versus Single Problem Training in Human Problem Solving." *Journal of Experimental Psychology*, 1954, Vol. 48, pp. 15–19.

Anderson, Richard C. and Richard M. Anderson, "Transfer of Originality Training," *Journal of Educational Psychology*, Vol. 54, 1963, pp. 300–304.

Anderson, Richard C., "Can First Graders Learn an Advanced Problem Solving Skill?" *Journal of Educational Psychology*, Vol. 56, 1965, pp. 283–294.

Atwater, S. K., "Proactive Inhibition and Associative Facilitation as Affected by Degree of Prior Learning," *Journal of Experimental Psychology*, Vol. 46, 1953, pp. 400–404.

Ausubel, David P., *The Psychology of Meaningful Verbal Learning*, New York, Grune and Stratton, 1963.

Craig, R. C., "Directed Versus Independent Discovery of Established Relations," *Journal of Educational Psychology*, Vol. 47, 1956, pp. 223–234.

Dorsey, M. W. and Hopkins, L. T., "The Influence of Attitude Upon Transfer," *Journal of Educational Psychology*, Vol. 21, 1930, pp. 410–417.

Duncan, C. P., "Transfer after Training with Single Versus Multiple Tasks," *Journal of Experimental Psychology*, Vol. 55, 1958, pp. 63–72.

Gagne, R. M. and O. C. Bassler, "Study of Retention of Some Topics of Elementary Nonmetric Geometry," *Journal of Educational Psychology*, Vol. 54, 1963, pp. 123–131.

Gagne, R. M. and E. C. Smith, Jr., "A Study of the Effects of Verbalizing During Problem Solving," *Journal of Experimental Psychology*, Vol. 63, 1962, pp. 12–18.

Gates, A. I., "Recitation as a Factor in Memorizing," *Archives of Psychology*, Vol. 6, 1917.

Gibson, Eleanor, J., "Improvement in Perceptual Judgments as a Function of Controlled Practice," *Psychological Bulletin*, Vol. 50, 1953, pp. 401–431.

Harlow, H. F., "The Formation of Learning Sets," *Psychological Review*, Vol. 56, 1949, pp. 51–65.

Haselrud, G. M. and Meyers, Shirley, "The Transfer Value of Given and Derived Principles," *Journal of Educational Psychology*, Vol. 49, 1958, pp. 293–298.

Hendrickson, Gordon and Schroeder, W. H., "Transfer of Training in Learning to Hit a Submerged Target," *Journal of Educational Psychology*, Vol. 32, 1941, pp. 205–213.

Hendrix, Gertrude, "A New Clue to Transfer of Training," *The Elementary School Journal*, Vol. 48, 1947, pp. 197–208.

Holland, J. G., "Response Contingencies in Teaching Machine Programs," *Journal of Programmed Instruction*, Vol. 3, 1965, pp. 1–8.

James, D. W., Johnson, M. L., and Venning, P., *Testing for Learnt Skill in Observation and Evaluation of Evidence*, London, Lancet, 1956.

Jones, R. S., "Integration of Instructional with Self-Scoring Measuring Procedures," Unpublished Ph.D. Dissertation, Columbus, Ohio State University, 1950.

Judd, Charles H., "The Relation of Special to General Intelligence," *Educational Review*, Vol. 36, 1908, pp. 28–42.

Judson, A. J., Cofer, C. N., and Gelfand, S., "Reasoning as an Associative Process, II, Direction in Problem Solving as a Function of Prior Reinforcement of Relevant Responses," *Psychological Reports*, Vol. 2, 1956, pp. 501–507.

Katona, George, *Organizing and Memorizing*, New York, Columbia University Press, 1940.

Kersh, B. Y., "The Motivating Effect of Learning by Directed Discovery," *Journal of Educational Psychology*, Vol. 53, 1962, pp. 65–71.

Klare, G. R., Mabry, J. E. and Gustafson, L. M., "The Relationship of Patterning (underlining) to Immediate Retention and to Acceptability of Technical Material," *Journal of Applied Psychology*, Vol. 39, 1955, pp. 40–42.

Krumboltz, J. D., "The Nature and Importance of the Required Response in Programmed Instruction," *American Educational Research Journal*, Vol. 1, 1964, pp. 203–209.

Lange, Phil C., "A Sampling of Composition Errors of College Freshmen in a Course Other than English," *Journal of Educational Psychology*, Vol. 42, 1948, pp. 191–200.

Luchins, A. S., "Mechanization in Problem Solving: The Effects of *Einstellung*," *Psychological Monographs*, Vol. 54, No. 248, 1942, pp. 1–4.

Luchins, A. S., and Luchins, Edith H., "A Structural Approach to the Teaching of the Concept of Area in Intuitive Geometry," *Journal of Educational Research*, Vol. 40, 1947, pp. 528–533.

Lumsdaine, A. A., Sulzer, R. L., and Kopstein, F. F., "The Effect of Animation Cues and Repetition of Examples on Learning from an Instructional Film." In *Student Responses in Programmed Instruction*, A. A. Lumsdaine (Editor), National Academy of Science, Washington, D.C., 1961.

Mager, R. F., and McCann, J., *Learner Controlled Instruction*, Palo Alto, California, Varian Associates, 1962.

Maltzman, Irving, "On the Training of Originality," *Psychological Review*, Vol. 67, 1960, pp. 229–242.

McNeil, J. D., "Concomitants of Using Behavioral Objectives in the Assessment of Teacher Effectiveness," Paper given at annual convention, American Educational Research Association, Chicago, 1966.

Morrisett, Lloyd Jr., and Hovland, Carl I., "A Comparison of Three Varieties of Training in Human Problem Solving," *Journal of Experimental Psychology*, Vol. 58, 1959, pp. 52–55.

Rothkopf, E. Z., "Some Theoretical and Experimental Approaches to Problems

in Written Instruction," In *Learning and the Educational Process*, J. Krumboltz (Editor), Chicago, Rand McNally, 1965.

Salisbury, Rachel, "Some Effects of Training in Outlining," *The English Journal*, Vol. 24, 1935, pp. 111–116.

Sassenrath, J. M., and Garverick, C. M., "Effects of Differential Feedback from Examinations on Retention and Transfer," *Journal of Educational Psychology*, Vol. 56, 1965, pp. 259–263.

Silberman, H. F., *Experimental Analysis of a Beginning Reading Skill*, Santa Monica, California, Systems Development Corporation, 1964.

Sipola, E. M., "A Study of Some Effects of Preparatory Set," *Psychological Monographs*, Vol. 46, 1935, pp. 28–37.

Stern, C., "Labeling and Variety in Concept Identification with Young Children," *Journal of Educational Psychology*, Vol. 56, 1965, pp. 235–240.

Thorndike, E. L., and Woodworth, R. S., "The Influence of Improvement of One Mental Function Upon the Efficiency of Other Functions," *Psychological Review*, Vol. 8, 1901, pp. 247–261, 384–395, 553–564.

Traub, R. E., "Importance of Problem Heterogeneity to Programed Instruction," *Journal of Educational Psychology*, Vol. 57, 1966, pp. 54–60.

Underwood, B. J., "Associative Transfer in Verbal Learning as a Function of Response Similarity and Degree of First List Learning," *Journal of Experimental Psychology*, Vol. 42, 1951, pp. 44–53.

University of Illinois Doctoral Dissertations as follows: E. D. Nicholas, 1956; Willis Ray, 1957; John D. Rowlett, 1960; Laurence Brown, 1962; Herbert Wills, 1967.

Ward, L. B., "Reminiscence and Rote Learning," *Psychological Monographs*, Vol. 49, No. 220, 1937.

Wittrock, M. C., "Set Applied to Student Teaching," *Journal of Educational Psychology*, Vol. 53, 1962, pp. 175–180.

Wittrock, M. C., "Verbal Stimuli in Concept Formation: Learning by Discovery," *Journal of Educational Psychology*, Vol. 54, 1963, pp. 183–190.

Wittrock, M. C., and Keisler, E. R., "Verbal Cues in the Transfer of Concepts," *Journal of Educational Psychology*, Vol. 56, 1965, pp. 16–21.

Woodrow, Herbert, "The Effect of Type of Training upon Transference," *Journal of Educational Psychology*, Vol. 18, 1927, pp. 159–172.

## Questions, Exercises, and Activities

1. Give an example of a learning situation in which both positive and negative transfer effects are operating.
2. Why is it difficult to differentiate transfer and retention, and to separate both from the application of what has been learned?
3. A child multiplies $2 \times 10$, $3 \times 10$, and so on, and determines that adding a zero to any whole number is the equivalent of multiplying by 10. Is this an example of transfer of learning? Give the arguments, for and against giving a pupil a series of such problems until he himself discovers the generalization as against telling him the rule.

4. In the previous chapter the term proactive inhibition was used. What is the difference between it and negative transfer?

5. What do you see about your own college training that reflects some of the misconceptions about transfer that were stated in this chapter?

6. What does teaching for transfer imply about the kind of teachers that are needed?

7. How do attitudes toward self, the self-concept, influence transfer of learning?

8. How would one determine in a given learning task whether the net transfer effect was positive or negative?

9. Discovery of principles and generalizations by pupils apparently promotes a significantly greater amount of transfer. Why?

10. The phrase "teaching for understanding" is sometimes glibly used without specifications of operations involved. Specify the operations necessary for the attainment of this kind of teaching, and the methods needed to ascertain whether or not it has been attained.

11. Design an experiment that could be used to determine the transfer effect (if any) that has resulted from having high school students engage in a series of six "brainstorming" sessions in one of their classes.

12. Study Table 13 carefully. Select the five generalizations regarding transfer of training which you believe to be of the highest value in managing the teaching process. Explain and defend your selection.

# Chapter 11

# The Social Psychology
# of Learning
# and Teaching

Teachers probably spend about 90 per cent of their classroom time working with groups. Yet, traditionally, little if any of their formal training is devoted to the understanding of groups. In this area, sometimes called group dynamics, there is probably more discrepancy between the requirements of the teacher's work and his training than in any other. The social psychologist, who studies the nature and operation of groups, has much to offer the teacher, for he has formulated laws and principles about human relationships, group interactions, and their products. The findings of social psychology (and related experimental applications in the classroom) are crucial for the instructor who wishes to promote the academic efficiency, happiness, and adjustment of pupils. Teachers may learn the principles and techniques which help in discovering and improving social interaction and social influences, particularly those within the classroom. This chapter will present a view of principles and research which bear upon this subject.

Paramount significance must be attached to social learnings when we consider that the most crucial problems of the world today revolve around interpersonal relations, and not around conquering the physical environment. Education in leadership and in working with others must assume a much more prominent role.

## THE IMPORTANCE OF SOCIAL
## CLIMATE IN SCHOOLING

The social climate in a classroom is based largely on the quality of the interpersonal relationships which exist there. These relationships are crucially important for a variety of reasons. They significantly affect the amount and kind of subject matter which is learned. Stormy, sullen, or passive emotional climates have dampening effects upon content learnings. These restrictive effects, unfortunately, are not limited to the kind and quality of current learnings. They tend to have continuing and pervasive effects on future learnings. Stimulating interpersonal relations not only promote desirable current content learnings but they also condition the student in ways that encourage continued systematic content learnings in the future.

Concomitant or collateral learnings are significantly affected by the social climate of the classroom. These learnings frequently represent the great covert or unrecognized agenda in the classroom. The English teacher thinks he is teaching "appreciation of literature" when actually his style of classroom leadership may be teaching a dislike of literature. The mathematics instructor knows he is teaching algebra when actually the meaningless (to the students), boring routine the students are compelled to go through each day results in a thorough job of teaching youngsters to hate mathematics. It is true the English teacher is making the learners know something about some plots and characters, while the mathematics teacher is requiring some familiarity with figures. However, the most significant learnings may be the development of a strong dislike for literature, or for mathematics, an aversion that may be so well learned that it will steer the student away from English or mathematics for the rest of his life. If a social climate does not build up a continuing desire for more and more contact with the subject matter field being studied it would have to be judged as having very limited and short-term values.

An intensive study of a single boy's day from the time he got up in the morning until he went to bed at night showed that about a fourth of the 712 episodes in his day occurred in the classroom. Of the 166 school room episodes, 70 per cent were marked by an interaction in some way with one or more persons.[1] Clearly an overwhelming amount of a child's total school experience involves social contacts with other pupils—contacts which produce many kinds of social learning and many and diverse influences upon his developing personality. Adverse social influences may manifest themselves in maladjustment, school failure, and unhappiness. A

---

[1] H. F. Wright, R. G. Barker, J. Nall, and P. Schoggen, "Toward a Psychological Ecology of the Classroom," *Journal of Educational Research*, Vol. 45, 1951, pp. 187–200.

major factor causing children to drop out of school is that many are unable to achieve a feeling of belonging to the group.[2] Still further evidence of the importance of social factors in schooling may be found in an appraisal of maladjusted students. In one such appraisal, the investigators found that the single major cause of students' difficulties was lack of social acceptance.[3]

Prior social experience may also have an influence upon various forms of cognitive learning. Persons who have learned to be authoritarian in their dealings with others tend to experience more difficulty in mastering material with a humanitarian content than persons with a more democratic orientation,[4] and persons who have learned to have social confidence seem to be more creative than those without such confidence.[5]

Social climate has been demonstrated to have significant effects on attitudes and values. Research suggests that these influences may be more crucial than changes in cognitive abilities and that even with gifted pupils an intensive program devoted almost exclusively to intellectual excellence may breed resentment and discouragement.[6] In following sections of this chapter, it is the intention to show how teacher perceptions, teacher-pupil relationships, interrelationships among pupils, the school's staff relationships, and other factors determine the social climate of the school, and how these factors influence learning.

When one looks at the whole school, instead of just at the classroom, the complexity of the social forces at work are even further magnified. Note in Figure 28 the schematic portrayal of some of the reciprocal social forces at work in a school when both internal relationships and those with other elements of the community are included.

## TEACHER PERCEPTIONS AND INTERPERSONAL RELATIONS

### Self-Perceptions and Interpersonal Relations

The understanding of one's self is possibly the most crucial of all understandings. Combs [7] has pointed out, "Perceptual psychology indicates that

---

[2] J. A. Lanier, "A Guidance-Faculty Study of Student Withdrawals," *Journal of Educational Research*, Vol. 43, 1949, pp. 205–212.

[3] S. D. Loomis and A. W. Green, "The Pattern of Mental Conflict in a Typical State University," *Journal of Abnormal and Social Psychology*, Vol. 42, 1947, pp. 342–355.

[4] A. F. Neel, "The Relationship of Authoritarian Personality to Learning: F Scales Combined to Classroom Performance," *Journal of Educational Psychology*, Vol. 50, 1959, pp. 195–199.

[5] L. G. Rivlin, "Creativity and the Self-Attitudes and Sociability of High School Students," *Journal of Educational Psychology*, Vol. 50, 1959, pp. 147–152.

[6] J. J. Gallagher, "The Influence of a Special School on Cognitive Style and Attitudes of Gifted Students," Unpublished Study, 1965.

[7] A. W. Combs, "The Personal Approach to Good Teaching," *Educational Leadership*, Vol. 21, March, 1964, pp. 369–377, 399.

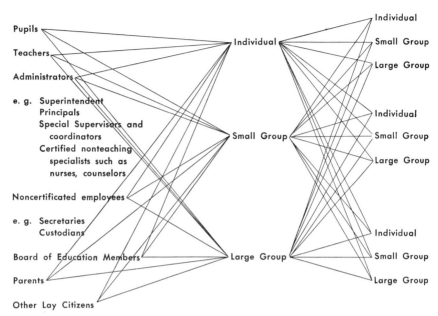

**Figure 28.** Some Educational and Social Group Interrelations. (From R. N. Bush, *The Teacher-Pupil Relationship*, Englewood Cliffs, N.J., Prentice-Hall, Inc.)

the behavior of the individual at any moment is a function of how he sees the situation and himself. . . . The behavior of a teacher, like that of everyone else, is a function of his concepts of self." The teacher's success in this basic area of interpersonal relations can be improved by examining and re-examining certain important issues the teacher may appropriately raise with himself:

1. Do I perceive my success as being closely tied up with the success of others? More specifically, do I see my professional success as being largely determined by the success of the pupils with whom I work? In art, authorship, or research the lone wolf may be very successful. However, it is very difficult to see how a teacher's success can be divorced from that of his students. The teacher who is smug and self-satisfied with "his high standards" when over 25 per cent of his students fail would not seem to meet the criterion suggested here.

2. Do I visualize myself as a crystallized, completed person or as an intellectually and behaviorally improving person? The former type of individual is likely to be so "mature" that his ideas are outdated and his intellectual outlook is backward. The active, professionally growing person, regardless of chronological age, not only will be critically examining new

events, but will also be an active learner who is challenged by the quantity and diversity of what he does not know, such as the infinite complexities of young people and their relationships with their peers and with adults. The teacher who perceives himself as one who has completed his learning and who sees his job as one of "dishing it out" is bound to slip backward. One cannot stand still. He who is not learning professionally is going to be deteriorating professionally.

Carl Rogers [8] suggests that the continuous becoming of an individual must include his willingness to be a "process that is ever changing." This becoming continues throughout the lifespan. Some mistakes will be perceived as an inevitable part of the learning process. The learning person is one who can take a disappointing situation and learn something useful from it.

3. Do I cultivate a flexible self-assurance in myself? After an extensive study of teachers with contrasting success records, Olander and Klagle [9] listed emotional maturity first among the four best predictive measures of success. It has been shown that teachers with an "integrative" pattern of conduct show significantly more spontaneity, initiative, voluntary social contributions, acts of problem solving, and fewer negative attributes, such as conflict with others and boredom.[10] The need for developing flexible self-assurance is very understandable, since the typical working day for teachers is more than nine hours, and more than half of this time the teacher is responsible for leading a dynamic working situation in a group of 20 to 40 active young people.[11] Myers [12] has described flexible self-assurance in the following fashion:

> The replacement of fears and anxieties by self-assurance which can accept good times and bad and yet remain intact gives one knowledge that the self-image can shift if the occasion demands and incorporate the shift into the changing perception of what it means to become. Teachers who have this flexible self-assurance which allows them to change to meet the new and ever changing classroom challenges, can help children achieve self-assurance.

---

[8] "What It Means to Become a Person," in C. E. Moustakes (Editor), *The Self*, New York, Harper, 1956.

[9] H. T. Olander and H. M. Klagle, "Differences in Personal and Professional Characteristics of a Selected Group of Elementary Teachers with Contrasting Success Records," *Educational Administration and Supervision*, 45, July, 1959, pp. 191–195.

[10] C. C. Anderson, and S. M. Hunka, "Teacher Evaluation, Some Problems and a Proposal," *Harvard Educational Review*, 33, Winter 1963, p. 73.

[11] NEA Research Bulletin, "Teacher Time Devoted to School Duties," *Education Digest*, Vol. 28, February, 1963, pp. 43–45.

[12] "Becoming: For Child and Teacher an Ever-Changing Self-Image," by Kent E. Myers. From *Childhood Education*, September 1964, Vol. 41, No. 1. Reprinted by permission of the Association for Childhood Education International, 3615 Wisconsin Avenue, N.W., Washington, D.C.

4. Do I perceive myself as a person who not only tolerates diversity of point of view and procedure but even welcomes it? Am I comfortable when two students disagree on a subject appropriate for class discussion or, even more crucial, when a student takes issue with me? Lack of appropriate perception toward diversity may be shown by irritation when controversial issues are discussed. Lack of tolerance for diversity of opinion may also be reflected in a desire to give quickly "the answer" in a discussion, rather than encourage the clash of differing perspectives and the probable accompanying sharpening of intellectual abilities.

With desirable perspective the teacher will encourage an atmosphere where each student will not be afraid of being labeled foolish if he proposes a creative or offbeat idea, even if it is extreme.

The teacher with a favorable perspective toward himself and diversity will avoid such expressions as: "The only way to teach _____ is _____." "The only good text in my field is _____." "The only way to solve the crisis in southeast Asia is _____." The traditions of democracy and the healthy search for the truth are not promoted by dogmatic assertions which reveal an intolerance for stimulating speculation and an honest search for the truth.

5. Do I see myself as a person able to discuss my own personal and emotional problems? Do I accept and even seek criticism as a part of my personal and professional development?

As the teacher looks inward upon himself he inevitably sees areas of doubt and uncertainty in his search for meanings and values. A comprehensive study by Jersild suggests that excessive personal tension may appear "in disproportionate resentment, competitiveness, discouragement, efforts to impress or placate, to play the game and play it safe." [13] The study further showed that most teachers when given the opportunity found discussion of their anxieties and doubts a very useful venture. Jersild's interpretation is this: [14]

> Facing the issue of anxiety meant, to them, a way of sharing a human situation with intimate personal meaning. The discussion of anxiety was a discussion of something that to them was *real*, even if painful. It was something that involved them personally, instead of telling them, as so many discussions in education do, how to do something to somebody else. It penetrated to some degree the wall of isolation that keeps people emotionally separate from one another.

### Self-Evaluation and Teacher Perceptions of Pupils

The preceding section has emphasized that the teacher's self-perception is strongly influential in determining his behavior. The teacher's needs,

---

[13] A. T. Jersild, *When Teachers Face Themselves*, New York, Bureau of Publications, Teachers College, Columbia University, 1955, p. 9.

[14] *Ibid.*, p. 64.

attitudes, tensions, and anxieties not only strongly condition his self-perceptions but also influence his perceptions of his pupils. Clarification and better understanding on the part of the teacher of his assumptions and perspectives with respect to his pupils are likely to decrease undesirable biases and distortions which would have adverse effects upon the teacher's leadership of learners. In this section we are concerned with issues that the teacher may appropriately raise with himself in better understanding his perceptions of his pupils.[15]

1. Am I sensitive to the private worlds of my students, particularly as these relate to me? In my interactions with them do I accept their perceptions, feelings, attitudes, beliefs, and understandings as extremely important? These issues are particularly significant to the teacher when a pupil's perceptions are at variance with his. Myers [16] suggests, "Teachers must be open to complete self-evaluations, for they must see themselves through children's eyes to evaluate the 'self' the children see. Children's evaluation is often an eye-opener for teachers who perceive themselves only through their own senses. . . . The critical examination of self is a difficult task, as self acceptance must be achieved."

The teacher should be aware that his complex perception of pupils and the related ongoing interaction of him with them will be conditioned by a number of processes which have been revealed by careful experimentation in social psychology. According to Secord and Bachman [17] these include (a) "the tendency to see persons as unchanging entities," (b) "the tendency to see the cause of a person's actions as lying in him rather than in the situation," (c) "the coloring of perceptions by favorable or unfavorable evaluations of the stimulus person," and (d) "the placing of persons in ready-made categories associated with sets of personal attributes." Knowing that these things happen can alert the teacher to prospective difficulties in relations with pupils, such as the danger of stereotyping as indicated by (d) above.

2. Am I primarily *person oriented* rather than thing or event oriented? A teacher's training all too frequently is almost exclusively tied in with things, such as history or mathematics. The current emphasis on things and events is usually accompanied in teacher training by a relatively small number of contacts with pupils of the age with which the teacher will later be working. Thus, it is very easy to get into the habit of giving excessive weight to things and events and insufficient weight to pupils and their perceptions.

---

[15] For a number of these issues the authors are indebted to Arthur W. Combs, "The Personal Approach to Good Teaching," *Educational Leadership*, Vol. 21, March, 1964, pp. 369–377, 399.

[16] *Ibid.*, p. 3.

[17] P. Secord and C. Bachman, *Social Psychology*, New York: McGraw-Hill Book Co., 1964, p. 90.

Not only is the good teacher person oriented but he likes persons. Keliher [18] states it this way: "He is interested in them (children), is intrigued by their way of doing things, likes to watch them grow in mind and body, enjoys their emerging accomplishments. This teacher knows about the rough edges of growth—that boys and girls need help and guidance. . . ."

In Ryans' six-year study,[19] which involved 100 separate research projects and over 6,000 teachers, he concluded that three of the key characteristics that differentiated between good and not so good teachers were: (a) the good teachers had attitudes favorable to pupils; (b) they enjoyed pupil relationships; and (c) they were generous in their appraisal of the behavior and motives of other persons.

3. Am I *meanings and significance* oriented rather than exclusively facts oriented? This question implies the need to learn more about the interpretations and meanings that pupils attach to some of the factual learnings. It suggests a need for the teacher to learn more about the perceptual experiences of his students, about why their perceptions may lead them to reject an assignment, about why the youngsters may believe that most of what they find in their texts is "phony." The growing teacher is concerned with how things seem to the pupils, for their ideas may turn out to be radically different from his own. This difference, if unperceived by the instructor, may seriously interfere with learning.

4. In my contacts with a pupil do I characteristically look for causes of his difficulties on which I can help him, rather than shrugging off his behavior with statements such as: "Look at his mixed-up family, what can you expect?", "His parents are divorced, he has no father, his mother works, you can't hope for much," or "He doesn't even know when to come in out of the rain"?

Much more constructive questions are ones like these: Why is the text I am using inappropriate for this pupil? Which reading material would be better for him? How might I modify the nature of my assignments, by giving optional ones, so that the pupil will perceive the study to be of value to him? I have perceived the pupil as "failing." In what respects am I as the classroom leader "failing"?

5. Do I regard each pupil as being capable? The traditional concept that each pupil in a particular class should be able to do "the work" of that class is an unfortunate legacy. It is a social vestige that prevents many teachers from dealing effectively with individual differences in varied goals, assignments, use of resources, and class procedures. When we really accept individual differences, we will recognize that the below average pupil

---

[18] A. V. Keliher, "Environment for Learning," *Education Digest*, Vol. 28, February 1963, pp. 12–15.

[19] D. G. Ryans, "Some Relationships Between Pupil Behavior and Certain Teacher Characteristics," *Journal of Educational Psychology*, Vol. 52, 1961, pp. 82–91.

can do as well *in terms of his abilities* as can the above average student.

Secord and Bachman [20] have concluded that "persons exhibit a general tendency to assume that others are similar to themselves." If a teacher denigrates his pupils or colleagues, there is a rather strong suggestion that he is unsure of his own abilities.

6. Does the personality I have developed encourage a love for learning? Possibly the greatest weakness in our schools today resides in our inability to do an effective job in instilling a love of learning in our pupils. This suggests that each teacher has the responsibility to study each aspect of his approaches to teaching and attempt to determine which of his behaviors are promoting a long-time interest in teaching and which, even though they are getting immediate results, are killing the desire to learn after the teacher is no longer around.

Two incidents reported by Hughes [21] illustrate contrary approaches: "A third grade child read to his class about dinosaurs, pronouncing the words, 'tyrannosaurus' and 'brontasaurus' without hesitation." After this feat the only response the teacher gave was, "You left out an 'and.'"

Contrast that incident with the second one: "One morning Charles clomped into Sister Teresa's second-grade, leaving a trail of large daubs of mud. He brought a bird with a broken wing held tenderly in his hand. After the bird's wing was attended to and the bird placed safely in the cage, Sister Teresa said, 'Charles, I know you are worried about the bird today but tomorrow you will take the mud off your shoes before you come into the classroom.'" The situational and perspective understanding illustrated here can contribute much to the fostering of a love for learning more about the great unknown.

### Teacher Perceptions of Differences and Similarities in Students

For the teacher to deal effectively with students he needs to have an understanding of various dimensions on which they are likely to differ and ones on which similarities may be expected. A significant study by Douvan and Adelson [22] suggest one type of background information which can be most helpful to the teacher.

Douvan and Adelson found, for example, that the adolescent crisis for boys and girls differs in almost every regard. They differ in the nature and

---

[20] *Ibid.*, p. 91.

[21] Marie M. Hughes, "Teacher Behavior and Concept of Self." From *Childhood Education*, September, 1964, Vol. 41, No. 1. Reprinted by permission of the Association for Childhood Education International, 3615 Wisconsin Avenue, N.W., Washington, D.C.

[22] Elizabeth Douvan and Joseph Adelson, *The Adolescent Experience*, New York, John Wiley and Sons, 1966.

sequence of developmental tasks and in the solutions available. Table 14 gives in capsule form the chief contrasts between boys and girls.

Other significant findings from Douvan and Adelson are suggested in the paragraphs following this table.

### TABLE 14
**Contrasts between Normative Responses of Girls and Boys in Adolescence
(Applies primarily to the large middle majority) ***

| Boys | Girls |
|---|---|
| Tend to focus on vocational future and their style is all business—concrete, crystallized, tied to reality if not always realistic. | Girls focus on the interpersonal aspects of future life—on marriage and roles of wife and mother. Steps toward goals are less concrete than boys! |
| Generally the jobs boys choose represent modest advances over their fathers' positions and are jobs with which the boys have had some personal contact. | Less concerned with real skills than boys. More concerned with social and interpersonal reality than boys. Job interests revolve around expressing feminine interests and getting a husband. |
| Boys without clear vocational plans are likely to show a current pattern of personal maladjustment. | Girls who specifically reject a feminine future are troubled adolescents. |
| Mobility aspiration is no idle dream but concrete and realistic in the light of his talent and opportunities. | Present and future more bridged with fantasy than with concrete plans. Steps toward goals ambiguous since they largely depend on "the man she marries." |
| Urge to be free is almost exclusively a masculine stirring and relates to integration of future concept, to upward mobility aspirations, to general achievement strivings, to current adolescent adjustment. | Mobility aspirations are less careful than boys; less cautioned by assessment of opportunity, more dreamlike. |
| Tend to hold allegiance to a peer group(s) as such, see group as offering support and as having authority. | To age 18 little press for independence is shown. Attitudes toward parental control do not relate very strongly to the nature or style of that control, are not tied to a peer group as such, nor sensitized to the pressure of "the gang" (except possibly in taste). More attracted to two-person friendships. The loyalty of best friend is sought and needed. Group is used to find individual friendships. Girls more highly developed in intimacy of friendships than boys. The interpersonal is a central area of growth for girls. A measure of interpersonal development is best predictor of ego integration in girls. |
| Masculine identity focuses about the capacity to handle and master nonsocial reality, to design and win for oneself an independent area of work which fits one's individual talents and taste and permits achievement of at least some central personal goals. Identity for the boy is a matter of individuating internal bases for action and defending these against domination by others. | |
| Areas of achievement, autonomy, authority, and control focus and express boys' major concerns and psychological growth. | Feminine identity is a process of finding and defining the internal and individual through attachments to others. The object relations—friendship, dating, popularity, and the understanding and management of interpersonal crisis hold the key to adolescent growth and integration for the girl. |

* Adapted from Douvan, Elizabeth and Adelson, Joseph, *The Adolescent Experience*, New York, John Wiley & Sons, 1966.

Those youngsters who are making adequate adolescent adaptations have a strong future orientation. A faulty time perspective characterizes those who are socially isolated.

The contrast between the products of democratic and authoritarian home background is striking. Democratic families allow much autonomy, include the child in important decisions affecting him, and tend to use psychological and verbal discipline. This social atmosphere tends to produce adolescents who are unusually self-reliant, poised, and effective. They are free to criticize and disagree with parents, but characteristically have a warm companionship with them.

Authoritarian parents set rules without consulting children, allow little autonomy, and tend to use physical techniques for enforcing discipline. These controls produce adolescents who are on the surface compliant; beneath the surface they are rebellious and impulsive. They tend to have externalized morality, to define morals as what one can get away with, and to lack effectiveness and poise.

By and large adolescent interests and activities, family patterns and moves toward independence are much the same in all regions of the United States and in all social classes. Among standard background variables, only religion yielded differences that are largely consistent and interesting.

## TEACHER BEHAVIOR AND LEADERSHIP ROLES

### Teacher Behavior Reflects Interpersonal Personality

Since a teacher's personality is reflected in his behavior, one method of examining his personality is to determine what his behavior reflects. That such behavior also affects children's behavior is illustrated in a study by Kounin and Gump [23] in which they selected three pairs of punitive versus nonpunitive first-grade teachers in three elementary schools. Each of the 174 children in these six teachers' classrooms was interviewed individually about what he thought was "the worst thing to do in school." He was also asked why he thought these misconducts were bad. The researchers concluded that, as compared with children who have nonpunitive teachers, children who have punitive teachers "manifest more aggression in their misconducts, are more unsettled and conflicted about misconduct in school, are less concerned with learning and school-unique values, show some, but not consistent indications of a reduction in rationality pertaining to school misconduct."

---

[23] J. S. Kounin and P. V. Gump, "The Comparative Influence of Punitive and Nonpunitive Teachers upon Children's Concepts," *Journal of Educational Psychology*, 52, February 1961, pp. 44–49.

Some indication of the relationships between pupil and teacher classroom behavior may be drawn from studies by Ryans.[24] He found that

> . . . for elementary school classes, *high* positive relationships were noted between observers' assessments of "productive pupil behavior" (e.g., assessments presumed to reflect pupil alertness, participation, confidence, responsibility, and self-control, initiating behavior, etc.) and observers' assessments of previously identified patterns of teacher behavior which seem to refer to understanding, friendly classroom behavior; organized, businesslike classroom behavior; and stimulating, original classroom behavior.
>
> For secondary school classes, *low* positive relationships appeared to obtain between productive pupil behavior and the above-named categories of teacher behavior, with a tendency for the stimulating, original teacher-classroom behavior pattern to show a slightly higher correlation with pupil behavior than the understanding, friendly or the organized, businesslike teacher behavior patterns.

It should be emphasized that while relationships have been established in such researches as Ryans' there is not yet proof of direct causal or producer-product relationships.

An additional type of semantic analysis is provided by Ryans in his teacher characteristics study.[25] One of the twenty-five dimensions of teacher behavior which he analyzed was the "harsh-kindly" dimension, and the following descriptions are provided by Ryans: [26]

| HARSH | KINDLY |
|---|---|
| 1. Hypercritical, faultfinding. | 1. Went out of way to be pleasant and/or to help pupils; friendly. |
| 2. Cross; curt. | |
| 3. Depreciated pupil's efforts; was sarcastic. | 2. Gave pupil a deserved compliment. |
| 4. Scolded a great deal. | 3. Found good things in pupils to call attention to. |
| 5. Lost temper. | |
| 6. Used threats. | 4. Seemed to show sincere concern for a pupil's personal problem. |
| 7. Permitted pupils to laugh at mistakes of others. | 5. Showed affection without being demonstrative. |
| | 6. Disengaged self from a pupil without bluntness. |

Although Ryans' listings and descriptions were made primarily for other purposes, they can be helpful to the individual teacher in self-evaluation of aspects of behavior that may significantly affect teacher-pupil relations.

Since Ryans' teacher characteristics study is the most impressive study

---

[24] Ryans, *op. cit.*

[25] D. G. Ryans, *Characteristics of Teachers* (Washington, D.C.: American Council on Education, 1960).

[26] *Ibid.*, p. 88.

of this type, the notable differences between the teachers rated high and those rated low are of significance. These have been summarized as follows:

There was a general tendency for high rated teachers to: be extremely generous in appraisals of the behavior and motives of other persons; possess strong interest in reading and literary affairs; be interested in music, painting, and the arts in general; participate in social groups; enjoy pupil relationships; prefer nondirective (permissive) classroom procedures; manifest superior verbal intelligence; and be superior with respect to emotional adjustment. On the other hand, low rated teachers tended generally to: be restrictive and critical in their appraisals of other persons; prefer activities which did not involve close personal contacts; express less favorable opinions of pupils; manifest less high verbal intelligence; show less satisfactory emotional adjustment; and represent older age groups.[27]

### Teachers' Leadership Roles

The kinds of roles which the teacher assumes have a profound effect upon the learning situation in the classroom. The way a particular pupil is regarded by his classmates is affected by the teacher's behavior toward him.[28] The high school teacher with undesirable teacher-pupil relations, who creates an atmosphere of fear and tension, and thinks primarily in terms of the *subject matter to be covered* rather than in terms of what the pupils need, feel, know, and can do, is more likely to fail pupils than an instructor who is able to maintain harmonious relations with his pupils and who is interested in pupils as pupils.[29] Teaching, in most situations, demands that the teacher assume a role of leadership, and it is through an analysis of the teacher's function as a leader that one sees most clearly how he affects the group.

THE AUTOCRATIC, LAISSEZ-FAIRE, AND DEMOCRATIC ROLES. What happens to a classroom when different kinds of leadership are imposed? Bearing upon this question is a study (one of the first major studies of group dynamics) in which the experimenter set out deliberately to produce two contrasting social climates.[30] In the study, there were two clubs of ten-year-olds who were engaged in making theatrical masks. In one club the leader operated as an autocrat (imposed his goals on the group, frustrated the group's goals and ideas, and was not objective in his comments about

---

[27] *Ibid.*, pp. 397–398.

[28] N. A. Flanders and S. Havumaki, "The Effect of Teacher-Pupil Contacts Involving Praise on the Sociometric Choices of Students," *Journal of Educational Psychology*, Vol. 51, 1960, pp. 65–68.

[29] P. D. Rocchio and N. C. Kearney, "Teacher-Pupil Attitudes as Related to Non-promotion of Secondary School Pupils," *Educational and Psychological Measurement*, Vol. 16, 1960, pp. 244–252.

[30] R. Lippitt, "Field Theory and Experiment in Social Psychology: Autocratic and Democratic Group Atmospheres," *American Journal of Sociology*, Vol. 45, 1939, pp. 26–49.

their work). In the other club the leader operated in a democratic manner by sponsoring group goals, and by giving friendly help and guidance, and objective praise and criticism. Both groups worked at the task of making theatrical masks for a period of three months under these two kinds of leadership. At the end of twelve weeks, the groups voted on (1) whether to continue, and (2) what to do with the masks they had made. All of the autocratic group voted to stop meeting, while most of the democratic group wished to continue. Children of the autocratic group wished to keep, as personal property, the masks they had made. In contrast, all children in the democratic group voted for a group disposal of at least one mask (i.e., to give it to the leader or put one on display). The significance of these findings should be apparent to the teacher. Children who work under the proper kind of leadership and group atmosphere seem to like their work, feel it to be important, and want more of the same or similar activities. Conversely, children whose needs are thwarted by rigid control tend to dislike school work.

In an extension of the above experiment, four groups of boys were organized into clubs and placed under three kinds of leadership: autocratic, democratic, and laissez-faire.[31] The leadership of the first two was like that described above, while the laissez-faire leadership gave unguided freedom to the group. (There were no rules, no apparent group or teacher goals, and little if any help or guidance initiated by the teacher.) Judged by the amount of work accomplished, the amount of identification with the group, group morale and "we feeling," and friendly relations with the leader, the democratic type of leadership was superior to either of the others, which were marked by such reactions as "scapegoating"[32] and attempts to resign from the group.[33] From this and similar studies emerges a picture of the kinds of leadership and the probable results of such leadership in terms of social climate. Table 15 presents a summary of the general findings.

It is apparent that a vital factor in class atmosphere is the way the leadership function of the teacher is used. Inflexible schedules, threats, and autocratic control cut off the communication of pupils with each other

---

[31] K. Lewin, R. Lippitt, and R. K. White, "Patterns of Aggressive Behavior in Experimentally Created 'Social Climates,' " *Journal of Social Psychology*, Vol. 10, 1939, pp. 271–300.

[32] "Scapegoating" is an adjustive mechanism, a kind of displaced aggression, in which people release their own hostility by attacking a person or group (usually weaker than they) not connected with the cause of their frustration.

[33] R. Lippitt and R. K. White, "The 'Social Climate' of Children's Groups" in R. G. Barker, J. S. Kounin, and H. F. Wright (Editors), *Child Behavior and Development*, New York, McGraw-Hill Book Company, 1943, pp. 485–506. (These three kinds of leadership have been depicted in a film, made during the experiments described in this reference. See "Films" at the end of this chapter.)

## TABLE 15
### Types of Leadership, Characteristics of Leaders, and Pupils' Reactions *

| Type of Leadership | Characteristics of This Type of Leadership | Typical Reactions of Pupils to This Leadership |
|---|---|---|
| Hard-Boiled Autocrat | 1. Constant check on students.<br>2. Expects immediate acceptance of all orders—rigid discipline.<br>3. Little praise is given as he believes this would spoil children.<br>4. Believes students cannot be trusted when on their own. | 1. Submission, but there is incipient revolt and dislike of the leader.<br>2. "Buck-passing" is a common occurrence.<br>3. Pupils are irritable and unwilling to cooperate and may indulge in "backbiting."<br>4. The work slips markedly when the teacher leaves the room. |
| The Benevolent Autocrat | 1. Is not aware that he is an autocrat.<br>2. Praises pupils and is interested in them.<br>3. The crux of his autocracy lies in the technique by which he secures dependence upon himself. He says, "that's the way *I* like it," or "how could you do this to me?"<br>4. Makes himself the source of all standards of class work. | 1. Most students like him, but those who see through his methods may dislike him intensely.<br>2. There is great dependence upon the teacher for all directions—little initiative on part of pupils.<br>3. There is submissiveness and lack of individual development.<br>4. Amount of class work may be high and of good quality. |
| The Laissez-Faire Teacher | 1. Has little confidence in dealing with pupils or a belief that they should be left alone.<br>2. Has difficulty in making decisions.<br>3. Has no clear-cut goals.<br>4. Does not encourage or discourage students, nor does he join in their work or offer help or advice. | 1. There is low morale and poor and sloppy work.<br>2. There is much "buck-passing," "scapegoating," and irritability among students.<br>3. There is no teamwork.<br>4. No one knows what to do. |
| The Democratic Teacher | 1. Shares planning and decision making with the group.<br>2. Gives help, guidance, and assistance to individuals gladly but not at the expense of the class.<br>3. Encourages as much group participation as possible.<br>4. Praise and criticism given objectively. | 1. Pupils like work, each other, and teacher better.<br>2. Quality and quantity of work are high.<br>3. Students praise each other and assume responsibilities on their own.<br>4. There are few problems of motivation whether teacher is in the room or not. |

* Adapted in part from L. P. Bradford and R. Lippitt, "Building a Democratic Work Group," *Personnel,* Vol. 22, American Management Association, Publisher, 1945, pp. 142–148.

and isolate the timid child from the group. These adverse influences may also create tension, irritability, and aggression among pupils. Also, autocratic control denies leadership training and training in social learnings to the pupils who need this kind of experience. In appraising his own leadership, the teacher might ask himself the following questions:

1. Do I help the group arrive at clearly stated goals and allow the group to have some part in planning these goals or ways of achieving them?
2. Have I helped all members of the class to find satisfaction in class membership through a gratification of social needs?
3. Do I have a sense of objectivity? For instance, do I give praise and reproof in terms of some standard rather than as "you have pleased me"?
4. Am I aware of my own ego needs, or must I dominate the class group or its members to satisfy these needs?
5. Do I encourage students to appraise their own and my activities and to seek improvement in group work?

THE DOMINATIVE VERSUS THE INTEGRATIVE ROLE. The effect which teachers may have upon a class over a period of time was illustrated by an intensive study [34] and comparison of the characteristics of second-grade children in the classes of two quite different teachers. One was a dominative teacher who more frequently than the other met aggression with aggression and "initiated" contacts with pupils rather than encouraging them to seek contacts with her. The other teacher, who was described by the investigators as "integrative," gave more friendly guidance, and encouraged pupils to join in class activities. At the end of a year there were fourteen statistically significant differences in behavior between the two classes, even though they were comparable in ability and background at the start of the first semester. These differences included such things as more voluntary suggestions, social contributions, and responsiveness in the integrative classroom. Teachers who dominate one class seem to retain this characteristic with other classes. Also it should be noted that the amount of conflict between pupils and dominative teachers does not seem to decline as the months of a semester pass. In fact conflict may increase. Even though teachers do not seem to change much semester after semester, it is fortunate that pupils do. When youngsters go from a dominative to an integrative classroom they tend to lose the characteristics which marked their previous behavior. However, when they go from an

---

[34] H. H. Anderson and J. E. Brewer, "Studies of Teachers' Classroom Personalities: II. Effects of Teachers' Dominative and Integrative Contacts on Children's Classroom Behavior," *Applied Psychological Monographs*, No. 8, American Psychological Association, Stanford University Press, June, 1946.

integrative to a dominative classroom, traits associated with domination are quickly assumed.[35]

## RELATIONS AMONG PUPILS

Another major factor in determining the school's social climate is the kind of relations which exist among pupils. Why is it that some youngsters crave to belong to a class group yet are rejected, others who might belong if they wish instead find undesirable groups outside the classroom, still others find a satisfaction of social needs within the classroom? The answer to these questions has been sought in studies involving observation, clinical analysis, sociometric tests,[36] and studies of personality and group dynamics.

One important finding is that a student may belong to a class group yet be relatively unaffected so far as its values are concerned, being instead affected by the standards and values of some other group (reference group). Or the group to which he belongs may influence him negatively, thus reinforcing a positive influence from an outside reference group. A boy may actually use his dislike of school as a reinforcement for feelings he has about his "gang."

Within a given group only those who conform with group norms have prestige within that group. Thus the boy who strives to be an outstanding scholar in school may be rejected by his peers who believe that school work is for sissies or girls. Many children's relations within the classroom are jeopardized because the school group or groups have values which conflict with values held by other groups of which they are members. Some children have never learned how to satisfy their social needs through contacts outside the home, while others have developed modes of behavior or personality traits which interfere with their relationships with other children. In some cases schools have failed to teach social skills which are necessary for effective group work. Furthermore, the traditional school has actually discouraged social interaction by allowing only individual work and by punishing children who attempt to talk with or help each other.

The way in which social learnings take place is an important consideration in the successful work of the teacher. Crime, insanity, divorce, inefficiency, and failure to learn are among the social catastrophes related to the failure of children to achieve a satisfactory place in social and

---

[35] H. H. Anderson, J. E. Brewer, and M. F. Reed, "Studies of Teachers' Classroom Personalities: III. Follow-up Studies of the Effects of Dominative and Integrative Contacts on Children's Behavior," *Applied Psychological Monographs*, No. 11, Stanford University Press, 1946.

[36] These tests are fully explained in Chapter 18.

work groups in the school and community. The following three questions indicate the kinds of information which a teacher needs in order to facilitate desirable interpersonal relationships among pupils.

1. What are the social needs of children, and how are they satisfied?
2. What are the factors in class organization, teaching, and the behavior and personality of children which lead to acceptance and rejection?
3. How can the teacher handle cases of rejection and isolation, and in general teach in such a way that desirable interpersonal relationships are facilitated?

The above questions are treated in the three subsections which follow.

### Social Needs

The reader will remember the earlier contention that social and ego needs are basic to human motivation. Children need acceptance by their age mates and by adults. They need to feel important and to have their accomplishments admired by others, and they need to feel that they are a part of a group, i.e., have a sense of belonging. They also need attention and affection. A social structure or other influence which denies these needs creates misery and maladjustment. Many of the factors which frustrate these needs are present in our schools. Excessive rivalry, limited rewards, favoritism, and retardation are examples of the many conditions which may militate against the satisfaction of social needs.

In the early work of Moreno (one of the first persons to use sociometric tests) many elementary school children were shown to have few if any friends in their classes and many others to be victims of unrequited friendship, i.e., desiring friendship with other youngsters who did not accept them as friends.[37] Some children are not only unpopular with other youngsters but also are odious to their teachers. In fact, more often than not, teachers and pupils agree on whom the problem children are.[38] Statements such as the following are not infrequently made by teachers: "I know I'm not supposed to feel this way, but I just can't like Carl. When he starts something with that smart-aleck sneer, I have to fight myself to keep from shaking him."

### Factors Related to Acceptance or Rejection

Research literature indicates that children with high social acceptance among peers tend to exhibit desirable and positive personality traits,

[37] J. L. Moreno, "Who Shall Survive?" *Nervous and Mental Disorders Monograph*, No. 58, 1934.
[38] S. L. Pressey and F. P. Robinson, *Psychology and the New Education*, New York, Harper and Brothers, 1944, p. 436.

while those of low social acceptance tend to lack such characteristics.[39] Those with high social acceptance also tend to participate actively and cooperate socially, while those who have low social acceptance do not. Children who are not socially accepted by their peers tend to display such undesirable characteristics as showing-off, attention seeking, nervousness, emotional instability, and restlessness. They also show less favorable teacher ratings, more resentment toward group control, and lack of self-control as shown by having temper tantrums.[40]

It is possible that the undesirable characteristics of the non-socially accepted are partially the cause of lack of social acceptance. It is also likely that a lack of social acceptance helps to produce much of the unacceptable behavior. This strongly suggests that one important role of the teacher is to break into the vicious cycle where lack of acceptance by peers helps produce unacceptable behavior and unacceptable behavior tends to generate lack of peer acceptance. The goal of guidance toward more appropriate behavior must be coupled with a generation of situations in which the unaccepted becomes more accepted by his peers.

Of great concern to teachers is the fact that some children seem always to be left out of things by their fellows. Disturbing also is the misery of the child who is actually rejected by his classmates. As mentioned earlier, the extent of acceptance and rejection in a classroom is often analyzed through a sociometric test. A summary of some sociometric results is shown in Table 16. The stars mentioned in the first category of Table 16 are pupils who received a large number of choices from other pupils on a sociometric test. The neglectees are individuals who received relatively few choices. And finally, the isolates are those who received no choices from their peers and who frequently are social outcasts in the classroom.

Clearly it behooves teachers to find out what characteristics are apt to lead to or be associated with unpopularity or rejection. In one study, when those who were rejected were compared with those who were highly acceptable to their peers, it was found that the former were more quarrelsome, complaining, nervous, aggressive, and dominating.[41] Other investi-

---

[39] M. Feinberg, M. Smith, and R. Schimdt, "An Analysis of Expressions Used by Adolescents at Varying Economic Levels to Describe Accepted and Rejected Peers," *Journal of Genetic Psychology*, Vol. 93, 1958, pp. 133–148. S. M. Goertzen, "Factors Relating to Opinions of Seventh-Grade Children Regarding the Acceptability of Certain Behaviors in the Peer Group," *Journal of Genetic Psychology*, Vol. 94, 1959, pp. 29–34. N. E. Gronlund and L. Anderson, "Personality Characteristics of Socially Accepted, Socially Neglected, and Socially Rejected Junior High School Pupils," *Educational Administration and Supervision*, Vol. 42, 1957, p. 335.

[40] N. M. Lorber, "Inadequate Social Acceptance and Disruptive Classroom Behavior," *Journal of Educational Research*, Vol. 59, 1966, pp. 360–362.

[41] H. H. Jennings, *Leadership and Isolation*, New York, Longmans, Green and Co., 1943, pp. 144–163.

## TABLE 16

### Percentage of Boys and Girls in the Star, Neglectee, and Isolate Categories on the Criteria of Seating Companion, Work Companion, and Play Companion in Forty Sixth-Grade Classrooms *

| Criteria (5 Choices Allotted on Each) | Percentage in Star Category | | Percentage in Neglectee Category | | Percentage in Isolate Category | |
|---|---|---|---|---|---|---|
| | Boys | Girls | Boys | Girls | Boys | Girls |
| Seating | 13 | 17 | 11 | 11 | 7 | 8 |
| Work | 12 | 15 | 12 | 11 | 7 | 8 |
| Play | 12 | 10 | 8 | 9 | 8 | 6 |

Note: There was an average of 16 boys and 16 girls in each classroom.

* Adapted from N. E. Gronlund, *Sociometry in the Classroom*, New York, Harper and Brothers, 1959, p. 99.

gators have summarized the positive traits associated with popularity as enthusiasm, daring, pleasing appearance, and cheerfulness.[42]

Youngsters prize qualities which match their concepts of that which gains prestige. For example, the twelve-year-old girl gives highest value in choosing friends to primness, sedateness, and ladylike behavior, while fifteen-year-old girls prefer glamour and being attractive to the opposite sex. Likewise, the boy of fifteen places high value upon physical skill, aggressiveness, and fearlessness. Woeful is the child who is minus these qualities.[43] In general, children who are highly chosen by their peers on a sociometric test tend to be more intelligent, to have higher scholastic achievement, to be younger in age, to have greater social and athletic skill, to participate more frequently in sports and social activities, to have a more pleasing physical appearance, to have more social and heterosexual interests, and to have more need-satisfying personality characteristics than children who receive few or no sociometric choices from their peers.[44]

Perhaps the most intensive analysis of children who are not acceptable to their classmates was made by Northway, who took twenty of the least frequently chosen children (on a sociometric test) and subjected them to special clinical study. These children grouped themselves into three patterns—the listless, recessive children; the quiet and retiring, socially unin-

[42] M. E. Bonney, "Personality Traits of Socially Successful and Socially Unsuccessful Children," *Journal of Educational Psychology*, Vol. 34, 1943, pp. 449–472.

[43] C. M. Tryon, "Evaluations of Adolescent Personality by Adolescents," *Monographs of the Society for Research in Child Development*, IV, Washington, D.C., National Research Council, 1939, p. 77.

[44] N. E. Gronlund, *Sociometry in the Classroom*, New York, Harper and Brothers, 1959, pp. 221–222.

terested children; and the noisy rebellious, socially ineffective children.[45] Gronlund concluded that pupils with low sociometric status are either overlooked by their peers (socially neglected) or are perceived by them as possessing an unpleasant appearance and socially ineffective and aggressive tendencies (socially rejected).[46]

There appears to be close agreement between sociometric results and the reputation an individual holds among his peers. The picture of the rejected child which emerges from these studies is that of a child who is seen by his fellows as different. He is one who does not conform to group norms of behavior, who retreats from social contact, and who attempts to satisfy social needs through the domination of others.

### Helping the Isolate and the Rejectee

Clinical psychologists recognize social isolates and rejectees as among the most serious of problem cases. Even if this were not true from the standpoint of adjustment and mental hygiene, it would be from an academic standpoint, as such children often lose the benefit of much class work because they are not active participants in the learning process. More specifically, improved social relations would appear to have the following beneficial effects on individual learning:

1. The security that arises from satisfying social relationships frees the pupil of emotional tension and enables him to concentrate more on his assigned learning tasks.
2. The social pressure arising from the feeling of being accepted by classmates increases the pupil's motivation to learn. This is partly due to the pupil's desire to maintain status in the group and partly due to his feeling of loyalty and responsibility to the group members.
3. The increased social contact accompanying peer acceptance aids in clarifying and reinforcing the pupil's classroom learning experiences by providing greater opportunity to exchange ideas with age mates.
4. The improved morale derived from satisfying social relationships in the classroom helps create in the pupil a favorable attitude toward the learning experience and toward the school in general.[47]

Psychological principles and the experiences of teachers and those who have worked with such children support the following techniques for helping rejected and isolated children achieve a place in the class group.

---

[45] M. L. Northway, "Outsiders, A Study of the Personality Patterns of Children Least Acceptable to Their Age Mates," *Sociometry*, Vol. 7, 1944, pp. 10–25.

[46] N. E. Gronlund, *Sociometry in the Classroom*, New York, Harper and Brothers, 1959, p. 174.

[47] Adapted from N. E. Gronlund, *Sociometry in the Classroom*, New York, Harper and Brothers, 1959, p. 235. Also see N. E. Gronlund, "Sociometry and Improved Social Relations in the Classroom," *High School Journal*, Vol. 48, 1965, pp. 391–395.

REGROUPING. In a classroom containing one or several social isolates, it is possible to reseat the class or restructure the work groups in such a way that children may be included in groups which are less likely to be antagonistic or indifferent to them. If sociometric data are available it is helpful to use the "choices" to seat children near those who have accepted them, even though it be on the basis of third-place votes. Unchosen children should not be placed near those who have rejected them. If possible, the teacher should place the isolate in a work group which has need for the particular skill which the unpopular child possesses.

FINDING GROUP JOBS. Much class work is of an individual nature, but there are some projects or work which really require group action, and involve a number of different kinds of skills. The isolate may receive much help if allowed to work with a group whose goals transcend petty personal considerations.

USING GRADUAL INDUCTION. Sometimes attempts to plunge a timid child into class work by direct questions, or by asking him to perform before the entire group, fail because the jump from his present withdrawn position to "total immersion" is too great a shock. Thus it may be wise to induct the child into the class group gradually. This may be done by letting him work with small groups at first, finding one person in class with whom he can feel at ease, or in extreme cases, letting him work with younger children for a time.

FINDING SPECIAL SKILLS. Most children have some skill in which they excel. Studies of intra-individual differences have shown that even dull children generally have some skills in which they approach or exceed average performance or potential. One thing which astonishes visitors to a feeble-minded institution is the high level of skills in many vocational areas which are exhibited by inmates. Full use of diagnostic tools ought to provide teachers with information about the interests and special abilities of the withdrawn child. In any class the variety of individual differences which pupils see as acceptable can be developed through an inventory of the skills of each class member. Once these are found, opportunity for the display of such skills should be given. This should do much toward giving needed self-confidence, and prestige in the eyes of peers.

TRAINING IN SKILLS. Children and adolescents often put a high value upon certain skills such as proficiency in games, and basic social skills such as dancing. These skills may take on exaggerated importance in the eyes of the deficient youngster. Thus one straightforward way to help the isolate achieve status is to provide special help in such skills, thus allowing him to participate in group activities on a par with other children.

DISCUSSION. Many times youngsters adopt habits, modes of behavior, and adornment which make acceptance by others unlikely. These characteristics may be retained simply because youths are not aware of the adverse effects of such behavior. Unfortunately young people do not readily change

simply as a result of a teacher's statement about such personal habits. They are much more apt to accept ideas about matters of this kind from each other. Hence, a discussion in which students are given a chance to air their views about desirable and undesirable traits (without names being mentioned) may be a worthwhile venture. There are available for teachers' use several films which will introduce such discussions.[48] In such discussions the teacher should make a careful attempt to involve the isolates and rejectees. Research has shown that many teachers can profit from a better distribution of their time and efforts among their charges. This is true not only in discussions but in other activities as well.

Certain learnings, particularly those in the area of attitudes, values, and understandings, can be promoted best through frequent exchanges with others. This conclusion underscores the importance of discussion as a valid and important teaching-learning technique.[49]

USING PEER HELPERS. Identifying and working with high status peers who are both respected and liked by hostile, rejected, or unmotivated pupils shows much promise as a technique. The teacher can take these peer leaders into his confidence and frequently reach and help pupils who would reject direct help from the teacher. Fox and others [50] have suggested several ways in which peer helpers can aid. Pairs of pupils may work on specific tasks, such as spelling words or correcting mathematics papers. Projects may be worked on by teams of students who share the results of their reading and interviewing with each other. Human leadership resources in a class can be surveyed by the teacher with the help of students, and a panel of experts can be ready to help any pupil requesting it. The learnings from a situation where a high status pupil helps an isolate, a rejectee, or a pupil having academic difficulties can be very profitable not only to the pupil who receives the help but also to the high status pupil. The latter with appropriate guidance from the teacher can develop both leadership skills and a sensitivity to the needs and difficulties of others who may be much less fortunate than he.[51]

PERSONAL GUIDANCE. A simple suggestion to a pupil may give him assistance in finding ways to join a social group. Some youngsters lack either the *savoir faire* or the self-confidence to break into a group. Often they hang back lest their egos be wounded by the rebuff which they so vividly

---

[48] Association Films, "You and Your Family," and "You and Your Friends," 79 East Adams Street, Chicago 3, Illinois; and Coronet Instructional Films, "How Friendly Are You?" and "Shy Guy," Coronet Building, Chicago 1, Illinois.

[49] L. W. Downey, *The Secondary Phase of Education*, New York, Blaisdell Publishing Company, 1965.

[50] R. Fox, M. B. Luszki, and R. Schmuck, *Tools for the Study and Diagnosis of Classroom Learning Atmospheres*, Ann Arbor, Michigan, Institute of Social Research, 1965.

[51] For additional suggestions on changing peer perception see R. Schmuck and M. Schmuck and M. Chesler, *Solving Interpersonal Problems in the Classroom*, Ann Arbor, Michigan, Institute for Social Research, 1963.

imagine will result from an overture of friendship. In such cases, teachers, counselors, or advisers may offer help by showing ways of getting a start socially. The following incident will illustrate how one instructor was able to help a social isolate.

> Mary was a freshman at a large state university. Since she had come to the university from a small town, she had no high school friends on campus. In talks with her freshman adviser she revealed that she was unhappy and would quit college if not for the disappointment it would bring her parents. She admitted that she had no friends—that her only recreation was going to the movies alone and taking walks. The only time she talked with others was when she and three other girls went from history to gym class. Further conversation revealed that all these girls lived on the other side of campus, while Mary had a room in the dormitory where swimming classes were held. The adviser suggested to Mary that she invite the other girls to hang their coats and clothes in her room, while swimming, thus saving them from having to jam their clothes in gym lockers. Mary adopted the suggestion and soon found a social group which accepted her wholeheartedly. Her adjustment to social life from that time on was adequate and her ideas about leaving the university disappeared.

## SCHOOL STAFF RELATIONS

Another set of relations which are significant in determining the social climate in any school is the quality of interaction among teachers, and between teachers and administrators. These are important relationships in that they may either lead to cooperative effort and progressive action or to dissension. When tensions are developed these are too often passed on down to the unfortunate pupil. How such tensions operate may be seen in the following record of a committee meeting of a junior high school staff.

Our committee is meeting in the late afternoon to consider the problem of homework. Present are Mr. Johnson, the principal; Miss Jones, English teacher and head of the department; Miss Martin, another English teacher; Mr. Brown, a social studies teacher; Miss Smith, mathematics; Mrs. White, physical sciences. (*Some of their thoughts and feelings, many of them unconscious, are given in italics within parentheses.*)

Mr. Johnson: "(*Another meeting, I hope there's no bickering. I'm always glad when the meetings are finished.*) Parents are complaining again about homework. One man called to say his son carried home thirteen pounds of books. Another feels he is doing the teaching teachers failed to do. Miss Jones, what happened when this problem was brought up at PTA?"

Miss Jones: "Many parents felt the school expects too much homework. Some thought this a lazy way of teaching. Others thought it unfair to have to help children do math problems because methods of working are different now. (*That was a swell chance to put Miss Smith in her place. She*

*acts like she owns the school.*) On the other hand, some parents thought that not enough homework was assigned, that students nowadays were spoiled in school. I'm glad to report these parents were in the minority."

Miss Smith: "The trouble with such a meeting is that the few parents with complaints speak so loudly that it looks as though the whole PTA agrees. Most parents are indifferent as to how their children get along. When you try to get their cooperation, you get picayune complaints. If we want to lower our standards, it will be easy to eliminate homework. (*Jones will take any side just so she gets on top. She's determined to run this school.*)"

Mr. Brown: "(*Here we go again. Smithy needs some support before she gets steam-rollered by Jones.*) It's easy enough to talk about eliminating homework. In schools where children have a fine home background, work can be completed during school hours. But with the mixture of children we have, it's impossible to expect standards to be upheld without supplementary study after class hours."

Miss Jones: "Every time we talk about homework, someone brings up standards. Some teachers maintain high educational standards without loading students down with extra homework at night. Good teaching makes children want to read so much that reading becomes pleasure and not homework. (*That shot told.*)"

Mrs. White: "The confusion comes from the lack of basic policy on the part of the school administration."

Mr. Johnson: "We want everyone to give his opinion. Miss Martin, what do you think?"

Miss Martin: "(*He must know that Jonesey pushes me around. She's making a grandstand play with her 'Good teachers don't need to assign homework' stuff. When she says in that sugar voice of hers, 'You don't have to read any of the books on this list but I know you'll all want to,' all her students know they had better read them or else. If I say what I really think about homework, Jonesey will make my life even tougher next month. But I don't like to let Mr. Brown and Miss Smith down.*) Perhaps part of the answer depends upon the subject studied. (*I hate Mr. Johnson for putting me on the spot.*)"

Mr. Johnson: "Now that you have expressed your opinions, I wonder if we shouldn't vote on a final decision."

Miss Smith: "I don't think this problem can be solved by voting. We must get at the real issue of educational standards."

Mr. Johnson: "(*This meeting is getting too hot. If I don't stop it, we'll never have any peace in this school.*) I wonder if we shouldn't appoint a subcommittee to study the problem and report back to us."

Miss Jones: "(*I'd better not let him pull that now. If we can get him to go on, we may get him to decide on less homework, which will put Smith*

*in her place.*) Don't you think, Mr. Johnson, we have most of the facts we need now? It seems to me we can come to a decision pretty soon."

Mr. Johnson: "I'm sure you'll agree that the sensible conclusion is to expect each teacher to make every effort to reduce homework requirements to the minimum. We will, I am sure, also maintain the high educational standards our school has always tried to uphold. If you wish, I'll be glad to tell the parents, at the next PTA meeting, of our decision."

Miss Smith: "(*We lost this fight. We'll lay for Jones until we get a swell issue where we can push her around.*)" [52]

It is appropriate here to ask what in this teachers' meeting prevented the formation of good working relationships and effective group judgment. An obvious first answer is that this group had little training in group work, and Mr. Johnson apparently was not trained to provide effective leadership. Furthermore, it is apparent that there was no prearranged plan of procedure, no delegation of tasks, and no satisfactory method for either understanding or solving the problem of homework. Likewise the group had developed no satisfactory method of handling the personal animosities and hostilities which subverted the main topic for discussion. Groups such as this one can improve the handling of their problems when they learn to apply the principles of social psychology to their work. Some of the principles which apply to group functioning are discussed in the last section of this chapter.[53]

## OTHER FACTORS IN SOCIAL CLIMATE

The teacher's personality and method of leadership, and the organization of interpersonal relationships within the class group are among the important factors in determining social climate. However, there are other factors such as the physical facilities of the school and classroom, the size and composition of the class, and the previous experience of pupils which may also have a decided effect upon social climate.

### Physical Facilities and Arrangements

Consider, for instance, the simple fact that there are dozens of ways in which thirty children may be placed or arranged in a classroom. They may be placed in rows of bolted down desks, sit around one large table, work in small groups of four to five pupils, sit in a circle facing each other, or

---

[52] K. Benne and B. Muntyan, *Human Relations in Curriculum Change*, New York, The Dryden Press, 1951, pp. 146–148.

[53] For additional ways of improving staff relations the reader is referred to Chapter 21, Professional Growth of the Teacher. Also see R. H. Simpson, *Teacher Self-Evaluation*, New York, Macmillan Company, 1966, Chapter 8, "Self-evaluation and Interpersonal Relations with Colleagues."

work at individual projects—as in a laboratory. When educators assumed that almost 100 per cent of a student's school time should be spent facing a teacher a somewhat rigid type of school setting was crystallized. With increasing attention in education to peer discussions, to small group work, to individual research and study (sometimes using machines), to increased student responsibility, significant changes have taken place in the physical arrangements that affect the social climate of a classroom. In general these changes have been toward greater flexibility in the use of space and facilities to implement the varied types of interpersonal relations that are emphasized.[54]

### Class Size

Besides the physical arrangement of the classroom, one must consider how the size of the class affects its social structure. It is apparent that the social climate in a classroom containing twenty students is different from one which contains fifty or a hundred students. Students are likely to feel freer to participate and take a more active role in group work when they are in small classes.[55] The crude fact that the amount of student participation is limited in the large class makes the small class more advantageous, especially when student participation is deemed an important part of the course. However, class size *per se* is probably of less importance than many other factors. It is probable that the effect of class size varies with the type of instructional method, the grade level of pupils, and the personality of individual teachers. There is some indication, for instance, that teachers are disturbed by the fact that large classes prevent them from knowing pupils well.[56] On the other hand, if a course consists almost entirely of lectures, class size might make little difference. Research studies indicate that class size should not be studied in isolation. Problems related to goals, curriculum, teacher skills, and class procedures must be considered in determining the effects of class size on learner growth.[57]

### Use of Groups and Grouping

Research data to date indicate that ability grouping by classes is not likely to be more than a first step in taking care of individual differences.[58]

---

[54] F. G. Cornell, "Plant and Equipment" in *Encyclopedia of Educational Research*, New York, The Macmillan Company, 1960, pp. 1008–1031.

[55] G. F. Castore, "Attitudes of Students Toward the Case Method of Instruction in a Human Relations Course," *Journal of Educational Research*, Vol. 45, 1951, pp. 201–213.

[56] H. L. Baker, "Class Size Does Make a Difference," *Nations Schools*, Vol. 17, 1936, pp. 27–28.

[57] J. I. Goodlad, "Classroom Organization" in *Encyclopedia of Educational Research*, New York, The Macmillan Company, 1960, pp. 221–226.

[58] J. H. Shores, "What Does Research Say about Ability Grouping by Classes?" *Illinois Education*, 47, 1964, pp. 169–172.

This suggests that within a particular class the teacher needs to be able to continually shift group gears by adapting group objectives, materials, and methods to significantly differing individuals within the classroom.

Many educators and psychologists have urged teachers to use small subgroups within a class, not only better to provide for individual differences, but also to allow all pupils an opportunity for maximum participation. Such schemes for subdividing a class into work groups also have a decided effect upon social climate and learning.[59] Herbert Thelen, who for several years has worked on the problem of how groups of pupils function, has suggested a principal of "least group size."

In speaking of the optimal size of groups, Thelen notes that the group should be "the smallest group in which it is possible to have represented at a functional level all the socialization and achievement skills required for the particular learning activity at hand." [60] As Thelen notes, an hour's class discussion in which thirty students are participating allows only two minutes per student for active interaction with others. The implementation of the principle of least group size is admittedly difficult in view of the incomplete knowledge presently available about the nature of socialization skills, and about the characteristics of various learning activities. But it is possible to make rough estimates of the optimal size of groups for specific purposes. For instance, when the learning activity consists of skill practice, the most appropriate size is probably two persons. For such tasks as creative thinking about the planning of an experiment or study, Thelen estimates that groups of from four to eight students would be needed. Apparently when groups are larger than needed to fulfill the essential conditions as stated, duplications of abilities and skills result, and there is less opportunity for a pupil to assume full responsibility in connection with a project.

A type of social organization which hundreds of American communities have been trying out recently is the non-graded school. A primary purpose of this type of grouping is to help pupils of varying intellectual and social abilities to move ahead unhampered by the lockstep of grade-school organization. Although research evidence on the values of this type of organization is quite limited there is some empirical evidence of reduced tensions in students, increased teacher awareness of individual differences in pupils, and of increased parental understanding of what the school is doing.[61, 62]

[59] S. L. Pressey and David C. Hanna, "The Class as a Psycho-Sociological Unit," *Journal of Psychology*, Vol. 16, 1943, pp. 13–19.

[60] H. A. Thelen, "Group Dynamics in Instruction, The Principle of Least Group Size," *The School Review*, Vol. 57, 1949, pp. 139–148.

[61] J. I. Goodlad and R. H. Anderson, *The Nongraded Elementary School*, New York, Harcourt Brace, and World, 1963.

[62] B. F. Brown, *The Nongraded High School*, Englewood Cliffs, N.J., Prentice-Hall, 1964.

### Readiness of Pupils for a Particular Social Climate

Success in using a particular kind of classroom social climate is highly dependent on current ability of pupils to adapt to such a climate. This adaptation depends much upon the kind of previous training which pupils have had. The child who has adjusted well to an autocratic type of control in previous classrooms or in the home may be much less able to accept or enjoy group work and interaction, and the responsibilities he is asked to share. In fact, when college students were asked to state their preference for permissive or directive sections in an introductory course in psychology, most of them chose the latter.[63]

Finally, there is the pervasive effect of goals, purposes, and objectives, and the way students believe their work will be evaluated. When a class knows that the goals of a course are centered around the learning of detailed facts which will be tested by recall of such facts on objective examinations, they are likely to prefer a directive, teacher-centered type of classroom. Contrariwise, students who see the objectives of a course as broad understandings and generalizations which will be evaluated by group and teacher not only on paper and pencil tests, but also through measures of performance, will be apt to prefer a permissive, student-centered type of class.

### Pupils' Attitudes Toward Teachers

Since students rate the teacher's personality and teaching methods as the most important factors in their enjoyment of classroom work,[64] teachers should know what children like and dislike about them. Helpful information was obtained through a national contest in which students were asked to write letters describing, "The Teacher Who Has Helped Me Most." The letters were analyzed to discover what characteristics of teachers were most frequently mentioned. Out of 12,000 letters written by children from Grades 2 to 12, the traits shown in Table 17 received the most mention. These may or may not be the chief characteristics of good teaching but they do represent what youngsters deem important. The wise teacher might well use such a list to partially gauge his own effectiveness.

## THE EFFECT OF SOCIAL CLIMATE ON LEARNING

The first part of this chapter was written to show the factors which produce the social-emotional climate of a classroom. It remains to be shown, once social climate is determined, what effects such classroom atmospheres have upon learning. For example, what happens to achievement in spell-

---

[63] L. G. Wispe, *op. cit.*, p. 184.

[64] W. B. Michael, E. E. Herrold, and E. W. Cryon, "Survey of Student-Teacher Relationships," *Journal of Educational Research*, Vol. 44, 1951, pp. 657–673.

## TABLE 17
### Traits of Well-Liked Teachers *

1. Cooperative Democratic Attitude
2. Kindliness and Consideration for the Individual
3. Patience
4. Wide Interest
5. Personal Appearance and Pleasing Manner
6. Fairness and Impartiality
7. Sense of Humor
8. Good Disposition and Consistent Behavior
9. Interest in Pupils' Problems
10. Flexibility
11. Use of Recognition and Praise
12. Unusual Proficiency in Teaching a Subject

* Paul Witty, "An Analysis of the Personality Traits of the Effective Teacher," *Journal of Educational Research*, Vol. 40, 1947, pp. 662–671.

ing, reading, or mathematics when the teacher is sarcastic or overcritical or in other ways abuses his position of leadership? What happens to a child's school work when his classmates reject or ridicule him? In extreme cases, adverse social climate may engender such profound feelings of inferiority, aggression, or boredom that learning (at least of subject matter) virtually ceases. Such effect is portrayed in the following case.

### CASE OF GRACE W.[65]

Grace had been ill with spinal meningitis when she was just learning to add. When she was well enough to return to school, she was promoted with her grade and was never taught how to borrow and carry. Now in the sixth grade, faced with applying her previous knowledge, she had resorted to a method which had been hastily taught her by her father, only to have the teacher ridicule it and send her back to her seat in disgrace. Being a sensitive child, and socially ill at ease, she quickly responded in a negative manner to such treatment and soon gave the teacher the impression that she was stupid. Later, faced with a mental test situation, the girl had retreated into herself and had remained uncooperative. The result was that the psychologist who tested Grace gave a report which tended to confirm Miss Jones' judgment about the child's inherent stupidity.

This girl was sent to a special class where the new teacher soon realized that here was a case of emotional rather than mental difficulty. Under the new permissive atmosphere, Grace began to learn and to participate with others in social life. Eventually she graduated from high school and obtained a supervisory position with a good salary.

---

[65] From Kimball Young, *Personality and Problems of Adjustment*, p. 440, Copyright, 1940, by Appleton-Century-Crofts, Inc., New York. Used by permission.

### Effects of Social Climate on Academic Learning

In general, the evidence for improving academic learning seems to favor the more flexible, democratically controlled classroom. The use of such procedures on a wide scale has been appraised in terms of the college achievements of high school graduates who have experienced teaching of this kind.[66] Unfortunately, studies which appraise a whole school, or school system, have the disadvantage of being so broad that it is difficult to isolate the various factors which may have had an influence in shaping their products.

More recently, paired classrooms or groups have been used to test the hypothesis that social climate is an important determiner of the quality of learning. Summarizing one such investigation, Flanders writes, "In all cases, the student's ability to name, elaborate, use, and recall principles in question was greater for learner-centered periods than for teacher-centered periods." [67]

Non-graded classes with their flexibility and departure from the lock-step of uniform goals, assignments, and materials seem to help produce favorable results. In Milwaukee, for example, test results on reading and personality adjustment slightly favored the non-graded group even though these pupils were a little younger and tested slightly lower in mental capacity.[68] A somewhat similar experiment in Appleton, Wisconsin, produced a median grade-placement achievement score of 4.57 for the graded groups and 4.83 for the non-graded groups. Administrative expediency in some school systems keeps a non-graded set-up from being adopted even when its potential values are recognized.

### Social Climate and Pupil Responsibility

The amount and types of responsibility which pupils assume in the teaching-learning situation are greatly determined by its social climate. Patton,[69] for example, found that students' acceptance of responsibility for learning is most likely to occur in learners who are both uncowed by traditional authority figures and high in need-achievement. Even preschool children have great capacity for assuming responsibilities if given appropriate guidance. There is danger these capabilities will be dampened or largely lost if the pupil has a long series of teachers who make all crucial decisions in the classroom.

---

[66] A report of a study of this kind (The Eight-Year Study) is shown in Chapter 20.

[67] N. A. Flanders, *op. cit.*, p. 105.

[68] Milwaukee Public Schools, *A Study of Primary School: Organization and Regular Class Organization in Eight Schools*, Milwaukee, Wisconsin, 1952.

[69] J. A. Patton, *A Study of the Effects of Student Acceptance of Responsibility and Motivation on Course Behavior*, Doctor's Thesis reported by W. J. McKeachie, "Students, Groups, and Teaching Methods," *American Psychologist*, Vol. 13, 1958, pp. 580–584.

There is research evidence that teachers can be trained to foster types of social climate which will result in greater pupil acceptance of responsibility. One study,[70] for example, showed that a teacher-training program could produce less authoritarianism in teachers and more responsibility in children.

### Problem-Solving

Problem-solving ability is learned best in permissive, learner-centered classrooms. For many purposes, considered group judgments are often better than an average of individual judgments. Also many problems, especially those which are significant, are the kind which require group action for their solution.[71]

Various elements of the problem-solving process have been found to be developed best in a democratic atmosphere. For instance, two classes in child study, one a teacher-centered class and one a group-centered class, were compared in terms of the amount they had learned. Although both classes were about equal in the number of facts learned, the group-centered class was superior in the use of evidence to support its views.[72] Likewise in sections from the second to the eighth grade (social studies), pupils in classes where teacher-pupil planning prevailed were better able to discriminate between valid and irrelevant reasons to support their views than were those in teacher-centered sections.[73]

Even children in primary grades can (and should) learn to solve problems through group processes. Following is an example of how a socially permissive, yet well-guided group of second graders solved an "ethical problem" during their regularly scheduled "Problem Period."

> Henry: "The other day I was painting at the easel. I left the easel to throw my paper in the basket and when I came back, Leland had my place. I tried to tell him that I just went to put my paper in the basket but he wouldn't listen to me. So today when I went up to the easel Leland came and wouldn't let me paint again. He said he just threw a paper in the basket. He made me let him have the easel the other day, but when I did the same thing today he still wouldn't let me paint. I don't think he's being fair about it."
> Sandy: "Leland, if you made Henry give it to you, you should have done the same thing when Henry wanted it."

[70] E. E. Levitt, "Effect of a 'Causal' Teacher Training Program on Authoritarianism and Responsibility in Grade School Children," *Psychological Reports*, Vol. 1, 1955, pp. 449–458.

[71] J. M. Seidman, *Readings in Educational Psychology*, Boston, Houghton Mifflin Company, 1965, pp. 57–59.

[72] H. V. Perkins, "Climate Influences Group Learning," *Journal of Educational Research*, Vol. 45, 1951, pp. 115–119.

[73] K. J. Rehage, "A Comparison of Pupil-Teacher Planning and Teacher-Directed Procedures in Eighth Grade Social Studies Classes," *Journal of Educational Research*, Vol. 45, 1951, pp. 111–115.

Leland: "Yes, but I had started to paint and I wanted to finish."
Teacher: "Henry wanted to paint, too."
Henry: "Leland, you could take your picture off and finish later."
Cynthia: "Henry, why didn't you put your name on the paper? Then no one could paint on it."
Teacher: "A very good suggestion, Cynthia."
Pamela: "Could we move the waste basket over near the easel? Then you wouldn't have to leave your place. I think it would be better anyway 'cause you wouldn't have to walk so far in quiet time."
Teacher: "We could try that. Leland, what do you think about this problem?"
Leland: "I think, maybe, I should have let Henry paint."
Teacher: "But you are not quite sure?"
Leland: "Yes, I am. If I did it to him, I should let him have it. I'll take my paper off, Henry, and finish later." [74]

These children were learning how to solve problems because the classroom atmosphere was permissive enough yet well enough guided so that pupil interaction and cooperative work were promoted.

## Social Learning

The kinds of attitudes, roles, characteristic modes of social adjustment, social skills such as taking part in a discussion, and emotional responses which are learned are further important products of classroom atmosphere. The question is how these social learnings come about, and how teaching can facilitate them.

Social interaction, either on the basis of working together toward group goals or in social situations, builds better interpersonal attitudes which may even transcend racial and religious prejudice. In an experiment comparing a group-centered with a leader-centered class, it was found that in the group-centered class there was a greater spontaneity and a better morale and cohesion.[75] Students in this class had a class party, and often remained after class in groups, and several students took part in small get-togethers during the semester following. In the teacher-centered class students were "only too anxious to leave the classroom." [76]

Perhaps attitudes toward people in general, a greater warmth in expression, and a greater readiness to accept people are products of group work which fosters widespread interaction. In other words, it is believed that permanent changes in personality may result from the kinds of social experiences made possible in classrooms. Even the way teachers feel about children may be a product of the kinds of class atmosphere which they

---

[74] A. Miel, "Children in Action," *Progressive Education*, Vol. 27, 1950, p. 156.

[75] A. J. Lott and B. E. Lott, "Group Cohesiveness and Individual Learning," *Journal of Educational Psychology*, Vol. 57, 1966, pp. 61–73.

[76] E. W. Bovard, Jr., "The Psychology of Classroom Interaction," *Journal of Educational Research*, Vol. 45, 1951, pp. 215–224.

have experienced in public school, and in their teacher-training institutions. In a controlled study of in-service teachers enrolled in a course in child development, those in group-centered classes were compared in several respects with those in leader-centered groups. It was found that individuals in the former class had more attitudes which were objective and warm, while in the teacher-centered class, the individuals' attitudes toward children were more often conventional, emotional, and cold.[77]

Extensive research on social learnings leads to these inferences: (1) when the aims of education are conceived to include social learning as an important outcome of education, then teaching methods must reflect and express the values associated with the democratic process; (2) the social climate of a classroom is the single most potent influence on the kind of social learning which occurs; (3) the social climate of the classroom and consequent social learning are products of the behavior of the group, which includes the teacher.[78]

### Effects of Social Climate on Attitudes

Some of the forces which affect attitudes may be seen from a report by Van Til.[79] After an analysis of about one hundred studies dealing with attitudinal changes in intercultural relations he concluded the following were crucial in getting such changes: (1) creation of a democratic atmosphere, (2) contact through situations involving cooperation, (3) recognition and change of the emotional facets of attitudes, (4) community surveys and audits, (5) actually working toward elimination of segregation and discrimination.

In changing attitudes the social climate is as important as the intellectual climate. It appears that the way a teacher sets up classroom groups may be an important determinant of attitudes.[80, 81]

### Group Discussion [82]

A final and most practical consideration regarding the effect of social climate on learning is its effect upon group discussion and other forms of group work. Good group discussion involves much more than a de-

---

[77] H. V. Perkins, op. cit., p. 116.

[78] G. M. Wingo, "Methods of Teaching" in Encyclopedia of Educational Research, New York, The Macmillan Company, 1960, p. 850.

[79] W. Van Til, "Intercultural Education" in Encyclopedia of Educational Research, New York, The Macmillan Company, 1960, pp. 722–724.

[80] K. M. Miller and J. B. Biggs, "Attitude Change Through Undirected Group Discussion," Journal of Educational Psychology, Vol. 49, 1958, pp. 224–228.

[81] J. M. Seidman, Readings in Educational Psychology, Boston, Houghton Mifflin Company, 1965, Part II, "Human Relations in the School."

[82] As it is not within the scope of this book to detail teaching methods, no attempt is made here to describe the educational techniques involved in group discussion. Rather this is intended as a presentation of some of the psychosocial factors which influence discussion. See bibliography at the end of the chapter for discussion methods.

cision by the teacher to have a group discussion. There are many forces at work within the group, and within the teacher's relation with the group which determine the nature and efficiency of discussion. Even training and practice in group discussion may fail to produce an efficient work group if social conflicts within the group remain unresolved.

Also the kind of appraisal which is used influences the nature of group work, as was demonstrated in the following study. Ten sections of five students each in an introductory psychology course were studied to find out what effect grading procedures would have upon group work. Five of the groups were told that each member would receive the same grade and that the grade would depend on how well the group did. The other five groups were told that each member would be rated against the other four in his group. All ten groups were then given significant psychological and social problems for discussion. The groups which were to be graded together (the cooperative groups) were superior in the communication of ideas, coordination of work, friendliness, and group pride.[83] Apparently, the rivalry within groups engendered by competitive ratings may be sufficient to interfere seriously with group discussion.

The emergence of student leadership and the acceptance of appropriate work roles in a discussion are necessary concomitants to good group discussion. These are factors over which the teacher may exercise some control as both leaders and followers must learn these roles in just such opportunities as group discussion provides.[84] On the other hand, teachers must realize that leadership is conferred by the group and not by the teacher. As one writer puts it, "the adult's choice of a certain child to be a leader may be a kiss of death to his leadership." In college classes, a group which was allowed to choose its own leader for a group discussion did a better job in a group discussion than a group for whom the leader was picked by the instructor, even though the latter student leader was superior intellectually.[85] It would appear that the teacher's job, rather than assigning roles in discussion, is to help the class pick its own leaders and assign other group positions. In this function the teacher should help the group assess its processes, select its leaders, and train its members.[86]

Unsatisfied needs and unresolved emotional tensions within a group may interfere with group goals. The reader will recall the teacher's meeting

---

[83] Morton Deutsch, "Social Relations in the Classroom and Grading Procedures," *Journal of Educational Research*, Vol. 45, 1951, pp. 145–152.

[84] See Kurt Lewin, "The Dynamics of Group Action," *Educational Leadership*, Vol. 1, 1944, p. 199, and Alice Miel, *Changing the Curriculum*, New York, Appleton-Century-Crofts, Inc., 1946, pp. 156–162, and J. M. Seidman, *Readings in Educational Psychology*, Boston, Houghton Mifflin Company, 1965, pp. 55–61.

[85] R. S. Jones, "A Procedure for the Appraisal of the Mechanics of Group Discussion," *Progressive Education*, Vol. 28, 1951, pp. 96–99.

[86] Ruth Cunningham and Associates, "Leadership and the Group," *National Education Association Journal*, Vol. 37, 1948, pp. 502–503.

Pupils feel accepted when they are able to make significant individual contributions to group projects. These pupils are gathering a variety of materials which will be used in a committee report on a social studies problem.

described earlier in this chapter. At that meeting, group goals were subverted by the attempts to use the discussion as a means of airing personal issues. The isolated, rejected child, and potential delinquent may not see the group discussion as a helpful activity. Their activities may be limited to attempts to use the discussion as means of gaining attention—of satisfying social needs. Likewise, the teacher's unsatisfied needs may easily interfere with group work. A study of junior high school students revealed that students were almost completely unaware of the nature of the teacher's social and status needs in the classroom. One student was heard to say, "I never thought about teachers having needs before." [87] The interdependence of pupils, and of pupils and teachers for a mutual satisfaction of needs, would seem to demand that each group receive training in understanding each other's social needs.

The criteria of the goodness of a group discussion are difficult to determine, as the evaluation of a group discussion has to be related to its objective and purposes. It has been suggested that some of the main purposes of group discussion are: "(1) the thoughtful solution of problems

---

[87] D. H. Jenkins, "Interdependence in the Classroom," *Journal of Educational Research*, Vol. 45, 1951, pp. 137–144.

considered important by the group; (2) the growth of individual members in the process of discussion in various insights and skills, particularly those essential to participation and cooperation in group thinking and action; and (3) the growth of the group as a group."[88] The following check list should help groups evaluate their progress.

### MEASURES OF GROUP PROGRESS

1. Does every member make contributions to the discussion?
2. Is every member intensely involved in the discussion at all stages?
3. Does the discussion move toward common agreements in terms of the solution of the problem being discussed? Do all members of the group understand and accept as important the problem being discussed?
4. Is the discussion oriented toward decision and action at all times?
5. Does the group accept and understand the conflicts encountered and move toward their resolution?
6. Does the group recognize its need for information? Does it know how to go about getting such information?
7. Does the group use resource persons or resource material as an aid to its own thinking, not as giving the final action-solution of its problem?
8. Is the group unduly dependent upon its leader or on some of its members? Does the group use its leadership as an aid to common solutions, not as a source of final solutions?
9. Is the leader accepted as a member of the group, with special functions to perform?
10. Is there an atmosphere of friendly cooperation in the group at all times, particularly when conflicts of ideas and points of view are encountered?
11. Does the group resent attempts at domination by its leader, one of its members, a clique of its members or by a visiting expert?
12. Is there a feeling of progress toward common goals?
13. Is the group "realistic" in its choice of problems and in setting its goals?
14. Does the discussion move readily toward decision when decision is required?
15. Does the group find it possible to dispense with the creaking machinery of parliamentary procedure? [89]

---

[88] K. D. Benne, L. P. Bradford, and R. Lippitt, "Stages in the Process of Group Thinking and Discussion" in Illinois Secondary School Curriculum Program, *Human Relations in Curriculum Change*, Bulletin No. 7, 1949, p. 78.

[89] *Ibid.*, pp. 79–80.

## SUMMARY

The way in which groups function, the manner in which members of groups interact, and the teacher's role in such activities are subjects which have paramount importance in the learning process. Most school learning takes place under conditions wherein the social-emotional climate of the classroom is a major determinant not only of the quality and amount of learning, but also of the way in which children react to class work, and the attitudes which they develop about school.

Social-emotional climate is the result of at least the following factors: (1) the kinds of teacher-pupil relationships which exist in the classroom; (2) the social interaction or relationships among pupils; (3) the relationships among members of the school staff; and (4) the physical characteristics of the classroom, class size, the previous experience of pupils, use of groups, pupils' social readiness, relative emphasis on cooperation versus competition, and pupils' attitudes toward teachers.

Analysis of teacher-pupil relationships has revealed that pupils like teachers who are cooperative, democratic, considerate, and who have patience, a breadth of interests, and a pleasing manner. When teachers abuse their position of leadership by being overly autocratic, or shirking responsibility through a laissez-faire manner, children are apt to become aggressive, and group morale is likely to be low.

The satisfaction of children's social needs is a crucial consideration for the teacher. The child who fails to achieve a place in the society of his peers is not only apt to become an educational casualty but a community problem as well. A summary of the skills which a teacher needs in order to help such children is: (1) ability to diagnose social needs, (2) ability to study the rejected child and the isolate to find causes of the behavior, and (3) proficiency in setting up programs and work which will allow the induction of such children into the class group.

Experimental evidence favors the flexible, democratically controlled classroom as a means of promoting both academic and social learning. Children under a more permissive type of classroom atmosphere have made as good or better school marks, and certainly have been found superior in ability to solve problems and take responsibility when they have been compared with children in conventional classrooms. Children in pupil-centered classrooms have also been shown to be more critical in their thinking than those in teacher-centered classes. Teaching methods which foster a high degree of interaction among pupils seem to offer unusual opportunities for important social learnings which are left untouched in many classrooms. Educators must find methods which teach children how to work together. Perhaps it is not an overstatement to say that the future of this civilization may depend upon how well children learn the social skills which will enable them to face the crises of tomorrow.

## References for Further Study

Amidon, E., and Simon, A. "Teacher-Pupil Interaction," *Review of Educational Research*, ol. 35, 1965, pp. 130–139.

Amidon, E., and Hunter, E. *Improving Teaching, The Analysis of Classroom Verbal Interaction*, Chicago, Holt, Rinehart and Winston, 1966.

Bany, Mary A., and Johnson, Lois V., *Classroom Group Behavior: Group Dynamics in Education*, New York, The Macmillan Company, 1964.

Brown, B. F., *The Nongraded High School*, Englewood Cliffs, N.J., Prentice-Hall, 1964.

Bush, R. N., *The Teacher-Pupil Relationship*, New York, The Macmillan Company, 1954.

Cartwright, D., and Zander, A. *Group Dynamics*, Evanston, Illinois, Row, Peterson and Company, 1953.

Chesler, M., and Fox, R. *Role Playing in the Classroom*, Ann Arbor, Michigan, Institute of Social Research, The University of Michigan, 1964.

Cunningham, R., and Associates, *Understanding Group Behavior of Boys and Girls*, New York, Bureau of Publications, Teachers College, Columbia University, 1951.

Fox, R., Luszki, M. B., Schmuck, R. *Tools for the Study and Diagnosis of Classroom Learning Atmospheres*, Ann Arbor, Michigan, Institute of Social Research, The University of Michigan, 1965.

Giles, H. H. *The Integrated Classroom*, New York, Basic Books, Inc., 1959.

Goodlad, R. I., and Anderson, R. N. *The Nongraded Elementary School*, New York, Harcourt, Brace, 1963.

Gronlund, Norman E. *Sociometry in the Classroom*, New York, Harper and Brothers, 1959.

Hare, P., Borgatta, E. F., and Bales, R. F. (Editors), *Small Group Studies in Social Interaction*, New York, Alfred A. Knopf, 1955.

Hartup, W. W. "Social Behavior of Children," *Review of Educational Research*, Vol. 35, 1965, pp. 122–129.

Harris, C. W. *Encyclopedia of Educational Research*, Third Edition, New York, The Macmillan Company, 1960, pp. 603–610, 848–850.

Henry, N. B. (Editor), *The Dynamics of Instructional Groups*, Fifty-ninth Yearbook of the National Society for the Study of Education, Part II, Chicago, The University of Chicago Press, 1960.

Kaufman, M., Schmuck, R., Lippitt, R. *Creative Practices Developed by Teachers for Improving Classroom Atmospheres*, Ann Arbor, Michigan, Institute for Social Research, University of Michigan, 1963.

Miel, A., and Associates, *Cooperative Procedures in Learning*, New York, Bureau of Publications, Teachers College, Columbia University, 1952.

Newcomb, T. M., Turner, R. H., and Converse, E. *Social Psychology*, Chicago, Holt, Rinehart and Winston, 1965.

Petrullo, L., and Bass, B. M. *Leadership and Interpersonal Behavior*, New York, Holt, Rinehart and Winston, 1961.

Selltiz, C., and Others. *Research Methods in Social Relations*, New York, Henry Holt and Company, 1959.

Sherif, M., and Sherif, C. W. *Reference Groups, Exploration into Conformity and Deviation of Adolescents*, New York, Harper and Row, 1964.

Simpson, R. H. *Improving Teaching-Learning Processes*, New York, Longmans, Green and Company, 1953.

Steiner, I. D., and Fishbein, M. (Editors), *Current Studies in Social Psychology*, Chicago, Holt, Rinehart and Winston, 1965.

Strang, R. *Group Work in Education*, New York, Harper and Brothers, 1958.

Thorpe, L. P., and Others. *Studying Social Relationships in the Classroom*, Evanston, Illinois, Science Research Associates, 1959.

White, R. K., and Lippitt, R. O. *Autocracy and Democracy: An Essay in Experimental Inquiry*, New York, Harper and Brothers, 1960.

Zapf, R. M. *Democratic Processes in the Secondary Classroom*, Englewood Cliffs, New Jersey, Prentice-Hall, 1959.

Note: The student will find past and current issues of the following periodicals of help in understanding the social psychology of learning and teaching: *Behavioral Science, Human Relations, Journal of Personality and Social Psychology, Journal of Conflict Resolution, Psychological Review, Educational and Psychological Measurement*, and *Sociometry*.

## Films

*Changes in Group Atmosphere*, Audio-Visual Aids Department, University of Iowa, Iowa City, Iowa. (15 mins.)

*Discussion in the Social Sciences*, Encyclopedia Britannica Films, 1150 Wilmette Avenue, Wilmette, Illinois. (22 mins.)

*Learning from Class Discussion*, Coronet Instructional Films, Coronet Bldg., Chicago I, Illinois. (11 mins.)

*Shy Guy*, Coronet Instructional Films, Coronet Bldg., Chicago 1, Illinois. (15 mins.)

*Social Climate of Groups*, Audio-Visual Aids Department, University of Iowa, Iowa City, Iowa. (15 mins.)

*You and Your Family*, Association Films, 79 East Adam Street, Chicago 3, Illinois. (11 mins.)

*You and Your Friends*, Association Films, 79 East Adam Street, Chicago 3, Illinois. (11 mins.)

*You and Your Parents*, Association Films, 79 East Adam Street, Chicago 3, Illinois. (15 mins.)

## Questions, Exercises, and Activities

1. Examine a book on sociometry such as N. E. Gronlund's *Sociometry in the Classroom* (New York, Harper, 1959) or a psychological dictionary and give the meaning of each of the following terms: (a) sociometric status, (b) group status, (c) sociometric or group structure, (d) sociogram, (e) isolate, (f) mutual choice, (g) sociometric clique, (h) sociometric cleavage, (i) social acceptability, (j) social frame of reference, (k) in-group, (l) psychegroup, (m) sociogroup.

2. Make a comprehensive list of all ways you can find for assessing the social climate of a classroom.
3. Consider differing kinds of social climate in the type of classroom in which you expect to teach. (a) Describe two contrasting kinds of class leadership roles which you might assume. (b) Also describe how you might experiment to help you determine the probable effects of each of these types of climate. Be specific and give details of how you would proceed in each class and how you would attempt to measure the effects of contrasting social climates.
4. (a) List separately adjectives describing each of the two teachers you have had in high school or college which you think have most favorably influenced your present attitudes toward teaching and learning. (b) Make a similar list for the two teachers who most adversely affected such attitudes. (c) Combine your lists with those of other members of a group of students in your class. (d) Summarize the key differences between the "favorable list" and the "adverse list."

# Chapter 12

## Discovering and Overcoming Special Difficulties in Learning

The slow learning pupil or the one who fails to learn basic essentials creates major problems for the teacher. The problems are intensified as class size and the range of individual differences increases. School populations are increasing at a greater rate than teacher populations, and school attendance laws are more stringent than in the past. Thus there are not only more children in school, but a greater proportion of them stay in school longer. A few decades ago, a child who had difficulty in learning to read, spell, or figure generally dropped out of school and went to work. Today such children tend to stay in school. The consequent increase in class size and in the range of abilities of children in school forces a greater and greater work load upon the teacher, who may feel that he must aim more and more of his work at the group as a whole rather than at individuals who need special consideration.

What to do with the slow reader, or the child with special deficiencies in arithmetic, spelling, speech, or English represents a major concern of teachers at both the elementary and secondary school levels. Teachers and

schools are attempting to find solutions for these problems in the use of special education for the marked deviate, and in the use of modern diagnostic and remedial methods in the classroom. This chapter is a survey of the principles, techniques, and tools which are being used to overcome special difficulties in learning.

## WHAT HAPPENS WHEN DIFFICULTIES REMAIN UNSOLVED?

The effects of difficulties in learning upon a pupil may be far out of proportion to the apparent seriousness of the problem because emotional pressures build up around his area of weakness. He may fall behind the level which his teachers, parents, or administrators have set up as a standard of performance. In reading and arithmetic as many as 10 to 15 per cent of the pupils in a class may be as much as two full grades behind the average grade level for their ages. This is inevitable. But when adults insist upon the achievement of an arbitrary standard for all children, not only will children have difficulties, but also they may suffer emotional disturbances and negative attitudes which can persist long after a given school subject is over. The problem of the slow learner is exaggerated by teachers and parents who cling to unrealistic standards of performance. Perhaps more difficult than the problem of the slow learner is that presented by the child who, as a result of unrealistic and arbitrary demands of the school, rebels and fails to learn even the bare essentials which are well within his capacities.

The number of children who drop out of school is mute testimony to the fact that the school and home have failed to help children solve their scholastic problems. The extent of this condition is indicated by the fact that approximately 14 per cent of the 24 million children from ages five to seventeen are not in school. Also it was recently noted that about 40 per cent of the students who begin high school never finish. In one city where a study of dropouts was made, students were asked why they dropped out. They listed as important reasons, general dissatisfaction, failure to see the value of material learned, and difficulties with subjects or with teachers.

Finally, the effect of unsolved difficulties in learning may be seen in the number of children who are seriously disturbed as a result of school failure. Many are so frightened and frustrated by the requirements of the schools that they may, and often do, suffer long-time maladjustment and feelings of inferiority. In cases such as these, parents and school have added to the usual difficulties of learning. It is to be hoped that the greater use of proper diagnosis and individualized remediation will continue to decrease the number of such cases in our schools.

## TYPES OF DIFFICULTIES AND
## CONTRIBUTING FACTORS

Slow maturation, fearfulness and aggression, poor teaching, illness, and bodily defects are samples of the many factors which may add to the problems of learning. Such factors are in addition to the difficulties of the learning itself which may contain inherent barriers that have to be overcome by all pupils. It has become popular in the past few years to speak of children who have some special difficulty as atypical children—but this is a "fuzzy" concept, for in a sense there is no typical child—each is unique in some way, and each has characteristics which make learning easier in some areas than in others. There are, however, certain children whose need for special attention is very apparent. Some of the more conspicuously handicapped types will now be discussed.

### The Slow Learning Pupil

Generally youngsters who are slow in learning lack either ability, interest, or experience. It is known, for example, that in large populations such as that represented by the group upon which the Stanford-Binet test was standardized (a sample of 2,904 children used) as many as 23 per cent had IQs of ninety or below and 3 per cent had IQs of eighty or below.[1] It is thus apparent that in the typical class there will be pupils who should not be expected to proceed at the rate of the average or superior pupil. When such children are ignored or unduly prodded, they may become "learning casualties."

As was shown in Chapter 8, some slow learning results from the fact that children may have little or no interest in the academic part of school. Interests and abilities are of course closely related, but it is quite possible to find in almost any class a child of high ability and an interest level so low that he learns very little about the formal class work (he probably learns a great deal about a number of other things).

The number of children who have suffered from extreme experiential deprivation is probably not large when this group is compared with those who have low ability or little interest in schooling. However, it is a sizable enough group to warrant serious consideration by teachers and the community as a whole. It may be recalled in this connection that in a study of the home life of poor readers, some were found to have come from homes which were almost "bookless."[2]

---

[1] Lewis M. Terman and Maud A. Merrill, *Stanford-Binet Intelligence Scale*, Boston, Houghton Mifflin Company, 1960, p. 18.

[2] M. C. Almy, "Children's Experience Prior to First Grade and Success in Beginning Reading," *Teachers College Record*, Vol. 51, 1950, pp. 392–393.

### Children with Sensory Defects

Unrecognized or untreated defects of vision or hearing are among the causes of failure to learn in school. About 30 per cent of all children of school age have some visual defect (most of which are easily corrected by glasses), and as many as 12 per cent may have some auditory defect.[3] In all such cases, early recognition, corrective measures, and special provisions in the classroom are essential. A failure to recognize such difficulties in early stages may cause the development of emotional disturbances which further interfere with the learning process. In Figure 29 is shown the *Keystone Visual Survey Instrument* which teachers or other school personnel may use to detect children with visual defects.[4]

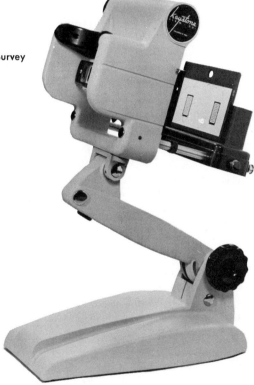

**Figure 29.** The Keystone Visual-Survey Telebinocular.

### Speech Defects

Speech defectives comprise one of the major groups of handicapped school children (about one to two per cent present serious problems).

---

[3] Nelson B. Henry (Editor), *The Education of Exceptional Children*, Forty-Ninth Yearbook of the National Society for the Study of Education, Part II, Chicago, The University of Chicago Press, 1950, p. 156.

[4] Distributed by the Keystone View Company, Meadville, Pennsylvania.

Speech is such an important part of the communication process, however, that regardless of how commendable the teacher's methods, there will probably be some adverse effects upon learning produced by defective speech. Teachers should know that four or five times as many boys as girls stutter in our culture, and that the majority of speech disorders probably arise from psychological rather than physiological causes. They should also know that the school may be the place where the problem comes into sharpest focus, and that because of attendant emotional involvement may interfere with learning and social adjustment.

### Orthopedic Cases

Various crippling diseases, accidents, and structural deviations may interfere with learning in devious ways. Often much school work is missed because of confinement or hospitalization. In other instances the handicap may prevent full participation in school activities. The scope of the problem is shown by the fact that about one person in 100 under twenty-one years of age is affected by some kind of crippling condition (about 550,000 in the U.S.), and about an equal number suffer from rheumatic heart.[5] In all such cases teachers may play an important role in identifying symptoms which point to the need for a medical examination. One authority writes:

> Among the most important sources of information regarding crippled children are the public schools. Countless undiscovered or neglected handicaps have been reported by alert classroom teachers who have recognized deviations in activity, responses or accomplishment and have related these to untreated physical handicaps.[6]

### Social-Emotional Maladjustment

As noted in Chapter 7, perhaps as many as a fifth of reading failures (to take but one subject) are clearly linked with emotional factors, and 80 per cent of cases of reading difficulties have been estimated to be accompanied by strong emotional disturbance. Thus emotional factors not only lead to difficulties of learning, but are a frequent accompaniment of learning difficulties which have other causes.

It is difficult to know how many children are handicapped by maladjustment. The incidence of severe behavior problems and other forms of maladjustment varies with the community or neighborhood and with the times. Undoubtedly there are some classrooms where as many as 20 or 30 per cent of the pupils are emotionally disturbed and upset, but in most situations the number would probably not exceed 5 to 10 per cent. Of these children, boys constitute about 85 per cent of the cases of aggressive

---

[5] Nelson B. Henry (Editor), *The Education of Exceptional Children*, Forty-Ninth Yearbook of the National Society for the Study of Education, Part II, Chicago, The University of Chicago Press, 1950, p. 197.

[6] *Ibid.*, p. 195.

behavior which results in delinquency and classroom disturbances.[7] However, it is probable that girls have just as serious problems but that the expression is more often in the form of withdrawal, fantasy, and nervous symptoms. In any event, adjustment problems constitute a very serious source of difficulty in learning. An entire section of this book is later devoted to such problems.

### Other Difficulties

There are many other factors which create educational casualties or produce difficulties which require special help. Malnutrition, frequent debilitating illness, and glandular disturbances are among those which should be mentioned. Sometimes, of course, the difficulty does not reside within the child, but is a result of previous unfortunate experiences. Parents who push the child too hard, or who pamper, overprotect, or neglect him may contribute to his learning failure, as well as teachers who use poor methods of instruction. Since much of this volume is devoted to just such considerations, discussion will not be given here. Nevertheless, it should be reemphasized that unfortunate attitudes, and bad habits which are learned at home or in the school, may interfere with learning to a great degree and for a long period of time.

### Summary of the Problem

Although there are no adequate or completely up-to-date figures, it is safe to estimate that there are at least 4,000,000 children in today's elementary schools who are in need of special help.

It is probable that at least one child in every seven is in need of a certain amount of individual teaching or assistance in addition to group work. Although special classes and other programs of special education take care of more serious cases, there still remains the borderline mental defective, the partially seeing pupil, the hard-of-hearing child, the slow academic achiever, and many others.

The problem then is of such scope that every teacher must be equipped to diagnose symptoms of slow or impeded learning, and trained to use those remedial techniques which practice has proven effective.

## EARLY RECOGNITION OF DIFFICULTIES

One of the most important principles both in the prevention and treatment of learning difficulties is that full-blown problems are preceded by behavioral symptoms or inadequacies, many of which are easily identifiable. The alert teacher should be able to anticipate difficulties and catch them before they become so extreme that there is great emotional involvement.

---

[7] *Ibid.*, p. 284.

Serious difficulties may, however, be overlooked. In a case known to the writer a child was in the sixth grade at school before a teacher discovered that his eyesight was so poor that not once in the past five years had he been able to read anything which had been written on the blackboard. His eyesight was only 20/200 in the best eye. In another case a freshman at the University of Illinois was astonished to find that he was nearly blind in one eye.

Routine examinations of vision, hearing, and other physical capacities are now a regular part of most schools' programs. Children with partial handicaps are thus identified early. A program of health examinations would seem a minimum essential in any school system. When it is not provided for by the school, however, teachers themselves should administer simple tests of vision and audition when these seem appropriate.[8]

Besides physical checks, it is recommended that children be surveyed in several areas of school achievement and in general ability level.[9] These surveys will reveal children who are having difficulty or are apt to have difficulty in learning.

Tests and checkups may give only a segment of the total picture of the child's problem, and besides some of the instruments may have questionable validity. Therefore, constant surveillance of a class and alertness for behavioral clues which may be signposts to difficulties are essential. A total list of such symptoms is difficult to compose as it would contain hundreds if not thousands of items. In Table 18, however, is presented a check list of some of the symptoms which might occur in the school room and indicate the need for further diagnosis.

## PSYCHO-EDUCATIONAL DIAGNOSIS
## IN THE CLASSROOM

Once a child has been identified as a slow or handicapped learner, it is necessary to establish the cause of the difficulty in order to do remedial teaching. In extreme cases the teacher relies upon agencies such as the health office and the psychological clinic. In many instances, however, the teacher must conduct a diagnosis himself. When he does so, he should keep in mind some of the principles and practices which will now be discussed.

In the first place, diagnosis of difficulties in school work should include a detailed study of the processes which erring pupils use. There is a marked difference between a survey test which simply shows the areas of weakness and a diagnostic test which traces the source of errors. Often tests made by

---

[8] For a description of the tests and devices which teachers may use to test for visual and auditory defects see G. M. Blair, *Diagnostic and Remedial Teaching*, Revised Edition, 1956, Chapter 3.

[9] See Chapter 17 for tests in these areas.

**TABLE 18**

**Symptoms Which May Point to Handicaps and Learning Difficulties \***

| Type of Defect | Symptoms |
|---|---|
| A. *Defects of Vision* | 1. Reading material held too close or too far away. (Normal close work about 8 inches.)<br>2. Squinting, frowning, or shutting of one eye.<br>3. Rubbing of eyes, eyes red, swollen, or eyelids red-rimmed.<br>4. Dizziness, headaches, nausea. |
| B. *Auditory Defects* | 1. High-pitched or flat voice (head turned to hear), posture.<br>2. Very poor spelling, or pronunciation.<br>3. Incorrect interpretation of a question.<br>4. Social withdrawal. |
| C. *Motor Defects* | 1. Uneven posture or gait.<br>2. Tremors.<br>3. Rigidity or stiffness of joints.<br>4. Incoordination.<br>5. Differences in size of limbs. |
| D. *Malnutrition* | 1. Puffiness under eyes.<br>2. Distended abdomen.<br>3. Lowered vitality and lack of energy.<br>4. Dull nails, hair, and skin. |
| E. *Speech Defects* | 1. Articulation (e.g., pay for play).<br>2. Fluency—i.e., jerky, slow, or irregular speech.<br>3. Loudness.<br>4. Voice pitch—monotones or very high pitch.<br>5. Hoarse, harsh, or nasal qualities. |
| F. *Neurological Disturbances* | 1. Chorea (St. Vitus's Dance).<br>2. Tics, such as a jerking of facial muscles.<br>3. Tremors (especially when fingers are tense).<br>4. Flights of attention.<br>5. Brief periods of loss of consciousness. |
| G. *Emotional Disturbances* | 1. Nail biting, twisting hair, thumbsucking, etc.<br>2. Crying easily.<br>3. Exaggerated fears and angers.<br>4. Responses out of proportion to stimuli.<br>5. Night terrors.<br>6. Symptoms of fatigue, such as backaches, tired eyes. |

\* Parts of this table were adapted from The National Society for the Study of Education, *op. cit.*, pp. 42, 43, 51, 52, 53, and 57.

the teacher for a particular case will give more diagnostic information than a standard test. Teachers should keep a record of the kinds of errors which given pupils make.

Worthwhile information may also be obtained through interviews with individual students. The amount of reliable information gained in such interviews is believed to be a function of the objectivity, acceptance, and rapport which the teacher is able to attain. Following are five rules for interviewing. (1) Do not talk too much. Studies of professional counselors

show that the ones who talk too much may discourage the client's talking, and make the interview less effective. (2) Begin the interview with innocuous material. An interview in which the teacher begins by criticizing or scolding a child will put him so much on the defensive that he will not open up; hence will not provide the information for which the interview is intended. Likewise pressing the child too hard or fast may cut off the flow of conversation. (3) Keep the interview pointed toward a central problem. If the talk gets painfully close to a subject (such as a child's feeling of inferiority about acne) the pupil may attempt to throw up a protective barrage of talk which is unrelated to any real issues. (4) Keep the material of the interview in complete confidence. There is no way to dry up the stream of information more quickly than to repeat to other students or parents the information which is given in confidence. (5) Accept what the child says. Censure or value judgments during the interview destroys the rapport which should be maintained. The child's perception of the interview situation as a warm permissive atmosphere should guarantee a decrease in his resistance.

## SOME GENERAL PRINCIPLES IN GIVING SPECIAL HELP

Following diagnosis, work should be set up to get the child back into class work. There will be a variation in the specific techniques used in different subject areas (as will be seen in the next section). However, there are some steps which apply in nearly every instance of remedial teaching.

One of the first of these is to remove negative emotional attitudes. Since a large percentage of learning difficulties are either caused by or accompanied by emotional disturbances it is clear that a major step is to alleviate this situation. A counterpart to alleviating emotional difficulties is to build up the child's self-confidence. A part of the problem of emotional disturbance is the effect upon youngsters of their view of themselves in relation to school work. Feelings of inadequacy in a particular field may persist long after the reason for it ceases to exist. Witness the number of students and adults who say, "I never was any good in arithmetic, I just can't do it."

A second important step is to find materials (in the area of weakness) which are interesting and commensurate with the child's readiness. A retarded reader might have great interest in comic books, and these might well be the media for beginning remedial instruction.[10] Thirdly, the remedial work must be such as to give close attention and guidance to learners

---

[10] Actually many comic books today are picture books. Ones such as *Classic Comics* and *Classics Illustrated* published by the Gilberton Company, New York, and *The Adventure Series* of the General Electric Company, Schenectady, New York, may be valuable supplementary reading materials. In Figure 30 children are shown reading this type of material.

**Figure 30.** Children Reading Highly Illustrated Versions of the Classics.

in early trials of any new kind of learning, or with new materials. Original difficulties, which may be caused by quite simple mistakes, may grow, become persistent, and affect whole areas of work. Finally, the child should be given an early opportunity to use and demonstrate his new-found skills. In this connection, however, care should be exercised so that the child who is undergoing remedial teaching is not thrown into a competitive situation too quickly, as it may undermine his growing confidence.

## DIFFICULTIES IN READING

More children seem to have difficulty with reading than with any other school subject. The causes of reading difficulty may be linked to any of the problems previously discussed, but in addition there may be specific difficulties which will become apparent only with detailed diagnosis. The report which follows is typical of the findings of a remedial reading clinic with respect to causes or concomitant factors in reading difficulties.

Fifty-four of the seventy pupils needed help in auditory discrimination, twenty were word readers, fifteen had a smart brother or sister. Eleven were troubled with chilling fears, nine thought they were "dumbbells," seven were suffering from insufficient sleep, seven could not see well, four came from broken homes, three had speech difficulties, eight had emotional difficulties due to too much parental pressure, neglect by the mother, overly strict father and a recent death in the family. Five were badly handicapped for physical reasons—thyroid imbalance, scarlet fever, rheumatic fever, bad tonsils, hearing defect, epilepsy, and cerebral palsy. One had learned the sound of individual letters but simply could not blend them.

345

*Diagnosis*

When children have unusual difficulty in reading, the following are perhaps minimum diagnostic procedures which should be undertaken.

1. The child should be given a non-verbal intelligence test. (A test which requires reading is obviously of no value in the case of a retarded reader, as such a test tells only what is already known, viz., that the child reads poorly.)
2. A check of vision and hearing should be made.
3. There ought to be some notation of the child's previous reading experiences. Such items as records of failures and parents' reactions should be included.
4. An appraisal of the child's interests and attitudes about school should be made. Information thus obtained may serve as a basis for the kind of remedial material that should be used.
5. Finally, the youngster should be given a good diagnostic reading test. Information about a child's reading abilities which may be obtained from various standard tests usually includes appraisal of reading speed and comprehension, and some measure of vocabulary; and often contains sections which test for special reading skills such as map-reading, use of an index, and reading of mathematical or other technical material.[11]

*Remedial Reading Instruction*

Remedial reading instruction aims to increase reading speed and comprehension by increasing reading enjoyment, and providing for practice with a wide variety of materials. The assumption is made, of course, in giving such instruction that a child is reading well below his level of ability. The slow learner, who is achieving well for his ability, simply needs to be guarded from the strain of intense competition and from emotional disturbance, and helped to find materials which are easy enough and enjoyable enough to keep his reading skills growing at a rate which is normal for him.

For the underachiever, on the other hand, a definite remedial or corrective program is necessary. Following are some suggested steps:

1. Go back to where the child is.
2. Build sight vocabulary and speed up recognition.
3. Teach self-help sounding.
4. Develop comprehension.
5. Secure much interesting reading at the child's present level.

---

[11] For more detailed discussion and illustration of diagnostic instruments see Chapter 17.

There are hundreds of remedial techniques which have been used successfully in both classrooms and clinics. Most are based on the principle of encouraging children to like reading by providing enjoyable practice. A frequent method of doing this is to make a game of learning. For example, Dolch has a device for improving sight vocabulary called "The Group Word Teaching Game," a sample card of which is shown in Figure 31.

Another method which is used with very difficult cases is described by Fernald.[12] First the child traces a word with "finger contact," saying each part as he traces it. He then writes the word himself, and uses it in a story. After the story is finished he makes a copy of the word on a file card and places it in an alphabetical card case. As a child progresses he is able to pick out new words, spell, and pronounce them without tracing them. Some teachers have used with success a method whereby the child tells a story, which is taken down by the teacher, transcribed and typed out, and given

| please | just | hold | keep | buy |
|--------|------|------|------|-----|
| today | | shall | why | |
| grow | try | H 5 | drink | kind |
| six | | use | well | |
| myself | pick | fall | | hot |

**Figure 31.** Group Word Teaching Game. Each card has 25 of the 200 words from Dolch's Basic Sight Vocabulary arranged in random order. The rules of the game are the same as in "Bingo." Successful participation necessitates a rapid recognition of words, both as they sound, and as they look. (Reproduced by permission of the author and The Garrard Press, Champaign, Illinois.)

---

[12] Grace Fernald, *Remedial Techniques in Basic School Subjects*, New York, McGraw-Hill Book Company, 1943, p. 35.

**Figure 32.** Child Learning to Read by the Tracing Method.

to the child to read. In Figure 32 a child is shown learning to read by using the tracing method. In Figure 33 the pupil is reading a story he has related to the teacher and which the teacher has typed for him.

One of the main objectives in remedial reading is to increase the child's self-confidence and decrease fear and anxiety. Fernald's clinic did this by starting a child with big words which gave him a sense of accomplishment and status, especially when he could use them in the presence of peers or even adults. The following anecdote related by Fernald illustrates this technique.[13]

Perhaps the most extreme case of positive reconditioning the writer has ever seen occurred at a teachers' institute meeting in California some years ago. Mrs. Helen Keller [14] was addressing the meeting on the subject of spelling. The children who were supposed to come for the demonstration had not arrived. When Mrs. Keller spoke with regret of the fact that she would be unable to demonstrate the remedial technique, a large and positive woman arose and asked, "Do you want the worst speller in the city for demonstration?" When Mrs. Keller said she would be delighted to have any school child help her out, the woman started down the aisle with a poor scared little eleven-year-old boy held firmly by the shoulder. Everyone gasped at the brutality of so disgracing the child.

Mrs. Keller shook hands with the boy in a matter-of-fact way and told

---

[13] *Ibid.*, pp. 15 and 16.
[14] Co-worker of Dr. Fernald.

**Figure 33.** Pupil Reading a Story He Has Composed and Which the Teacher Has Typed for Him.

the mother to sit down in the audience. Within a few moments Mrs. Keller had determined how he could best learn words. She then proceeded to teach him *development, university, department, education.*

All the fear and self-consciousness disappeared. As the boy finished the word *education* he turned and grinned at his mother who was staring at the performance in open-mouthed amazement. The audience broke into loud applause. The school reported later that the emotional transformation was complete and permanent. Mrs. Keller worked with the boy and his teacher until they were ready to go on with spelling by the new method. Each day the boy gloated over the words he had learned and went on to new conquests.

IMPROVEMENT OF VOCABULARY AND COMPREHENSION. Regardless of the cause, poor readers are frequently retarded in vocabulary, and are often unable to recognize even the most common words. For beginning readers one of the important first steps is the provision of a simple sight vocabulary. From 50 per cent to 75 per cent of ordinary reading matter is made up of 220 very common words immediately recognized by any capable reader. These words are presented in Table 19.

When pupils have difficulties with any of the words from this list, they need practice which will build up their ability to recognize immediately those which they have missed. These words have been printed on flash cards for use with either individual pupils or with groups, and they have been made into games as is shown in Figures 31 and 34.

Probably the most effective method of developing both vocabulary and comprehension is through wide reading in a variety of subject matter areas.

## TABLE 19
### A Basic Sight Vocabulary of 220 Words *

| | | | | |
|---|---|---|---|---|
| a | don't | if | out | these |
| about | down | in | over | they |
| after | draw | into | own | think |
| again | drink | is | | this |
| all | | it | pick | those |
| always | eat | its | play | three |
| am | eight | | please | to |
| an | every | jump | pretty | today |
| and | | just | pull | together |
| any | fall | | put | too |
| are | far | keep | | try |
| around | fast | kind | ran | two |
| as | find | know | read | |
| ask | first | | red | under |
| at | five | laugh | ride | up |
| ate | fly | let | right | upon |
| away | for | light | round | us |
| | found | like | run | use |
| be | four | little | | |
| because | from | live | said | very |
| been | full | long | saw | |
| before | funny | look | say | walk |
| best | | | see | want |
| better | gave | made | seven | warm |
| big | get | make | shall | was |
| black | give | many | she | wash |
| blue | go | may | show | we |
| both | goes | me | sing | well |
| bring | going | much | sit | went |
| brown | good | must | six | were |
| but | got | my | sleep | what |
| buy | green | myself | small | when |
| by | grow | | so | where |
| | | never | some | which |
| | had | new | soon | white |
| call | has | no | start | who |
| came | have | not | stop | why |
| can | he | now | | will |
| carry | help | | take | wish |
| clean | her | of | tell | with |
| cold | here | off | ten | work |
| come | him | old | thank | would |
| could | his | on | that | write |
| cut | hold | once | the | |
| | hot | one | their | yellow |
| did | how | only | them | yes |
| do | hurt | open | then | you |
| does | | or | there | your |
| done | I | our | | |

* E. W. Dolch, *A Manual for Remedial Reading* (Second Edition), p. 438. Copyright, 1945, by The Garrard Press, Champaign, Illinois.

**Figure 34.** Child Learning Sight Vocabulary by Utilizing a Word Wheel Which His Teacher Has Constructed.

Words learned in context are much better remembered and also more clearly understood than those learned in isolation. Especially desirable materials for this purpose are those which have immediate usefulness and which help the pupil answer questions and solve problems.

Supplementary methods of improving vocabulary include word study (using dictionaries or building a class dictionary), a study of the derivation of words, and a study of prefixes. The list in Table 20 should be useful in connection with the study of prefixes.

IMPROVEMENT OF READING SPEED. Generally reading speed increases as children read more, and as they come to enjoy reading. When reading speed does remain relatively slow, it is usually a symptom of difficulty in comprehension, poor mechanics of reading, or of a lack of motivation. In the writers' opinion the best way to increase a child's reading speed is to help him find easy-to-comprehend materials which he will enjoy, and encourage him to read rapidly. In those few cases where slow reading is due to bad habits which are persistent (such as pointing with finger to reading material, or regressive eye movements) a series of corrective exercises under the individual guidance of the teacher should be undertaken.

Speed of reading is, of course, closely linked with comprehension. Many children who read slowly do so because they do not really understand

**TABLE 20**

**Prefixes Occurring Most Often in the
20,000 Words of the Thorndike\* List †**

| Prefix | Meaning | Frequency |
|--------|---------|-----------|
| ab | from | 98 |
| ad | to | 433 |
| be | by | 111 |
| com | with | 500 |
| de | from | 282 |
| dis | apart | 299 |
| en | in | 182 |
| ex | out | 286 |
| in | into | 336 |
| in | not | 317 |
| pre | before | 127 |
| pro | in front of | 146 |
| re | back | 457 |
| sub | under | 112 |
| un | not | 378 |

(These fifteen prefixes account for 82 per cent of the total prefixes in Thorndike's word list.)

\* E. L. Thorndike, *Teachers List of 20,000 Words*, New York, Bureau of Publications, Teachers College, Columbia University, 1932.

† R. G. Stauffer, "A Study of Prefixes in the Thorndike List to Establish a List of Prefixes that Should be Taught in the Elementary School," *Journal of Educational Research*, Vol. 35, 1942, pp. 453–458.

many of the words they are asked to read. Likewise slow readers may not have learned (because of insufficient neural maturation or poor training) to respond to reduced cues, or to use their perceptual abilities effectively. Symptomatic of inadequate perceptual ability are poor performance on flash-card drills and poor eye movements while reading. Training to produce better understanding and to increase perceptual skills may involve a comprehensive program which enriches the child's experience with words and meanings, and provides exercises such as flash-card drills and reading acceleration. Acceleration has been made possible through the use of machines which uncover printed material at a predetermined rate. One such device, The Reading Accelerator, is shown in Figure 35. This machine adapts itself to all sizes of books or pamphlets, and operates in such a way that the pupil is forced to read at speeds which are appropriate for him.

Another scheme for improving speed of reading is known as the *push-*

**Figure 35.** The Reading Accelerator. (Courtesy of Science Research Associates, Chicago, Illinois.)

*card method.* In using this technique, the teacher should first determine the pupil's rate of reading by timing him while he reads a few pages of a book or other selection. For example, it might be found that a given pupil requires, on the average, five seconds to complete a line of print. After ascertaining this fact, the teacher should ask the pupil to continue his reading of the given material. As soon as he has read a line or two the teacher should begin moving a large card down the page, one line at a time, and at a rate of speed that will force the pupil to read at a faster than usual tempo. Since the pupil in our example reads a line in about five seconds, the teacher might begin by moving the card at the rate of four seconds per line. This will make it necessary for the pupil to speed up his reading to keep ahead of the card. With a little practice, the teacher will find that it is possible to count at a rate which will correspond to one second per count. Some teachers have found that by counting to themselves and saying "one-thousand-one," "one-thousand-two," "one-thousand-three," "one-thousand-four," etc., they are able to count out seconds. Pupil assistants, who have learned the technique of using the push-card method, may substitute for the teacher in using this device. Figure 36 shows one girl helping another increase her speed of reading with the push-card method.

**Figure 36.** Increasing Speed of Reading by Means of the Push-Card Method.

Often youngsters, and adults for that matter, can read more rapidly than they actually do without any loss of comprehension. In fact, increased speed of reading frequently is accompanied by an increase in comprehension. Since persons are generally not aware that they do have the potential to read more rapidly, devices such as that shown in Figure 35 serve the dual purpose of demonstrating to the individual that he can read more rapidly, and at the same time provides him training in more rapid reading.

IMPROVEMENT OF INTEREST IN READING. Many children lose interest in reading because of the type of material which they are forced to read, and because reading materials are of a single-difficulty level in a classroom in which reading ability varies as much as seven- or eight-grade levels (see Chapter 6). One obvious way to heighten interest in reading, therefore, is to provide a variety of reading materials representing not only several levels of reading ability but also several areas of interest. Studies have been made of youngsters' reading interests, including the interests of retarded readers, and books which have been preferred have been listed for the use of classroom teachers. One such list appears in Table 21. Some older children who show no interest in reading books can often be induced to read newspaper-type material if the vocabulary is simple enough. Teenagers will often read *My Weekly Reader* and other news materials which are of elementary school difficulty. In any reading improvement program, the classroom library holds a key position. The children in Figure 37 are shown

## TABLE 21
### Easy Reading Books for Older Children *

1. The Aviation Readers (first three books). The Macmillan Company, New York
   *Straight Up, Straight Down, Planes for Bob and Andy*
2. The Core Vocabulary Readers, The Macmillan Company, New York
   *The Ranch Book, Rusty Wants a Dog, Smoky the Crow*
3. The Unit Reading Series, The Macmillan Company, New York
   Booklets to go along with readers for first three grades, many of them of older interest and without pictures of children.
4. The Fairy Tale Series, Chas. E. Merrill Company, Columbus, Ohio
   *First Fairy Tales, Giants and Fairies, Magic Tales*
5. The Pleasure Reading Series, The Garrard Press, Champaign, Illinois
   *Fairy Stories, Famous Stories, Bible Stories*, and others.
6. The Walt Disney Books, D. C. Heath, Boston
   An unmarked series of readers from Primer on, with the Disney animal characters.
7. *Robinson Crusoe for Young Folks*, Beckley Cardy Company, Chicago, Illinois
8. Picture Scripts, E. M. Hale Company, Chicago, Illinois
   Booklets in Literature, Science, and Social Studies
9. Science Education Series, Row, Peterson and Company, Evanston, Illinois
   Four Primary Booklets, *Spring Is Here, Summer Is Here*, etc.
10. The beginning books of other science series such as by Charles Scribner's Sons, Ginn and Company, Singer Publishing Company
11. Childhood of Famous Americans Series, Bobbs-Merrill Company, Indianapolis, Indiana

    | | | |
    |---|---|---|
    | *Abe Lincoln* | *Boy of Old Virginia* | *Alex Hamilton* |
    | *Robert Fulton* | *Mark Twain* | *Ben Franklin* |

12. American Adventure Series, Wheeler Publishing Company, Chicago, Illinois

    | | | |
    |---|---|---|
    | *Davy Crockett* | *Kit Carson* | *Buffalo Bill* |
    | *Daniel Boone* | *Chief Black Hawk* | and others |

13. Easy Reading Books by Scott, Foresman and Company, Chicago, Illinois

    | | | |
    |---|---|---|
    | *The Box Car Children* | *Eight Treasured Stories* | *When Washington Danced* |
    | *Lorna Doone* | *Six Great Stories* | *Moby Dick* |
    | *Tom Sawyer* | | |

14. Real People Series, Row, Peterson and Company, Evanston, Illinois
    Booklets of 36 pages, each about some person prominent in American history
15. Meadowbrook History Stories, T. Y. Crowell and Company, New York
    *On Indian Trails, The First Year, Shipboy with Columbus*
16. The Real Book Series, Garden City Books, Garden City, New York
    Animals, sports, pets, inventions, hobbies, etc.
17. The "Initial Biography" Series, Charles Scribner's Sons, New York
    Washington, Lincoln, Jackson, and others.

* E. W. Dolch, Unpublished Material, Urbana, College of Education, University of Illinois.

reading what interests them from the tables and shelves of their own classroom library.

In summary, it might be said that an excellent remedial reading program always possesses two important characteristics. The first is *motivation*. Children must want to learn to read. The second is *materials*. They must have a wealth of exercises and reading matter upon which to practice. In Table 22 a wide variety of materials and teaching aids useful in a remedial reading program is presented.

**Figure 37.** Utilizing the Classroom Library to Improve Reading Skills.

## REMEDIAL SPELLING

One of the basic skills of good communication is spelling. At one time, this skill was probably overemphasized in our schools. The winner of one of the state "spelling bees" in Illinois two decades ago was given individual tutoring by his teacher for three years. During this time the two of them tried to cover the entire unabridged dictionary. Although spelling has been relegated to a position of less prominence in today's schools, it is still essential if understandable writing is to be achieved.

Teachers at all grade levels are aware that they face a real problem in their attempt to bring their pupils up to a satisfactory level of spelling proficiency. Recently an eighth-grade teacher asked her pupils to write a short paragraph on the subject "What I would do tomorrow if I had a vacation." She showed these papers, which contained numerous misspellings, to the writer. One boy of good general ability wrote as follows:

> if I had a vaccation on tusiday I would finish my choirs and start putting rings in my moter and nount it on the watter pump. after I finest that I would laid the top floor of the barn.

Another boy wrote:

> I am going to St. Lious to buy a new suit where my boitaday moeny. We are going to seen the hole day over there. . . .

356

**TABLE 22**

**Materials and Teaching Aids Useful in a Remedial Reading Program** *

| Title | Publisher |
|-------|-----------|
| Dolch Games (Selected titles) | Garrard, Champaign, Illinois |
| Puzzle Pages | Garrard, Champaign, Illinois |
| Conquests in Reading | Webster, St. Louis, Missouri |
| Eye and Ear Fun | Webster, St. Louis, Missouri |
| Vocabulary Development | Macmillan, New York, N. Y. |
| Word Clues | Educational Developmental Laboratory, Huntington, N. Y. |
| Tach-X Tachistoscope | Educational Developmental Laboratory, Huntington, N. Y. |
| Controlled Reader | Educational Developmental Laboratory, Huntington, N. Y. |
| Skimmer | Educational Developmental Laboratory, Huntington, N. Y. |
| Shadowscope Reading Pacer | Psychotechnics, Inc., Chicago, Illinois |
| Tachomatic | Psychotechnics, Inc., Chicago, Illinois |
| Reading Accelerator | Science Research Associates, Chicago, Illinois |
| Word Analysis Practice | Harcourt, Brace and World, New York, N. Y. |
| Speech-to-Print Phonics | Harcourt, Brace and World, New York, N. Y. |
| Working with Sounds | Barnell Loft, Rockville Centre, N. Y. |
| Using Context | Barnell Loft, Rockville Centre, N. Y. |
| Word Analysis (Spectrum of Skills) | Macmillan, New York, N. Y. |
| Conquests in Reading | Webster, St. Louis, Missouri |
| The Magic World of Dr. Spello | Webster, St. Louis, Missouri |
| Remedial Reading Drills | Wahr, Ann Arbor, Michigan |
| Structural Reading Series | Singer, Syracuse, N. Y. |
| Ways to Read Words | Bureau of Publications, Teachers College, New York |
| Ways to Read More Words | Bureau of Publications, Teachers College, New York |
| Breaking the Sound Barrier | Macmillan, New York, N. Y. |
| Word Attack | Harcourt, Brace and World, New York, N. Y. |
| Building Reading Power | Charles Merrill, Columbus, Ohio |
| Building Reading Skills | McCormick-Mathers, Wichita, Kansas |
| Phonics We Use | Lyons and Carnahan, Chicago, Illinois |
| Time for Phonics | Allyn and Bacon, Boston, Massachusetts |
| Developmental Reading Worktexts | Bobbs-Merrill, Indianapolis, Indiana |
| Reader's Digest Skill Builders | Reader's Digest, Pleasantville, N. Y. |
| Power Builders, Reading Laboratories | Science Research Associates, Chicago, Illinois |
| Rate Builders, Reading Laboratories | Science Research Associates, Chicago, Illinois |
| Standard Test Lessons in Reading | Bureau of Publications, Teachers College, New York |
| Practice Exercises | Bureau of Publications, Teachers College, New York |
| Practice Readers | Webster, St. Louis, Missouri |
| Advanced Skills in Reading | Macmillan, New York, N. Y. |
| Reading for Significance | American, New York, N. Y. |
| Reading with Purpose | American, New York, N. Y. |
| Following Directions | Barnell Loft, Rockville Centre, N. Y. |
| Getting the Facts | Barnell Loft, Rockville Centre, N. Y. |
| Locating the Answer | Barnell Loft, Rockville Centre, N. Y. |
| Reading Comprehension | Macmillan, New York, N. Y. |
| How to Study | Science Research Associates, Chicago, Illinois |
| How to Be A Better Student | Science Research Associates, Chicago, Illinois |
| Learn How to Study | Science Research Associates, Chicago, Illinois |
| Learning How to Use the Dictionary | Macmillan, New York, N. Y. |
| Reading Latitude from Maps | McGraw-Hill, New York, N. Y. |

* (Adapted from materials prepared by William R. Powell, University of Illinois, 1968.)

There were six other papers from this class of 40 pupils in which the spelling was on the same general level as that shown in the two previous illustrations. What to do with children who spell poorly causes teachers much concern.

Poor spellers are easily located, but the causes are not readily apparent. Unlike deficiencies in other school subjects, the major cause does not appear to be closely related to low ability. Fernald claims that most poor spellers are the direct result of poor teaching practices, viz., (1) formal spelling periods, (2) monotonous and uninteresting repetition of meaningless content, (3) lack of adequate attention to spelling, and (4) the use of methods by which certain children cannot learn.[15]

As in other areas, there is available to teachers, a wealth of research material upon which diagnosis and remedial teaching can be based. Besides a number of good diagnostic tests, there are several spelling lists which include words commonly needed by the average person. For example, Dolch has composed a list of 2000 words which comprises about 95 per cent of the words needed for ordinary writing.[16] Also there are studies of the kinds of words with which children may be expected to have difficulty. In the Gates list,[17] for example, not only are frequency of errors reported, but also the kinds of errors are indicated so that teachers may know what to stress in their teaching. The list of words in Table 23 comprises the 100 words most often misspelled by elementary school children as shown by one study. The sample was taken from school children in forty-eight states, including 190 school systems, and a total of 14,643 children. Words are arranged in the order of their frequency of misspelling. The most misspelled word was *their* (964 times) and the least *money* (54 times).

Any remedial teaching of spelling must take account of the basic fact that children have different kinds of word imagery. Some form visual images, others auditory, and still others motor (the way the word feels when spoken or written). Successful remediation usually entails adding practice in various ways of perceiving words. The most stubborn cases, for example, who have failed to spell using the sight or phonics approach, may show immediate and marked improvement when given practice in tracing words. In all such cases, important basic causes, such as emotional disturbance, negative conditioning, and physical or mental handicaps must also be given careful consideration.

One who has studied the principles of learning and of transfer of training would be forced seriously to question the value of formal spelling

---

[15] Grace Fernald, *op. cit.*, pp. 186–192.

[16] E. W. Dolch, *The 2,000 Commonest Words for Spelling*, Champaign, Illinois, The Garrard Press, 1945.

[17] A. I. Gates, *A List of Spelling Difficulties in 3876 Words*, New York, Bureau of Publications, Teachers College, Columbia University, 1937.

**TABLE 23**

**One Hundred Words Most Often Misspelled by Children of the Elementary Grades ***

| their | because | swimming | it's | all right |
|---|---|---|---|---|
| too | thought | first | started | happened |
| there | and | were | that's | didn't |
| they | beautiful | than | would | always |
| then | its | two | again | surprise |
| until | went | know | heard | before |
| our | where | decided | received | caught |
| asked | stopped | friend | coming | every |
| off | very | when | to | different |
| through | morning | let's | said | interesting |
| you're | something | mother | wanted | sometimes |
| clothes | named | another | hear | friends |
| looked | came | threw | from | children |
| people | name | some | frightened | an |
| pretty | tried | bought | for | school |
| running | here | getting | February | jumped |
| believe | many | going | once | around |
| little | knew | course | like | dropped |
| things | with | woman | they're | babies |
| him | together | animals | cousin | money |

* L. W. Johnson, "One Hundred Words Most Often Misspelled by Children," *Journal of Educational Research*, Vol. 44, 1950, pp. 154–155. A similar study has been made of high school spelling. First reports are contained in Thomas C. Pollock, "Misspelling in the Twelfth Grade," *Teachers Service Bulletin in English*, New York, The Macmillan Company, Vol. 6, No. 1, November, 1952.

exercises in which pupils commit lists of words to memory. In the first place, words so studied are out of context, and, as already shown, material is more easily and effectively learned when in a meaningful context. Secondly, the pupil's goal may be simply to learn the list and keep the spellings in mind long enough to repeat them to the teacher. Finally, it is certain that all children do not need practice in spelling the same words. It would thus appear that the most effective program, and one which might prevent difficulties in spelling, would be to concentrate on spelling as an integral part of the pupil's written work. For example, a daily systematic check by the teacher and/or other pupils of all written work done by a particular child should provide a list of misspelled words for him. Work by each child on his own list might avoid much repetitious and needless practice, and in turn increase interest in spelling.

## REMEDIAL SPEECH

Defective speech deserves consideration in its own right, but in addition needs special consideration because of its adverse effect upon other school

learnings. Furthermore, speech disorders are frequently accompanied by emotional difficulties. The importance of speech is well put by Johnson who writes:

> Children and adults, in school and out, do more speaking than either reading or writing. Speech is the most used of all language functions, and the most fateful, day in and day out, in the social and workaday relationships of people everywhere. What is done about speech, and especially speech disorders in our schools is, therefore, of utmost importance to the pupils as individuals and to society which they will help to create as they become adult citizens.[18]

Speech disorders include those of articulation, stuttering or stammering, and voice problems. As there are a number of disorders, so there are a number of causes, including illness, organic defect, hearing loss, injury through the misuse of the voice, and psychological factors. Stuttering, which is probably the most dramatic and common of the classroom disorders is believed to be almost entirely a result of psychological factors. Children who stutter are in many cases made to do so by parents, early teachers, or other persons having a formative influence upon the child. Parental anxiety about speech and the focusing of undue attention upon the normal non-fluency of children are common causes. It is not uncommon for parents to label, as a stutterer, a child who is having no more than the expected amount of speech difficulty. Speech may, in such cases, become a focal point for children's anxieties and feelings of inadequacy. A speech disorder becomes closely linked with emotional life, and may be made more serious by events which increase emotional tension. Emotional strain may magnify the disorder, especially in social or group situations.

A leading expert in the psychology of speech has given as general principles for classroom teachers the following points.[19]

1. No classroom teacher or school administrator should ever diagnose any child as a stutterer.
2. Speaking should be fun (a high degree of criticism of speech is bad).
3. Speaking should be encouraged (not forced).
4. Conditions affecting speech adversely should be minimized. In general a more informal, socially permissive classroom is less apt to cause speech difficulty. The more formal, threatening recitation or oral quiz is apt to do little to help and may actually interfere with the adjustment of the speech-handicapped person.

---

[18] National Society for the Study of Education, *op. cit.*, p. 176.
[19] National Society for the Study of Education, *op. cit.*, pp. 188–192.

## REMEDIAL ENGLISH

Studies on a national scale have helped show the frequency of various kinds of errors in written and spoken expression. For example, one survey showed that somewhat over one-half the errors in oral English are in verb forms. A sample list (which in the twelfth grade comprised 70 per cent of all errors) was: [20]

| | | |
|---|---|---|
| ain't | has rang | done-did |
| he don't | have did | can-may |
| I seen | is-are | drawed |
| have saw | sit-set | blowed |

Surveys such as these not only provide teachers with guides to material which should be stressed, but also serve as guides for analyses of errors within their own class. Identification of common errors and of the pupils who make them is a first step in gearing the teaching program to individual abilities, needs, and handicaps.

Errors of pupils in English expression (especially spoken) are apt to be persistent even in the face of efforts by the school to correct them. Ways of expression and colloquialisms from community and family are formed over a long period of time. Furthermore, pupils are apt to see school English and out-of-school English as unrelated. In spite of the effects of early training, and strong attitudes on the part of some pupils against changing to better English usage, there is much that the school can do in remedying poor English. The following points should be fundamental to any remedial program.

1. Give constant examples of correct spoken and written English in a variety of situations. Class discussions, class reports, school clubs, and social events will offer opportunities for the use of English which the student may begin to emulate. Youngsters are much more apt to accept change of English expression and attitudes about English from their peers than they are from their teachers.

2. Provide students with a knowledge of specific errors. Show pupils the correct expression and give a rule they can follow in finding it in the future. A paper which is returned with such notes as: "Too many incomplete sentences," "Punctuation poor," or "Capitalization of wrong words" will be of little help to the student who does not realize the specific errors of punctuation, capitalization, and sentence structure he is making.

3. Work on minimum essentials first. Glaring errors such as "He seen

---

[20] G. M. Blair, *op. cit.*, p. 328.

them" should be the targets of beginning instruction. Only after the rules which govern such common mistakes are understood and properly applied should teachers begin to stress the niceties of English. If these latter details are pressed too hard, and before the student is ready for them, the whole program may break down.

4. Above all, follow the principles of motivation (Chapters 7 and 8). Have English learned in context; relate it to presently existing interests and needs. The theme topic, selected entirely by the teacher, and covering a subject such as "My Favorite Grandparent," is still widely used in teaching English composition. Such assignments may be justified occasionally, but when they are the only kind which are made, there is little chance that all students will be interested.

5. Enlist the aid of other teachers in the school. English, reading, spelling, speech, and arithmetic are important to all teachers. Learning these things should be considered as a venture for the entire school rather than the responsibility for only one class.

## REMEDIAL MATHEMATICS

Perhaps in no other academic subject are deficiencies so persistent and so needless as in arithmetic. Many surveys have shown that students fail to learn the fundamental essentials of arithmetic even though they have sufficient ability and are not hampered by emotional disturbances. The idea that "I just can't get arithmetic" is common among college students as well as among those in the lower grades who face arithmetic problems daily. There is little doubt that in the schooling of many pupils there have been some experiences with mathematics which have built up habits of avoidance toward any problem or situation which involves even the simplest arithmetic. It is therefore crucial that early identification and remedial work be undertaken before such adverse attitudes are formed. In this task the teacher will find many useful diagnostic tools. Some of the tests available identify the specific processes involved in the several skills in each of the basic computational areas. A good example is the Buswell-John Teacher's Diagnostic Chart for Individual Difficulties in the Fundamental Process of Arithmetic, which is shown in Figure 38.

There is no substitute for practice in learning the essential combinations in arithmetic. Practice of these combinations in a pleasant, non-threatening atmosphere is the mainstay of remedial work in this field. In order that this activity be specific to the student's weaknesses, it is advisable for teachers to keep an individual record of students' errors. To make the work pleasant, teachers should know of a variety of exercises and games which might appeal to the student who needs special help. Some of the schemes which have been developed for this purpose are: (1) self-practice workbooks with graded step-by-step exercises (available for all levels from

Teacher's Diagnosis

for pupil _____

Published by the
Public School Publishing Co.,
Bloomington, Illinois
Printed in U. S. A.

**TEACHER'S DIAGNOSTIC CHART**
FOR
**INDIVIDUAL DIFFICULTIES**

**FUNDAMENTAL PROCESSES IN ARITHMETIC**
Prepared by G. T. Buswell and Lenore John

Name_____ School_____ Grade_____ Age_____ IQ_____

Date of Diagnosis:_____ Add._____; Subt._____; Mult._____; Div _____

Teacher's preliminary diagnosis_____

**ADDITION:** (Place a check before each habit observed in the pupil's work)

| | |
|---|---|
| ___ a1 Errors in combinations | ___ a15 Disregarded column position |
| ___ a2 Counting | ___ a16 Omitted one or more digits |
| ___ a3 Added carried number last | ___ a17 Errors in reading numbers |
| ___ a4 Forgot to add carried number | ___ a18 Dropped back one or more tens |
| ___ a5 Repeated work after partly done | ___ a19 Derived unknown combination from familiar one |
| ___ a6 Added carried number irregularly | ___ a20 Disregarded one column |
| ___ a7 Wrote number to be carried | ___ a21 Error in writing answer |
| ___ a8 Irregular procedure in column | ___ a22 Skipped one or more decades |
| ___ a9 Carried wrong number | ___ a23 Carrying when there was nothing to carry |
| ___ a10 Grouped two or more numbers | ___ a24 Used scratch paper |
| ___ a11 Splits numbers into parts | ___ a25 Added in pairs, giving last sum as answer |
| ___ a12 Used wrong fundamental operation | ___ a26 Added same digit in two columns |
| ___ a13 Lost place in column | ___ a27 Wrote carried number in answer |
| ___ a14 Depended on visualization | ___ a28 Added same number twice |

Habits not listed above_____

(Write observation notes on pupil's work in space opposite examples)

| (1) | | (5) | |
|---|---|---|---|
| 5  6<br>2  3 | | 6 + 2 =<br><br>3 + 4 = | |
| **(2)** | | **(6)** | |
| 2  8<br>9  4 | | 52   40<br>13   39 | |
| **(3)** | | **(7)** | |
| 12  13<br>2  5 | | 78   46<br>71   92 | |
| **(4)** | | **(8)** | |
| 19  17<br>2  9 | | 3  8<br>5  7<br>8  9<br>2  7 | |

**Figure 38.** A Diagnostic Chart in Arithmetic. (From Buswell-John *Diagnostic Test for Fundamental Processes in Arithmetic*, Test Division of Bobbs-Merrill Company, Inc., 4300 West 62nd Street, Indianapolis, Indiana. Used by permission of the original publishers.)

early elementary grades through adult levels), (2) number combination flash cards, (3) games using basic combinations in the four arithmetic areas: addition, subtraction, multiplication, and division, and (4) play situations (make-believe stores or banks) which allow practice in a pleasant and meaningful context.

The verbalization (working the problem out loud) by the pupil of the

processes he uses in arithmetic gives the teacher an insight into the way he goes about his problem-solving. Also, it gives the child a better understanding of what he is doing. Equally important is the use of concrete objects in beginning arithmetic experience. Subtraction (at least for the majority of children) should be learned by taking some things away—not just by taking away an abstraction which may have no root in the concrete experience of the youngster. Likewise, problems (especially the so-called thought problems) should be geared to the meaningful experiences of pupils.

## USE OF AVAILABLE RESOURCES

Throughout this chapter there have been references to specific tests and instructional materials for use in diagnostic and remedial work. No teacher can be expected to know of all the tools which are available. He should, however, know where he can find out about them and the general psychological principles involved in their use. Some of the sources available are the following.

### Free and Inexpensive Materials

Booklets, posters, maps, recordings, scripts and other resources are available for little or no cost to the teacher who cares to write for them. Comprehensive lists of such materials have been published.[21] Also several book companies have free professional-service bulletins, as well as supplementary materials for classroom use.

### Bibliographic Materials

In every subject matter field in elementary school and in most of those in high school there are books which give specific techniques of remedial work for that particular subject (see the references at the end of this chapter). In addition there are professional journals, indexes, encyclopedias, and abstracts which should be available in the school's professional library. In planning the school or classroom library so that it will offer materials suitable for all abilities and interests, the teacher should know also that there are several good annotated bibliographies of books for children.

### Other Facilities and Agencies

In several of the writers' classes in educational psychology the question has arisen regarding local, state, and Federal agencies which are available

---

[21] Examples of such lists are: Division of Surveys and Field Service (George Peabody College for Teachers, Nashville, Tennessee), *Free and Inexpensive Learning Materials*, 1967, and Educators Progress Service, *Elementary Teachers Guide to Free Curriculum Materials*, J. G. Fowlkes and D. A. Morgan (Editors), Annual Editions, Randolph, Wisconsin.

to help teachers with special problems. For the most part, teachers show a surprising lack of awareness of such facilities (even in their own community). The U.S. Office of Education, The National Education Association, The Office of Vocational Rehabilitation, the U.S. Public Health Service all make publications available through the Superintendent of Public Documents. Most states offer consulting service and printed information through their state departments of public instruction, plus information and help through child welfare and juvenile research organizations.

Assistance which may be obtained in most communities includes consultative help from local physicians, ministers, and employers. Information may also be obtained from local offices of juvenile research or child welfare agencies, and from social case workers. These are but suggestive of the resources of which a teacher may avail himself. Often feelings of helplessness which accompany a very serious problem case could be overcome and remedial work undertaken if available resources were known and put to use.

## SUMMARY

A sizable percentage of the school-age population is either not in school or profits little from its school experience. Many of the latter group (perhaps as many as 40 per cent) will drop out before they finish high school. In the face of increasing class size, teachers may feel they are forced to give less time to individual pupils even though the range of abilities has probably increased in the past few decades.

Although there is no single answer to the problem of educational casualties, it is virtually certain that many pupils, who would otherwise have failed or dropped out of school, are being helped by teachers who have discovered children's difficulties early enough and have provided appropriate remedial teaching. Alert teachers have recognized that anything which interferes with reception of stimuli (sensory defects in vision and hearing), the child's responses (such as disease, low mental ability, or injury), or with motives and energy (such as negative attitudes and emotional instability) interferes with learning. Any such interference whether it be a speech defect, a slight loss of hearing, or a feeling of rejection must be recognized and treated before the child's full potential is released. Remedial teaching begins with a discovery of pupils who are having or are apt to have difficulties. Once these cases have been identified, a more thorough diagnosis to discover the cause of the difficulty is undertaken.

Learning difficulties may be detected by routine physical checkups, mental tests, achievement tests, and clues which the teacher may notice in observing children at work.

The causes of difficulties are found through a more intensive analysis which includes the use of diagnostic tests, interviews, and case studies. It is especially important in this step that teachers study the *processes* which pupils use in solving problems or in going about their work.

Principles of diagnosis and remedial teaching apply to all subjects and grade levels. But there are individual problems in each of the school subjects. In the teaching of reading, for example, there are common errors such as reversals, regressive eye movements, and inability to discriminate between letters and words. In each subject, the teacher should apply the basic principles of remedial teaching, but in addition should make use of the special techniques which research has found to be effective. Remedial teaching in essence is just good teaching which takes the learner where he is, and through well-motivated activities leads him to increased competence in his areas of weakness.

### References for Further Study

Algeo, J., "Why Johnny Can't Spell," *English Journal*, Vol. 54, March, 1965, pp. 209–213.

Anderson, Verna D., *et al.*, *Readings in the Language Arts*, New York, The Macmillan Company, 1964.

Balow, Bruce, "The Long-Term Effect of Remedial Reading Instruction," *Reading Teacher*, Vol. 18, April, 1965, pp. 581–586.

Bamman, Henry A., "Organizing the Remedial Reading Program in the Secondary School," *Journal of Reading*, Vol. 8, November, 1964, pp. 103–108.

Barbe, Walter B. (Editor), *Teaching Reading: Selected Materials*, New York, Oxford University Press, 1965.

Blair, Glenn M., *Diagnostic and Remedial Teaching*, Revised Edition, New York, The Macmillan Company, 1956.

Bond, Guy L., and Tinker, Miles A., *Reading Difficulties: Their Diagnosis and Correction*, 2nd Edition, New York, Appleton-Century-Crofts, 1967.

Bond, Guy, and Wagner, Eva Bond, *Teaching the Child to Read*, Fourth Edition, New York, The Macmillan Company, 1966.

Brown, Edward T., "Programmed Reading for the Secondary School," *The High School Journal*, Vol. 49, April, 1966, pp. 327–333.

Brueckner, Leo J., and Bond, Guy L., *The Diagnosis and Treatment of Learning Difficulties*, New York, Appleton-Century-Crofts, Inc., 1955.

Buswell, G. T., "Arithmetic" in *Encyclopedia of Educational Research*, Third Edition, New York, The Macmillan Company, 1960, pp. 71–72.

Dallman, Martha, *Teaching the Language Arts in the Elementary School*, Dubuque, Iowa, William C. Brown Company, 1966.

Dawson, Mildred A., and Bamman, Henry A., *Fundamentals of Basic Reading Instruction*, New York, Longmans, Green and Co., 1959, Chapters 12, 13.

DeBoer, John J., and Dallman, Martha, *The Teaching of Reading*, Revised Edition, New York, Holt, Rinehart and Winston, 1964.

Drewes, Ruth H., Fischer, Winifred, and Round, Lorna, *Practical Plans for*

*Teaching English in the Elementary Schools*, Dubuque, Iowa, William C. Brown Company, 1965.

Dutton, Wilbur H., *Evaluating Pupils' Understanding of Arithmetic*, Englewood Cliffs, New Jersey, Prentice-Hall, Inc., 1964.

Friedman, Silvia S., "Remedial Therapy with a Twelve-Year-Old Incarcerated Delinquent," *Reading Teacher*, Vol. 19, April, 1966, pp. 483–489.

Frostig, Marianne, "Corrective Reading in the Classroom," *Reading Teacher*, Vol. 18, April, 1965, pp. 573–580.

Gildston, Phyllis, "Stutterers' Self-Acceptance and Perceived Parental Acceptance," *Journal of Abnormal Psychology*, Vol. 72, February, 1967, pp. 59–64.

Gray, William S., "Reading" in *Encyclopedia of Educational Research*, Third Edition, New York, The Macmillan Company, 1960, pp. 1128–1135.

Harris, Albert J., *How to Increase Reading Ability*, Fourth Edition, New York, Longmans, Green and Company, 1961.

Harris, Theodore L., "Handwriting" in *Encyclopedia of Educational Research*, Third Edition, New York, The Macmillan Company, 1960, pp. 621–624.

Hellmuth, Jerome (Editor), *Learning Disorders*, Vol. 2, Special Child Publications, Seguin School, Inc., 71 Columbia Street, Seattle, Washington, Bernie Straub and Jerome Hellmuth Co-publishers, 1966.

Higgins, C. and Rusch, R. R., "Remedial Teaching of Multiplication and Division: Programmed Textbook Versus Workbook, A Pilot Study," *Arithmetic Teacher*, Vol. 12, January, 1965, pp. 32–38.

Horn, Ernest, "Spelling" in *Encyclopedia of Educational Research*, Third Edition, New York, The Macmillan Company, 1960, pp. 1347–1354.

Johnson, G. Orville, *Education for the Slow Learners*, Englewood Cliffs, New Jersey, Prentice-Hall, Inc., 1963.

Kasbohm, Mary C., "Remedial Reading Materials," *Elementary English*, Vol. 43, March, 1966, pp. 209–213.

*Language Programs for the Disadvantaged*, National Council of Teachers of English, 508 South Sixth St., Champaign, Illinois, 1965.

McElravy, A., "Handwriting and the Slow Learner," *Elementary English*, Vol. 41, December, 1964, pp. 865–868.

Mintz, Natalie and Fremont, Herbert, "Some Practical Ideas for Teaching Mathematics to Disadvantaged Children," *The Arithmetic Teacher*, Vol. 12, April, 1965, pp. 258–260.

Money, John and Schiffman, Gilbert, *The Disabled Reader*, Baltimore, The Johns Hopkins Press, 1966.

Otto, Wayne and McMenemy, Richard A., *Corrective and Remedial Teaching*, Boston, Houghton Mifflin Company, 1966.

Powell, William R., "Changing Times in Reading Instruction," *Education*, Vol. 86, April, 1966, pp. 451–453.

Robbins, Melvin P., "Delacato Interpretation of Neurological Organization," *Reading Research Quarterly*, Vol 1, Spring, 1966, pp. 57–78.

Ross, Ramon, "A Description of Twenty Arithmetic Underachievers," *The Arithmetic Teacher*, Vol. 11, April, 1964, pp. 235–241.

Roswell, Florence and Natchez, Gladys, *Reading Disability: Diagnosis and Treatment*, New York, Basic Books, Inc., 1964.

Sarason, Seymour B., *Psychological Problems in Mental Deficiency*, Third Edition, New York, Harper and Brothers, 1959.

Scott, Louise B., and Thompson, J. J., "Helping Children Who Stutter" in *Speech Ways*, St. Louis, Webster Publishing Company, 1955, Chapter 8.

Shaw, P., "Individualization of Instruction in Freshman English," *Journal of Developmental Reading*, Vol. 7, Spring, 1964, pp. 150–158.

Shores, J. Harlan, "What Does Research Say About Ability Grouping by Classes?" *Illinois Education*, Vol. 53, December, 1964, pp. 169–172.

Shores, J. Harlan, "Are Fast Readers the Best Readers?—A Second Report," *Elementary English*, Vol. 38, April, 1961, pp. 236–245.

Spiegler, Charles G., "If Only Dickens Had Written About Hot Rods," *English Journal*, Vol. 54, April, 1965, pp. 275–279.

Stahl, Stanley, *The Teaching of Reading in the Intermediate Grades*, Dubuque, Iowa, William C. Brown Company, 1965, Chapter 5.

Strang, Ruth, *Diagnostic Teaching of Reading*, New York, McGraw-Hill Book Company, 1964.

Van Riper, Charles and Butler, Katharine G., "Helping Children with Speech Defects in the Classroom," in *Speech in the Elementary Classroom*, New York, Harper and Brothers, 1955, Chapter 10.

Webster, Staten W. (Editor), *The Disadvantaged Learner*, San Francisco, Chandler Publishing Company, 1966.

Woodby, Lauren G. (Editor), *The Low Achiever in Mathematics*, Washington, D.C., U.S. Government Printing Office, 1965.

Zintz, Miles V., *Corrective Reading*, Dubuque, Iowa, William C. Brown Company, 1966.

### Films

*Education of Exceptional Children*, Division of University Extension, University of Illinois, Urbana, Illinois. (25 mins.)

Coronet Films, Coronet Building, Chicago 1, Illinois, have several excellent instructional films which are useful in remedial teaching. Among those available are the following: *Improve Your Pronunciation* (10 mins.), *Improve Your Reading* (10 mins.), *Improve Your Spelling* (10 mins.), *Improve Your Handwriting* (11 mins.).

*Why Can't Jimmy Read?* Syracuse University, Syracuse, New York. (20 mins.)

### Questions, Exercises, and Activities

1. Do you agree with the idea that every teacher should be a teacher of reading regardless of what subject he teaches? Defend the position you take.
2. It has been estimated that 20 to 30 per cent of the pupils who enter senior high schools in this country read so poorly that it is difficult for them to engage in required reading activities. Make a list of the causes of this situation. What can or should be done about it?
3. Do pupils in our elementary and secondary schools read as well as they

did 50 years ago? What is your opinion? Do you have any evidence to support your conclusion?

4. What are the values of spelling rules, if any, in improving the spelling abilities of pupils? Do you know of any spelling rule that does not have exceptions?

5. Read an article or research report from a current periodical or journal which deals with "remedial reading," "remedial spelling," "remedial arithmetic," "remedial handwriting," or "remedial speech." Evaluate the soundness of the article and point out the implications for teaching.

6. In some schools, pupils are sectioned to classes according to their abilities to read or do arithmetic. This is called homogeneous grouping. Do you believe this is a sound practice? What psychological evidence supports this procedure? Are there any good reasons why homogeneous groupings may be harmful? What does research on this subject show? See such sources as the Shores article in the list of references at the end of this chapter.

7. Teachers are often at a loss to know how to grade pupils who are in remedial classes. If a retarded pupil makes excellent progress in such a course, should he be given a grade of "A," "B," "C," "D," or what? Defend your answer. Also make an investigation of what some of the better schools are doing with this problem.

# PART FOUR

## Adjustment and Mental Hygiene

# Chapter 13

## Basic Processes
## of Adjustment

Every person, man or child, spends twenty-four hours a day satisfying or attempting to satisfy his physical, social, and personality needs. We see people eating, drinking, resting, striving for social approval, seeking affection, trying to achieve mastery of a vocation, and striving for independence. Anyone who observes small children will note that they are always wanting something. Older children and adults are always on the go, attempting to reach the goals which will reduce the tensions created by their needs. It is important for teachers to recognize that every activity of the child or pupil satisfies some need. Whenever a pupil is restless, aggressive, impudent, uncooperative, delinquent, or in fact doing anything, he is making an adjustment to life. The adjustment he makes may not be a good one so far as society is concerned, but it is an adjustment just the same, and its purpose is to satisfy some organic or personality need of the individual.

### FUNDAMENTAL HUMAN NEEDS

Many lists have been given of human needs. Murray divided all needs into two groups: (1) viscerogenic needs, and (2) psychogenic needs. His list of viscerogenic needs includes: air, water, food, sex, lactation, urination, defecation, avoidance of injury, etc. His list of psychogenic needs includes: achievement, recognition, autonomy, affiliation, and some twenty-two others which could well be grouped under two or three basic needs. Freud in his later years advanced the notion that man has two basic drives—the

life instinct and the death instinct. The life instinct includes all sexual impulses as well as the urges for self-preservation. The death instinct would include not only self-destruction tendencies but also aggressive and hostile feelings toward others. Alfred Adler made the desire for status the key urge in man. People want to be important, and most of their life activities are devoted to satisfying this need, he believed. Herbert Carroll has stated that the preservation and enhancement of the phenomenal self are achieved through satisfaction of four fundamental needs: the need for physical security, the need for emotional security, the need for achievement, and the need for status.[1] Other lists could be given. In previous chapters of this book (Chapters 2, 3, 4, and 7) discussions of the needs of children have been presented together with a listing of some of the basic needs. Most lists of needs overlap each other to a great extent and there is usually considerable overlapping between the needs presented on a single list. It is most important, however, for the teacher to have some list in mind when analyzing the behavior of children. It helps the teacher realize that all behavior is motivated, and assists in clarifying the causes of behavior.

### A List of Human Needs

The major physical needs (drives) include:

1. Hunger
2. Thirst
3. Activity-rest cycle
4. Sex
5. Temperature regulation
6. Evacuation (urination and defecation)
7. Avoidance of pain and injury

It is somewhat more difficult to draw up a satisfactory list of social and personality needs, but there is general agreement that individuals, at least in our culture, exhibit the following:

1. Need for status
2. Need for security
3. Need for affection
4. Need for independence
5. Need for achievement

In addition to these somewhat universal physical and social needs, every individual develops habits of a personal nature which possess driving force and act in much the same fashion as a basic need. A person who has learned

---

[1] Herbert A. Carroll, *Mental Hygiene*, Fourth Edition, Englewood Cliffs, New Jersey, Prentice-Hall, Inc., 1964, pp. 16–35.

to drink coffee, play golf, or attend the opera possesses a series of drives to action which differ from those of a person who has not developed these particular habits. In understanding why children are motivated to do what they do, the teacher must take into account not only the fundamental physical and social needs (drives) of all children, but also the particular habits and interests of each individual child.

### How Needs Operate

When a need exists and is unsatisfied, the individual becomes restless and tense. He seeks some goal which will reduce the state of imbalance which exists within him. The hungry person seeks food, the thirsty individual wants liquid, the tired person craves rest, the cold individual seeks warmth, the unnoticed person strives for attention and status, the unloved one wants affection, and the overprotected individual desires and strives for independence. When a need is completely satisfied, a temporary or momentary state of equilibrium is established and activity toward the appropriate goal ceases. After eating a hearty meal, the individual does not crave food for several hours. A student who has been complimented by his teacher or peers for some worthy performance may not need further vocal approval for several hours or even days. He does, however, need to feel constantly that he belongs, has status, and is a worthwhile person. Most of the social and personality needs remain in a somewhat unsatisfied state. Seldom does a person achieve too much status, security, affection, or achievement.

## CONDITIONS WHICH CREATE FRUSTRATION

In many ways this world is unfriendly to man and the satisfaction of his needs. Too much rain or too little rain may result in flood or drought which may create a shortage of food. Extreme heat and cold are also examples of physical factors which may thwart the satisfaction of man's needs. Society has passed many regulations which may or may not be good for the group as a whole, but which invariably restrict the satisfaction of the needs of some individuals. Laws which discriminate between races, requirements of admission to medical schools, standards of what constitutes appropriate dress in the summer time, all are examples of situations which may cause frustration. In some communities on the warmest days men are required to wear their coats on occasions when they would be much more comfortable with them off. School regulations which insist that all pupils meet certain prescribed levels of achievement may be very thwarting to children of limited background or ability. Poverty may seriously limit what a person may do, and thus create numerous frustrations which must be met by some sort of adjustment.

The individual with a personal defect or physical ailment may not be

able to engage in activities open to others. Poor eyesight, lameness, a damaged heart, all may produce frustrations of a serious nature for some persons. Conflict with resulting frustration inevitably ensues also when an individual strives to attain two goals which are not compatible. The student who desires to be a playboy and a Phi Beta Kappa candidate at the same time may run into difficulties as will the individual who tries to please two groups which have widely differing ideals. The Biblical statement that "Ye cannot serve God and mammon" is true from a mental hygiene viewpoint. A final source of frustration results when an individual's moral standards, which have been developed as a child, come in conflict with subsequently developed behavior patterns. Thus the child who has been taught that it is wrong to smoke, dance, or play cards may have severe guilt feelings when he engages in these activities as a college student. The Hebrew child who has been taught that he should not eat pork may spend a sleepless night after having partaken of this food, and the Seventh Day Adventist child may feel very worthless and uncomfortable after having played ball or attended a movie on Saturday.

## ADJUSTING TO FRUSTRATING CONDITIONS

As has been stated earlier, the individual whose needs are thwarted is tense and uncomfortable. He is in a state of disequilibrium. Some adjustment must be made to reduce this state of hypertension and make the situation tolerable for him. There are numerous adjustment mechanisms which are typically used by persons who are thawarted in reaching their goals. These include aggression, direct and indirect; compensation; sublimation; identification; rationalization; projection; repression; reaction formation; egocentrism; negativism; withdrawal; regression; developing physical ailments; and expiation or atonement. The neurotic or psychotic person, in addition, has ways of behaving in the face of frustration which include hysterias, amnesias, obsessions, phobias, hypochondria, delusions, and hallucinations.

## ADJUSTMENT MECHANISMS

### Aggression

A typical reaction to frustration is aggression. In fact, the thesis is held by Dollard *et al.* that aggressive impulses are inevitably set in motion by frustration. The individual does not always show overt aggressive responses, but instead may suppress and restrain them. It is very normal, however, to attack directly the frustrating object. The boy who is insulted by a classmate not uncommonly attacks his tormentor physically. School yard fights may not be as much in evidence as formerly, but they have by no

means become extinct. Children from the lower social classes tend to exhibit their aggressive feelings somewhat more directly than those from the middle and upper classes. The psychologist Karen Horney has indicated that to repress all hostile and aggressive feelings is bad from a mental hygiene viewpoint. The repression of such feelings may lead to anxiety and neurosis. She would suggest that it is good for a person to express his hostile feelings occasionally, to blow off steam.

Much aggression, however, is not direct. Particularly in middle class culture the pattern is to relieve aggressive feelings in indirect ways. The man who is humiliated by another man may not suggest that the two of them have a fight. Instead, he may take out his feelings of hostility by making disparaging and critical remarks regarding the man he dislikes. Innocent bystanders are often the targets for people who have aggressive feelings which must be relieved. The teacher who has had an argument with her husband before coming to school in the morning may vent her aggressive feelings upon the children in her room. The boy who has been thwarted by his teacher in the classroom may, during the recess period, push into a mud puddle some child he chances to see on the playground. People who are frustrated also frequently relieve their feelings of aggression by attacking inanimate objects. We have all seen people break dishes, kick chairs, or slam a door as a means of releasing pent-up feelings of aggression.

Students of social psychology have suggested that aggressive feelings also form one of the bases for prejudice toward certain minority groups. A large group of people or given individuals who are frustrated may make attacks or show unfavorable attitudes toward some group which has never done them any harm. A scapegoat is made of the minority group as a means of reducing the tensions resulting from group or personal frustration.

Every individual will have aggressive feelings at times. The teacher should expect to encounter this behavior on the part of pupils. It is perfectly normal. Hilgard and Russell comment on aggression as it affects the classroom teacher as follows:

> Every child needs to find some way to give expression to anger, hostility, and destructiveness which arise out of the thwartings which he faces. . . . One of the lessons to be learned is that we do not, as teachers, always achieve the consequences we seek by an overemphasis upon wholesomeness, propriety, and adult standards of cleanliness and order. . . . Occasional permissiveness, that allows a frank expression of resentment, that takes feelings at their face-value rather than forcing their denial or disguise may result in a child's coming out more spontaneous and friendly and in the end, actually more socially conforming.[2]

---

[2] Ernest R. Hilgard and David H. Russell, "Motivation in School Learning," Forty-Ninth Yearbook of the National Society for the Study of Education, Part I, *Learning and Instruction*, Chicago, The University of Chicago Press, 1950, pp. 41–42.

Some of the socially acceptable channels for relieving aggressive feelings which can be used by the school include athletic contests, finger painting, dramatic plays, and so on. The pupil who has no socially acceptable outlet for his hostile feelings will either repress them and possibly develop anxieties, or he may become aggressive in non-socially acceptable ways and find himself in trouble with constituted authority.

### Compensation

Every individual must feel important. If he cannot attain distinction in one way, he will try to attain it in some other way. The boy who is a failure in his course in Latin may save his ego or self-esteem by making a success of his efforts in athletics. The boy who has suffered as a child from infantile paralysis may not go out for athletics but instead become unusually proficient as a writer or speaker. The boy who cannot dance may brag of his prowess in football, and the pupil who is never given any scholastic recognition may attain distinction as the school's biggest rowdy. The term compensation as used in the foregoing illustrations really means substitution. Attainable goals are substituted for non-attainable goals or goals difficult to attain.

The term compensation has also been used to apply to the situation where a person attempts to succeed in the very line where his handicap lies. Thus a child with a speech defect may, through outstanding effort, become famous as a speaker. A weakling may through strenuous training become a great athlete. A man with very ordinary ability may through hard work rise to the top of his profession. Examples of this type of compensation are numerous. It has been reported that such outstanding athletes and "strong men" as Eugene Sandow, Charles Atlas, Bernarr Macfadden, and Johnny Weissmuller were sickly in their youth. Glenn Cunningham was crippled by burns when he was seven years old, yet he was able to overcome his physical handicap to become one of the greatest mile runners of all time.

Both types of compensation which have been mentioned serve to satisfy the individual's ego and make it possible for him to atone for inferiority feelings he may have. It is generally accepted that compensation is a mechanism which grows out of a feeling of inferiority. Since everyone feels inferior at times it is inevitable that everyone compensates. The person who is relatively secure, however, probably does not engage in compensatory activities to as great an extent as the very insecure individual. It should be stressed, nevertheless, that compensation may be a valuable aid to adjustment. It reduces tensions and anxiety feelings and promotes in many cases good mental health. Teachers should help pupils find activities in which they can excel and thus compensate for weaknesses they may possess. The child who is a success in something is much more apt to be developing in a wholesome manner than one who has been continuously

thwarted in reaching his goals. It is important, however, that socially approved compensatory activities be resorted to rather than those which are disapproved. The child with inferiority feelings may compensate by engaging in delinquent acts to gain the attention he desires, or he may satisfy his fundamental need for status by putting forth effort to succeed in worthwhile activities. The way the child is treated by the school will to a great extent determine which type of compensation he will employ.

### Sublimation

Sublimation is really a form of compensation. As used by the Freudians the term meant the substitution of a socially accepted non-sexual goal for a goal which is sexual in nature. The individual who was thwarted sexually might resolve his frustration by developing interests in art, sports, scientific research, social service work, etc. More recently, the term has been used in a somewhat broader sense. Cameron and Magaret define sublimation as "the substitution of socially approved reactions, particularly if they have an altruistic flavor, for socially discredited or taboo behavior." This latter definition, of course, would include the substitution of non-sex activities for sex activities. Children of adolescent age according to the Kinsey report are by no means sexless. Sex curiosity and sex drive probably reach their peaks during the teens. In our society with its prolonged period of adolescence, young people need many non-sexual outlets to relieve sex tensions which are built up. Schools with their programs of athletics, social dancing, music and art, woodworking, etc., undoubtedly contribute activities which serve this purpose. The child who is kept busy in such ways has considerably less energy to devote to direct sexual activity or to fantasy in this realm. Helping children develop hobbies, scientific interests, and vocational plans are also among the things the school can do to assist children in sublimating their basic sexual drives.

### Identification

Identification is a mechanism by which an individual satisfies certain of his basic needs by allying himself emotionally with or feeling himself one with another person, group of persons, or institution. The individual may have many personal limitations and be quite unsuccessful in reaching his own goals, but by associating himself with successful people or institutions he may receive some reflected glory.

Children often identify themselves with their parents, a successful relative, or with characters in movies, novels, or plays. Through this process adventure may be had, and the desire for power and status may be partially gratified. A common sight around a high school is a non-athletic youth walking arm in arm with a successful athlete or at least trailing close behind. Individuals like to talk about the important people they know or have met. Graduate students when asked what professors they have studied

under, give the names of the most distinguished professors and omit the less distinguished. People strive to shake the hands of famous personages or to collect their autographs. It is a great source of pride to the citizens of a community to be able to say that the governor of the state lives in their town or that Abraham Lincoln once slept there. To be associated with a famous business firm, if only in a very minor capacity, or to be a student at a well-known university gives the individual involved a sense of prestige and importance and helps reduce any feelings of inferiority he may have. Colleges with successful athletic teams or with distinguished faculties have little trouble drawing students.

Individuals want to be important. If they cannot achieve distinction in their own right they can at least identify with someone who has. When a child identifies himself with a given person or group the tendency is for him to emulate the characteristics of that person or group. Identification thus becomes a powerful dynamism in the formation of personality and character. The school by providing worthwhile models in the form of teachers, personages in literature and science, and appropriate school traditions can do much to assist pupils in making proper identifications. The child who identifies with characters from the realm of gangsters, hoodlums, and rich gamblers is likely to turn out to be quite a different person from one who establishes strong emotional ties with respected and worthwhile people.

### Rationalization

It is very difficult for one to admit that he has failed to reach a cherished goal or that his behavior falls short of what is expected of him by others or himself. The situation of not achieving one's goals or not living up to one's expectations may leave the individual not only frustrated but also with feelings of guilt. This is, of course, very undesirable for the person's state of mental health. An adjustment mechanism which is widely used to reduce guilt feelings and tensions arising from this condition is known as *rationalization*. Rationalization has been defined as a mechanism by which the individual justifies his beliefs or actions by giving reasons other than those which activated or motivated him. By rationalization the individual is able to excuse his shortcomings and maintain the defense of his ego.

The pupil who fails in his school work may insist that his teachers are unfair or that a recent illness was the basis of his difficulty. The student who fails to gain admission to medical school may take the position that he did not want to be a doctor anyway—since the work is so strenuous and unpleasant. The girl who is unsuccessful in being invited to join a sorority may argue that sororities are snobbish and not worth belonging to. This type of rationalization has been referred to as the *sour grapes* mechanism. It gets its name from the story of the fox in Aesop's Fables

who saved his pride by insisting that the unattainable grapes were sour and hence not worth the effort required to reach them.

Another form of rationalization bears the name of *sweet lemon* or Pollyanna mechanism. The individual is unsatisfied with what he has attained but maintains that everything is lovely. A school teacher may have taken a position which is most grueling and unpleasant, yet he may maintain that he likes his work immensely and that he would not change to another position for anything. A man may buy an automobile which is so inferior that inwardly he is most unhappy. Outwardly, however, he may argue that it is a fine car—one of the best on the market. The pupil who is given a minor part in a school play, though secretly disappointed, may loudly proclaim how happy he is with the type of role he has obtained.

Everyone rationalizes his failures to some extent. If people did not do so the world would contain many more people in poor mental health than it now has. Rationalization is a face saving device which keeps people in a relatively sound state of mind who otherwise would be quite unhappy and maladjusted. As with most other adjustment mechanisms, however, it may be overused. The college student who plays twenty-seven holes of golf every day while receiving failing grades in his courses, may rationalize that one's health should always come first. Yet this student's approach to his problem is far from being realistic, and greater conflict and frustration may result in the future if he does not change his routine of college life. Many problems and situations in life have to be met directly and solved rather than rationalized away.

### Projection

Another method used by individuals to excuse their shortcomings and relieve guilt feelings is known as projection. This is a mechanism by which an individual may ascribe to others his own weaknesses, faults, and impulses. The individual judges others by himself. The stingy person more often than would be expected by chance will accuse others of being stingy. The person with a weakness for alcohol will call attention to this defect in others. The dishonest person will assume that everyone else is dishonest.

The term projection is also used to apply to the process by which an individual blames other people or inanimate objects for his own failures. In this sense, projection is essentially another form of rationalization. A school boy involved in a fight will usually blame the other boy for starting the fight. The tennis player who drives the ball into the net will look at his racket as if something were the matter with it. The person involved in an automobile accident almost invariably accuses the other person of being responsible for the mishap. School children caught committing offenses frequently reply, "George made me do it." Projection is an age-old method of shifting responsibility and passing the buck which goes back to the garden of Eden when Adam blamed Eve for his own deficiencies.

Although projection is extremely common and undoubtedly reduces tension in the frustrated individual, its constant use is by no means to be commended. In the first place, it does nothing to solve the basic problem or difficulty, and in the second place, when carried on in an extreme form, its use may eventuate in hallucinations. School teachers should aid children to make adjustments which will protect and enhance their egos in ways other than those which involve projection. The child who makes excessive use of this mechanism can appropriately be thought of as needing help.

### Repression

Repression is a dynamism which is fundamental in the Freudian system of psychology. It is a process by which the individual attempts to protect his ego by pushing into the unconscious those thoughts and experiences which are in conflict with his moral standards or which are painful to contemplate. Freudians account for much forgetting in terms of repression. Experiences which end in failure or humiliation, or which cause the person to have guilt feelings are more frequently forgotten than those which are of a more happy nature. The individual escapes from his troubles and conflicts by forgetting them.

Redl and Wattenberg have given an example of how repression is used by children to bury feelings of guilt and anxiety. They say:

> Nothing is more normal than occasional feelings of rivalry or hostility between brothers and sisters. Under ordinary circumstances youngsters will be aware of these emotions, express some of them openly but gain control of their more harmful wishes just as they gain command over anger-producing inclinations in other areas. In some cases, however, where parents put such a heavy demand on "loving" a brother or sister, the child cannot even allow himself to perceive such hostile feelings as he may have. He will have to repress them all. That means he will not be aware of having them even when they color his actual behavior or appear disguised in his dreams.[3]

There is no question but that repression is used by all individuals at times as a tension-reducing mechanism. It is generally believed, however, that this method is one of the most undesirable of the adjustment devices. Although it may provide temporary relief, it ultimately serves to perpetuate the emotional disturbance by concealing it. It may also be possible that repressing hostile feelings is a chief cause of anxiety and eventually neurosis.

So far as the school is concerned the point should be made that repression may be minimized by providing for children a permissive atmosphere —one in which fear and personal threats are largely eliminated. This will

---

[3] Fritz Redl and William W. Wattenberg, *Mental Hygiene in Teaching*, Second Edition, p. 64. Copyright, 1959, by Harcourt, Brace, New York.

give children a chance to work out their problems rather than forget them or deny their existence. Carroll has suggested that "children should be taught not to force back their desires, not to try to forget their fears and the experiences which they have had which have been accompanied by feeling of guilt, but to face their needs frankly and to work out socially acceptable means of satisfying them." [4] In any event, opportunities should be provided for children to let off steam once in a while, to give vent to their pent-up emotions. The successful teacher will allow pupils to disagree with him on occasion and to express openly contrary opinions and feelings. It is possible for children to develop self-control without the harmful consequences which may result from continually repressing or bottling up normal emotions.

### Reaction Formation

Reaction formation or reversal formation, as it is sometimes called, is the process of substituting an opposite reaction for one which is frustrating or anxiety-inducing. A mother, for example, originally wished very much not to have a baby. The baby was born nevertheless. The mother disliked the baby and rejected it. This rejection, however, aroused in her serious feelings of guilt, for mothers are not supposed to dislike their babies. She repressed these emotions of hatred toward her baby, and substituted in its place an extremely overprotective attitude. She guarded the baby's health with the greatest of care. As the child got older, she insisted that he always be kept absolutely clean. She would not let him play with other children for fear that he would get dirty or would be hurt. She took him to school regularly when other children his age were able to go alone and showered him with excessive affection and attention. Some people might regard this woman as being a wonderful mother. Her overprotection which resulted from reaction formation, however, actually made the child feel insecure and led to his social maladjustment.

Whenever an individual is observed to go to great extremes in expressing a viewpoint or advocating a course of action—when he is all steamed up over a situation which is of relatively little concern to average adjusted persons, the presence of reaction formation may be suspected. The individual who is extremely prudish, inordinately polite, or outstandingly sanctimonious, may actually be covering up for powerful feelings in the opposite direction. The writer once knew of a minister in the West who preached every Sunday morning for a period of several months on the evils of women wearing short skirts and low necked dresses. He emphasized that such attire was dragging America to its doom, and was the basis for most sexual crimes in our society. He seemed to be unusually concerned

---

[4] Herbert A. Carroll, *Mental Hygiene*, Fourth Edition, Englewood Cliffs, New Jersey, Prentice-Hall, Inc., 1964, p. 212.

over this particular subject. It was not long, however, after this series of lectures was delivered that this particular preacher was expelled from the denomination he represented because he was found guilty of numerous sexual indiscretions. Another person of the writer's acquaintance, a young man 33 years of age, died of acute alcoholism after having suffered numerous attacks of delirium tremens. When he was sober he had been a powerful temperance lecturer. Neither of these persons was insincere. Each was trying desperately to repress undesirable feelings he recognized in himself and used the mechanism of reaction formation to help him succeed in this task.

School children are sometimes observed to be extremely favorable toward or opposed to certain types of behavior which is just the opposite of their repressed feelings. A high school boy, for example, may declare that it is disgraceful for boys and girls of high school age to have dates or to walk around arm in arm. Actually this is exactly what he would like to do if his conscience or circumstances would permit it. School teachers should be on the alert to detect such individuals and help them if at all possible to release their fundamental feelings more appropriately.

### Egocentrism

The individual who feels insecure will often strive to establish himself as the center of attention. He may show off, ask numerous questions, talk loudly, try to be witty, and play all types of mischievous pranks. School children who fit this description are numerous and are not difficult to identify. The writer knows of a ninth-grade youngster who released a snake in the back of the room while his English class was in session. Needless to say he received attention not only from his classmates but also from his teacher who soon arrived on the scene. This particular boy had been very unsuccessful in his English course, largely because of low scholastic ability and poor home background. As the course was taught there were very few ways, if any, that he could attract attention through normal channels. Engaging in the type of prank he played was, however, well within his abilities and it gave him a feeling of importance to be noticed.

Everyone, of course, needs regular and satisfying reinforcement of his ego. School activities and curricula should be so designed that every child has some opportunity to receive attention and acclaim for creditable achievement. If this is done, many so-called misbehavior problems will automatically disappear from classrooms.

### Negativism

Another ego enhancing and attention getting device is known as negativism. The individual may be opposed to almost everything. In school when a group decides upon a course of action the negativistic child may stubbornly refuse to go along with the decision. He will often sulk, rebel

against authority, and refuse to be bound by rules. Negativistic behavior in the home is also a frequent reaction of children who feel thwarted or insecure. Such children may refuse to eat, to talk, or follow any idea propounded by a sibling or their parents. Negativism on the part of children is difficult to deal with but may be lessened by teachers and parents if such rules as the following are adhered to:

1. Avoid situations which are known to produce conflict.
2. Do not make issues of minor sources of disagreement.
3. Reward positive behavior when it occurs.
4. Look at one's own behavior to see if it may possibly be the type which is producing negativistic reactions. Teachers and parents frequently assume that the blame rests with the child. Actually, the alteration of adult behavior will tend to produce marked changes in the child's behavior insofar as negativism is concerned. When a child refuses to do an assignment required by the teacher, the teacher might well analyze the assignment in terms of its relevance to the child's needs, interests, and capabilities.

### Withdrawal

In the face of thwarting and distressing situations some individuals find that the easiest way out is to withdraw. Withdrawing probably does not take as much energy as some of the other adjustment mechanisms, e.g., aggression or compensation. One merely removes himself from the world of action and conflict and obtains the satisfaction of his needs in less strenuous ways. Among the several forms of withdrawal are daydreaming, becoming sleepy or drowsy, escaping into work, and using alcohol or other narcotics.

In the process of daydreaming the individual achieves a certain amount of relief from tension and frustration through imaginative thinking. The boy who has failed his course in algebra may imagine that he is a successful boat captain or aviator, and that throngs of people are waiting to give him acclaim as he steps from the parlor car of the Century Limited. The girl who has failed to get a date for the high school dance may sit for hours dreaming of her success as an opera singer or dancer. Everyone daydreams to some extent and no harm may result if the person keeps in good touch with reality. An individual, however, who habitually achieves his successes in the world of fantasy is in for trouble. He may withdraw into the world of dreams to such an extent that he does not recognize that people are around him. He may develop hallucinations and carry on the major part of his living in a world of make-believe.

The case of a boy who was given to excessive daydreaming but who was helped by his teacher to overcome this tendency is described by Bernard as follows:

The danger of excessive daydreaming is apparent in the case of a boy who wanted to be a hero in the eyes of his playmates. His conception of the hero role was that of an outstanding athlete. As his participation in the boys' games did not bring him immediate stardom, he forsook the difficult route of actual accomplishment for the easier path of daydreaming. Withdrawing from the group, he devoted his time to the construction of imagined successes on the playing field. Here his success was unchallenged. Since he controlled all the imaginary players, he could always assume the hero's role, and he dreamed that he received the adulation and praise which he desired. Luckily, he came into contact with a teacher who was concerned with his withdrawal and was willing to help attack the problem. By slow stages the teacher secured the confidence of the lad, learned of his daydreams, and used them constructively, showing the boy the necessity of going through a learning period preparatory for successful participation in sports. He helped him develop his latent capacities and the boy actually did become competent, though not a star. After a time, the degree of accomplishment afforded enough satisfaction so that the boy gave up his world of fantasy for the thrill of real participation.[5]

Individuals who have an unpleasant or distressing task to perform also are known to try to escape from it by becoming drowsy and falling asleep. Students occasionally are found sound asleep in a class which has been a source of frustration. Students who have examinations scheduled for the next day and who plan to study on the evening before the examination, often report that they become very tired right after supper and have to go to bed early.

Other escapes from trying situations which were mentioned earlier involve going to the movies, devoting oneself to hard work, and using narcotics. Our motion picture theaters and taverns are full of people every evening, and on Saturdays and Sundays, who are trying to get away from themselves or from some problem they face. To stay at home would be most painful because time would be provided to think of their troubles and to rehash their old anxieties. Alcohol and other narcotics may so benumb the thought processes that worry is impossible for a period of several hours. Some individuals who throw themselves into hard work whenever spare time is available do so as a means of escaping from a personal problem which generates conflict.

Some of these withdrawal devices which have been mentioned are, of course, more hazardous for the personality than others. All of them, however, may be highly non-adjustive in character in that the real source of the difficulty is left untouched. The individual who can be induced to face and solve his problems probably obtains more satisfaction from living and is of more use to society than the one who withdraws in order to escape the perplexities of living.

---

[5] By permission from *Toward Better Personal Adjustment*, by Harold W. Bernard. Copyright, 1951, McGraw-Hill Book Company, New York, p. 317.

### Regression

Another form of retreat which might well have been included under the heading of withdrawal is regression. It is a mechanism by which an individual returns to a less mature level of development or adjustment in order to maintain his personal integrity. An adult unable to solve the problems that face him may resort to childish or adolescent tactics in an effort to get what he wants. Adolescents may use childish methods, and children may take on characteristics which served them well as babies.

The process of regression in a young woman is illustrated in the following case:

> A young girl was in love and very anxious to marry. The young man she loved was not ready to marry. He wanted to run around and have what he considered a good time for a while before he settled down. This led the girl to fear the consequences of marriage with such a care-free youth and, aided by the disapproval of her fiancé expressed by her relatives and friends, she tried to decide that she would stay single. Yet she could not bear the thought of remaining single indefinitely. She was in a strange dilemma. She wanted to marry and she was afraid to do so. This led to the wish that she did not have any of the tendencies toward love life. If she were only a child again she would not want to marry and the trouble would be at an end. So she tried again to be a young innocent girl who knew nothing of love. She took the same attitude toward the whole affair that she would have taken when she was a preadolescent girl, and she seemed to get satisfaction from this for a time. When this satisfaction did not continue, her physiological maturity eventually forcing her to recognize that she was a woman, she attempted to commit suicide. After gaining insight into what she was doing, the girl adjusted her attitude, took a forward view instead of wishing to revert to a childish stage, and has made a satisfactory adjustment ever since.[6]

Adults have been known to cry and throw temper tantrums when they do not get what they want. Boys and girls of adolescent age sometimes lisp or engage in "baby talk" as a means of securing attention or affection which they feel is denied them. Living in the past is also a form of regression widely used by individuals whose present successes are not satisfying. This is known as the Old Oaken Bucket Delusion. To the individual, things were better in the old days. This technique may be of value to people getting along in years because the review of successes of earlier days helps to maintain and reinforce their egos. The discouraged person may also derive some sense of encouragement by retrospecting on his past successes. In young people, however, such tendencies should be viewed with suspicion. Regression and all other forms of withdrawal, when carried to extremes, may be symptomatic of such a future behavior disorder as schizophrenia. Regarding this point, Morgan states:

---

[6] John J. B. Morgan, *The Psychology of the Unadjusted School Child*, pp. 144-146. Second Edition, The Macmillan Company, New York. Used by permission.

Since regression often begins at the age of adolescence, the teacher should be on the lookout for first signs. Early discovery is especially important in this disorder on account of the fact that in later stages the patient may become so inaccessible that no one can do anything for him.

In the mildest type of schizophrenia, known as *simple schizophrenia*, the onset is hard to discern. The symptoms may appear gradually in a boy or girl who has been getting along satisfactorily in school. At first there is seen a lack of interest in things; the child ceases to go out and associates less and less with other children. There comes over him a general listless, apparently lazy and tired-out attitude toward life. Lessons are neglected and the child begins to fail in his studies. . . .

Even if this form does not progress into more severe forms, the adult that is produced finds it very difficult to adapt himself to life. It is quite likely that a great many criminals, hoboes, prostitutes, pseudo-geniuses, cranks, and eccentrics of various types are cases of permanent and non-progressive simple schizophrenia.[7]

### Escape Through Physical Ailments

The individual who is in conflict or in a difficult situation may make a somewhat graceful withdrawal by developing symptoms of physical disability. Technically this adjustment mechanism is known as *hysteria*. In the neurotic person the symptoms of paralysis, blindness, deafness, and invalidism may appear. Being ill provides a way out for the individual. There is, of course, nothing organically wrong, but the illness may persist until the personal problems of the individual are solved. Minor forms of hysteria are sometimes referred to as *hysteroid reactions*. School teachers have ample opportunity to observe such reactions on the part of their pupils. On the day of an examination some children will become so ill that it is necessary for them to return to their homes. The day after the examination they will be perfectly well. Students scheduled to make a talk before a class or before the other students in the auditorium have been known mysteriously to lose their voices and be unable to appear. As soon as the crisis period is over the physical ailment disappears.

Redl and Wattenberg have stated that "one thing for teachers to remember is that a child who has frequent absences, especially when parents report that doctors are having a hard time finding the cause, is probably emotionally troubled. To punish him for his absences or to make school more unpleasant for him is more likely to add to his troubles than to solve them."[8]

Teachers should be sympathetic to pupils who develop headaches, eye trouble, sinus trouble, colds, sore throats, and fainting spells in their at-

[7] John J. B. Morgan, *The Psychology of the Unadjusted School Child*, Revised Edition, pp. 228–229. Copyright by The Macmillan Company, New York. Used by permission.

[8] Fritz Redl and William W. Wattenberg, *Mental Hygiene in Teaching*, Second Edition, New York, Harcourt, Brace, 1959, p. 81.

tempts to avoid unpleasant situations. At the same time, every effort should be made to make pupils feel so competent and adequate that such defense mechanisms will be unnecessary. The child who has a major or minor success with a school examination or with a talk before the class is on the road to developing such personal adequacy that hysteroid reactions in such situations will be unlikely to appear.

### Expiation or Atonement

A final mechanism used by many individuals to establish personal adjustment and to relieve guilt feelings is referred to as expiation or atonement. Challman says that "when other means fail to alleviate painful conflict over an act that is repugnant to the conscience, the individual may endeavor to find a way of atoning for it. The difficulty involved in many forms of restitution, however, is that the individual is subjected to social disapproval. Thus he seeks a way of solving the conflict without running this risk." [9]

Pupils who have neglected their studies or who have violated school regulations may be severely worried over their misdeeds. Some relief has been obtained by such individuals through the process of punishing themselves in one way or another. Individuals have been known to do penance such as fasting for a week to compensate for wrongs they have committed. The writer knew of a high school boy who had extreme guilt feelings which resulted from his practice of masturbation. This boy reported that he had pricked his arm with a pin until it bled in several places in an effort to ease his guilty conscience.

The method of atonement as a reducer of tensions is probably used by all individuals at times. The man who brings his wife flowers when he has been late at the office, or the student who studies unusually hard after having failed an examination are examples of individuals who are expiating for their shortcomings. Atonement produces some sort of a balance for the individual, since good deeds are substituted for bad deeds. Like all compensatory mechanisms its use can probably be overdone. It would, of course, be much better if the individual could so steer his life that he did not have many shortcomings for which it would be necessary to atone. Making appropriate restitution, however, is to be preferred to carrying around a load of guilt and the inevitable anxieties that result from the conflict between the person's ideals and his behavior.

## NEUROTIC AND PSYCHOTIC ADJUSTMENTS

The fourteen adjustment mechanisms which have been described in the previous pages are all used by normal people to a greater or lesser degree

---

[9] R. C. Challman in Gates, *et al.*, *Educational Psychology*, Third Edition, New York, The Macmillan Company, 1948, p. 678.

in response to the various frustrations of living. The more serious the frustration the more one may depend on some escape mechanism to relieve pent-up tensions. Neurotics and psychotics employ the usual adjustment devices in much the same manner as do so-called normal people. The extent to which they use them, however, greatly exceeds that of normal individuals. The neurotic, for example, may withdraw into complete invalidism in order to escape from a conflict situation, whereas a more normal person might develop only a temporary and much less severe physical ailment. The psychotic may have delusions that he is Napoleon or Alexander the Great, whereas a normal person might only think of himself "more highly than he ought."

Despite the fact that neurotics and psychotics are subject to the general laws of behavior the same as anyone else, these individuals do develop somewhat unique techniques and symptoms in the process of solving their problems of adjustment which should be mentioned. The average teacher will probably not encounter a great many neurotic or psychotic children in his classes, although from time to time, some may be identified. Such children should be referred to the school psychologist if one is available, or to medical personnel. It should be remembered that neurotics and psychotics were all once normal individuals. The teacher who can prevent minor maladjustments from becoming more serious and who can detect incipient cases of neurosis or psychosis is one who can make a great contribution to the mental hygiene program of a school.

### Neurotic Adjustments

The neurotic or psychoneurotic, as he is sometimes called, maintains his ego by developing certain functional disorders. These include hysteria, obsessions, compulsions, phobias, hypochondria, and anxiety disorders.

HYSTERIA. It was mentioned earlier that normal individuals may sometimes develop physical ailments of a minor sort to escape unpleasant situations. The neurotic may go to great extremes in this respect. Menninger cites the case of a little girl who developed hysterical lameness:

> There was a dispute among the doctors over the case of a pretty little nine-year-old girl. The girl had developed a limp in one leg and it appeared to be hip-trouble. Along with it she had become pale and lost weight. She complained of pain in the hip, and the X-rays suggested some changes in the bony structure. It looked very much as if she might have tuberculosis of the hip-joint. For this reason some of the doctors advocated a plaster cast.
> Certain things about the case, however, gave some of the doctors another notion about it. For example, the child complained of a variety of pains, and sometimes when touched ever so gently by her mother she would scream out of all proportion to the justification. She would have limp spells in which she would drop into her mother's arms and lie motionless. At other times she would grow bitter toward her mother, make faces at her, and even throw things at her.

The mother was sure the child had tuberculosis of the hip as some of the doctors had suggested. This we assured her was not true. A week after the child had been placed under treatment the leg was perfectly well! [10]

The treatment consisted of helping the little girl become adjusted to a very difficult home situation in which "the father and mother had staged any number of dramatic fights in front of all the children."

A case of hysterical blindness is reported in the *Journal of the American Medical Association* as follows:

Helen D., a charming, curly-headed girl of 14, was the only daughter in a rather large family of boys. On her shoulders fell the drudgery of housework. She resented doing the dishes and the cleaning, and came home every day from school unwilling to perform her tasks. One day she was scolded by her mother; she replied sharply, and received a stinging smack across the face. Immediately she became blind.[11]

This again is an example of a person solving a personal problem by escaping into a disability. In the case of the person suffering from hysteria, nothing is organically wrong. When the individual personal conflict is solved, the disability disappears.

Other symptoms sometimes exhibited by persons suffering from hysteria are paralysis of the arms or legs, deafness, loss of voice, continuous vomiting, fits, sleep walking, and loss of memory.

OBSESSIONS. An obsession is an irrational idea which keeps recurring to the individual. It may persist until the person develops a feeling of subjection to it and until he cannot do much useful thinking or work. Thorpe has illustrated an obsession in the following case:

The nature of obsessional neurosis may be seen in the case of a seventeen-year-old high school student who could not keep from repeating the phrase, "I am not wicked." He was unable to concentrate on his studies and would mutter this phrase to himself hundreds of times a day. A study of the boy's case showed that he had been treated harshly since early childhood by his father, a dominating, sarcastic man who showed him no affection, and who frequently threatened to lock him out of the house if he did not do as he was told. To add to his troubles, the boy had some years previously been severely scolded and whipped for playfully moving his younger sister's chair at dinner with the result that she fell and fractured her back. During her three-month stay in the hospital and for some time afterward the boy dwelt morbidly on the incident, continually blaming himself for his sister's partial paralysis. For years afterward he could not keep from repeating the phrase, "I am not wicked." Following several months of therapy, during which he was given

---

[10] Karl A. Menninger, *The Human Mind*, Third Edition, pp. 142–143. Copyright, 1945, by Alfred A. Knopf, New York.

[11] J. Fetterman in the *Journal of the American Medical Association*, Vol. 91, No. 5, p. 317.

the opportunity of talking freely about his sister's accident and other unhappy experiences, as well as being assured of the full respect of the thera-
pist, he was able to make an almost complete recovery.[12]

COMPULSIONS. Some neurotics feel compelled to carry out certain acts
regardless of the fact that they are unreasonable. When leaving the house,
the neurotic may go back several times to see whether the front door is
locked or the gas heater has been turned off. Some people feel they have
to touch all the gate posts they pass, or step on every crack that appears
on the sidewalk. One neurotic endured for years the compulsion of dressing
and undressing three times before he felt comfortable in his clothes. Another neurotic had to wash his hands with soap, and then with alcohol
every time he touched a doorknob. The writer knows of a neurotic who
hates to see medicine wasted. Every time half a bottle is left around the
house by any member of the family, he feels compelled to finish it. Some
people will not throw away anything. A little old lady who recently died
left among her belongings a little box which was neatly labeled "string too
short to use."

There is a group of compulsive reactions which are referred to as *manias*.
Among the well-known manias are *kleptomania, pyromania, dipsomania,
nymphomania*, and *homicidal mania*. Kleptomania is characterized by an
overpowering impulse to steal; pyromania, by an irresistible urge to set
fires; dipsomania, by an uncontrollable desire for alcoholic beverages;
nymphomania, by excessive sexual desires in females; and homicidal mania,
by a compulsion to kill.

Compulsive reactions have been described by Cameron and Magaret [13]
as "techniques of controlling intermittent anxiety reactions. They are the
product of incomplete repression, and they provide only temporary control
of intolerable anxiety." In treating compulsive disorders it does little good
to deal directly with symptoms. Instead it is necessary to discover the conflicts and frustrations of the individual and attempt to help him resolve
them.

PHOBIAS. Phobias are irrational fears. There is virtually no end to the
list of objects and situations that may bring panic or fear to some neurotics.
There is *acrophobia*, fear of high places; *agoraphobia*, fear of open places;
*claustrophobia*, fear of closed places; *misophobia*, fear of contamination;
*ochlophobia*, fear of crowds; *toxophobia*, fear of poisons or being poisoned;
*zoophobia*, fear of animals or of some particular animal; and *phobophobia*,
fear of fear, fear that one will be afraid.

The writer knows a young man who has an irrational fear of cats. When-

---

[12] Louis P. Thorpe, *The Psychology of Mental Health*, pp. 385–386. Copyright, 1950,
by The Ronald Press, New York.
[13] Norman Cameron and Ann Magaret, *Behavior Pathology*, Boston, Houghton Mifflin Company, 1951, pp. 358–359.

ever a cat or even a little kitten is met on the street this person crosses over to the other side of the street in great haste. This individual could not possibly bear to be in the same room with a cat.

Unreasonable fears are usually explained in terms of early unfortunate experiences with the object feared, or in terms of some personality conflict or anxiety which expresses itself in the form of a fear.

HYPOCHONDRIA. The person suffering with hypochondria is abnormally preoccupied with his health. He wakes up in the morning feeling exhausted. He runs from one doctor to another without being benefited. His medicine cabinet is usually full of patent medicines. He can be said to be a person who enjoys his ill health. He may bitterly resent anyone telling him that he looks well. The hypochondriac's imagined illness serves as an escape mechanism to relieve him of anxieties which result from personal frustrations. Hypochondriacs whose lives have been reorganized and whose personal problems have been solved are known to have improved miraculously so far as their health is concerned.

ANXIETY NEUROSIS. The person suffering with an anxiety neurosis is in an almost constant state of fear, apprehension, and worry. He is afraid he will lose his money, that he will not be successful in his work, or that he will go "crazy." If he is a student, he may worry unduly about his grades or his ability to make friends or get a girl or boy friend. The neurotic with acute anxiety feelings will go to great lengths to protect himself from his anxieties. Karen Horney [14] has pointed out that the neurotic tries to protect himself from his anxiety in four principal ways:

1. By securing affection—He has an inordinate need for this type of reassurance. His motto seems to be: "If you love me you will not hurt me."
2. By being submissive—The neurotic argues: "If I give in, I shall not be hurt."
3. By trying to achieve power, possessions, and status—He reasons: "If I have power, no one can hurt me."
4. By withdrawing—His motto is: "If I withdraw, nothing can hurt me."

In addition to these methods, the neurotic suffering from severe anxiety may try to escape from his worries by overeating, overworking, or resorting to alcohol or other narcotics.

### Psychotic Adjustments

The neurotic is characterized by possessing minor nervous disorders. He usually goes about his work and does not cause his friends or his family too much trouble. He is in relatively good touch with reality and very seldom is treated in a mental hospital. Many of our greatest inventors,

---

[14] Karen Horney, *The Neurotic Personality of Our Time*, New York, W. W. Norton & Co., Inc., 1937, pp. 96–99.

poets, and scientists who have been pronounced neurotics have compensated for their inferiority and anxiety feelings by producing something outstanding. The *psychotic*, on the other hand, possesses a major mental derangement. His mental functions are so profoundly disturbed that he is unable to participate in everyday activities. He is usually confined to a mental hospital. One of his chief characteristics is loss of contact with reality. He may almost totally retreat into a world of make-believe and receive his satisfactions through delusions and hallucinations. Space will not permit detailed discussion of the adjustment mechanisms of the psychotic. A few of the characteristics and symptoms of this group of maladjusted persons will, however, be mentioned.

### Schizophrenia

Schizophrenic disorders are syndromes of disorganization and desocialization, in which delusion and hallucination are prominent, and in which behavior is dominated by primary fantasy. For many years this functional psychosis was known as dementia praecox because it was believed that it was an adolescent disorder. When it was discovered that this maladjustment was not limited to young people, the older term dementia praecox was dropped in favor of the newer term schizophrenia which means "split mind." Schizophrenia has usually been divided into four somewhat overlapping types: simple, hebephrenic, catatonic, and paranoid.

SIMPLE SCHIZOPHRENIA. The simple type shows lack of interest in human affairs, has little ambition, and ultimately withdraws from practically all social contacts. He may become careless about his dress, refuse to shave or bathe, and give himself over to daydreaming. The child who is extremely shy, lethargic, and withdrawn in school should be particularly a cause of concern to teachers, and every effort should be made to cause him to participate socially. Children of this type may ultimately develop simple schizophrenia.

Bruno Bettelheim [15] describes the case of Joey, a schizophrenic boy who converted himself into a "machine" in order to escape from the problems of living. "Entering the dining room, for example, he would string an imaginary wire from his 'energy source'—an imaginary electric outlet—to the table. There he 'insulated' himself with paper napkins and finally plugged himself in. Only then could Joey eat, for he firmly believed that the 'current' ran his digestive apparatus." He could not drink except through straws built into an elaborate piping system. His behavior at school became so bizarre that he had to be removed for specialized treatment. In Figure 39 is shown a drawing which Joey made of himself.

---

[15] Bruno Bettelheim, "Joey: A 'Mechanical Boy,'" *Scientific American*, Vol. 200, March, 1959, pp. 116–127.

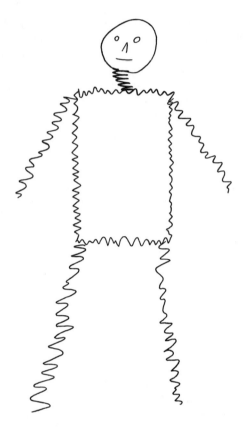

**Figure 39.** Self-Portrait of a Schizophrenic Boy. (This drawing by Joey shows a robot made of electrical wires. The figure symbolizes the child's rejection of human feelings. Reared by his parents in an utterly impersonal manner, he denied his own emotions because they were unbearably painful.)

HEBEPHRENIC SCHIZOPHRENIA. This type is characterized by giddiness, silliness, various tics, and some hallucinations. He may laugh foolishly when describing the death of his best friend or weep when explaining how well he feels. One hebephrenic claimed that he received daily radio messages from Moscow, Russia, through the gold fillings in his teeth. Some hebephrenics regress to childish behavior, crawl on all fours, urinate on the floor, and show little or no concern for others. The hebephrenic comes close to filling the layman's conception of "crazy" or "insane."

PARANOID SCHIZOPHRENIA. This form of psychosis is characterized by delusions. The individual so afflicted may either have delusions of persecution or delusions of grandeur or both. The individual who feels persecuted may hold to the belief that people are trying to follow him, poison him, or undermine his character. He is suspicious of everyone. The person af-

flicted with grandiose delusions may claim that he or she is Christ, Queen Victoria, or some other famous personage. Through these delusions the individual attains some of the satisfactions of his basic needs, e.g., status, that have been denied him in real life. The writer had a college student in his class who developed extreme disorganization of his thought process and delusions of persecution and grandeur. Before the course was over it was necessary for him to be committed to a state mental hospital. An example from a note he wrote to the writer while in the course is reproduced as follows:

> I and God (one spiritually) reveal from prophetically sealed scriptures my dreams from the perfect subconscious mind that knows, observes, interprets, and records all phenomena as no man can and never will, as I do now . . . I wrote to the admirals next and told them to hide the great navy and to hold Australia for a base, to march across the River Euphrates with me and the liberated princes of the East to the battle of Armageddon to knock out the 10 restored major powers at the very hub of 3 continents. "To win," I said, "you will still need me or else lose." Pal, some day I will tell how the world runs—means my sex life. You can never tell what is walking in a man's pants. They will never believe you. But you will believe us and see. Look at the movies and the mice. Break them all up. Dirt on all of them.

After leaving the university and while in the mental hospital this man sent the writer numerous disorganized letters which were signed in such ways as the following: George Washington, Valley Forge, c/o Mother MacCrea; Julius Caesar, Appian Way, Rome, Italy; Montezuma of the White Incas, Atlantic, Michigan.

Although teachers do not often encounter cases as serious as this in their classes, it is important for them to have some knowledge of this type of maladjustment in order to recognize children whose symptoms may be drifting in this direction.

CATATONIC SCHIZOPHRENIA. The catatonic is characterized by negativism, phases of excitement and stupor, muscular rigidity, stereotyped and impulsive behavior, and some hallucinations. Some catatonics can be pushed around as one would push a dummy. In the condition known as *waxy flexibility* the individual's arms, legs, or other parts of his body may be placed in the most grotesque positions and these positions may be maintained for long periods of time. With regard to the prevention of catatonia, Morgan makes the following statement:

> If teachers and parents are to detect the symptoms of this disorder in its early stages it will necessitate a careful study of the nature of the emotional cycles of the children in their care. If the excitement and depression are highly emotional in nature and if the child gives other evidence of be-

ing extrovertive then the procedure should be to help him adjust to his source of conflict. If on the other hand the evidence points to an introvertive reaction, a sort of senseless activity or meaningless stuporous withdrawal from the environment, effort should be directed toward making the individual more extrovertive. This can be accomplished by managing affairs so that it will be to his advantage to mix with others. Teach him to get pleasure from his social contacts and, insofar as this is successful, he is being guarded against any tendency to withdraw into himself.[16]

### Other Forms of Psychosis

Besides schizophrenia other recognized types of psychosis include manic-depressive disorders, involutional melancholia, and (true) paranoia. The manic-depressive swings from the highest levels of elation to the lowest levels of despair. When in the excited phase the individual may be hilarious, extremely talkative, unable to sit still. When he swings to depression he becomes very slow in his responses. If a question is asked him it may be two or three minutes before he answers. He may sit and weep for long periods of time and accuse himself of all sorts of wrongdoing. An involutional melancholic is a person who is perpetually sad and depressed. His feelings of dejection, hopelessness, and sorrow may reach the point where suicide seems to him the only way out. The paranoid individual reacts in some respects much like the person afflicted with schizophrenic paranoia. His delusions which are usually of a persecutory nature, however, are much more highly systematized than the schizophrenic paranoid. He is a most suspicious individual but may otherwise appear quite normal. Teachers should be on the alert to detect children who are developing paranoid tendencies. Such children should be immediately referred to a clinical psychologist or child psychiatrist who may be able to suggest measures to arrest the development of this serious disorder.

## SUMMARY

Human beings, adults and children alike, possess a great array of needs which are constantly demanding satisfaction. Some of these are physical, others are psychological and social. The physical needs are generated by deficits in the organic structure and chemical balance of the body, the psychological and social needs are learned. Both types of needs create tension in the individual which lead to action (goal seeking). When an individual is blocked in reaching a goal, he may seek to reach the goal with renewed vigor, adopt a substitute goal, try to reach the original goal by devious means, or withdraw into a world of fantasy.

---

[16] John J. B. Morgan, *The Psychology of Abnormal People*, Second Edition, pp. 564–565. Copyright by Longmans, Green and Co., New York.

When a teacher observes a child using to an excessive degree such mechanisms as aggression, compensation, identification, rationalization, projection, or daydreaming, he may be sure that the child is trying to satisfy some need which has been thwarted. Since all individuals are thwarted to some extent in satisfying their needs, the various adjustment mechanisms can be observed in everyone at times. The adjustment devices described in this chapter are not all necessarily bad since they do relieve to some extent tensions which have been built up, and help restore equilibrium.

Teachers, however, should assist pupils to set realistic goals which can be achieved. Too great frustration or habitual and exaggerated use of a defense mechanism may greatly reduce an individual's social effectiveness and also his personal happiness. Extreme and prolonged frustration is also believed to be the forerunner of neurotic and psychotic behavior.

## References for Further Study

Bandura, Albert and Walters, Richard H., *Social Learning and Personality Development*, New York, Holt, Rinehart and Winston, 1963.

Carroll, Herbert A. *Mental Hygiene*, Fourth Edition, 1964.

Coleman, James C. *Abnormal Psychology and Modern Life*, Third Edition, Chicago, Scott, Foresman and Company, 1964.

Janet, Pierre, *The Major Symptoms of Hysteria*, New York, Hafner Publishing Company, 1965 printing.

Jourard, Sidney M. *Personal Adjustment*, Second Edition, New York, The Macmillan Company, 1963.

Kaplan, Louis, *Foundations of Human Behavior*, New York, Harper and Row, 1965.

Kisker, George W., *The Disorganized Personality*, New York, McGraw-Hill Book Company, 1964.

Lawrence, P. J. (Editor). *Mental Health and the Community*, Canterbury Mental Health Council, Christchurch, New Zealand, 1963.

Lindzey, Gardner and Hall, Calvin S. *Theories of Personality: Primary Sources and Research*, New York, John Wiley and Sons, 1965.

Ohmer, Milton. *Behavior Disorders*, J. B. Lippincott Company, 1965.

Rosen, Ephraim and Gregory, Ian. *Abnormal Psychology*, Philadelphia, W. B. Saunders Company, 1965.

Sawrey, James M. and Telford, Charles W. *Dynamics of Mental Health*, Boston, Allyn and Bacon, 1963.

Torrance, E. Paul and Strom, Robert D. *Mental Health and Achievement*, New York, John Wiley and Sons, 1965.

Wepman, Joseph M. and Heine, Ralph W. (Editors). *Concepts of Personality*, Chicago, Aldine Publishing Company, 1963.

White, Robert W. *The Abnormal Personality*, Third Edition, New York, The Ronald Press, 1964.

## Films

*Conflict*, New York, McGraw-Hill Book Company. (10 mins.)
*Facing Reality*, New York, McGraw-Hill Book Company. (12 mins.)
A *Clinical Picture of Claustrophobia*, Central Film Library, U.S. Veterans Administration, Washington 25, D.C. (31 mins.)

## Questions, Exercises, and Activities

1. Define a need. How does it differ from a drive or an interest?
2. Do you agree with Adler that the desire for status or power is the chief urge in man? Why?
3. One authority has stated that the school is partly responsible for juvenile delinquency. Do you agree? Explain your answer.
4. Is aggressive behavior on the part of school children always bad? Give examples to explain your answer.
5. Should teachers help pupils compensate for inferiorities they have? If so, tell how this can be done.
6. Give several concrete examples from your own experience of ways children use the mechanism of identification to satisfy their needs.
7. George cannot dance well, but constantly brags of his prowess in football. Which one of the following mechanisms is he using: (a) rationalization, (b) sublimation, (c) compensation, (d) aggression?
8. Why may the child who withdraws be a more serious adjustment problem than one who is disobedient?
9. Distinguish between a neurosis and a psychosis. Are children ever neurotic and psychotic?
10. Are some of the adjustment mechanisms discussed in this chapter useful for maintaining good mental health and others harmful? Justify your answer and make a list of useful and harmful mechanisms.
11. It has been said that most of our greatest inventors and creative artists have been individuals who were markedly neurotic. Do you agree with this? Defend your answer. If this is true, what is the psychological explanation?
12. Research seems to indicate that psychotic behavior runs in families to some extent. Does this indicate that such behavior is inherited? What is your interpretation of this finding?

# Chapter 14

## Problems of School Discipline

Many types of maladjusted children are found in our classrooms. The symptoms they exhibit are numerous. These include shyness, suspiciousness, untruthfulness, tattling, cruelty, bullying, cheating, truancy, impertinence, tardiness, stealing, profanity, boisterousness, showing-off, masturbation, heterosexual activity, and all sorts of classroom disorderliness. In this chapter and the one to follow practical suggestions will be given for dealing with a wide range of behavior problems of children. The present chapter will concern itself with behavior problems which might be labeled disciplinary.

### TEACHERS VIEW DISCIPLINE PROBLEMS

The National Education Association asked 1,125 high school teachers from every section of the United States to answer a four-page questionnaire on disciplinary problems.[1] From this mountain of data the following conclusions were among those reached:

1. The larger the class and the larger the school system the greater are disciplinary problems.
2. Fewer disciplinary problems arise in foreign language classes than in science, mathematics, and English.

---

[1] See "Discipline in the High School Today," *Phi Delta Kappan*, Vol. 47, October, 1965, pp. 103–104.

3. Fourteen teachers reported that students had committed acts of physical violence upon them during the school year studied.
4. Twenty percent of the teachers report that there is widespread cheating on tests.
5. Forty-four percent of the teachers blame parents for school disciplinary problems.
6. Some other causes listed by teachers for unacceptable behavior were: increased availability of automobiles (28.3 percent), lack of special attention for academically retarded students (18.6 percent), and undesirable comic books and magazines (8.6 percent).

The above are just a few examples of what teachers think about discipline in the schools. There is no question but that many teachers view the keeping of discipline as their number one problem.

## CLASSROOM PRACTICES—PAST AND PRESENT

Although the importance of discipline in schools has never seriously been doubted, marked changes have taken place over a period of years in the methods of keeping discipline, and in an understanding of the psychological principles underlying the process.

Horace Mann described the method of keeping discipline in his day as follows:

> In one of the schools . . . consisting of about two hundred and fifty scholars, there were 328 separate floggings in one week of five days, or an average of 65 each day. In another, eighteen boys were flogged in two hours in the presence of a stranger.[2]

An elderly man who had formerly been a school teacher told the writer that the first day he taught school he whipped every boy in the room. Thrashings were very common in the public schools attended by the writer during the period 1914–1922. On one occasion a sixth-grade woman teacher and a large unruly boy wrestled on the floor in full view of the rest of the class.

In 1848, a secondary school in North Carolina published a list of punishments which were in effect in the school.[3] A few of them were:

| | |
|---|---|
| 1. Boys and girls playing together | 4 lashes |
| 2. Quarreling | 4 lashes |
| 3. Playing cards at school | 10 lashes |

---

[2] This quotation taken from Pickens E. Harris, *Changing Conceptions of School Discipline*, New York, The Macmillan Company, 1928, p. 53.
[3] Taken from S. L. Pressey, *et al.*, *Life: A Psychological Survey*, New York, Harper and Brothers, 1939, p. 91.

4. Telling lies                                 7 lashes
5. Swearing at school                        8 lashes
6. For drinking liquor at school           8 lashes
7. For wearing long finger nails           2 lashes
8. For blotting your copy book             2 lashes
9. For not making a bow when going home    2 lashes

In 1928 an article [4] appeared in the *Elementary School Journal* which listed seventeen different types of school offenses and recommended specific punishments for each type. The author stated, "It is not intended that all punishments listed under an offense should be used at each violation. The punishments are arranged in order of severity and should be used in order as far as it is necessary to control the situation." Some examples of the disciplinary procedures which are recommended in this article are as follows:

1. Truancy
    a. Keep pupil in after school to make up work
    b. Report case to parents
    c. Report case to public officer
2. The "show-off" attitude
    a. Put offender in place by a remark that will enlist pupils on your side
    b. Removal of privileges
    c. Public acknowledgment of fault
3. Dishonesty in assigned work
    a. Removal of credit
    b. Assignment of extra work
    c. Seat pupil apart from the group
4. Overzealousness in recitation
    a. Assignment of extra work
5. Bullying
    a. Oral reproof
    b. Removal of privileges

The other twelve types of misbehavior listed in the article are handled in an equally unsound psychological manner as those which have just been presented. It is hard for a student who has been trained in the principles of mental hygiene to conceive that such an article could have been written by a professional educator at so recent a date.

A more up-to-date description of how teachers handle disciplinary problems can be gathered from an examination of Table 24.[5] The material

---

[4] H. W. James, "Punishments Recommended for School Offenses," *Elementary School Journal*, Vol. 29, October, 1928, pp. 129–131.

[5] Frank Slobetz, "Elementary Teachers' Reactions to School Situations," *Journal of Educational Research*, Vol. 44, October, 1950, pp. 81–90.

## TABLE 24
### How Teachers Met Classroom Behavior Problems

| How Situations Were Met | Frequency |
|---|---|
| Physical Force (spanked, shook, tied in seat, etc.) | 134 (1%) |
| Censure (scolded, warned, shamed, hushed, used sarcasm, embarrassed, soaped mouth, etc.) | 1088 (11%) |
| Overtime or Extra Work | 486 (5%) |
| Deprivation (deprived recreational time, isolated, rearranged seating, removed from class, etc.) | 1044 (10%) |
| Sent or Referred to Office | 65 (0.6%) |
| Penalties (demerits, money fines, non-promotion) | 99 (1%) |
| Rectification or Reparation (required payment, required giving up of personal article, etc.) | 214 (2%) |
| Ignored or Did Nothing | 512 (5%) |
| Verbal Appeal (used reasoning, reminded, requested cessation, in behalf of the group, etc.) | 2586 (25%) |
| Group Reaction | 143 (1%) |
| Constructive Assistance (tried to create opportunity for successful participation, conferred with parent, assigned special responsibility, arranged for play with peers, etc.) | 3167 (31%) |
| Commendation (personal, public, etc.) | 57 (0.6%) |
| Searched for Reasons of Behavior | 620 (6%) |
| Tried Many Things Unsuccessfully | 29 (0.3%) |

presented in this table is based upon the replies of 290 elementary teachers representing eighty-six counties in a mid-western state. Although this study was reported in the year 1950, it is clear that teachers still used many outmoded and psychologically unsound procedures. Physical force, censure, and penalties of one sort or another are much in evidence and probably used more often than the situations would justify. It is encouraging to note, however, that constructive measures were employed in a substantial proportion of the cases.

In the past, discipline in the classroom was too often maintained by using essentially police methods. The child who misbehaved was regarded as "bad" and in need of punishment to make him "good." The newer point of view with respect to discipline gives cognizance to the basic processes of adjustment which have been outlined in the preceding chapter. Children are not regarded as being naturally bad or depraved, but as individuals that have definite needs which must be met in one way or another. Whenever a child misbehaves the teacher should ask himself such questions as: What is it the child is gaining by this particular behavior? or What needs of the child are being met by doing what he is doing? Teachers should realize that there are causes behind every type of behavior exhibited by children.

In many schools a typical method of dealing with misdeeds is to keep the offending pupils after school. If a pupil is tardy he is kept after school, if he

doesn't do his geography lesson he is kept after school, if he whispers he is kept after school, if he throws paper wads he is kept after school. There is obviously no connection in these instances between the offenses and the punishment. Such a procedure is similar to that followed by old time doctors who prescribed little pink pills for the patient regardless of what ailed him.

If a pupil is tardy, the teacher should try to find out why. Perhaps the family does not own an alarm clock. Maybe the child works before school, or the mother is ill and the child must do the dishes. If the pupil doesn't do his geography lesson, the teacher should again try to find out the reason. Perhaps he cannot read, or has lost his book. Maybe he doesn't see how studying geography will do him any good anyway. If he whispers, there is a reason also. Perhaps he has nothing to do. Maybe the work is too difficult for him. Perhaps he is uninterested or bored. Maybe he whispers to attract attention. Or maybe he is whispering to find the answer to an important question which he must have in order to proceed with his work. If the pupil throws paper wads, there is also a reason. People just do not throw paper wads for nothing. Some pupils secure attention and recognition in this manner which is denied them in more legitimate activities. If a pupil cannot succeed in conjugating Latin verbs, he may achieve distinction among his peers as the roughest and toughest pupil in the room. Other pupils will look up to him. That makes him somebody.

In the sections to follow, illustrations of classroom disciplinary problems, and the methods used by teachers in dealing with them are presented.

## ILLUSTRATIVE DISCIPLINARY PROBLEMS

### A SHOW-OFF IN THE ALGEBRA CLASS

Mr. Smith was teaching his first day of school in a medium sized high school. The subject was Algebra I. Mr. Smith began to call the roll. All went well until he came to the name of Max Howard. When this name was called a large boy began to wave his arms in the air and shouted with ear splitting volume: "I'm here, see I'm right here—old Max Howard is right here." All the rest of the class began to laugh and general disorder temporarily swept over the classroom. The next day when roll was called, the same incident took place. The teacher then sent the pupils to the blackboard to do some problems. Max again began to talk in loud tones which could be heard all over the classroom and even in adjoining rooms. Mr. Smith was greatly worried about what to do. He, however, said nothing to Max about his behavior, but when an opportunity was presented later in the period to speak to Max privately, Mr. Smith asked him if he would like to come in for a little visit later in the day during his conference hour. Max was told that all the pupils in the class were to make similar visits. Max said he would come, and sure enough he kept his appointment.

When Max entered Mr. Smith's room for his private conference, the first thing he said was, "You know, I am a pretty tough customer, I ran a teacher out of the high school I attended last year." Mr. Smith made no comment. Max went on talking. He said, "You know, I have a very loud voice." Mr. Smith replied that he didn't particularly mind loud noises as he used to work in a box factory and had become accustomed to noise. Max then said, "You know, I can also talk softly if I want to." Mr. Smith did not comment directly but gave the impression that he was not particularly concerned with how loudly a pupil spoke. He told Max that he just wanted to get acquainted and help him plan his future or assist him with any problem he might have. He also told Max that he thought it was unnecessary to call the roll every day and wondered if it wouldn't be better to make a seating chart as a means of checking the roll. Max agreed that this might be a good idea. Mr. Smith then asked Max if he would be willing to take charge of the seating chart and make a record of attendance for the ensuing week. Max consented to do this.

The next day, Max took over his duties in connection with taking the roll. His behavior changed remarkably. Mr. Smith reported to the writer that from that time on Max ceased entirely his loud talking and became a very cooperative pupil.

### DISORDER IN THE STUDY HALL

Pandemonium reigned very frequently in the study hall at Oakville High School. Miss Steiner, the teacher in charge, was doing her best to provide a quiet place for pupils to study, but her efforts were futile. On one occasion a mouse was brought into the room and released. On another, a "stink bomb" was burst. During such periods the entire study hall was in an uproar. Miss Steiner's procedure was to try to locate the culprit in each case. She would dash to the section of the room where the disorder seemed to break out and would look for a pupil who gave the appearance of being guilty. When she spotted a promising suspect she would often pounce upon him and give him a good shaking or send him from the room. The children loved this, for seldom did she ever apprehend the real culprit. When she could not find a guilty looking pupil she would turn upon the entire group with threatening statements of what would happen if such disorder should happen again.

Each study hall period began to degenerate into an exciting game of seeing what Miss Steiner would do next. She tried to police the room, but it was so large and there were so many pupils that she simply could not cover her "beat." Finally one day Miss Steiner did not appear at school. The principal received a report that she had had a nervous breakdown and probably would be gone for the rest of the year.

A new teacher was brought in to take over the study hall—a Miss Wilson. Miss Wilson's concepts of disciplinary methods differed radically from

those of Miss Steiner. After introducing herself to the pupils, Miss Wilson explained that she had no fixed ideas on just how a study hall should be run. She said that she wanted the type of conditions and atmosphere in the study hall which were desired by the pupils. She asked them if they would like to elect a committee to draw up procedures which all could follow. The pupils liked the idea, and suggested that the elected committee submit their tentative plan when finished to all the pupils in the study hall for their approval or amendment. This course of action was carried out and rules of conduct for the study hall were developed entirely by the pupils. Miss Wilson then made it clear that she was not at all interested in serving as an officer to carry out the rules which the pupils had enacted. She suggested that the pupils design a system for enforcing the rules they had made. The pupils set about to do this, and finally came forward with a system which included a standing committee on study hall procedure. A separate committee was elected for each period of the day. Pupils who were dissatisfied with any condition existing in the study hall were encouraged to report their grievances to this committee which would recommend appropriate action. Membership on the committee was rotated in such a way that many pupils were given the opportunity to serve. Cases of improper study hall conduct on the part of pupils were vigorously dealt with by this committee. Strong social pressure soon developed among the pupils to maintain a place of study that was in line with their expressed wishes.

Many suggestions for improving the physical appearance and educational facilities of the study hall were also sent in to the committee from time to time by pupils. As a result, bookshelves were built along one entire wall of the previously bare hall and these were filled with newspapers, magazines, and numerous interesting books. Some movable tables and chairs were added and potted plants were placed in appropriate places. The pupils began to take an interest in their study hall. So far as discipline was concerned, it ceased to be any real problem at all. Miss Wilson continued to work in the study hall, but her duties consisted of helping pupils with whatever problems they cared to bring to her. She worked with the pupils and not against them.

### The School Building Is Defaced

Arriving at Union High School one morning, pupils and teachers found red paint smeared all over the white pillars which stood at the entrance of the building. Several light globes in the front of the high school were also broken. Investigation produced evidence that this was the work of George Stevens, a high school junior, who was considered a general nuisance and problem around school. When confronted with the evidence George admitted his guilt, but was unable to give a reason for his behavior. A group of teachers met with the principal that evening after school to decide what

to do with George. It was suggested by several teachers that this was the last straw to break the camel's back. George had committed so many misdemeanors that there was no use putting up with him any longer. A recommendation was made that he be expelled from school. One teacher, however, disagreed with the group and refused to concur in this recommendation. She stated that in her opinion, George was a boy who had been beaten down around school, had been unsuccessful in his studies, and had received nothing in the way of commendation for even the small efforts he had made to do well. She maintained that his desire for recognition and status had been almost entirely thwarted in every avenue of the school's activities. "What George needs," she said, "is a chance to be significant and worthwhile in some activity connected with the school." What activity this might be she was unable to see. One of the other teachers, however, now came to the rescue and stated that there was a need for an assistant to help the regular janitor of the building. Some small compensation would be made available for this work. After much discussion it was agreed that this idea be presented to George for his reaction. This was done and George accepted the job with great enthusiasm. The principal who related this incident to the writer stated that the next morning after George had received this appointment he (George) arrived at the school building one hour before classes began and insisted that every pupil wipe off his shoes before entering the building. George had now found an activity which satisfied his need for attention and status.

### Joe—A Slow Learner and Bully [6]

"Joe was larger than his classmates, a fact he was never allowed to forget. Nor was he allowed to forget that he was less intelligent than his classmates. The brilliant method used by Joe's teacher to 'keep him in line' was to send him to the board to do an arithmetic example beyond his mental reach. A carnival air always permeated the classroom during these incidents. Joe would slouch to the board and try the impossible. Then, accompanied by much giggling, a 10-year-old girl would be sent up to complete the example. Joe would slink to his seat with hatred in his heart and another little piece of his soul destroyed. He naturally became quite bullyish and tried to achieve success the only way he thought he could.

"When Joe left school he found that he was no longer physically superior to his associates and his 'education' had convinced him that he was mentally inferior to everyone. What hope had he? More money than his companions was one possibility which he tried to accomplish by stealing. This led to his being sentenced to life imprisonment when he was 19— and a fourth offender. Obviously there were many other contributing fac-

---

[6] Paul E. Chapman, "Sarcasm: Pedagogical Poison," *The Clearing House*, Vol. 23, December, 1948, pp. 219–220.

tors—but is there any doubt but that some of Joe's sentence should be served by that teacher?"

### Miss Henry Is Upset

Miss Henry was an English teacher about fifty years of age. Her students considered her to be a very poor teacher and almost completely scatter-brained. She was referred to as "the ol' battle ax." On several occasions students asked each other—"Wonder what color the ol' lady's hair is gonna be today?" The university student who described this case to the writer stated that the class spent more time laughing at her than trying to learn anything.

At any rate, one day the phone rang. The phone, as it happened, was in a small closet-like affair that served both as Miss Henry's wardrobe and as a phone booth. Miss Henry got up to answer the phone and closed the closet door halfway so that the students could not hear what she was saying.

The half-opened door and the entire set-up proved to be a temptation which Jim Hansen could not resist. Stealthily he crept from his desk and on noiseless feet he worked his way up behind the door. In a moment he had slammed the door and snapped the lock. The students who had been sitting in silence during this escapade now burst into a tremendous uproar, applauding what he had done and howling like a pack of coyotes.

Soon the expected banging from the inside of the booth and the frenzied voice of the teacher were heard. She first demanded, and then implored that the students open the door immediately and set her free. Her pleas fell on deaf ears. Some of the pupils began to feel sorry for her and would have unlocked the door but the social pressure from the group kept them from doing so.

Finally after a considerable length of time, Jim unlocked the door and got back to his seat so quickly that Miss Henry had no notion who had done it. When she emerged she was close to being hysterical. Her hair was flung about her in strings and knots; plainly she had been sobbing, and her movements showed that her nervous restraint was nearly gone. "Who did this?" she demanded. "Who dared do such a thing? Why you could have killed me, locking me in there with no air." "Class" (and now she changed her tone), "we are going to have to maintain discipline. You're all going to have to be good little children and mind what I tell you or I'm going to do something drastic." She pointed to the window which was on the third floor of the high school. "If you ever misbehave again I'm going to open that window and throw myself out. Then you'll be sorry for what you have done."

Details are somewhat lacking with respect to further events that took place in this classroom. There is, however, no record that Miss Henry ful-filled her threat. Instead, she continued to nag, make other threats, and have occasional crying spells until the semester finally came to an end.

## GUIDING PRINCIPLES FOR KEEPING DISCIPLINE

Teachers should bear in mind that children generally behave in about the only way it is possible for them to behave considering the hereditary characteristics they possess, the kinds of experiences they have had, and the social pressures which are operating upon them at the moment. This is another way of saying that *behavior is caused.* This statement also indicates some of the causes. This principle implies that teachers have an opportunity to alter the behavior of children by helping them restructure their environment and by creating new social arrangements. Teachers are in a strategic position to assist pupils to develop new ideals and patterns of conduct. Realization of the fact that children behave in about the only way they can considering the factors in their backgrounds and present conditions surrounding them, should cause teachers to be sympathetic toward misbehaving children. Seeking for the cause of the misbehavior should replace the pronouncement of blame.

E. K. Wickman [7] has given a succinct explanation of why children misbehave. He says: "Behavior can best be explained in terms of discrepancies between the individual's capacities to behave and the requirements for behavior that are imposed upon him by social forces. By capacities we refer not only to biological (physical and mental) capacities but also to experiential factors (conditioned responses, social attitudes, etc.) that extend or limit the individual's possible behavior responses." A seventh-grade teacher, for example, who expects all the children in the room to do work requiring an intellectual level of, say, twelve or thirteen years, is inviting disciplinary episodes. Those children who fall considerably below this level of ability may respond to these excessive requirements by truancy and aggressive behavior or they may withdraw and become introvertive. Similarly children whose abilities far exceed the twelve- or thirteen-year-old levels may respond to the discrepancy between their capacities and the requirements by exhibiting symptoms of boredom or engaging in many types of annoying behavior.

It has been mentioned earlier that all children desire to be significant and to achieve status in the eyes of their peers, teachers, and other members of their society. The teacher who can help children reach this goal will have few if any problems of discipline.

Teachers should remember furthermore that older children and adolescents can take considerable responsibility for their own discipline if given a chance. Recently the writer visited a classroom from which the teacher

---

[7] E. K. Wickman, *Children's Behavior and Teachers' Attitudes,* New York, The Commonwealth Fund, p. 151.

Disciplinary problems seldom arise when pupils are engaged in stimulating activities which are of real value to them.

was temporarily absent. She had stepped down the hall to make a telephone call. The pupils continued to work on their projects just as if the teacher were present. This teacher left the room whenever the occasion demanded it. She never expected disciplinary problems. The children knew she trusted them and considered them responsible people. Other teachers in the same building did not dare leave their classes unattended. They had treated their pupils as immature individuals and as a result got immature behavior from them.

Some generalizations and suggestions for keeping discipline which seem to be valid are the following:

1. Praise and social approval are more effective in promoting good standards of conduct than are censure, blame, and punishment.
2. It is unwise to punish a whole group for the misconduct of an individual or a small group.
3. Sarcasm should be used sparingly if at all. Children are sensitive and may become severely hurt by such procedure.

4. The teacher should never consider misconduct as a personal affront. Instead the teacher should adopt the attitude that his interests and those of the pupil go in the same direction. The teacher should work with pupils, not against them.
5. Whenever possible, necessary rules and regulations should be formulated either by the pupils or by the pupils assisted by the teacher.
6. Discipline is most difficult to maintain unless pupils sense the real worth of the activities in which they engage.
7. Whenever disciplinary episodes arise, the teacher should ask himself such questions as: What is wrong with the course of study? What is wrong with my teaching methods?
8. When a child misbehaves, he should be studied in an effort to determine which of his needs have been thwarted. An attempt should be made to make the child's school experiences satisfying to him.
9. A child may misbehave because he is physically ill or suffering from a glandular disorder. Some restless and annoying children may have hyperthyroidism which needs medical attention.
10. Prevention of disciplinary situations is to be preferred to remedying difficulties that arise. If pupils have sufficient readiness for their work, are highly motivated, and if they are given sympathetic and understanding treatment by their teachers and peers very few problems of a disciplinary nature will develop.

## SUMMARY

Teachers consider the keeping of discipline to be their number one professional problem. More teachers probably fail in their work because of inability to maintain a well-ordered classroom than for any other single reason. Although the importance and need for providing a classroom atmosphere that is conducive for effective learning has never been doubted, methods of keeping discipline have changed radically over the years. Formerly, it was considered standard practice to bring an offender into line by corporal punishment, ridicule, or the removal of privileges. Discipline was something imposed upon the child by the teacher. Today, the goal is to avoid clashes between pupils and teachers by making the children as responsible as possible for their own behavior and by providing learning experiences which are highly motivated.

When children misbehave there is a reason. The teacher should try to find out what it is. Children frequently show-off in class, are impudent, or are negativistic because they want attention. The wise teacher will attempt to see that such children obtain the attention they crave from more fruitful types of activities. As a matter of fact, frustrated children may show almost any number of unhealthy symptoms which indicate that needs are not

being met. When disciplinary episodes arise, the teacher should make a study of the children involved in order to determine their motivations. He should also carefully evaluate his own teaching methods, and the curricular arrangements of the school to ascertain to what degree they are responsible for creating frustration in children.

The need for keeping discipline will diminish when children are happy and are busily engaged in activities that appear to them as being of real worth. Disciplinary problems will increase when the goals of children and the goals of the school are at cross purposes.

### References for Further Study

Amsterdam, Ruth, *Constructive Classroom Discipline and Practice*, New York, Comet Press Books, 1957.

Barnes, Donald L., "An Analysis of Remedial Activities Used by Elementary Teachers in Coping with Classroom Behavior Problems," *Journal of Educational Research*, Vol. 56, July, 1963, pp. 544–547.

Bonney, Merl E., *Mental Health in Education*, Boston, Allyn and Bacon, Inc., 1960, Chapter 4.

Bowman, Herman J., "A Review of Discipline," *National Association of Secondary School Principals Bulletin*, Vol. 43, September, 1959, pp. 147–156.

Canning, Ray R., "Does an Honor System Reduce Classroom Cheating? An Experimental Answer," *Journal of Experimental Education*, Vol. 24, pp. 291–296.

Chamberlin, Leslie J., "Group Behavior and Discipline," *The Clearing House*, Vol. 41, October, 1966, pp. 92–95.

Cutts, Norma E., and Moseley, Nicholas, "Four Schools of School Discipline —A Synthesis," *School and Society*, Vol. 87, February 28, 1959, p. 87.

Dreikurs, Rudolph, and Soltz, Vicki, "Your Child and Discipline," *NEA Journal*, January, 1965.

Gnagey, William J., "Effects on Classmates of a Deviant Student's Power and Response to a Teacher-Exerted Control Technique," *Journal of Educational Psychology*, Vol. 51, February, 1960, pp. 1–8.

Gnagey, William J., *Controlling Classroom Misbehavior*, What Research Says to the Teacher, American Educational Research Association of the National Education Association, 1201 Sixteenth Street, N.W., Washington, D.C., 1965.

Howard, Alvin W., "Discipline: Three F's for the Teacher," *The Clearing House*, Vol. 39, May, 1965, pp. 526–529.

Hymes, James L., Jr., *Behavior and Misbehavior*, Englewood Cliffs, New Jersey, Prentice-Hall, Inc., 1955.

Kounin, Jacob S., Gump, Paul V., and Ryan, James J. "Explorations in Classroom Management," *Journal of Teacher Eductaion*, Vol. 12, 1961, pp. 235–246.

Krall, George M., "What About Discipline," *The Clearing House*, Vol. 34, May, 1960, pp. 534–536.

Laughlin, Richard L., "Controlling a Class," *National Association of Secondary School Principals Bulletin*, Vol. 42, November, 1958, pp. 107–111.

Parody, Ovid F., *The High School Principal and Staff Deal with Discipline*, New York, Bureau of Publications, Teachers College, Columbia University, 1958.

Punke, Harold H., "Corporal Punishment in the Public Schools," *National Association of Secondary School Principals Bulletin*, Vol. 43, September, 1959, pp. 118–138.

Reynolds, James A., "Classroom Discipline," *School and Community*, Vol. 46, April, 1960, pp. 10–12.

Rogers, John R., *et al.*, "Discipline," *National Education Association Journal*, Vol. 47, September, 1958, pp. 367–381.

Seidman, Jerome M. (Editor), *Educating for Mental Health: A Book of Readings*, New York, Thomas Y. Crowell Company, 1963, pp. 264–274.

Sheviakov, George V., and Redl, Fritz, *Discipline for Today's Children and Youth*, Washington, D.C., Association for Supervision and Curriculum Development, NEA, 1956.

Wittenberg, Rudolph M., *Adolescence and Discipline*, Association Press, 291 Broadway, New York, 1959, Chapter 14.

Woodruff, Asahel D., "Discipline" in *Encyclopedia of Educational Research*, Third Edition, New York, The Macmillan Company, 1960, pp. 381–385.

## Questions, Exercises, and Activities

1–5. Following are given five statements about discipline in the classroom. Indicate which are true and which are false. Also, tell why you marked the item true or false.

    _____ A. The first thing a teacher should do when beginning a course is to show the children who is boss.

    _____ B. If a pupil should be impertinent or show-off in class, the teacher should ask him to apologize to the class.

    _____ C. When classroom requirements are too difficult for pupils, disciplinary episodes are likely to occur.

    _____ D. If a child misbehaves he should be studied.

    _____ E. Keeping children after school is probably the best method of eliminating tardiness and truancy.

6. Some teachers have their pupils help formulate the rules for conduct which will be followed in the classroom. What do you think of this idea? Write a paragraph giving your reaction.

7. In some high schools and colleges, the teacher leaves the room when an examination is given. These schools are operating on what is known as the honor system. Do you know of any such schools? Do you think it helps eliminate cheating on examinations?

8. If you were placed in charge of a study hall, how would you proceed to maintain discipline?

9. Do you favor a classroom which is absolutely quiet or do you prefer one in which there is a certain amount of noise? Justify the position you take.

10. In terms of learning theory, explain why punishment has an effect in modifying behavior. Is the avoiding of punishment reinforcing to the individual? What are some of the bad side effects that may result from learnings produced by punishment? Discuss the relative merits of punishment vs. reward as a procedure for controlling conduct. See Chapter 7.

# Chapter 15

---

# Promoting the
# Personal and Social
# Adjustment of Pupils

The preceding chapter has given attention to some maladjustments of children which give rise to disciplinary problems in the classroom. There are, however, many children who do not create overt classroom disturbances but who are none the less unhappy, insecure, and maladjusted in various ways. Teachers should have an understanding of these children—should be able to diagnose as far as possible their troubles and should in addition be able to create situations designed to improve their condition.

Information from the White House Conference on Child Health and Protection would indicate that one out of every three school children is maladjusted in one way or another. It has also been estimated that 12 per cent are so emotionally upset as to require the services of guidance specialists and psychiatrists.[1]

## HOW TEACHERS VIEW ADJUSTMENT PROBLEMS OF PUPILS

Forty years ago, E. K. Wickman [2] found a marked discrepancy between

---

[1] C. Morley Sellery, "An Organized Mental-Hygiene Program in the Schools," *NEA Journal*, Vol. 37, p. 586. Also see Thomas E. Jordan, *The Exceptional Child*, Charles E. Merrill Books, Inc., Columbus, Ohio, 1962, p. 239 for an extended listing of studies on the extent of emotional difficulties among school children.

[2] E. K. Wickman, *Children's Behavior and Teachers' Attitudes*, New York, The Commonwealth Fund, 1928.

the ratings of teachers and mental hygienists on the relative seriousness of behavior problems in school children. Wickman reported that "teachers stress the importance of problems relating to sex, dishonesty, disobedience, disorderliness, and failure to learn. For them, the problems that indicate withdrawing, recessive characteristics in children are of comparatively little significance. Mental hygienists, on the other hand, consider these unsocial forms of behavior most serious and discount the stress which teachers lay on anti-social conduct."[3] More recently, however, the Wickman study has been repeated by Stouffer.[4] He finds that today's teachers and mental hygienists are in much closer agreement as to the seriousness of children's behavior problems than they were back in 1928. The extent of the present agreement can be seen from an examination of Table 25. The actual degree of correlation between the teachers' rating and those of the psychological experts was found to be .61. The fifty classroom behavior problems listed in Table 25, although not of equal seriousness, are all ones which require the attention of teachers. None of them can be said to be entirely unimportant. The well-trained teacher should be prepared to deal with each using the best psychologcial techniques available.

## DETECTING MALADJUSTMENT

There are a number of tests, rating scales, and inventories which are useful to teachers and school psychologists in the process of discovering children who are personally and socially unadjusted. Among these are the *Haggerty-Olson-Wickman Behavior Rating Schedules*,[5] the *Bell Adjustment Inventory*,[6] the *California Test of Personality*,[7] the *Rogers Test of Personality Adjustment*,[8] the *Mooney Problem Check List*,[9] the *SRA Youth Inventory*,[10] and *Getting Along*.[11]

Many symptoms of maladjustment are readily observed by watching the child. His facial expression may indicate unhappiness or anxiety. He may be restless, hyperactive, tense, give evidence of being neglected, seem self-conscious about physical defects, be easily upset, depressed, or angered by frustration, have nervous habits such as twitching or nail biting, or be

---

[3] *Ibid.*, p. 129.

[4] George A. W. Stouffer, Jr., "Behavior Problems of Children as Viewed by Teachers and Mental Hygienists: A Study of Present Attitudes as Compared with Those Reported by E. K. Wickman," *Mental Hygiene*, Vol. 36, April, 1952, pp. 271–285.

[5] Published by the World Book Company, Yonkers, New York.

[6] Published by the Stanford University Press, Stanford University, California.

[7] Published by the California Test Bureau, Los Angeles, California.

[8] Published by the Association Press, 347 Madison Avenue, New York.

[9] Published by the Bureau of Educational Research, Ohio State University, Columbus, Ohio.

[10] Published by Science Research Associates, 57 West Grand Avenue, Chicago.

[11] For grades 7, 8, 9. May be obtained from Dr. Trudys Lawrence, 6117 N. Rosemead Blvd., Temple City, California.

## TABLE 25

**Rank-Order Comparison of the Ratings by Mental Hygien-
ists and Teachers of the Seriousness of 50 Behavior
Problems of Children ***

| Behavior Problem | Ranking by Mental Hygienists | Ranking by Teachers |
|---|---|---|
| Unsocial, withdrawing | 1 | 6 |
| Unhappy, depressed | 2 | 3 |
| Fearfulness | 3 | 23 |
| Suspiciousness | 4 | 35 |
| Cruelty, bullying | 5 | 4 |
| Shyness | 6 | 34 |
| Enuresis | 7 | 30 |
| Resentfulness | 8 | 11 |
| Stealing | 9 | 2 |
| Sensitiveness | 10 | 24 |
| Dreaminess | 11 | 40 |
| Nervousness | 12 | 18 |
| Suggestible | 13 | 13 |
| Over critical of others | 14 | 27 |
| Easily discouraged | 15 | 10 |
| Temper tantrums | 16 | 16 |
| Domineering | 17 | 15 |
| Truancy | 18 | 7 |
| Physical coward | 19 | 33 |
| Untruthfulness | 20 | 5 |
| Unreliableness | 21 | 1 |
| Destroying school material | 22 | 12 |
| Sullenness | 23 | 32 |
| Lack of interest in work | 24 | 22 |
| Cheating | 25 | 9 |
| Selfishness | 26 | 17 |
| Quarrelsomeness | 27 | 28 |
| Heterosexual activity | 28 | 14 |
| Restlessness | 29 | 45 |
| Inattention | 30 | 36 |
| Impertinence, defiance | 31 | 8 |
| Tattling | 32 | 47 |
| Slovenly in personal appearance | 33 | 31 |
| Obscene notes, talk | 34 | 29 |
| Laziness | 35 | 20 |
| Stubbornness | 36 | 37 |
| Attracting attention | 37 | 43 |
| Thoughtlessness | 38 | 41 |
| Imaginative lying | 39 | 46 |
| Disobedience | 40 | 19 |
| Carelessness in work | 41 | 25 |
| Masturbation | 42 | 26 |
| Impudence, rudeness | 43 | 21 |
| Inquisitiveness | 44 | 44 |
| Disorderliness in class | 45 | 39 |
| Tardiness | 46 | 38 |
| Interrupting | 47 | 48 |
| Profanity | 48 | 42 |
| Smoking | 49 | 49 |
| Whispering | 50 | 50 |

* Adapted from Stouffer.

constantly engaged in daydreaming, or again, the maladjusted child may be a truant. The social activities of the child will also reveal much. He may be left out of play groups; he may bully or be bullied by other children. He may be resentful of criticism, be fearful, quarrelsome or defiant, or be given to temper tantrums.

The teacher may sometimes find out what is bothering a child by having him tell a story or write a theme on such topics as "What I Dreamed Last Night," "If I Had Three Wishes," and "When I Was Most Afraid." Sociometric questions such as "With whom would you like to sit?" "With whom would you like to work?" or "With whom would you like to attend a movie?" when answered by pupils may give the teacher an indication of whom the isolates or rejected children in a room are. The child who steals, cheats, lies, or engages in disapproved heterosexual activity sooner or later identifies himself by becoming involved in conflicts with other people.

## CAUSES OF MALADJUSTMENT

In previous chapters it has been pointed out that every child in order to develop in a normal and wholesome manner must achieve reasonable satisfaction of his physical, social, and personality needs. Problem behavior, delinquency, and personal unhappiness are fundamentally due to frustration of these needs. There are, of course, numerous conditions in and out of the school which create frustrations which lead to maladjustment. Included among these are poverty, broken homes, personal inadequacies, rejection or over-protection by parents, and numerous unhygienic school practices.

### Poverty

Sociological studies [12] have shown the close connection which exists between poverty and personal maladjustment. Not all children who come from underprivileged homes are problems by any means, but statistically speaking low socio-economic status breeds conditions unfavorable to sound adjustment. How this works is illustrated in the case of two brothers, Gene and Clyde.

Our acquaintance began when two forlorn little fellows were brought in by the police for stealing from a neighborhood grocery store. Gene was the elder by a year, but it is hard to remember that because he has never been as large as his brother. Undersized, Gene was also undernourished and an extremely nervous little fellow with facial twitches, a shoulder and arm that jerked involuntarily, and he could never sit still. Clyde was not so under-

---

[12] Sheldon Glueck and Eleanor Glueck, *Unraveling Juvenile Delinquency*, New York, The Commonwealth Fund, 1950. Also see Daniel Schreiber, "The School Dropout," in *The Sixty-sixth Yearbook of the National Society for the Study of Education, Part I,* Chicago, The University of Chicago Press, 1967, pp. 211–236.

nourished as Gene, but was a moody, sensitive boy. He cried easily, and could not face censure, expressed or even implied, and he was never to blame. He felt insecure and unloved, said the boys at school picked on him and called him names that he hated. Even then, at the age of ten, Clyde was smarting under the injustice of his lot. Other boys had better homes; other fathers had better jobs. They could have things Clyde and his brother could not have; and their folks were not beaten by life. With very superior intelligence, neither boy was interested in school nor was either doing more than barely passing work. At home the situation was dispiriting. . . . When Clyde's father worked, it was at housecleaning jobs that Clyde and his brother were ashamed. Resenting the necessity and the implications of charity the family complained bitterly about the amount and character of the aid given them by the county. Health conditions were perilous. The mother was found to have active tuberculosis, and Gene's undernourished condition threatened to develop into the same disease. The parents were listless and indifferent. The school and welfare department complained that they were uncooperative. Keeping the house clean and looking after the children was too heavy a burden for the always-tired mother, but she and her husband could forget about it all when they had had enough alcohol to deaden their sensibilities.[13]

### Broken Homes

Statistics have shown that children who come from homes which have been broken by death, divorce, desertion, and separation are more often maladjusted than children who come from more stable homes. In reporting on delinquent boys, Glueck and Glueck state that "no fewer than six out of every ten of the homes of the delinquents, as compared with three of the homes of the nondelinquents, had been broken by separation, divorce, death, or the prolonged absence of one of the parents." [14] It is, of course, the insecurity caused by the breaking of the home that has the deleterious effect upon children. Homes which are not broken but in which there is much parental conflict also provide more than their quota of nervous, unhappy, problem children. To understand why some children behave as they do, it is essential for teachers to engage in home visitation. Such experiences will be most rewarding to the teacher and will furnish a perspective for dealing with the child which cannot be obtained in any other way.

### Personal Inadequacies

The child who is physically or mentally inadequate for tasks which are expected of him is certain to experience frustration. Equally frustrated is the child who sets goals for himself which he cannot reach. One important

---

[13] Maud A. Merrill, *Problems of Child Delinquency*, pp. 80–82. Copyright, 1947, by Houghton Mifflin Company, Boston.

[14] Sheldon Glueck and Eleanor Glueck, *Delinquents in the Making: Paths to Prevention*, New York, Harper and Brothers, 1952, p. 60.

function of the teacher is to help each child set aspiration levels which are commensurate with his abilities.

The child who is crippled or disfigured has problems of adjustment to face which are more complicated than those of the average child. Barker and his co-workers state that "studies by means of interviews, observations, and reports of informants indicate rather consistently that physically disabled persons are more frequently maladjusted than physically normal persons." [15] They point out that the resulting maladjustment may take such forms as the following:

a. Withdrawing, retiring, reticent behavior
b. Shy, timid, self-conscious, fearful behavior
c. Serious, thoughtful behavior
d. Refusal to recognize real condition, concealment, delusions
e. Feelings of inferiority
f. Emotional and psychosexual immaturity
g. Friendless, isolated, asocial behavior
h. Paranoid reactions, sensitivity, suspiciousness
i. Craving for affection, love of praise, seeking attention
j. Too high goals
k. Extremely aggressive, competitive behavior
l. Anxiety, tension, nervousness, temper tantrums

Sheldon [16] in one of his studies has noted the fact that delinquents are not as high in the *t* factor (a measure of good looks) as non-delinquents.

Children and adolescents are very sensitive about being different from what is considered typical or normal. They want to be like their peers. The teacher who can make each child feel significant regardless of whether he is tall, short, crippled, or disfigured can do much to alleviate inferiority feelings created by what the child may consider to be personal inadequacies. It is not the condition *per se* which causes maladjustment, it is the way the child views himself that determines his reactions. The teacher can cite many examples to show that people with all sorts of deficiences have made outstanding successes of their lives. This approach may help the child to forget some of his personal limitations and aid him to make the most of his positive characteristics.

### The Rejected Child

Many children come from homes where they are neither loved nor valued by their parents. Such treatment threatens the child's need for

---

[15] Roger G. Barker, Beatrice A. Wright, and Mollie R. Gonick, *Adjustment to Physical Handicap and Illness: A Survey of the Social Psychology of Physique and Disability*, New York, Social Science Research Council, 1946, pp. 72–73.

[16] William H. Sheldon, *Varieties of Delinquent Youth*, New York, Harper and Brothers, 1949, p. 762.

affection and security and may leave him feeling helpless and alone. The forms that parental rejection may take are many. These include neglect of the child; separation from the child; witholding gifts from the child; threatening, nagging, and punishing the child; humiliating him before other people; and comparing him unfavorably with other children in the family.

Children who are rejected by their parents may show a variety of un-healthy symptoms when in the classroom or in other situations. One of these is excessive attention-getting behavior. Many a child who is hyper-active, restless, and who seeks attention through non-conformity or wise-cracking is merely striving in the classroom to attain the satisfaction of a need which has been denied him at home. Symonds has pointed out that children who are much neglected or harshly treated by their parents may develop psychopathic and unstable tendencies. He describes the behavior of the psychopathic child as follows:

> The psychopathic child is one characterized by utter disregard of rules and conventions of society, by shallow feeling, by lack of reactions of guilt, and by emotional instability. He has not learned self-control nor developed behavior which is socially acceptable. Rejected children have low frustration tolerance. Since the parents have not exercised restraint or control, the child himself acquires no conscience or restraints from within. His superego is embryonic and consequently he is without feelings of guilt or remorse.[17]

The child who feels rejected also very often tends to be withdrawn or if he is able to find a friend, he may be extremely jealous of him and desire that no one else share his affection.[18] Children who have met with little or no emotional response on the part of parents, more often than not, have the greatest difficulty in forming genuine attachments for anyone. It is hard for them to give affection when they are not certain that it will be reciprocated.

Although teachers are not in a position to do much to alter parent-child relationships, they can do much to make children feel accepted, loved, and significant when at school. Acceptance by any adult who is respected by the child or by the child's own peers may at least partially compensate for rejection experienced in the home. This source of need satisfaction may help many a child from becoming a severe behavior case.

### The Over-protected Child

Just as children may be rejected, they may be overindulged by their parents. Parents who are themselves insecure and anxious often lavish

---

[17] Percival M. Symonds, *The Dynamics of Parent-Child Relationships*, New York, Bureau of Publications, Teachers College, Columbia University, 1949, pp. 27–28.

[18] For a discussion of "rejection versus acceptance" and the effects upon children see Henry Clay Smith, *Personality Adjustment*, New York, McGraw-Hill Book Company, 1961, pp. 511–515.

affection and attention upon their children. They crush the child with solicitude and excessive gratification. Every whim of the child is catered to. He may eat whenever he wants, or may have any toy or other material object he desires. He, however, may be protected and restricted from playing with other children or from going out into the weather because his parents feel he may suffer thereby.

Children who are overindulged show numerous characteristic behavior traits. These include selfishness, aggressiveness, lack of responsibility, and general infantile behavior. Children who are over-protected often exhibit such nervous habits as thumb sucking, enuresis, and temper tantrums. "The overindulged child has poor social adjustment. He is known as the child with bad manners, the impolite child who will say the saucy thing and who will be rude and boorish. He is also known as the undisciplined child, and parents and teachers call him disobedient. When they make a request of him, he will obey it or not according to his whim and if it is something disagreeable, he may become impudent when an attempt is made to coerce him. With other children he is demanding, bossy, selfish, cocky, and a show-off." [19]

The over-protected child is greatly in need of socialization. The school can do much to help him take responsibility and overcome his self-centered infantile behavior. He will receive many hard knocks both from teachers and other children but it will be greatly to his advantage if he can learn to develop tolerance for frustration. This is something that he has never developed at home and something which he will greatly need in life if he is to be successful. Care should be taken, however, that his rough edges are not removed more quickly than he can stand. He will need sympathetic but firm and realistic treatment. Over a period of years the overindulged child through association with individuals outside the family may develop socially acceptable behavior.

### Unhygienic School Practices

There is no question but that unfavorable home conditions play a large part in maladjustments which children exhibit at school. It is not so apparent, however, that conditions existing in the school may also contribute much to a child's unwholesome development. Teachers who are inadequately trained in psychology and mental hygiene unwittingly commit many serious errors and carry forward practices which are extremely detrimental to the good mental health of their pupils. Requiring all children in a given grade to satisfy the same requirements regardless of their abilities is one such practice. For example, a twelve-year-old child with a mental age of eight may be required to undertake tasks which are appropriate only

---

[19] Percival M. Symonds, *op. cit.*, p. 55.

for normal children of his age. In this case, the child's response to these excessive requirements may be expressed either by withdrawing (e.g., daydreaming) or by attacking the situation (e.g., disobedience). Many children are made to feel insecure, uncertain, and afraid because the teacher constantly threatens them with unexpected examinations or with failure in the course.

Many teachers use stringent autocratic controls in their classrooms which have the unfortunate effect of reducing children's resourcefulness and initiative. Children who are impertinent or who "show-off" are publicly humiliated and forced to make apologies. Children who are tardy or who play truant are required to stay after school. Children who lie or steal are accused and threatened with expulsion from school.

Altman describes a teacher who told her pupils that "everything in the classroom was charged with electricity, and that they might be electrocuted at any moment if they misbehaved because she, the teacher, could pull a switch to kill them all." He also related a case of an eight-year-old boy who developed a severe case of St. Vitus's Dance, because of his fear of his teacher. The boy's nervous symptoms entirely disappeared when he was transferred to another school.[20]

Healy and Bronner have suggested that the school may in some instances directly contribute to the delinquency of children. A quotation from their discussion of what makes a child delinquent will show how this may occur.

> Slurs, taunts, cutting remarks, evidences of social and racial prejudice may arouse or accentuate feelings of inferiority which in turn, are reflected in reckless antisocial behavior. If a teacher, without thinking, asks in the classroom, "Why doesn't your mother send you to school cleaner?" or "Are you a placed-out child?" or "What does your father do for a living?"—questions that possibly imply social inferiority—he little realizes how the child may be touched to the quick. We could give vivid illustrations of how such remarks have set off whole trains of explosive behavior. A strong, determined boy of thirteen, already sensitive about his home life, met a teacher's slurs about his mother's lack of care for his appearance with immediate truancy. He stubbornly evaded school for weeks, steadily refusing to return to this teacher's room. When the principal rejected the idea of transferring him to another school, he ran away, made his way to Texas, and was gone a whole year. Returning while still of school age, he continued to be truant, committed other delinquencies and was always embittered about the earlier school experience.[21]

---

[20] Emil Altman, "Our Mentally Unbalanced Teachers," *The American Mercury*, Vol. 52, April, 1941, pp. 391–401.

[21] William Healy and Augusta F. Bronner, "What Makes a Child Delinquent?" in *Forty-Seventh Yearbook of the National Society for the Study of Education, Part I, Juvenile Delinquency and the Schools*, Chicago, University of Chicago Press, 1948, pp. 37–38.

Wendell Johnson has pointed out that in some schools "children are singled out as defective, and even though no official announcements are made, the children themselves, their schoolmates, their families and neighbors become vaguely aware of what they feel to be an unsavory and disturbing label. Then nothing constructive is done. They simply wait and worry. The simple fact is that branding a child as defective and then ignoring or neglecting him intensifies his problem both for him and his family." [22] The practice of labeling children as "dumb," "bad," "stubborn," "disobedient," or a "stutterer" may actually contribute toward making a child display the characteristics of his label.

Many additional examples could be given of school procedures which promote poor mental health on the part of pupils. The picture, however, is not all dark. As was shown in the study by Stouffer, cited earlier in this chapter, teachers are becoming more conscious of mental hygiene than ever before and as a result the number of unhygienic school practices are undoubtedly decreasing.

## DEALING WITH SPECIFIC TYPES OF MALADJUSTMENT

In Table 25 which was presented earlier in this chapter are listed fifty types of behavior problems encountered by teachers. It will be impossible to discuss ways and means of dealing with each of these. As a matter of fact, there is no specific technique that applies to one that may not apply to others as well. These fifty problems are largely symptoms which indicate that all is not well with the pupils who exhibit them. A child who shows one or more of these symptoms should be studied. This study should attempt to discover what is back of the behavior—what needs of the child are thwarted, etc. Frequently many symptoms or problem behaviors of a child can be traced to one given cause.

In this section a few typical behavior problems will be discussed. It is hoped that these illustrations will present a point of view that may be useful in dealing with other similar problems of adjustment.

### The Child Who Steals

Behind the act of stealing there is always a cause or motive. The teacher should try to find out what need or needs of the child is being met by this type of behavior. A child may steal because he is hungry, needs clothes, or because he needs money to impress his friends. Perhaps he can buy the

---

[22] Wendell Johnson, "Teaching Children with Speech Handicaps" in Forty-Ninth Yearbook of the National Society for the Study of Education, Part II, *The Education of Exceptional Children*, Chicago, University of Chicago Press, 1950, p. 184.

social approval of other children if he has money to procure gifts for them. Sometimes children steal in order to get revenge upon another child or the teacher, or to vent hostile feelings toward their parents. Just what should be done in the case of the child who steals would depend upon which of the foregoing motives were operative. The child who steals because he is hungry should certainly first of all be supplied the necessities of life. The child who steals in order to buy gifts which will win him acceptance into a social group needs help in gaining social recognition through more legitimate channels. The child who steals in order to express feelings of hostility toward his teacher probably needs more affection and response from his teacher and opportunity to release his emotions in such activities as school plays, music, art, or athletics. From the mental hygiene point of view it would be very unwise to demand a confession from a child who steals or to publicly accuse him of such an act. Such procedures do not get at the basic cause of his trouble and may only aggravate the case by causing him to lie or gain a bad reputation for an act he may not commit again.

### The Child Who Cheats

Cheating on the part of pupils is a problem which confronts a great many teachers. It is true, however, that children cheat in the rooms of some teachers, but do not do so in their other classes. Children cheat for a variety of reasons. Thorpe has suggested four possible causes of this behavior. They are as follows:

1. The task is too difficult
2. Parent, teacher, or child standards are too high
3. Parent, teacher, or child has placed a premium on marks or grades rather than on understanding
4. Child feels inadequate or insecure in many situations [23]

The child who cheats is usually under severe pressure to make good or has a fear that he will fail in his studies. The teacher who gears learning tasks to the abilities and interests of pupils will find that cheating drops off drastically. Many times children do not see how the subject they are studying will help them personally. They thus take the shortest possible route to secure a passing grade. Units of work and problems directly related to real life activities often so intrigue pupils that the possibility of cheating never occurs to them. Much cheating can, however, be expected in dull and tense classes where a premium is placed upon the acquisition of subject matter which has doubtful value in the minds of the pupils. Even

---

[23] Louis P. Thorpe, *The Psychology of Mental Health*, New York, The Ronald Press, 1950, p. 538.

in such situations, the honor system as employed by some schools, has had a marked effect in reducing cheating. When children are given full responsibility for their own conduct and when peer group pressures are brought to bear, it is a rare child who will break the rules of the game. Under the honor system there may be thirty or forty pairs of watchful eyes supervising an examination instead of just one pair of eyes—those of the teacher.

### The Lazy Child

It is not uncommon to hear teachers characterize certain of their pupils as being "lazy." The writer once taught a high school geometry class. In this class was a big husky boy named Bill who seemed to be about the most "lazy" pupil the writer had ever encountered in his several years of public school teaching. Bill never did his assignments, and during class periods he would drape himself over the desk in a most lackadaisical manner. One Saturday, however, the writer had occasion to do some shopping at a large chain grocery store. Whom should he see but his geometry pupil, Bill, directing the operations of one of the departments of the store. Although Bill was only a junior in high school, he had been placed in charge of one of the largest divisions of the store. The writer asked the manager how Bill was getting along with his Saturday job. He was told that Bill was one of the most efficient, energetic, resourceful, and ambitious students the store had ever employed. The writer blinked his eyes in amazement. It seemed impossible. Bill apparently was not "lazy" at all. About all that could be said was that he was unmotivated when it came to studying geometry.

Many so-called lazy children come to life and exhibit real enthusiasm and competence when school activities are slanted toward goals which the children themselves consider to be important. Too often, however, the goals of the school and the goals of pupils are at cross-purposes. In such situations there will inevitably be many unmotivated or "lazy" pupils on the class rolls.

### The Truant

According to Table 25, truancy is ranked seventh in order of seriousness by teachers. It is, however, ranked only eighteenth by mental hygienists. Teachers consider truancy, for example, to be a more serious behavior problem than fearfulness, shyness, enuresis, nervousness, and suspiciousness. Mental hygienists, on the other hand, rate all these symptoms above truancy. The truant is an individual who just does not want to go to school and makes plans to do something else. He may go fishing, attend a movie, visit the circus, take a trip, or work on some interesting project in a friend's basement. He may or may not have a serious problem of personal adjust-

ment. It is clear, however, that he has a real problem of school adjustment. If the activities at school challenged him as much as those outside school, it is certain that he would be no truant. Basketball coaches have no problem of truancy among their players. In fact, they often have great difficulty keeping the boys out of the gymnasium even when practices are not scheduled. The child who is successful in school—whose needs are being met—is unhappy if events prevent him from attending his classes. Teachers should consider truancy on the part of pupils a sign that something is wrong with the school as well as with the pupil. When changes have been made in school programs, truancy has been known to drop off. One teacher commented upon one of her boys as follows: "K. is one of our truants. We have previously had great difficulty in keeping him in school. He is now in one of the remedial reading clubs where he is responsible for telling other children when the group meets. His truancy first disappeared on the days the club met, but recently he has been attending every day." [24] This boy cannot afford to be absent from school because he would then miss the opportunity of being a valued member of his reading club.

### The Unsocial, Withdrawing Child

Of all the problem types of classroom behavior, mental hygienists rate this one the most serious. Teachers are also becoming conscious of the unsocial, withdrawing child in their midst as is seen by the fact (Table 25) that they now rate this problem sixth in importance out of a list of fifty behavior deviations. The shy child, although he causes the teacher no inconvenience, may be most unhappy and suffering from feelings of insecurity and inadequacy. He may daydream excessively, refuse to mix with other children, and withdraw into a world of his own. It is this type of child, mental hygienists believe, that is in the most danger of developing schizophrenia if nothing is done to check his unsocial trend. All shy children, of course, do not become psychotic; perhaps only a few do. Yet the fact that some may and that others often develop into adults who are socially ineffective and unhappy is sufficient cause for concern.

An example of such a child is Dodie, a fourteen-year-old girl, who is described by Buhler as follows:

> Dodie was an unobtrusive and quiet girl. In school she passed from grade to grade as an average to good student until now she was in the ninth grade of a junior high school. Nobody had paid much attention to her except one physical education teacher who had asked her, in front of all the children, why she had inferiority feelings about games and athletics. This was an unfortunate remark in the circumstances.

---

[24] Marion Monroe and Bertie Backus, *Remedial Reading: A Monograph in Character Education*, Boston, Houghton Mifflin Company, 1937, pp. 155–156.

Dodie never talked in class unless asked to. She went around with one or two girls whom she called her friends. She never talked with boys and never participated in group activities or was elected to any office.

The first time any teacher concerned herself with Dodie was when her grades began to drop considerably. The teacher discovered that in the ninth grade Dodie sat daydreaming and rarely spoke to anyone or participated in class.

Calling the mother to discuss Dodie's work, the teacher learned to her surprise that the mother a few weeks earlier had taken the child to a doctor and to a psychologist, but had not wanted the school to know because she felt the school might think there was "something wrong" with Dodie. (This unfortunate idea that the school might be prejudiced against a child seen by a psychologist is not unfrequently encountered in parents.)

The teacher was now interested and worked with mother and psychologist to understand this child. She learned that Dodie, after coming home from school, never talked to anybody outside the house if she could help it. She participated in no games with the many neighbor children as did her brothers and sisters. . . .

Most of her time was spent among books and magazines; she liked to draw dress models and model dolls. She put much imagination into these drawings and her absorption let the mother feel that Dodie, who herself was plain, identified with these beautiful models in her long periods of daydreaming. When asked whether she wanted to be a dress designer, she declared that she just wanted to marry and have children. As she refused to meet anyone, particularly to date with boys, or to talk with them, her marriage wish appears an unreal dream similar to her dreams about beauty and models.[25]

Children like Dodie are not at all uncommon in the classrooms of this country. Efforts to socialize them should definitely be made by teachers. The kindly, sympathetic, and understanding teacher is in a position to maneuver things so that the withdrawn child is drawn into more school and social activities. If such a child can experience one success in a group activity, a good start is made. The isolated child needs to feel that he is essential to the happiness of others—that he is a valued member of some group. If satisfaction can be achieved in real life activities, there is no need for the child to withdraw into the realm of dreams to satisfy his basic wants. The wise teacher may observe that a withdrawing child has some special competence or ability that can be used in a group activity. By indirection the child may be induced to participate. If his contribution is appreciated by the other children, he will be encouraged to repeat his successful performance in group situations. The writer knows of a home economics teacher who induced one of her very shy and poorly adjusted girls to have a cooking party in her home. Other children in the class were invited. The success of the enterprise greatly increased the girl's confidence

---

[25] Charlotte Buhler, *et al., Childhood Problems and the Teacher*, pp. 141–142. Copyright, 1952, by Henry Holt and Company, New York.

in herself and resulted in a changed attitude of the other children toward her.[26]

## SCHOOL PROGRAMS WHICH AID PUPIL ADJUSTMENT

### The Case Study Conference

Some schools have worked out a plan whereby time is set aside each week for the careful analysis of a given pupil's adjustment problem. At this time all the pupil's teachers gather along with such other interested individuals as the principal, counselor, school nurse, and school social worker. All the pertinent information available regarding the pupil and his problem is presented, and a recommendation is made which is designed to facilitate the pupil's adjustment. This device not only serves to alleviate problems of children but provides valuable in-service training for teachers.

### The Delaware Human Relations Class

One of the widely known plans for aiding pupil adjustment is the Delaware Human Relations Class. Bullis has described how this operates in the following words:

> Our weekly class generally starts with the teacher reading a stimulus story which features emotional problems. The students are then encouraged to discuss freely the emotional problems presented in the stimulus story, to give an appraisal of the story, and then most important of all to indicate from their own personal experiences parallel situations to those presented in the story. In this retelling of emotional experiences—often bringing out into the open problems they have never discussed before—a better understanding of their actions often results. The students also gain insights by listening to their classmates tell freely of how they meet certain emotional problems.[27]

The Delaware program has been designed especially for use in grades seven, eight, and nine. The originator of the plan (H. E. Bullis) has prepared and published three teachers' handbooks—*Human Relations in the Classroom*, Courses I, II, and III.[28] Each book contains thirty lesson plans and six teacher aids together with additional information for conducting the classes.

---

[26] For other suggestions see C. H. Patterson, "The Classroom Teacher and the Emotional Problems of Children," in *Readings in Educational Psychology*, Second Edition (J. M. Seidman, Editor), Boston, Houghton Mifflin Company, 1965, pp. 66–69.

[27] H. Edmund Bullis, "A Positive Mental Health Program," *American Journal of Public Health*, Vol. 40, September, 1950, p. 1114. For description of the Delaware program also see H. Edmund Bullis, "Are We Losing Our Fight for Improved Mental Health?" *Progressive Education*, Vol. 30, February, 1953, pp. 110–114.

[28] These may be obtained from the Delaware State Society for Mental Hygiene, Wilmington, Delaware.

### The Tulsa Personal Relations Course [29]

This course is designed for boys and girls at the eleventh-grade level. Among the topics covered are: "Understanding Ourselves," "You and Your Family," "Boy and Girl Friendships," and "Looking Toward Marriage." It is suggested by the designers of the program that the teacher may stimulate interest in the first of these topics, for example, by:

1. Having students list personal adjustment problems
2. Discussing behavior observed, or conversations overheard, which indicate adolescent problems
3. Showing and discussing films, slides, or recordings which present adolescent problems

The work of the course involves a thorough consideration of the basic principles of mental hygiene and their application to everyday living. Regular credit is given for the course. Over the years, the course has been so popular with pupils that many ask to repeat it a second time without additional credit.

### Remedial Classes

Children who are extremely retarded in reading, arithmetic, English usage, and other tool subjects often find themselves bewildered, frustrated, and discouraged in regular classes which are geared many levels too high for them. Theoretically a master teacher with unlimited resources in materials and small classes, could minister to the needs of these children. Actually, however, this is very difficult to accomplish. As a result the very slow learning child is frequently humiliated to such an extent that he develops aggressive, withdrawing, and other anti-social behaviors. A great number of schools have set up remedial classes to fit the needs of such children.[30] By giving the slow learner success experiences rather than failure experiences a big step is taken toward rebuilding his morale and integrating his personality. Reports indicate that as a result of remedial classes many resistant children have become cooperative, apprehensive children have become self-confident, discouraged children have become hopeful, and socially maladjusted children have become acceptable to the group.

In teaching such classes it is imperative, however, that teachers create an atmosphere which makes their pupils feel important and significant and not inferior to other pupils. The pupils should be made to feel that they

---

[29] Course in Personal Relationships, Eleventh Grade, Tulsa Public Schools, Tulsa, Oklahoma. An excellent outline of a program in personal and family relationships for pupils in grades 7–12 can be found in *Home Economics Education*, Illinois Curriculum Program, Subject Field Series, Bulletin D-7, Office of the Superintendent of Public Instruction, Springfield, Illinois, 1966, pp. 47–76.

[30] For description of remedial classes in schools see Glenn M. Blair, *Diagnostic and Remedial Teaching*, Revised Edition, New York, The Macmillan Company, 1956.

are normal—that every individual is good in some things and not so good in other things. If it is a special class in reading, the teacher should convey the idea that anyone can learn to read just like anyone can learn to tap dance or play the piccolo. The teacher might cite cases of famous men such as President Andrew Johnson who did not learn to read until after he was married. If a pupil is really made to believe that there is nothing peculiar about him, he will generally be enthusiastic about improving his reading skills even if the lessons are conducted in a class especially designated for that purpose. On the other hand, if teachers and school administrators tend to regard special classes for poor readers as essentially "dumbbell" classes, the pupils quickly sense this and very unsatisfactory results are bound to occur. Under such circumstances, slow learning pupils would probably be better off in regular classes.

If properly taught and administered, however, these unfortunate results need not occur. The writer has visited special classes in which children were beaming with success. They were finding out for the first time in their lives that they could learn to read, write, spell, and do arithmetic. Such achievement had a marked effect upon their self-confidence and their entire outlook on life.

## USEFUL TECHNICS AND MATERIALS

### Technics

The major part of this chapter has been devoted to consideration of ways and means of helping the maladjusted child. Essentially the technique advocated has been that of understanding what his needs are and providing a school atmosphere and curriculum which will make possible their satisfaction. This, of course, is fundamental and all devices utilized should have as their aim a similar purpose. Techniques reported in the literature which have been used or suggested for use by classroom teachers to aid maladjusted children include group therapy,[31] play therapy,[32] non-directive counseling,[33] and psychodrama.[34] Teachers who desire to improve their skills in dealing with maladjusted children should make a careful study of these methods by reading the available literature and pursuing specialized courses in these areas.

---

[31] Henry S. Maas, "Group Therapy in the Classroom," *Mental Hygiene*, Vol. 35, April, 1951, pp. 250–259.

[32] Virginia Mae Axline, *Play Therapy*, Boston, Houghton Mifflin Company, 1947.

[33] Kathleen Fawcett, "Psychotherapy in Your Classroom," *Texas Outlook*, Vol. 32, August, 1948, pp. 19–20. For detailed description of this method see Carl R. Rogers, *Client-Centered Therapy; Its Current Practice, Implication, and Theory*, Boston, Houghton Mifflin Company, 1951.

[34] Robert B. Haas, *Psychodrama and Sociodrama in American Education*, New York, Beacon House, 1949.

An example of how play therapy was used by one teacher to help a disturbed, little boy is reported by Liss.[35]

### JOHN

John was a sturdy, handsome eight-year-old with a violent temper. One of the big causes of friction in his home was his inability to read. He was continually reminded of his inadequacy and his reaction was usually a temper tantrum in which he smashed his own play things and stormed and screamed. . . . He tried this same behavior in school, demanding immediate attention whenever he had any difficulty and tearing up his pictures or breaking his clay or wooden handwork when there was any delay in getting help. He did beautiful handwork and was very proud of it so its destruction was a measure of his troubled twisted thoughts. His sullen face and bursts of anger kept him from having any friends. He was a most unhappy little boy.

John's teacher induced him to make puppets as a means of releasing his tensions and developing status among his classmates. This method apparently worked for after a few months it was noted that his class work was improving, he was beginning to read, and his personality was changing for the better. He lost his sullenness and fiery temper and became a friendly, well-liked, sociable boy.

Haas [36] has described how troubled pupils may be helped by the use of psychodrama. The following procedures were suggested to aid the adjustment of a boy and a girl.

1. Boy calls on a girl in the home of her parents. He is instructed to ask her for a date to a coming school dance.
2. A girl comes into a school room and discovers two of her friends in a violent gossip session about her. The nature of the gossip is varied to suit the level of the pupil.

Those who advocate the use of psychodrama in schools feel that through the process of acting out a situation (role playing) there will be a release of tension on the part of the pupil and a more complete understanding of his problem. Psychodrama has been recommended for all grade levels of the school.

---

[35] Florence Liss, "How Puppets Helped John," *Childhood Education*, Vol. 26, January, 1950, pp. 214–216.

[36] Robert B. Haas, *op. cit.*, pp. 101–102. Also see Harold W. Bernard, *Mental Hygiene for Classroom Teachers*, Second Edition, New York, McGraw-Hill Book Company, 1961, p. 394. How the technique of the sociodrama is used to aid the adjustment of mentally retarded adolescents is described in A. Edward Blackhurst, "Sociodrama for the Adolescent Mentally Retarded," *The Training School Bulletin*, Vol. 63, November, 1966, pp. 136–142.

## Materials

An increasing number of good books and films are being produced which can be used in mental hygiene programs of the school. Books which have been prepared for pupils include: *Getting Along with Others,*[37] *How Personalities Grow,*[38] *Personality and Youth,*[39] and *Ways to Improve Your Personality.*[40]

Films that may be used include such titles as *Developing Self-Reliance, Shy Guy, Developing Your Character, Developing Friendships,*[41] *The Other Fellow's Feelings,*[42] *Understanding Yourself,*[43] and *You and Your Family.*[44] Films such as these may frequently be rented from state or university visual aid libraries.[45]

## THE SCHOOL PSYCHOLOGIST AND GUIDANCE COUNSELOR

Many schools have a psychologist or guidance counselor on the regular staff. This person helps to supplement the mental hygiene program of the school. He works with teachers, assists with the testing program, and may consult with individual children who are seriously disturbed. Although he may render extremely valuable service of a specialized nature, he is just one cog in the total program. Teachers in the classroom will always have to do much of the counseling and guidance work regardless of whether a specialist is or is not available. When mental hygiene principles are extensively applied in classroom practice the number of children needing the attention of a psychologist will become progressively fewer. The well-trained teacher should be able to recognize children whose problems are of such a nature that outside help is needed.

In some communities there are child guidance clinics which may be used by schools with limited specialized personnel. These clinics are often directed by a psychiatrist who has psychologists on his staff. Severe problem

---

[37] Published by Science Research Associates, 57 West Grand Avenue, Chicago, Illinois. This publisher has a whole library of Life Adjustment Booklets which have been designed to help teenagers solve their problems.

[38] Helen Shacter, *How Personalities Grow,* Bloomington, Illinois, McKnight and McKnight.

[39] Louis P. Thorpe, *Personality and Youth,* Dubuque, Iowa, William C. Brown Company.

[40] Virginia Bailard and Ruth Strang, *Ways to Improve Your Personality,* New York, McGraw-Hill Book Company.

[41] These first four are all Coronet Films.

[42] Young America Films, Inc.

[43] Church Screen Productions.

[44] Association Films.

[45] The Audio-Visual Aids Department of the Division of University Extension, University of Illinois, Urbana, Illinois, carries many films of this type.

cases which require deep psychotherapy should be referred to such agencies.

## SUMMARY

Not all maladjusted children create disciplinary problems for the teacher. Some children who are unsocial, withdrawing, unhappy, depressed, suspicious, fearful, and nervous, actually attract very little attention to themselves. These children, according to mental hygienists, need as much if not more sympathetic help from teachers as do the "trouble makers."

The causes of personal unhappiness, inferiority feelings, shyness, and other socially ineffective behavior can be traced to the same sources of conflict that create more aggressive types of maladjustment. Both the shy child and the aggressive child have thwarted needs, but each adopts a quite different method of resolving his problem. Conditions in the environment which create frustrations leading to personal maladjustment are poverty, broken homes, personal inadequacies, rejection by parents, over-protection, and certain unhygienic school practices.

In this chapter some common types of cases encountered by teachers are discussed, and suggestions are given for helping personally and socially unadjusted children. The truant, for example, is described as being a child who finds few satisfactions at school. School is such an unpleasant place to go that non-attendance is preferred. Truancy, however, can be made to disappear when the child finds that he is really needed at school and that what he has to offer is appreciated by others. Likewise the shy and socially ineffective child can be made to show more confident behavior and to take part in more group activities when arrangements are made for him to experience success rather than failure in connection with social activities.

Schools are beginning to give increased attention to problems of mental hygiene. In some instances, special classes or programs have been developed which deal directly with adjustment problems of children. Examples of these are the Delaware Human Relations Class and the Tulsa Personal Relations Course. Teachers, as a result of more sound psychological training, are becoming increasingly skillful in using therapeutic devices which formerly were employed only by a few experts. Such procedures include group therapy, play therapy, non-directive counseling, and psychodrama.

Problems such as have been presented in this chapter obviously require for their solution the highest levels of psychological training and insight. How to deal with children who present personality difficulties is a skill which must be mastered by all who would succeed in the difficult task of teaching.

## References for Further Study

Carroll, Herbert A., *Mental Hygiene*, Fourth Edition, Englewood Cliffs, New Jersey, Prentice-Hall, Inc., 1964, Chapter 13.

Cruickshank, William M., *Psychology of Exceptional Children and Youth*, Second Edition, Englewood Cliffs, New Jersey, Prentice-Hall, Inc., 1963.

Donahue, George T., and Nichtern, Sol, *Teaching the Troubled Child*, New York, The Free Press (Macmillan Company), 1965.

Ekstein, Rudolph, "Puppet Play of a Psychotic Adolescent Girl in the Psychotherapeutic Process," in *The Psychoanalytic Study of the Child*, Vol. 20, New York, International Universities Press, Inc., 1965, pp. 441–480.

Holmes, Donald J., *The Adolescent in Psychotherapy*, Boston, Little, Brown and Company, 1964.

Kounin, Jacob S., Friesen, Wallace V., and Norton, A. Evangeline, "Managing Emotionally Disturbed Children in Regular Classrooms," *Journal of Educational Psychology*, Vol. 57, February, 1966, pp. 1–13.

Lawrence, Trudys, "An Evaluation of the Emotional Health of Secondary School Pupils," *The Journal of School Health*, Vol. 35, September, 1965, pp. 327–332.

Orr, Douglass W., *Professional Counseling on Human Behavior*, New York, Franklin Watts, Inc., 1965.

Sachs, Benjamin M., *The Student, the Interview, and the Curriculum: Dynamics of Counseling in the School*, Boston, Houghton Mifflin Company, 1966.

Slavsow, S. R., *A Textbook in Analytic Group Psychotherapy*, New York, International Universities Press, Inc., 1964.

Sutherland, Robert L., and Smith, Bert K., *Understanding Mental Health*, Princeton, New Jersey, D. Van Nostrand Company, Inc., 1965.

Ullmann, Leonard P., and Krasner, Leonard, *Case Studies in Behavior Modification*, New York, Holt, Rinehart and Winston, Inc., 1965.

Verville, Elinor, *Behavior Problems of Children*, Philadelphia, W. B. Saunders Company, 1967.

Weldon, Lynn L., "Cheating in School: Teachers Are Partners in Crime," *The Clearing House*, Vol. 40, April, 1966, pp. 462–463.

## Questions, Exercises, and Activities

1. Why is it that many children who come from poverty stricken homes or from broken homes are well-adjusted personally and other children who come from these same types of homes are poorly adjusted?

2. Describe some practices in the elementary or secondary school you attended that violated good principles of mental hygiene.

3. The text lists several specific types of maladjustment, e.g., stealing, cheating, being truant, and withdrawing, and suggests methods of dealing with them. Select one other specific type, discuss it, and tell what a teacher should do about it.

4. Do you know of a child or young person who is emotionally disturbed? Describe his symptoms, explain the cause of his behavior. and tell what steps should be taken to alleviate his condition.
5. Read an article on group therapy, play therapy, non-directive counseling, or psychodrama. Summarize it and give your opinion of its worth.
6. What types of information should teachers have regarding pupils who are personally maladjusted? In what way should these data be used? Are teachers competent to counsel children with emotional disturbances?
7. Did the high school you attended have a guidance program? If so, describe it and evaluate its effectiveness.

# Chapter 16

## Studying the Individual Child

In a sense this whole book is a study of children—how they develop, learn, and adjust. This chapter, however, will focus upon the study of the individual child rather than deal with facts about children in general. No child is simply a summation of many traits, characteristics, interests, and ideals. Rather each is a unique, indivisible organism and each must be appraised separately and *in toto*. A leading authority in the psychology of personality aptly expressed the need for individual study when he wrote: "The only way to make a certain prediction of effect from cause is to study the life in which the causes operate and not a thousand other lives." [1]

This chapter will present the need for child study, some of the sources of information avaliable to teachers and others who work with children, and the methods and tools which psychologists and teachers have found useful.

### THE NEED FOR CHILD STUDY

The need for child study, especially the intensive study of individual children, becomes clearly apparent in those cases where teachers make judgments and take action with insufficient knowledge about a child. The pathos of some such mistakes is illustrated in two cases which follow.

[1] G. W. Allport, *The Use of Personal Documents in Psychological Science*, New York, Social Research Council, 1942, p. 210.

In the first case, the teacher who was giving a timed test told the class that when she said "go" all pupils should begin immediately. All pupils started work on the signal except Mary who delayed a few seconds and (according to the teacher) gave her an impudent stare. The teacher collected all the papers, passed them out a second time, and again said "go," but Mary was still late in starting. At this turn of events, the teacher slapped Mary's face several times. Shortly afterward, a medical examination diagnosed Mary's case as "post-encephalitic epileptiform behavior." In short, damage to motor nerves made this girl's reaction time slow. She would have been unable to start on the word "go" no matter how hard she tried.

The second case was that of a girl, Doris, who was accused of stealing from her classmates' lunch boxes. Investigation revealed that large quantities of sandwiches and fruit had had been hidden in the school's basement, and Doris was found guilty. The teacher was aggravated by this apparent willful waste of food and suspended the girl from class. A clinical study of this case turned up the fact that Doris was extremely malnourished. Her lunches generally were nothing more than an ungarnished slice of bread or a few saltines. Other children had made fun of her lunch and she retaliated by taking tidbits and hiding them. When she was asked why she had not eaten any of the sandwiches, apples, and other "goodies," she replied, "Eat their lunches, that would be stealing." [2]

### Each Child Is Unique

Even though people have much in common, there is also much which makes each unique. Children with identical IQs may be very different in other traits and may even be radically different in the distribution of their mental abilities. For example, two children may both score an IQ of 120 on the *Stanford-Binet* test. Yet one may be an excellent reader and the other almost a non-reader. One of these children may have unusual musical talent and the other possess almost none. Furthermore, on the IQ test itself, one child may score highly on the memory items while the other child will make his strongest showing on the problem-solving tasks. Even identical twins may, and generally do, have different personalities. [3] When identical twins are reared apart, differences in temperament and personality may be even more pronounced. [4]

---

[2] D. E. Lawson, "Development of Case-Study Approaches," *Educational Forum*, Vol. 16, March, 1952, pp. 311–317.

[3] Evelyn Troup, "A Comparative Study by Means of the Rorschach Method of Personality Development in Twenty Pairs of Identical Twins," *Genetic Psychology Monographs*, Vol. 20, 1938, pp. 461–556.

[4] H. H. Newman, F. N. Freeman, and K. J. Holzinger, *Twins: A Study of Heredity and Environment*, Chicago, The University of Chicago Press, 1937, p. 192.

## Children Have Individual Problems

The most useful way to answer the question as to "why" a child is behaving in a certain way is to study that particular child. "A problem child is one who has a problem that has not been solved." [5] That child and that problem are unique. An illustration of the way in which individual study and treatment may help youngsters solve their problems is shown in the following case described by Thornley. [6]

The boy, who was 17, had a mental age of 14.3, and an IQ of 89. His achievement test scores were: vocabulary 5.4; [7] reading comprehension 7.9; arithmetic reasoning 8.3; arithmetic fundamentals 6.1; language 5.3; and total grade equivalent 6.2. Intensive individual interviews with this boy revealed that he had considerable drawing ability, and that he wanted to study women's clothing design but was hesitant to make this known. With encouragement from the teacher, he began making sketches and drawing designs. Presently, the teacher suggested that he go to the clothing teacher and talk with her about designs but he found that he was unable to understand her, and returned to the English teacher somewhat discouraged. It was then suggested that he read about design and clothing, and make a list of words that he did not understand. He did this and continued his drawing. Within a few months, he had produced several dress designs which, according to the clothing teacher, were better than the commercial designs which she was buying. Not only had this boy gained self-confidence, and made achievement in this specific area, but in the short space of a semester read nearly 2000 pages—a feat which was unduplicated in his previous work.

The case just cited illustrates that even though the educational deficiencies clearly pointed to a need for action, further information was needed and the seeking of it actually led, as it often does, to the individual attention so badly needed by some children. [8]

## PITFALLS TO BE AVOIDED IN CHILD STUDY

The arch enemy of good child study is the "typing" of children on the basis of too limited data. Contrary to the specific information which comes from individual study is the kind of generalization which is implied in such remarks as: "all smart kids are like that." By pigeonholing people, it is

---

[5] T. L. Torgerson, *Studying Children*, New York, The Dryden Press, 1947, p. 26.

[6] W. R. Thornley, "Unlocking Resources of Retarded Students," *The English Journal*, Vol. 39, 1950, pp. 302–306.

[7] "Vocabulary 5.4" means that the boy achieved in vocabulary as well as the average pupil in about the middle of the fifth grade.

[8] The reader who wishes to find examples of such cases is referred to G. M. Blair, *Diagnostic and Remedial Teaching*, Revised Edition, New York, The Macmillan Company, 1956, Chapter 13.

possible to brush off differences and treat all children alike. The reaction of
a school principal to types of children, and the consequent distortion of his
perceptions about the individual children involved is illustrated in the following incidents described by Hollingshead.[9]

Elmtown High was having trouble with tardiness so decided all children
should get "detention" for further infractions, and that there would be no
excuses. So a decision to this effect was made, and announced to the school
and to the office staff. The following Wednesday morning Frank Stone,
Jr. (Class I) [10] parked his father's Cadillac in front of the high school at a
quarter after eight. When he came into school, the principal said:
"What's the story this time?"
. . . "I didn't wake up, I guess."
The boy was told to report for detention. He failed to do so and when
the principal called his father (a very prominent man in the community),
the son was sent to school, but the superintendent interceded and got him
off, with the mild warning that he try not to let it happen again.
Three weeks later, "Boney" Johnson who was a Class IV boy came late.
Before "Boney" could say a word the principal said:
"So my pretty boy is late again! . . . I suppose you took a bath last
night too. New shoes and they're shined." "Boney" said nothing, but his
face flushed and he bit his lip. The principal walked back to his desk, sat
down, and wrote out an admission slip. He put "Boney's" name on the
detention list and handed over the excuse with the remark, "I want to see
you in detention tonight. Now go on up to class and show the girls what a
pretty boy you are."
After the boy left the principal said:
"Now there's a hot one. He's one of our *wise guys*. He thinks he's a *hot
shot*. His old man is a laborer out at the fertilizer plant, and the kid thinks
he's someone umph! He'll be on the W.P.A. if they have one twenty
years from now. There's one guy I'm going to see put in detention."
That night after school when "Boney" tried to escape, the principal
seized him and when the boy tried to fight loose, hit him several times.
The superintendent who was also on hand joined in and together they threw
"Boney" out the front door with the threat not to come back till he brought
his father. After he was gone, the principal and superintendent spoke of
"Boney" as a "sassy kid," a "trouble making type," a "smart kid."
"Boney" quit school. Undoubtedly some might add that he was the type
who would.

Here was a case in which prejudgment based on typology, plus sarcastic action were probably influential in producing an educational casualty

---

[9] The incidents described here were taken from A. B. Hollingshead, *Elmtown's Youth*,
New York, John Wiley and Sons, Inc., 1949, pp. 188–192.

[10] In Elmtown, the fictitious name of an actual town in Illinois, there seemed to be
five distinct socio-economic classes. Class I represented the moneyed land-owning
group, Class V were the impecunious "squatters" who worked irregularly and who
lived for the most part in homes which were more like shacks than houses. "Boney"
Johnson was in the Class IV group, which rated just a little higher than the Class V
group just described.

which could have been averted by individual attention and study. Likewise, the case of Frank Stone, Jr., although on the surface he fared better, was nevertheless shrugged off on the basis of typology. That "kid" was the "rich" type about whom the school could do nothing. Some of the dangerous and misleading kinds of typing which are sometimes employed by teachers are given in the next five paragraphs.

### IQ Typing

Frequently used terms are "dull," "average," and "bright." These are based on an arbitrary criterion such as an IQ score. Teachers should know that the error of measurement on tests could easily throw a person from one class into another. Also it must be remembered that there are great differences within the individual, and typing on the basis of IQ might have little connection with abilities in other areas. Another source of error is that excessive weight is given to single items of behavior or single scores. The way to avoid this kind of typing error is to fight the "halo" [11] effect by the use of objective tools of appraisal, the recognition of the limitations of tools of measurement, and the avoidance of the use of stigma words with regard to children who lack one kind of academic proficiency.

It should be recognized, of course, that categorizing children by IQ may be a necessary arrangement for grouping them for special classes. For example in many states a child with an IQ below 75 or 80 and above 50 is eligible for enrollment in a special class. When the IQ is below 50, children may be designated as uneducable, but possibly "trainable." But even at these lower levels of ability, category designations are somewhat arbitrary, and it is well to remember that membership in a certain category is not immutable. Kirk's study of the effects of preschool experience upon the mental functioning of the mentally handicapped showed that the intensive early training resulted in 70% of the children gaining in their tested levels from 10 to 30 IQ points.[12]

### Hereditary Typing

"He'll never amount to anything, look at his father. He's shiftless, and the boy's a chip off the old block." Statements such as these illustrate a kind of erroneous thinking which certainly should not be practiced by school teachers. Attributing bad characteristics to the influences of heredity may be a convenient way to shrug off a difficult case, but it does not solve any problems.

---

[11] The halo effect is an error of judgment about a person which results from over-generalizing on the basis of a limited amount of specific information. For example, a youngster who has committed one misdemeanor may be viewed as a "bad" boy, or a child who makes one high score may be seen as having overall high ability.

[12] Samuel A. Kirk, *Early Education of the Mentally Retarded*, Urbana, Illinois, University of Illinois Press, 1958, p. 205.

### Associational Typing

This kind of typing represents a variety of thinking which is characteristic of the generalizations of small children. It is exemplified by such reasoning as: "One man with a mustache cheated me, therefore all men with mustaches are cheaters." Although no teacher should be guilty of this kind of logic in dealing with children, one suspects that this kind of overgeneralization was working when teachers made these statements: [13] "Dirty children are careless in school," and "aggressive boys are girl-crazy," or the statements that children who masturbate are "mentally unbalanced" or "usually dull and thin."

### Social Class Typing

No one can question that there are relationships between social class and behavior. But to judge behavior on social class alone is wrong because there is considerable variation of behavior of children coming from a given social class. Much of the cause of misbehavior is probably due to just such typing and the rejection and unfairness it creates. For the most part, teachers are middle-class persons with the values and mores of that group. It is thus difficult for them to look at behavior of lower class children objectively. There is a tendency to excuse the lack of study of such children by the implicit belief that it would be hopeless anyway.

### Racial and Religious Typing

This is a most pernicious and psychologically unsound kind of typing. Nevertheless it is sometimes used by teachers as is shown by these statements:

Negro children remind me of an odor.
Jewish children think they are better than other children.

From a group of nearly 200 teachers who completed the sentence "Italian boys _____" the following responses were not rare:

have a hot temper
are handsome
are busybodies
are dirty and nasty
are cute
are usually fine athletes, and not too bright

Undoubtedly ethnic and religious backgrounds may have an influence upon personality development. To deny these influences is just as unscien-

---

[13] Unpublished data collected by E. L. Gaier, Urbana, Illinois, Psychology Department, University of Illinois, 1951.

tific as it is automatically to ascribe personality and behavioral traits solely on the basis of membership in a certain group.

The effect of typing of lower-class Negro children is pointed out by Clark,[14] who, speaking of theories about social deprivation, asks: "to what extent do they offer acceptable and desired alibis for the educational default: the fact that these children, by and large, do not learn because those who are charged with the responsibility of teaching them do not believe they can learn, do not expect that they can learn, and do not act toward them in ways which help them to learn?"

## WHICH CHILDREN SHOULD BE STUDIED?

All children should receive some degree of individual study. The intensity or thoroughness of the study should be a function of the following criteria:

1. The degree to which present behavior is likely to affect adversely a child's development
2. The amount of help the child will probably need in solving his problems
3. The amount of competence the teacher has in dealing with such problems
4. The degree to which the problem behavior interferes with the work of the teacher and of the class

The choice of children for study may be biased by the social class to which they belong, although it is obvious that this is not a valid criterion for deciding whom to study. Another factor (number one above), the seriousness of the behavior, is probably the one most frequently used. This is as it should be. However, many teachers probably do not know which varieties of problem behavior are the most serious, and often make their choice of children to study on the basis of number four above, which is probably the least important factor.[15]

The beginning teacher may be aided by knowing what kinds of problems to expect. Relevant here is a survey made by Torgerson. He found in a study of 1,270 pupils from Grades 1 to 8 the following percentages of children having these difficulties: [16]

31 per cent had scholarship difficulties
27 per cent suffered from reading disabilities

---

[14] Kenneth B. Clark, *Dark Ghetto Dilemmas of Social Power*, New York, Harper and Row, 1965, p. 131.
[15] See the discussion of the work of E. K. Wickman and George A. W. Stouffer, Jr. in the preceding chapter.
[16] T. L. Torgerson, *op. cit.*, p. 45.

20 per cent had social behavior problems
15 per cent had speech problems
13 per cent had health problems and physical disabilities

An extensive investigation of behavior problems (as contrasted with scholastic problems) was conducted by Peterson.[17] Out of 427 representatively chosen cases at a child guidance clinic, he selected the 58 most common reasons for referral. The list included items such as:

thumb sucking
restlessness, inability to sit still
doesn't know how to have fun; behaves like a little adult
crying over minor annoyances and hurts
dislike for school
nausea, vomiting
temper tantrums
excessive daydreaming
uncooperativeness in group situations

These 58 items were built into a scale used by teachers to rate 831 kindergarten and elementary children, and a factor analysis of the results was obtained. Two factors emerged with reliability and clarity:

1. Conduct Problems (impulses against society)
2. Personality Problems (low self-esteem, moodiness, and social withdrawal)

When boys and girls were compared at different ages, it was found that boys had more conduct problems (factor 1) at all ages, and in kindergarten and primary levels boys also had more personality problems. At the middle and upper elementary grades, however, girls had more personality problems than boys.

The kind of child who is studied is probably also determined by the types of problems which teachers expect, and the sorts of "problem" behavior for which they search. For instance, the referrals from a traditional school, which followed strict routines, and in which there was a crowding of pupils, were almost all disciplinary cases or subject matter failures. A "progressive school" with which the former was compared sent to the school psychologist considerably more cases in which children suffered from fear, shyness, and social maladjustment.[18]

Finally, it is interesting to note that the sex of children often enters into the question of whom should be studied. In a survey of 1,357 children in

---

[17] Donald R. Peterson, "Behavior Problems of Middle Childhood," *Journal of Consulting Psychology*, Vol. 25, 1961, pp. 205–209.

[18] R. G. Anderson, "Two Schools and Their Problem Cases," *Progressive Education*, Vol. 11, 1934, pp. 484–489.

Detroit about one per cent were classed as having serious behavior problems, and 85 per cent of these serious cases were boys.[19] In referrals to clinics for problems of reading, speech, and delinquent behavior, boys lead. It is to be noted that the aggressive behavior which leads to study is less likely to occur among girls, who nevertheless may be having other difficulties which are just as serious. In the writer's classes over the past few years, when teachers have turned in case studies of their problem pupils, well over 90 per cent have been studies of boys.

## SOURCES OF INFORMATION

Where do teachers obtain information about the child? This is an important, but none the less difficult question. A child may act very differently in various situations. Furthermore, there are places and ways of obtaining information which are often overlooked in the study of a child.

A child may be extremely aggressive in a permissive play situation and well-controlled, even over-inhibited, in the classroom or home.[20] The model child at his mother's knee might, when mother is not around, be the one who would be found squeezing his little brother's fingers with a pair of pliers. To acquire data for a dependable child study requires the gathering of material from many places and in various circumstances. This section will attempt to show how a study of the home, community, and school may furnish information about a child's problems.

### Parents and Home Conditions

One of the most successful teachers the writer knows is one who regularly visits the homes of every pupil in her class. This teacher has a third grade in the "toughest" section of a large industrial city, yet she has fewer disciplinary problems than most teachers in the city, and is well-liked by both pupils and parents. This teacher attributes her success to knowing how the parents and children live, and dealing with the problems of each child in the light of the information thus collected.

An important question is what to look for in the home, and what to find out from parents. Parents can be a rich source of information, but simply going to a home or talking to parents will not automatically unlock this source. The teacher may be so busy trying to avoid being called "nosey" or concealing the shock he feels on seeing bad conditions in a home that he misses some of its important psychological characteristics.

In teachers' visits to homes, classroom visits by parents, interviews with

---

[19] H. J. Baker and V. Traphagen, *The Diagnosis and Treatment of Behavior-Problem Children*, New York, The Macmillan Company.

[20] A. F. Korner, *Some Aspects of Hostility in Young Children*, New York, Grune and Stratton, 1949, p. 167.

parents, and in group meetings, teachers should be alert to and seek for information in the following areas:

1. The emotional reactions of the parents toward the child
2. The parents' understanding of the child and his problems
3. The parents' ideals, values, and aspirations with respect to the child
4. The parents' control techniques and disciplinary measures
5. Parents' attitudes toward the school, teacher, and learning

Successful work with parents hinges on the same psychological principles which operate in dealing with the problems of motivation, readiness, and individual differences of pupils. Just as children can be alienated by unfavorable comparisons, harsh criticisms, and sarcasm, so parents may become emotionally disturbed and refuse to give information or cooperate when these techniques are used.[21]

### Community

At first glance it would appear that a teacher might easily acquire information about a community simply by virtue of living in it. Not so for the middle-class teacher who may see the community and its neighborhoods through middle-class eyes. Even small towns may have a number of fairly distinct subcultures each with its own values, ideals, and ways of living. In one town of only 6,200, for example, there appeared to be at least five separate socio-economic classes and about eight rather distinct neighborhoods.[22]

In studying communities and neighborhoods, teachers should ask these questions:

1. How does the community feel about itself? Does it consider itself to be composed of distinct classes?
2. What are the community's influences upon its youth? What youth serving agencies are there? What do the people who staff these agencies think about the community?
3. Who are the community leaders and how do they feel about the community?
4. How does the school fit into the community? How do the citizens feel about the school?
5. How does the child feel about his community and neighborhood?

---

[21] For a good discussion of "The Teacher's Work With Parents" see Charlotte Buhler, Faith Smitter, Sybil Richardson, Franklyn Bradshaw, *Childhood Problems and the Teacher*, New York, Henry Holt and Company, 1952, Chapter 12, especially page 251.

[22] A. B. Hollingshead, *op. cit.*, p. 462.

## Observations

Direct observation of a child under a number of different circumstances has promise of offering more valuable information for the time spent than any other diagnostic activity. On the other hand, when observations are biased or incomplete, they may be worse than useless, as they may lead to either the wrong action on the part of the teacher or give a distorted notion to others when reports of the behavior are made. Two teachers can look at the same behavior in the same child and make very different reports and interpretations of the child's behavior.

The accuracy of perception of observed behavior as well as the empathy which a teacher has for a child's problems and behavior are both important in observation and the action which follows. Ways of improving the accuracy of observation as well as increasing identifications (empathy) with a particular child are suggested in the numbered points which follow.

1. Observations should be planned. One way of implementing the planned nature of observations is to time-sample behavior. This means that at planned (and randomized) intervals observations of a certain length (e.g., 15 minutes) be made of a given child. If such a formalized planning is not feasible for the teacher, it is suggested that he might plan to observe a little of the behavior of the child in each of the various activities during the day on various days of the week for a period of time.

2. Interpretation should *follow* the collection of data. Tentative interpretation, before the data are in, especially when it is made explicit in writing or discussion may ego-involve the observer so that he makes future observations conform to the original diagnosis. In this regard, the teacher could take a tip from the advice given counselors and clinicians, "Only when he has all the data he is going to have, should he make his public commitment on paper or to the patient or in any other communicated form." [23] Even such an apparently small consideration as the order in which a teacher obtains information may color the interpretation of observed behavior.[24]

3. A written record (if one is to be made) should be made directly after an observation. The longer material is kept in mind, the more details are lost and the greater is the tendency for distortion. But as shown in 2 above, this record should not, at least initially, contain interpretive material.

---

[23] N. L. Gage, *Explorations in the Understanding of Others,* Paper read at the Sixteenth Annual Guidance Conference at Purdue University, Lafayette, Indiana, April 10, 1951.

[24] S. E. Asch, "Forming Impressions of Personality," *Journal of Abnormal and Social Psychology,* Vol. 41, 1946, pp. 258–290.

4. Teachers ought to learn how to play the role of the child, i.e., put themselves in the child's place. This was neatly expressed by Cottrell, who wrote:

> Just the simple device of saying to himself, "Now I am X facing this situation and having to deal with this problem," seems to enhance the observer's comprehension of the perspectives, attitudes, and overt behavior of his subject. Deliberate role-taking practice also seems to increase these observational skills.[25]

5. One should look for symptoms of difficulty. H. B. English, who for many years has regularly required the study of an individual child by students in his classes in child psychology, recommends that they look especially for: the "child's relationship with other people," and he adds, "anything that makes the child a little different is always interesting and important." [26]

### Interviews

A special kind of observation is the interview. Here the teacher tries to observe the child's behavior (mainly verbal) in a face-to-face relationship. Some interviews are counseling sessions in which the main goal is one of therapy, but most conferences in the classroom are for the purpose of gaining information which will help in cooperatively planning learning experiences that are not necessarily therapeutic. The educator may not be a psychotherapist, but at the same time he may have more powerful tools for influencing the social setting of the classroom than does the psychotherapist.

Careful analyses of interviews and of the interaction in counseling situations have revealed that the amount and validity of the information obtained is governed to a degree by the rapport or good relationship existing between the client and counselor—or in this case between the teacher and pupil. It should also be noted that interviews may be useful for shedding light on a variety of problems extending from process errors in arithmetic to deep seated problems of maladjustment or personality disorders.

Too common is the notion that a conference with a pupil means having the youngster "on the carpet." In fact there is some question that a teacher can play the dual role of grader and "boss," and at the same time be a confidant of a troubled pupil. Much depends not upon the interview alone, as it does in clinics where the counselor and child meet for the first time, but on the kind of relationships which previously existed in the classroom. In this sense, an interview is merely an extension of an everyday relationship, and should offer no problem for the good teacher.

---

[25] L. S. Cottrell, Jr., "Some Neglected Problems in Social Psychology," *American Sociological Review*, Vol. 15, 1950, pp. 705–712.

[26] H. B. English, *Child Psychology*, New York, Henry Holt and Company, 1951, p. 21.

OPENING THE INTERVIEW. This is a very important phase, for it may set the stage for resistance or open the way for a warm relationship and the gaining of much information. Following are some examples of interviews poorly started and those well-opened:

| POOR OPENINGS | GOOD OPENINGS |
|---|---|
| Well, I guess you know why you're here, John. | Won't you sit down here, John. |
| Take off your hat. | Hello, Mary. Come in and help me move this desk off the light cord. |
| Did you forget about the rules we had made, Mary? | Well, I'm glad to see you, Edward. Have a seat. |

One should avoid putting a child on the defensive in the beginning of an interview as this closes off the source of information. If the purpose of the interview is to discuss some misbehavior, one should not refer to this immediately. Since an interview is not a "third degree," a teacher should never overly press a point when emotional disturbance is detected.

SECURING INFORMATION. Teachers must listen! They may learn very little by talking, but may learn a great deal about a child by listening to everything he has to say. They must also avoid too rapid probing. The creation of a warm, permissive, and confidential atmosphere will help more than anything else in facilitating the flow of information. The surest way to create resistance and bewilder a child is to ask him a question he is unable or afraid to answer. (Many times teachers ask questions which no one could answer.) The writer recently heard a teacher tearfully ask, "How could you do this, Mike?" To ask a seven-year-old, "Why did you do such a terrible thing?" not only is a threat, but also may force a response which has only protective purposes. The child may learn to try to escape rather than to face problems.

RESISTANCE. How well the interview is going can be estimated by the amount of resistance which is produced. Some of the indicators of resistance which practiced counselors have noted are: (1) the avoidance of detail or specific plans, (2) use of monosyllables, (3) intellectual discussion of topics, (4) rejection of the teacher's ideas, (5) hostility, (6) apathy, (7) blocks in thinking, and (8) attempts to leave before the interview is concluded.[27] The teacher, as a professional interviewer, ought to become familiar with these symptoms of resistance, and know that they are signals which indicate the need for less probing.

---

[27] F. P. Robinson, *Principles and Procedures in Student Counseling*, New York, Harper and Brothers, 1950, p. 107.

### Gaining Information From Creative Activities

Unwittingly and without conscious awareness children may reveal many of their needs and much of their frustration through such things as themes, stories, drawings, paintings, and play. In fact, young children who are not able to verbalize well, or to use abstractions, may have no other means of telling adults their problems. Such is the case of Carl—who made the sketch shown in Figure 40.

**Figure 40.** Pencil Sketch Made by an Emotionally Disturbed Twelve-Year-Old Boy.

Carl, just under age twelve when he made the above sketch, was a pupil in a special classroom for retarded children. He was one of four boys in a lower middle-class family. The mother was very much disappointed because Carl was a boy, and often expressed her resentment by dressing him

as a girl. She had kept him in long curls and dresses for several years after his birth, and even continued the practice up to the time of the incidents described here. Carl's tested IQ was 75 on the Stanford-Binet and 72 on the Grace Arthur Point Scale. In a Progressive Achievement Test most of his scores were just below the third-grade level. A description of Carl written by his special-class teacher follows:

> When Carl first came to us he was a trouble maker, and still frequently reverts back to his bad behavior. He is large for his age, height 61 inches and weight 102 pounds. He tried to gain recognition by crawling around on the floor, whining, snickering, and acting very immature. He shoves, pushes, tattles, is destructive, inattentive, denies failures, bullies, acts smart, teases, giggles excessively, is nervous and restless, and indulges in temper tantrums.

The sketch shown in Figure 40 was but a sample of many such sketches and drawings,[28] made by Carl dealing with the same theme. These drawings portrayed Carl killing, boxing, hanging, shooting, frightening Jerry, and other younger children, especially effeminate boys and girls. In these drawings Carl always allied himself with the most masculine boys in class.

If Carl has been able to verbalize what his problems were, he would probably have said something like this:

> I hated being treated like a girl when I was younger. I should have hated my mother for doing this to me, but I know children must love their parents. The least I can do now is to prove that I am not a girl in any way— not like Jerry who is a big sissy. I'm like Bill and John. We are tough guys.

It seems obvious that Carl was releasing tension and fighting against a girl's role which had been thrust upon him. In Carl's mind Jerry had come to symbolize the type of boy which represented the femininity which his mother had tried to create in him.

In creative activities one should look for such mechanisms as projection, compensatory activities, and daydreams. In this way the teacher may begin to get a glimpse of a child's real needs, which may emerge only briefly out of his disturbed emotional depths.

## TOOLS AND METHODS FOR CHILD STUDY

The exploitation of the sources of information described in the previous section is facilitated by the use of appropriate tools and methods. What are the tests, rating scales, inventories, and records which will most ef-

---

[28] In one water color Carl and his pal John were shown shooting down Jerry in a plane over Korea (Carl's story). In another Carl depicts himself as a ghost chasing several younger children most of whom were girls.

ficiently provide teachers the information they need in working with children?

### Home and Community Rating Scales

Some professional workers have found a standard rating scale [29] for appraising the socio-economic level of the home or community a helpful device. This is probably too formal a procedure for most teachers' purposes. However, some of these scales can be administered to pupils without the necessity for a home visit, and they seem to have considerable reliability when so used.[30] One such scale, *The Kerr-Remmers American Home Scale* has items such as the following: [31]

Does either of your parents belong to a parent-teacher
organization? . . . . . . . . . . . . . . . . . . . Yes  No
Does your family own (not rent) the home in which
you live? . . . . . . . . . . . . . . . . . . . . Yes  No
Does your family have an automobile? . . . . . . . . Yes  No

Another scale which is filled out by pupils themselves is the *Sims SCI Occupational Rating Scale*.[32] It contains listings of various occupations and the student is asked to rate his own family level as the same, lower, or higher than the social class represented by the given occupations.

Somewhat less formal than the above scales is one suggested by English [33] as a guide for the teacher or case worker who wishes to study the home. This *Items-in-the-Home-Index* asks questions such as:

Is there an electric or gas refrigerator in the home?
Is there a bathtub in the home?
Does the family leave town every year for a vacation?
Does the child have his own room at home?
How many books does the family have?

Socio-economic rating covers but one aspect of the home. The most difficult and important task is that of appraising the psychological climate of the home, and there is no way of doing this simply by administering a questionnaire to the child. Direct observation of the goings-on in the home is the best method, but if this is impossible a teacher may be able to

---

[29] An example is the "Home Environment Inventory" of T. L. Torgerson, *op. cit.*, pp. 136–139.

[30] H. H. Remmers and N. L. Gage, *Educational Measurement and Evaluation*, Revised Edition, New York, Harper and Brothers, 1955, p. 468. The Kerr-Remmers American Home Scale is published by Psychometric Affiliates, Box 1625, Chicago 90, Illinois.

[31] *Ibid.*, pp. 439–440.

[32] Published by World Book Company, Yonkers-on-Hudson, New York, 1952.

[33] H. B. English, *op. cit.*, p. 45.

get pertinent information from the child, interviews with parents, neighbors, social case workers, and other adults who know the family.

For the unusual case in which a really intensive study is made, there are scales which can be used to rate many factors in parents' relationships with children. Such an instrument is the *Fels Parent Rating Scale*. One of the ten paragraphs from this scale is shown here: [34]

### PARAGRAPH IV

How emotional is the parent's behavior where the child is concerned? Is the parent highly emotional; or is he/she consistently cool and objective?

A. Constantly gives vent to unbridled emotion in reaction to child's behavior.

B. Controlled largely by emotion rather than by reason in dealing with the child.

C. Emotion freely expressed, but actual policy seldom much disorganized.

D. Usually maintains calm, objective behavior toward child, even in the face of strong stimuli.

E. Never shows any sign of emotional disorganization toward child, either directly or in policy.

Other instruments for assessing parental attitudes and practices are: (1) *Parent Attitude Research Instrument* (PARI),[35] (2) *The Pattern Study Scales*,[36] and (3) the *Porter Scale of Parental Acceptance*.[37]

### Behavior Inventories and Rating Scales

When people try to force the description of a child into a check list of adjectives (which may only add to an already existing bias) there may be a danger of defeating the very purpose of the child study. For example, note the following items which might have been taken from any one of several rating scales: [38]

|  |  |
|---|---|
| _____Bluffs in class | _____Scowling |
| _____Excitable | _____Excessive giggling |
| _____Acts "smart" | _____Temper tantrums |
| _____Quarrelsome | _____Selfish |

All these items require a qualitative judgment by the rater. Raters without training will not reliably use such instruments, as one rater will describe a

---

[34] From H. B. English, *op. cit.*, p. 493.

[35] E. S. Schaefer and R. Q. Bell, "Development of a Parental Attitude Research Instrument, *Child Development*, Vol. 29, 1958, pp. 339–361.

[36] R. R. Sears, Eleanor Maccoby and H. Levin, *Patterns of Child Rearing*, Evanston, Ill., Row-Peterson, 1957.

[37] B. M. Porter, "Measurement of Parental Acceptance of Children, *Journal of Home Economics*, Vol. 46, 1954, pp. 176–182.

[38] These items were taken from a rating form used by a school counseling service (name withheld for obvious reasons).

behavior as excitable, while another may label the same behavior as aggressive, or as a temper tantrum. Thus, if such scales are to be used it is essential that caution be employed, and that raters agree beforehand with regard to the behavioral referents of the terms which are used in the scale.

Some rating schemes have been developed which attempt to overcome such errors.[39] By and large, however, they have not yet been adapted to use for rating children, and for the present, the most profitable way of improving ratings would seem to be in providing proper training of teachers who will make ratings.

The most common errors in the use of rating scales are: *personal bias errors*, the tendency to place all individuals at about the same position on the scale (the rater may be overly generous or severe or place everyone in the middle); *halo effect errors*, previously discussed; and *logical errors* resulting from the mistaken assumption that a correlation exists between rated traits when in fact no such relationship may exist.[40]

### Systematic Records of Behavior

Each semester, teachers in the writer's classes discuss problem children they have encountered in their classrooms. In one instance, a teacher described a boy who had a temper tantrum. Without further description, the writer asked all students in the class (most of them teachers) to jot down what a temper tantrum was, and what, in the case under discussion, this behavior was likely to have been. In essence they were asked to give a "mind's eye" picture which the term temper tantrum had evoked in this case. When the papers were collected, no two had like definitions or descriptions. One student's description was, "I'd say he fell to the floor screaming, kicking and waving his arms." Others believed that he might have struck the teacher, run from the room, or attacked other children. Very revealing was the description of the behavior as it actually occurred. In the words of the teacher who had originally used the term temper tantrum, the boy had "torn up a test paper on which he had received a low grade."

It should become apparent immediately that one of the purposes of good objective records of behavior is to facilitate communication. Teachers are members of a professional staff, much as are a group of doctors in a hospital. Both groups have the problem of communicating their findings and observations to others if they expect to receive the benefits of this staff relationship.

---

[39] There are graphic, numerical, man-to-man, and forced-choice rating schemes. The student who wishes to study the details of such scales is referred to H. H. Remmers and N. L. Gage, *op. cit.*, pp. 365–376, and E. B. Greene, *Measurements of Human Behavior*, New York, The Odyssey Press, 1952, pp. 455–472.

[40] N. E. Gronlund, *Measurement and Evaluation in Teaching*, New York, The Macmillan Company, 1965, pp. 321–324.

It was previously noted that data must be recorded, and recorded without delay, if they are to be accurate and contain the necessary detail. Informal records of observed behavior are often referred to as "anecdotal records." Several summaries and descriptions of these records have been made,[41] and rules have been devised for their use. Some of the principles which have been suggested for increasing skill in the use of anecdotal records are:

1. Start by selecting one or two cases for intensive study.
2. Describe as many significant events each week as possible.
3. Do not try to interpret every incident. Make a summary analysis at convenient periods and look for developmental trends.
4. Concentrate on describing those types of conduct problems of cause-effect relationship which you know have a bearing on the child's difficulties.[42]

There is little reason to believe or even hope that mere lip service to a kind of record keeping will bring any significant change in the quality of child study, nor is there anything especially unique about anecdotal records. There are other ways of securing behavioral records. Inventories and rating scales have already been mentioned. A self-rating or record kept by the child might also be useful. A diary or log kept jointly by the teacher and pupil to record what each perceived to be significant experiences is used in some schools. Whatever form the record takes, the cardinal rule is that it contain description of behavior, and not merely a series of descriptive adjectives which are often once or twice removed from what the child actually does.

### Cumulative and Personnel Records

Behavioral records (anecdotal or otherwise) plus all other pertinent material which is available should be included in the pupil's personnel folder. This record should be cumulative and developmental, and its accretion a planned process rather than the business of stuffing into the folder anything which happens to come along. Since records from a psychological and educational standpoint are so important, the authors would argue that records should be kept even if pupils have to help write them themselves. One system has been described for having each pupil fill out a record card

---

[41] Summaries of the description and uses of anecdotal records may be found in A. E. Traxler, *The Nature and Use of Anecdotal Records*. Supplementary Bulletin C., New York, Educational Records Bureau, 1939; and L. L. Jarvie and Mark Ellingson, *A Handbook of the Anecdotal Behavior Journal*, Chicago, University of Chicago Press, 1940. For a discussion of how anecdotal records help in "Knowing the Child" see Helen Bieker, "Using Anecdotal Records to Know the Child" in *Fostering Mental Health in Our Schools*, Washington, D.C., Association for Supervision and Curriculum Development, National Education Association, 1950.

[42] T. L. Torgerson, *op. cit.*, p. 85.

once each semester in his home room. The card contains a good many details, yet any pupil of junior high school age should be able to fill it out. It has spaces for courses taken, grades, reaction to school activities, readings, vocational choices, and the like.[43]

### The Case Study or Case History

When the causes of children's difficulties, either in school work or in adjustment, are not readily apparent from the usual data contained in personnel records, a more intensive study should be made either by the teacher or the school psychologist to whom the child is referred.

There is little virtue in making a case study just to be making a case study. A case study should have a definite direction and purpose, and the details included should have relevance to the behavior which initiated the study. Nearly a dozen sources [44] give as essential material to include in a case study the following:

1. Data about the family, neighborhood, and community, and the sources from which such information is obtained
2. Physical characteristics and selected items from the medical record of the child
3. The developmental history of the child (mental and physical)
4. The school record (academic, extracurricular, and behavioral)
5. Sociometric and other test data
6. Recommendations

In addition to such data as these, it is equally important to obtain information about:

1. The child's needs and the barriers which thwart them
2. A record of the action taken as a result of the case study, and a follow-up report at later periods

Material which combines the information specified in the eight points above is presented in the following Case Study Outline. As will be seen, the major focus is upon the child's unfilled needs, and the plans for action which will help him overcome his deficits. Taking stock of what a child lacks is a prerequisite to helping a child overcome his difficulties.

Teachers in the writer's courses have, over a period of several years, submitted case studies of selected children in their classes. Since these studies are under scrutiny of their classmates and the instructor, they may not be representative of what teachers actually do. On the other hand, they il-

---

[43] E. C. Roeber, "Cumulative Records Plan Lifts Burden from Teachers," *The Clearing House*, Vol. 24, 1950, pp. 534–535.

[44] Good examples of case studies and suggested outlines for making them are found in the Buhler, English, and Young references at the end of this chapter.

## CASE STUDY OUTLINE

### I. Basic Personal Data

A. Name _____ Age _____ Sex _____ Grade _____

B. Number of Siblings _____, Their Ages, _____

C. Address _____ Type Home _____ Community Rating_____

D. Father's Occupation _____ Mother's Occupation.

E. Brief statement about the family structure, the place of the family in the community, and the parent's attitudes toward the child and school.

### II. Statement of the Problem

A. Give a brief summary of the problem, and the reason for making this study.

B. Make a list of the behaviors of this child that need to be changed. Be specific and report in behavioral terms, e.g., "Talks out loud when other children have the floor."

### III. Standard Diagnostic Information

A. Give the results of diagnostic and aptitude tests. (List by type and in chronological order.)

B. Specify additional diagnostic information that should be collected.

### IV. Previous School Record

A. Academic (Include grades and previous teachers' comments)

B. Behavioral (Include précise of any anecdotal records)

C. Samples of written work.

D. Record of previous and current treatment of the present problem and of treatment for similar and/or other problems in the past.

### V. Deficit Analysis

This analysis of the child's needs is of the greatest importance. It should cover the extent of his needs in each of the following areas: physical, cognitive-perceptual, ego, emotional, social, and motivational. The case report should include a description of how the deficits were determined.

### VI. Etiology of Deficits

List here all items in point V that have been checked as extreme or great, and judge whether the deficits have arisen mainly from (a) the child's personal inadequacies (b) the child's own deviate behavior (c) external forces in the school, community, or family.

### VII. Recommended Action to Correct Personal Inadequacies

### VIII. Recommended Action to Alter External Forces which produced the Deficiencies

### IX. Recommended Program for Treating Deviate Behavior

### X. Follow-up:

A. Changes in observed behavior in the classroom

B. Parental reactions

C. Improvement in school work

D. Changes in scores on standard tests, sociometric tests, etc.

Signature of person preparing report _____

lustrate certain strengths and weaknesses which may provide insights for other teachers. A summary of some of the things which were done poorly and some which were done well is given in the following analysis.

### ANALYSIS OF CASE STUDIES WRITTEN BY TEACHERS IN A GRADUATE COURSE IN MENTAL HYGIENE

#### THINGS DONE POORLY IN CASE STUDIES

1. Inadequate or missing diagnosis. Even when diagnosis was given, the cause was not probed.
2. Little evidence about pupils' peer relationships.
3. Seldom were other teachers contacted about the child.
4. Too little use of a behavioral record—too much opinion.
5. Very little about the child's interests and wishes (or anything positive about the child).
6. Virtually no criticism by teachers of the school, its practices, or of their own teaching methods.
7. Practically nothing about children's needs and how they were fulfilled or thwarted.
8. Rarely were the child's own feelings and ideas about his problems noted.

#### THINGS DONE WELL IN CASE STUDIES

1. Statement of the school problems encountered by the youngster.
2. Recommendations were good and practical.
3. General home conditions of the child were fairly well described.
4. Presentation of measurement data done reasonably well.

What teachers did, they did well for the most part, but their omissions were numerous. Largely these omissions resulted from failures to exploit all the sources of information about the child and his teachers. Many of these sources were close at hand. Pupils' relationships with each other, the reaction of other teachers, and the way the child himself feels are important materials which can be secured if an effort is made.

Some specific errors in collecting information and in writing case studies are illustrated below:

1. *Failure to follow leads.* Teacher's Report—"However, on one home visit the mother told me Carole was terribly afraid of her father." This was the only reference to this matter in the whole case history. In the writer's opinion, this glimmer of information was of sufficient importance to warrant further pursuit. This illustrates the point that a case study involves more than a passive reception of information. It is an active seeking of that information which is important.
2. *Burying important matter.* Teacher's Report—"Monte is not a behavior problem in any way, shape, or form. He only earned one and

one-half credits in his entire freshman year. His grade in those subjects were only D's. *He seldom smiles or is happy.* He is of a serious
nature, but is a gentleman in every respect." The writer italicized what
is probably the most important bit of data about Monte. The teacher
in his complete report made no further mention or use of the fact that
Monte was unhappy, but dealt exclusively with his academic difficulties.

3. *Use of opinion in place of evidence.* Teacher's Report—"I think he is
   well-liked by his classmates." or "He seems to understand what I want
   him to do, but I think he just doesn't care." Some opinion in a case
   study is desirable, especially in the interpretation and recommendations, but in the factual presentation opinions should be held to a
   minimum.

4. *Overly abbreviated presentation.* Teacher's Report—"In talking with
   Carmen about her typing she made known the following:
   1. She was tense at the machine—was trying too hard.
   2. She enjoyed her typing, but was getting discouraged with her in-
      ability to do as well as she wanted to.
   3. She wanted to do office work when she finished school."

Here the report of the interview might well have provided some of the
actual statements of the girl.

Lest the presentation of these errors and omissions discourage the reader,
it should be said that most of the hundreds of case studies which teachers
have submitted to the writer were excellent, and stand as evidence that
many teachers are well-equipped to study individual cases intensively, make
diagnoses, and take the remedial or therapeutic action which is indicated.
On the other hand, most of the studies could have been improved if some
of the suggestions of this chapter had been more widely utilized.

The most frequent objection which teachers raise regarding the case-
study method of studying children is that it takes too much time—more
time than is available in the working day. However, there are methods
which will reduce the amount of time necessary to collect and interpret
information. In the first place, it is probable that too little attention is
given to training children how to assume the responsibility for self-evaluation. Children's own self analyses could well become an integral part of a
case study. Secondly, it would seem feasible and desirable for schools to set
aside regular meeting times when teachers could have staff conferences in
which they would pool information about various children.

## SUMMARY

Intensive, individual child study enables the teacher or other professional worker to probe for the causes of a child's behavior—causes which

often exist in the form of motives or needs not clearly apparent on the surface. When problems of behavior, either in school learning or adjustment, are treated by teachers who have not given sufficient study to a case, the corrective measures may do more harm than good. Individual study is necessary because each child is a distinct individual who cannot be judged on the basis of what holds true for another child.

Anathema to good child study are the biases or prejudices which may either cause a teacher to pick the wrong children for intensive study, or distort the studies which are made. Often these errors occur when teachers "type" children as "dull" or "lower class," or over-generalize about children on the basis of limited data.

One must learn *how* to collect accurate information about a child. In the task of probing for information, the teacher can find help in a variety of recommended instruments and methods. Standard rating scales to appraise the home, the parents' relationships with the child, and the child's behavior are available. The use of such scales necessitates training of the teacher in making ratings, however, as all are somewhat subjective in nature. Also of value to the teacher are anecdotal behavior journals, and cumulative records which are a collection of all pertinent material about a child.

The case study generally includes information about the child's home and family, his physical and mental characteristics, his school record, a statement of his problem, and the recommendations which result from a study of these materials. When teachers make case studies, they are apt to give too little information about causes of behavior, reaction of other teachers, the child's relationships with other pupils, or the child's own feelings and ideas about himself.

No teacher can expect to fulfill his obligations in the modern classroom if he is unacquainted with methods of studying individual children. This does not mean that teachers should be amateur psychiatrists, but it does mean that teachers should learn to look for and study basic causes of behavior. This cannot be done without adequate information regarding each child.

## References for Further Study

Almy, Millie, *Ways of Studying Children: A Manual for Teachers*, New York, Bureau of Publications, Teachers College, Columbia University, 1959.

Bingham, Walter V. D., and Moore, Victor B., *How to Interview*, Fourth Edition, New York, Harper and Brothers, 1959.

Buhler, Charlotte, Smitter, Faith, and Richardson, Sybil, *Childhood Problems and the Teacher*, New York, Henry Holt and Company, 1952.

Engel, Mary and Raine, Walter J., "A Method for Measuring the Self-Concept

of Children in the Third Grade," *Journal of Genetic Psychology*, Vol. 102, 1963, pp. 125–137.

English, H. B. and Raimey, Victor, *Studying the Individual School Child*, New York, Henry Holt and Company, 1941.

Gordon, Ira J., *The Teacher as a Guidance Worker*, New York, Harper and Brothers, 1956.

Gordon, Ira J., *Studying the Child in School*, New York, John Wiley and Sons, Inc., 1966.

Jensen, Dale E., *Socio-psychological Analysis of Educational Problems: Readings in Diagnostic Theory*, Ann Arbor, Edwards Letter Shop, 1957.

Mann, Frank A., "The Frequency of Unmet Emotional Needs as Evidenced in Children's Behavior," *Journal of Educational Sociology*, Vol. 24, 1951, pp. 414–432.

Marzolf, Stanley S. *Psychological Diagnosis and Counseling in the Schools*, New York, Holt-Dryden, 1956.

Millard, Cecil V., and Rothney, John W. M., *The Elementary School Child: A Book of Cases*, New York, Holt-Dryden, 1957.

Strang, Ruth, *The Adolescent Views Himself*, New York, McGraw-Hill Book Company, 1957.

Thomas, R. Murray, *Aiding the Maladjusted Pupil*, New York, David McKay Co., 1967.

White, Verna, *Studying the Individual Pupil*, New York, Harper and Brothers, 1958.

Young, Kimball, *Personality and Problems of Adjustment*, New York, F. S. Crofts and Company, 1946, Appendix, pp. 819–824.

## Questions, Exercises, and Activities

1. In previous chapters, the urge to conform, especially in adolescence, was portrayed as a forceful motivation. How then is it possible for each individual student to have unique and individual characteristics and problems?
2. What are the logical errors that lead to the typing of children?
3. Why is it sometimes difficult to obtain from the child himself useful information about his problems?
4. Give various ways pupils themselves may be helpful in the process of studying an individual child.
5. Describe your own home community, giving its characteristics, cultural levels, etc., that are important in shaping the personalities of its children. If someone else in your class comes from the same community, compare your descriptions.
6. Many communities have child study clinics, or similar agencies staffed by professionally trained diagnosticians. What criteria should be used in determining which children should be referred to such agencies?
7. Write a self-case study. Use the outline suggested in the chapter, or even better one of the more detailed outlines suggested in one of the references at the end of the chapter. In appraisal of the study of yourself, what notable gaps in information are apparent?

8. In what ways does child study bring beneficial effects of and in itself even though no further action is taken?
9. Studying children takes time. Suggest various ways in which time for this activity may be obtained.
10. Suppose, as is most often the case, the study of a child reveals that his difficulties come mainly from bad home conditions. What is the school's responsibility in such cases? If it has a responsibility, what are some of the things the teacher and school can do?

# PART FIVE

## Measurement and Evaluation

# Chapter 17

# Diagnostic Tools

When early in the century Edward L. Thorndike said, "Anything that exists can be measured," he became a spokesman for a movement which ushered in a new era in education. At first, tests were crude and covered only a few aspects of behavior, but in the years that followed, literally thousands of diagnostic tools were constructed by educators, psychologists, and personnel workers. At present, standardized tests of intelligence, achievement, personality, and interests are accepted as an essential part of the school's materials and equipment.

An average of five standardized tests a year is probably taken by each of the 56,000,000 students enrolled in schools in the United States.[1] In addition an increasing number of such tests are being given to adults, and the number of teacher-constructed tests is many times the estimated 270,000,000 standardized tests given to school children. *The Fifth Mental Measurements Yearbook* lists 957 commercially available tests—educational, psychological, and vocational—published in English speaking countries during the years 1952–1958.[2] The comparable figures for the years 1959 to mid-1964 are 1,219, an increase of 27.2 per cent in a shorter span of time.[3] Included in *The Sixth Mental Measurements Yearbook* are "95 critical test reviews by 396 reviewers, 97 excerpts from reviews of tests which appeared in 30 journals, and 8,001 references for specific tests."[4] In the same source is a

---

[1] *Carnegie Quarterly*, Vol. 14, Number 2, 1966, p. 3.
[2] O. K. Buros (Editor), *The Fifth Mental Measurements Yearbook*, Highland Park, New Jersey, The Gryphon Press, 1959.
[3] O. K. Buros (Editor), *The Sixth Mental Measurements Yearbook*, Highland Park, New Jersey, The Gryphon Press, 1965.
[4] *Ibid.*, p. xxx.

vast array of types of tests. There are tests of bookkeeping, Latin achievement, English progress, nursing, sensory acuity, coordination, sales aptitude, handwriting, etiquette, sex knowledge, health, religion, honesty, and a host of other skills and aptitudes. Every teacher should be aware of the great number of diagnostic tools which can assist him in his work.

To test simply for the sake of testing, however, has little virtue. It is not the purpose of this chapter to encourage the indiscriminate use of tests. Indeed, the very fact that there are so many different tests—so many ways of carrying on diagnostic work—makes it essential that teachers be critical in their selection of appropriate methods of measurement. It should be apparent that the teacher needs to understand the purposes of tests and the information which they yield. It should be remembered that the basic purposes of diagnostic tools are to help determine what is needed for the pupil and to assess the effect of various teaching procedures in achieving the teacher's and pupil's goals.

The following sections of this chapter will contain discussions of intelligence tests, achievement tests, measures of character and personality, measures of interests and values, and the appraisal of study skills. Also brief mention will be made of certain other useful diagnostic devices. Suggestions will then be given for selecting the appropriate diagnostic tools. Finally, consideration will be given to tests which the teacher himself constructs.

## INTELLIGENCE TESTS

Intelligence tests are designed primarily to determine a person's capacity to learn, or his ability to adapt to life's tasks. For practical purposes, mental tests in school are generally used to estimate how well children will achieve in school work.

Essentially, such tests are made up of items or tasks which are designed to elicit the quality or efficiency of an individual's behavior in situations for which he has not been specifically trained. The first intelligence scale to appear anywhere in the world was devised by two Frenchmen, Binet and Simon. This test, which was brought out in 1905, contained among other things material for the measurement of word meanings and for the evaluation of memory through the repetition of digits. The original purpose of the test was to screen out youngsters who could profit little or not at all from regular Paris schools. Since the time of Binet and Simon, literally scores of intelligence tests have been devised. Some of these are complete batteries of tests which can be administered to only one individual at a time; others can be given to large groups; still others have been designed especially for the measurement of the deaf, the blind, the illiterate, and peoples of various ages from early infancy to senescence.

In a sense, of course, intelligence tests are nothing more than achievement tests. They differ from regular achievement tests in that they attempt to sample those achievements which are somewhat independent of formal schooling. The reader may obtain an idea of the contents of intelligence batteries by examining the following lists of points which are covered in well-known intelligence tests:

| | |
|---|---|
| 1. Following directions | 9. Memory of form |
| 2. Ideational memory | 10. Analogies |
| 3. Vocabulary | 11. Number series |
| 4. Space perception | 12. Aesthetic judgment |
| 5. Memory of numbers | 13. Drawing |
| 6. Memory of sentences | 14. Abstract reasoning |
| 7. Memory of stories | 15. Completion |
| 8. Abstract ideas | 16. Reorganization |

## Individual Intelligence Tests

Perhaps the most widely used individual test of intelligence is the *Stanford-Binet Scale.* The first Stanford revision of the Binet test was published in 1916, a second in 1936, and a third in 1960. The test now comes in three forms (L, M, and L-M) and has been standardized on a large group of children carefully selected from eleven states and from representative geographical areas and cultural levels. The kinds of behaviors measured may be seen in the following sample items taken from the 140 on Form L-M of this scale. The items shown are some of those which are given at the two-year-old, eleven-year-old, and the Superior Adult II levels.

**FORM L-M—YEAR TWO** [5]

*Test 1.* THREE-HOLE FORM BOARD (Must precede Three-Hole Form Board: Rotated, Year II–6, A)

*Material:* Form board 5″ × 8″ with three insets for circle, square, and triangle.

*Procedure:* Present the board with the blocks in place. Place the board so that the base of the triangle will be towards the subject. Say, "*Watch what I do.*" Remove the blocks, placing each on the table before its appropriate recess on the side toward S. Then say, "*Now put them back into their holes.*" Allow two trials. Return the blocks to the board for a second trial and repeat the procedure.

*Score:* 1 correct. All three blocks must be placed correctly in one of the two trials.

---

[5] Lewis M. Terman and Maud A. Merrill, *Stanford-Binet Intelligence Scale,* Boston, Houghton Mifflin Company, 1960, pp. 67–68.

*Test 3.* IDENTIFYING PARTS OF THE BODY
*Material:* Large paper doll.
*Procedure:* Show the paper doll and say, *"Show me the doll's hair."*
*Same for mouth, feet, ear, nose, hands, and eyes.*
(a) Hair, (b) mouth, (c) feet, (d) ear, (e) nose, (f) hands, (g) eyes.
*Score:* 4 correct. The child must clearly indicate the parts on the paper doll.

*Test 5.* PICTURE VOCABULARY
*Material:* Eighteen 2" × 4" cards with pictures of common objects.
*Procedure:* Show the cards one at a time. Say, *"What's this? What do you call it?"*
*Score:* 3 correct.

### FORM L-M—YEAR ELEVEN [6]
*Test 2.* VERBAL ABSURDITIES IV
*Procedure:* Read each statement and, after each one, ask, *"What is foolish about that?"* The response is frequently ambiguous. If it is not clear that the subject sees the absurdity say, *"Why is that foolish?"*
(a) "The judge said to the prisoner, 'You are to be hanged, and I hope it will be a warning to you.'"
(b) "A well-known railroad had its last accident five years ago and since that time it has killed only one person in a collision."
(c) "When there is a collision the last car of the train is usually damaged most. So they have decided that it will be best if the last car is always taken off before the train starts."
*Score:* 2 correct.

*Test 3.* ABSTRACT WORDS II
*Procedure:* Say, *"What is . . . ?"* or *"What do we mean by . . . ?"*
(a) Connection, (b) compare, (c) conquer, (d) obedience, (e) revenge.
Responses defining abstract words are often ambiguous. In asking for a further clarification, say, *"Yes, but what do we mean by . . . ?"* or *"Yes, but what is . . . ?"*
*Score:* 3 correct.

*Test 6.* SIMILARITIES: THREE THINGS
*Procedure:* Say: *"In what way are . . . . . . . . , . . . . .     and . . . . . alike?"*
(a) *Snake, cow, sparrow.*
(b) *Rose, potato, tree.*
(c) *Wool, cotton, leather.*
(d) *Knife-blade, penny, piece of wire.*
(e) *Book, teacher, newspaper.*
A little urging is sometimes necessary to secure a response. If S hesitates or says he doesn't know, urge him to try by repeating the question or asking, *"How are they alike?"*
*Score:* 3 correct.

---

[6] *Ibid.*, pp. 97–99.

FORM L-M—SUPERIOR ADULT (SECOND LEVEL) [7]

*Test* 2. FINDING REASONS III

*Procedure:* Say:

(a) *"Give three reasons why some people use typewriters which cost so much when they could get pen and ink for a few cents."*

(b) *"Give three reasons why a man who commits a serious crime should be punished?"*

*Test* 3. PROVERBS II

*Procedure:* Say: *"Here is a proverb, and you are supposed to tell what it means. For example, this proverb, 'Large oaks from little acorns grow,' means that great things may have small beginnings. What does this one mean? If another set has preceded, say, "Here is another proverb. What does this one mean?"*

(a) *"The mouse that has but one hole is easily taken."*

(b) *"You must not throw pearls before swine."*

*Score:* 1 correct.

*Test* 5. ESSENTIAL DIFFERENCES

*Procedure:* Say, *"What is the principal difference between . . . . . and . . . . . ?"* Repeat for each item.

(a) Work and play.

(b) Ability and achievement.

(c) Optimist and pessimist.

*Score:* 3 correct.

When one is buying shoes for a school age child he does not order them by chronological age. Rather he gets a size that depends primarily upon the length and width of the child's foot. On a much more complex scale, but in a roughly comparable fashion, the learning tasks which are appropriate for a particular child depend on several mental dimensions. One dimension is called the mental age. On the *Stanford-Binet Scale* the tests are grouped according to the age at which a majority of children pass the test. For example, the Verbal Absurdities test, IV, described above (Form L-M—Year Eleven, Test 2), has been passed by over fifty per cent of a sample of eleven year old children. A child with a mental age of eleven is judged, overall, to be able to do mental tasks as well as the average eleven-year-old. Although the concept of mental age is valuable, as are other measures, it has limitations. As a child grows older the mental age units represent a decreasing degree of development. For example, between the ages of three and five years there is a much greater increase in mental ability than between the ages of sixteen and eighteen. Also, a child of five with a mental age of eight is likely to be quite different from a child of eleven with a mental age of eight. Because of the plateauing out of mental abilities in the late teens, the concept of mental age becomes rather meaningless be-

---

[7] *Ibid.,* pp. 116–117.

yond the mid-teens. However, if a teacher recognizes its limitations, the concept of mental age can be helpful to the elementary and the junior high school teacher in adjusting learning tasks to a child's ability.

Another mental dimension of help to the teacher is the child's rate of mental development, whether the child is developing more or less rapidly than the average child. An approximate indicator of rate of mental development is the IQ. This is obtained by dividing the child's mental age by his chronological age and multiplying by 100. Suppose a twelve-year-old child could do mental tasks as well as the average nine year old child. His IQ would be:

$$\frac{MA}{CA} \times 100 \text{ or } \frac{9}{12} \times 100 = 75.$$

The score is meaningful, of course, only insofar as the child's performance can be judged to be well-motivated. Also, if the score is to mean anything, certain other assumptions such as the absence of verbal limitations, correct administration, and the absence of disturbing emotional factors must be met. It cannot be too strongly emphasized that IQ scores are but suggestive guides or estimates of ability, that they are subject to error, and that they should not be taken as a final judgment about a child. When used with these limitations in mind, they can provide valuable diagnostic information.

Sometimes schools wish to test youngsters with speech or hearing difficulties, or other verbal disabilities. In such cases, the Stanford-Binet, or other tests which rely heavily upon verbal skills, are not appropriate. Hence there are a number of performance tests which require a minimum of verbal facility. These tests require youngsters to fit pieces into puzzles, construct designs, draw pictures and designs, use building blocks, etc. A battery of such tests is the *Arthur Point Scale of Performance Tests*.[8] This battery is often used to test children who are suspected of having difficulty with words and also is frequently used as a check when a child's obtained IQ with one of the other tests is out of line with the judgment of the teacher or school psychologist. In Figure 41 a teacher is shown administering a non-verbal type intelligence test to a sixth-grade pupil.

For upper level high school students, and particularly for adults, the Stanford-Binet scale may have limitations, as the scale was devised for younger children. There is, however, an excellent instrument, the *Wechsler-Bellevue Intelligence Scale*,[9] which can be used with its two extensions for ages from five to seventy.

---

[8] G. Arthur, *Arthur Point Scale of Performance Tests*, Chicago, C. H. Stoelting Company, 1925–1947.

[9] D. Wechsler, *Wechsler-Bellevue Intelligence Scale*, New York, The Psychological Corporation, 1947. (*Wechsler Intelligence Scale for Children*, WISC, 1949. Adult Scale, 1955.)

**Figure 41.** Testing a Pupil With a Nonverbal Intelligence Scale.

For children with serious verbal or motor disabilities a test like the *Columbia Mental Maturity Scale* [10] is particularly appropriate since it calls for no verbal response and only for a minimum of motor response on the child's part. The *Peabody Picture Vocabulary Test* [11] estimates a subject's verbal intelligence through measuring his hearing vocabulary. Besides giving a quick estimate of intelligence for normal subjects, it can be used with special groups, e.g., persons with reading problems, speech problems, brain damage, cerebral palsy, mental retardation, or emotional withdrawal. The pictures encourage children to cooperate in the testing. The Arthur adaptation of the *Leiter International Performance Scale* [12] can be administered by pantomime, and may be used with children from various cultures who speak different languages.

All of these scales which must be given individually are widely used and were introduced only after the most careful selection of items and standardizing procedures. Each has been the subject of intensive research, so that in the hands of a trained examiner they will provide not only an IQ score, but a wealth of other diagnostic clinical information.

---

[10] B. B. Burgemeister, L. H. Blum, and I. Lorge, *Columbia Mental Maturity Scale*, Yonkers, New York, World Book Company, 1954.

[11] L. M. Dunn, *Peabody Picture Vocabulary Test*, Minneapolis, Minnesota, American Guidance Service, Inc., 1959.

[12] G. Arthur, *Leiter International Performance Scale: Arthur Adaptation*, Chicago, C. H. Stoelting Co., 1955.

### Group Intelligence Tests

The major advantage of group intelligence tests is that they permit the examination of large numbers of individuals. Also, the administration of a group intelligence test takes somewhat less training than the administration of an individual test.

To give the reader an idea of the types of directions and questions which may be asked in a group intelligence test, examples from the *California Short-Form Test of Mental Maturity* are shown in Figure 42. This test which takes fifty-two minutes to administer is designed to measure mental abilities in the following areas: spatial relationships, logical reasoning, numerical reasoning, and verbal concepts.

The test from which examples are given in Figure 42 yields two main scores—language and non-language. The *language* score gives an indication of how well the individual understands relationships expressed in words, such as instructions, conference discussions, statements of logical principles on courses of action, and the like. *Non-language* results are designed to indicate how well the individual understands relationships among things or objects when no language or a minimum amount of language is involved, such as physical or mechanical relationships. The manual which accompanies the test gives extensive suggestions for use of various combinations of the subtest scores.

One of the ever-present problems in the measurement of intelligence is the difficulty of determining how much the performance is due to innate potential and how much is due to cultural factors. It is known, for example, that middle-class children make higher scores on the Stanford-Binet scale than do lower-class children. Is this an artifact of the selection of items which favor middle-class children, or do they in fact possess a higher potential? Psychologists and teachers are concerned about the possibility of "cultural bias" in items on intelligence tests.

Several group intelligence tests represent attempts to avoid unfairly penalizing the child from low socio-economic home surroundings. One of the most recent of these is the *Purdue Non-Language Test* which requires subjects to select unique elements from sets of geometric designs.[13] The *Davis-Eells Games* represents another attempt at a "culture fair" test which has been widely used. It has 62 sets of questions related to pictures.[14] A third illustrative attempt to secure freedom from contamination by cultural-learning effects is the IPAT *Culture Fair Intelligence Test*.[15] Each of the three tests mentioned above represent commendable steps in the direction

---

[13] J. Tiffin, A. Grubner, and K. Inaba, *Purdue Non-Language Test*, Chicago, Science Research Associates, 1958.

[14] A. Davis and K. Eells, *Davis-Eells Games*, Yonkers, New York, World Book Company, 1952.

[15] R. B. Cattell and A. K. S. Cattell, IPAT *Culture Fair Intelligence Test*, Champaign, Illinois, Institute for Personality and Ability Testing, 1933–1963.

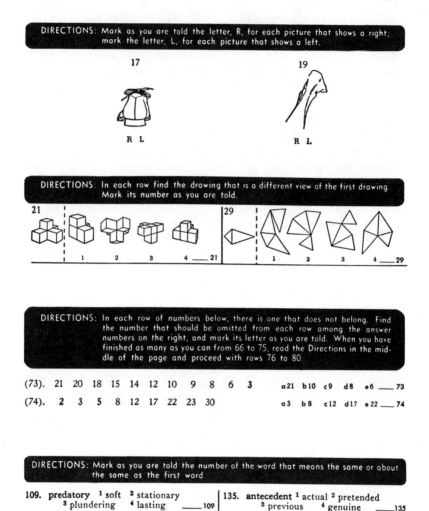

**Figure 42.** Excerpts from the California Short-Form Test of Mental Maturity. (Courtesy of the California Test Bureau, Los Angeles.)

of a test that is culturally fair. However, since experiential impoverishment early in life inhibits intellectual development, it is debatable how much compensatory experience in later years will help. Therefore, it is questionable whether any test of latent potential can produce a score that is essentially free of cultural "contamination."

Since there are dozens of group tests of mental abilities, it is not practical to attempt to discuss each one. Most of these, as the three just discussed, have distinctive features which make them appropriate for certain purposes. For example, the *Cooperative School and College Ability Tests*,

(SCAT) [16] and the *Ohio State University Psychological Test,*[17] are measures of mental ability which are particularly useful in predicting academic success in college. The *Differential Aptitude Tests* (DAT) [18] are helpful in educational and vocational guidance. Other tests which are widely used in schools are the *SRA Tests of Educational Ability,*[19] the *Henmon-Nelson Tests of Mental Ability,*[20] the *Kuhlmann-Anderson Intelligence Tests,*[21] the *Terman-McNemar Test of Mental Ability,*[22] the *Kuhlmann-Finch Tests,*[23] and the various forms of the Otis group intelligence tests.[24]

As has been suggested by the preceding discussion, understanding of human intelligence and its testing is quite a complex process. Moreover, the term most closely associated among laymen with intelligence testing, IQ, has frequently been misunderstood as illustrated by two brief stories.[25]

> A few years ago, one of my neighbors came home from a PTA meeting, remarking: "That Mrs. So-And-So, thinks she knows so much. She kept talking about the 'intelligence *quota*' of the children; 'intelligence *quota*'; imagine. Why, everybody knows that IQ stands for 'intelligence *quiz.*' "
>
> The other story comes from a little comic strip in a Los Angeles morning newspaper, called "Junior Grade." In the first picture a little boy meets a little girl, both apparently about the first-grade level. The little girl remarks, "I have a high IQ." The little boy, puzzled, said, "You have a what?" The little girl repeated, "I have a high IQ," then went on her way. The little boy, looking thoughtful, said, "And she looks like such a nice little girl, too."

The sheer complexity of the human intellect, as visualized by psychologists, is illustrated by Figure 43. Along one dimension are found the various kinds of operations, along a second one are the various kinds of products, and along the third dimension are the various kinds of content. In Figure 43 are 120 cells, each of which represents a factor of intellect. There is not space here to suggest possible educational implications of a model of this sort but it should help us avoid the danger of thinking of intelligence as one unanalyzed factor.

## ACHIEVEMENT TESTS

In nearly every field of study or school subject there are achievement tests available. Of the 2969 tests listed in the last three mental measure-

---

[16] Published by the Educational Testing Service, Princeton, New Jersey.
[17] Published by the Ohio College Association, Columbus, Ohio.
[18] Published by The Psychological Corporation, New York, N.Y.
[19] Published by Science Research Associates, Chicago, Illinois.
[20] Published by the Houghton Mifflin Company, Boston, Massachusetts.
[21] Published by The Personnel Press, Princeton, New Jersey.
[22] Published by the World Book Company, Yonkers, New York.
[23] Published by the American Guidance Service, Minneapolis, Minnesota.
[24] Published by the World Book Company, Yonkers, New York.
[25] J. P. Guilford, "Three Faces of Intellect," *The American Psychologist,* Vol. 14, 1959, p. 469.

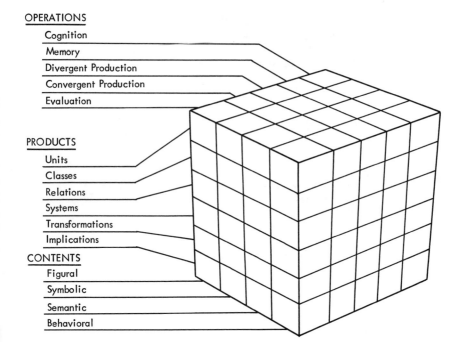

**Figure 43.** A Cubical Model Representing the Structure of Intellect. (From J. P. Guilford, "Intelligence: 1965 Model," *The American Psychologist,* Vol. 21, 1966, p. 21.)

ments yearbooks (793 in 1953, 957 in 1959, and 1219 in 1965) well over half are achievement tests distributed as indicated in Table 26.

Some of these tests have been carefully drawn up and standardized, while others, which also may be useful for some purposes, are in less refined stages of development. Expert reviews of many of these appear in the three most recent yearbooks.[26,27,28]

### Achievement Batteries

Some of the tests listed in Table 27 are designed to give a general overall picture of the pupil's achievement in a great variety of skills or subjects. These tests are called achievement batteries. Because of the wide and extremely varied nature of what an achievement test battery might include,

---

[26] O. K. Buros (Editor), *The Fourth Mental Measurements Yearbook,* Highland Park, New Jersey, The Gryphon Press, 1953.

[27] O. K. Buros (Editor), *The Fifth Mental Measurements Yearbook,* Highland Park, New Jersey, The Gryphon Press, 1959.

[28] O. K. Buros (Editor), *The Sixth Mental Measurements Yearbook,* Highland Park, New Jersey, The Gryphon Press, 1965.

## TABLE 26
### Numbers of Achievement Tests Listed in Various Fields in the Three Most Recent Mental Measurements Yearbooks

| | | | |
|---|---|---|---|
| Achievement Batteries | 26 | 21 | 27 |
| English Tests | 30 | 31 | 39 |
| Composition Tests | 2 | 4 | 7 |
| Literature Tests | 18 | 12 | 14 |
| Spelling Tests | 15 | 11 | 10 |
| Vocabulary Tests | 16 | 9 | 17 |
| Art Tests | 6 | 1 | 2 |
| Music Tests | 6 | 12 | 8 |
| Foreign Language Tests | 34 | 40 | 77 |
| General Mathematics Tests | 15 | 24 | 30 |
| Algebra Tests | 18 | 18 | 11 |
| Arithmetic Tests | 24 | 38 | 39 |
| Geometry Tests | 17 | 10 | 11 |
| Miscellaneous Mathematics Tests | 2 | — | — |
| Trigonometry Tests | 3 | 1 | 3 |
| Agriculture Tests | 2 | — | 1 |
| Business Education Tests | 21 | 26 | 29 |
| Etiquette Tests | 4 | 3 | 0 |
| Health Tests and Physical Education | 13 | 16 | 17 |
| Home Economics Tests | 12 | 5 | 4 |
| Industrial Arts Tests | 2 | 4 | 3 |
| Philosophy Tests | 2 | 1 | 2 |
| Psychology Tests | 3 | 3 | 2 |
| Religious Education Tests | 3 | 5 | 8 |
| Listening Comprehension | — | 2 | 2 |
| Driving and Safety Education Tests | 5 | 3 | 6 |
| Reading Tests | 50 | 72 | 74 |
| Study Skills Tests | 11 | 13 | 12 |
| Science Tests | 7 | 17 | 20 |
| Biology Tests | 11 | 11 | 12 |
| Chemistry Tests | 16 | 19 | 24 |
| General Science Tests | 7 | — | — |
| Geology Tests | 1 | 1 | — |
| Miscellaneous Science Tests | 2 | — | 5 |
| Physics Tests | 11 | 11 | 12 |
| Social Studies Tests | 8 | 15 | 16 |
| Economics Tests | 4 | 1 | 3 |
| Geography Tests | 5 | 6 | 6 |
| History Tests | 19 | 35 | 18 |
| Political Science Tests | 10 | 0 | 8 |
| Sociology Tests | 2 | 3 | 2 |
| Specific Vocations (Chiefly Achievement Tests) | 31 | 50 | 178 |
| Speech | — | 2 | 11 |
| Handwriting | — | 2 | 3 |
| Test Programs | — | — | 8 |
| Multi-aptitude Batteries | — | — | 16 |
| Contemporary Affairs | — | — | 8 |

many differences exist between what is included in one battery and what is included in another. For example, in Table 27 note differences in the contents of two widely used achievement batteries.

**TABLE 27**
**Comparison of Subtests of Two Widely Used Achievement Batteries**

| Iowa Tests of Basic Skills * (Grades 3–9) | Metropolitan Achievement Tests † (Grades 5–6, 7–9) |
|---|---|
| 1. *Vocabulary* | 1. *Word Knowledge* |
| 2. *Reading Comprehension* | 2. *Reading* |
| 3. *Work-Study Skills* including map reading, reading graphs and tables, knowledge and use of reference materials | 3. *Spelling* |
| 4. *Basic Language Skills* including punctuation, capitalization, usage, spelling | 4. *Language* including usage, parts of speech, punctuation and capitalization |
| 5. *Arithmetic Skills* including arithmetic concepts and arithmetic problem solving | 5. *Language Study Skills* |
| | 6. *Arithmetic Computation* |
| | 7. *Arithmetic Problem Solving and Concepts* |
| | 8. *Social Studies Information* |
| | 9. *Social Studies Study Skills* |
| | 10. *Science* |

* E. F. Lindquist, A. N. Hieronymus, and Others, *Iowa Tests of Basic Skills*, Boston, Houghton Mifflin Company, 1964.

† H. H. Bixler, W. N. Durost, G. H. Hildreth, K. W. Lund, and J. W. Wrightstone, *Metropolitan Achievement Tests*, World Book Company, Tarrytown, New York, 1958–1962.

Each of these batteries may do a good job of measuring what it measures. Whether either of these batteries or any of the other two dozen achievement batteries measure the complex abilities which a particular school or teacher believes should be measured depends largely upon the educational goals and educational philosophy held.

### Achievement Tests in Specific Subjects

Subtests of achievement batteries are sometimes used, or expanded and used, to measure achievement in specific subjects such as arithmetic, reading, spelling, handwriting, and English usage. There are other achievement tests which are set up without relation to any achievement battery. An example of one such tool is the *Diagnostic Test of Achievement in Music*.[29] Its subtests include diatonic syllable names, chromatic syllable names, number names, time signatures, major and minor keys, note and

[29] M. Lela Kotick and T. L. Torgerson, *Diagnostic Tests of Achievement in Music*, Los Angeles, California Test Bureau, 1950.

rest values, letter names, signs and symbols, key names, and song recognition. This test has to do with the rudiments of music and contains mostly factual material. One of the serious difficulties in this type of test is that only a part of what constitutes musical ability may be measured. When one attempts to measure global capacities, such as musical ability, he must recognize that specific knowledge and mechanical skill are but a part of the total picture. There are other important factors such as musical appreciation, rhythm, aural perception, and mental imagery. It is probable that most subject matter fields involve many factors presently not adequately measured. For example, one important factor common to most fields is the ability to study which is probably not measured in most achievement tests. (A later section of this chapter will show tools used to measure study skills.)

The *Nelson Biology Test* in the *Evaluation and Adjustment Series* [30] is another illustration of a subject achievement test. In it an attempt is made to blend together the gist of traditional biology with the modern approaches as represented for example by the *Biological Sciences Curriculum Study* (BSCS). Considerable attention is given to creative enquiry, and three major cognitive categories are encompassed. These are: (1) knowledge, considered fundamental, (2) comprehension, and (3) application. Comprehension "embodies the ability to interpret facts and ideas expressed in unfamiliar terms, to extrapolate and make intelligent predictions or judgments, to recognize trends, and to understand the implications and relationship of ideas. Application involves a utilization of knowledge and comprehension in dealing with the problems of real or hypothetical situations." [31]

Since tests tend strongly to influence course objectives and procedures, a test with the types of goals implied in the preceding paragraph is likely to have a healthy influence on course objectives and activities.

As can be seen in Table 26, there is no dearth of achievement tests for the specific teaching fields. The teacher of art, foreign languages, home economics, business education, or in fact almost any other subject in the elementary and secondary curricula will find tests of use to him in his work.

## MEASURES OF CHARACTER AND PERSONALITY

The importance of diagnosing personality and character cannot be questioned. But difficulties involved in making appraisal in this area are probably greater than in the field of achievement testing. Nevertheless, during the past twenty years tremendous advances have been made in assessing

---

[30] Clarence H. Nelson, *Nelson Biology Test: Evaluation and Adjustment Series,* Grades 9–15, Harcourt, Brace and World, Inc., 1965.

[31] *Ibid.,* Manual, p. 3.

personality and character traits. The increasing attention which psychologists and educators are giving to personal and social development is indicated by the fact that there are 196 tests (76 per cent new, revised, or supplemented) in *The Sixth Mental Measurements Yearbook*.[32]

The measurement of character and personality has been attempted in four basic ways, viz., through the use of (1) inventories or questionnaires answered by the person himself, (2) rating scales, (3) situational tests, and (4) projective techniques. Each of these methods, together with examples, will now be discussed.

### Personality Inventories and Questionnaires

There are currently available over three hundred character and personality tests designed to measure a multitude of factors such as aggressiveness, emotional adjustment, curricular adjustment, level of aspiration, sociability, social adaptability, home adjustment, dependability, generosity, creativity, grace, psychosomatic symptoms, and attitude toward a disciplinary procedure.

Generally such tests ask questions about a person's feelings, behavior, and attitudes in an attempt to measure personality and adjustment. For example, note the following items taken from the *Personal Index*.[33]

| | | |
|---|---|---|
| Do you like to tease people till they cry? | YES | NO |
| Do you find school a hard place to get along in? | YES | NO |
| Do any of your teachers mark examinations too severely? | YES | NO |
| Do you ever wish that you were dead? | YES | NO |

A test similar in form to the *Personal Index*, but with slightly different emphasis, is the *Washburne Social-Adjustment Inventory*.[34] It is designed to test the degree of social and emotional adjustment and gives scores on truthfulness, happiness, alienation, sympathy, purpose, impulse-judgment, control, and wishes. Each of the 122 items in the eight-page booklet is answered by "yes" or "no." Illustrative questions are: "Did you ever act greedily by taking more than your share of anything?" and "Do you sometimes enjoy the sight of an animal or a person being hurt?"

The breadth of material which may be covered by various questionnaires may be sensed by comparing the two questionnaires just illustrated with a very different kind of instrument—the *Social Distance Scale*.[35] This test,

---

[32] O. K. Buros, *op. cit.*, p. xxxi (1965).

[33] G. C. Loofbourow and Noel Keys, *Personal Index*, Minneapolis, Educational Test Bureau, Inc., 1933.

[34] John N. Washburne, *Washburne Social-Adjustment Inventory*, Ages 12 and over, non-timed, takes about 30–50 minutes, Yonkers, New York, World Book Company, 1932–1940.

[35] Emory S. Bogardus, *Social Distance Scale*, Ages 15 and over, takes about 25 minutes to administer, 3518 University Avenue, Los Angeles, 1925–1951.

together with its adaptations, is probably the most used single test of social attitudes. The test itself is one of the simpler of those now available. Original instructions went like this: "According to my first feeling reactions, I would willingly admit members of each race (as a class, and not the best I have known nor the worst members) to one or more of the classifications under which I have placed a cross: (1) To close kinship by marriage, (2) To my club as personal chums, (3) To my street as neighbors, (4) To employment in my occupation in my country, (5) To citizenship in my country, (6) As visitors only to my country, (7) Would exclude from my country." [36] Under these seven points as column headings are spaces to rate a large number of ethnic and nationality groups.

Another type of questionnaire has been used to differentiate between students who are unduly swayed by false consensus in a discussion group and those who are admirably independent in their judgments. Eight illustrative questions from one such questionnaire are shown below.[37]

1. I like to fool around with new ideas, even if they turn out later to be a total waste of time. (True)
2. The best theory is the one that has the best practical applications. (False)
3. Some of my friends think that my ideas are impractical, if not a bit wild. (True)
4. The unfinished and the imperfect often have greater appeal for me than the completed and the polished. (True)
5. I must admit that I would find it hard to have for a close friend a person whose manners or appearance made him somewhat repulsive, no matter how brilliant or kind he might be. (False)
6. A person should not probe too deeply into his own and other people's feelings, but take things as they are. (False)
7. Young people sometimes get rebellious ideas, but as they grow up they ought to get over them and settle down. (False)
8. Perfect balance is the essence of all good composition. (False)

In parentheses after the eight items are the responses made significantly more often by the "independents" than by the "yielders." Responses from studies of this type suggest that "independents" are more open to innovation and to the challenge presented by apparent imbalance and imperfection on the surface of things.

This test like most other questionnaires depends on voluntary self-description by the person being tested. If for some reason or another he does

[36] E. S. Bogardus, "Measuring Social Distances," *Journal of Applied Sociology*, Vol. 9, May–June, 1925, pp. 299–308.
[37] F. Barron, "The Psychology of Imagination," *Scientific American*, Vol. 199, 1958, pp. 156–157.

not want to cooperate, the results are useless. Hence, proper rapport between tester and subject is of prime importance.

While most questionnaire-type personality measures are easy to score, and deal with important information about a child, they also have serious limitations. Little claim can be made for high validity of such instruments,[38] and they are appropriate only for children old enough and bright enough to have a clear understanding of the questions.

### Rating Scales

Personality questionnaires ask for self-ratings which, as noted above, may be unreliable (give inconsistent results) and of questionable validity. Another method of securing information about a child is by having teachers or other persons make the ratings. One such scale, which is suitable for appraising young children as well as grown-ups is the *Vineland Social Maturity Scale*.[39] It is made of of 117 items of performances "in respect to which children show a progressive capacity for looking after themselves and for participating in those activities which lead toward ultimate independence as adults." The functions measured are: self-help (general, eating, dressing), self-direction, locomotion, occupation, communication, and social relations. A person who knows the subject well answers the interviewer's questions on the subject's demonstrated performance of the 117 items included in the scale. Test results will yield a social age and a social quotient if these are desired. It also has value as an interviewing device with parents.

Probably the most widely used rating scale for school children is the *Haggerty-Olson-Wickman Behavior Rating Schedules*.[40] In two schedules, this rating form combines a check list and a graphic rating scale. There are spaces in Schedule A for checking how frequent is the occurrence of such behaviors as cheating, lying, bullying, and sex offenses. In the second part, Schedule B, is a series of 35 questions set up as follows:

| Is his personality attractive? |
|---|
| Repulsive   Disagreeable   Unnoticed   Colorful   Magnetic |
| Colorless |

All rating devices are subject to errors some of which were discussed in Chapter 16. Chief among these is the error due to over-generalization (halo effect). There is a tendency for a teacher who rates a child high or

---

[38] Albert Ellis, "The Validity of Personality Questionnaires," *Psychological Bulletin*, Vol. 43, 1946, pp. 385–440.

[39] Edgar A. Doll, *Vineland Social Maturity Scale*, Ages, birth to maturity, 1 form, Minneapolis, Educational Test Bureau, 1935–1947.

[40] Published by the World Book Company, Yonkers-on-Hudson, New York.

low on one trait to continue to rate him the same on other traits. Furthermore, it has been shown that four or five independent ratings are necessary in order to secure adequate reliability and validity.

### Situational Tests

Situational tests are measures of actual conduct in the face of difficulty, or when the stimulus situation is such that character traits are revealed by the choice or reaction which a child makes. These tests have been useful in the measurement of such behaviors as stealing, lying, sharing, cheating, and reactions to such conditions as psychological stress, pain, shock, and humor.

For example, in a very extensive investigation of children's character, Hartshorne and May [41] devised such test items as:

1. A situation in which a storekeeper returns too much change to a child.
2. Arithmetic problems involving the use of coins. Coins were placed in boxes each of which contained an identifying mark (not apparent to the child). Since children were not aware that boxes could be identified, many kept some of the money.
3. A situation in which children score their own papers, unaware that the teacher had scored them the night before.

As with other types of personality and character measurement, there are difficulties in the use of conduct measures. It is hard to obtain a representative sample of behaviors and still retain the experimental or test controls which are necessary to make comparisons among children. Also, the time spent in devising situations and in observing each child in these situations is great. However, in the final analysis, segments of actual behavior under controlled conditions probably offers a type of information which can be obtained in no other way. [42]

### Projective Tests

One of the most interesting approaches to personality measurement is the projective method. There are now available over fifty such tests of character and personality. In the projective test a highly unstructured or ambiguous set of stimuli is presented to the individual. In such a situation, the person being tested is encouraged to bring his own unique meanings and organization to the situation. He does not know what inferences the

---

[41] H. Hartshorne and M. May, *Studies in Deceit*, New York, The Macmillan Company, 1928.

[42] For a comprehensive discussion of measures of typical behavior in the areas of personality, attitude, and interest see L. J. Cronbach, *Essentials of Psychological Testing*, New York, Harper and Brothers, 1960, Chapter 15 through 19.

tester intends to make, and so may reveal some of the hidden reaches of his personality.

The *Rorschach Test*, the best known and most widely used projective test, makes use of ten cards each of which contains an ink blot similar to that shown in Figure 44. The person being tested is given the following instructons:

**Figure 44.** One of the Ten Ink Blots from the Rorschach Test. (From H. Rorschach, *Psychodiagnostics*, Hans Huber Publishers, Berne and Stuttgart.)

You will be given a series of ten cards, one by one. The cards have on them designs made up out of ink blots. Look at each card, and tell the examiner what you see on each card, or anything that might be represented there. Look at each card as long as you like; only be sure to tell the examiner everything that you see on the cards as you look at them. When you have finished with a card, give it to the examiner as a sign that you are through with it.[43]

The Rorschach Test has been used to diagnose a wide variety of character and personality traits. One version of the test, designed to differentiate between creative and non-creative individuals has been developed by Barron.[44] An item from this test is shown in Figure 45.

While the teacher should know about Rorschach-type tests, it should be emphasized that it is a technique to be used only by thoroughly trained clinicians. In this type of test, the interpretive work of the examiner is as important as the test itself.

Another widely used projective test is the TAT (*Thematic Apperception Test*).[45] In this test the subject is asked to interpret a series of twenty

---

[43] S. J. Beck, *Rorschach's Test*, New York, Grune and Stratton, 1944, p. 2.

[44] F. Barron, "The Psychology of Imagination," *Scientific American*, Vol. 199, September, 1958, pp. 150–166.

[45] H. A. Murray, *Thematic Apperception Test*, Ages 4 and over, individual, non-timed but takes about 120 minutes, Cambridge, Massachusetts, Harvard University Press, 1944.

### Common Responses of Random Sample

1. An African Voodoo Dancer
2. A Cactus Plant

### Responses of Creative Individuals

1. Mexican in Sombrero Running Up a Long Hill to Escape from Rain Clouds
2. A Word Written in Chinese

**Figure 45.** Item from a Projective Test of Creativity. (Adapted from Barron)

pictures by telling a story about each—what is happening, what led up to the scene in the picture, and what will be the outcome. As in the Rorschach Test, the subject is required to set up his own answer structure. The person projects himself into each picture and presumably brings to it his own problems, conflicts, wishes, needs, and attitudes toward self. In addition to evaluating stories themselves, the examiner observes the subject during the test. Behavior shown may indicate emotion, eccentricities, habits in problem attack, and other cues pertinent to an analysis of personality. As with the Rorschach Test, use of the TAT without much training and guided experience is unwise.

A projective test, similar to the TAT, is the *Children's Apperception Test* [46] which uses pictures of animals instead of people to elicit the stories. Other projective tests designed specifically for children are mentioned in the following numbered points. (1) *The Blacky Pictures: A Technique for the Exploration of Personality Dynamics*.[47] This test uses eleven cartoons of a dog, Blacky, and is used to test the child's psychosexual development. (2) *The Driscoll Play Kit*.[48] This kit is a cutaway of an apartment

---

[46] Published by the Psychological Corporation, New York, N.Y.
[47] *Ibid.*
[48] *Ibid.*

and contains furniture and a doll family which the child can manipulate. It is believed useful for revealing family relationships. It has a dual purpose of providing both diagnostic information and material for play therapy. (3) *The Machover Draw-a-Person Test.*[49] This test requires only 10 to 20 minutes to administer. The child is asked to draw a person, and then to draw another of the opposite sex. It is believed that conflicts and personality characteristics may be revealed in the drawing of bodily parts.

The importance of creativity and imagination in education cannot be over-emphasized. These personality dimensions are, or at least should be, some of the most treasured and cultivated by teachers. Two interesting types of tools for diagnosing these traits are indicated in Figures 46 and 47. Incidentally, the use of such tools as these has produced some tentative conclusions that may challenge the conventional ideas of those of us who are teachers. Some conclusions regarding creative artists and perhaps creative scientists are summarized at the top of page 487.

**Figure 46.** Figure Preference Test. Individuals are required to express a preference, or lack of preference, for line drawings on cards. Subjects chosen at random tend to prefer drawings such as the two at the left; creative individuals, drawings such as the two on the right. The sketches are from the Welsh Figure Preference Test, published by the Consulting Psychologists Press, Palo Alto, California. (Adapted from F. Barron, *op. cit.*)

---

[49] Published by Charles C Thomas, Publisher, Springfield, Illinois, 1949.

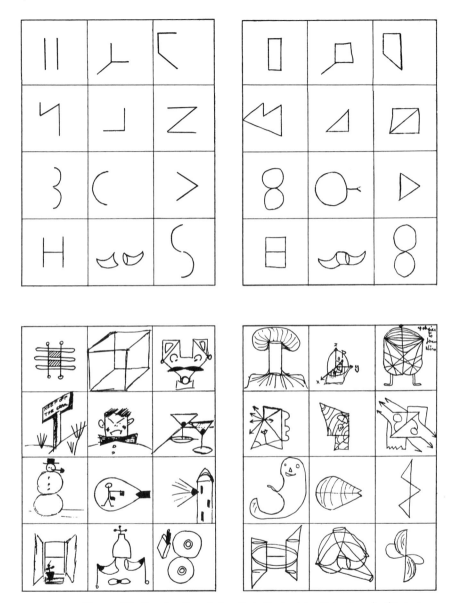

**Figure 47.** Drawing-Completion Test. Devised by Kate Franck, this test requires subjects to elaborate on the simple figures at top left. At top right is a typical response of a person chosen at random. At bottom left and bottom right are the responses of creative individuals. (From F. Barron, *op. cit.*)

Creative people are especially observant, and they value accurate observation (telling themselves the truth) more than other people do.

They often express part-truths, but this they do vividly; the part they express is the generally unrecognized; by displacement of accent and apparent disproportion in statement they seek to point to the usually unobserved.

They see things as others do, but also as other do not.

They are thus independent in their cognition, and they also value clearer cognition. They will suffer great personal pain to testify correctly.

Their universe is more complex, and in addition they usually lead more complex lives, seeking tension in the interest of the pleasure they obtain upon its discharge.

They have more contact than most people do with the life of the unconscious—with fantasy, reverie, the world of imagination.

They have exceptionally broad and flexible awareness of themselves. The self is strongest when it can regress (admit primitive fantasies, naive ideas, tabooed impulses into consciousness and behavior), and yet return to a high degree of rationality and self-criticism. The creative person is both more primitive and more cultured, more destructive and more constructive, crazier and saner, than the average person.[50]

It is probably not an overstatement to say that in all of a child's creative work (writing, drawing, making things) there are elements of projection. There are ways in which he puts himself into the task at hand. Thus a child's English theme, an oral story he tells, or a game he plays with imaginary companions may reveal much about his needs, conflicts, and personality. Sims clearly recognized this in his thought provoking article, "The Essay Examination Is a Projective Technique," in which he defines an essay test as follows:

> The essay examination is a relatively free and extended written response to a problematic situation or situations (question or questions), which intentionally or unintentionally reveals information regarding the structure, dynamics and functioning of the student's mental life as it has been modified by a particular set of learning experiences.[51]

Although most projective tests are of recent origin, they do represent an approach to the study of personality which has great promise. With further refinement of scoring methods and continuing efforts to establish their validity, the time may not be far off when they may be widely used in classrooms. Already school psychologists are employing them to a limited extent in helping teachers better understand their children.

---

[50] F. Barron, "The Psychology of Imagination," *Scientific American*, Vol. 199, 1958, p. 155.

[51] V. M. Sims, "The Essay Examination Is a Projective Technique," *Educational and Psychological Measurement*, Vol. 8, 1948, p. 17.

## MEASURES OF INTERESTS AND VALUES

Since changing interests and values frequently become a significant goal in many subjects such as music, mathematics, art, literature, and science, the measurement of interests and values is increasingly recognized as important to teachers. As has been indicated in Chapter 8, teachers can capitalize for instructional purposes on knowledge of pupils' interests and values which are indicators of attitudes. Also interest and value measurements are important in predicting the reactions and adjustment of pupils in certain school programs and in future occupational activities. Some technics for measuring interests and values are based on non-verbal behavior such as the amount of student time or money spent on specified activities; [52] however, most measurement approaches have depended upon verbal indices, the individual's responses to questions. A brief description of several devices follows:

*What I Like to Do—An Inventory of Children's Interests* [53] through the use of 294 yes-no items is designed to indicate what a pupil in Grades 4 through 7 would like to do, would not like to do, or neither like nor dislike to do. Interests in the following areas are measured:

Art:           preference for arts and crafts activities and appreciation of the fine arts
Music:         appreciation for all kinds of music and liking for musical activities
Social Studies: social awareness and curiosity, ranging from the pupil's own group to the world—past and present

The *Study of Values* is based on the assumption that the personalities of men are best known through a study of their values or evaluative attitudes. After a student provides 120 answers it is possible to see the relative prominence he gives to each of six basic interests or motives in personality: the theoretical, economic, aesthetic, social, political, and religious. This classic instrument first published in 1931 and revised in 1951 [54] is designed primarily for use for college students and adults who have had some college (or equivalent) education.

In addition to the guided response tests asking for expressions of opinion on verbal items, a wide variety of self-reports on what happened and how

---

[52] For example, see H. G. Shane and E. T. McSwain, *Evaluation and the Elementary Curriculum*, New York, Henry Holt and Company, 1951, pp. 428–435, for behavorial indices of good citizenship.

[53] L. P. Thorpe, C. E. Meyers, and M. R. Sea, *What I Like to Do: An Inventory of Children's Interests*, Chicago Science Research Associates, 1954–1958.

[54] G. W. Allport, P. E. Vernon, and G. Lindzey, *Study of Values*, Boston, Houghton Mifflin Company, 1931–1960.

a pupil felt are available to the teacher. These include such tools as the diary, free discussion, check lists, dream reports, and self-evaluation reports.

Vocational interest tests are widely used for occupational guidance. The *Kuder Preference Record—Vocational,*[55] one of the interest tests frequently employed with high school students, is used, for example, to (a) point out vocations with which the student may not be familiar but which involve activities of the type for which he has expressed preference, and (b) check on whether a person's choice of an occupation is consistent with the type of thing he ordinarily prefers to do.

The unusual form and appearance of the booklets and the special "pin-prick" device for marking responses have considerable interest value for students and aid in getting careful and thoughtful responses. In the test, the pupil is asked to choose which of certain activities are preferred. For example, he is asked to choose which of the activities in this triad he most prefers and which he least prefers: (a) visit an art gallery, (b) browse in a library, and (c) visit a museum. The Kuder form which has been most used gives eleven scores: mechanical, computational, scientific, persuasive, artistic, literary, musical, social service, clerical, outdoor, and verification. The manual classifies occupations according to the profiled interest areas. Such classifications are to be considered tentative and suggestive for guidance purposes only.

The most recent *Kuder Preference Record* is designed to give evidence of how closely the subject's responses typify each of 22 different occupational groups.[56] In one of the triads from this form the subject is asked which of the following activities he would like most and which he would like least: (a) visit an exhibit of famous paintings, (b) visit an exhibit of various means of transportation, and (c) visit an exhibit of laboratory equipment.

A second widely used vocational interest inventory is the *Vocational Interest Blank for Men,* Revised.[57] This test indicates whether subjects mark the test the way successful people in various occupations mark it. There are now fifty-seven scorable categories of which the following are examples: artist, psychologist, osteopath, veterinarian, mathematician, production manager, aviator, mathematics-physical science teacher, policeman, certified public accountant, purchasing agent, mortician, realtor, and presi-

---

[55] G. F. Kuder, *Kuder Preference Record—Vocational,* Grades 9–16 and adults, IBM; editions 3; time to administer—about 50 minutes; Chicago, Science Research Associates, 1934–1962.

[56] G. F. Kuder, *Kuder Preference Record—Occupational,* Grades 9–16 and adults, IBM; time to administer—about 30 minutes; Chicago, Science Research Associates, 1956–1963.

[57] E. K. Strong, *Strong Vocational Interest Blank for Men,* Revised, Ages 17 and over; 57 scoring scales (47 occupations, 6 occupational group scales and 4 nonvocational scales); Palo Alto, Consulting Psychologists Press, 1927–1963.

dent of a manufacturing concern. There is also a form of this test for women which rates interest in twenty-eight occupations.[58]

The instrument is very time consuming to score, unless machine scoring is used.[59] It can be a valuable instrument for vocational counseling if used as a supplement to other significant types of data such as demonstrated level of mental ability or special proficiency in given fields of study.

A final word of caution is probably appropriate. Neither the Strong blank, nor the Kuder record, nor any other vocational interest inventory is designed to show into what occupation a person should go. They are only intended to give a picture of vocational *interests*. There are many other facts which should be carefully considered when vocational choices are made.

## STUDY SKILLS TESTS

Children no longer spend a whole year reading one book as they did in the days of the McGuffey Reader. Instead, in the average classroom today, pupils are bombarded with multiple texts, supplementary readings, magazine articles, and newspapers. There are a number of different study skills required to meet the demands placed upon the present-day learner. Thus the evaluation of a student's study habits is a matter of great importance. Fortunately a number of methods for diagnosing study skills are now available to teachers.

Traxler's *Survey of Study Habits* [60] is one such device. It not only gives the pupil a basis for analyzing his own study habits but also serves as a basis for counseling by the teacher. The survey consists of 85 items grouped under the following 17 headings:

| | |
|---|---|
| Keeping in physical condition for study | The prompt completion of work |
| Understanding the assignment | Persistence in overcoming difficulties |
| Planning a study schedule | Paying attention in class |
| Efficient finding of the necessary materials | Participation in class activities |
| Applying one's self consistently | Reviewing |
| Fixing material in mind | Memorizing |
| Reflecting | Increasing vocabulary |
| Working independently | Improvement of reading rate |
| | Maintaining an attitude of study |

---

[58] E. K. Strong, *Strong Vocational Interest Blank for Women*, Revised, Ages 17 and over, Palo Alto, Consulting Psychologists Press, 1933–1962.

[59] Schools may have their Vocational Interest Blanks machine scored by Testscor, 1554 Nicollet Ave., Minneapolis 3, Minnesota, or by several other testing agencies and university testing bureaus located throughout the country.

[60] Arthur E. Traxler, *Survey of Study Habits, Experimental Edition*, Grades 8–14, nontimed—30 minutes, New York, Educational Records Bureau, 1944.

In the Traxler survey the items are statements which do or do not characterize the pupil. He responds by checking "seldom or never," "sometimes," or "usually or always." The total score is not nearly so important as the diagnostic information which the test reveals.

A tool for analyzing a quite different type of study skill is the *Interpretation of Data Test*.[61] In this test the learner in Grades 7–12 is presented with various sets of data and asked to discriminate, on a 3-point scale, whether the accompanying statements are (1) true, (2) false, or (3) uncertain as to the truth or falsity because of insufficient information in the data. The test is designed to reveal such factors as a pupil's accuracy, tendency to be overcautious, tendency to be undercautious and go beyond the data.

Although scoring and interpretation is somewhat more difficult than with most tests, the *Interpretation of Data Test* does provide a unique and educationally stimulating departure from traditional methods of pupil evaluation. The use of this type of test can provoke a healthy reexamination of educational goals and procedures.

A basically different type of instrument is the Brown-Holtzman *Survey of Study Habits and Attitudes*.[62] This inventory for high school and college students is designed to identify those students whose study habits and attitudes differ from students who do well in academic work. It also provides a basis for aiding the students so identified through counseling and improvement of study methods. In addition, the instrument has some value in predicting academic success in high school and college. The authors have found that study attitudes seem to be more highly related to academic success than items assessing the mechanics of studying. Hence, a valuable and somewhat unique feature of this inventory is its probing of motivation for study and attitudes toward academic work. This is *not* a test, and frankness of response is crucially important if the inventory is used for either screening or diagnostic purposes.

Other valuable tests for appraising study skills are:

*Spitzer Study Skills Test: Evaluation and Adjustment Series*, Grades 9–13, 6 scores: dictionary, index, graphs—tables—maps, sources of information, note taking, total for subtests 1–4, World Book Company, Yonkers, New York, 1954–1955.

*SRA Achievement Series: Work Study Skills Supplement*, Grades 4–6,

---

[61] Evaluation Staff (R. W. Tyler, Director) of the Eight-Year Study of the Progressive Education Association, *Interpretation of Data Test: General Education Series*, Grades 7–12, 12–14, 40 minutes to administer, Princeton, New Jersey, Cooperative Test Division, Educational Testing Service, 1939–1950.

[62] W. F. Brown and W. H. Holtzman, *Brown-Holtzman Survey of Study Habits and Attitudes*, New York, The Psychological Corporation, 1953–1956.

6–9, 2 scores: references, charts, Science Research Associates, Chicago, Illinois, 1954–1963.

*Stanford Achievement Test: Study Skills*, Grades 5–7, 7–9, checks practical interpretations or uses of data in charts, tables, maps, dictionaries, indexes, and other sources of information, World Book Company, Yonkers, New York, 1953–1964.

*Watson-Glaser Critical Thinking Appraisal*, Grades 9–16, 6 scores: inference, assumptions, deduction, interpretation, arguments, total, World Book Company, Yonkers, New York, 1942–1964.

The teacher who is considering the use of any of the tools listed above would do well to acquire and carefully examine a specimen set including the manual, one or more forms of the test, and the key. Before ordering any large number of tests it is frequently wise to try out the test with a small number of pupils to see whether in actual practice it meets the needs of teacher and puipls.

## OTHER DIAGNOSTIC TOOLS

For practically every psychological trait or characteristic, one or more tests are available. The teacher who is interested in diagnosing the behavior of his pupils in any specific area should consult the catalogues of test publishers [63] and bibliographies of tests such as those of Buros.[64] No attempt can be made here to give a complete listing; however, to illustrate the range and variety of tests available some illustrative tools are briefly described.

### Vision

*Eames Eye Test*, Grades Kgn.–16 and adults; 8 pass-fail scores: visual acuity, lens, near vision, coordination fusion, astigmatic chart (optional), eye dominance (optional), total; 1 form; Thomas H. Eames; World Book Company, Yonkers-on-Hudson, New York, 1938–1950.

### Clerical

*Minnesota Clerical Test*, Grades 8–12 and adults; 2 scores: number comparison, name comparison; 15 minutes to administer; Psychological Corporation, New York 17, New York, 1933–1959.

### Listening

*Brown-Carlsen Listening Comprehension Test*, Grades 9–13; listening skills measured: immediate recall, following directions, recognizing

---

[63] See references at the end of this chapter.
[64] O. K. Buros (Editor), *Tests in Print*, Highland Park, New Jersey, The Gryphon Press, 1961.

transitions, recognizing word meanings, and lecture comprehension; 2 forms; about 50 minutes to administer; World Book Company, Yonkers, New York, 1953–1955.

### Mechanical Ability

*Revised Minnesota Paper Form Board Test*, Grades 9–16 and adults; IBM; 2 editions; original test by D. G. Paterson, R. M. Elliott, L. D. Anderson, H. A. Toops, E. Heidbreder; revision by Rensis Likert and William H. Quasha; Psychological Corporation, New York 18, New York, 1930–1955.

### Education

*National Teaching Examinations.* For applicants for teaching positions and prospective teachers; an examination program for use in selection of teachers and the appraisal of teachers-in-training; designed to measure some of the knowledges and abilities expected of teachers; 2 parts; tests administered in February at centers established by Educational Testing Service; application form and bulletin of information may be obtained from publisher; prepared under the direction of the Staff of Educational Testing Service with the consultation of the Committee for the National Teacher Examinations; Educational Testing Service, Princeton, New Jersey.

## SELECTING THE APPROPRIATE TEST

Out of the thousands of available tests, the teacher must find those which are the most appropriate for his purposes. Before tests are chosen, a necessary first step is that of defining clearly the objectives which the teacher or school is trying to attain. Such objectives must be specific and straightforward if one is to have a reasonable basis for selecting tests. Relatively meaningless phrases such as, "an understanding of," or "an appreciation of," may be of little use in describing the school's aims unless the educator spells out in detail what he wants children to understand and appreciate. When tests are selected on the basis of poorly conceived or over-generalized objectives, the results of measurement are apt to be disappointing both to the teachers and pupils.

Each teacher or school administrator will have to solve for himself the problem of selecting from the vast array of available diagnostic instruments, those which are most related to his goals. However, there are a number of criteria which will aid him in making wise choices. The questions which follow should provide some of the important criteria to be used in finding the appropriate test.

### Is the Test Reliable and Valid?

Most good standard tests have a high consistency of measurement (reliability), and measure or discriminate well in the areas which they are supposed to cover (validity). In the examiner's manual accompanying most tests there is usually some statement of the test's reliability.[65] Also there is usually some evidence about its validity. Validity, however, involves the appraisal of educational outcomes which are themselves very difficult to measure. Thus in many cases, a test will have a high reliability, but there will be incomplete evidence as to its validity. In such cases, the teacher will have to scrutinize the test itself to find out if it gives a useful index of the outcomes which he wishes to measure. For example, an English teacher may wish to measure appreciation of literature. If the test he surveys contains only factual items about literature, the test is probably not valid for this purpose, since it is possible for a pupil to have considerable information about novels, poetry, and stories, and still hate literature. The question of the validity of a test is not only of highest importance, but is also a most difficult one to answer. Sometimes the best a teacher can do is to try out the test with a small group of students. Results on the trial run can then be appraised to see if they yield the type of diagnostic information which will be helpful.

### Does the Test Have Alternate Forms?

In some situations, it is helpful to the teacher and pupil if one form of the test can be given early in the learning experience for diagnostic purposes, and a second form administered after a period of training or development. This second test can then provide a basis for evaluating the effectiveness of the instruction which took place. Also in cases of error, or when the results of a test seem out of line with what the teacher knows about a child, it is good to have a second form to administer.

### What Is the Cost of the Test?

Even tests which are quite similar in content may vary greatly in cost. One reading test may be twice as expensive as another without yielding better results. In estimating the cost of a test, however, there is more than just the cost of the test booklets to be considered. Some tests are answered directly on test booklets, so that new tests must be purchased for each class. Others are so constructed that the blanks can be used over and over again, since students' answers may be put on separate answer sheets. It may

---

[65] This is usually given as a correlation coefficient such as .93. There are several formulae used to calculate the degree to which a test gives consistent results. It should be emphasized that although most standard tests have a high reliability, .90 or above, they may have little or no validity. The latter, of course, is the more crucial factor.

be possible for a teacher to get one complete set of test booklets and mimeograph answer sheets. Such a procedure permits the school to use many more tests at less cost than is involved if a new test is purchased for each student.

### What Competence Is Needed for Administration?

The administration of most achievement tests does not require extensive training. However, it is well for the teacher to study a test manual before giving a test. Also it may be helpful in anticipating difficulties if the teacher himself takes the test.

### What Is the Interest Value of the Test?

Most tests depend for their accuracy of measurement upon highly motivated performance of pupils. Test makers generally take this into account by trying to write items which have a high interest value. For younger children, tests may even be set up as a game. It should be noted, however, that what is interesting for one age group may not be for another. Hence, a test of achievement or intelligence for retarded children may be inappropriate, in that items were chosen to match the interests of a younger group. Likewise a test for his own age group may be of little interest to a pupil of superior ability.

### How Much Time Is Required for the Test?

Typically this information is given in the test catalogue and certainly in the test manual, and should be investigated before purchase of more than a sample of the test. Some tests require an amount of time that is difficult to fit into the school schedule. Most schools seek tests which can be administered during one class period or can be broken into parts which fit into a class period.

### Is the Difficulty Level of the Test Appropriate?

A test may be labeled as appropriate for a given group, but if a teacher has a very accelerated class, the test may be too easy for most of the pupils. On the other hand, if the teacher has a relatively retarded group of pupils, most of the test items may be much too difficult. Sometimes, actual administration of the test is necessary, at least to one of the best and one of the poorest students, in order to estimate the difficulty range of the instrument.

### How Many Pupils Can Be Tested at One Time?

Most achievement tests can be given to fairly large groups of students. Some tests, however, such as reading readiness tests, may require exten-

sive supervision and the breaking of the class into smaller groups which are tested one at a time.

### Are There Likely to Be Difficulties in Scoring?

Tests vary greatly with respect to ease of scoring. The teacher should, therefore, before ordering the test in large numbers, score a sample test or two to determine how long the scoring will take and how difficult it will be. Some tests have quick scoring stencils and answer keys which reduce the work of correcting papers to a fraction of that required for other tests.

### In What Form Are Test Results Given?

Frequently, this question is not investigated by the teacher until after the test is given, but it is a matter of sufficient importance to be considered before tests are ordered. Some tests provide a helpful record form which gives a profile of achievement. All test manuals should give a clear description of the test's norms and the group used to standardize the instrument. Most of the better tests provide both grade norms and percentile norms.

### Does the Test Measure Extraneous Factors?

A mathematics test, for example, may have in its questions many words which the student may not understand. Hence, the student may get a low score not primarily because of weakness in mathematics, but because of the vocabulary used in the test.

### How Diagnostic Is the Test?

Some comprehensive achievement tests give a single score in reading, a single score in arithmetic, and a single score in other aspects of achievement which are tested. This type of result although useful for survey purposes does not provide the specific information needed for certain teaching purposes. It is often desirable to break down achievement in reading, for example, into various kinds of reading, such as getting the facts, interpreting what has been read, vocabulary, and critical reading. One way of appraising the diagnostic value of a test is for the teacher to plan in advance the ways in which he can use the information provided by a given test.

The wise selection of measuring instruments which will appropriately promote teaching and learning is a very complex process. There are many excellent sources of help for the teacher in his selections. The Buros yearbooks have already been mentioned. Among others Traxler's [66] *Introduction to Testing and the Use of Test Results in Public Schools* helps answer in more detail many of the questions which have already been raised.

---

[66] A. E. Traxler, R. Jacobs, M. Selover, A. Townsend, *Introduction to Testing and the Use of Test Results in Public Schools*, New York, Harper and Brothers, 1953.

## TEACHER-CONSTRUCTED TESTS

Regardless of the fact that there are hundreds of commercially available diagnostic tools, the teacher is frequently faced with the task of making some of his own evaluative instruments. In the following paragraphs suggestions are given for helping the teacher construct such tests.

### Preparing to Construct Tests

To do a sound job of constructing tests for educationally defensible purposes, the teacher should first identify the specific behavioral goals that a particular course or set of learning experiences is supposed to achieve. Unless this is first done, testing is likely to be a hit or miss affair without any well-defined orientation. Sometimes it is helpful if the general goals for a specific class or set of educational activities are defined and then more specific behaviors are listed under each of the general goals.

In preparing to construct a test, it is desirable to consider the possible types of test approaches which might be used. Sometimes testing can be done in the actual situation where the behavior occurs. For example, teachers might observe whether good citizenship is being practiced by noting whether paper is being thrown on floors of the hall rather than in wastebaskets. Likewise the effect of a safety education program could be judged by keeping a record of traffic violations committed by students.

It cannot be too strongly emphasized that much of the work of constructing a test should take place before any items are written, or before any specific instrument is planned. As previously stated one must first determine the objectives of the course. Secondly, and also very important, a content analysis of the course or unit should be made. This analysis should include (1) the major facts and principles of the course or learning unit, (2) the skills which should be provided, (3) the behavioral changes which are intended to occur as a result of the course, and (4) common misconceptions, errors, or trouble spots which exist in the field being measured. Only when such an analysis is completed does the teacher have a sound basis for making out a test plan and beginning the construction of test items. In other words, items should not be chosen because they are easy to write or score, but because they definitely fit into the analysis which has been made of the goals and content of the course of study.

Tests will be more closely related to the goals of schooling and to the important content of school subjects when pupils are given an opportunity to help with the analysis described in the above paragraph. If pupils and teachers plan assignments together, and if pupils are given an opportunity to help set goals for themselves, the preparation of tests may well become a joint project.

### Directions for the Test

The problem of test directions assumes importance inasmuch as the pupil's orientation for the test or his mental set is likely to be determined by the type of directions that are given.

Travers suggests that the directions to the students should contain statements concerning the following matters: "(1) the purpose of the test, (2) the time allowed for answering questions, and the speed at which the student should work, (3) the extent to which the student should guess or not guess when he is not sure of the answer, (4) instructions concerning the way in which the student is to record his answers." [67] In addition to these four minimum essentials, directions might also be improved by including sample items in the testing instructions and by explaining what the student should do if he encounters unclear or ambiguous items.

### General Principles of Test Construction

It is difficult in a brief space to discuss all the important issues involved in the construction of tests. Several volumes and hundreds of journal articles have been devoted to the problems of constructing and analyzing tests. However, every teacher must be prepared to construct instruments of appraisal, and there are some principles of such major importance that all should apply them in their evaluative work. The suggestions which follow, if applied by teachers, should result in a marked improvement in the quality of their measuring instruments.

1. Choose items whose difficulty level is appropriate for the task at hand. Items at the 50 per cent difficulty level (half of those answering the item pass and half fail) give maximum discrimination. For teaching purposes, it may be appropriate to have items of greater ease. However, youngsters will generally find a test more interesting if it is sufficiently difficult to challenge them.

2. Occasionally have two or three students take a test in advance of its general use. Ask these students to explain each step in the solution of a problem and to give detailed oral reasons for their answers. Such a procedure may be very helpful in revealing ambiguities or other unanticipated flaws in the instrument.

3. Avoid insofar as possible all of the following: (a) trivial details, (b) textbook phrases, (c) phrases which may unintentionally give clues to the correct answer such as "always" and "may" in true-false questions, (d) trick or catch questions so phrased that the correct answer depends upon a single, obscure key word, (e) questions which give answers to other questions in the test, (f) items which have no answer

---

[67] Robert M. W. Travers, *How to Make Achievement Tests*, New York, The Odyssey Press, 1950, p. 132.

upon which experts will agree, and (g) questions which depend strictly upon rote memory.
4. Constantly strive to improve existing tests. By going over tests with a class after they have been scored, a teacher will find questions which are ambiguous or for other reasons poor. Such questions should be deleted or revised. Many test experts recommend keeping a file of good test questions on file cards. Data such as the number of pupils who missed the item or other forms of item analysis [68] may be included on this card.
5. Use various types of test items. Some pupils do better on one type of item than on another. Furthermore, the use of a variety of types of test items is apt to result in better testing of a variety of skills and understandings than is a single type.

### Preparing True-False Items

There are special precautions to be followed in connection with different types of test items. True-false items are widely used in schools but have serious limitations as well as some unique advantages. When to use true-false items and how to phrase such items are important points to be kept in mind by teachers who make their own tests. Greene has stated that true-false items are most appropriately used in the following situations.

1. If one is faced with a situation in which time is short for composing, administering and scoring a test.
2. If the test will have to be scored by clerical helpers who are ignorant of the subject.
3. If complexity of thinking and recall of information are not considered as important as a wide range of information.
4. If occasional chance successes and failures are not too serious.[69]

Suggestions for constructing true-false items are as follows:

1. Avoid excessively long and involved statements, and make the average length of true items and false items approximately the same.
2. If items which express opinions are included, attribute the opinions to some source.
3. In arranging the items, do not establish a pattern or rhythm of true and false answers. For example, do not make every other item true.
4. Avoid double negatives and use single negatives very sparingly if at all.

---

[68] For an excellent discussion of item analysis, see N. E. Gronlund, *Measurement and Evaluation in Teaching*, New York, The Macmillan Company, 1965, pp. 208–215.
[69] E. B. Greene, *Measurements of Human Behavior*, New York, The Odyssey Press, 1952, pp. 61–62.

5. Double-barreled statements in which one part is true and one part is false should not be used.
6. Do not use ambiguous statements which may be either true or false depending upon the interpretation which is made.
7. Have the number of true items and the number of false ones approximately equal.
8. Although the time required for scoring is greatly lengthened, a highly desirable procedure is to provide space following each question, and request pupils to tell why the item is true or false.

### Writing Completion Test Items

In completion test items, words or phrases are omitted and these are to be supplied by the person taking the test. To be useful, such a test must involve a nice balance between what is given and what is omitted. In scoring, complete adherence to a set key is unsound. The following procedures should improve the construction of completion items.

1. Avoid the omission of too many words. Long phrases, particularly, should not be left out. Frequently in a short sentence, only one key word should be omitted.
2. Statements should not be taken verbatim from textbooks, particularly ones the students being tested have used. A test should not encourage blind memorization of phraseology.
3. Avoid making the items merely a test of general reasoning or intelligence, unless these are the factors which the test is designed to measure.
4. Make a key when the test is constructed. Revise the key, adding alternative, acceptable answers as experience with the test item is gained.
5. Leave enough space for writing responses, but do not tailor the space to the length of the answer.

### Constructing Multiple Choice Questions

The multiple choice type of test item usually includes the presentation of three or more words, phrases, or sentences from which the best or most logical alternative is to be selected. Items may also be constructed which ask the pupil to select the worst or poorest alternative. Use of the following suggestions will help teachers in constructing multiple choice questions.

1. Many items should present problems which require critical thinking on the part of the pupil.
2. Distractor alternatives (wrong answers) should be sufficiently plausible and attractive so that uninformed pupils will frequently select them. Farfetched and patently wrong answers should be avoided.
3. In general, the correct alternative in a test item should be about the same length as the incorrect ones.

4. The position of the best answer should be varied. That is, it should not almost always be first, last, or in the middle.

## Making Essay Examinations

The much maligned essay examination has again achieved status in the eyes of measurement specialists. It is realized that certain outcomes of education can be more validly assessed by this technic than by any so-called objective test items. Some of the values of the essay examination have been summarized by Sims in the following statement:

> The essay examination appears to be particularly well-suited for obtaining evidence related to certain "higher order" intellectual outcomes of education. Although most essay testing actually done is primarily concerned with the recall of information learned, the value of the essay for testing ability to organize, relate, and "weigh" materials learned has been long appreciated.[70]

In making specific test questions of the essay type, the teacher may find the following recommendations useful.

1. First, write down what is to be measured and then phrase questions to evaluate this.
2. Phrase questions so as to permit a relatively free response, but be specific enough so that pupils know what they are supposed to do.
3. The problems posed in an essay question should have a "reasonable" separation from the students' original learning situation.
4. The student answering the questions should be encouraged to use his own "frame of reference," to reveal his method of reasoning, to show reasons for his choice of material, and defend any position he takes.
5. So far as possible, arrange questions in order of difficulty with the easier questions appearing first.

Most of the criticism leveled against essay examinations has centered around problems of scoring. Under certain circumstances, tests of this type have proved to be very unreliable. However, adherence to the following suggestions in scoring should increase both the reliability and validity of the tests.

1. Do not have pupils write their names on their papers but instead have them use an identifying number. This will help the teacher maintain objectivity in scoring the test.
2. Some teachers feel that more accurate results are obtained by marking question one for all pupils before moving to question two, etc.
3. First scan a few papers to obtain an estimate of the quality of an-

---

[70] V. M. Sims, "The Essay Examination Is a Projective Technique," *Educational and Psychological Measurement*, Vol. 8, Spring, 1948, pp. 15–31.

swers. This will help to preclude the possibility of the first papers read being more rigorously scored than succeeding ones.

4. Determine a scale of points in advance of the reading which will be used to rate the quality of the answers. For example, an outstanding response might be given a value of five points, a superior response four points, and so on to zero points for an omitted question.

For additional suggestions on test construction the teacher will find six of the books listed below in "References for Further Study" of particular value—those by E. J. Furst, J. R. Gerberich, J. A. Green, N. E. Gronlund, O. J. Rupiper, and D. A. Wood.

## SUMMARY

Teachers who have not made a special study of tests and measurements would be very much surprised at the number and scope of evaluative and diagnostic instruments which are available at all levels and in all fields of education. One bibliography lists over 5000 tests and rating scales. Although the existence of intelligence and achievement tests is relatively well known to teachers and laymen alike, the availability of devices for measuring such aspects of behavior as character, critical thinking, study skills, and interest patterns is not so generally known. Regardless of the field in which a teacher works, he will find helpful measuring tools at his disposal.

In this chapter, some of the better tests in the following areas have been presented and evaluated: (1) intelligence (group and individual), (2) achievement (batteries and special subject matter examinations), (3) character and personality, (4) interests and values, and (5) study skills. Various types of tests and their uses have also been discussed. These include rating scales, inventories, situational tests, and projective tests. Sources the teacher may consult in connection with testing problems were also recommended.

Throughout the preceding pages it has been emphasized that the indiscriminate use of tests, simply for the sake of testing, is undesirable. Each test that is used should contribute to the attainment of some specific goal of education. A set of criteria which teachers may use to enable them to select appropriate tests was included.

Although a wealth of standardized and published tests is available, teachers will still have to construct many of their own evaluative devices. Suggestions for doing this constituted the concluding section of the chapter.

### Publishers of Tests

American Guidance Service, Inc., 720 Washington Avenue, S. E., Minneapolis, Minnesota 55414.

Bureau of Publications, Teachers College, Columbia University, New York, New York 10027.

California Test Bureau,* Del Monte Research Park, Monterey, California 93940.

Consulting Psychologists Press, Inc., 577 College Street, Palo Alto, California 94306.

Cooperative Test Division, * Educational Testing Service, Princeton, New Jersey 08541.

Harcourt, Brace & World, Inc.,* 757 Third Avenue, New York, New York 10017.

Houghton Mifflin Company,* 2 Park Street, Boston, Massachusetts 02107.

Personal Press, Inc., 188 Nassau Street, Princeton, New Jersey 08541.

Science Research Associates, Inc., 259 East Erie Street, Chicago, Illinois 60611.

The Psychological Corporation,* 304 East 45th Street, New York, New York 10017.

The reader is also urged to consult a good sampling of the headings in the *Education Index*, which are listed at the end of Chapter 18.

The series of six yearbook volumes edited by Oscar K. Buros deserves special mention and is particularly important for the educator wishing to make a survey of the published tests available. The six volumes give pertinent information and reviews on almost all published English language tests. The first yearbook was published in 1938 and the sixth in 1965. Volumes one, two, and three were published by the Rutgers University Press; volumes four, five and six by the Gryphon Press, Highland Park, New Jersey. *Tests in Print*, published by the latter firm, serves as an index to *The Mental Measurement Yearbooks* and is a comprehensive bibliography of tests for use in education, psychology, and industry.

### References for Further Study

Ahmann, J. S., and Glock, M. D., *Evaluating Pupil Growth*, Boston, Allyn and Bacon, Inc., 1963.

Blair, G. M., *Diagnostic and Remedial Teaching*, Revised Edition, New York, The Macmillan Company, 1956.

Bloom, B. S., *Stability and Change in Human Characteristics*, New York, John Wiley and Sons, Inc., 1964.

Buros, O. K. (Editor), Mental Measurement Yearbooks, Highland Park, New Jersey, The Gryphon Press, 1953, 1959, 1965.

---

* All publishers will provide, *gratis*, catalogues of their current tests. An asterisk (*) indicates the company also provides on request free bulletins on testing and the use of test results.

Cronbach, L. J., *Essentials of Psychological Testing*, New York, Harper and Brothers, 1960.

Furst, E. J., *Constructing Evaluation Instruments*, New York, Longmans, Green and Co., 1958.

Gerberich, J. R., *Speciment Objective Test Items*, New York, Longmans, Green and Co., 1956.

Green, J. A., *Teacher-Made Tests*, New York, Harper and Row, 1963.

Gronlund, N. E., *Measurement and Evaluation in Teaching*, New York, The Macmillan Company, 1965.

Harris, C. W. (Editor), *Encyclopedia of Educational Research*, Third Edition, New York, The Macmillan Company, 1960. See major articles and bibliographies listed in the index of this encyclopedia under these headings: Abilities, Achievement, Achievement Motive, Achievement Tests, Aims and Objectives, Aptitude Tests, Attitude Scales, Comprehensive Examinations Diagnosis, Essay Test, Evaluation, Individual Differences, Intellectual Abilities, Intelligence, Interests, Kindergarten Evaluation, Man-to-Man Rating Scale, Motor Ability Tests, Musical Abilities, Observational Techniques, Self-Evaluation, Stanford-Binet Test.

Lindeman, Richard H., *Educational Measurement*, Glenview, Illinois, Scott, Foresman and Company, 1967, Chapter 4.

Noll, V. H., *Introduction to Educational Measurement*, Boston, Houghton Mifflin Company, 1957.

Remmers, H. H., Gage, N. L., and Rummel, J. F., *A Practical Introduction to Measurement and Evaluation*, New York, Harper and Brothers, 1965.

*Review of Educational Research*, Volume 35, February 1965, pp. 4–100.

Rupiper, O. J., *Item Writing: A Programmed Text for Writing Objective Type Test Items*, Norman, Oklahoma, Harlow, 1964.

Simpson, R. H., *Improving Teaching-Learning Processes*, New York, Longmans, Green and Co., 1953, Chapters 5, 7, 8, 11.

Taba, H., and Others, *Diagnosing Human Relations Needs*, Washington, D.C., American Council on Education, 1951.

Terman, L. M., and Merrill, M. A., *Stanford-Binet Intelligence Scale*, Third Revision, Boston, Houghton Mifflin Company, 1960.

Thomas, R. M., *Judging Student Progress*, New York, Longmans, Green and Co., 1960.

Thorndike, R. L., and Hagen, E., *Measurement and Evaluation in Psychology and Education*, New York, John Wiley and Sons, Inc., 1961.

Wood, D. A., *Test Construction*, Columbus, Ohio, Charles E. Merrill Books, Inc., 1960.

Wrightstone, J. W., Justman, J., and Robbins, I., *Evaluation in Modern Education*, New York, American Book Co., 1956.

## Questions, Exercises, and Activities

1. Make a list of the standardized tests available in your teaching area. If tests or test catalogues are not available write to four or five companies requesting a copy of the test catalogue of each. Below the name of each test and its publisher indicate:

    a. The purposes of the test.

    b. The uses you might consider making of results of the test.

2. Find the names and descriptions of three non-subject matter tests you might consider using. Below the name and publisher of each test indicate what use you might consider making of it.

3. From the *References for Further Study* find one of the books on testing and list some of the key information on testing which you think you, as a teacher, should keep in mind.

4. Make up five true-false questions, and two essay questions covering important parts of this chapter. Review the part of the chapter on test construction and indicate how your questions line up with the suggestions there.

5. Do you think "intelligence" tests are sometimes misused by teachers? Discuss this problem, pointing out instances and situations where harm may be done to children by improper interpretation or utilization of such tests.

6. What advantages and disadvantages do you see in a schoolwide testing program? Under what circumstances might more improvements in education result if the resources spent on such a program were allocated to teachers for use in getting whatever tests and test supplies they thought they could use to improve their teaching?

# Chapter 18

## Interpreting
## and Using
## Test Results

Proper selection, administration, and scoring of tests may be of little value unless there are appropriate interpretations and uses of test results. Consider, for instance, a large school system, known to the writer, which gave a comprehensive, standardized achievement test to all of its seventh-grade pupils in the spring of the year. Results from the test indicated that the median (middle) grade equivalent of the seventh graders taking the test was 9.2. This means that half of the pupils taking the test in this school system did as well or better than a typical (median) ninth grader in the country as a whole does in October. Since the median-grade level of an average group of seventh graders in April would be 7.7, on the surface, it appeared that the pupils tested in this school system were 1.5 grades above pupils upon whom the test had been standardized. As the result of this showing, self-satisfaction verging on smugness was the typical reaction of both teachers and administrators in the schools of this system.

However, when some of the factors which produced these results were carefully examined by outside test consultants serious doubts were raised regarding the quality of the educational achievement in the school system. What had happened was that the teachers and school administrators failed to take into account numerous conditions which may have influenced test results. They neglected to ask several important questions, which if answered, would have accounted for the seeming superiority of the pupils on

the test. In the next few pages some of the factors which this school system should have examined, and which should be kept in mind by any educator using test results, will be discussed. Following this, suggestions are given for effectively employing achievement tests and sociometric measures in classroom situations.

## CAUTIONS IN INTERPRETING TEST RESULTS

An essential first step in properly interpreting and wisely using information given by tests is to know what factors influence test performance and test scores. It is obviously unfair to compare two children or two classes on the basis of an improperly administered test. Likewise it is ridiculous to consider seriously the IQ earned by a retarded reader on a test which requires much reading ability. The person giving a test, school policy which determines who will be in school to take the test, the attitudes of pupils toward testing, and the conditions under which the test is given are some of the variables which alter test scores. Cautions in test interpretation related to these and other factors will now be discussed.

### Teacher Motivation and School Policy

ARE TEACHERS GIVEN PAY RAISES ON THE BASIS OF TEST RESULTS? Some superintendents, principals, and supervisors, casting about for an objective basis for giving promotions or salary increases, have settled on the idea of giving monetary rewards to those who can produce the best test results. The goal of giving salary increases on the basis of merit is admirable but this particular method has resulted in many unprofessional practices which should be eliminated in any place where they exist. In the school system used in our illustration, the school supervisor apparently did give the pay increases to those whose pupils had the highest median scores. This was particularly unfair to teachers in schools serving pupils of low socio-economic status and poor home background.

IS THE PRIMARY GOAL OF THE TEACHERS TO HELP THE PUPILS OR TO GET GOOD TEST RESULTS? In some school systems it is unfortunately true that in the struggle to have "my class" come out on top the teacher has almost forgotten the primary purpose of education, to help the learner. In these schools, test results have, unfortunately, sometimes tended to become an end in themselves. When this occurs, "good" test results may be accompanied by basically poor education.

HAS THE ATTENTION OF THE TEACHER BEEN FOCUSED ON IMPROVING THE TEST RESULTS OF THOSE JUST BELOW THE MEDIAN AT THE EXPENSE OF THE RAPID AND SLOW LEARNERS? If a teacher knows that his group and his teaching are likely to be evaluated on the score of the middle learner (median score) of his group, he may gear his teaching to the level of the middle third of the group, feeling that the highest third will get fairly good scores

anyhow and that the lowest third or at least the lowest fifth will in all probability have little effect in moving the median upward.

HOW MUCH RETARDATION IS THERE IN THE SCHOOL? It is quite possible for a school system that is doing a relatively poor instructional job to reach or even to exceed the national norms on tests by having a rigid policy of promotion. For example, the writer is familiar with a school system which takes great pride in its "standards." With very few exceptions no pupil is promoted until he has reached the "norm" for his grade on a standardized achievement test. This means that a child in the fifth grade is not promoted to the sixth grade until he can make a score equivalent to 6.0 on the comprehensive achievement test. This policy has resulted in excessive retardation with about 50 per cent of the seventh-grade pupils being held back at least one year. Obviously, a comparison of the median score of this group with the younger group on which the norms of the test were based is unsound. With excessive administrative retardation even an inefficient school system may seem to have a good achievement record when its results are compared with national grade norms. One way of determining the amount of administrative retardation is to see how many pupils are over-age for their grade.

HOW MUCH ELIMINATION IS THERE IN THE SCHOOL? Some schools have a deliberate policy of "weeding out" the weakest pupils, particularly in the upper grades; other schools just fall into the habit. Consider two schools each of which originally had 200 pupils entering the first grade. In school A only 60 per cent, or 120 pupils, ever reached the seventh grade—the others were eliminated in one way or another. In school B 95 per cent, or 190 pupils, entered the seventh grade. Since it usually is the poorer achievers who are eliminated in a school such as A, it is obvious that school B with a lower median score than A might still be doing a much better job of educating the children in its community. The holding power of a school needs to be carefully considered in interpreting test results. The twin evils of excessive elimination and excessive retardation demand thoughtful consideration, and test makers and publishers should be encouraged to give figures indicating the extent of the elimination and retardation in the schools on which norms are based. Actually, in the school system described at the opening of this chapter, there were both unusual "holding back" and elimination. In some elementary schools in the system there were fourteen-year-old students languishing in the third grade. If only the average or above average students are measured in the seventh grade, a basically poor school can look good insofar as test results are concerned.

### Learner Background and Training for Test

DID THE TEACHERS TEACH THE TEST DIRECTLY OR INDIRECTLY? It may seem undignified even to suggest that such an unprofessional practice might be carried on. But in certain school systems the practice *is* carried on by some

teachers, and those who interpret test results need to be aware of this possibility. Of course, any time a group of learners is coached on a test the use of norms accompanying the test becomes meaningless. Unfortunately some administrators and supervisors have unwittingly encouraged this practice, partially through the procedure, already discussed, of tying teacher promotions to the test results obtained by their pupils. One type of teaching of the test which borders on questionable practice may involve teaching exactly the same kind of items as the test is expected to contain.

An example of what can happen if this caution is not observed recently came to the writer's attention. In an air force base in Texas a test of 275 items was developed from a longer list of several thousand items. Scores on this test were highly correlated with bombardier performance in actual combat. After the test had been used with several classes on the base, test results on the new groups were again matched with combat efficiency. This time the correlations turned out to be low. Further investigation revealed that bombardier instructors were teaching the test items to their students. A test can thus become worthless or even lead to disastrous consequences if improperly used.

HOW MANY YEARS HAS THE TEST BEEN GIVEN IN THE SCHOOL? Undue familiarity with a particular test will tend to produce artificially high results on that test. For example, the writer is familiar with a school which, twice a year, has used some form of the same test for five years, which means that some of the pupils in the upper grades in that school may have had ten very simliar tests and some repetitions of the same test. Too great familiarity with a test will indicate the need for using a different test. In the school system described earlier the *Metropolitan Achievement Tests* had been used for some ten years. This school obviously should make use of some of the other excellent achievement tests available.

WHAT IS THE POTENTIAL ABILITY OF THE LEARNERS AS COMPARED WITH THOSE UPON WHOM THE TESTS WERE STANDARDIZED? While this probably cannot be determined exactly, some clues to the answer can be obtained through the use of good intelligence tests, particularly ones which do not themselves depend upon reading or other achievement skills for successful performance. The occupational level and socio-economic status of the parents will also frequently give a very rough indication of the answer.

WHAT ARE THE PRIMARY MOTIVATORS OF THE STUDENTS? Threats, fear of punishment, marks, extrinsic rewards, and the like can produce what seem to be fairly good temporary results but the net result is likely to be undesirable in the long run. An extreme illustration of this was reported to the writer by one of his students. A teacher of American history had given his final examination, the scores of the examination were quite acceptable to the teacher, and the final marks in the course had been prepared. On the final day of school when the report cards were passed out the pupils in a dramatic demonstration of their attitude toward American history tore

their history books to bits and tossed the pieces of paper out of the school windows. When high test scores are obtained through motivation that produces antagonistic attitudes, the scores themselves may be of minor significance.

WHAT HAS BEEN THE EFFECT OF HOME TRAINING, TRAVEL, AND OTHER NONSCHOOL FACTORS? Some schools take credit for doing a great deal more than they are responsible for. Schools with learners coming from homes with good "educational opportunities" should give the home credit for many learnings which the pupils demonstrate. A healthy community environment including a well-run public library, where youngsters have many opportunities for informal educational experiences outside both the school and the home, may have considerable influence on achievement test results.

WHAT IS THE ANNUAL AMOUNT SPENT PER CHILD FOR EDUCATION? The time spent with the child and the wherewithal for educating him should be considered in evaluating and interpreting test results. For example, in some school districts in the United States over $1600 per child per year is spent. In others the amount is below $200. Obviously one could not reasonably expect similar results in two districts where one spends eight times as much per child as does the other.

ARE TEST RESULTS IN CERTAIN LEARNINGS BEING ACHIEVED AT THE EXPENSE OF OTHER EQUALLY IMPORTANT LEARNINGS? The basic importance of this point cannot be over-emphasized. In the preceding paragraph attention was called to differences in the amount of money spent by the community for education. Here the focus is on the emphasis the school gives to different kinds of learnings. There are schools where the teaching is so slanted by standardized tests, that many learnings not touched by the tests, but considered at least equally important by outstanding educators, are being neglected. This neglect may produce negative and undesirable attitudes as illustrated by the book-tearing episode described earlier. Such neglect may also produce anti-social pupils, or ones who take a passive attitude toward teachers in general, schools, testing, or specific subjects.

In one school the methods of a mathematics teacher were appropriately questioned, even though his pupils scored very high on achievement tests, because it was determined that none of the students he had taught went on to take another mathematics course. The short term asset learnings, as shown by relatively high achievement test scores, were more than overbalanced by the liability learnings, indicated by a violent dislike of mathematics which was apparently engendered by student contact with this teacher.

ARE ADVERTISING CLAIMS JUSTIFIED? The teacher needs to examine critically the advertising claims for various tests. Criticism has already been made of the use of the term culture-free tests. In a recent widely distributed letter from a prominent publishing firm the claim was made that the four

standardized tests being advertised "offer THE TEACHER an entirely objective measure for evaluating student achievement." No achievement measure is entirely objective. Crucial subjective judgments always enter into decisions relating to such questions as: What particular areas should be covered in the test? Should the test emphasize speed or power? What should be the difficulty level of the vocabulary in the test? How difficult should the questions themselves be made? What form (i.e., true-false, matching, multiple choice) should the questions take? What should be considered a passing score? Perhaps the best safeguard here is a careful study of some of the excellent books on testing and evaluation which are available.[1]

### Administration and Scoring Problems

WAS TEST ADMINISTERED IN STANDARDIZED MANNER? In some schools "standardized" tests are given in a very unstandardized fashion either through lack of knowledge of sound testing procedures or because the person administering the test desires to influence the results. If lack of knowledge of good testing procedures is the difficulty, study of test administration is, of course, strongly indicated. If directions are only partially read or not followed, if the timing is inaccurate, or if unauthorized help is given to testees, then the norms for the test become meaningless and it is probable that much pupil and teacher time has been wasted.

WHAT WERE CONDITIONS UNDER WHICH TEST WAS TAKEN? Some of the conditions against which the teacher must guard are: excessive noise, frequent interruptions by outsiders, inappropriate desk equipment for writing, and too high or too low temperatures in the testing room.

WAS THE STANDARDIZED TEST SCORED ACCORDING TO DIRECTIONS IN MANUAL? Most test manuals give complete directions for scoring a test. These must be followed carefully if the test results are to be meaningful.

ARE THE METHODS OF EXPRESSING TEST SCORES UNDERSTOOD? To make a pupil's test score meaningful it is usually necessary to convert the raw score into some type of standard score. There are several systems, with which the teacher should be familiar, of expressing standard scores in order to reveal the relative status of an individual within a normative group. The basic equivalence of the most popular standard score procedures is shown in Figure 48.

There is not space here to detail the methods used to convert raw scores to the scales shown in the figure. However, the use of various scales can be seen by considering the pupil whose raw score places him two standard deviations above the mean on the normal curve. What is his comparable standing on each of the other scales? From Figure 48 we see that 98 per

---

[1] See References for Further Study at the end of the preceding chapter.

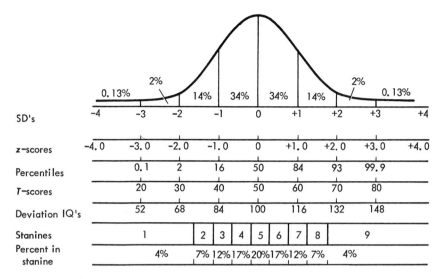

**Figure 48.** Corresponding Standard Scores and Percentiles in a Normal Distribution. (From N. E. Gronlund, *Measurement and Evaluation in Teaching*, New York, The Macmillan Company, 1965, p. 291.)

cent of the normative group score below him. Also, he has a 98th percentile rating, a +2.0 z score, a 70 T-score, a 700 *College Entrance Examination Board* score, a 140 *Army General Classification Test* score, a 9 Stanine, a 16 Wechsler intelligence subtest score, and an IQ of 130 on the Wechsler test.[2]

### Reliability and Validity of the Test

In both standardized and unstandardized tests the concepts of test reliability and test validity must be considered. As an extreme example consider a teacher who claimed he had a new measure of intelligence—the circumference of the head. Since a test and subsequent retest would probably show similar results on a particular individual, the test would have a high degree of reliability, i.e., consistency from one measurement to another. However, if head circumference for individuals were compared with some accepted criterion of intelligence little relationship would be found. Hence, one would say the new test is not valid. Reliability indicates how consistently a test measures what it does measure. Validity represents the accuracy with which a test measures what it is supposed to measure. A reliable test that is not valid is likely to be useless.

---

[2] For more detailed consideration of such scales as these see a test and measurement book such as N. E. Gronlund, *Measurement and Evaluation in Teaching*, New York, The Macmillan Company, 1965.

## USING ACHIEVEMENT TEST RESULTS

The improvement of teaching and learning activities should, of course, be the primary purpose for understanding the uses to which tests may be put. Every teacher has a responsibility for knowing some of the uses which may be made of test results. To aid the reader in recognizing some of these possibilities, a summary of actual scores from one reading test is given in Table 28. This material is based upon data gathered in a class of thirty-four sixth-grade pupils.

The teacher who is to use such data as presented in Table 28 might well, at the outset, ask himself the following questions: (1) How can the test results help in analyzing the major strengths and weaknesses of the class as a whole? (2) What are some ways of planning improvement on a class-wide basis? (3) How can the test results facilitate individual learner diagnosis? (4) How can the results of the individual diagnosis help individual learner improvement? (5) How can the test results be used to stimulate school-wide diagnosis and plans for improved teaching and learning?

### Finding Strengths and Weaknesses of Class as a Whole

Each teacher, or even better a teacher-learner committee, can find the average grade score for students on each test and each subtest to see on which tests the students as a whole are high and on which tests the students as a group are low.

When the data from Table 28 are summarized and averages are computed, material is available for making a class profile. Such a profile has been drawn in Figure 49 for the class under discussion.

The profile reveals some interesting things about the class. It is strongest in the "Use of the Index" and weakest in "Vocabulary," and has an overall reading grade level of 6.0.

A very helpful procedure is also to compare the results on a reading test with achievements in other areas. For example, another class profile which included reading along with arithmetic, spelling, handwriting, English usage, and other aspects of the school program would be of much assistance to the teacher in understanding the overall progress being made by a class.

The data in Figure 49 answer some questions regarding pupil's reading abilities but not all. The teacher and pupils also need to raise such questions as these: What are the attitudes of the majority in this class toward reading? To what extent is the reading ability demonstrated on the test actually being used in situations where the reading might appropriately be used? What interest do the youngsters take in reading out of class where the ordinary school pressures are not being exerted? To what extent are they able to find and select appropriate reading materials for particular problems and in particular situations? What are the processes which they

## TABLE 28
### Iowa Silent Reading Data for One Room of Sixth Graders *

| Pupil Number | Actual Age | Reading Age | Grade Level | | | | | | | | |
|---|---|---|---|---|---|---|---|---|---|---|---|
| | | | General Reading | Reading Rate | Reading Comprehension | Directed Reading | Vocabulary Level | Central Idea | Development | Sentence Meaning | Use of Index |
| 1 | 12–4 | 13–2 | 8.4 | 9.6 | 6.3 | 9.0 | 5.6 | 10.6 | 6.6 | 7.3 | 10.8 |
| 2 | 12–8 | 12–10 | 8.0 | 4.2 | 5.3 | 10.6 | 12.0 | 8.7 | 7.3 | 4.5 | 9.8 |
| 3 | 11–10 | 12–5 | 7.6 | 7.5 | 7.5 | 7.6 | 6.6 | 7.3 | 9.6 | 7.3 | 12.0 |
| 4 | 11–10 | 12–5 | 7.6 | 6.9 | 8.2 | 12.0 | 6.6 | 8.7 | 8.0 | 7.8 | 8.2 |
| 5 | 14–3 | 12–4 | 7.5 | 5.7 | 7.5 | 7.3 | 4.7 | 10.6 | 6.6 | 8.4 | 8.2 |
| 6 | 12–8 | 11–10 | 6.9 | 6.6 | 6.9 | 7.6 | 5.1 | 7.3 | 5.5 | 6.9 | 5.6 |
| 7 | 12–9 | 11–10 | 6.9 | 6.5 | 5.7 | 8.0 | 5.1 | 8.7 | 7.3 | 5.1 | 5.9 |
| 8 | 12–6 | 11–8 | 6.9 | 5.5 | 6.3 | 6.6 | 6.9 | 5.9 | 8.0 | 5.1 | 12.0 |
| 9 | 12–7 | 11–7 | 6.6 | 6.2 | 6.9 | 6.2 | 4.6 | 8.7 | 7.3 | 6.6 | 9.0 |
| 10 | 12–6 | 11–7 | 6.6 | 7.1 | 5.7 | 6.8 | 4.7 | 8.7 | 6.6 | 5.1 | 6.2 |
| 11 | 12–6 | 11–5 | 6.5 | 5.5 | 6.3 | 7.1 | 4.0 | 8.7 | 6.6 | 3.9 | 9.8 |
| 12 | 13–9 | 11–4 | 6.3 | 5.2 | 4.5 | 6.8 | 5.9 | 4.8 | 6.6 | 6.9 | 8.0 |
| 13 | 12–2 | 11–4 | 6.3 | 5.5 | 9.0 | 7.3 | 7.3 | 7.3 | 9.6 | 4.6 | 4.0 |
| 14 | 12–11 | 11–1 | 6.2 | 6.9 | 5.7 | 7.3 | 5.5 | 4.8 | 7.3 | 5.5 | 8.2 |
| 15 | 11–9 | 11–1 | 6.2 | 6.2 | 6.9 | 6.2 | 7.8 | 8.7 | 7.3 | 6.0 | 5.6 |
| 16 | 12–10 | 11–1 | 6.2 | 8.0 | 4.1 | 7.1 | 3.4 | 4.7 | 3.8 | 6.6 | 7.6 |
| 17 | 14–7 | 11–1 | 6.2 | 6.5 | 3.4 | 5.7 | 5.6 | 7.3 | 6.6 | 7.8 | 5.2 |
| 18 | 11–11 | 11–0 | 6.0 | 6.6 | 4.5 | 6.5 | 4.8 | 7.3 | 6.0 | 4.6 | 5.6 |
| 19 | 12–2 | 10–10 | 5.9 | 4.7 | 5.7 | 6.8 | 5.9 | 7.3 | 6.6 | 5.7 | 4.0 |
| 20 | 12–10 | 10–10 | 5.9 | 6.2 | 5.7 | 9.0 | 5.1 | 4.8 | 6.6 | 5.5 | 8.2 |
| 21 | 13–9 | 10–10 | 5.9 | 3.8 | 6.3 | 6.5 | 6.2 | 7.3 | 5.5 | 3.6 | 4.5 |
| 22 | 14–10 | 10–10 | 5.9 | 6.9 | 7.5 | 5.7 | 6.2 | 4.8 | 6.6 | 5.5 | 6.2 |
| 23 | 12–2 | 10–10 | 5.9 | 6.2 | 5.7 | 4.7 | 5.5 | 7.3 | 7.3 | 4.8 | 12.0 |
| 24 | 11–10 | 10–8 | 5.7 | 6.0 | 6.9 | 5.2 | 6.0 | 6.0 | 6.6 | 5.2 | 5.6 |
| 25 | 13–7 | 10–9 | 5.7 | 5.5 | 5.7 | 6.5 | 4.0 | 5.9 | 6.0 | 5.5 | 5.2 |
| 26 | 15–8 | 10–5 | 5.3 | 3.6 | 4.9 | 6.0 | 4.7 | 5.9 | 6.2 | 7.8 | 8.2 |
| 27 | 12–7 | 10–0 | 4.9 | 4.2 | 5.3 | 6.0 | 5.1 | 3.9 | 5.5 | 4.0 | 6.6 |
| 28 | 14–12 | 9–6 | 4.5 | 4.5 | 4.1 | 5.7 | 3.9 | 5.9 | 6.0 | 4.2 | 4.8 |
| 29 | 12–0 | 9–5 | 4.4 | 3.6 | 4.1 | 4.7 | 3.3 | 5.9 | 3.9 | 3.9 | 6.2 |
| 30 | 14–11 | 9–5 | 4.4 | 3.4 | 4.9 | 5.2 | 3.0 | 4.7 | 3.8 | 4.5 | 3.7 |
| 31 | 15–6 | 9–3 | 4.2 | 8.2 | 4.9 | 3.9 | 3.1 | 1.0 | 2.0 | 4.5 | 5.2 |
| 32 | 15–9 | 9–3 | 4.2 | 3.4 | 6.3 | 3.7 | 3.6 | 4.8 | 6.0 | 3.6 | 4.8 |
| 33 | 14–3 | 8–10 | 3.9 | 4.2 | 4.1 | 5.7 | 3.7 | 5.9 | 6.0 | 3.7 | 4.7 |
| 34 | 14–6 | 8–5 | 3.5 | 2.0 | 4.1 | 3.4 | 4.8 | 3.8 | 4.4 | 4.1 | 3.4 |
| Average | 13–2 | 10–9 | 6.0 | 5.7 | 5.8 | 6.6 | 5.0 | 6.6 | 6.4 | 5.5 | 6.9 |

\* Scores from two subtests, Poetry Comprehension and Selection of Key Words, are omitted because of space limitations.

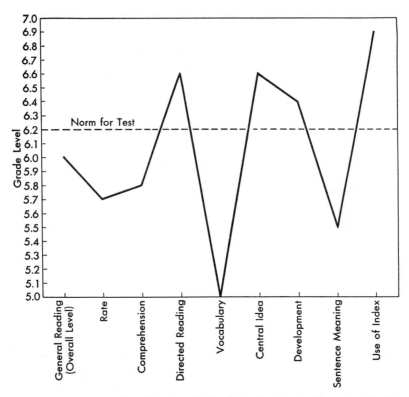

**Figure 49.** Profile of Reading Skills of the Sixth-Grade Class Described in Table 28.

use in reading (as opposed to the products of reading shown on the test)?

Teachers interested in ways of utilizing such data as presented in Table 28 may wish to study such additional questions as the following:

1. Out of 34 pupils listed in Table 28, how many are reading up to actual age? (Use Columns 2 and 3.)
2. How many have average beginning seventh-grade reading ability or more?
3. What is the range of ability in vocabulary?
4. What is the range in the use of the index?
5. What is one of the first things that should be done to meet such great individual differences?
6. What does the table indicate about using the same texts and materials for everybody in the same grade?
7. How many grade levels of material are needed for this class?

8. How many in this group can now read average seventh-grade material with comprehension?
9. What level of material does pupil 26 need? Pupil 30? Pupil 1?
10. Which of these youngsters probably reads too fast for his comprehension?
11. Which pupils should probably be encouraged to speed up their reading?
12. Which of these youngsters apparently needs training in using the index?
13. In the light of these and other data, what would it be reasonable to expect of pupil 20 with respect to reading improvement this year? What is a reasonable goal for him? What might be a reasonable goal for pupil 32?
14. What types of professional problems does it appear the teacher of this class should be studying?

### Planning Improvements on a Class-wide Basis

The average levels of attainment as shown on different reading scales and the class profile and individual profiles may indicate some of the places or points where instruction has been strong or weak (at least, as compared with classes on which the test was standardized). The teacher, as well as students, should be able to act in the light of such information by engaging in activities designed to correct areas of weakness.

The elimination of the weaknesses revealed by the test may involve many activities, some of which will now be discussed. (1) A study of how other teachers in the same school have worked on such problems. (2) A study of relevant published materials. Extensive use of the *Education Index* and the *Psychological Abstracts* will probably be desirable. Annual summaries of reading studies are given in the *Journal of Educational Research*. For example, in Volume 59, February, 1966, there is a "Summary and Review of Investigations Relating to Reading" covering July, 1964 to July, 1965.[3] Other helpful sources are the summaries and bibliographies printed by the Educational Records Bureau, 437 West 59th Street, New York 19, New York. These summaries and annotated bibliographies are of value in helping the teacher find studies which relate to a particular reading problem such as developing reading interest, activity programs in reading achievement, developmental reading, and remedial and corrective teaching of reading. (3) Finally, weaknesses spotlighted by the tests may be eliminated through revised teaching methods. Those methods which are effective should be capable of validation by a continuous testing program.

For instructional purposes some teachers and teacher-pupil planning groups may find it advisable to group children for particular types of read-

---

[3] By T. L. Harris, pp. 243–268.

ing or other learning activities. Referring back again to Table 28, the question might be asked: What subgroups may be organized to facilitate the learning of various reading skills? Pupils may be grouped according to the areas of the greatest need as indicated by a study of the diagnostic test results. Subgroups should vary according to the pupil's needs in the different school subjects and their membership should shift as conditions change.

In the matter of grouping it should be kept in mind that some pupils need to develop into leaders in the community and one way of promoting such development is to help individuals assume some responsibility in handling groups. Simply to turn the leadership job over to the student is not enough. The teacher must systematically make a study of ways of developing students leaders [4] and actively engage in promoting the process.

### Diagnosis of Individual Difficulties

The teacher should make a systematic study of outstanding strengths and weaknesses of each pupil with the aim of giving appropriate individual help. Questions such as the following point the way toward the effective use of test results for individual diagnosis: Do a pupil's answers on a test indicate that he is weak in following directions? Does his test show that he works quite accurately but too slowly? Does he seem to reverse words or letters and read them from right to left rather than left to right? An analysis of the pupil's errors and the processes he used in making them often sheds much light on the type of remedial work needed.

Another important factor to keep in mind in the diagnosis of individuals is the need to study achievement not in terms of an absolute standard but rather in terms of expected and reasonable *individual* achievement. As reading has consistently been used as an illustration in this chapter, one might pursue the matter of reading achievement a step further by asking who are retarded readers? Can the question be answered from the data shown in Table 28? Some years ago the writer asked several teachers and administrators to define retarded readers. The answers, as will be shown by the following illustrations, were far from constant.

"A retarded reader is one behind his age norm in comprehension and speed in reading ability." If this definition were used, approximately 50 per cent of the youngsters in our schools would always be retarded since the norm simply represents the average achievement at a particular age or grade. Other definitions were: ". . . one who may be in the fourth grade, but has the reading ability of the average second grader." ". . . one who is at least a grade level below his class norm when given a standard test." ". . . one who does not read as well as the average member of his class."

---

[4] See Ruth Cunningham, *Understanding Group Behavior of Boys and Girls*, New York, Teachers College, Columbia University, 1951.

Each of the four definitions given in this paragraph implies that every child should be up to average. This is certainly an impossible and unrealistic goal.

What, then, should be meant by the term a retarded reader? Consider three students aged 11 years, 2 months, who are all in the sixth grade. Mary has a reading age of 9.5; John's reading age is 11.4; and Jean has a reading age of 12.5. It is difficult to tell which of these is retarded in reading until the approximate mental age or *reading capacity* of each is known. When mental test data are included the following figures are obtained:

| Pupil | Chronological Age | General Reading Age | Mental Age [5] |
|-------|-------------------|---------------------|---------------|
| Mary  | 11–2              | 9.5                 | 9.5           |
| John  | 11–2              | 11.4                | 11.6          |
| Jean  | 11–2              | 12.5                | 15.0          |

Assuming that both the reading test and the capacity test are reasonably valid, we are now in a position to say that Mary, the poorest reader, is reading apparently about as well as should be expected in view of her mental test score; John is slightly retarded; and Jean, who is the best reader of the three, shows the greatest amount of basic retardation. Thus, the slowest and poorest reader may actually be the least retarded, while the fastest and best reader is apparently retarded about three grades in reading ability.

Before we can intelligently approach remedial reading, we must know which youngsters are most retarded. That child is most retarded whose reading achievements are farthest below his reading capacities. He is the child whom someone has neglected or trained improperly in reading. He is the child who now needs remedial assistance with particular emphasis on the kinds of reading in which he is weakest.

### Helping Pupils Improve

Achievement test results combined with some measure of basic intellectual capacity will help give a more realistic basis for determining appropriate class, course, and other educational goals. From the achievement tests can be secured an indication of present accomplishments; from mental capacity tests come an approximation of the *speed* with which one may expect the pupil to progress. With these factors in mind it should not be expected that a sixth-grade youngster whose mental capacity is much below average and whose present achievement level is that of the average fourth

---

[5] It should be understood, of course, that mental age as measured by intelligence tests is not a perfect indication of reading capacity, especially if the mental test requires the subject to read. Nevertheless, measured mental ability adds an important ingredient to the study of the so-called retarded reader.

grader will be able to do *average* sixth-grade work. Neither should one expect him to be ready to begin *average* seventh-grade work one year later.

For instance, in an activity such as reading, the average reading grade level of a pupil can be used as a basis for helping him select and use reading materials. This would mean that each classroom would need to have available for use reading materials which vary in difficulty and in areas of interest to the same extent as the reading capacities and interests of pupils. Likewise, diagnostic arithmetic tests may be used to find levels of arithmetic experience which are needed and will be meaningful for each pupil. In essence, the optimum usefulness of diagnostic tests can be achieved only when a major share of the assignments and exercises represent a planned follow-up of the individual test results.

For recreational reading it is at times desirable for the pupil to have reading materials which are considerably easier than those he can comprehend as indicated by test results. For sheer enjoyment and to promote the desire to do much reading, it is sometimes desirable to have materials which are so easy that the pupil does not have to struggle with new words in his reading.

The great spread of ability within each grade level, as indicated by tests, means that if the development of each pupil is to be provided for, the teacher must gear instruction to several grade levels within his class. The data which were shown in Table 28 are typical of what would be found in classrooms the country over—and similar data would be found in subjects other than reading. Within one grade, a range of ability of eight or nine grades frequently appears on test results. It is apparent that a teacher should not only be familiar with materials and methods suitable for *average* pupils of his grade, but should also know about materials and be able to use methods adapted to both less and more mature pupils. This is, obviously, an extremely difficult task, but one which can be faced with considerable optimism if the teacher is willing to study and experiment, and if the teacher is willing to use the learners themselves, so far as is possible, in diagnosing their own difficulties, and in planning their own activities.

## USING TESTS TO FACILITATE SOCIAL RELATIONSHIPS

The previous section of this chapter showed some of the many ways in which achievement tests could be used as a basis for improving teaching. If learning were governed strictly by capacity for achievement, an explanation of the use of achievement and mental tests might suffice. However, successful school work depends equally as much upon such characteristics as the pupils' personal adjustment, attitudes, and social or group skills. It is therefore essential that teachers know how to measure and interpret these personal and social factors, and to use the test results in planning classroom

activities. One of the most practical and useful types of evidence about children is obtained by appraising their interpersonal relationships.

The term which is generally used to describe a study of patterns of inter-relation existing in a group of people is *sociometry*. From the measure of interrelationships it is possible to draw up a chart which gives a pictorial representation of some aspects of interpersonal relations. As with any other type of testing procedure, the purposes and uses of the technique are matters of major concern. In the initial part of this section procedures for gathering sociometric data will be discussed. Following this an illustrative sociogram will be presented. Finally, uses which may be made of sociometric approaches will be listed and briefly discussed.

### Gathering Sociometric Data

In collecting sociometric data it is desirable not to suggest to pupils that they are taking a test. A superior procedure would be to begin with a statement such as the following:

> Yesterday it was decided by our class that we should set up some com-mittees for various purposes in our next unit of work. There are various ways in which these committees might be set up, but it is desirable that you have an opportunity to work on committees with students whom you feel you work with best. If each of you will put on one of these sheets of paper your own name and names of three other students with whom you would like to work I will attempt to summarize these over the weekend and set up some committee groups based on the recommendations which our planning committee made today.

Obviously the information gained from the voting for committees sheds light on the kind of interpersonal relationships existing within a class. Any number of additional questions could be phrased and presented to the pupils for their reactions. Following are some questions which teachers have found useful:

> Will you write on a piece of paper the names of your three best friends?
> With which classmates (two or three) do you like best to play?
> Whom would you like to have sit next to you in class?
> With whom would you like to discuss personal problems?
> Who is your choice as a student leader for this class?
> Whom would you like most to invite home to dinner?
> With whom would you like to go to a party?

In this type of testing it is extremely important that the pupils be frank in stating what their preferences are. One way of assuring this, of course, is for the teacher to keep information so gained in strictest confidence. Usually it is wise for the teacher to mention that these data will not be shown to other students in the room or revealed to any other individual.

There is some difference of opinion among experts as to whether it is ever wise to ask for negative reactions or dislikes on the part of pupils. One argument for attempting to get such information is that if there are dislikes it is well to know whether they exist and against whom they are directed so that something can be done to better the situation. If it is decided that it is wise to attempt to obtain sociometric rejections, then any of the questions already suggested could be used by placing "not" appropriately in each question. Statements like the following may also be used:

What three pupils do you like least?
Who are the pupils nobody likes very much?
Which children get into a lot of trouble?
Which children are afraid of everything?
Which children do you think are bossy?
Which children act like sissies?
Which pupils cause you trouble?

In the primary grades where pupils are too young to write the names of other children, teachers may obtain similar information through personal interviews with the youngsters themselves. When this is done it is clear that such interviews should be conducted outside of the hearing of other pupils.

Finally, the teacher should keep in mind the following suggestions. It is well to: (1) build up desirable relationships with pupils before requesting the information; (2) collect and use sociometric measurement in situations where the need for such data is or can be made obvious to the pupils; [6] (3) word questions so that they can easily be understood by the pupils.

### Pictorial Representation of Interpersonal Relationships

After students' nominations have been collected, the teacher will want to convert the data into some usable form. There are many possible ways of graphically representing the information gathered.[7] One such plan is presented in Figure 50.

The diagram in Figure 50 is constructed to show *mutual relationships* between pupils in the same grade and *mutual relationships* with pupils in other grades. Each child in Grades 4 to 8 was asked to indicate: (1) with whom would he like best to play; (2) with whom would he like best to work; and (3) whom would he like best to have sit next to him. Three choices were possible for each question, although this number was not

---

[6] For illustrations of such situations see the *Ohio Social Acceptance Scale* published by the Ohio Scholarship Tests and Division of Elementary Supervision, State Department of Education, Columbus, Ohio.

[7] For an excellent analysis of sociometric approaches see N. E. Gronlund, *Measurement and Evaluation in Teaching*, New York, The Macmillan Company, 1965, pp. 335–342.

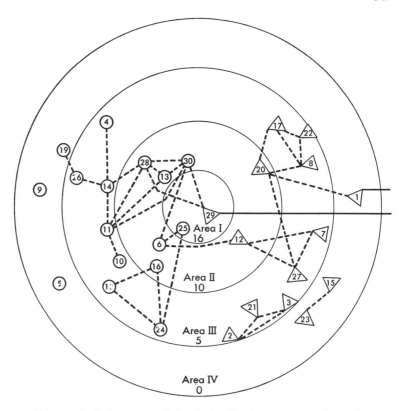

**Figure 50.** Sociogram for Thirty Eighth-Grade Pupils. This shows the mutual relationships with pupils in same grade (broken lines) and the mutual relationships with pupils in other grades (straight lines). Small circles represent boys; triangles, girls. Area I includes pupils chosen as friends by other children 16 or more times; Area II, pupils chosen 10–15 times; Area III, pupils chosen 5–9 times; and Area IV, pupils chosen fewer than 5 times. (From E. A. Flotow, "Charting Social Relationships," *Elementary School Journal,* Vol. 46, May, 1946, pp. 498–504.)

required. On the basis of the answers of the eighth-grade group, the sociogram in Figure 50 was constructed. The dotted lines in the diagram show reciprocated choices—that a pupil not only likes a pupil but is liked by him in return. These are mutual relationships. Pupils are placed in one of four concentric circles according to the extent of their popularity.

Six of the facts or implications indicated by this sociogram follow. (1) Pupils 5 and 9 not only are chosen fewer than five times but their own choices of other students were in no instance reciprocated. Although pupils 19, 15, 23, and 1 were also chosen less than five times, at least one mutual choice was found in each case. Two of these five pupils, 15 and

23, chose each other. One of these pupils, 1, had his choice reciprocated by a pupil in another grade. (2) In or near Area II seem to be found the pupils with the most satisfactory mutual relationships. (3) One pupil, 29, although receiving more than fifteen votes apparently has no reciprocated friendship with any other girl in her own classroom and crossed room boundaries to establish a mutual relationship with another girl. (4) Most of the social relationships are with pupils of the same sex. (5) The boys seem to represent a somewhat more tightly knit group than the girls. (6) In general, pupils who receive the most choices also have the greater number of reciprocated relationships.

The teacher of the pupils shown in Figure 50, with these and other data available such as marks and intelligence test scores, should be able to develop and study other facts and hypotheses and gain insights not mentioned in the points above. The way a teacher will pictorially represent data will depend primarily on what relationships he is trying to study.[8]

### Uses of Sociometric Data

It is a well known fact that teachers are poor judges of the social roles of many of their pupils. Teachers frequently feel that if a child is bright and doing excellent academic work he is also equally effective in his social relationships. By means of sociometric procedures teachers can get some checks of their own impressions regarding the social relations in their classrooms. Sociometric procedures help the busy teacher avoid the danger involved in neglecting children who are rejected or ignored by their classmates.

In the following list are specific values the teacher can derive from various measures of interpersonal relationships. Sociometric data can:

1. Help the teacher identify cliques and cleavages in class groups.
2. Focus the attention of the teacher on social goals and on tangible ways in which interpersonal relations can be improved.
3. Help improve pupil understanding of social relations and problems, if discussed with class without names on sociogram.
4. Help identify rejected pupils—those who are actively disliked by some or many classmates.
5. Detect pupils who *feel* themselves to be social outcasts in the classroom. (This feeling may not, of course, be accurate, but may still have educational significance.)

---

[8] For other illustrations of sociogram construction see (1) Horace-Mann Lincoln School of Experimentation, *How to Construct a Sociogram*, New York, Bureau of Publications, Teachers College, Columbia University, 1947; (2) E. Forsyth and L. Katz, "A Matrix Approach to the Analysis of Sociometric Data," *Sociometry*, Vol. 9, November, 1946, pp. 340–347; (3) N. E. Gronlund, *Sociometry in the Classroom*, New York, Harper and Brothers, 1959, Chapter 3.

6. Give teacher a basis for comparing class with published social norms.[9]
7. Indicate those who are out-of-school leaders but do not show leadership in school. (Such pupils would frequently have great potentialities as classroom leaders if teacher guidance were appropriate in this regard.)
8. Provide clues as to ways of dealing with disciplinary cases. (Can show with whom the problem case would like to work and whom he respects.)
9. Show how newcomers in a school or class are faring and can help the teacher check on the effectiveness of various procedures for integrating newcomers into classroom groups.
10. Show which students have friends in the classroom but are also thoroughly disliked by one or more students.
11. Help identify the isolates in the classroom—those who are ignored by peers and who have no friends in the classroom.
12. Help identify those who are presently classroom leaders. (These individuals can be taught to assume some of the roles now assumed only by the teacher in many classrooms.)
13. Aid in determining interracial or interreligious relations and problems.
14. Show the direction of changes in interpersonal relationships which are continually taking place in classroom groups.
15. Show degree of individual maturity on one dimension by indicating level of interest in those of the other sex.
16. Help the teacher through pretests and post-tests to determine the effects of specific procedures which have been tried out in the classroom.
17. Give the teacher significant data upon which formal or informal research may be based.
18. Show how many mutual or reciprocated choices of friends there are in the classroom.
19. Show which class members are in greatest demand as friends.

The values of sociometric testing can be realized only when tests are followed by further diagnostic work or appropriate remedial action. As already noted, sociometric data should point out isolates, rejected children, potential leaders, cliques, and perhaps the general conditions of group morale and group interaction. Some of the uses of such information may be implemented by the techniques described in the following paragraphs.

---

[9] H. H. Jennings, *Sociometry in Group Relations*, Washington, D.C., American Council on Education, 1948, p. 21. Also, for an analysis of the distribution of sociometric choices of a normative sort see N. E. Gronlund, *Sociometry in the Classroom*, Chapter 4.

First of all, the data may provide a means for reseating or reconstituting groups within the classroom. If two near isolates choose each other, for example, it would seem desirable to see that these two youngsters be given the opportunity to work together. Group work of some sort is essential if the full value of sociometry is to be achieved.

Secondly, the information gleaned from sociometric voting should provide a basis for further diagnosis. Interviews, diaries kept by pupils, personality measures, observations, and case studies may be indicated in cases where children are very unpopular. The unpopular child who is identified early in his school career may be helped immeasurably. The writer knows a case in which a girl was rejected almost unanimously by her classmates. She was most unhappy and maladjusted. Further study showed her to be the unfortunate product of an oversolicitous mother who went so far as to bring this teenage youngster to class each day, and to wait for her after school outside the classroom door. The teacher followed sociometric testing by interviewing the girl and her classmates, and eventually, through the use of group work and several parties which were held at the rejected girl's home, helped her achieve a place in her peer group.

Finally, sociometric information may be used in a more general way to make changes in group procedures and to involve the class in problems which sociograms bring to light. Such matters as needed recreational activities, prejudices, personal inadequacies, tightly knit cliques, and the like are problems which youngsters themselves can help solve. Class discussions in which pupils are encouraged to raise such problems may be one solution. Also, group project work in which youngsters investigate the very problems which exist in their group may lead to better self-insight. The key to good group morale is in the hands of the teacher. Whenever sociograms show an inordinate amount of rejection and group disintegration, the teacher needs to take account of his own teaching methods. Youngsters who are handled in a democratic fashion, who are challenged by significant problems, and who feel that they are making an important contribution to the class are most likely to have a high degree of group morale.

In addition to sociometric techniques for assessing interpersonal relations, the teacher should also consider other peer appraisal approaches such as the "guess who" technique. In this approach each pupil is given a series of brief behavior descriptions and he is asked to name those pupils who best fit each description. Two descriptions are illustrative of this approach:

1. This person usually comes up with very good ideas.

2. This classmate talks too much without thinking enough about what is said. The "guess who" method is easy to administer, and scoring simply involves counting the number of nominations received by each pupil. Through analysis of results and diagnosis and development of personality characteristics, character traits, and social skills can be improved.

## SUMMARY

The giving of standardized tests of many sorts has become an almost universal practice in the schools of this country. So far as many schools are concerned the giving of the tests constitutes an end in itself with little thought being given to the uses to which they may be put. Other schools use their test results, but commit serious errors in so doing.

Those who use tests for instructional and guidance purposes need to observe many precautions. In the first place, the validity of any test used should be questioned. Is there evidence that the test measures what it purports to measure? Many tests on the market claim to measure certain important outcomes of education, but in reality appraise something quite different from that announced in their titles. A test of critical thinking, for example, should measure something other than general intelligence or reading ability. In the second place, the reliability of each test employed should be given careful scrutiny. Does the test give consistent results? A reading test which places a pupil at the fifth-grade level one day and at the seventh-grade level the next, is obviously very unreliable.

In this chapter numerous common uses and misuses of tests have been considered. Also included are detailed illustrations of specific help which teachers may obtain from diagnostic achievement tests and sociometric devices.

The perspectives of educators must go beyond the view of a test simply in terms of its accuracy or technical construction. Useful interpretations of test results depend not only upon the soundness of the test, but also upon a careful appraisal of the whole school program and of the children whom the test is supposed to measure. When teachers teach test items, or bring undue pressure to bear upon children's performance, or when schools have a large amount of retardation and elimination, the consequences are clearly mirrored in test results. In short, all testing must be viewed in its relation to the objectives, methods, and administrative policies of the school.

The modern teacher must know much about tests and instruments of appraisal if he is to succeed in his work. He must understand how tests can contribute to effective learning, and how they can point the way to satisfactory individual and group guidance. Testing devices in the hands of inexperienced or inadequately trained teachers may in many instances do much more harm than good. When cautiously and intelligently employed, however, many of the testing devices now available may become indispensable aids in teaching.

### References for Further Study

Instead of listing all of the excellent articles in educational periodicals on tests and their uses, the writer recommends for this chapter that students

obtain practice in locating these by using the *Education Index*. The following headings, taken from the *Education Index*, are illustrative of ones which merit exploration:

*Attitudes*, Tests and scales
*Behavior*, Tests and scales
*Educational measurements*
*Evaluation*
*Higher education*, evaluation
*Intelligence*
*Intelligence quotient*
*Intelligence tests*
*Interest (psychology)*, Test and scales
*Personality tests*
*Practice teaching*, evaluation
*Prognosis of success*

*Psychological tests*
*Public schools*, rating
*Questionnaires*
*Readability tests*
*Reading*, tests
*Research*, educational evaluation
*Self appraisal*
*Social acceptability tests*
*Sociometry*
*Surveys*
*Testing programs*
*Tests and scales*

Also see subhead, Tests and scales, under school subject, e.g., *Reading*, Tests and scales; *Music education*, Tests and scales; *Science*, Tests and scales.

The Index Numbers of *Psychological Abstracts*, December issues of each year, are excellent sources.

The *Encyclopedia of Educational Research*, C. W. Harris (Editor), Third Edition, New York, The Macmillan Company, 1960, represents a useful source of ideas and references on many problems related to diagnostic tools and their uses.

Cronbach, L. J., *Essentials of Psychological Testing*, New York, Harper and Brothers, 1960, Chapters 3, 16.

Cunningham, Ruth, and Others, *Understanding Group Behavior of Boys and Girls*, New York, Teachers College, Bureau of Publications, Columbia University, 1951.

Gronlund, N. E., *Measurement and Evaluation in Teaching*, New York, The Macmillan Company, 1965.

Gronlund, N. E., *Sociometry in the Classroom*, New York, Harper and Brothers, 1959.

Henry, N. B. (Editor), *Individualizing Instruction*, Chicago, The University of Chicago Press, 1962.

Proctor, C. H., and Loomis, C. P., "Analysis of Sociometric Data" in Part II of *Research Methods in Social Relations*, S. W. Cook, and Others, New York, The Dryden Press, 1951, pp. 561–585.

Seidman, J. M. *Readings in Educational Psychology*, Boston, Houghton Mifflin Company, 1965.

Simpson, Ray H., *Improving Teaching-Learning Processes*, New York, Longmans, Green and Co., 1953, Chapters 5, 7, 8, 12, 14.

Thomas, R. M., *Judging Student Progress*, Second Edition, New York, Longmans, Green and Co., 1960.

Thomas, R. M., and Thomas, S. M., *Individual Differences in the Classroom*, New York, David McKay Company, 1965, Part II, Intellectual Dif-

ferences, Part III, Artistic and Motor Differences, Part IV, Psychophysical Differences.

In addition, most of the books listed at the end of the preceding chapter contain material very useful to the teacher in interpreting and using test results.

## Questions, Exercises, and Activities

1. Find one of the books on tests and measurements listed at the end of Chapter 17. Make a list of suggestions for test interpretation which you gather from the book.
2. Study the results from a test given to an elementary, high school, or college class. What suggestions or implications for the teacher do you think are contained in the results?
3. List uses a teacher may make of each of the following types of tools: (a) interest inventories, (b) attitude inventories, (c) value inventories, (d) personality inventories, (e) readability tests, (f) social acceptability tests, (g) sociometric diagrams.
4. Take two of the types of tools mentioned in question 3 above and discuss possible misuses of the instruments by teachers.
5. Discuss the pros and cons of using objective types of tests exclusively. What are the advantages of sometimes employing teacher-made essay-type questions for diagnostic purposes?

# Chapter 19

## Marking, Reporting, and Pupil Placement

Of all school practices, those involved in marking and reporting seem most shrouded in confusion, misinterpretation, and misunderstanding. Confusions and difficulties involve not only pupils and their parents, but also teachers.

The writers have heard numerous teachers state that they would enjoy teaching if they did not have to make out and issue grades. Much of the difficulty is due to the fact that many teachers are never quite sure what purpose the grades are supposed to serve, as is indicated by the following comments: "I gave John a low mark because he continually irritates me in class. . . ." "Jane doesn't learn much but she tries so hard I just can't discourage her by giving her a low mark." "Thorn almost always gets the highest score on the test, but since he never seems to do any work I feel guilty in giving him a high mark for doing no studying."

The objectives of this chapter are to aid current and prospective teachers to: (1) appreciate more clearly the complex problems and issues involved in marking and reporting, (2) perceive some of the purposes which marking and reporting may serve, (3) understand misuses of marking and reporting, (4) visualize guides for improvement, and (5) consider psychological factors related to pupil placement or promotion, an area closely intertwined with marking and reporting.

Much of the difficulty in current marking and reporting methods arises

from the failure to identify and to resolve the crucial issues that generate stress and misunderstanding. Many times as previously noted it is not clear what the grade on a test, or the final mark in a course, is supposed to do. They may be used to indicate progress relative to a pupil's classmates, they may be based on some arbitrary standard previously determined by the teacher, or they may be estimates of the degree to which a child measures up to his capabilities. Moreover there is some confusion about how specific these marks and grades ought to be. Sometimes teachers give a single letter grade or number, but in other schools teachers write long reports to the parents explaining in detail what the child's progress has been, and what future steps should be taken by the school and parents. Finally there is lack of agreement about how the mark or grade should be interpreted to the pupil. In some situations, marks are assigned during an individual conference with each student; in others, getting the child's opinion of his own progress is considered entirely beside the point, and it is assumed that the meaning of his grade is obvious. These are but a few of the questions and issues encompassed by this phase of the school's task. Many others will become apparent in the balance of the chapter.

## VALUES OF MARKS AND REPORTS
## TO VARIOUS GROUPS

If marking and reporting systems are to make a contribution to the work of the school, it is of utmost importance that a careful study be made of the possible purposes which they may serve. Due to differences in communities, in school systems, in backgrounds of pupils and teachers, as well as to other factors, a marking or reporting system that is appropriate for one school system might be quite inappropriate for another system where the combination of factors is different. This means, in effect, that when one considers a desirable reporting system for a particular school or community, he must take into account the present level of development of those affected by the marking or reporting system. For example, a group of schools which has been experimenting with different marking and reporting systems might profit greatly from descriptive reports to students and parents in lieu of traditional letter grades. However, in a system where only letter grading has been used in the past, an abrupt change to descriptive reporting would probably be unwise. Parents, students, and teachers would all be accustomed to a certain type of marking and reporting, and it would seem to be sound in terms of readiness for those concerned to move gradually from the older system to the newer one. If changes are to be effective they cannot be imposed by administrative decision but should result from study of the problems by teachers, pupils, and parents.

There are various ways in which the purposes of marking or reporting systems might be considered. The organization in the following section of

this chapter is based on the fact that marking is designed to serve particular individuals or specified groups. For example, a reporting system designed to inform parents about the school's objectives, activities, changes, and proposed changes has a decidedly different purpose from a system which aims only at informing parents about the relative standing of their son or daughter. Likewise, a mark indicating a learner's progress in relation to his ability has a quite different aim than a mark designed to show how a child's achievement compares with others. Consequently, marking purposes may be in conflict with each other. Those who get and use marks, if they are to use them intelligently, must recognize the aims of the system. Otherwise, marks intended to mean one thing by the maker may be misinterpreted to mean something quite different by the user.

There are at least three groups whom marks and reports serve: pupils, teachers and administrators, and parents. Variations in reporting to meet the needs of these groups will now be discussed.

### Marks and Reports Serve the Student

Frequently the teacher's purpose in giving a mark to the pupil is simply to inform him of his status. Too often the instructor has in mind no planful procedure as to how youngsters can or should constructively use such information. There are several ways in which teachers, through marks, may impart information to pupils. One of the most common is to show the pupil his level of achievement, as compared with others in his class or with pupils who comprised the population used to standardize a test. For example, the mark may tell the pupil that he was in the lowest one-tenth of his class on a test in critical reading.

The mark may also show the youngster the amount of progress he has made in a designated period of time. The well-designed report card should, furthermore, make it possible to keep the pupil constantly informed about his progress in a wide variety of behaviors. If the child has improved in his ability to handle fractions, or in his skill in word attack, he should be made aware of this fact.

The instructor may also attempt to communicate to the student his progress in relation to his estimated ability. For example, consider the following data on two students:

|  | IQ | Year's Progress in General Reading Ability |
|---|---|---|
| James | 100 | 1.3 average grade levels |
| Robert | 102 | .5 average grade levels |

A report on James might indicate satisfactory progress in general reading ability while the report for Robert might raise questions as to why he, with average ability, had apparently only made about half as much progress in

this skill as does the average student. In giving such information to the student, the teacher must recognize that the figure on estimated ability is difficult to determine with great accuracy. Intelligence tests, measures of socio-economic background, measures of amount of time the pupil spends in school, and other similar factors will give some basis for helping the teacher determine what might be reasonably expected of a particular learner.

MARKS AS MOTIVATORS OF LEARNING. Teachers often use marks or reports in an effort to stimulate the learner to improve his work. A very common but questionable practice from a psychological standpoint is to punish, discipline, or penalize the learner by giving him poor grades for past mistakes. Such a procedure has to be used on the assumption that the pupil will work harder when his past failures are emphasized. But such an assumption is not warranted by existing evidence.

In an experiment by Sears,[1] the work of subjects who experienced continuous failure steadily deteriorated while a group with success experiences made steady and persistent gains. This type of experiment throws much doubt on the belief frequently held by teachers that continuously failing a student will improve his learning.[2]

In the hands of some teachers, a red pencil becomes a whiplash used to keep pupils tractable, docile, or "in line." Low grades are often a last ditch attempt at motivation. When marks are used as threats, they typically indicate a failure by the instructor to help the pupil see basic or intrinsic values he may obtain from his work. Marks used in this fashion are usually found in autocratically controlled classrooms.

A much more defensible use of grades for motivating pupils is one in which the teacher capitalizes on the diagnostic values of marks by guiding the pupil to see his own strengths and weaknesses. The goal of such a diagnosis will be to stimulate future study through helping the learner identify behaviors needing improvement. To be effective, this type of reporting needs to be rather specific. For example, it probably is not very helpful to the pupil for the teacher to indicate a weakness in sportsmanship. On the other hand, if the teacher can indicate those behavioral aspects of sportsmanship in which the learner is strong and those in which he is weak, there will be a better basis for the learner to plan activities, to capitalize on the strengths, and to eliminate the weaknesses. The following are illustrations of behaviors which might be given attention under the heading of sportsmanship: To what extent (1) does the pupil observe game rules? (2) is he a good loser? (3) does he treat visiting players and officials with respect? Generally, when the diagnostic function is uppermost in the mind of the

---

[1] R. R. Sears, "Initiation of the Repression Sequence by Experienced Failure," *Journal of Experimental Psychology*, Vol. 20, 1937, pp. 570–580.

[2] See M. J. Loomis, "Elementary School Nonpromotion and Individual Potential," *Theory into Practice*, Vol. 4, 1965, pp. 85–87.

teacher, he will attempt to maintain a balance in emphasis between the weak and strong points of individual pupils. Excessive emphasis on weaknesses may lead to discouragement, and continued failure will result. Conversely, excessive emphasis on an individual's strong points may either lead to self-complacency, or give him little indication of where self-improvement is needed. When detailed diagnostic information is emphasized in a reporting system, it may be said to be *future oriented*. When the emphasis is on punishment, discipline, or penalties, the system is *past oriented*.

When pupils are encouraged to see report cards or progress reports as diagnostic aids for learning they are likely to develop desirable self-evaluative abilities. Hence, marking and reporting usually need to be related to goals which pupils have helped to set for themselves.

GIVING THE STUDENT PRACTICE IN REPORTING HIS OWN PROGRESS. Too frequently students' descriptions of their school work denote a very superficial view of their own progress, and probably indicate that they have had little practice in reporting their own achievement. The following brief excerpt from a dinner conversation illustrates this superficial view of events in school.

"Well, what did you do at school today, Jack?"
"Oh, the same thing as usual. Please pass the meat."
"What happened in your science class?"
"Well, two of the kids didn't have the assignment done so they had to stay in after school."
"What are you studying in your English class now?"
"Oh, some of that jazz about predicate nominatives and participial phrases—nobody seems to know what it's for."

Some teachers have thought of reporting functions as the exclusive responsibility of the teacher. However, in some schools students have also been given certain opportunities and responsibilities for recording and reporting their own progress. Following are excerpts from a weekly report which was written by Frank, a pupil in a ninth-grade mathematics class:

During the past week I have been working on the values and costs of different kinds of car insurance. Since I completed driver's training last semester Mr. Hall (the mathematics teacher) and I together decided this would be a good math problem for me to tackle. . . .

In addition to doing quite a bit of figuring this week I have learned such things as the following: My dad's insurance policy is no good if I am driving. This must be changed right away even if I have to use some of the money I make setting pins (in the bowling alley) to pay the extra amount. A $50 deductible policy now means something to me. Some states require every driver to have insurance. . . .

I find I need more practice in doing percentages and must give more study to the different kinds of insurance policies and their purposes. Next week I want to do some figuring on car maintenance, depreciation, trade in

values of various makes, miles per gallon of various makes in town and in country driving. . . . Over the weekend I must try to get dad in a good humor and then get him to see the local agent about changing our car policy so I can drive! This report should pave the way.

Reports of this sort have several values. They give the student practice in writing on subjects of concern to him. They give parents some picture of what the child and the school are trying to do. They can improve public relations and they can easily be included in the pupil's permanent record. Perhaps even more important, they can help the youngster assume additional responsibility for his own learning. They give both the pupil and the teacher a basis for evaluating past work and for planning future work. Pupils' goals and purposes tend to become clear. These goals, when defined and more clearly structured, form a basis for future educational, vocational, and recreational activities.

When a youngster is encouraged to take a hand in recording his own progress and appraising his own work, his personal adjustment is likely to be improved. For example, if he is having difficulties in interpersonal relations, his troubles may be alleviated by writing a description of the situation as he sees it. He may also try to indicate what types of things he might consider doing to improve the situation. The self-report also gives him practice in verbalizing his difficulties and in expressing them in such a way that others may give him help.

### Marks and Reports Serve Teachers and Administrators

Teachers sometimes use marking and reporting to make life easier for themselves. In some cases, grades or unfavorable reports are used to purge pupils who are difficult to handle. Some teachers feel that unless a student is docile in obeying without question their directions, he should not receive a high mark. From a psychological standpoint, a use of marking for the convenience of the teacher is extremely questionable if not actually dangerous.

One of the writers once visited a large midwestern high school to talk with a principal about his school problems. During the conversation, the principal proudly drew from his desk a report which he was just getting ready to submit to the school board. This document gave the name of each teacher, the subject he taught, the percentage of pupils in his course who "passed" the subject for the semester just closed, and the percentage who "failed." He commented regarding three algebra teachers who were listed. The first teacher, a Miss Olson, had "failed" 53 per cent of her pupils. He remarked that she was a fine teacher—one with high standards. The second, a Miss Burnham, had failed only 26 per cent of the members of her class. He noted that she was also quite acceptable. The third teacher, Mr. Brownfield, however, was not held in high repute! The principal pointed

to the fact that he had only "flunked" 8 per cent of his algebra pupils. He stated that nearly any pupil could pass his course. In general, the principal was proud of his teaching staff because they maintained one of the highest records of "washing out" students to be found anywhere in the state.

An extremely high percentage of failures in a class can usually be traced to one or more of the following causes: (1) improper placement of pupils in the class in the first place, (2) inappropriate course content for individual students, (3) unsound standards or goals which take no account of individual differences, and (4) poor teaching. The reader will note that each of these four contributing causes of failure is primarily if not entirely in the hands of the teacher or school.

At times teachers boastfully may use marks as indicators of their own teaching ability. Sometimes there is overemphasis on pencil and paper tests and little concern for individual needs, goals, and important skills not easily measured by current tests. It should be emphasized that grades in such a situation indicate how well the learner did in relation to teacher-structured assignments. The mark or report frequently does not indicate how well the pupil could do if he were ego-involved. Unknown under these circumstances is the level which might be achieved if the student were permitted to have a considerable share in setting up his study goals and those of the class and in helping to plan activities needed to achieve these goals.

Administrators or teachers sometimes use grades to determine the eligibility of students for sports, musical activities, other extracurricular activities, the honor roll, or an honor society. When so used care must be taken lest the pupil be excluded from activities in which he can succeed in school. Forcing a pupil to spend all of his time on activities in which success is unlikely may cause him to leave school too early, or result in other adverse effects.

Potentially, one of the most valuable, but frequently overlooked, uses of marks is that of helping the teacher evaluate his own work, his strengths and weaknesses. For example, the teacher might find that pupils did well on certain individual tests, but rather poorly in group discussion or in other group activities. Such information might well constitute a challenge which would lead to systematic study by the teacher. If this value is to be achieved marks must be based on rather detailed analysis of various aspects of student behavior.

### Pictorial Reporting Facilitates Communication Between Teachers, Pupils, and Administrators

As has been suggested in the preceding pages the importance of appropriate standards, goals, and reporting *for the individual pupil* cannot be overemphasized. How can we devise reporting techniques that on the one

hand keep the slow learner from becoming discouraged because of unrealistic expectations and on the other keep the talented child from developing improper work attitudes and self-perceptions because too little is expected of him? The diagram in Figure 51 suggests one pictorial framework for facilitating the study of individual pupils.

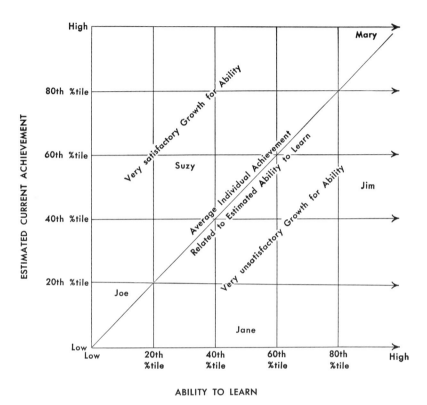

**Figure 51.** Chart for Reporting Relation Between "Ability to Learn" and "Current Achievement." (The course is mathematics. Ability to learn measured by the *California Capacity Test.* Achievement measured by the *Metropolitan Achievement Test—Mathematics Section.*)

The diagram may be used either as a part of the permanent record of the individual student or as a chart on which the teacher can study a group of students on two dimensions, achievement and ability.[3] Two percentile

[3] Since the correlation between school achievement and IQ is only approximately .50, this scheme should be used with extreme caution. IQ is only one of the factors affecting school grades. Such a report as this obviously should not be sent home to parents.

ratings for each student are needed to locate him on the chart. One percentile gives a comparative estimate of the individual's intelligence and should be based preferably on the results of more than one intelligence test. The other percentile should be based on results from as valid a measure as is available of the student's achievement in the specified subject.

Let us examine five cases which have been plotted on the chart in Figure 51. Joe's location indicates achievement in the lowest 20 per cent of the normative population but also indicates very limited mental capacity or "ability to learn"; hence, there may be no great cause for alarm. Suzy and Mary, while achieving at quite different levels both seem to be doing reasonably well in view of their differing mental capacities and the fact that each is achieving above average for her respective mental abilities.

In marked contrast to Suzy and Mary it would appear that Jim and Jane are not being appropriately challenged in the subject on which achievement has been measured. Jane with about average mental capacity is apparently achieving only about as well as the lowest 10 per cent of students. Jim, whose achievement is about average, still is apparently growing at a rate far below his potential.

From the pictorial reporting in Figure 51 then it would appear that three students, Joe, Suzy, and Mary are each making satisfactory or superior progress. Conversely, a more thorough study should be made of Jane and Jim to determine whether their inadequate achievement comes from their own attitudes and habits or from a failure of the school and particularly the teacher or both.

### Marks and Reports Serve Parents

Good reporting practices should improve relations between the school and the home. The effective report will not only show a youngster's status and progress but should also at least implicitly attempt to show changing school goals, procedures, and techniques. Such things as new methods, revised grouping procedures, or reasons for using various texts may be explained through the reporting system. Through such school reporting it is also possible to emphasize school needs in terms of personnel, salaries, equipment, and school buildings. Such a continuous interpretation going to the home provides parents some evidence which can be used in evaluating the work of the school and tends to promote more sympathetic attitudes on the part of parents.

In some schools letters from the teacher to the parent make up for some of the deficiencies of older report forms. Vredevoe and Lindecamp concluded after an extensive study of recording and reporting pupil progress in the secondary school "that no part of the program of communication with parents is of greater importance or influence than that which attempts

to report achievement, growth, or progress of the individual pupil in the school." [4]

When a detailed report of a pupil's behavior is given, information should be of such a nature that it helps the parent assess strengths and weaknesses of his child. This can facilitate appropriate child guidance at home. Indications of specific ways in which the parent can help the child are also desirable. Some schools attempt to use the reporting system as a motivational lever for the parent. Generally speaking, the goal here is to provide the parent with a basis for giving guidance to his youngster. Appropriate information might help the parent answer such questions as the following: In what subjects has the child shown a particular interest? What are occupational areas for which the child probably has particular aptitude? Should the boy or girl go to college? If so, to what kind of college? If he goes to college, what course of study would it probably be desirable for him to consider taking?

After an extensive study of reporting practices Traxler [5] concluded that: Home letters are now a common way of reporting by elementary school teachers even in school systems that lay no claim to progressive methods, but the use of this way of reporting is still rather rare in secondary schools. Traxler found certain trends which are indicated in shortened form below.[6]

1. There is considerable dissatisfaction with systems of marking that encourage comparisons of pupils with one another.
2. For years, there has been a trend in report cards away from percentage marking toward a scale with fewer points.
3. There is at least a slight trend toward the reporting of pupil progress in relation to ability.
4. There is a widespread tendency for report cards to include an evaluation of traits other than subject matter achievement alone.
5. There is a clear tendency to use descriptive rather than quantitative reports.
6. In some secondary schools and in many elementary schools, formal reports are being replaced by notes or letters to parents.
7. Noteworthy attempts are made in some of the more recent report cards to analyze and diagnose a pupil's achievement in terms of the objectives of the school.

---

[4] L. E. Vredevoe and C. D. Lindecamp, "How Shall We Make the Recording and Reporting of Pupil Progress More Meaningful?" *Bulletin of the National Association of the Secondary School Principals,* Vol. 37, April, 1953, pp. 179–185.

[5] A. E. Traxler, *Techniques of Guidance,* Revised Edition, New York, Harper and Brothers, 1957.

[6] *Ibid.,* pp. 236–239.

8. Reports are being sent at less frequent intervals, and in some schools only when there is specific occasion for communication with the home.
9. There is also a trend toward shorter report forms. (This trend is not clear-cut.)
10. Parents are being asked to cooperate in building (and revising) report cards and also to take part in plans of reciprocal reporting in parent-teacher conferences.
11. In some schools, pupils cooperate in devising report cards and in evaluating their own achievement.
12. Elementary schools are freer "to experiment with new and novel procedures," and they are "less conventional and less formal." Proof that one is better than another is not now available. Maybe needs are different at different age groups.
13. Finally, there is a recognizable trend toward better administration of procedures of reporting to parents. (Rotation of sending of reports so those for different students are made out at different times. Time is given for work to do a good job.)

A natural extension of the report that goes to parents is the ensuing conferences that the teacher holds with parents. Often the success of such conferences will hinge upon how well the school has been able to break the stereotype that such conferences are held only when a child has misbehaved or has made a low grade. Helpful guidelines to such conferences are given in the following list.[7]

1. Establish a friendly atmosphere free from interruptions.
2. Be positive—begin and end the conference by enumerating favorable points.
3. Be truthful, yet tactful.
4. Be constructive in all suggestions to pupils and parents.
5. Help parents to achieve better understanding of their child as an individual.
6. Respect parents' and children's information as confidential.
7. Remain poised throughout the conference.
8. Be a good listener; let parents talk.
9. Observe professional ethics at all times.
10. Help parents find their own solutions to a problem.
11. Keep vocabulary simple; explain new terminology.
12. If you take notes during the conference, review them with parents.
13. Invite parents to visit and participate in school functions.

---

[7] Louis Romano, "The Parent-Teacher Conference," *National Education Association Journal*, Vol. 48, December, 1959, pp. 21–22.

14. Base your judgments on all available facts and on actual situations.
15. Offer more than one possible solution to a problem.

## PITFALLS IN MARKING AND REPORTING

A major reason why improvement in marking and reporting systems is difficult is because of the hold which tradition has upon teachers, pupils, and parents. While many teachers feel that they would like to have improved marking and reporting systems, they maintain, sometimes with justification, that it is extremely difficult to change because parents and other teachers are not in sympathy with any type of change.

The hold of tradition is further illustrated by the attitude on the part of many parents, and even teachers, that there is some magic in terms of passing or failing, or about a score of 70 or 80 per cent right on a test. Those suffering under such a delusion certainly have not clearly analyzed the fact that a teacher can make a test on which no pupil will make more than 70 per cent correct. And the same teacher can make another test for the same group of learners in which all students will make more than 70 per cent correct on the particular test. The idea of a fixed yardstick or absolute measure for marking purposes disregards the essential fact that marks always depend to a high degree upon subjective factors such as the types of questions which the teacher constructs, the areas covered by the questions, the difficulty of the questions, and the directions given to learners prior to and while taking the test. These are but a few of the subjective factors which influence the eventual numerical score which the pupil gets.

Marks frequently are not adjusted to individual differences in needs, abilities, and goals. Sometimes the teacher's goals and standards are based largely upon his own experience in school. A high school instructor, for example, may base the standard of achievement he expects in a particular class upon what he himself could do without too much difficulty when in high school. Such a point of view was expressed by one teacher who said: "Well, I didn't have any trouble doing that in high school. I didn't have to work overly hard. It's plain that 60 or 70 per cent of my students are just plain lazy. If they would get down to work and really tackle these problems, they would not have difficulty. Consequently, I am justified in giving them failing marks." Since most teachers were undoubtedly superior pupils when in school and differed in many other important respects from many of the pupils they teach, the practice just described is clearly most unrealistic.

The unreliability of teachers' marks on examinations is well known. In classic experiments conducted by Starch and Elliott, two final examination papers for ninth-grade English were graded independently by 142 English teachers. On the first paper marks ranged from 64 to 98 with a total of nine grades above 95 and five grades below 75. On the second paper there were eight marks above 90 and fourteen marks below 70. The range on the

second paper was from 98 down to 50. Using a somewhat similar approach, grades on a final examination paper in geometry marked by 114 mathematics teachers ranged from a high of 92 to a low of 28. The latter is particularly significant in view of the fact that one might expect that papers in mathematics could be marked with precision. Marks on a history examination treated in a similar fashion and scored by seventy history teachers ranged from 43 to 90.[8] More recent experiments on marking have tended to support the conclusion that teachers' grades are extremely unreliable.[9]

It must be recognized that the great emphasis upon marks has focused attention upon extrinsic values in which pupils are much more concerned about labels [10] put upon learning rather than upon the real values of the course. Thus, one of the pressing problems educators face in attempting to study marking and reporting systems is how to swing the attention of the learner away from the symbols represented by marks and toward the intrinsic values and achievements which can be obtained from his schooling.

Finally, a major criticism that can be directed toward present marking and reporting systems is that they result in a large number of emotional upsets on the part of pupils. According to research studies [11] fear does not seem to be a particularly desirable motivating device and yet in too many school systems the student is plagued continually with failure or the fear of failure. This excessive strain militates against educational effectiveness. The emotional atmosphere which surrounds examinations, marks, and reporting has tended to upset many students and make them nervous. If the emotional tension thus induced led to improved learning, it might be justified. But the evidence seems to be that anxiety is likely to produce just the opposite results. Pupils are encouraged to try to get by, to see if they can fool the teacher, and to worry over past experiences in connection with marks rather than to plan intelligently for future improvement in learning and evaluative activities. If marks produce many emotional disturbances, and the evidence seems to be that they do, then it would appear that attention should be given by teachers, administrators, and students to ways of eliminating these undesirable concomitants which sometimes accompany marking and reporting.

---

[8] D. Starch, *Educational Psychology*, New York, The Macmillan Company, 1924, Chap. 22.

[9] P. Hartog and E. C. Rhodes, *An Examination of Examinations*, London, Macmillan and Company, Limited, 1935; A. E. Traxler, "Note on the Accuracy of Teachers' Scoring on Semi-Objective Tests," *Journal of Educational Research*, Vol. 37, 1943, pp. 212–213.

[10] Such as marks, awards, stars, ribbons, and honor lists.

[11] For example, see R. R. Sears, "Initiation of the Repression Sequence by Experienced Failure," *Journal of Experimental Psychology*, Vol. 20, 1937, pp. 570–580. Also see G. T. Korwitz and C. M. Armstrong, "The Effect of Promotion Policy on Academic Achievement," *Elementary School Journal*, 1961, pp. 435–443.

## IMPROVING MARKING AND
## REPORTING PRACTICES

Marking and reporting are integral parts of the total instructional process. They not only reflect what teachers consider important but also direct the activities of students. More specifically, school and course purposes tend to be reflected in the type of marking and reporting practices which are used. Such practices also are likely to reflect the amount of attention or lack of attention given to individual differences. The clarity with which the instructor has thought through his goals in a particular course is likely to be shown by the report or record of progress. For example, if a report card only contains spaces for letter grades in academic subjects this would appear to indicate that the school's objectives are very limited in scope. On the other hand, if space is provided for evaluating such behaviors as critical thinking, social adjustment, and study habits, it is evident that the school is concerned with a much broader set of objectives.

In the past too much attention has been given to grades and report cards as instruments for looking at the present status of the pupil rather than as ways of influencing his behavior in the future. Suppose a superior pupil gets A grades without very much work. Another student gets D's or F's after hard work. The first youngster soon acquires the idea that he can get good marks without work. The second child is likely to develop an attitude of defeatism, that even with hard work it is impossible for him to get recognition. Obviously neither situation is desirable. Whatever marks are used or grades given, they should serve to encourage the child to work better in the future rather than to discourage him and force him into repeated failure.

### An Example of a Secondary School's Reporting Forms

Attention should be given to such factors as the student's capacity to learn, his attitudes, his purposes, his readiness for a particular kind of activity, and his probable needs in connection with the area being studied. A number of marking difficulties would be resolved if both teaching and marking took account of individual differences. An illustration of a science course report which presents some individual diagnostic information to youngsters and to their parents is shown in Figure 52.

In University High School, University of Illinois, where the form in Figure 52 was developed, teachers, students, and parents have persistently worked to improve the reporting system. The present form represents one stage in the evolution of the report and it is expected that subsequent modifications will take place as changing perspectives and needs indicate improvements are necessary.

The form, used with pink and green carbon copies, is the same for all

| | |
|---|---|
| PROGRESS REPORT            SCIENCE<br>University of Illinois High School<br>Urbana, Illinois<br><br>Science I    Biology    Chemistry    Physics    Advanced Problems<br><br>  ____ 1st quarter–November      ____ 3rd quarter–April<br>  ____ Semester–February         ____ Final Report–June | |

RATING SCALE:   + Outstanding   S Satisfactory   U Unsatisfactory   O Inadequate basis for judgment.

         S   U   O      Respects rights, opinions and abilities of others
         S   U   O      Accepts responsibility for group's progress
         S   U   O      Is careful with property
         S   U   O      Uses time to advantage
         S   U   O      Is attentive
         S   U   O      Follows directions
         S   U   O      Makes regular preparations as required

    +   S   U   O      Evidences independent thought and originality
    +   S   U   O      Seeks more than superficial knowledge
    +   S   U   O      Shows ability to define problem areas and locate sources of information
\*   +   S   U   O      Makes accurate and selective interpretation of data
    +   S   U   O      Shows increasing self-direction
    +   S   U   O      Displays mastery of factual information

| ACHIEVEMENT | EFFORT |
|---|---|
| The grade below is a measure of achievement with respect to what is expected of a pupil of this class in this school, and in relation to what is expected in the next higher course in this subject. | The grade below is an estimate, based on evidence available to the teacher, of the individual student's effort. |
| ____ 5 excellent    ____ 2 passing, but weak | ____ 5 excellent      ____ 2 weak |
| ____ 4 very good    ____ 1 failing | ____ 4 very good     ____ 1 very weak |
| ____ 3 creditable    ____ 0 inadequate basis<br>                         for judgment | ____ 3 creditable     ____ 0 inadequate basis<br>                         for judgment |

COMMENTS:



    \*This section of report for science only.
    See Figure 53 for other subjects.         Teacher: _____

**Figure 52.** Example of a Progress Report in Science.

school subjects except for the part to the right of the bracket and, of course, the name of the subject. Characteristics rated in four other subjects are shown in Figure 53.

The list for each subject represents not only criteria on which students are rated, but it also suggests the goals and objectives which teachers, students, and parents believe are of major importance in the subject. Thus, the report form serves a double purpose, to show significant goals in a subject and to help a student understand his strengths and weaknesses, thereby providing a springboard for new learnings.

The University of Illinois High School staff believes non-course activi-

ties have a significant place in a school which serves students from the seventh through the twelfth grades. Some of the educational goals of such activities are suggested in Figure 54. Ratings on the form shown there also provide a picture of areas where growth is needed.

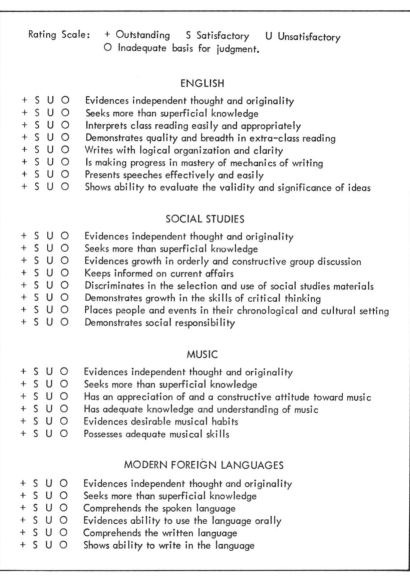

Rating Scale:   + Outstanding   S Satisfactory   U Unsatisfactory
                O Inadequate basis for judgment.

ENGLISH

+ S U O   Evidences independent thought and originality
+ S U O   Seeks more than superficial knowledge
+ S U O   Interprets class reading easily and appropriately
+ S U O   Demonstrates quality and breadth in extra-class reading
+ S U O   Writes with logical organization and clarity
+ S U O   Is making progress in mastery of mechanics of writing
+ S U O   Presents speeches effectively and easily
+ S U O   Shows ability to evaluate the validity and significance of ideas

SOCIAL STUDIES

+ S U O   Evidences independent thought and originality
+ S U O   Seeks more than superficial knowledge
+ S U O   Evidences growth in orderly and constructive group discussion
+ S U O   Keeps informed on current affairs
+ S U O   Discriminates in the selection and use of social studies materials
+ S U O   Demonstrates growth in the skills of critical thinking
+ S U O   Places people and events in their chronological and cultural setting
+ S U O   Demonstrates social responsibility

MUSIC

+ S U O   Evidences independent thought and originality
+ S U O   Seeks more than superficial knowledge
+ S U O   Has an appreciation of and a constructive attitude toward music
+ S U O   Has adequate knowledge and understanding of music
+ S U O   Evidences desirable musical habits
+ S U O   Possesses adequate musical skills

MODERN FOREIGN LANGUAGES

+ S U O   Evidences independent thought and originality
+ S U O   Seeks more than superficial knowledge
+ S U O   Comprehends the spoken language
+ S U O   Evidences ability to use the language orally
+ S U O   Comprehends the written language
+ S U O   Shows ability to write in the language

**Figure 53.** Special Rating Criteria Used on Report Form for Indicated Subjects. (These, for each subject, are in addition to the nonbracketed parts in Figure 52.)

```
ACTIVITY EVALUATION
University of Illinois High School
Urbana, Illinois

Activity_____

Office held_____          Date_____
```

| Rating scale: | + Outstanding | S Satisfactory | U Unsatisfactory | NA Not applicable |
|---|---|---|---|---|

| Student rating: | (Use of student self rating is optional for the Sponser) | Sponsor rating: |
|---|---|---|
| + S U NA | Makes wise use of time when self-directed. | + S U NA |
| + S U NA | Shows independence and orginality in thought and action. | + S U NA |
| + S U NA | Contributes to success of group. | + S U NA |
| + S U NA | Respects rights, opinions and abilities of others. | + S U NA |
| + S U NA | Makes persistent effort to attain a goal. | + S U NA |
| + S U NA | Performs routine obligations. | + S U NA |

Comments:



Sponsor _____

**Figure 54.** An Activity Report Form.

### Enlisting Support of Pupils and Parents

Descriptive marking and reporting help the student see the intrinsic values of the material being learned. When marking and reporting systems become more diagnostic they also tend to emphasize meaningful situations and goals for the individual pupil. Increasingly, diagnostic descriptions in marking and reporting are likely to decrease the emphasis upon grades *per se* and increase the emphasis upon learning for intrinsic values and for the improvement and self-satisfaction that can be attained through study.

Real improvement in a school's marking and reporting program requires that teachers join efforts to study the program intensively. For example, if teachers decide that more attention should be given to pupils' social development, a study should be made of the behavioral characteristics which indicate desirable or undesirable social development. Next, pupils and teachers should work together in determining specific goals in this area.

Plans can then be made for teachers and pupils to report progress toward the achievement of these goals.

One of the major sources of help in improving marking and reporting practices, which has been relatively little utilized in most schools, is the enlistment of the help of pupils. Youngsters can cooperate not only in helping to set up goals but can also assist in measuring and reporting progress toward these goals. Pupils can be helped to see how the achievement of the goals will help them individually, and they can also be aided in setting up check lists and other types of measurements for determining the extent to which their own goals are being achieved. Such practice helps the learner to appreciate what is being attempted in the school and in the particular class. It also teaches him to do the types of things that he needs to know how to do if he is to continue systematic learning after school is over.

Such self-progress reports also give tangible bases for reviewing and evaluating what has been done in past school activities, and such evaluation can form a basis for a realistic planning of future activities upon the part of both the student and the learning groups of which individual students are a part. If teachers try to monopolize reporting and evaluative activities, it is doubtful whether major improvements can be made in marking and reporting systems. On the other hand, if teachers are willing to work with the students and train them in diagnosing their own needs, in keeping a record of progress that they have made toward these goals, and in planning future work on the basis of descriptions of what has been done in the past, then we can be optimistic about the amount of improvement which can be expected in current marking and reporting systems.[12]

As indicated before, the "report card" can be improved if a space is given for parents' comments. If such has not been done before in a community, it would be desirable to educate parents as to uses that might be made of such a space. One way of doing this is through mass guidance sessions with parents. In these sessions teachers can indicate to parents types of comments which would facilitate the work of teachers in helping their children. Another way to encourage such parent comment is to have on the report card specific questions which each parent may be asked to answer. Short answers to such questions can lead into more extensive comments on the part of parents and gradually develop into a two-way communication system.

Schools need to educate the public about school and course purposes and how particular marking and reporting systems are designed to help the individual child. Obviously each parent is interested in the welfare of his own child. If he can be shown how a particular system will help his child, he should be in a better frame of mind to reveal his reactions and to co-

---

[12] For example, see W. Wallace, J. Chreitzberg, V. M. Sims, *The Story of Holtville*, Deatsville, Alabama, Holtville High School, 1946, pp. 63–65, 74–83.

operate with the school. If the mark is designed to indicate progress of the individual child in relation to his ability, then both parent and learner should be conscious of this and not misinterpret the mark. Unless such steps are taken many parents are likely to think that the mark represents the standing of the learner in relation to other learners in his class. If the latter mistake occurs, then the report on a relatively slow learner who does well in terms of his ability may give his parents the impression that he has the ability to become a doctor or to enter some other professional occupation. Actually the mark may simply indicate that this learner is doing well in terms of what seems to be his potential ability. To mark in relation to ability seems to be desirable from many standpoints, but it may have undesirable repercussions if both parents and the learner himself are not clear as to what purpose the mark is designed to serve. In some reports both status and progress in relation to ability are shown on the report. Status marks, indicative of educational achievements and sometimes based largely upon standardized tests, can be extremely valuable when parents and teachers are trying to help the pupil decide what his future educational plans will be.

Rapid changes in reporting practices can be made if appropriate public education is carried on before, during, and subsequent to the changes. For example, in one school system [13] teachers and administrators decided that trying out a new card in only one grade at first and using it in an additional grade each year would only give the opponents of change more ammunition to block progress. School leaders reasoned that in many homes both the new and the old cards would be arriving simultaneously and this, it was believed, would make public acceptance of the revised reports more difficult. Acceptance of the new reporting system was promoted through the school board, PTA meetings, parent-teacher conferences, and bulletins answering parents' questions. The emphasis in the discussions was on ways in which the new reporting system helped parent and child more than the old.

### An Illustration of a Dual Reporting System

A large number of school faculties have decided that one school mark to show both (1) level of achievement reached, and (2) progress in relation to *individual* ability to achieve is quite unsatisfactory. Hence, these faculties are experimenting with *two* marks for each pupil in each subject: one indicating the pupil's achievement against the achievements of other pupils, the other representing the pupil's achievement as measured against his ability to achieve. Such an approach gives encouragement to real effort regardless of potential, but also helps the student and his parents see his level of achievement in proper perspective.

---

[13] Walter Crewson, "Boldness Sells Hamilton's New-Type Report Card," *The Clearing House*, Vol. 26, November, 1951, pp. 146–148.

NAME_____Grade_____

A number rating is given for each main subject, each habit, and each special area. This number shows your child's progress in relation to his ability. An X indicates the need for improvement in the particular skill so marked.

Code:
I — outstanding
2 — doing well
3 — satisfactory
4 — unsatisfactory

| | First Report | Second Report | Third Report | Fourth Report |
|---|---|---|---|---|
| **READING** | | | | |
| Reads with understanding | | | | |
| Works out new words | | | | |
| Reads to others | | | | |
| Reads independently for enjoyment | | | | |
| **LANGUAGE (Writing, Speaking, Listening)** | | | | |
| Listens thoughtfully | | | | |
| Speaks clearly and distinctly | | | | |
| Expresses ideas orally | | | | |
| Expresses ideas in writing | | | | |
| Uses correct English | | | | |
| **SPELLING** | | | | |
| Learns words in spelling lessons | | | | |
| Spells correctly in written work | | | | |
| **HANDWRITING** | | | | |
| Forms letters correctly | | | | |
| Writes legibly with ease | | | | |
| **ARITHMETIC** | | | | |
| Knows number facts and processes (addition, subtraction, multiplication, division) | | | | |
| Shows growth in solving problems | | | | |
| Is accurate in work | | | | |
| **SOCIAL STUDIES, SCIENCE, HEALTH, SAFETY** | | | | |
| Is gaining in knowledge and understanding of our historical heritage and geographic resources | | | | |
| Is learning the responsibilities of citizens in a democracy | | | | |
| Is growing in knowledge of scientific facts and methods | | | | |
| Is growing in use of study materials such as books, maps, diagrams | | | | |
| Is learning to follow good health practices | | | | |
| Is learning to follow good safety practices | | | | |

**Figure 55.** An Example of a Dual Reporting System. It emphasizes: (1) progress in relation to individual ability, and (2) progress in relation to other children.

|  | First Report | Second Report | Third Report | Fourth Report |
|---|---|---|---|---|

## SPECIAL AREAS

MUSIC (interest and participation)................................
ART (interest and creative participation)..........................
PHYSICAL EDUCATION (knowledge and skills)..................

## HABITS

Respects the rights and property of others.....................
Accepts and profits from suggestions...........................
Takes effective part in class and school activities.............
Takes his share of responsibilities..............................
Cooperates in school regulations...............................
Makes good use of time and materials..........................
Shows initiative ..............................................
Does neat and careful work.....................................
Follows directions .............................................

| **ATTENDANCE** | First Report | Second Report | Third Report | Fourth Report |
|---|---|---|---|---|
| Times Late |  |  |  |  |
| Days Absent |  |  |  |  |

A check (√) shows your child's progress in relation to other children in the grade.

|  | First Report | | | Second Report | | | Third Report | | | Fourth Report | | |
|---|---|---|---|---|---|---|---|---|---|---|---|---|
|  | Above Average | Average | Below Average | Above Average | Average | Below Average | Above Average | Average | Below Average | Above Average | Average | Below Average |
| Reading |  |  |  |  |  |  |  |  |  |  |  |  |
| Arithmetic |  |  |  |  |  |  |  |  |  |  |  |  |
| Language |  |  |  |  |  |  |  |  |  |  |  |  |

(Reproduced with the permission of the Department of Education, Baltimore, Maryland.)

A useful example of the trend toward a dual reporting system is that now used in the Baltimore Public Elementary Schools. Two pages of the reporting form are shown in Figure 55. On a third sheet and on the back of the second page are spaces for "COMMENTS OF TEACHER" and "SIGNATURE AND COMMENTS OF PARENT." Note that the main part of the report is designed to help the pupil see areas of strength and weakness so that he will know points for improvement. The emphasis in the first three-fourths of the card is on "your child's progress in relation to his ability." The last section of the card gives the pupil a picture of his actual achievement level. This latter perspective is particularly important for later educational and vocational guidance.

### Criteria for Evaluating a Marking and Reporting System

When individual instructors or teacher committees wish to study and improve a marking and reporting system, a set of evaluative criteria is sometimes a helpful starting device. An illustrative set of criteria for doing this has been drawn up by the writer.

1. Does the system clearly reflect the specific educational objectives of teachers and learners?
2. Does the current system represent an improvement over the one(s) used in the last few years?
3. Have both students and parents helped to formulate the present system?
4. Is the reporting procedure a two-way communication system (school to home, home to school)?
5. Does the system put emphasis upon areas for future development of the student rather than on errors of the past?
6. Is sufficient working time given teachers for adequate marking or reporting in the system currently being used?
7. Is the behavior of learners desirably affected by the system?
8. Does the marking and reporting system put sufficient emphasis on social and emotional development?
9. Are the specific purposes which the system is designed to serve clearly understood by those affected (i.e., pupils, parents) by the marking and reporting?
10. Does the system give sufficient attention to *ways* the student is learning as well as to what he has learned?
11. Does the system encourage thinking rather than memorization?
12. Are the marks and reports sufficiently diagnostic in nature?
13. Are the differences among individual students in purposes, abilities, and needs adequately handled by the system?
14. Does the marking and reporting system tend to encourage learners to overcome weaknesses rather than discourage added effort?

15. When weaknesses of the learner are stated, are they accompanied by suggested ways of improving?
16. Does the system help the student plan for future vocational activities?
17. Does the system promote self-evaluation on the part of the student?
18. Does the marking and reporting system promote desirable public relations?

## FACTORS OF IMPORTANCE IN PUPIL PLACEMENT

As a general policy it is well to keep in mind that what is commonly called promotion should be thought of as placement rather than as reward. Before judgments are made regarding placement such questions as the following should be raised: What promotion decision is likely to be best for the individual student, taking into account all significant factors in the situation? With what placement is the student likely to learn most profitably in the next year? How is this placement likely to affect other pupils? How are teachers likely to react to a particular placement? What will be the probable reaction of parents?

The child's attitude toward retention, promotion, or double promotion is of utmost importance. The possibility, of course, should be kept in mind that the child's attitude can be changed. If steps are taken sufficiently early the child will sometimes see that being retained is actually the best thing for him, and he may accept this as being quite desirable. On the other hand, if pupils have been trained to think of lack of promotion as a stigma, it is difficult to use this placement policy without modifying their attitudes. When it appears desirable to retain a pupil, groundwork for retention must be laid through conferences with him. Too great attention cannot be given to the morale of the learner. "Nothing fails like failure," and certainly if the child believes that his placement is an indication of failure he is not in a very good mental state to carry on learning activities profitably in a subsequent year.

Although the effect of each of the various alternatives in connection with promotion upon the individual learner is unquestionably of primary importance, attention must always be given to the likely effect of the placement of a particular learner upon other students. If pupils have been taught that the youngsters in a particular class should reach the same standards regardless of ability, they may feel that promotion of a particular child is a compromise with the "standards" of the school. If the school seriously attempts to base promotion policies upon good placement practices for learning purposes, then pupils must be helped to understand this policy.

The probable effect of promotion, retention, or acceleration upon each teacher with whom the pupil might be placed also demands serious consideration. This must be done because the new teacher can "make or break"

the child. If an instructor is likely to be irritated or to react adversely to the placement of the learner, then the latter is placed in an extremely difficult position and successful learning is not likely to ensue.

In considering placement alternatives this question must be faced: If a below-average child is promoted does the prospective teacher's method provide for individual differences? If a sixth-grade teacher, for example, expects all learners to read the same text regardless of the fact that reading ability is likely to range from average second-grade level to average tenth-grade level, a sound placement policy for the fifth-grade English teacher becomes very difficult. On the other hand, the problem becomes easier if the fifth-grade teacher knows that the sixth-grade teacher not only recognizes individual differences but is able to a considerable degree to meet these in such activities as assignment making, standard setting, testing, and use of resources. Similar considerations need to be kept in mind when a given child is retained for two years in one grade. A realistic promotion policy must always take into account the fact that there are great variations among teachers in their ability to operate classes in terms of individual differences.

How is "passing" a course or grade likely to be interpreted by administrative officials? Will they conclude that passing a particular course or grade implies achievement of a particular standard? The attitudes of administrative officials and department heads are of significance in deciding on promotion or retention of a particular learner.

What are likely to be parental attitudes toward promotional practices in general? What are likely to be particular parents' reactions toward the promotion or retention of their child? These are types of questions which finally need to be considered. It should be kept in mind of course that parental attitude toward promotion and toward the possible stigma of non-promotion can be definitely altered if the school starts soon enough to develop, and does develop, a desirable type of communication with parents. Obviously parents are primarily concerned about the welfare and growth of their children and can usually be helped to see and approve of an appropriate placement policy if parental education on this point starts when Johnny enters school.

Extensive research on the problems of retention leads one to conclude that

repetition of grades has no special educational value for children; in fact, the educational gain of the majority of non-promoted students subsequent to their non-promotion is smaller than that of their matched age mates who were promoted. Similarly, the threat of failure has no appreciable positive effect on the educational gain of those threatened. The personal and social adjustment of regularly promoted students is better than that of students who have experienced non-promotion, and the average level of student achievement tends to be higher in school systems with high promotion rates.

A high rate of non-promotion does not decrease the variability of student achievement and thus does not free the teacher from the important task of adapting instruction to individual differences.[14]

In facing some of the problems discussed in the preceding paragraphs some school systems have established non-graded schools for certain age groups. In such schools, for example, there is no first, second, or third grade and a particular youngster may stay on the primary level as long as seems wise, possibly two, three, or four years. An intensive effort is made to provide a program which will encourage continuous progress for each child, a program geared to his capacities, background, and growth rate with standards appropriate to him as an individual.[15]

In conclusion it should be stated that there is no easy answer to the question of whether a pupil should be retained, promoted, or accelerated. Each individual case must be handled on its own merits. All relevant factors should be considered, and then an attempt should be made to place the learner where he is likely to get the most out of his schooling. The important consideration is not promotion or non-promotion as such, but rather what is done with individual pupils in the classes where they find themselves.

## SUMMARY

There is a great deal of confusion about the aims and values of various marking and reporting practices. Much of the confusion stems from a failure to realize that marks and reports can serve various groups such as children, parents, and teachers in different ways. The values one group may hope to secure from marks and reports may conflict with those desired by another group. Hence clarity of purpose in using these evaluative devices in particular situations is a consideration of utmost importance.

Marks may militate against desirable educational activities if used for unsound purposes. For example, when marks and reports are used to punish a child for misbehavior, to make the life of an harassed teacher easier, and to help teacher and pupil escape from serious consideration of the intrinsic values of courses, they are likely to be harmful. On the other hand, if grading and reporting procedures are used to orient future work, to give young-

---

[14] H. J. Otto and D. M. Estes, "Accelerated and Retarded Progress" in *Encyclopedia of Educational Research*, Third Edition, New York, The Macmillan Company, 1960, p. 8. Also see "Elementary School Nonpromotion and Individual Potential," whole issue of *Theory into Practice*, Vol. 4, 1965, pp. 85–128.

[15] See F. R. Dufay, *Ungrading the Elementary School*, West Nyack, New York, Parker Publishing Company, 1966. Also see B. F. Brown, *The Appropriate Placement School: A Sophisticated Nongraded Curriculum*, West Nyack, New York, Parker Publishing Company, 1965.

sters practice in evaluating and expressing themselves, to establish two-way communication with parents, to individualize goals and procedures, and to focus attention on significant intrinsic values of courses, they can be extremely valuable.

Placement policies should be designed to place the pupil in the class or grade that will be best for him rather than to punish or reward him for past activities. In deciding on placement for a particular pupil the emphasis should be upon looking forward rather than backward.

### References for Further Study

Ahmann, J. S. and Glock, M. D., *Evaluating Pupil Growth*, Boston, Allyn and Bacon, Inc., 2nd edition, 1963, Chapter 17.

Dimond, S. E. and others, "Promotion Policies in Our Schools, A Symposium," *National Education Association Journal*, Vol. 49, April 1960, pp. 15–23.

Goodlad, J. I., "Some Effects of Promotion and Nonpromotion upon the Social and Personal Adjustment of Children," *Journal of Experimental Education*, Vol. 22, 1954, pp. 301–328.

Goodlad, J. I. and Anderson, R. H., *The Nongraded Elementary School*, revised edition, New York, Harcourt, Brace, 1963.

Gronlund, N. E., *Measurement and Evaluation in Teaching*, New York, The Macmillan Company, 1965.

Harris, C. W. (Editor), *Encyclopedia of Educational Research*, Third edition New York, The Macmillan Company, 1960. See the following articles: Accelerated and Retarded Progress, pp. 4–11; Examinations, pp. 857–858, 1502–1514; Marks and Marking Systems, pp. 783–788; Nongraded School, pp. 222–223; Objective Type Tests, pp. 1506–1508; Promotion of Students, pp. 8, 428, 423–439, 1250; Report Cards, pp. 1253, 1439–1440; Retention, pp. 1269–1270, 1277–1279.

Henry, N. B. (Editor), *Individualizing Instruction*, Chicago, The University of Chicago Press, 1962.

Lindeman, Richard H. *Educational Measurement*, Glenview, Illinois, Scott, Foresman and Company, 1967, Chapter 6.

Loomis, M. J. (Editor), "Elementary School Nonpromotion and Individual Potential," *Theory into Practice*, Vol. 4, 1965, pp. 85–128. (Includes 45-item bibliography.)

Noll, V. H., *Introduction to Educational Measurement*, Boston, Houghton Mifflin Co., 2nd edition, 1965.

Nunnally, J. C., *Educational Measurement and Evaluation*, New York, McGraw-Hill Book Company, 1964.

Remmers, H. H., Gage, N. L. and Rummel, J. Frances, A *Practical Introduction to Measurement and Evaluation*, New York, Harper and Brothers, 2nd edition, 1965.

Ross, C. C. and Stanley, J. C., *Measurement in Today's Schools*, New York, Prentice-Hall, Inc., 1954, Chapters 13 and 16.

Rothney, J. W. M., *Evaluating and Reporting Pupil Progress, What Research*

*Says to the Teacher*, Washington, D.C., National Education Association, 1955.

Seidman, J. M., *Readings in Educational Psychology*, Boston, Houghton Mifflin Company, 1965, Chapter 12, "Marking, Reporting, and Pupil Placement."

Shores, J. H., "What Does Research Say About Ability Grouping?" *Illinois Education*, Vol. 27, 1964, pp. 169–172.

Strang, Ruth, *Reporting to Parents*, New York, Teachers College, Columbia University, 1958.

Traxler, A. E., *Techniques of Guidance*, New York, Harper and Brothers, 1957, pp. 233–265.

Wrinkle, W. L., *Improving Marking and Reporting Practices in Elementary and Secondary Schools*, New York, Rinehart and Company, Inc., 1947.

The reader is also encouraged to use the following headings in the *Education Index*:

| | |
|---|---|
| Acceleration | Promotions |
| Failures | Report cards |
| Marking systems | Reports and records |
| Marks, students | Reports to parents |

## Questions, Exercises, and Activities

1. Visit schools in and near your home community. From the principal or other administrative officer request a copy of the reporting forms used in each school system. Study a sampling of these forms and those collected by your classmates and try to answer these questions about each form.
   (a) What are its strong and questionable points in view of what you have learned in this chapter?
   (b) How does it compare with the University of Illinois High School forms and with the Baltimore Public Elementary School forms shown in this chapter?
2. A few systems have set up "Non-graded Schools." (For examples see J. I. Goodlad and R. H. Anderson, the *Nongraded Elementary School*, New York, Harcourt, Brace, 1959.)
   (a) List possible advanatges for challenging learners of varying abilities, attainments, and interests which you see for this organizational approach.
   (b) List potential disadvantages, dangers, or limitations.
3. What difficulties would you visualize for a school system which *only* shows a pupil how he is achieving in relation to other students in the same school? What problems would face a school that *only* reports to a pupil how well he is progressing in relation to his ability to learn?
4. After examining a number of reporting forms formulate one yourself which you think incorporates the best features of those which you have studied. (Use forms you and your classmates have collected. Also gather ideas from "References for Further Study" and the *Education Index*.)
5. Assume that you are a teacher and that near the end of a unit you gave a

four-answer multiple choice test consisting of one-hundred items. The table below indicates the scores, in grouped form, received by the pupils:

| SCORE | NUMBER | SCORE | NUMBER |
|-------|--------|-------|--------|
| 80–89 | 2      | 40–49 | 12     |
| 70–79 | 5      | 30–39 | 10     |
| 60–69 | 15     | 20–29 | 3      |
| 50–59 | 20     |       |        |

Discuss the following questions and defend your answers:

(a) Does this test tell you anything about your teaching success?

(b) What does it tell you about the pupils in the class?

(c) What marks would you give the pupils? Tell how many should receive each mark.

# Chapter 20

# Appraising
# the Work
# of the School

The ultimate criterion of the effectiveness of schooling is not to be found in test papers, rating scales, or the teacher's grade book, but must be sought in the school's broader contributions to the community at large. No problem which educators face is more difficult than that of appraising the effectiveness of various educational procedures. Opinion and belief, based upon tradition alone, are poor substitutes for experimental evidence and systematic appraisal; yet much of what is done in today's schools finds no other justification. The world struggle and criticisms of current education challenge teachers to reappraise what they are doing.

Far too little experimentation and study have been devoted to the validation of educational procedures, but a number of technics, which have been used to appraise certain aspects of the school's work, do offer some valuable leads for immediate action and for further study. Such experimentation and study have given firm support to the break with many traditional teaching methods. It is hoped that the reader will find, in the studies and examples which follow, enough evidence so that he will be able to appraise more critically not only his own teaching, but also the broader school policies which he does or should help to formulate.

In the balance of this chapter there will be presented some of the technics teachers may use in gathering useful data for appraisal, some of the

ways in which educators and psychologists have attempted to appraise the schools, and finally some of the difficulties in making such appraisals.

## EVALUATING THE EFFECT OF TEACHING ON OUT-OF-SCHOOL BEHAVIOR

Some instructors are almost exclusively concerned with in-school behaviors, particularly those demonstrated by writing on a piece of paper in response to questions formulated by a teacher. The importance of such responses is not questioned. However, many educators are becoming increasingly concerned with the improvement of out-of-school behaviors. Such concern has resulted in the development of evaluative techniques for estimating the extent to which goals related to out-of-school behaviors are being achieved.

One of the major difficulties in developing evaluative devices related to these goals is the commonly accepted way of describing course purposes. Unfortunately such expressions in statements of objectives as "understanding of . . . ," "appreciation of . . . ," "recognition of . . . ," and "considerable familiarity with . . ." when only couched in vague and general terms, do not encourage teachers to objectify their goals by stating them in behavioral terms. Since teachers should be concerned with what their students do after school, on weekends, in the summer, and after they permanently leave school, it is vital that the specific behaviors to be produced or improved be clearly identified. In addition to the identification of the behaviors, procedures are needed for continuous checking in the community on the extent to which desirable behaviors are actually being demonstrated.

The issue may be clarified through the description of one part of the experience of an agricultural education teacher who became concerned with the "carry-over" effectiveness of his teaching. He set up a comprehensive list of the out-of-school behaviors he had been trying to develop in his students. Then, with some of his current students, he visited the farms of all of the last year's high school seniors who had taken his courses, and a check was made on the extent to which they were practicing what he thought (or hoped) they had learned. Some of the results were encouraging. Others were both disappointing and at the same time challenging. For example, one of his goals had been to teach the boys to build guard rails around the farrowing pens to protect new-born pigs from being crushed when the sow lies down.[1] An actual check of the pens on farms of recent high school graduates who had taken vocational agriculture showed that only 20 per cent of pens had the guard rails. Interviews further revealed that even these rails apparently had been put up because of the influence of the county farm agent, not because of school training. The check revealed *no*

---

[1] About 10 per cent of the new-born pigs probably would be killed without such rails.

favorable effect on any graduate in this respect. Needless to say this agriculture teacher changed many of his approaches to teaching agriculture as a result of his use of an out-of-school evaluative device.

Another illustrative study of out-of-school behavior was one in which data on community reading were collected and analyzed.[2] The teachers who carried on this study questioned the assumption that if the child *could* read well when he left school he *would* necessarily read often and well after he left school. These teachers in a midwestern junior high school decided they needed to try to get (1) some check on the extent to which their teaching goals were being achieved in the community, (2) some clarification of their out-of-school reading goals, and (3) some indication of the degree to which home situations are likely to facilitate the achievement of reading goals. With these general objectives in mind a committee of teachers set up a list of fifteen specific goals on which they could initially agree. They also listed forty-one questions to be asked of parents by means of a questionnaire.

How these parents, acting for their families, responded to two of the questions is shown in Table 29. The table shows there was a marked dif-

**TABLE 29**
**Survey of Community Reading**

| Questions | Junior High School | | | | Senior High School |
|---|---|---|---|---|---|
| | A | B | C | D | |
| Subscribe to bulletins telling how to choose best value for your money? | 19% | 39% | 31% | 30% | 10% |
| Average number of plays read per family per month? | 0.5 | 0.7 | 0.3 | 0.7 | 0.7 |

ference between the responses from junior and senior high school families to the question: "Do you subscribe to any magazine, report, or bulletin which emphasizes how to tell the value of any given article, and how to choose the best for your money?" Since reading of this type had been emphasized in the junior and not in the senior high school, it would appear that the specific instruction given was having at least an immediate effect on out-of-school behavior. In this community the teachers were spending considerable time teaching drama in the schools. The results showing play reading behavior (or its lack) in the families caused some of the teachers to reconsider and re-evaluate the effectiveness of their drama teaching. This led to the trying out of revised teaching procedures.

Teachers were found to vary greatly in their ability to get and use mean-

---

[2] Ray H. Simpson and K. L. Camp, "Diagnosing Community Reading," *School Review*, Vol. 61, 1953, pp. 98–100.

ingfully results of this sort. As with most technics the value of such a procedure depends greatly upon the resourcefulness of the teacher using it.
One teacher emphasized and thoroughly explained the purpose of the
questionnaire to the pupils before sending the forms home. This teacher
and class decided that they would study the returns, using the results as one
measuring stick in planning their future literature work. This teacher reported that the amount of zeal and zest which his students showed in
planning new literature units alone made the study well worth the time
and effort.

## APPRAISING COMMUNITY SATISFACTION
## WITH THE SCHOOLS

The degree of satisfaction which pupils, parents, and other community
members have with respect to the school's goals and procedures has a significant bearing on the improvement of teaching-learning situations. In the
long run, as Leonard[3] has pointed out, parents probably get the kind of
school program they really want, including winning teams—if they want
them badly enough. Possibly parents and other community members need
to take a new look at their own attitudes toward learning and intellectual
activities.

That there are indeed regional differences in the perception of the public
school's task has been clearly demonstrated in a study by Downey,[4] who
had several thousand people from different sections of the United States
and Canada rate the importance of such goals of the school as knowledge,
creativity, patriotism, and vocational preparation. Figure 56 gives the
trends of this survey. There it may be seen that the Midwestern United
States assumed what might be called a middle-of-the-road position; the
West leaned toward those goals that had to do with socialization and civic
responsibility; the South seemed to attach greater importance to physical
and moral development; the East to world citizenship; and Canada placed
a high premium upon aesthetic and intellectual goals.

Some of the community attitudes can, of course, be obtained and appraised through informal talks with parents, pupils, and other interested
individuals. However, to depend entirely on such non-systematic technics is
not sufficient. There are now available several types of technics for determining attitudes toward schools which are designed to substitute systematic consumer research for guessing. Unless youngsters and their parents
understand and largely agree with what schools are doing, basic progress in

---

[3] G. B. Leonard, Jr., "Schools Reflect the Public" in C. W. Scott, C. M. Hill, and
W. H. Burns (Editors), *The Great Debate*, Englewood Cliffs, New Jersey, Prentice-
Hall, Inc., 1959.

[4] L. W. Downey, *The Task of Public Education*, Chicago, Midwest Administration
Center, The University of Chicago, 1960.

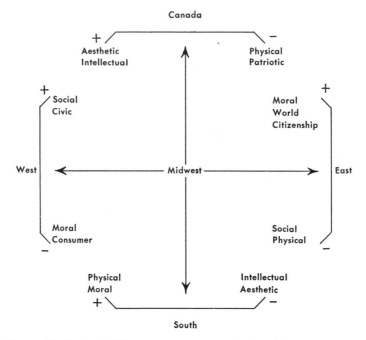

**Figure 56.** Regional Differences in Perception of the Public School's Task.

the improvement of education is extremely difficult if not impossible. A thorough appraisal of existing attitudes reveals not only the degree of dissatisfaction or satisfaction, but also the specific areas in which attitudes have crystallized.

What are some of the dimensions to be investigated in getting evidence of parent satisfaction and dissatisfaction with the schools? Hand,[5] for example, has developed specific questions to investigate parent attitudes toward some twenty-three aspects of the school's work. Illustrative of the areas covered are the following: (1) treatment of children by other youngsters, teachers, and other school officials, (2) discipline, (3) help in resolving personal problems, (4) value of school work, (5) adequacy of the school's offerings, (6) participation in student activities, (7) homework, (8) teaching methods, (9) overcrowded school buildings, (10) most liked feature of the school, (11) most disliked thing about the school, and (12) overall rating of satisfaction or dissatisfaction.

The attitudes of children toward what goes on at school—in the class, on the playground, and in the library—are of major importance. Hand [6] has listed nineteen components of pupils' satisfaction-dissatisfaction. Some of

---

[5] Harold C. Hand, *What People Think About Their Schools*, Yonkers-on-Hudson, New York, World Book Company, 1948, pp. 33–44.

these are: (1) feeling of "belonging," (2) pupil-teacher bond, (3) fair treatment by teachers, (4) attitudes toward discipline, (5) relationship of school work toward real life needs, (6) work requirements in school courses, (7) most liked feature of the school, (8) most disliked feature of the school, and (9) general rating of satisfaction. To measure attitudes toward school, Hand has devised a check list. On this form is also provided space for constructive suggestions.

What are some of the specific questions which may be asked in assessing pupil and parent (and teacher if this is desired) attitudes in such areas as those indicated in the preceding paragraphs? Three illustrations of questions used and data gathered from a senior high school in an Illinois community [7] are given in Table 30.

Many implications may be gathered from these and similar data. For example, they may indicate that more attention should be given to public relations, and perhaps to adult education. They also may suggest some new emphasis which would improve the work of the school. The answers to item 2 in Table 30 imply that more effort should be made to take care of individual differences in needs, abilities, and interests through different amounts and types of assignments for pupils, even for those in the same class. Such

### TABLE 30
#### Some Reactions of Parents, Pupils, and Teachers Toward Their Schools *

1. In general, is the discipline in your school too strict or not strict enough?

|  | Pupils | Parents | Teachers |
|---|---|---|---|
| Too strict | 20% | 5% | 0% |
| About right | 66% | 58% | 34% |
| Too lax | 13% | 27% | 63% |
| No reply | 1% | 10% | 3% |

2. How much are you (or your child, or your pupils) getting out of your (or his, or their) schoolwork?

|  | Pupils | Parents | Teachers |
|---|---|---|---|
| All one could reasonably expect | 74% | 56% | 44% |
| Less than one could reasonably expect | 26% | 41% | 51% |
| No response | 0% | 3% | 5% |

3. How much work do you (or your child, or your pupils) have to do in order to "keep up" in your (or his, or their) studies?

|  | Pupils | Parents | Teachers |
|---|---|---|---|
| Too little | 5% | 9% | 19% |
| About the right amount | 59% | 61% | 74% |
| Too much | 36% | 20% | 1% |
| No response | 1% | 10% | 6% |

* Adapted from Hand, op. cit., pp. 143–147.

---

[6] *Ibid.*, pp. 48–57.
[7] *Ibid.*, pp. 143–147.

data at least give the school a fairly adequate picture of where it stands with parents and pupils.

## COMMUNITY SELF-APPRAISAL PROJECTS

Community school appraisal studies have become widespread since World War II. The basic method in these studies has been described as "the active use of democratic processes in stimulating citizens to examine their communities, to define major community problems, to work out some plan for grappling with at least some of these problems and then actively attempt their solution." [8]

Such projects may appropriately be thought of as adult educational enterprises. In the early stages a check list is sometimes used to get citizens thinking about community needs and to identify some of the problems which they should be cooperatively facing. From a fifty-four item check list five of the items, together with the scales used, and one citizen's responses are shown in Table 31.

### TABLE 31
#### Sample Items From a Citizen Check List with Illustrative Responses *

| Item | Most Serious and Pressing Needs | Needed in Near Future | Desirable but Not Seriously Needed | Probably Not Needed; Pure Luxury | Not Needed at All | Do Not Know | Presently Adequate |
|---|---|---|---|---|---|---|---|
| Public Library | | | | | | X | |
| Handling of Juvenile Delinquency Problem | X | | | | | | |
| Adult Education Services | | | X | | | | |
| Handling of Minority Group Problems | | | | X | | | |
| Counseling Service for Children and Adults | | | X | | | | |

\* Excerpted from W. K. Beggs and D. K. Hayes, *The Nebraska Community Education Project*, Lincoln, Nebraska, Teachers College, University of Nebraska, 1957.

The community that wishes to make a more analytical self-study may find the Metropolitan School Study *Council Report Card* [9] a useful device.

---

[8] Truman M. Pierce, *The Nebraska Education Project—The Expansion Year*, New York, The Carnegie Corporation, 1958.

[9] The Metropolitan School Council, *Council Report Card*, New York, Teachers College, Columbia University, 1958.

The Card provides sixteen measures that are known to be related to educational quality, and includes detailed directions for quantifying such things as community characteristics, financial climate, spending policy, and staff characteristics.

## CASE STUDIES OF CLASSES

Evaluation of class operations may be facilitated if the teacher, with the help of his students, makes a careful record of what happens in a class. The study of such a record of plans and procedures in ongoing class work should not only provide a foundation for additional planning in the immediate class, but can also form a substantial basis for future improvement in teaching and learning.

### Preplanning for Class Case Study

In preparing for a class case study it is desirable for the instructor to lay some initial groundwork. For example, he might very profitably write down the assumptions upon which he will attempt to operate. In doing this, one teacher developed the following guiding principles:

1. Usefulness of knowledge in life situations should be a primary criterion for their selection.
2. Pupils should study those problems which they recognize as being worthy of their efforts. (One important role of the teacher is to try to make student problem identification and selection increasingly wise.)
3. What, for each learner, is an appropriate learning experience should be given primary weight. "Ground to be covered" should be de-emphasized.
4. The development of effective ways of identifying and solving problems is to be expected as a product of method.[10]

This type of approach may, of course, be used cooperatively by a group of teachers or even by the whole school staff. Preplanning not only helps the teacher plan more effectively for the immediate course, but also forms a partial framework for evaluation of the course after it is over. Such evaluation, if persistently employed, will tend to produce improved teaching and learning.

### Keeping a Record of What Happens

In addition to having a record of the plans of both teacher and student, it is desirable to secure a follow-up of what happens in order to evaluate

---

[10] Adapted from E. A. Waters, A Study of the Application of an Educational Theory to Science Instruction, New York, Bureau of Publications, Teachers College, Columbia University, 1942.

how well plans have been carried out. Such records can be kept by the teacher or the student or, preferably, by both.

The teacher's record is probably most useful if kept on a day to day or week to week basis. It should usually contain a record of such things as: the long-time and immediate goals, resources used by teacher and pupils, ways in which class procedures were planned and how these succeeded. Also, suggestions for modifications of goals, plans, procedures, and resources in subsequent classes might be included.

The pupil's record may be similar to that of the teacher but should be geared to the purposes of the youngster who is keeping the record. It may be a daily or weekly summary of plans or activities or it may involve a comprehensive summary of one or more years of work. Inspection of such summaries can help the teacher improve in his work. The following paragraphs are excerpts [11] from one year of a three-year report by a senior in high school:

> This year I did not go to school the first few weeks of the first semester. I worked for the school, operating farm machinery. The work is a help to our community and to other communities. The machinery has been out of the county. The machines the school now has are three tractors, a binder, threshing machine, combine, hay baler, peanut picker, power spray, two distributors, a cutaway harrow, and a flat-bottomed plow. I have worked with them all. This fall we worked at the Dam, Lightwood, Deatsville, Coosa River, Elmore, and Crenshaw. Almost all of these machines made this round. They have even gone as far as Millbrook. We baled about 500 tons of hay this year besides the peanut vines we baled behind the peanut picker. We picked off 82 tons of peanuts. We threshed about 20,000 bushels of oats and wheat. The binder didn't go far from this community, but we cut about 200 acres of wheat and oats.
>
> We have been plowing some for the community, cutting and turning land. We turned the school farm and planted vetch.
>
> With the power spray we sprayed several hundred peach trees in the spring. We spray them for scale, worms, and dry rot. We spray them with oil emulsion mixed with water for scale, arsenate and lime for worms, and sulphur and water for dry rot.
>
> I started to school in November. I made my plans as follows: first block, agricultural mathematics; second block, current history, and English; third block, biology; and fourth block, feed mill.
>
> Our mathematics class has been working on adding, subtracting, and dividing of fractions; dairying; feeds; soil fertility; percentage, and formulas.
>
> Students in our current history group have been discussing the world today, the wars, and the foreign countries. I wrote a report on Nova Scotia and on England at war, which was part of English work. I have also worked on English in a workbook. I have worked on parts of speech and their uses in a sentence, capital letters, and paragraphs. I am now writing more reports on history work. . . .

---

[11] W. Wallace, J. Chreitzberg, and V. M. Sims, *The Story of Holtville*, Deatsville, Alabama, Holtville High School, 1944, pp. 132–135.

The fourth block of time I worked at the feed mill, where we have a feed mixer, a hammer mill, and a grist mill. I have learned to operate these. With the feed mixer we can mix our own chicken feed, which is cheaper than the ready-mixed feed. We crush different kinds of feed such as corn, beans, hay, and peanut vines. We can take a hard feed and crush it into a meal. . . .

I have accomplished more this year by working out with the farm machinery than I would have by being in a classroom, because I take an interest in that kind of work. I can operate all of the machines which the school has. This is a help to the community because these modern machines do not take so much labor. When you do work with these power machines, people can cooperate and help each other. This will save them from hiring labor. These power machines not only take less labor, but they are also faster. You can take a power hay press and bale 250 to 300 bales of hay a day, whereas a mule-drawn press would bale only 100 to 125 bales a day. I did this work to learn and to get experience. It helps me in English, as I have to meet the public and speak correctly. At the feed mill, especially, we have lots of figuring to do in selling feed by the pound, and we meet and deal with lots of people there.

Looking back at my work, I think I did not get as much English as I would have liked. In that and some other things I think I could have done more book work. Working does not give you as much book knowledge as being in classes all day, but it gives you experience. You really should have both.

I feel that my schooling has fitted me for farming and for living a successful and happy life. I am in the draft age now and would have gone to the Army, but because I was needed to farm I was deferred. Farming is the basis of all our war effort. If we did not raise food, everyone would starve. Food is not the only thing that farm products are used for. If all the farms were stopped, everything would stop.

### Drawing Some Conclusions

To reap most benefit from the types of data which have been mentioned, the teacher will want to draw some conclusions after a course is over. These conclusions can form a sound basis for continuous improvement in teaching. One high school English teacher reached the following conclusions:

*Goals.* The formal grammar work does not seem to appreciably affect pupils' speech and writing. A consultant we had at one of our faculty meetings said research has indicated a similar thing. I am going to give more attention to the functional speaking and writing (expression, punctuation, spelling, and speech in realistic situations) and see if this will not give better results.

*Resources.* We need to plan to get and use more easy reading material. The regular text was too difficult for about 60 per cent of my last class. I am afraid that instead of appreciating literature some of the students were actually turned against it because I started them out on too difficult material.

*Class Procedures.* The small group discussions of "a short story I like and why" worked out well and served to arouse much interest in reading. Attempts at improving speech for actual situations through role playing of

these situations seem to have many possibilities. I must study this procedure more myself and plan for trying out more types of situations.

Although I feel I made progress in getting individuals and groups to help set up their goals, plans and activities, I still do too much dictating and am front-center-stage too much of the time for democratic class operation. Perhaps some study of democratic leadership and group dynamics would help both me and the other students.

## THEN AND NOW STUDIES

In most communities questions like the following are periodically raised: "Are not the schools deteriorating with the introduction of fads and frills?" "Why don't the schools teach the 3R's like they did when I was in school?" "Since it is obvious that graduates today don't know how to read or spell like graduates once did, why don't we make teachers discipline their pupils and teach them like we were taught?" The alert teacher must be able to answer these and similar questions. This requires him to know the facts which have been gathered through careful investigations.

The criticisms of schools and schooling now being made are not new at all. Perennially parents have cast a nostalgic look behind to the schools of their youth. Even in ancient times they were complaining.

> A clay tablet of great antiquity records the lament of a merchant whose son has come home from school into the shop. Alas, the boy cannot keep the money and accounts straight, cannot write his hieroglyphic legibly, cannot deal with customers. The money spent on his schooling has been wasted. . . .[12]

In 1894 a committee on composition and rhetoric reporting to the Board of Overseers of Harvard said:

> At Harvard, as the committee demonstrates, the unhappy instructors are confronted with immature thoughts, set down in a crabbed and slovenly hand, miserably expressed, and wretchedly spelled, and yet the average age of admission is nineteen.[13]

Systematic studies of actual student achievements would seem to provide a better basis for judgment than armchair speculation based on a few cases or schools which may be highly atypical. When the results of dozens of research studies are examined, the overwhelming weight of evidence indicates that not only are children learning the traditional fundamental subjects better than they ever did before, but they are also learning more of other

---

[12] W. H. Burton, "Get the Facts: Both Ours and the Other Fellow's!" *Progressive Education*, Vol. 29, 1952, p. 89.

[13] *Ibid.*, p. 90.

subjects such as art and music than ever before. Certainly there are many areas where our schools badly need improvement, but is the answer to look backward, as some popular journalists, historians, and scientists are periodically suggesting? The pattern of tryout of teaching approach, systematic appraisal, tryout of planned, revised approach, reappraisal, and so on, is a sounder procedure than one based largely on emotional appeals for the good old schools of yesteryear.

## STUDIES COMPARING TWO METHODS

If education is effective it changes behavior. One persistent and continuing problem the teacher faces is that of attempting to compare the relative effectiveness of different methods in producing desired behavior. Techniques employed by Bavelas [14] and Lewin [15] are suggestive of a type of informal study which teachers or groups of teachers might successfully employ in evaluating their work.

Acquiring knowledge alone may suffice for pencil and paper test purposes, but may be totally inadequate for more significant behaviors. Recognizing this, Lewin and Bavelas set up an investigation to determine which of two methods of teaching, the lecture or the group decision method, would produce more changes in certain food habits. The immediate goal of the teaching in this experiment was to produce greater use of three types of food (kidneys, brains, and hearts) against which there was known resistance.

Six groups of women were used in the experiment, two of low economic level, two of middle, and two of high economic level. Each of three of the groups, one from each economic level, participated in a discussion led by a skillful teacher with an expert nutritionist as consultant. Members of these groups were led to regard the subject being discussed as important to themselves, and began to assume responsibility for carrying forward the discussion. Finally, after some of their objections and attitudes had been talked over, they reached a decision concerning action to be taken.

In the other three groups the lecture method was used. The expert nutritionist in charge talked for approximately half an hour about the nutritional advantages of using the meats, and described how the meats could be prepared in order to avoid unpleasant odors, textures, and appearance. Visual aids were used by the lecturer to emphasize the vitamin and mineral

---

[14] A. Bavelas, *Group Decision*, paper read before a meeting of the S.P.S.S.I., 1943.

[15] K. Lewin, *The Relative Effectiveness of a Lecture Method and a Method of Group Decision for Changing Food Habits*, Washington, D.C., Committee on Food Habits, National Research Council, June, 1942. (Mimeographed.) Also see R. H. Simpson, "Attitudinal Effects of Small Group Discussions: Shifts on Certainty-Uncertainty and Agreement-Disagreement Continua," *The Quarterly Journal of Speech*, Vol. 46, 1960, pp. 415-418.

value of the meats. The amount of time used in each of the six groups was the same. Mimeographed recipes were distributed to the members of all six groups.

The relative effects of the lectures and the group discussions were tested seven days after the experiment began. Through an interview at home with each participant a determination was made of the extent to which the foods were actually served, and what the reactions of the families were.

Although the frequency of using these meats by the participants of the two groups was about equal *before* the experiment, striking differences appeared at the end as shown in Table 32.

### TABLE 32
**Effects of Two Procedures in Changing Food Habits ***

| Method of Inducing the Change in Food Habits | Group Decision | | | | Lecture | | | |
|---|---|---|---|---|---|---|---|---|
| Economic Level | Low | Middle | High | Total | Low | Middle | High | Total |
| *Number of Participants* | 17 | 16 | 13 | 44 | 13 | 15 | 13 | 41 |
| % of individuals serving one or more of the three meats | 35 | 69 | 54 | 52 | 15 | 13 | 0 | 10 |
| % of individuals serving a meat they had *never* or *hardly* ever served before | 20 | 53 | 54 | 44 | 0 | 8 | 0 | 3 |
| % of individuals serving a meat they had never served before | 13 | 36 | 50 | 32 | 0 | 8 | 0 | 3 |
| % of participants serving one or more new meats who had *never* served *any* of the three meats before the experiment | | | | 29 | | | | 0 |

* Adapted from Lewin, op. cit.

Note that after the experiment 52 per cent of the discussion group members served one or more of the three meats, while only 10 per cent of those in the lecture group did so. Thirty-two per cent of those who had been in the discussion groups, and only 3 per cent of those who had been in the lecture groups served a meat they had never served before. In short, this investigation seemed to show that the discussion approach was much more effective in producing changed behavior than the lecture technique.[16]

[16] It is possible the "lecture group" women might have made as good or even better scores on a pencil and paper test on nutrition than the "discussion-group" women. The educator continuously faces the problem of considering what kind of behavior he is trying to produce. Considerations regarding short-time school behaviors should not crowd out consideration of equally or more important out-of-school behaviors.

## LONGITUDINAL STUDIES

### The Eight-Year Study

Appraisal of long-time, comprehensive aims of education may require co-operative planning by representatives of a large number of educational institutions, and may demand inquiry over a period of months, semesters, or even years. Illustrative of such an investigation is the Eight-Year Study. This study, initiated in 1930, represented an extensive attempt to answer, upon a factual basis, such questions as the following: Can secondary schools be trusted to use wisely their freedom from traditional college requirements? How can improvements be made in high schools without jeopardizing students' chances of being admitted to colleges or of doing well after admission to college? Is the commonly made assumption sound that success in a college depends upon the study in high school of certain subjects for certain periods of time? How well do high school students who went to college from experimental schools succeed?

PROCEDURES. At the outset, a planning committee selected thirty representative high schools who were willing to experiment educationally provided their students would be freed from the usual college entrance requirements. Starting in 1933 plans for changes in curriculum, organization, and procedure were set up in these schools. Representatives of the thirty schools met annually for mutual stimulation in thinking and planning.

When the study started the schools all sought to adapt work to individual needs, and to provide for greater mastery of skills, and for release of creative energy. More continuity in learning and greater unity of school experiences were also provided. Two major principles guided the work of the thirty schools. The first was that the general life of the school and methods of teaching should conform insofar as possible to what is now known about the ways in which human beings learn and grow, and the second was that the high school in the United States should re-discover its chief reason for existence. Leaders in the study concluded that the school itself should become a *demonstration* of the kind of life in which this nation believes. They felt that the spirit and practice of experimentation and exploration should characterize secondary schools in a democracy. The Thirty Schools [17] early in the study became known as experimental schools. Much attention from the beginning was given to recording and reporting the results of their work. Special emphasis was given to the development of testing instruments to meet new purposes of teachers and administrators. Devices designed to appraise critical thinking, sound attitudes, and social sensitivity were among the many which were constructed.

RESULTS. Graduates of the thirty schools were studied to determine how

---

[17] This was the name given in the study to the schools which agreed to experiment.

well they succeeded in college. A basis of comparison was established by matching, with utmost care, the graduates from the thirty high schools with graduates from high schools not participating in the study. This latter group had met the usual college entrance requirements. Factors included in the matching were college attended, sex, age, race, scholastic aptitude scores, home and community background, interest, and probable future.[18]

In a careful comparison of the 1,475 matched pairs which were intensively studied, the College Follow-up Staff found that the graduates of the Thirty Schools surpassed the non-experimental group in many ways. Some of the findings were as follows:

1. Earned a slightly higher total grade average
2. Earned higher grade averages in all subject fields except foreign languages
3. Specialized in the same academic fields as did the comparison students
4. Did not differ from the comparison group in the number of times they were placed on probation
5. Received slightly more academic honors in each year
6. Were more often judged to possess a high degree of intellectual curiosity and drive
7. Were more often judged to be precise, systematic, and objective in their thinking
8. Were more often judged to have developed clear or well-formulated ideas concerning the meaning of education—especially in the first years in college
9. More often demonstrated a high degree of resourcefulness in meeting new situations
10. Did not differ from the comparison group in ability to plan their time effectively
11. Had about the same problems of adjustment as the comparison group, but approached their solution with greater effectiveness
12. Participated somewhat more frequently, and more often enjoyed appreciative experiences, in the arts
13. Participated more in all organized student groups except religious and "service" activities
14. Earned in each college year a high percentage of non-academic honors (officership in organizations, election to managerial societies, athletic insignia, leading roles in dramatic and musical presentations)
15. Did not differ from the comparison group in the quality of adjustment to their contemporaries

---

[18] W. M. Aiken, *The Story of the Eight-Year Study*, Harper and Brothers, 1942, p. 109.

16. Differed only slightly from the comparison group in the kinds of judgments about their schooling
17. Had a somewhat better orientation toward the choice of vocation
18. Demonstrated a more active concern for what was going on in the world.[19]

While some of the indicated differences in favor of the experimental schools were not large, they were consistent for each class. When one finds even small margins of differences for a number of large groups, the probability greatly increases that the differences are not due to chance alone. When judged by college standards, by the students' contemporaries, or by the individuals themselves, it appeared that the students from the experimental schools did a somewhat better job on the average in college than students with similar backgrounds and basic abilities who were trained in traditional high schools.

The graduates of the "most experimental schools" were strikingly more successful than their matchees. Differences in their favor were much greater than the differences between the total Thirty Schools and the comparison group. Conversely, there were no large or consistent differences between the "least experimental graduates" and their comparison group.

The College Follow-up Staff commenting on these facts stated:

> If the proof of the pudding lies in these groups, and a good part of it does, then it follows that the colleges got from these most experimental schools a higher proportion of sound, effective college material than they did from the more conventional schools in similar environments. If the colleges want students who have developed effective and objective habits of thinking, and who yet maintain a healthy orientation toward their fellows, then they will encourage the already obvious trend away from restrictions which tend to inhibit departures or deviations from the conventional curriculum patterns.[20]

### Identification of Talent and Follow-up of High School Graduates

Dr. George D. Stoddard, formerly President of the University of Illinois, once said that the perennial debate on the current status of education in various subject areas could "be properly answered if, and only if, a comprehensive examination could be administered regularly to all persons at about their eighteenth birthdays." A study that promises to give some answers to questions about the long-term effects of schooling and about the country's talent and its training is being conducted by the American Institute for Research, largely under the sponsorship of the U.S. Office of Education. All students in Grades 9 through 12 of a carefully chosen

---

[19] *Ibid.*, pp. 111–112.
[20] *Ibid.*, p. 113.

sample of 1,100 high schools throughout the United States were given an extensive battery of mental and achievement tests during January and February, 1960. These half-million students will be studied intensively for the next twenty years. The pool of information yielded by both the testing and especially the follow-up should be of tremendous value in appraising the schools.[21]

## COMMUNITY COMPARISONS

One helpful technique which has been used to a limited extent is to compare the educational results in two communities whose population and ability to support education are similar but whose educational practices differ strikingly. Illustrative of such studies is one by Wrightstone [22] who made an extensive appraisal of achievement of pupils under described experimental teaching practices in one group of communities, and compared their achievement with that of matched pupils under conventional teaching situations in similar communities. In addition to using conventional tests of knowledge, instruments were designed to measure work skills, abilities to organize, interpret and apply facts, and such variables as civic beliefs and attitudes.

Because of the complexity of the study a complete picture of it or of all the results obtained will not be given here.[23] However, the implications of the findings are well summarized by its author who notes, "The comparative measurement of certain intellectual factors, dynamic factors, and social performance factors in selected experimental and conventional schools (in matched communities) indicate *equal or superior* achievement for the experimental practices. Such evidence may be interpreted as tentative proof of the validity of the educational theory and principles upon which the newer-type practices in the selected schools are established." [24] While the matched community procedure is a technique which has been used for research it should be emphasized that it could be misused. It is difficult to match communities. Intercommunity comparisons may cause jealousies and other complications. What one community can or should do may not necessarily be best for another community. However, the results from carefully designed community comparisons may give clues as to the effectiveness of certain educational procedures.

---

[21] Warren G. Findley, "The Impact of Applied Problems on Educational Research" in *Educational Research*, Bloomington, Indiana, Phi Delta Kappa, 1960, p. 51.

[22] J. Wayne Wrightstone, *Appraisal of Experimental High School Practices*, New York, Bureau of Publications, Teachers College, Columbia University, 1936.

[23] *Ibid.* For descriptions of conventional and experimental practices see pages 3–116. For appraisal of conventional and experimental practices see pages 117–194.

[24] *Ibid.*, p. 193.

## REVIEW OF RESEARCH SUMMARIES

Also fruitful, for the time spent, is the review of research reports which summarize a number of experimental studies. In such summaries an attempt is made to analyze and partially "digest" for the reader dozens of individual studies. An illustration of the research summary is one made by Leonard and Eurich with the cooperation of others which summarized the results of 154 investigations of progressive practices in teaching.[25]

Probably the most extensive and thorough synthesis of research of interest to teachers is to be found in the *Review of Educational Research*[26] which periodically covers such topics as: "Educational and Psychological Tests," "Methods of Research and Experimentation," and "General Aspects of Instruction, Learning, Teaching and the Curriculum." Also of value to the teacher is the *Encyclopedia of Educational Research*,[27] which brings together in one volume the accumulated research on educational problems of the past half century.

A balanced picture of the "pros and cons" on many controversial issues is contained in the very readable book, *The Great Debate*.[28]

## UNDERSTANDING AND APPRAISING NEWER CURRICULA

One of the most striking recent developments in education has been the emergence of more modern subject matter. Regardless of teaching grade level or subject matter area, each teacher needs to give thought to this change and concomitant appraisal problems. Over nine million students in the United States are currently using the newer curricula, and the number is steadily increasing.[29]

The newer curricula have been initiated by interested scholars and teachers, who after much arduous conferring and committee work over an extended period of time decided what should represent the most advanced thinking in the subject matter field under consideration. Financial support has come largely from Federal grants and from private foundations. The primary goal is not to get complete coverage of a field (an impossible job),

---

[25] J. P. Leonard and A. C. Eurich (Editors), *An Evaluation of Modern Education*, New York, D. Appleton-Century Company, 1942.

[26] American Educational Research Association, National Educational Association, 1201 Sixteenth Street, N.W., Washington 6, D.C.

[27] Chester W. Harris (Editor), *Encyclopedia of Educational Research*, Third Edition, New York, The Macmillan Company, 1960.

[28] C. W. Scott, C. M. Hill, and H. W. Burns (Editors), *The Great Debate*, Englewood Cliffs, New Jersey, Prentice-Hall, Inc., 1959.

[29] G. Saslow, Review of "New Curricula" in *Contemporary Psychology*, Vol. 10, 1965, p. 174.

but rather to emphasize the relatively few basic conceptions which it is felt students should obtain. There is not a complete consensus as to what these basic conceptions are. For example, there are at least two types of new mathematics curricula and three types of new biology curricula being tried in the schools.

Basic conceptions in each field are developed in the mind of the student by having him explore, experiment, or create in a fashion which attempts to simulate what the scholar or artist does. Much use is made of films, laboratory experiments, collateral reading, and tests designed primarily for learning, not marking, purposes.

Since the newer curricula frequently involve radically changed emphasis in goals, procedures, and appraisals from traditional approaches, additional training for experienced teachers is most desirable. Year-long, summer-long, and in-service institutes have been widely used for this purpose. Teachers who try them nearly always (92–99 per cent) find the new curricula preferable to the old, and students apparently do as well as those traditionally educated, even when tested by traditional examinations.[30] Significant changes in teacher training programs are beginning. Programs for future teachers also need to take into account the newer programs in mathematics, science, English, social studies, foreign languages, and industrial education.

Newer programs are set up to be changed, as continuous feedback is obtained on tentative texts and other materials, experiments, and course outlines. The feedback that comes from weekly, monthly, or unit appraisals from students and teachers goes to planning and writing committees of scholars and teachers who make revisions of materials, in whole or in part, as these seem needed.

While the cost of each new curriculum is from one to five million dollars, the total cost of all money for research or education is only a fraction of one per cent of the annual education expenditure in the United States of twenty-four billion dollars.[31] Procedures involved in the newer curricular developments seem to be a social invention which should help deal with the problem of obsolescence in education. The hope lies in sustained interaction between scholars, teachers, and research and development personnel.

One of the most outstanding aims of modern curriculum reform movements is to help students organize their learnings around basic principles in the subject matter field. Communicative, associative and distributive laws of mathematics and the concept of tropism in biology are examples of fundamental ideas. This new curriculum trend was started in 1951 when Beberman and his University of Illinois Committee on School Mathematics (UICSM) organized the first of the newer project-type curriculum

---

[30] *Ibid.*, p. 174.
[31] *Ibid.*, p. 176.

improvement efforts. Since Sputnik I, other mathematics educators have developed additional "new maths." New appraisal challenges have been presented by these programs. The previously developed tests, which at one time served well, are no longer as appropriate as they once were, largely because of different teaching goals and procedures. In addition to new tests for use with new texts, evaluators have been concerned with such things as methods for reporting class observations, analyses of objectives, study of teacher held objectives, comparison on achievement of classes taught the "new math" with control classes which were more conventionally taught, and follow-up studies of students in college.

Three series of standardized tests developed for appraisal of "new math" learnings are:

Contemporary Mathematics Test, Forms for Grades 3 & 4, 5 & 6, 7–9, 8 & 9 (algebra), 9–12 (advanced). Monterey, California, California Test Bureau, 1965. Designed to assess knowledge of concepts unique to the several most widely taught modern mathematics programs.

Stanford Modern Mathematics Concepts Test, Forms for Grades 5 & 6, 7–9. New York, Harcourt, Brace & World, 1965. Designed to cover concepts, vocabulary, and operations commonly included in modern arithmetic courses.

Modern Math Understanding Tests, Grades 4–6, 6–8, 8–9. Chicago, Science Research Associates, 1966. Based on a study of over twenty modern mathematics programs, an attempt was made to be impartial to any one program. Each test encompasses foundations of mathematics. Measured are four facets of understanding: knowledge and computation, elementary understanding, problem solving and application, and structure and generalization.

A characteristic of a healthy science curriculum is its changing character. Rapidly expanding subject matter knowledge and improved understanding as to how students learn best are two reasons for needed changes. As in the newer mathematics, the newer science tends to put emphasis on principles, particularly the methodological principles which are shared by all sciences, even though the frequency of use of such principles may be very different between sciences and even within a science at different times. An example of a newer type science test is:

Biological Sciences Curriculum Study, Comprehensive Final Examinaiton in First-Year Biology, New York, The Psychological Corporation, 1965. Particularly related to BSCS goals, but may be used with other modern biology curricula. Primarily for instructional uses.

Although most major efforts in curricular change have been in the natural and physical sciences, some significant attempts have been made in

Second Grade Pupils Learning the Initial Teaching Alphabet (I.T.A.) Which Has Been Developed to Minimize Early Reading Problems.

other fields. In social science for example, there is an attempt to create awareness of who social scientists are, the methodology of social science is emphasized, the phenomena of cultural differences, social power, and group decision making are investigated, actual behavioral data are studied, and scientific reports are being rewritten at appropriate reading levels. Students try out the processes of investigation used by the historian, the economist, the professional geographer, and the political scientist.[32] Obviously appraisal of progress must be quite different from, for example, the conventional history test.

Some progress in new curricula and their appraisal has also been made in modern languages. The "new English" may involve use of programed books for self-instruction, more interest in the art of communication and less concern for traditional formal grammar, more emphases on techniques for mastering words unknown to the student, attempts to help students understand the language and how it changes—not just how to use it—and the provision of sufficient variety of material to meet the wide range of individual differences. The widespread experimentation with the Initial Teaching Alphabet should also be noted.[33] In the newer foreign language instruction there is likely to be less memorizing of declensions and vocabulary and more use of language laboratories, which enable an entire class to practice simultaneously speaking aloud, with less emphasis on reading and writing. Foreign language teaching has also moved into the grades. Both English and foreign language teachers are gradually giving more attention

---

[32] See E. Fenton (Editor), *Teaching the New Social Studies in the Secondary Schools,* New York, Holt, Rinehart, & Winston, 1966.
[33] Pitman Publishing Company, 20 E. 46th Street, New York.

577

Pupils Utilizing the School's Language Laboratory. Through the Audio-Lingual Method, Listening and Speaking Skills in English and Foreign Languages Are Best Developed.

to experimental evidence and less exclusive emphasis to intuitive or armchair speculation on the effectiveness of different approaches.

## DIFFICULTIES IN ANALYZING MERITS OF DIFFERENT APPROACHES

The technics which have just been described represent attempts to base educational procedure upon fact rather than merely on opinion. It must be recognized that no appraisal technic or procedure gives a final or complete answer to the educational questions that teachers want to have answered. Some of the practical difficulties which must be kept in mind in assessing the results of most technics will now be discussed.

### Goals Differ

One of the major difficulties in comparing different educational approaches is that teachers, pupils, parents, and communities are not agreed with respect to the goals of particular educational procedures. It is very difficult to compare the results of teaching which stresses the learning of detailed, factual material with the results obtained when teaching emphasizes critical or analytical thinking, unless it is known which is the more desirable.

For example, how should one assess the results of German education in the first half of this century? It helped produce outstanding physical scientists, mathematicians, and military leaders. But, in view of two world wars and the brutal extermination of some 5,000,000 members of a minority

group, were the educational assets gained at the expense of too little attention to human values?

### Experimentation May Stimulate Teacher Creativity

In attempting to assess the comparative values of older and newer methods the results have typically indicated some advantage of the newer method over the older method. This does not necessarily mean that the newer method is in and of itself superior to the older method. It may be that the teacher who tries out a new procedure is stimulated to work harder and to be more creative than he otherwise would be. If this hypothesis is correct, administrators, supervisors, and others might encourage teachers to try out new approaches with the idea that by so doing their teaching will be invigorated.[34]

It is also possible that the type of teacher or the kind of school staff which tries new or different approaches may be of better quality than those who do not try out innovations. Such complications as these make it extremely difficult to evaluate the effectiveness of schools using different approaches.

### Adequate Description of Teaching-Learning Situation Difficult

While most experimenters who try to determine the relative merits of two or more educational approaches attempt to describe as adequately as possible the differences between the competing approaches, it must be recognized that such descriptions are extremely difficult. In fact, it may be almost impossible to describe adequately the multitude of factors which can have a vital bearing on the success of an educational venture. Because of this fact, the student or teacher reading about the results of experiments must be extremely cautious in making interpretations and drawing conclusions.

### Readiness of Participants for a New Method

Most educational psychologists recognize that there is probably no best method for all situations and all conditions. One reason for this fact is that those involved in a particular teaching-learning situation may not be ready for a specified method. For example, if neither teachers, learners, nor parents are ready for a particular method to be used, it is obviously impossible to give this method a fair trial. Readiness of participants for a certain method or for aspects of the method is hard to determine. Consequently,

---

[34] For an example of how experimentation may stimulate new understanding on the part of a teaching staff see Ralph Tyler, "Symposium Discussions" in *Educational Research*, Bloomington, Indiana, Phi Delta Kappa, 1960, pp. 110–111.

an approach that may appear to give inferior results initially may, if persisted in, give better results later on.

### Short-Term and Long-Term Gains

It is sometimes difficult to assess the efficacy of a given educational method or organizational plan because there may be a conflict between immediate and longtime goals. For example, the learner who has been practicing tennis for three years while holding his racket the "wrong way" may find that he cannot hit the ball at first after he is shown how to hold his racket in the "right way." Unless the teacher and learner are willing to give a procedure or method a fair tryout it may be eliminated too quickly because it is "too confusing," "too frustrating," "too disorganized," or "too time consuming." Also, studying a subject in a particular way may make it possible for a pupil to pass a particular kind of test immediately after the study, but may cause him to dislike the subject and thus militate against future learning in the area. In assessing the results of educational experience, it is critically important to attempt to identify both short-term and long-term gains and losses.

### "Newer Methods" Vary Widely

Sometimes an attempt is made to differentiate between newer methods and older methods. In general, of course, there probably can be established certain major differences between what might be labeled the new emphases in education and the older points of view. However, it must be clearly recognized that newer methods differ widely among themselves and that even two classes believed to be using the same procedures may actually differ considerably in the teaching-learning situations involved. Differing teacher and pupil perceptions, furthermore, create differences in situations where no difference would be noticed by an outside observer.

### Schools Vary Immensely

A pronounced characteristic of schools in the United States is their diversity. Even if something is true in one or a few schools with which we are familiar it may be true for only a very small percentage of schools. To get a comprehensive picture of our schools is very difficult because of their very diversity. This suggests a need for caution in reaching and publicizing conclusions.

## SUMMARY

Evaluating the total effects of schooling upon children's immediate and later behavior is one of the most difficult and complicated processes the educator faces. The marks which are registered in the principal's office only partially indicate important changes which have been made in children's

behavior. In order to appraise the effectiveness of their programs, schools should employ a wide variety of measuring devices and approaches.

In this chapter, techniques for evaluating some of the broader and less easily measured outcomes of education have been described. These include measures of out-of-school behavior following formal instruction, scales for determining pupil and community attitudes toward school practices, case studies of classes, and matched community comparisons. Much information regarding what is superior educational practice may also be secured from such longitudinal investigations as the Eight-Year Study, "then and now" studies of achievement, comparisons of teaching methods reported in the professional literature, and research summaries such as those found in the *Review of Educational Research* and the *Encyclopedia of Educational Research*.

Some of the sources of difficulties likely to be encountered in appraising different educational approaches are: (1) Goals of educators may differ, (2) A new method may stimulate a teacher to be more creative, (3) Adequate description of a teaching-learning situation is difficult, (4) Participants in a new method may differ in readiness for it, and (5) Conflicts may exist between short-term and long-term goals and gains.

Pencil and paper tests given in school have their place in an appraisal program. However, the ultimate appraisal must be made on the basis of the out-of-school behaviors of those whom the school seeks to influence.

### References for Further Study

Aiken, W. M., *The Story of the Eight-Year Study*, New York, Harper and Brothers, 1942.

Banghart, Frank W. (Editor), *Educational Research*, Bloomington, Indiana, Phi Delta Kappa, 1960.

Brun, O. G., Goslin, D. A., Glass, D. C., Goldberg, I., *The Use of Standardized Ability Tests in American Secondary Schools and Their Impact on Students, Teachers, and Administrators*, New York, Russell Sage Foundation, 1965.

Chamberlin, D., and Others, *Did They Succeed in College?* New York, Harper and Brothers, 1942.

Gibson, R. L., and Others, *A Comparative Study of the Academic Achievements of Elementary Age Students of the United States and the British Isles*, University of Toledo, Toledo Research Foundation, USOE Project Number 2177, 1965.

Goslin, D. A., Epstein, R. R., Hallock, B. A., *The Use of Standardized Tests in the Elementary Schools*, New York, Russell Sage Foundation, 1965.

Gronlund, N. E. *Measurement and Evaluation in Teaching*, New York, The Macmillan Company, 1965.

Hawes, G. R., *Educational Testing for the Millions*, New York, McGraw-Hill Book Company, 1964.

Progressive Education Association (Informal Committee on Evaluation of Newer Practices in Education), *New Methods vs. Old in American Education*, New York, Bureau of Publications, Teachers College, Columbia University, 1941.

Scott, C. W., Hill, C. M., and Burns, H. W. (Editors), *The Great Debate*, Englewood Cliffs, New Jersey, Prentice-Hall, Inc., 1959.

Terman, Lewis M., and Others. *Genetic Studies of Genius*, Stanford, California, Stanford University. Vol. 1, Mental and Physical Traits of a Thousand Gifted Children, 1925; Vol. 2, The Early Mental Traits of Three Hundred Geniuses, 1926; Vol. 3, The Promise of Youth: Follow-up Studies of a Thousand Gifted Children, 1930; Vol. 4, The Gifted Child Grows Up: Twenty-Five Years Follow-up of a Superior Group, 1947; Vol. 5, The Gifted Group at Mid-Life, 1959.

Wallace, W., Chreitzberg, J., and Sims, V. M. *The Story of Holtville*, Deatsville, Alabama, Holtville High School, 1944.

West, Charles K., "Theoretical and Instrumental Intervention or 'The Medium is the Message,' " *Perceptual and Motor Skills*, Vol. 24, 1967, pp. 753–754.

The student is also urged to study current issues of educational and psychological periodicals. The following are illustrative of magazines which sometimes have articles on appraising the work of the school:

*Educational and Psychological Measurement*

*Elementary School Journal*

*Journal of Educational Psychology*

*Journal of Educational Research*

*Journal of Experimental Education*

*Journal of Experimental Psychology*

*Journal of Personality and Social Psychology*

*Journal of Psychology*

*Journal of Social Psychology*

*Review of Educational Research*

*The School Review*

## Questions, Exercises, and Activities

1. List arguments for and against an elementary or secondary school teacher being concerned about, and working to improve, the quality of education in each of the following:
   (a) Other classrooms in his school.
   (b) Other schools in his community.
   (c) Other schools in his state.
   (d) Other schools in other states.
   (e) Schools in other countries.
2. If comprehensive school-wide standardized tests show excellent results in two subject areas and very unsatisfactory results in two other subjects, what are some specific things that might be done about the latter two subjects? *Who* should be responsible for getting these things done?
3. Using one or more of the approaches suggested in this chapter, make a survey of some community attitudes toward the schools. A committee or group of students may want to plan what will be investigated and how it will be done. Plan to report to the class on what you find.

4. Question a group of your friends, acquaintances, and/or strangers with this query: How do you think the schools compare today with those of thirty years ago? Write down and bring to class a complete record of the replies together with your conclusions regarding the findings.
5. In the library find a study comparing two approaches to education and make an abstract of the purposes, procedures, and results of the study. (Possibly you will want to use the *Education Index*.)
6. List five changes in post-school behavior which you think teachers in your area should work harder to produce.

# PART SIX

## The Psychology of the Teacher

# Chapter 21

## Professional
## Growth
## of the Teacher

Educational psychology is just as much a psychology of the teacher as of the pupil. The professional growth of the teacher involves not only a continuous effort to understand children better, but also constant self-appraisal in which the teacher carefully scrutinizes methods of increasing his own learning. The teacher's professional growth, or lack of it, will be reflected in his methods, in his willingness to change, in his working relationships with children, and in his overall efficiency as a teacher. It is clear that children's behavior as individuals, and more especially as individuals interacting with the teacher and with other pupils, will depend to a great extent upon the kind of a teacher they have.[1] The teacher whose intellectual growth terminates upon graduation from college or whose work is stultified by monotonous, inflexible routines, will most certainly be an unhappy and ineffective classroom leader. A professionally maturing teacher, on the other hand, is not only better able to diagnose and meet his own needs, but also sets a worthwhile example of growth and learning for students with whom he works.

In the following paragraphs a picture will be given of: (1) some be-

---

[1] Ray H. Simpson, *Teacher Self-Evaluation*, New York, The Macmillan Company, 1966, Chapter 7.

haviors that characterize a professionally growing teacher, and (2) some specific areas for professional appraisal and growth.

## BEHAVIORS OF A PROFESSIONALLY GROWING TEACHER

### The Teacher Continues as a Learner

As a professional person, a teacher's learning should continue throughout his professional life. However, even in teacher-training institutions some of the practices seem to indicate that there may be two quite distinct concepts of the role of the teacher as a learner. The one concept is based on the implicit but frequently unrecognized assumption that the teacher practically finishes his systematic learning as soon as the coveted degree or diploma is obtained. The opposing concept is based on the assumption that the instructor's own systematic learning is only well-started when he is graduated from his formal program of teacher training. Only the latter approach can be supported by educational psychology and it implies training for continued learning.

The genesis of the differences in these concepts can probably best be understood by considering the differing emphases in college courses, depending upon which point of view the instructor supports. In the one case the course is highly structured by the instructor; in the other case considerable attention is given to helping the student learn how to plan his own systematic learning. The college instructor who assumes that systematic learning will be finished at the end of the teacher-training program must attempt to impart all information the student (potential teacher) will need on the job. The instructor who is greatly interested in training the future teacher for systematic learning after the course is over is not only concerned with building up the student's informational background, but he is also equally concerned that the prospective teacher develop the attitudes, skills, and abilities necessary continuously to increase and appraise his store of information while he is on the job. Too often the traditional teacher largely completed his education when he graduated. The modern teacher is one who looks upon his teacher training as preparation to start teaching, and *preparation to continue systematic learning after his formal course work is over.*

There are many reasons why the modern teacher cannot afford to stop growing professionally once he gets on the job. In the first place, stagnation may lead to grumpiness, unhappiness, and irritation. Furthermore, there is danger that continuous repetition of the same assignments and discussions will make the teaching job a boring one instead of the challenging one it can be. Continuous systematic learning by the instructor can make teaching a very pleasant and exhilarating experience.

Not only does the assumption of an active role as a learner give great satisfaction to the teacher, as has already been indicated, but such a role is also indispensable in setting an example for students. It is probable that the teacher in most situations has more influence on learners through his example than through the precepts he expounds or the information he teaches. Pupils can usually sense the basic attitudes the teacher takes toward learning. Does the teacher believe enough in systematic learning to practice it himself? Does the teacher who encourages pupils to read actually use his own skill in reading in order to do a better job of teaching? Pupils quickly catch the enthusiasm of a teacher who is constantly growing in knowledge and in its utilization. Some educational administrators, keenly aware that teachers should grow on the job, aid them in doing so by helping them develop in-service training programs and professional libraries. Financial recognition is also given in some school systems for continued professional development.

### The Teacher Assesses His Personal Characteristics

In a comprehensive study involving 2,043 teachers, 978 elementary and 1,065 secondary, Ryans [2] identified and studied three major patterns of teachers' classroom behaviors. These were:

Pattern X—(Friendly, understanding) versus (Aloof, egocentric, and restricted).

Pattern Y—(Responsible, businesslike, systematic) versus (Evading, unplanned, slipshod).

Pattern Z—(Simulating, imaginative, surgent) versus (Dull, routine).

The classroom behaviors of all the teachers were assessed by trained observers. The teachers also completed a self-report type inventory which included 300 multiple-choice and check-list-type items relating to such things as personal preferences, self-judgments, and biographical data. Then the 67 teachers rated by observers as "high" on all three of the patterns, X, Y, and Z were compared on their inventory responses with the 37 rated "low" on the patterns.[3]

Some of the responses to the inventory that were characteristic of the "high" group and that significantly contrasted them from the "low" group are shown in Table 33, and those that characterized the "lows" as contrasted with the "highs" are given in Table 34.

---

[2] David G. Ryans, "Some Correlates of Teacher Behavior," *Educational and Psychological Measurement*, Vol. 29, Spring, 1959, pp. 3–12.

[3] High and low were defined to include those teachers who were one standard deviation or more above or below the mean as determined by the observers who used Patterns X, Y, and Z as scoreable dimensions.

## TABLE 33
### Personal Characteristics of Teachers with High Ratings *

Elementary-Secondary Teachers Combined

A. "High" Group members more frequently (than "Low"):
  1. Manifest extreme generosity in appraisals of the behavior and motives of other persons; express friendly feelings for others.
  2. Indicate strong interest in reading and in literary matters.
  3. Indicate interest in music, painting, and the arts in general.
  4. Report participation in high school and college social groups.
  5. Judge selves high in ambition and initiative.
B. "High" Group on the average (compared with "Low" Group):
  1. Indicates greater enjoyment of pupil relationships (i.e., more favorable pupil opinions.)
  2. Indicates greater preference for non-directive classroom procedures.
  3. Is superior in verbal intelligence.
  4. Is more satisfactory with regard to emotional adjustment.

* Adapted from David G. Ryans, "Some Correlates of Teacher Behavior," *Educational and Psychological Measurement*, Vol. 19, Spring, 1959, pp. 9–10.

## TABLE 34
### Personal Characteristics of Teachers with Low Ratings *

Elementary-Secondary Teachers Combined

A. "Low" Group members more frequently (than "High"):
  1. Are from older age groups.
  2. Are restricted and critical in appraisals of the behavior and motives of other persons.
  3. Value exactness, orderliness, and "practical" things.
  4. Indicate preferences for activities which do not involve close contacts with people.
B. "Low" Group on the average (compared with "High" Group):
  1. Is less favorable in expressed opinions of pupils.
  2. Is less high with regard to verbal intelligence.
  3. Is less satisfactory with regard to emotional adjustment.

* *Ibid.,* p. 11.

Ryans concluded that the abstract models of teachers, partially pictured in Tables 33 and 34, show "Several rather marked characteristics, notable among which is the general tendency for 'high' teachers to be extremely generous in appraisals of the behavior and motives of others; to possess strong interests in reading and in literary affairs; to participate in social groups; to enjoy pupil relationships; to prefer non-directive classroom procedures; to manifest superior verbal intelligence; and to be above average in emotional adjustment. Turning to the other side of the coin, 'low' teachers tend generally to be restricted and critical in their appraisals of other persons; to prefer activities which do not involve close personal contacts; to express less favorable opinions of pupils; to manifest less high

verbal intelligence; to show less satisfactory emotional adjustment; and to represent older age groups." [4]

On most of the characteristics listed in Table 34 it is possible for the teacher to improve if he is willing to give the time and effort necessary.

### The Teacher Uses Books and Periodicals to Help Solve Professional Problems

The well-trained teacher is one who increasingly appreciates that the more competent he becomes, the more challenging problems he will recognize. Professional magazines and books offer an excellent resource for meeting this challenge. Margaret Mead, world famous anthropologist, has remarked: "For those who work on the growing edge of science . . . only a few months may elapse before something which was easily taken for granted must be unlearned or transformed to fit the new state of knowledge." [5] Those who use knowledge and teach knowledge must keep up with new knowledge in their fields. The new experimental studies with potential implications for teaching must be continuously assayed.

Practically every problem a teacher meets has been met with some success by hundreds of other teachers. The key to viewing the experiences of other instructors is often available through the medium of professional reading.[6]

When the issue of reading disabilities is discussed, educators sometimes forget that they themselves may suffer from such liabilities. For example, in a large urban school system it was found that 3 per cent of the twelfth-grade pupils actually read better than 100 per cent of the teachers.[7] This conclusion was reached after the teachers and administrators, who were planning a reading improvement program, asked one of the writers to administer to them a comprehensive reading test. It was also found that 75 per cent of twelfth-grade pupils read better than 15 per cent of these administrators and teachers. The educators were found to be particularly low on these subtests of the Iowa Silent Reading Test: Selection of Key Words, Use of Index, and Directed Reading.

An even more challenging picture was revealed in this same study when an analysis was made of the reading these school men and women did during a typical month.[8] A reasonable amount of leisure-time reading was done, but little or no professional reading to help solve school problems

---

[4] *Ibid.*, p. 8.

[5] M. Mead, "Why Is Education Obsolete?" *Harvard Business Review*, Vol. 36, 1958, pp. 23–30.

[6] For many teachers professional writing constitutes an important activity. Two primary values of such expression are these: (1) it helps the teacher clarify what he believes, what he is doing, and how he can improve; and (2) it can stimulate other teachers to attempt to improve through the tryout of new ideas.

[7] Ray H. Simpson, *Teacher Self-Evaluation*, The Macmillan Company, 1966, p. 18.

[8] *Ibid.*, pp. 18–19.

was engaged in by the typical teacher or administrator. *Even those teachers who scored high on the reading test, which indicated they knew how to read well, made little if any more professional use of this ability than did those who scored low.*

The crux of the matter is that many teachers and administrators know *how* to read on a satisfactory level but make extremely little use of this skill in attacking professional problems. In a study of 746 teachers and administrators made by one of the writers, the following results related to professional reading were revealed for a particular month:

| | |
|---|---|
| No magazine articles read | 14 per cent |
| One magazine article read | 10 per cent |
| Two magazine articles read | 13 per cent |
| Three to five magazine articles read | 29 per cent |
| More than five magazine articles read | 34 per cent |

40 per cent had not even looked at one professional book.
17 per cent had sampled one book.
24 per cent had read parts of two books.
15 per cent had read parts of three to five books.
 4 per cent had read parts of five or more books.

CAUSES OF FAILURE TO READ PROFESSIONAL LITERATURE. Why do teachers and school administrators not make more use· of reading? The following causes may partly account for this situation:

1. The experiences of many school men in colleges and universities have led them to think that their professional growth ends when the coveted degree is received. This doctrine stunts growth.
2. Many administrators and teachers are hired largely on the basis of past credit-getting rather than on present abilities and upon probable self-education and growth on the job.
3. Many administrators have not expected their teachers to continue to grow professionally while on the job.
4. Teachers and administrators have not been taught how to get the printed materials which will be of definite help in solving their day-to-day problems.

IMPROVING PROFESSIONAL READING HABITS. Administrators with the aid of their school boards can improve the professional reading habits of teachers by utilizing the following suggestions:

1. Set aside a small sum of money each month for professional materials.
2. Establish with the aid of the teachers and librarians active professional libraries in each school.

3. Make salary increases partially contingent upon evidences of professional growth. One evidence of this would be a consistent use of professional materials.
4. In faculty meetings and elsewhere encourage the discussion and consideration of new ideas relating to methods, materials, and evaluation which are being tried in other school systems.
5. Help teachers isolate the specific professional problems which they feel are the most pressing and make it a point to suggest some reading sources from which they might get help.
6. Ask individual teachers periodically what they are reading and what ideas they are using from such reading.
7. Encourage publishers to send notices of new professional materials to librarians and teachers for their consideration.
8. Make provisions in work schedules of teachers so that some time each week can be utilized for studying new practices and trends.

## TEACHER SELF-APPRAISAL

It is apparent that the development of the teacher and improvement in what he does necessarily involve changes. It is also clear that not all change results in improvement. To set the stage for systematic change in activities which will result in improvement, it is desirable for the instructor continually to diagnose what he is doing, why he is doing it, and how it is succeeding. The remainder of this chapter suggests specific approaches the teacher may use in diagnosing and improving some of his behaviors.

### The Teacher's Diagnosis of His Own Classroom Activities

If the idea is accepted that the chances of happiness and success as a classroom teacher are enhanced by continuous self-diagnosis of his own behavior, then the question immediately arises: What are possible ways of planning such a diagnosis? There is much variety in approaches which may be used with profit.[9]

Some procedures for encouraging self-evaluation are illustrated in Table 35.[10] It is not, of course, implied that every teacher should use all of the seventeen types of diagnosis suggested in the checklist. The list, however, does show the wealth of approaches available and it is recommended that each teacher experiment with one or more of the tools not tried heretofore.

---

[9] It should be emphasized that the approaches discussed here are recommended for the self-improvement of the teacher, not specifically for pay or promotion ratings. The latter problem area may be studied in such references as V. M. Rogers, *Merit Rating for Teachers*, Syracuse, New York, Syracuse University, 1959.

[10] Ray H. Simpson, "Evaluation of College Teachers and Teaching," *Journal of Farm Economics*, Vol. 49, No. 1, Part II, February, 1967, pp. 295–296.

**TABLE 35**

**Self-evaluation Procedures Listed in Order of Number of 5,303 Professors
Who Have Used Them and Found Them Valuable**

| Item No. | Procedure | Used and Found Valuable | Used and Found of Doubtful or No Value | Success Ratio[a] | No. of Non-users Who Might Be Interested in Trying |
|---|---|---|---|---|---|
| 1. | Comparative check on your efficiency using one teaching approach vs. your efficiency in using another approach | 2,813 | 196 | 14.4 | 897 |
| 2. | Voluntary and contining colleague discussions or seminars by teachers of a particular course | 2,231 | 91 | 24.5 | 1,073 |
| 3. | Open-ended, relatively unstructured, evaluation by students | 2,101 | 737 | 2.9 | 841 |
| 4. | Visiting in a colleague's class for the purpose of evaluating and improving your own classes | 1,999 | 146 | 13.7 | 1,191 |
| 5. | Self-constructed evaluative questionnaires or checklists to be filled out by your students | 1,780 | 577 | 3.1 | 1,254 |
| 6. | Yearly written recap. of own activities and an assessment of the strong and weak aspects of such activities | 1,499 | 133 | 11.3 | 1,191 |
| 7. | Published teacher evaluative instruments | 1,225 | 408 | 3.0 | 1,710 |
| 8. | Planned meetings with colleagues for the purpose of evaluation of your own and others' teaching | 1,120 | 98 | 11.4 | 1,465 |
| 9. | Soliciting the help of administrators or supervisors in evaluating one's own teaching | 1,109 | 159 | 7.0 | 901 |
| 10. | Systematic search in printed sources for diagnostic tools and procedures for self-evaluation | 1,064 | 93 | 11.4 | 1,034 |
| 11. | Tape recording or TV recording of regular class sessions and then feedback analysis on your part | 682 | 96 | 7.1 | 1,877 |
| 12. | Comparative ratings by your students on specified dimensions of your instruction vs. that of other instructors | 456 | 307 | 1.5 | 1,290 |
| 13. | Regular luncheons to discuss evaluations of own and others' teaching | 392 | 112 | 3.5 | 1,214 |
| 14. | Student evaluation committee to provide feedback to the teacher | 392 | 191 | 2.1 | 1,296 |

[a] Success ratio is determined by dividing the number of successful users by the number who found the procedure to be of "doubtful or no value."

**TABLE 35 (Continued)**

| Item No. | Procedure | Used and Found Valuable | Used and Found of Doubtful or No Value | Success Ratio [a] | No. of Non-users Who Might Be Interested in Trying |
|---|---|---|---|---|---|
| 15. | Other action research, in addition to that in No. 1 above, to test teaching efficiency | 281 | 39 | 7.2 | 438 |
| 16. | Tape recording of an evaluative class session in which strengths and limitations of classes are analyzed (This discussion to be led by the instructor, by a student, by a panel of students, or by a colleague) | 202 | 61 | 3.3 | 1,320 |
| 17. | Cooperating colleague who near the end of a semester or quarter leads a discussion in your class of strong points and weak points of the class with you absent | 97 | 79 | 1.2 | 1,233 |

### Keeping a Record of What Happens

A comprehensive record of what goes on in the classroom furnishes one of the best sources for a diagnosis of strengths and weaknesses in the teacher's classroom activities. In connection with this record it is helpful for the teacher to keep a list of his own recognized difficulties encountered from day to day.

A systematic collection of student reactions to class activities and methods employed can also be studied for clues as to ways of improving the teaching-learning situation. Methods for administering and interpreting questionnaires which solicit student reactions to teaching procedures have been described by Simpson.[11] Although students may not be competent to assess a teacher's methods, their perceptions are important to the teacher, even if he thinks they are wrong. A study of such reactions can stimulate the teacher to rethink and reconsider some of the approaches he has been using.

### Some Results of Self-Diagnosis

What will a teacher's diagnosis of classroom activities likely show? What areas frequently are revealed as being in need of improvement? Each teacher in the writer's classes during one summer session was asked the

---

[11] Ray H. Simpson, *Teacher Self-Evaluation*, The Macmillan Company, 1966, pp. 20–22.

question: "What are specific weaknesses which you think have characterized your most recent teaching and learning?" A summary of the results indicated that the following nine areas were mentioned as ones where improvement is much needed. For each category one example of a teacher's comments is given.

SMUGNESS OR COMPLACENCY. "Since I have been teaching, I have utilized the 'information giving and checking method' exclusively and have been complacent with its use. A teacher usually teaches as he has been taught, and I was subjected only to this method when I was a student. Perhaps I should not blame myself too much for starting out as I did, but I cannot excuse myself for not continuing to learn professionally and systematically since I should be setting an example to my pupils. I plan to study and improve my procedures."

OBJECTIVES AND STANDARDS. "Perhaps my most serious weakness is that of unconsciously attempting to standardize my group of fifth graders. I set up a standard that I expected all pupils to meet, yet I now realize this puts undue pressure on the lower group and does not provide a rich enough program for the upper group."

CLASS CONTROL. "As a teacher of history, it is somewhat ironic that I have *talked* so much about democracy and have been so clearly *practicing* extreme autocratic control in the direction of assignments and class activities. I am going to study how to make my practices more consistent with the theories I have so assiduously expounded."

ASSIGNMENT MAKING. "Too often this past year my assignments filled no need other than keeping students busy in study hall. In some cases, particularly in the grammar unit, I was even guilty of 'page to page' assignments."

PLANNING CLASS ACTIVITIES. "In my classes the planning for activities has been done entirely by myself. I can see now that pupils could not be expected to gain much self-control as long as I held a monopoly on the making of decisions."

CLASS ACTIVITIES. "In the past my students have been required to absorb the information presented to them through the media of formal lectures and teacher assigned outside readings. The activities of students in class have tended to be characterized by passive absorbing of information rather than by active participation in a variety of cooperatively planned activities."

TAKING CARE OF INDIVIDUAL DIFFERENCES. "My neglect of individual differences was shown by my:

1. Presenting the same subject matter to all pupils
2. Giving the same assignments to all pupils
3. Requiring the same reading of all pupils
4. Using the same standards of evaluation for all pupils."

RESOURCES. "In my science classes I have made assignments from two textbooks. The pupils have received no experience in finding their own references and in evaluating resources. I have not encouraged pupils to use sources other than these two textbooks."

EVALUATION. "Another weakness of which I have been guilty is that of not letting pupils evaluate themselves or their group when working on a problem or when they have completed it. The evaluation is usually done entirely by me. In receiving his grade the pupil has no idea what his weaknesses were if his grade was low and what his strong points were if his grade was high. Being kept in this type of darkness the pupil has no knowledge of how he can improve himself. If each pupil kept his own record and helped evaluate himself as well as the others this would lead to more learning and a more complete understanding of what was being done."

## IMPROVEMENT OF THE TEACHER'S CLASS ACTIVITIES

After a teacher has made a tentative diagnosis of his own classroom activities, what can he do to eliminate weaknesses? The points of attack for each teacher will vary depending on such factors as his present practices, the type of self-diagnosis made, and the perceptions of the teacher regarding the areas where improvements are both needed and feasible. Some changes teachers can make will now be discussed.

### Assignment Making

One of the areas which study reveals to be in need of improvement is assignment making. Improvement in this activity frequently involves moving from assignments exclusively planned by the teacher toward assignments cooperatively originated by the teacher and learners. For example, one instructor reports:

> After consideration of my assignment-making practices I am forced to admit they are clearly autocratic and dictatorial. Learners have usually done the work, but apparently the motivation has been almost entirely a desire to get a respectable grade and pass the course. There is little evidence the students have really understood *why* they were studying particular assignments. There has been a rather passive interest in the work. I have started to involve the learners in the planning of assignments. This, I believe, will result in more active interest on their part in the work. We are attempting to have assignment-making more democratic.

When learners are given some opportunities to help plan their work, a movement away from the same assignment for everyone usually occurs. Individual differences in such factors as purposes, goals, reading abilities,

needs, interests, and mental capacities are likely to result in multiple rather than uniform assignments. For example, Jim Martin, after listing the words he had misspelled in his written work during a particular week (the teacher and other students helped him identify these words) decided with the guidance of his teacher that this list should constitute his spelling assignment for the following week. Increasing responsibility is placed upon the individual learner to help decide what assignment is best for him at a given time. Children in the upper grades and in high school are particularly competent to assist in such activities. Incidentally, such emphasis helps prepare the student for increasing self-responsibility in initiating learning activities.[12]

### Control of Activities

Many teachers are fearful that unless they keep strict control, pupils may get out of hand. However, strict control does not give pupils the share in planning activities which is educationally defensible. Beginning teachers often report discipline as a major problem. Improvement in discipline usually involves some shifts in class control. As with assignment making, control of many classes has been clearly autocratic. Improvement here typically involves study and experimentation designed to give students considerable practice in managing individual and small group activities and in analyzing the advantages and disadvantages in various plans of action. With more student responsibility for what is done in classes comes more active interest in learning activities. As a consequence of acquired student dependence on teachers and lack of teacher familiarity with democratically operated class procedures, improvement may come slowly at first.

### Uses of Resources

Improvement in the use of resources is intimately related to the ways in which a teacher handles individual differences. The teacher should ask himself the following questions: Have I given students sufficient practice in learning how to select and *acquire* books, magazines, and other resources they will need for individual and group-learning activities? Have I put too much dependence upon a single text, particularly when it was probably inappropriate for certain pupils in each class? Have I underemphasized the use of such non-reading resources as films, pictures, and the wealth of resources found in community activities? Has the money spent on texts or

---

[12] For assignment-improving suggestions, made and rated by groups of teachers, see Ray H. Simpson and Eugene L. Gaier, "Assignments Can Be Improved," *Illinois Education*, Vol. 47, May, 1959, pp. 382, 392–393. Also see Ray H. Simpson, *Teacher Self-Evaluation*, The Macmillan Company, 1966, Chapter 5, "Self-Evaluation in Developing Goals and Procedures."

other resources resulted in a plethora of a few resources and a paucity of varied resources? Have I told learners too often exactly what resources to use, giving them little or no practice in making such decisions themselves?

### Evaluation

Systematic evaluation in the classroom has long been considered the exclusive job of the teacher. Such control of evaluative processes has led to extreme pupil dependence on the teacher for evaluative activities. It has also resulted in the learner being ill-equipped to evaluate for learning purposes. Evaluation for learning purposes involves practice in setting up objectives, in diagnosing needs through measurement, and in planning future activities. Improvement of teacher activities in this regard will involve helping learners (1) determine their own goals in various areas; (2) diagnose their own individual and group needs; and (3) set up plans for learning activities designed to mitigate or eliminate weaknesses revealed by the diagnosis. The teacher's role in this improvement will shift from one of complete responsibility for evaluation to one of helping students improve their learning through increased facility in self-evaluation. Jim Martin, the boy referred to on a previous page who had a hand in planning his spelling assignments, also learned how to evaluate his success in learning to spell the words he used. Each week a fellow classmate pronounced Jim's individual spelling list to him. Jim checked the words he misspelled and practiced on these the following week.

## IMPROVING TEACHER-TEACHER RELATIONS

In times past it has been assumed by too many teachers that the only major front for improvement of professional activities was in the classroom. While it is true that the teacher's behavior in the classroom is of paramount importance, it is now recognized that there are key areas outside the classroom where potentialities are great for professional improvement. One of these is the working relationships between teachers.

Let us contrast the attitudes of teachers toward each other in two school systems. In the one school a general spirit of cooperation prevailed. Materials were generously shared, including professional books and magazines. Staff members discussed the problems of their pupils. Teachers told others what they were doing in their classes, the difficulties and successes they were having. Things sometimes did not run smoothly in the school, but an attitude of mutual helpfulness characterized the working relationships within the staff. This attitude, incidentally, also seemed to be contagious and favorably affected teacher-learner and teacher-administrator relationships as well.

In the other school the characteristic interpersonal attitudes existing within the staff ranged from an outright antagonistic attitude to one of watchful neutrality. Each teacher's motto seemed to be: "If you keep out of my way, we will get along fine." Below the surface in staff meetings there was an air of suspicion. A teacher would occasionally drop hints to students that certain other teachers took too much student time, or were too easy markers, or that they let pupils get away with too much. There was little sharing of ideas and materials. Some teachers talked as if their subject was the only one of real importance. This lack of cooperation was also spread to teacher-learner relationships. Students quickly sensed that all was not well. Many disciplinary problems developed. In general the atmosphere was not a happy one in which to work.

Much of the success of the modern school depends upon the willingness and the ability of its teaching staff to work together. There are many areas which demand such cooperation. One of these is curriculum revision. Unless the educational experiences of a student are continuously coordinated it is possible that the experiences encouraged by one teacher may work at cross purposes with those recommended by another. For example, it is a too common experience in some schools for a student, particularly one of below average ability, to have an amount of homework assigned which makes it impossible, if he takes all of the assignments seriously, for him to have time for adequate recreation, outdoor activity, and sleep.

Teachers also need to cooperate in dealing with such problems as marking, promoting, and reporting the activities of pupils. Continuous improvement in a school program involves gradual changes in the purposes and specific goals in teaching-learning situations. Such changes can and should be reflected in the bases upon which marks are given and in the school's reporting and promoting practices.

The initial training of most teachers has usually placed all too little stress on the importance of working with other teachers and on developing the skills necessary to work with teaching peers successfully. There is presently an increasing tendency to give added attention to this social aspect of educational psychology. Fortunately, the arousal of interest in interpersonal relations among teachers has developed concurrently with increased research related to the functioning of groups.[13]

Contribution to the improvement of the professional activities of colleagues has too frequently been neglected by teachers. Reciprocal training by teachers of each other has unlimited possibilities as an approach to educational advance.

---

[13] For example, see K. Benne and B. Muntyan, *Human Relations in Curriculum Change*, New York, The Dryden Press, 1951.

## IMPROVING TEACHER-ADMINISTRATOR RELATIONS

### Causes of Difficulties

Whenever difficulties in interpersonal relations are encountered, it is natural to project the troubles on someone else.[14] Bradford and Sheats [15] found that administrators were likely to try to place failure of staff meetings upon teachers. Teachers tend to reciprocate by blaming administrators for lack of cooperation. A more sound approach from a psychological standpoint is to say: What weaknesses on my part have contributed to the difficulties I have in working with administrators (or teachers)? Such a self-diagnosis can pave the way for eliminating many of these weaknesses and for developing needed interpersonal skills which may have been neglected in early professional training.

### Active Role Needed

If the teacher feels professional relations with the administrator need improvement he may decide to take a more active role in the operation of the school. Such a role is likely to bring the teacher into more working contact with the principal or superintendent. Evidence from social psychology suggests that such cooperative work is one of the best ways of establishing mutual respect. The teacher sees in most cases that it is possible to work with the administrator after all. The principal (or superintendent) finds that the teacher is a worker who sometimes makes mistakes, as he does, but who is willing to try to help improve the school program. Each is a bit more tolerant of the other as he gets more acquainted with the other's point of view.[16]

### Exposing of Weaknesses

When mutual respect and cooperation between teacher and administrator have been developed each is willing to divulge some of his weaknesses to the other. Fear that such exposure may itself be labeled a weakness is minimized. Each begins to see that it is through mutual trust and cooperative attack on these weaknesses that they can be gradually eliminated. One clue as to the quality of teacher-administrator relations lies in the answer to this question: Is the teacher willing to expose some of his weaknesses to

---

[14] See p. 381 for a discussion of projection.

[15] L. Bradford and P. Sheats, "Complacency Shock as a Prerequisite to Training," *Sociatry*, Vol. 2, 1948, pp. 38–48.

[16] For an additional discussion on this point see Roberta Green, "The Obstacles to Democratic Administration as Seen by a Teacher," *Progressive Education*, Vol. 30, 1952, pp. 35–37.

the administrator so that he can give help or suggest where such may be found? In many situations the principal is to the teacher as the teacher is to the child. If the administrator is to help the teacher in professional learning, he must treat confidentially many matters which have been discussed with him.

## IMPROVING TEACHER-COMMUNITY RELATIONS

Teachers not only need to establish good rapport with pupils, other teachers, and administrators but also to create sound relationships with parents and other community members. Such relations are likely to have considerable effect upon the success of student efforts and upon the effectiveness and happiness of the teacher. Without appropriate school-home understanding and communication the learnings teachers are trying to encourage in school may actually be discouraged, directly or indirectly, by the parents. Poor or inadequate school-home relations too frequently result in a lowering of respect for the role of the teacher and are likely to decrease the financial support the community will give to its schools. Obviously this latter result is likely to keep the salaries of teachers at a low level. Thus, we see that healthy school-home relations not only contribute to better education for learners but also tend to make the status of the teacher a more desirable one.

### School Program and Community Needs

Nothing gives a school a sounder foundation for the development and establishment of appropriate relations with the community than to have a dynamic program attuned to community needs. School activities are likely to become more meaningful if students receive guided practice in attacking community problems.[17] The probability of getting transfer of learning from school situations to out-of-school activities is also greatly enhanced. The following are some of the problems which schools in various communities have found useful as vehicles for increasing motivation, getting transfer of learning, and improving school-community relations: How can an unsanitary waterway in the community be changed to improve health and recreation? What improvements can and should be made in parks and playgrounds? How might race relations be bettered? What are ways of getting more active participation in civic activities?

### Homework

Instead of being a profitable learning experience for the student and a contribution to improved school-home relations, homework has frequently

---

[17] For a description of successful joint school and community practices from kindergarten through adult education see E. G. Olsen, *School and Community Programs*, New York, Prentice-Hall, Inc., 1949.

damaged such relations. Parents are too commonly kept in the dark about the purposes of homework. The child himself is in no position to help the parent understand the work when the purposes of assignments are not clear to him. This lack of understanding by either the parent or child often results from the common practice of having all assignments autocratically imposed on the learner rather than having them developed through teacher-pupil cooperation. Ventures by the teacher in the direction of democratically developed assignments will go a long way toward helping students, and in turn their parents, appreciate the school's objectives. In addition such changes may improve motivation and interest in school work through eliminating busy work and non-meaningful activities.

Frequently the homework can complement rather than merely duplicate the in-school work. For example, if the meaning and skills involved in multiplication are being studied, the pupil might be asked to determine such things as the cost of the bread to be bought by his family in the next week. This will probably involve determining the cost per loaf and multiplying this by the number of loaves purchased.

Sometimes the parent can be given an opportunity to cooperate in guiding the homework. The parent might be asked, for example, if he would state the amount of bread or other items to be purchased and let the child determine the cost per item at the grocery store. Budget-making, figuring income tax, planning purchases, using consumer research data are other illustrations of problems where skills can be developed through parent-teacher cooperation.

### Using Criticism

All teachers can develop the ability to use criticism in a constructive fashion. Too often suggestions given in a friendly fashion are taken as personal affronts rather than as clues for needed change. Because of their close contact with children, parents can sometimes supply such clues if they feel teachers welcome them. Teachers also need to study how to offer constructive criticism in such a way that parents and colleagues accept and use it rather than resent the teacher's suggestions. Even open disagreement of a friendly sort may be a healthy sign at times.

### Adult Use of School Facilities

If the community is to get its money's worth out of the big investment it has in its school plant, such facilities must not be unused three whole months a year plus Saturday, Sunday, and weekday nights. One way of improving school-community relations is for teachers to take the lead in promoting adult use of school facilities. For example, one group of teachers was interested in furthering good reading in the community. They arranged to have the school library open several nights a week. This led to discussion or "seminar" groups being formed. The community thought

more highly of its school and the educators in charge of it when the school started giving taxpayers more for their money.[18]

### Other Ways of Improving Communication and Understanding

Use of parents' nights, fathers' nights, and parent-visiting weeks have been found helpful in some communities.[19] Of course, parents should always be welcome in the school but special invitations are not out of place.

Active parent participation in such organizations as the Parent-Teachers Association is to be encouraged. To be virile, PTAs must be willing to face and grapple with significant issues even though at times the matters may be of a controversial nature. Too often such meetings have been innocuous and boring affairs attended out of a sense of duty.

Surveys of community problems jointly conducted by parents and teachers, as well as active participation by students in local projects outside the school are additional ways in which healthy relationships between the home and school can be promoted. In the last analysis, good professional development demands that teachers so involve themselves in community affairs that school work meets the needs and best interests of pupils. There is perhaps no better way to attain this involvement in the community than to make studies of community problems and local issues a regular part of school work.

## PROGRAMS FOR TEACHER IMPROVEMENT

The primary responsibility for improvement always rests with the individual teacher. However, formal and semi-formal institutional programs can facilitate professional growth. Three of these are discussed in the following paragraphs.

### In-Service Training Programs

For the interpersonal relations within a school staff to remain on a healthy and constructive level some type of in-service training program is most desirable. What form it should take for the individual teacher and for the school staff will, of course, depend to a considerable degree upon the backgrounds of the individuals involved. However, some characteristics of a useful in-service program can be pointed out.

In the first place it should be thought of as a cooperative staff effort designed to bring about specific improvements in the school activities. Mere courses or lectures for the staff will not fill the real need. Active study

---

[18] *Ibid.*, pp. 63–73.
[19] *Ibid.*

by teachers and attacks on actual school problems is needed if substantial improvement is to result.

Those working on a particular problem may be the whole staff or this group may divide itself into smaller subgroups, each of which studies and plans improvements. Illustrative problems are these: How can we improve the curriculum in our school? What are ways of meeting individual differences in more effective ways? How can the basic causes of disciplinary cases be identified and eliminated? How can we improve our marking and reporting practices?

The individual teacher, to profit most from the program, must not only be able to accept but should also welcome ideas and suggestions of fellow teachers concerning ways to improve his teaching and other professional activities. A permissive air should be developed in which the teacher is willing to expose some of his difficulties, weaknesses, and confusions so that others can help him eliminate these.

Individuals involved in an in-service training program will find it desirable to study ways of improving their functioning in groups. This is particularly true, since many teachers in their preservice training have had little or no careful study of the social psychology underlying the behavior of individuals in groups. Furthermore, most teachers have had insufficient practice in working democratically with peers on important professional problems. For example, too many teachers in a group situation tend to have too great a dependence on the group leader.[20] There is a tendency to sit back and wait for the leader to initiate and carry through the activities of the group. Other teachers with all good intentions sabotage group activities since they have only trained themselves to study and plan individually and have not developed the skills and abilities necessary for desirable professional activity.

Finally, in considering the psychological soundness of an in-service program we may ask such questions as these: Do teachers in a friendly fashion continuously exchange constructive criticism, involving professional goals, plans, and procedures? Does each teacher budget a certain amount of time each week for work with other teachers to get and give professional help? Do teachers realize the fact that helping other teachers learn may be more economical teaching than only teaching pupils? Committee work and departmental meetings offer the teacher opportunities for gathering and giving professional ideas. Trading ideas on an informal basis can constitute a profitable source of professional stimulation. Helping new teachers adjust to the multitude of problems which inevitably face and sometimes threaten

---

[20] K. D. Benne and B. Muntyan, *Human Relations in Curriculum Change*, New York, The Dryden Press, 1951, pp. 251–257. Also see Ronald Lippitt and colleagues, "The Teacher as Innovator, Seeker, and Sharer of New Practices," in *Prospectives on Educational Change*, R. I. Miller (Editor), New York, Appleton-Century-Crofts, 1967, pp. 307–324.

to overwhelm them is a service which not only may help the new teacher but can also provide new points of view for the more experienced teacher.[21]

### Workshops and Preschool Planning Conferences

Those studying in workshops are likely to come from more than one school. Members of the preschool planning conference are usually from a single school or school system. However, the purposes and procedures of workshops and preschool planning conferences tend to be similar. The general purpose of both of these approaches to in-service training is to improve the educational program through concentrated staff study on realistic school problems. The work of each teacher is pointed toward the solution of problems which he has encountered or visualizes he will encounter in his professional work.[22] Both the workshop and the preschool planning conference are based on the assumption that teachers learn best when they work together in an atmosphere which encourages critical thinking, free discussion, and systematic planning for future activities.

One of the chief values of workshops and preschool planning conferences is that they encourage teachers to work with and get the points of view of teachers in other subjects and on other levels. The mathematics teacher may study underlying causes of disciplinary problems with the English teacher. The social studies teacher may study and plan how to improve pupil reading abilities with the fifth-grade teacher. The interaction of teachers which characterizes preschool planning conferences and workshops tends to broaden the points of view held by the individual teacher.

Generally workshops and preschool conferences are run on a more democratic basis than more conventional institutes. Instead of being fairly passive participants in an imposed program, the teachers themselves help formulate the framework in which they study and plan. After activities have started the individual teacher has an important role in helping to determine the problems he will attack and the procedures he will use in furthering his study and planning.

Many of the participants of a workshop or planning conference are likely to continue their study during the ensuing school year. Tentative plans resulting from study are to be tried out on the job. The amount of transfer of training from the study situation to the teaching situation should be greater than from the ordinary professional class or course.

---

[21] For an excellent and detailed picture of goals, procedures, and evaluation of in-service programs see N. B. Henry (Editor), *In-Service Education for Teachers, Supervisors, and Administrators,* Fifty-sixth Yearbook of the National Society for the Study of Education, Chicago, The University of Chicago Press, 1957.

[22] E. C. Kelley, *The Workshop Way of Learning,* New York, Harper and Brothers, 1951, pp. 6–11.

## SUMMARY

Teaching is a professional field where changes are constantly taking place. New discoveries in psychology and in methods of teaching are the rule rather than the exception. The graduate of a teacher-training institution of ten years ago, if he has not kept up to date, would be astonished by advances which have been made even in that short time in the techniques of his profession. Changes and new developments in subject matter fields also are moving ahead at a fast pace. The teacher who is to be a challenging leader of children must learn how to keep abreast of such changes and in a very real sense continue to be a learner after his formal education has been completed.

In this chapter, methods have been presented which enable the teacher to appraise and evaluate his professional activities and teaching procedures. Suggestions are given for improving teacher-pupil relationships, teacher-teacher relationships, teacher-administration relationships, and finally teacher-community relationships.

The professionally maturing teacher is one who not only reads widely in journals dealing with teaching methods and his field of specialization, but also keeps closely in touch with expanding knowledge in all fields. He learns to be a critic of his own performance, and stimulates progress among his colleagues and other professional workers. Most important of all, the continually developing teacher affects the behavior of his pupils who learn by example and profit from the enriched and up-to-date program of studies which almost inevitably ensues.

### References for Further Study

Amidon, E. and Hunter E., *Improving Teaching, The Analysis of Classroom Verbal Interaction*, Chicago, Holt, Rinehart and Winston, Inc., 1966.

Barnes, Fred, *Research for the Practitioner in Education*, Washington, D.C., NEA Department of Elementary School Principals, 1964.

Barnes, John B., *Educational Research for Classroom Teachers*, New York, G. P. Putnam's Sons, 1960.

Biddle, B. J. and Elena, W. J., *Contemporary Research on Teacher Effectiveness*, Chicago, Holt, Rinehart and Winston, Inc., 1964.

Carlson, R. O., *Adoption of Educational Innovations*, University of Oregon, Eugene, Oregon, The Center for the Advanced Study of Educational Administration, 1965.

Combs, A. W., *The Professional Education of Teachers*, Boston, Allyn and Bacon, 1965.

Department of Classroom Teachers, *What Research Says Series*, American Educational Research Association of the NEA, Washington, D.C., National Education Association, 1953 to the present time. Consists of a con-

stantly growing series of valuable research summaries by national authorities. Some of the areas included in the *What Research Says Series* are: Teaching Reading, Evaluating and Reporting Pupil Progress, Science in the Elementary Schools, Class Organization for Instruction, Teaching Arithmetic, Teaching Spelling, Reading in the High School, The Gifted Child in the Elementary School.

Gage, N. L. (Editor), *Handbook of Research on Teaching*, Chicago, Rand McNally and Company, 1964.

Gardner, John W., *Self-Renewal: The Individual and the Innovative Society*, New York, Harper and Row, 1965.

Harris, C. W. (Editor), *Encyclopedia of Educational Research*, Third Edition, New York, The Macmillan Company, 1960. See such headings as: Criteria of Teacher Effectiveness, pp. 1482–1485; In service Education, pp. 702–708, 831–832, 1250; Leaves of Absence for Teachers, pp. 1362–1363; Merit Rating, p. 1179; Professional Associations for Teachers, pp. 1491–1495; Professional Education, pp. 1056–1060; Promotions of Teachers, pp. 1365–1366; Social Status, p. 1361; Teacher Attitudes Toward Teaching, pp. 1359–1360; Teacher Effectiveness, pp. 1481–1491.

Henry, N. B. (Editor), *In-service Education for Teachers, Supervisors and Administrators*, Fifty-Sixth Yearbook of the National Society for the Study of Education, Chicago, The University of Chicago Press, 1957.

Kerlinger, F. N., *Foundations of Behavioral Research*, Chicago, Holt, Rinehart and Winston, 1964.

Miel, A., and associates, *Cooperative Procedures in Learning*, New York, Teachers College, Columbia University, 1952.

Miles, M. B. (Editor), *Innovation in Education*, New York, Bureau of Publications, Teachers College, Columbia University, 1964.

Shumsky, A., *The Action Research Way of Learning*, New York, Teachers College, Columbia University, 1958.

Shumsky, A., *Creative Teaching in the Elementary School*, New York, Appleton-Century-Crofts, 1965.

Simpson, Ray H., *Improving Teaching-Learning Processes*, New York, Longmans, Green and Company, 1953.

Simpson, Ray H., *Teacher Self-Evaluation*, New York, The Macmillan Company, 1966.

Wiles, Kimball, *Teaching for Better Schools*, Englewood Cliffs, New Jersey, Prentice-Hall, Inc., 1959.

The reader is also urged to utilize the following headings in the *Education Index:*

*College professors and instructors*, Rating, Rating by students
*Orientation programs for teachers*
*Principals and teachers*
*Professional books and reading*
*Professional education*
*Professional growth*
*Public relations*
*Social adjustment and development*
*Teacher training*

*Teacher training in service*
*Teachers,* Rating, Rating by students
*Teachers' Workshops*
*Teaching methods;* also subhead Teaching methods under school subject, e.g., Human relations—Teaching methods.

## Questions, Exercises, and Activities

1. Assume you will have 28 students in a class next year. The range in IQs is from 80 to 140. A standardized test shows an achievement range of at least six grade levels.
   (a) Using the index of this book, list headings, and the pages indicated for each, which you think might refer you to helpful ideas on the problems related to this situation.
   (b) Using the *Education Index,* list headings which might be helpful. Also, note at least two relevant and specific references in periodicals you think might be helpful.
   (c) Select one of the "References for Further Study" given above and list additional ways you as a professional person might go about getting ideas to help you face the situation more wisely.
2. List reasons why *you* think too few teachers try to grow professionally in a systematic fashion.
3. Consider what you have written under question number 2 above. Describe what you think you personally should do in your next teaching situation to grow professionally. Be specific.
4. Talk to one or two men or women in each of two or three professions other than teaching and ask each what he does to keep up-to-date in his field. Compile a summary list. (This may be done by three, four, or five students working together.) What implications or suggestions do you see here for teachers?
5. Compile a list of professional journals in education and psychology which you think give the teacher help in understanding and working with pupils. After the name of each give a few sentences indicating such things as the kinds of articles, the understandability of the writing for you and your general appraisal of the journal.

# Chapter 22

## Personal and Emotional Adjustment of the Teacher

If psychology has any practical value, it ought to help teachers with their own personal adjustment. Teachers need this help. It has been noted that, "All day long, the teacher is dealing with emotionally toned activities—hostility, defiance, dependency, demands, destruction of property, dishonesty. . . ." [1] The energies of children and the turmoil of the classroom inevitably create tensions within the teacher. These tensions must find healthy release in work and recreation. Teachers who are unable to discover mechanisms of release are apt to become irritable, emotionally disturbed, and maladjusted. The teacher who screams, cries, threatens, or ridicules pupils is the one who has failed to attain other means of relieving pressure and uses the children in his classroom as scapegoats for his own frustrations.

This chapter will present the problem of maladjustment among teachers, the causes and effects of this maladjustment, and finally suggest ways in which teachers may remain in good mental health.

### THE PROBLEM

Because of the emotionally toned and tension-producing activities which teachers daily encounter, it is not too surprising to find "that the incidence

---

[1] Forty-Ninth Yearbook of the National Society for the Study of Education, Part I, *Learning and Instruction*, Chicago, University of Chicago Press, 1950, p. 180.

of mental disturbance among teachers seems higher than among persons in other occupations." [2] A study by Smith and Hightower indicated that of 1164 patients studied at the Mayo Clinic, teachers were diagnosed as having the highest percentage (55%) of neurosis of all occupational groups. The percentages for some other occupational groups were: physicians, 17%; farmers, 19%; dentists, 30%; lawyers, 36%; housewives, 36%; clergymen, 39%; and nuns, 42%. [3]

Thus it appears that in the population as a whole, and particularly among teachers, personal problems and maladjustment take an alarming toll in impaired efficiency and unhappiness. But unlike many other groups, teachers' mental health is an integral part of the job itself. In no other work is good mental health more essential than in teaching. The profession demands stability—a capacity to withstand pressures, and most important the skill of working aggressions off into channels different from the work situation. In other words, the teacher must learn to keep his aggressions and personal difficulties out of the classroom. Most teachers succeed, but a sizeable percentage, to some degree, allow personal maladjustment to interfere with their work. The number of teachers who succumb to pressures of work, or fall victim to nervous disorders, and the form which these deviate behaviors take will now be discussed in greater detail.

### How Many Teachers Are Maladjusted?

The various studies of the condition of mental health and adjustment of teachers have differed to a considerable extent in their findings. All seem to agree that many experienced teachers could profit from psychological or psychiatric assistance. Table 36 outlines the results of some of the major studies of teachers' adjustment. It is clear that although samples used, methods, and findings differ, there is an agreement that a significant percentage of the teacher population is so maladjusted that teaching suffers.

Perhaps the most comprehensive study of any shown in Table 36 was that of Fenton. Both Fenton and Hicks (the first study shown in the table) estimated that about 20 per cent of the teachers in their sample were in need of mental hygiene assistance. More serious disturbances—those which would warrant immediate study and therapy—are spotted by Blair and by Altman as comprising a group somewhere between 4 and 8 per cent. These data would tend to support the conclusion that one-fifth or more of teachers need psychological help while as many as five out of a hundred are mental cases, and need immediate professional treatment. The extremely high percentage of maladjustment found in the Mayo Clinic study can be partly attributed to the fact that this was not a random sampling of teachers.

---

[2] J. T. Shipley, *The Mentally Disturbed Teacher*, Philadelphia, Chilton Company, 1961, p. 6.

[3] H. L. Smith and N. C. Hightower, "Incidence of Functional Disease (Neurosis) Among Patients of Various Occupations," *Occupational Medicine*, Vol. 5, 1948, pp. 182–185.

**TABLE 36**

**Incidence of Maladjustment of Teachers as Reported in Several Investigations**

| Investigation | Findings | Sample | Method |
|---|---|---|---|
| Hicks [*] | 17.5 per cent of teachers unduly nervous or psycho-neurotic. 10.5 per cent had had nervous breakdowns. | 600 teachers 124 men 476 women | Analysis of questionnaire filled out by teachers themselves. |
| Peck [†] | About 17 per cent in need of psychiatric service. | 100 women teachers | Administered the Thurstone Personality Schedule. |
| N.E.A. Yearbook Committee [‡] | 37.5 per cent subject to persistent worries. | 5,150 teachers | Analysis of questionnaire filled out by teachers. |
| Altman [§] | 4 per cent described as mental cases. 13 per cent in need of treatment. | 35,000 New York teachers | Estimate from clinical practice. |
| Fenton [‖] | 22.5 per cent in need of mental hygiene help and 15.4 per cent handicapped in their work by maladjustment. | 241 teachers from small communities | Conferences with supervisors, and classroom observation of all teachers in the sample. |
| Blair [¶] | 8.8 per cent maladjusted to such an extent that they should be screened for psychological study. | 205 experienced teachers | Administered the Multiple-Choice Rorschach. Used the Harrower-Erickson norms to determine a cutting score. |
| Smith and Hightower [**] | 55 per cent of teachers applying for examination at Mayo Clinic showed emotional illness. | 106 female teachers, 16 male teachers | Examination by doctors. |

[*] F. R. Hicks, "The Mental Health of Teachers," *Contributions to Education*, No. 123, Nashville, Tennessee, George Peabody College, 1934.

[†] Leigh Peck, "A Study of the Adjustment Difficulties of a Group of Women Teachers," *Journal of Educational Psychology*, Vol. 27, 1936, pp. 401–416.

[‡] Ninth Yearbook of the National Educational Association, Department of Classroom Teachers, *Fit to Teach*, Washington, D.C. 1938, p. 77.

[§] Emil Altman, "Our Mentally Unbalanced Teachers," *The American Mercury*, Vol. 52, April, 1941, pp. 391–401.

[‖] Norman Fenton, *Mental Hygiene in School Practice*, Stanford University, California, Stanford University Press, 1943, p. 288.

[¶] G. M. Blair, "Personal Adjustment of Teachers as Measured by the Multiple-Choice Rorschach Test," *Journal of Educational Research*, Vol. 39, May, 1946, pp. 652–657.

[**] H. L. Smith and N. C. Hightower, *Occupational Medicine*, Vol. 5, 1948, pp. 182–185.

## How Is Maladjustment Manifested?

The personal difficulties of teachers are often revealed in their treatment of pupils. One investigator found the following examples of cruel and unusual punishments being practiced by experienced teachers:

1. A child jerked from his seat by his hair.
2. Kicking child.
3. A child forced to push chalk around the room with his nose.
4. Child forced to apologize on his knees.
5. Mimicry of stuttering child.
6. Coining of descriptive names such as "spaghetti, lard, garbage, and tattler." [4]

Such examples lead one to believe that further training of many teachers is necessary. But when teachers lose control or resort to almost sadistic forms of punishment there is little doubt that their behavior springs not from lack of training but from emotional instability. Altman described a case in which a teacher in a frenzy of rage attacked a girl of nine and came very close to severing her jugular vein. In still another of Altman's cases, a teacher, clearly a psychotic, believed that the school janitor was trying to freeze her, so she insisted on wearing her overcoat in the school room. In fact, according to Altman one teacher commuted back and forth to her school from a mental hospital where she was being treated.[5] These are clear-cut cases of profound disturbance. But not all personal problems and emotional disturbances so clearly manifest themselves in the classroom. Many teachers complain of persistent worries, sleeplessness, and nervousness. In the comprehensive study of the N.E.A. Yearbook Committee shown in Table 36, teachers listed nervousness as the third highest ailment in a list of seventeen.[6] And in a survey of 300 beginning high school teachers in Illinois, it was found that 20 per cent had difficulties which they were unable to solve.[7] Apparently many teachers are beset by difficulties which do not markedly interfere with their teaching but nevertheless do interfere with their adjustment and happiness. And it is safe to say that such difficulties, if they remain uncorrected, may eventually lead to more serious disturbances which will certainly manifest themselves in the classroom.

### Early Symptoms of Maladjustment

What are danger signals in the behavior of the teacher which indicate maladjustment or emotional immaturity? How can an observer or the teacher himself be alerted to the symptoms which indicate a need for precautionary mental hygiene measures? Such questions are crucial since it is well recognized that preventive steps are more effective than later therapy.

---

[4] C. R. Adams, "Classroom Practice and the Personality Adjustment of Children," *Understanding the Child*, Vol. 13, June, 1944, pp. 10–15.

[5] Emil Altman, *op. cit.*, pp. 391 and 396.

[6] *Fit to Teach, op. cit.*, p. 77.

[7] H. L. Wellbank, "The Teacher and His Problems," *Educational Administration and Supervision*, Vol. 38, 1952, pp. 491–494.

Crossness and general irritability are perhaps the most general and frequent early symptoms. Loss of temper is sometimes a reflection of underlying emotional difficulties. For example, the teacher who says: "Who made that noise? You won't tell? All right, all of you will stay in one hour after school," is probably showing either poor judgment or is allowing his work to create mental health hazards. Indulging in sarcasm or incessant scolding, or subjecting children to cruel or unusual punishments are, as previously noted, clues which indicate unhealthy reactions to difficult or frustrating conditions.

The teacher who finds fault with other staff members or departments frequently suffers from a lack of personal security which he tries to give expression to by attempting to tear down the reputations of others. Such a teacher also frequently feels too insecure to experiment and try out teaching innovations, and may make fun of colleagues who attempt to improve teaching-learning situations. Sometimes such behavior is accompanied by an attitude of cynicism toward the world in general and toward the possibilities of improvement in education in particular. Such teachers not only try little to improve themselves but may actually strive to keep others from improving.

Sometimes teachers' mental ill health is also reflected in an inability to accept normal aggressions of youngsters. One who cannot stand noise or horseplay, or who becomes unduly disturbed over the exaggerated braggadocio which many adolescents display, should consider a career other than teaching.

A complete list of the symptoms which disturbed teachers might exhibit would be difficult to compose. The few which have just been listed are representative of those which the alert school administrator or teacher should be able to recognize. As a general guide, it might be stated that bizarre methods of striving to be important or loss of emotional control are symptomatic of maladjustment.

## EFFECT OF TEACHER MALADJUSTMENT ON PUPILS

That many personally maladjusted teachers are to be found in our classrooms no one will deny. The extent to which such teachers affect the lives of the children under their tutelage, however, has not been fully determined. Several research studies conducted to date seem to indicate that the effects may be very far-reaching. For example, an early study by Boynton and others [8] carried out in the classrooms of 73 fifth- and sixth-grade teachers

---

[8] P. Boynton, H. Dugger, and M. Turner, "The Emotional Stability of Teachers and Pupils," *Journal of Juvenile Research*, Vol. 18, 1934, pp. 223–232.

showed that pupils of the teachers in the best mental health were more stable than pupils in classes taught by teachers who were rated as being in poor mental health. In a somewhat more recent study [9] it was shown that kindergarten children, taught by a teacher considered to be poorly adjusted, changed for the worse while a comparable group, taught by "an adjusted teacher," suffered no such loss. Baxter's [10] investigation clearly showed that the way teachers conducted their classes was reflected in the security and freedom from tension of pupils, and that much of the teacher's behavior appeared to be tied up with factors of adjustment.

The fate of a pupil who had the misfortune to have a maladjusted teacher is presented by Wallin.[11] This case is described by the individual involved some years after the unfortunate incident occurred.

My friends are always talking about my inferiority complex. I have always considered myself dumb and had little confidence in my ability to get high grades or to achieve much in school, in spite of the fact that I continue to find my university courses very interesting. I think my inferiority feelings sprang up in the third grade, when I had a teacher whom I hated. She is the one who mocked and made fun of my thumb sucking. . . . She said I was naughty, inattentive, and unable to get my work, and kept me in the third grade for three years, while my classmates with probably no more ability than I had were advanced. When the fourth-grade teacher got hold of me and became aware of the injustice done me, she shoved me on as fast as she could, so that I made up about a year that way. Although I advanced a grade every year thereafter, as long as I was in that particular school I always felt I was a dumbbell. When I transferred to another school, where I had no bad record, I worked with real zest and during the last few years of grammar school I was among the first six or seven in the class. But this did not entirely eliminate my deeply implanted inferiority feeling. In my heart I felt I was dumb but the teachers in this school didn't know it, and I felt I was putting something over on them. My inferiority feeling is still with me, although my later successes have helped some to overcome it.

In summarizing numerous studies of the effects of teacher adjustment on child development, Snyder [12] states that there is no question but that the teacher's state of mental health influences the behavior of children under his care. He goes on to say:

[9] M. Nichols, J. Worthington, and H. Witmer, "The Influence of the Teacher on the Adjustment of Children in Kindergarten," *Smith College Studies Social Work*, Vol. 9, 1939, pp. 360–402.

[10] Bernice Baxter, *Teacher-Pupil Relationships*, New York, The Macmillan Company, 1941.

[11] J. E. W. Wallin, *Personality Maladjustments and Mental Hygiene*, Second Edition, New York, McGraw-Hill Book Company, 1949, p. 105.

[12] William U. Snyder, "Do Teachers Cause Maladjustment," *Journal of Exceptional Children*, Vol. 14, December, 1947, pp. 76–77.

Adjusted teachers do much to bring about pupil adjustment, and the converse is also true. Probably the most satisfactory way of measuring whether or not a classroom is smooth-running and effective would be to measure the degree of personal adjustment of the teacher.

Some interesting case studies bearing on this point have been collected by the psychologist Laycock [13] who visited 157 different classrooms in an effort to study the effect of the teacher's personality on the behavior of pupils. Although his data do not permit of statistical treatment, Laycock ventures the opinion that "the effect of many teachers on the mental health of their pupils is definitely bad." Two of the fifteen cases he described are reproduced as follows:

### TEACHER A

This man is an elderly veteran. He is dirty and untidy. He is nervous, jittery and dashes about. He berates pupils who don't know the answers. He complained about the pupils to the superintendent. His teaching is didactic and authoritarian. He makes no attempt to develop his class as a cooperative group. The pupils appear fearful, timid, insecure, and repressed. The teacher's mental health is obviously so bad that he should not be permitted to continue in the classroom.

### TEACHER B

This teacher is in charge of Grades one to four. Her attitudes are not suited to children. She frowns a great deal and never smiles. She is un-animated, prosaic, and unenthusiastic. She does not appear to be a happy, well-adjusted person. She does not appear to like her pupils or to enjoy teaching. She drives her pupils and may succeed in getting them to acquire certain facts and skills. Her "discipline," judged by the standards of a generation ago, was good. The pupils appeared repressed and unhappy. The general effect of the teacher on the mental health of the children is judged to be poor.

There probably is little doubt but that the friendly, enthusiastic, secure, and well-adjusted teacher can contribute much to the well-being of his pupils. On the other hand, the irritable, depressed, hostile, tired, and neurotic teacher can create tensions which are disturbing to pupils, and which may permanently alter their outlooks on life.

## CAUSES OF TEACHER MALADJUSTMENT

Teachers become maladjusted and develop mental ill health in the same manner as do pupils or other individuals. The fundamental cause is frustration resulting from blocked goals. Teachers have all the needs of other

---

[13] S. R. Laycock, "Effect of the Teacher's Personality on the Behavior of Pupils," *Understanding the Child*, Vol. 19, April, 1950, pp. 50–55.

people. They desire security, recognition, new experience, and independence, for example, and become tense when these needs remain unfulfilled. The school teacher who does not feel that he is appreciated by the school administration may relieve himself of his tense emotions by gossiping about other teachers or engaging in daydreams which give imaginary success experiences. The teacher who has had a violent quarrel with her husband before coming to school may take out her hostile feelings on children in her classes. The many adjustment mechanisms described in Chapter 13 all apply to teachers.

### Special Occupational Hazards

There are frustrating conditions in any occupation or profession. The traveling salesman must not only "put-up" with all types of odd and unreasonable customers, but must also run the risk of missing trains and failing to obtain hotel reservations. The doctor must leave the football game or party he is attending, or get up at all hours of the night to minister to the needs of patients. The ticket agent in a railroad station or clerk in the post office must answer thousands of unreasonable questions and try to be serene when he is insulted by some members of his public. Employed people in many walks of life complain that their work is mentally fatiguing and that they very much need prolonged vacations if they are to avoid mental breakdowns.

School teaching is thus not unique in providing an atmosphere which may be conducive to poor mental health or nervous disorders. Living itself is hazardous, and whether a person succeeds in meeting the problems he faces depends not only on the problems themselves but also how he regards them and how he adjusts to them. Nevertheless, there are special restricting conditions in teaching which may lead to frustrations not encountered equally often in certain other professions. Kimball Young [14] has drawn up a list of ways in which communities attempt to regulate the lives of their teachers. Some of these are as follows:

1. Frequent indication as to preference of the kind and location of residence.
2. Prescription of appropriate dress, facial make-up, and use of cosmetics.
3. Close definition of leisure-time activities; drinking alcoholic beverages, smoking, dancing, and card-playing are especially taboo in some communities.
4. Restrictions of association between teachers and members of the opposite sex who may be students, townspeople, or other teachers.

---

[14] Kimball Young, *Personality and Problems of Adjustment*, Second Edition, New York, Appleton-Century-Crofts, Inc., 1952, p. 445.

5. Considerable pressure to take part in religious or other community-approved activities.
6. Expectation that teachers will give strong support to any extracurricular functions which the community likes, such as competitive sports and musical festivals.
7. Restrictions in many communities on the frequency of trips to other localities during weekends.
8. Taboos against joining labor unions and running for political office or otherwise participating in local politics.

School communities, of course, vary greatly with respect to the degree to which they supervise the private affairs of teachers. In larger cities teachers often have the freedom of almost any citizen, while in smaller places rules and regulations which teachers must follow may be unusually severe. The writer was recently told of a young woman teacher who was dismissed from a small Illinois high school because her landlady found an ash tray in her room. Another teacher in a midwestern town lost his job because he bought his new car from a dealer in a community eighteen miles away. Beale [15] has reproduced a contract which one community required its teachers to sign. It read as follows:

> I promise to take a vital interest in all phases of Sunday school work, donating of my time, service, and money without stint for the uplift and benefit of the community. I promise to abstain from all dancing, immodest dressing, and other conduct unbecoming a teacher and a lady. I promise not to go out with any young men except in so far as it may be necessary to stimulate Sunday school work. I promise not to fall in love, to become engaged or secretly married. I promise to remain in the dormitory or on the school grounds when not actively engaged in school or church work elsewhere. I promise not to encourage or tolerate the least familiarity on the part of my boy pupils. I promise to sleep at least eight hours a night, to eat carefully, and take every precaution to keep in the best of health and spirits in order that I may be better able to render efficient service to my pupils. I promise to remember that I owe a duty to the townspeople who are paying me my wages, and that I owe respect to the school board and the superintendent that hired me, and that I shall consider myself at all times the willing servant of the school board and the townspeople and that I shall cooperate with them to the limit of my ability in any movement aimed at the betterment of the town, the pupils, or the schools.

Frustrations which beset teachers do not all come from the community. Some come from professional relationships with other teachers and administrators, and some from the pupils themselves. One writer [16] has stated that:

---

[15] Howard K. Beale, *Are American Teachers Free?* New York, Charles Scribner's Sons, 1936, pp. 395–396.

[16] Margaret J. Synnberg, "Why Teachers 'Blow Their Tops,'" *The Nation's Schools*, Vol. 41, March, 1948, p. 47.

Despite tenure, regardless of contracts, many teachers live in a state of perpetual insecurity. They are fearful of the principal, of the superintendent, of the head of the department, of examiners, of tests, of their failure to meet teaching norms, of unexpected demands, of new arrangements, and of impending changes. Some of them are afraid of their students.

Three hidden hazards in teaching have been suggested by Crescimbeni and Mammarella.[17] They are: (1) Since most teachers spend their professional lives with members of one particular age group, there is danger the teacher's view of life will be frozen at the level of the students he teaches, (2) The teacher may face loss of courage when his high, idealistic hopes of combining self-fulfillment and social contribution are frequently dashed by a series of restraints which he can do little about, and (3) The teacher's sense of humor may be threatened by his assuming an overly serious role.

The fact that teachers are usually not in a position to fight back when they are unjustly accused, mistreated, or dismissed from their positions, causes many to adopt a very submissive attitude which in the long run may be at the bottom of a great many "anxiety neuroses." The psychiatrist Karen Horney [18] believes that one of the surest ways to develop deep-seated fears and anxieties is to repress hostile feelings. From this point of view, teachers who would remain in good mental health should not continually give in to pressure groups or to superiors, but should at times stand up for their own rights. Expressing hostile feelings once in a while is believed to have excellent therapeutic value.

## SUGGESTIONS TO TEACHERS FOR KEEPING IN GOOD MENTAL HEALTH

Since there are many causes of maladjustment among teachers, there are also many ways in which their personal and emotional difficulties may be alleviated. Progress toward better mental health is a goal which must be sought not only by teachers and educational organizations, but also by the community as a whole.

Perhaps no point has been more greatly stressed in this volume than the principle that needs, wants, and drives must come to fruition if people are to be well-adjusted. Consequently, the starting point for helping teachers maintain good mental health must be the determination of their drives and goals. Two needs immediately stand out as important in the job of teaching. The first is that teachers want to be liked and respected by their pupils. The second is that teachers need to feel a sense of professional accomplish-

[17] Joseph Crescimbeni and Raymond J. Mammarella, "Hidden Hazards of Teaching," *NEA Journal*, Vol. 54, January, 1965, p. 31.
[18] Karen Horney, *The Neurotic Personality of Our Time*, New York, W. W. Norton & Co., Inc., 1937, pp. 60–78.

ment. As previously shown, several things stand in the way of the satisfaction of such needs. Pupils are not aware of the needs of teachers. To some extent, they share the community's stereotype about teachers as being a group apart—a little different from other people. Under such circumstances, it might be wise for teachers to make known to pupils what some of their own needs are. Perhaps the simple statement by the teacher that he wants all pupils to like him, and wants help from the class when he does things which the pupils do not like, would be an effective first step.

A further barrier which blocks the attainment of professional goals is that teachers may have erroneous notions about the way in which such goals may be achieved. It is apparent that teachers ought to know the characteristics of teachers which children like.[19] It is also clear that a failure to realize professional goals calls for a re-examination of the teaching situation and one's objectives, as was pointed out in the preceding chapter.

Much of the progress toward the better mental health of teachers is in the hands of the larger community whose dictums about salary, teachers' conduct, school buildings, and the size of classes determine not only the kinds of teachers that are recruited, but also the morale of those presently engaged in this profession. Great strides have been made toward bettering the teacher's social status and working conditions in the past twenty years. But even under good teaching conditions there are many problems which teachers must learn to solve for themselves. These are feelings of pressure and inferiority, gnawing anxieties, fears and depressions, and inevitable frustrations and conflicts.

There is no panacea for the solution of these problems, yet much is known about the general conditions which foster good mental health. Principles from the field of mental hygiene would seem to support the following suggestions to teachers:

1. Recognize that differences of opinion are healthy and learn how to use the criticisms of others constructively.
2. Expect a certain amount of aggression and rebellion in young people. Such expression is a normal developmental pattern in our culture.
3. If you do not feel well get a medical examination. Some of your aches and pains may be real.
4. Become so absorbed in teaching and avocational activities that there is little time for worrying about petty problems and engaging in unhealthy preoccupation with yourself.
5. Put yourself periodically into a position where you must learn something new. It may be typing, ping pong, a foreign language, or anything else which keeps you active.
6. Become a member of some organization—church, community, civic,

---

[19] See Chapter 11.

or professional. Belonging to a group tends to make one feel secure and to satisfy a need for belonging and status.

7. Develop some close personal friends. Complete self-sufficiency is undesirable.
8. Learn how to converse with, and work with, different kinds of people.
9. Work actively to help the teaching profession deserve and attain a higher status than it now enjoys.
10. Express hostile feelings once in a while. Repressing them may lead to anxiety.
11. Make a plan for your life, but do not be overly ambitious. Over-ambition can be just as harmful as underambition. Cut the world down to your size. Do not aspire for things beyond the level where you have a reasonable chance for success.
12. Develop a satisfying philosophy of life. Believe in something.
13. Be yourself. Although there is always room for improvement in personality, you are probably not too bad a person as you are. No one is perfect. Excessive attempts to ape other people kill individuality, and lead to unhappiness.

## SUMMARY

Psychology is a basic tool in the work of the teacher. Much of this book has shown how the principles which this discipline offers may be used in improving teaching and learning. But psychology can also help teachers solve personal and emotional problems. All evidence suggests that teachers, although relatively stable when compared with other professional groups, need assistance in improving their mental health. This need takes on added importance when the undesirable effects upon pupils of teacher maladjustment are considered.

Research dealing with the incidence of maladjustment among teachers has shown that about a fifth of teachers have personal difficulties, the solution of which would improve their teaching, and that as many as five teachers out of a hundred are sufficiently maladjusted to warrant immediate professional help.

The effects of mentally unbalanced teachers upon pupils is to be found in the instability, anxieties, dislikes, and feelings of inferiority which are found among pupils who are unfortunate enough to have a maladjusted teacher. Some of these characteristics and behaviors of children are inevitable, but there is little denying that such children and behavior traits are found in greater numbers in the classrooms of unbalanced teachers. On the positive side, there is little question that well-adjusted and stable teachers have helped many disturbed children achieve good adjustment.

The causes of maladjustment among teachers have been shown basically to be the same as the causes for maladjustment of children, viz., frustrated

drives and needs. In addition, however, it has been noted that special hazards occur in teaching. Stringent demands by the community for strict codes of conduct, low salaries, poor materials and teaching facilities, and the pressures of handling the emotionally toned activities of children are among the many conditions which may disturb teachers. Most teachers are able to handle these pressures, but some succumb and vent their insecurity and emotion upon children. The fact remains that there are still teachers who scream, cry, threaten, and who subject children to bizarre forms of humiliation and punishment.

Adjustment is a relative matter. No one is entirely free from some peculiarities and eccentricities. The successful teacher, however, should strive to maintain as high a level of personal adjustment as possible. Suggestions for doing this include the development of appropriate personal and professional goals, and a philosophy of life which gives direction and meaning to teaching and living.

### References for Further Study

Barron, Frank X., *Creativity and Psychological Health: Origins of Personal Vitality and Creative Freedom*, Princeton, New Jersey, Van Nostrand, 1963.

Bernard, H. W., *Mental Hygiene for Classroom Teachers*, New York, McGraw-Hill, 1961.

Bruce, W. F. and Ellena, W. J., Jr., *The Teacher's Personal Development*, New York, Holt, 1957.

Combs, A. W., *The Professional Education of Teachers*, Boston, Allyn and Bacon, 1965.

Crow, L. D., *Mental Hygiene for Teachers: A Book of Readings*, New York, Macmillan Company, 1963.

Huggett, A. J. and Slinnett, T. M., *Professional Problems of Teachers*, New York, Macmillan, 1963.

Jersild, Arthur T., *When Teachers Face Themselves*, New York, Bureau of Publications, Teachers College, Columbia, University, 1955.

Malamud, D. J. and Machover, S., *Toward Self-Understanding: Group Techniques in Self-Confrontation*, Springfield, Illinois, C. C Thomas, 1965.

Powell, M. and Ferraro, C. D., "Sources of Tension in Married and Single Women Teachers," *Journal of Educational Psychology*, Vol. 51, April 1960, pp. 92–101.

Redl, Fritz and Wattenberg, William W., *Mental Hygiene in Teaching*, Second Edition, New York, Harcourt, Brace, 1959, Chapter 18.

Rogers, C. R., *On Becoming A Person*, Boston, Houghton Mifflin, 1951.

Schneiders, A. A., *Personality Dynamics and Mental Health: Principles of Adjustment and Mental Hygiene*, New York, Holt, Rinehart and Winston, 1965.

Shipley, J. T., *The Mentally Disturbed Teacher*, Philadelphia, Chilton Co., Book Division, 1961.

Stevenson, George S. and Milt, Harry, "Ten Tips to Reduce Teacher Tension," in *Readings in Educational Psychology*, Second Edition, (J. M. Seidman, Editor), Boston, Houghton Mifflin Company, 1965, pp. 85–88.

## Questions, Exercises, and Activities

1. Why is it that a teacher may be well-informed about mental hygiene and blind to his own emotional difficulties and maladjustment?
2. If one of your colleagues seemed to be emotionally unstable and maladjusted, and this condition seemed to be affecting his pupils, what would you do?
3. After reading this chapter, it should occur to you that a good deal of this material has implications for teacher-training institutions. Give some of these implications. What is your own institution doing along these lines?
4. Describe a maladjusted teacher whom you have had at any point in your schooling. What were the symptoms that in retrospect led you to this conclusion? What were your reactions at the time?
5. Although some special "psychological" hazards exist in the profession, there are also certain therapeutic characteristics in it. Why? How can these characteristics be maximized?
6. Although the evidence is not complete nor clear-cut, it is believed that teachers' maladjustment may have an adverse effect upon children's personalities and behavior. What kinds of maladjustments are likely to have the most severe consequences? In what way may teachers' maladjustments affect pupils?
7. What administrative practices in schools should be developed or changed so as to insure optimum mental health for teachers?
8. Do you believe that teachers as a group are more maladjusted than other professional groups such as doctors, lawyers, or accountants? What evidence do you have to support your opinion?
9. Do you feel that the personal conduct of a teacher should be on a higher level and subject to restrictions not applied to other professional groups in the community?
10. In this chapter there is a list of thirteen suggestions to teachers for keeping in good mental health. Study this list and then write a fourteenth suggestion based upon your knowledge of teaching and principles of mental hygiene.

# Indexes

# Author Index

# Subject Index

ET    50    7